Signs of the Flesh

Signs of the Flesh

AN ESSAY ON THE EVOLUTION
OF HOMINID SEXUALITY

Daniel Rancour-Laferriere

INDIANA UNIVERSITY PRESS

Bloomington & Indianapolis

 The paper used in this publication meets the minimum requirements of American
National Standard for Information Sciences--Permanence of Paper for Printed
Library Materials, ANSI Z39.48-1984.

Manufactured in the United States of America

Library of Congress Cataloging-in-Publication Data

Rancour-Laferriere, Daniel.
        Signs of the flesh : an essay on the evolution of hominid
    sexuality / Daniel Rancour-Laferriere.
              p.   cm.
        Reprint. Originally published: Berlin ; New York : Mouton,
    c1985. Originally published in series : Approaches to semiotics ; 71.
        Includes bibliographical references (p.   ) and index.
        ISBN 0-253-20673-1 (alk. paper)
        1. Sex (Psychology) 2. Sex role. 3. Sex differences (Psychology)
    I. Title.
    BF692.R265   1992
    306.7--dc20
                                                                    91-6785

    1 2 3 4 5 96 95 94 93 92

Preface

There is something for everybody in this book. Human sexuality is a vast, fascinating, and disturbing realm. I suspect that most people approach such topics as female orgasm, penis envy, incest, the double standard, etc. with a mixture of curiosity and trepidation. Nobody is indifferent to sex.

Because of the universal human interest in sex, there is no shortage of theories on the subject. But in this book I attempt to make testable or falsifiable claims, that is, claims that are scientific in the Popperian sense (Popper 1959). I realize, though, that there is more to science than falsifiability. In order to come up with falsifiable claims, one has to speculate. There is much interdisciplinary speculation in the following pages, and many of my speculations have not been tested or perhaps are not yet testable. So the book is not science, properly speaking, but is headed in that direction. It is an essay in the etymological sense of the word.

The book is also not meant to be prescriptive. I do not advance a theory of what the relations between (and within) the sexes *should* be, now or in the future. I am only human, however, so the reader may detect now a trace of male chauvinism, now a bit of feminist tendentiousness.

I begin with female sexuality, focusing on the female orgasm. After arguing that female orgasm is a mechanism which helps a female to choose a male who is committed to her and to her offspring, I turn to the ontogenetic background of this mechanism and find that the female's experience of her father plays a crucial role. A female's ideal mate represents the devoted father in her past. But, complementarily, a male's ideal mate represents the mother in *his* past. One of the major behavioral features to emerge in hominid phylogeny has been mate-choice based on experience of the opposite-sex parent in early ontogeny. Various mechanisms have developed to prevent increasingly dependent young hominids and their increasingly attentive parents from engaging in incestuous relations, but the very inclination to incest has become the basis for adult mate-choice.

Having developed a psychoanalytically inspired notion of mating in to-day's hominids, I move on to the sociobiologically indispensable topic of altruism. Typically, though not necessarily consciously, a male renders altruism to a female and her offspring in order to retain access to her as a reproductive resource and to facilitate the survival of replicas of his genes in her offspring. At the same time the female — who is free of doubts as to the maternity of her offspring — is ordinarily expected to behave in a way that gives the male some confidence of paternity of the offspring. This she can do by emitting signs of being faithful to him, such as having orgasms during intercourse with him or being a virgin upon marrying him. The altruism he renders may make it worth her while to give off such signs, even if they are false (fake orgasms, fake virginity). He, on the other hand, is also capable of pretense, and may abandon her and her offspring after having appeared to her to be a good bet for long-term altruism.

Deception is not as rampant, however, as this sociobiological scheme would lead one to believe. Love, for example, has a role to play. I argue that love is one of the major mechanisms keeping male and female 'locked' together over an extended period of time, with the advantageous result that offspring receive various kinds of altruism from two parents rather than one. I try to show that both males and females acquire the knack of loving primarily from early interaction with their mothers, roughly at the same time as they acquire their 'mother tongue.'

Love and language have much in common in my theory (e.g., baby talk can facilitate lovemaking). But language turns out to be useful for a variety of other things too. Since most languages are inherently sexist, for example, they tend to foster male control over females. At the same time the speech of females tends to be more oriented toward eliciting altruism than the speech of males. Male domination thus goes hand in hand with a perceived obligation to render altruism to females.

After reviewing the abundant evidence for a power asymmetry between the sexes, I argue that the chief sexual signifier of this asymmetry is the male organ. A man has a penis, and he typically has power. A woman does not have a penis, and she typically does not have power. When a man's penis does not function properly he is literally im-potent, without power, overwhelmed by what psychoanalysts mean by castration anxiety. And just as a woman uses her orgasms to judge whether a man is a reliable altruist for her, so too a man uses his sexual potency to judge whether the altruism he renders is compensated for in the form of power over her.

Of course, some men may not be potent with women at all, and some women may not respond sexually to men. But I attempt to show that homosexuals too have ways of rendering altruism that are profitable for their genes.

The final sections of the book deal with two somewhat symmetrical phenomena: penis-envy in the female and male envy of the female's ability to have babies. Although the evidence for penis-envy is not nearly as extensive as that for male envy of female reproductive functions, I believe nonetheless that the two envies constitute yet another mechanism for 'locking' couples together and thereby making it more likely that their offspring receive altruism of maximal quantity and quality.

As I said at the start, there is something for everybody in this book. In other words, I have little respect for the boundaries between disciplines. Sexuality enters very many areas of human life, and I did not want to lose the sexual trail no matter where it led me. More importantly, the thematic and disciplinary diversity of this book is the result of a conviction I have steadfastly held: when it comes to sexuality, no one academic discipline has cornered the market on the truth (or more scientifically, the market on falsifiable hypotheses). Every major sexual topic in this book is therefore treated from the perspectives of at least three different disciplines: psychoanalysis, semiotics, and evolutionary biology. More often than not other perspectives are considered as well: physiological-anatomical, experimental psychological, sociological, paleontological, anthropological, linguistic, etc.

Most of the literature on human sexuality is of a narrowly specialized nature. This is to be expected, given the vastness of the subject. What bothers me is the academic provincialism that specialization fosters. Most of the psychoanalytic work, for example, displays an ignorance of neo-Darwinian evolutionary paradigms. Most Darwinians, on the other hand, have hardly the faintest idea of what psychoanalysis is all about. But Darwinians and Freudians stand to learn a lot about sexuality from one another. Likewise, psychologists can learn something from specialists in sexual folklore, anthropologists can profit from research on reproductive physiology, and so on.

In a word, I think the specialists in human sexuality need to communicate with one another, and a purpose of this book is to encourage such communication.

I cannot of course assume that any one reader has a knowledge of the diverse fields which are here brought to bear on human sexuality. Accordingly, I have provided some "Preliminaries" (pp. 1-62) which will help the reader get acquainted with basic concepts and terms in each relevant discipline. Specialists can without loss skip over those introductory sections that deal with their own discipline. The general or lay reader, on the other hand, will probably want to risk the tedium of reading all the "Preliminaries" before tackling *Signs of the Flesh* proper.

Some portions of this book appeared in earlier versions in the following journals: *Psychoanalysis and Contemporary Thought, Journal of Social and Biological Structures, Versus: quaderni di studi semiotici, Ars semeiotica,* and *Academe.*

It is a pleasure to acknowledge the assistance I received from many people while writing. Most important to me were the comments of someone who will be referred to as "my lawyer" in the text. She is Barbara A. Milman, who is in fact an attorney specializing in the investigation of political corruption, and who is therefore uniquely qualified to advise me on the sexual politics described in this book. Special thanks also go to Paul D. MacLean who has been encouraging my excursions into theoretical biology for some years now. Donald Symons and Michael Ruse provided very useful socio-biological comments. Allen Jossey-Bass and Thomas Sebeok deserve thanks for their good advice on publishing matters. Others to whom I am grateful for constructive oral and/or written criticism include: Richard Alexander, Robert Amorocho, Steve Armstrong, Glen Clark, Brett Cooke, Martha Cornog, Lucy Day, Gonzalo Diaz-Migoyo, Alan Dundes, Susan Erickson, H. J. Eysenck, Brand Frentz, Jim Gallant, Lynette Geyer, Ben Hart, Gordon W. Hewes, Bob Hopkins, Seymour Howard, Simon Karlinsky, Mary Keller, Melvin Konner, Karl Menges, Sarah Meyers, George Munro, Peter Richerson, Janet Shibamoto, and Harvey Wheeler. Faye Vierra of Shields Library helped me obtain some of the more obscure articles and books on human sexuality which are listed in my bibliography. Gay Baldwin and Heinz Fenkl made cogent comments even as they typed the manuscript. Finally, I appreciate the three successive years of faculty research grants which were provided by the University of California at Davis.

D. Rancour-Laferriere

February, 1985
Davis, California.

Contents

Signs of the Flesh

Preliminaries

A. Minimal Semiotics

One of the fields which potentially has much to offer to an understanding of human sexuality is semiotics. I will limit the discussion to only the barest bones of current semiotic theory. For further, more technical treatises the reader may wish to consult: Eco 1976; Silverstein 1976; Sebeok 1976b; Chomsky 1979. Those with great patience and a bent for highly abstract reasoning will find rewarding the *Collected Papers* (1965-66) of the great American pioneer in logic and semiotics, Charles Sanders Peirce (1839-1914).

Semiotics is not an easy thing to define. Some say it is a fad. They are correct, but it is not only a fad. Some say it is a field. But it is really too early to support such a claim. Some say it is a fraud. But who would seriously believe that there exists an international conspiracy to perpetrate fraudulent scholarship?

Semiotics is not new. It may be a fad, but it is not new. It is in fact an old topic which, having lain dormant for centuries, is now receiving new vigor. It goes back at least as far as a gentleman of the Stoic persuasion named Chrysippus, who lived during the third century before the birth of Christ.

One of the things the Stoics were interested in was how the world is represented by human beings to other human beings. According to the Stoics, representations of objects and events in the world are *signs.* Semiotics is the study of signs, i.e., of those entities which effect communication between interpreters of signs. Quite a variety of things can function as signs. A word, a sentence, a gesture, a facial expression, a photograph, a diagram, etc., are all signs because we, their interpreters, are more concerned with what they stand for or represent than with what they are merely in themselves. Semiotics thus does not study any particular thing — the way a mineralogist, for example, studies specifically rocks and minerals, or a biologist studies specifically living organisms — rather, semiotics studies a wide variety of things, but only insofar as they enter into a relationship in which they stand for something else.

The Stoics seem to have been the first to invent a terminology for the various events and processes which take place when something is used to stand for something else. Perhaps the most interesting is the Stoic notion of *lekton,* which basically refers to the hidden process which must take place in an interpreter when one thing (*sēmaion*) is understood to take the place of or represent another thing (*tugchanon*). This process permits the interpreter to make what would otherwise (in a nonsemiotic situation) be the absurd assumption that one thing somehow *is* another thing. Evidently the Stoics thought of the *lekton* as a quite concrete or physical process, however hidden from direct view. It was definitely not an idea or concept. The noted neurophysiologist Warren McCulloch put it, "what's in the brain is the Stoic *lekton*" (1965, 390).

This latter claim, which is of a type that tends to horrify professors of philosophy, pretty accurately represents what is happening at one segment of the leading edge of semiotics today. Researchers into the problem of aphasia, for example, have been able to make some very specific correlations between defects in the use of *verbal signs* and lesions in brain tissue (e.g., Geschwind 1970; below, section 33). Or, to take a *nonverbal sign,* it has been found that display of the erect penis, which is a sign of dominance and aggression in such primates as squirrel monkeys, is controlled by very precisely specifiable brain areas (MacLean 1973a). Such specifically neuro-behavioral discoveries as these are important to the semiotician, though they are often made by researchers who have no particular interest in the theory of signs. Indeed a wide variety of researchers — neurologists, linguists, ethologists, anthropologists, sociobiologists, psychologists, philosophers, literary theoreticians, language pedagogues, and others — are constantly finding out things that are relevant to semiotics. Just as a medical researcher interested in a cure for cancer might make a real contribution to theoretical biology, or the biographer of a novelist might stumble on some important fact for the literary scholar who studies the works of that novelist, so too a scholar engaged in some not particularly semiotic enterprise might discover something of direct relevance to semiotics. The difference is that semioticians seem to practice this kind of "parasitism" more extensively than do other kinds of scholars, especially since the academic scene today is compart-mentalized in such a way as usually to exclude a specifically semiotic compartment (for more on the politics of semiotics in American academia, see Laferrière 1979).

The proper object of semiotic scrutiny is the sign. Colors, for example, can be signs. Biologists know that the perceived green color of a leaf is in some sense a "sign" of chlorophyll in the leaf. Chemists know that the blue color of litmus in some sense "signifies" an alkaline solution. Astronomers know that a red shift in the spectrum of light emanating from a star is in some sense a "sign" that the star is moving away. But biologists, chemists, astronomers, and various other scientists are "semioticians" only in a rather banal meaning of the word. The relationships these scientists study can perfectly well exist without them, i.e., without interpreters to semioticize such relationships.

Not so with the relationships studied by the professional semiotician. The latter is interested in the functioning of signs in an interpreter (or interpreters) other than himself (unless he is studying himself objectively, as another interpreter). Thus, for example, a semiotician might study how biologists make connections between the colors of leaves and their notions of the chemicals in the leaves. That is, it is possible to do a semiotics of scientific interpretation. More commonly, however, the semiotician studies signs that are imputed within a complex cultural code rather than signs which result from scientific discoveries. Thus a semiotician might take an interest in how the color green came to be associated with the command "go!" at a traffic intersection. Or he may try to determine how and why green came to represent the psychological state of envy in English (cf. Russian, which uses green to represent fury instead, as in "On pozelenel ot zlosti" ["He turned green with fury"]). Or he might become interested in why so many of the characters portrayed in Chagall's paintings have green faces (*I and the Village, The Poet, Jew in Green, The Green Violinist*, etc.).

The essential ingredient in the semiotician's studies, as opposed to the studies of a biologist, a chemist, etc., is the interpreter. Whereas light of a wavelength perceivable as green is related to chlorophyll, whether or not the biologist is present, such light does not signify "go!" at a traffic intersection unless there is an interpreter present behind the wheel of an automobile entering that intersection. No semiosis takes place in the absence of an interpreter. The tree falls in the forest whether or not an interpreter is present, but the fall does not *signify* anything without an interpreter. Semiotics, then, is not merely the study of signs, but is the study of how interpreters actualize the many potential semiotic relationships that exist in the universe.

If semiotic theory is going to be applied specifically to the subject of human sexuality, a few terminological clarifications first have to be made. But this is not an easy thing to do, given the exceedingly complex history of semiotic theorizing across a number of different cultures and languages — from the Stoics, the Medieval Schoolmen, Locke, Peirce, de Saussure, Morris, and a number of other historical figures right down to the present-day babel of terminologies emanating from the Soviet semioticians, the Parisian Left-Bank school, the American neo-Peirceans, etc. To be frank, much of what passes for "semiotics" today is unfalsifiable fluff, and not at all what E.O. Wilson called it in his famous introduction to sociobiology, i.e., "the *scientific* study of communication" (1975, 594, emphasis added). I therefore intend to use semiotic terminology very sparingly, and to recur to just a few very simple but important and widely accepted semiotic notions such as:

1) A *sign* is anything that can be used to stand for or represent something else – *aliquid stat pro aliquo,* in the transparent formulation of the Medieval Schoolmen.

2) A sign that stands for something else by reason of a perceived similarity is termed an *icon.* Examples: drawings, photographs, diagrams, imitative gestures, onomatopoetic words.

3) A sign that stands for something else because of some relationship of existential contiguity to that something else is termed an *index.* Examples: the act of pointing, use of past tense, use of words such as "here," "there," personal pronouns, etc.

4) A sign that stands for something else purely by convention is a *symbol.* Examples: most of the words in language (including nouns, adjectives, verbs minus tense, pronouns minus indexicality, etc.).

5) In much of the semiotic literature a sign is understood to be the union of both that which does the signifying (called a *signifier* [cf. Latin *signans,* French *signifiant*]) and that which is signified (called the *signified* [cf. Latin *signatum,* French *signifié*]). I will simply use the English terminology – signifier vs. signified – and will sometimes use "sign" interchangeably with "signifier".

6) The entity which is responsible for relating the signifier to the signified is called the *interpreter.* In this book the interpreters of primary interest will be evolving hominids, including humans.

7) The internal (i.e., mental or neurophysiological) correlates of the signifier and signified in the interpreter will not be of much concern in this book, though they do exist and probably have been acted upon by natural selection in the course of hominid evolution. For example, if a woman perceives her mate as an icon of her father, then there must have been internal schemata (the Stoic *lecta*?; the neurologist's cell assemblies or holographic juncture patterns?) which have been selected for to produce such a perception in significant numbers of females.

The professional semiotician will of course recognize that I have made some extreme simplifications here, and have left out much. However, Peirce's fundamental trichotomy of icon/index/symbol is still recognizable, as is Saussure's dyadic conception of the sign. When necessary – e.g., when I attempt to relate linguistic complexities to human sexuality – more terms will be introduced. Otherwise I will proceed with a minimal load of semiotic vocabulary.

B. The Evolutionary Perspective

Semiotics can be a big help for understanding human sexuality as it exists today, but today's sexuality is only one result of several million years of progressive biological (and eventually cultural) change in the hominid line. An evolutionary as well as a semiotic perspective is necessary for understanding how today's hominids engage in sexual relationships.

Various components of hominid sexual behavior, including sexual signs, had to have been under the influence of natural selection over long periods of geologic time. At the very least natural selection has insured that sexual behavior took place in our hominid ancestors — else we obviously would not be here. Genital sexuality, in other words, is at least partially under the control of genes, though such an assertion also implies partial control by environmental circumstances in the development (ontogeny) of the individual as well.

This brings up the old problem of genes vs. environment ("nature vs. nurture"). No evolutionist believes that a gene completely "determines" a structure or function, because every single structure and function in an organism, no matter how "close" to genes, exists in an environment, including the remaining structures and functions of the organism itself. Thus a standard textbook on evolutionary theory defines evolution in terms of both genes and environment: "organic evolution is a series of partial or complete and irreversible transformations of the genetic composition of populations, based principally on altered interactions with their environment" (Dobzhansky *et al.* 1977, 8).

Sociobiology is a form of evolutionary biology that has recently elicited some sharp debate on the gene/environment dichotomy. Sociobiologists like to say that various social behaviors are "determined" by genes. For example, the leading spokesman for sociobiology today, E. O. Wilson, speaks of the genes which "determine" altruistic or beneficient acts in humans (1976, 342). To this Ashley Montagu objects:

But do genes "determine" altruistic acts? They may do so in insects on which Wilson is an authority, but as an anthropologist I consider it more than doubtful that they do so in humans. Surely, common experience tells us that some individuals are quite incapable of an altruistic act, and that variability in this is as great as it is in any other human behavior?
... as Harlow and his co-workers have shown, monkeys who have been isolated or inadequately socialized are, in later life, altogether wanting in anything resembling a capacity for altruistic behavior. The same is true of humans who

have suffered similar deprivations in infancy and childhood. That altruistic behavior has a genetic basis I have not the least doubt. I have repeatedly set out the evidence for this, and it has recently been confirmed in babies and infants whose altruistic behavior has long been known to some if not to others. What is, however, clear is that environmental factors play a decisive role in determining whether such behaviors will be developed or not. (1980, pp. 6-7).

But this is sheer misunderstanding of sociobiology on Montagu's part. Thinking that he is rebutting a central argument of sociobiology, he is in fact restating what sociobiologists say. He is granting that genes are a necessary but not sufficient condition for human altruism. Environmental factors are also crucial. Yet any evolutionary biologist, including a sociobiologist, will grant the importance of environment in the development of something that is "determined" by genes. Contrary to what Burian (1981-2, 49) says, sociobiology can have "bite" and still permit the environment to play a decisive role: "... if sociobiology is to be of any general interest, it must maintain that the behaviors it studies are rather tightly controlled by the genetic constitution of the organism under investigation" (*ibid.*, 62). This statement is false because 1) sociobiology, judging from the proliferation of publications alone, has proven to be of "general interest," and 2) it has done so without, in the majority of instances, claiming that behaviors are "tightly controlled" by genes (cf. Hardin 1978, 185).

What could be more genetically "determined," for example, than the structure of the human eye? Yet that structure can be modified to the point of blindness if there just happens to be an overabundance of oxygen in the *environment* of the newborn child. Or, to take an example more relevant to the subject matter of this book: the ejaculation of semen from the penis is something that is obviously "programmed" to occur when the erect penis is in the vagina, yet there are in fact quite a few contextual and developmental circumstances that prevent ejaculation from occurring in a vagina (see section 45, below).

Everything about an organism develops only within certain environmental limits. What Montagu and other anti-sociobiologists (e.g., Sayers 1982, ch. 4) tend to overlook is something sociobiologists and psychologists studying human evolution call "prepared" (or "primed") learning (e.g., Seligman and Hager 1972; Wilson 1978), or what ethologists call "a faculty to acquire" (see Reynolds 1981, 22). Human altruism, for example, is "primed" by the genes in such a way that the human organism (in significant numbers, and in a typical environment for ontogeny) is following the path of least selective resistance in developing altruistic traits.[1] Put differently, altruistic features

---

1. As Alexander (1979b, 120) points out, Wilson is occasionally guilty of playing down

may be controlled by an "open" genetic program (cf. Mayr 1982, 598-99). Some individuals may in fact do little to benefit others at their own personal expense, but the sociobiologists argue that it is in part genes that prevent such things from happening in uncharacteristically large numbers (see Alexander 1979b, 89ff. and Pulliam and Dunford 1980 for particularly clear discussions of the heritability versus learnability of traits).

Another controversial topic raised by the evolutionists is adaptation. As I see it, to take an evolutionary approach to human sexuality is, among other things, to be inclined to look for the adaptive value of observable sexual behaviors and attitudes. In other words: how might a given sexual trait in the present possibly have resulted from natural selection in the past? Darwin of course did not believe that natural selection was the *only* means whereby organisms change over geologic time. As Gould and Lewontin have shown (1984 [1978]), there are alternatives to the "adaptationist programme" in evolutionary biology. One can, for example, attempt to explain a given instance of change as due to genetic drift, allometrical correlation, phenotypic plasticity, or some other non-selective process. But Darwin did believe that natural selection was the *main* means of evolutionary modification, and I think it especially useful to ask how a cross-culturally typical sexual trait *might* have been produced by natural selection. There may not necessarily be an answer to the question. But the question itself can lead to considerations that might otherwise not have been raised. Also, in many cases the question is worthwhile if only because it is being asked for the first time. For example, no one has apparently ever thought about castration anxiety in adaptationist terms before. This is true not only because evolutionists tend to be ignorant of psychoanalysis, but also because the subject mater itself is quite repulsive. It is difficult to have a theory — never mind an adaptationist theory — about something that tends to be unthinkable. It behooves the scholar of human sexual evolution to ask again and again: Am I abandoning the search for an adaptive explanation of feature X because the explanation is inherently unwarranted, or because I would just rather not have to think about feature X? Trying to understand why men have such powerful feelings about their own penises is not quite the same thing as trying to explain the zig-zag commissures of clams.

---

developmental processes which "prime" an organism in the direction of a behavioral trait as much as genes do. In other words, Wilson's practice is not always perfectly consistent with what, ideally, sociobiology ought to be (cf. Barkow 1980, 178). I would not (nor would Alexander) throw out the sociobiological baby with this particular wash, however — any more than I would throw out psychoanalysis because Freud did not always follow certain ideals of psychoanalysis.

Some critics of the adaptationist approach like to ridicule the "just-so stories" told by their colleagues (see Gould 1980). But, as a literary scholar, it is my impression that all scientists tell stories. What is a scientific research article, if not a story? The narrative character of the historical sciences is especially indispensable. Anyone who attempts to narrate the evolution of something over geologic time is telling a story. For Gould to borrow Kipling's pejorative epithet "just-so" is only to indicate disapproval of certain kinds of stories. But a story is not falsified by scorn. It is falsified by other stories. In particular, a given adaptationist story stands until falsified by the evidence embedded in another story — including a non-adaptationist story, if such can be created. In the end, evolutionary biology is the survival of the fittest story.

C. Sociobiology and Psychoanalysis

If sociobiologists sometimes convey the mistaken idea that everything in an individual's life is controlled only by the complement of genes present at conception, psychoanalysts often convey an erroneous notion that everything in an individual's psychical life is controlled only by events that have taken place by about age five (the end of the "Oedipal" phase). But although the impressions people get on these matters are mistaken in similar ways, there are in fact some substantial similarities and overlaps between sociobiology and psychoanalysis. It is no accident that much of the theory of human sexuality developed in this book draws heavily on these two fields in particular. The best in psychoanalytic thinking, like the best in sociobiological thinking, recognizes the importance of both genes and environment. The British analyst D. W. Winnicott (1960, 588) says, for example: "... the inherited potential of an infant cannot become an infant unless linked to maternal care."

E. O. Wilson declares that "psychoanalytic theory appears to be exceptionally compatible with sociobiological theory" (1977, 135; cf. Ruse 1979, 186). In agreement, the historian of science Frank Sulloway claims that Wilson's pathbreaking treatise *Sociobiology: The New Synthesis* (1975), "despite its differing theoretical premises, is fully in keeping with the general spirit of Freud's own views on social behavior" (1979, 367). Similarly, the sociobiologist David Barash writes that "there are several interesting parallels between [Freud's] thought and the theories of modern sociobiology" (1979, 213). From a somewhat different perspective, the psychiatrist Robert Jay Lifton speaks of an "interesting convergence of ideas" between his own psychoanalytically grounded theory of "biological immortality" and Wilson's evolutionary theory of "ultimate causation" (1976, 62-63). A curiously negative lumping of sociobiology with psychoanalysis appears in a remark by the anthropologist Marvin Harris. He attributes to both of them (along with structuralism) a "weakness" whereby "universal components of human nature are said to account for a remarkably variable set of institutions" (1979, 264). On the other hand, the anthropologist Jerome Barkow does not seem to feel that there is anything despicable in the fact that both sociobiology and psychoanalysis postulate *covert* processes behind a great variety of outward social manifestations (1978a, 7). Pierre Van den Berghe (1978; 1979) seems to be alone among the sociobiologists in categorically rejecting psychoanalysis.

It seems to me that there are basically two ways in which all biological (including sociobiological) and psychoanalytic theorizing can overlap. One way has to do with what Ernst Mayr (1961) and others (e.g., Wilson 1975, 23; Sulloway 1979, 365; Alexander 1978, 198; Symons 1979, 5) call the *proximate* causation of behavior, while the other concerns what these scholars call *ultimate* causation: "proximate causal analyses are attempts to explain *how* animals come to develop and exhibit behavior patterns; ultimate causal analyses are attempts to explain *why* animals exhibit behavior patterns" (Symons 1979,5). Proximate causal analysis takes the organism's genetic constitution as a given, and it applies at the level of a very short span of time, geologically speaking. Ultimate causal analysis, on the other hand, attempts to explain how (some aspect of) the organism's genetic constitution actually came into being over relatively much longer spans of geological time. The proximate cause of a wife's infidelity to her husband, for example, could be any one of a number of psychological or physiological factors in her, while the ultimate cause would be the genetic advantages of having offspring by a different father or possibly obtaining a better source of paternal investment in offspring.

A good example of an overlap of proximate-cause biology specifically with psychoanalysis is Chapter VII of *The Interpretation of Dreams*, where Freud (*SE*, vol. V) brings his knowledge as a neurologist to bear upon his new theory of dream processes. In this chapter Freud's conception of how certain parts (primarily neurons) of the human organism work is related to his conception of how dreams work. As Sulloway (1979) shows, Freud eventually abandoned such proximate causal analysis. But the impression Freud left in this area was great. Pribram and Gill (1976) demonstrate, for example, that Freud's theories are important even to modern-day neurology (cf. Konner 1982, 130-36; Rancour-Laferriere 1980).[2]

Sociobiologists engage in ultimate-cause theorizing insofar as they try to construct explanations of how social behavior evolves over geological time. Although it is not in principle necessary that sociobiologists deal only with

---

2. Probably the most important and most currently relevant of Freud's contributions to neurophysiology and neurolinguistics are: 1) the notion of cathexis (*Besetzung*), which is neurologically "the amount of local nonpropagated neural excitation which leads to impulsive, transmitted excitation only under certain special circumstances" (Pribram 1962, 264; cf. Pribram and Gill 1976, 63); 2) the distinction between two kinds of cathexis, namely the thing-presentation (*Sachvorstellung*), which is a neurological signified, and the word-presentation (*Wortvorstellung*), which is a neurological signifier (Freud, *SE* XIV, 159-215; Laferrière 1978, 13); 3) the distinction between primary process, which is a feedback-controlled neuronal discharge (error processing), and secondary process, which need not be feedback-controlled (information processing) (see Pribram and Gill 1976, Ch. I; Pribram 1978, 80-81).

ultimate causal analysis,[3] the most significant and interesting work in socio-biology has in fact been oriented toward explaining the ultimate causes of given social behaviors. That is, the best sociobiology has been evolutionary biology, and Wilson refers to his major book (1975) as "an attempt to codify sociobiology into a branch of evolutionary biology" (p. 4).[4]

But evolutionary biology is precisely the kind of biology Freud turned to after his initial explorations in proximate causal analyses (primarily neurology). In Sulloway's recent book *Freud: Biologist of the Mind* (1979, 361-415), there is a detailed study of how evolutionary biology helped Freud to resolve three major problems: (1) the nature of repression and morality, (2) the sexual etiology of the neuroses, and (3) the choice of neurosis as the central concern of psychoanalysis. Rather than trying to summarize all the evidence Sulloway amasses in his insightful discussions of each of these core psychoanalytic concerns (see also Schur and Ritvo 1970; Gould 1977, 155-64), I will point out the two (related) evolutionary premises Freud consistently reverts to in writing about them (cf. Waddington 1960, 158). The first is Ernst Haeckel's famous biogenetic law, which states that "ontogeny is the short and rapid recapitulation of phylogeny" (1866, Vol. II, 300; translated by Sulloway 1979, 199). The second is Lamarckism, that is, the belief that traits acquired during an individual organism's lifetime can be inherited (Sulloway calls Freud a "psycho-Lamarckian"; Freud's Lamarckism has of course been discussed by other scholars, such as Derek Freeman, Ernest Jones and John Bowlby). The following passage from *The Ego and the Id* illustrates how these two basic evolutionary premises infiltrate Freud's psychoanalytic thinking:

The experiences of the ego seem at first to be lost for inheritance; but, when they have been repeated often enough and with sufficient strength in many individuals in successive generations, they transform themselves, so to say, into experiences of the id, the impressions of which are preserved by heredity. Thus in the id, which is capable of being inherited, are harboured residues of the existences of countless egos; and, when the ego forms its superego out of the id, it may perhaps only be reviving shapes of former egos and be bringing them to resurrection. (*SE* XIX, 38; quoted also by Sulloway, 1979, 375).

In this conception, the id/ego/superego triad is a structural complex capable of registering the *acquired* features of hordes of ancestral egos

---

3. Wilson defines sociobiology only as "the systematic study of the biological basis of all social behavior" (1975, 4). The "biological basis" could presumably be either proximate or ultimate in Mayr's sense of these terms.
4. It is the consistently evolutionary orientation of sociobiology that chiefly distinguishes it from the older tradition of ethology. Alexander says: "in an important sense the Lorenzian ethologists never bridged the gap between evolutionary biology and behavioral analysis" (1975, 79).

(Lamarckism) and of *recapitulating* the phylogenetic development of these hordes (biogenetic law). Among the features so registered and recapitulated are what Freud called the "primal phantasies":

I believe these *primal phantasies,* as I should like to call them, and no doubt a few others as well, are a phylogenetic endowment. In them the individual reaches beyond his own experience into primaeval experience at points where his own experience has been too rudimentary. It seems to me quite possible that all the things that are told to us today in analysis as phantasy − the seduction of children, the inflaming of sexual excitement by observing parental intercourse, the threat of castration (or rather castration itself) − were once real occurrences in the primaeval times of the human family, and that children in their phantasies are simply filling the gaps in individual truth with prehistoric truth. I have repeatedly been led to suspect that the psychology of the neuroses has stored up in it more of the antiquities of human development than any other source. (*SE* XVI, 371; cf. Sulloway 1979, 386).

One could hardly ask for more explicit ultimate causal analysis. The question is: Is it also good sociobiology? Is it even correct biology?

Sulloway's assumption (and most biologists[5] today would probably agree) is that it is neither. Sulloway speaks of Freud's "erroneous biogenetic logic" and says that "Freud's theories reflect the faulty logic of outmoded nineteenth-century biological assumptions" (*ibid.,* 497; see Gould [1977] for a detailed study of the relations of ontogeny to phylogeny). Yet Sulloway also claims that Wilson and other sociobiologists are "rediscovering" many biological and psychological notions which Freud and his contemporaries took for granted. As examples of a Freudian "return of the repressed," Sulloway enumerates the following themes from Wilson's book *On Human Nature* (1978):

... The biological nature of incest taboos, with their intimate relationship to the genetics of outbreeding; the adaptive and hereditary nature of childhood phobias; the role of man's constitutional bisexuality in homosexuality; the importance of facial expressions in the biology of social behavior; and the theory that myth and religion are mass "illusions" helping to cement the loyalties of the group. (1979, p. 500).

Perhaps many biologists before sociobiology was invented did indeed repress

---

5. Outside of biology, implicit acceptance of the biogenetic law is still often encountered. Jerome Bruner (1972, 700), for example, makes some proposals about the evolution of language on the basis of language development in the child. Even sociobiologists (e.g. Crook 1980, 140) will occasionally suggest that ontogeny can be used as an indicator of phylogenetic stages. Konner points out that the grain of truth in the biogenetic law is that "... ontogeny recapitulates not the adult phases of ancestral forms but, to some extent, the early ontogeny of these forms" (1981, 15).

these topics, and perhaps sociobiology is to some extent reinventing the psychoanalytic wheel. But not *all* of the "pre-sociobiological" biologists were isolated from psychoanalysis. For example, *The Ethical Animal* (1960), by the British geneticist C. H. Waddington, has an entire chapter devoted to a careful consideration of the psychoanalysis of ethical behavior. Another example is the classic book *Mankind Evolving* (1962), where the evolutionary biologist Theodosius Dobzhansky devotes several pages to psychoanalysis (pp. 63-68). He states: "despite the frankly environmentalist bias of many of its [psychoanalysis'] exponents, the discoveries of Freud and his successors are probably amenable to interpretation in agreement with concepts of modern genetics" (66); "psychoanalytic or depth psychology and genetics are not necessarily incompatible despite the fact that the contrary opinion is rather widespread in psychoanalytic circles" (64). By "contrary opinion" Dobzhansky is suggesting, in his non-Freudian language, the possibility that psychoanalysts have been repressing biology (especially genetics) for a long time (with a few exceptions, such as Sandor Ferenczi and Lipot Szondi).

It is of course rather comical to think that psychoanalysts, the supreme theoreticians of repression, should have repressed so important an entity (the anti-biology of the so-called "French Freud" school of Lacan, Derrida, and others is the most extreme example [see Rancour-Laferriere 1980]). Yet repression is what seems to have taken place, for how else are we to explain the deletion of biology from so much of psychoanalytic theory after Freud? At the heart of psychoanalysis, as Freud conceived it, was biology: "we must recollect that all our provisional ideas in psychology will presumably someday be based on an organic structure" (*SE* XIV, 78). Sulloway (1979) marshals an impressive array of evidence that Freud was a "biologist of the mind." The fact that Freud's biology was often "bad" ("outmoded" [Waddington 1960, 158]) biology is not enough to explain why biology disappeared from much of psychoanalysis (a biologist like Wilson is willing to take Freud seriously, even after having labeled his theories of the primal father, the primal horde, and the origins of the incest taboo as "poor" sociobiological hypotheses [1977, 135-136]). Freud's "bad" (i.e., Lamarckian, biogenetic) evolutionary biology no more makes Freud less of a biologist than Hippocrates' "bad" (from a modern viewpoint) medicine made Hippocrates less of a physician, or Ptolemy's "bad" astronomy made Ptolemy less of an astronomer.

D. Sociobiology and the Unconscious

> The proper study of mankind is sham.
> *Michael T. Ghiselin*

So both biologists and psychoanalysts have been less than receptive to each other's insights in the past. What sociobiology offers, I think, is one way to break down this barrier that has grown up between biologists and psychoanalysts. Or rather, sociobiology is in a position to serve as a kind of functional interface between biology and psychoanalysis.

Now, sociobiology is obviously open to biology. Most writing that claims to be "sociobiology" is by professional biologists. But is sociobiology really open to psychoanalysis (after eliminating, that is, the "bad" biology from psychoanalysis)?

A good test is to consider how the fundamental psychoanalytic notion of the unconscious fares in the sociobiological literature. I use the noun phrase "the unconscious" here, rather than the mere adjective "unconscious" (see Lifton 1976, 77). Even the staunchist anti-Freudian would probably grant that some acts involve "unconscious" components − e.g., aiming a spoon precisely at one's mouth, speaking a sentence that has a complicated syntactic structure, knowing ahead of time which foot will step up onto the curb on the other side of the street, etc. But to grant the existence of some *entity* that is somehow topographically isolated from what we consciously experience is something else altogether (see Chapter VII of *The Interpretation of Dreams*, nicely summarized by Foulkes 1978, 76-85; cf. also Ellenberger 1970 for a historical study, and Rancour-Laferriere 1980 for semiotic considerations). Behaviorists in the West, such as Watson and Skinner, could not countenance such an entity as the unconscious. The Pavlovians had little use for it, though recently there has been resurgence of interest in the Freudian unconscious in the Soviet Union (see the four-volume work *Bessoznatel'noe* [*The Unconscious*] edited by Prangishvili, Sherozia, and Bassin 1978). The Gestaltists, such as Köhler and Koffka, did not incorporate any notion of an unconscious into their theoretical edifice. Current cognitive psychology (as represented, for example, by Neisser [1967; 1976]) seems to have no intrinsic need for the unconscious as an entity, though Foulkes (1978) has made use of cognitivist constructs in his preliminary reanalysis of Freud's dream theory. Piaget (e.g., 1977, 55-59) pays only lip service to the idea of the unconscious because he seems to be, as Foulkes says, "relatively uninterested in the kinds of phenomena which fascinated Freud" (1978, 123).

But sociobiology is in principle at least capable of making the unconscious an integral feature in its account of human behavior, and is thus at one level a truer continuation of the psychoanalytic tradition than are many schools of psychology. Wilson says: "if the essence of the Freudian revolution was that it gave structure to the unconscious, the logical role of sociobiology is to reconstruct the evolutionary history of that structure" (1977, 135). In his speculative study of human sociobiology, *The Whisperings Within*, David Barash writes: "There seems little doubt that the unconscious, although poorly understood, is real, and that in certain obscure ways it influences our behavior. We can therefore predict that it is a product of our evolution, and, especially insofar as it is widespread and 'normal,' that it should be an adaptive product as well" (1979, 211; cf. Lockard 1980a). For Barash, the unconscious is one of the genetically programmed "whisperings within" each and every human organism. The unconscious has evolved basically as a result of the collective advantages of an organism's being able to *lie* to itself, and to others. If, Barash says, all the dangerous ideas stored in an individual's unconscious were permitted to become conscious (and to possibly be acted out) in real life, then that individual would in various ways be discriminated against by society, and would thus be less likely to propagate its genes than an individual equipped with a properly functioning unconscious.

J. H. Crook, in his sociobiologically oriented treatise *The Evolution of Human Consciousness* (1980, 279-284), sees the ontogenetic origin of the unconscious primarily in the conflict of the child with a parent (usually the mother). Most of the thoughts that would cause an adult to fail in interactions with other adults are already banned from consciousness before adulthood by the child in its highly charged, give and take interaction with its mother. Furthermore, since the child's brain (especially the cortex) is still quite underdeveloped in its early relationship with the mother, ontogenetically early experiences tend to be laid down in phylogenetically "older" brain areas, such as the limbic system, and thereby tend to be isolated from the consciousness associated with parts of the brain which develop later (note the recapitulationism implicit in this argument; see Lockard [1980a] for a different proximate model of self-deceptive behavior; Sackeim 1983 for a sophisticated combination of psychoanalytic and neurological perspectives on self-deception; Lopreato 1981 for an argument that the *soul* is one cultural result of the natural propensity for self-deception).

Richard Alexander says that there has been selection for those humans who repress from consciousness their fundamentally (i.e., reproductively) selfish inclinations (1975, 95-97; 1977, 134; cf. Waddington 1960, 172-173). Alexander arrives at a remarkable sociobiological reformulation of the psychoanalytic notion of *resistance*: "We can recognize a triple paradox that the only organism capable of at least a feeble analysis of its own attributes must use the very attributes to be analyzed to carry out the analysis, when a central one of those attributes is a rather strong tendency to reject the results of all such analysis!" (1975, 96; cf. 1979b, 4-5).

There are of course many species of animals (other than humans) which prevaricate in their relations with members of their own species or of other species (Sebeok [1976b, 143-147] reviews some of the literature in this area; see also Wilson [1975, 119] and Desmond [1979, 198-205]). Thus chimpanzees will falsely signal each other in order to obtain food. Carnivorous female fireflies of one species will falsely signal a sexual response to males of another species, and then devour them. The whole issue of prevarication in nonhuman organisms is very complex, and shades into that other traditional topic of evolutionary biology — mimicry. In Julian Huxley's classic book *Evolution: The Modern Synthesis*[6] (1942) biological mimicry is taken as one of the chief forms of evidence for the existence of adaptation:

The field worker rightly laughs at the disbelievers in the adaptive significance of mimetic or protective coloration or of threat behaviour. I have been deceived in Africa by the resemblance of a mimetic spider to the ants with which it associates; have spent vain hours on a Surrey common searching for a nightjar's nest, so perfect was the bird's cryptic coloration, before stumbling accidentally upon it; have nearly fallen out of a tree when a wryneck on its eggs simulated a hissing snake. That the examples of protective coloration, afforded by the leaf-insect, the woodcock, the dab, or the twig-like larvae of geometrid moths, should be hackneyed is no argument against their biological validity. (413).

The most elaborate form of mimicry in nonhuman organisms, brood parasitism in cowbirds, cuckoos, and other birds (Wilson 1975, 364-368), seems to rival even the human ability to prevaricate. Yet humans have an advantage possessed by no other organism: *language*. It is precisely because linguistic signs are capable of conveying much more (and much more complex) information than the semiotic systems of other species that it is also capable of conveying much more (and much more complex) misinformation than other natural semiotic systems. The sociobiologist W. D. Hamilton says: "as language becomes more sophisticated there is also more opportunity to pervert its use for selfish ends: fluency is an aid to persuasive lying as

---

6. From the title alone, Huxley's book is clearly a major "subtext," as the literary scholars would say, for Wilson's *Sociobiology: The New Synthesis* (1975).

well as to conveying complex truths that are socially useful" (1975, 135; quoted also by Symons 1979, 48; cf. Caws 1969, 1380; Sebeok 1976b, 144).

The key here is, I think, *persuasive* lying. When the organism lies to others, or to itself, there has to be complete sincerity (cf. Ghiselin 1980, 188). Any "leakage" of the truth is too likely to be detected by so intelligent a primate as a human being, and can ruin an interaction that is potentially advantageous for the liar. A mechanism for consistently making certain things unconscious appears to be just the adaptive device necessary to ensure sincerity. We can calmly go about the business of looking out for our own (genetic) self-interests, or of damaging the self-interests of others, if we can truly believe (and can appear to others to believe) that we are being altruistic (more on this term in Section E).

Of course it is easier to discuss the unconscious as a theoretical entity than to discuss concrete examples of the way the unconscious works. This is because the very examples are by definition likely to trigger the proximate mechanism which makes things unconscious − as Alexander (1975) understood. Sexual matters in particular are likely to set off the mechanism. But psychoanalysts have developed ways of dealing with materials which tend to make one, initially at least, "resist," i.e., drive back into the unconscious, those materials. I am not saying, however, that one has to actually have the experience of being psychoanalyzed ("didactic analysis") in order to think clearly about the materials in question. If truly interested, one just becomes "hardened" to the materials, much as one who is truly interested in human anatomy gets used to dissecting a corpse.

Let me give, then, a fairly mild hypothetical example of the kind of material I have in mind. An 18-year-old boy is typically programmed (genetically) to be sexually aroused, under certain circumstances, by attractive young females of his own species. But if he is in the presence of his attractive 16-year-old sister, it is advantageous to his genes that arousal not take place (see below, section 19, on incest avoidance). Evidently, if the boy and his sister have grown up together, such arousal is not likely to occur. I would suggest that part of the mechanism which inhibits incestuous advances by the boy includes the "lies" he tells himself (or others): "It was *not* my sister that I dreamed of last night" (negation); "It is really *my sister's girlfriend* that I am interested in" (displacement); "It is my *best friend* who wants to sleep with my sister" (projection); etc. All the "lies" the boy tells himself are probably just the linguistic tip of an iceberg of affective conflicts, but such lies probably make it much easier for him to live with these conflicts.

Or, consider the same boy's death wish toward his siblings, who competed for his mother's attention. Keeping such a wish unconscious, i.e., lying to himself, in some way helps prevent his ever carrying out the wish, i.e., exterminating duplicates of his own genes which necessarily reside in his siblings.

Obviously it would be possible to cite examples of other mechanisms of the unconscious that do *not* necessarily enhance genetic fitness. But sociobiologists work with relative frequencies of items in populations. Individual examples do not really prove anything, one way or another. But the task of classifying all the unconscious defense mechanisms (initiated with considerable precision by Suppes and Warren [1975]) and of then discovering their relative frequencies in the behavior of human populations is formidable, and is not likely to be accomplished in the near future. In addition, it will be necessary to construct complex hypotheses relating frequencies of unconscious defense mechanisms to gene frequencies. Only when this work has been done will it be possible to say for certain whether or not the unconscious, as psychoanalysts know it, is relevant to evolution, as sociobiologists know it. In the meantime, there is at least the pleasure of speculating on this topic, a pleasure that I freely indulge in here, and a pleasure that most sociobiologists thus far seem very reluctant to indulge in.

For example, such psychoanalytically familiar instances of the workings of the unconscious as those I gave above tend to be absent from the sociobiological literature. Most sociobiologists do not yet seem to have delved very deeply into the psychoanalytic literature. When sociobiologists do come around to discussing specific psychoanalytic claims, they are more often than not rejected. Thus Barash (1979, 70) includes Freud's theory of the Oedipus complex among those which are "woefully unconvincing" for accounting for the psychological differences between the sexes. Wilson rejects Freud's interpretation of human aggression as the outcome of (what Wilson characterizes as) "a drive that constantly seeks release" (1978, 101, 105: cf. Sipes 1973).[7] As pointed out above, Wilson also views the major premises of *Totem and Taboo* as "poor" (1977, 135-136).

I am not saying whether sociobiologists are right or wrong in these particular brushes they have had with Freudian theory. What I am saying is that they have not really grappled with psychoanalysis, or have at least failed to treat in detail any of the truly significant contributions of

---

7. Both Sipes and Wilson (not to mention Barash 1979, 214) appear to be unaware that, in his writings after 1920, Freud largely abandoned notions of tension reduction or drive reduction in his theorizing about instinct (cf. Sulloway 1979, 407).

psychoanalysis. And I suspect that this is at least partially explained by a failure of most sociobiologists to "harden" themselves against the materials that would have to be considered if psychoanalysis were to be taken seriously.

E. From Altruism to Identification

A frequently encountered topic in the sociobiological literature is *altruism* (or "donorism" [Alexander and Borgia 1978] or "beneficient behavior" [Clutton-Brock and Harvey 1976]). Much of human sexual behavior is related to altruism (or *is* altruism), and it will therefore be necessary to explain some of the current evolutionary thought on this matter.

Wilson defines altruism as "the surrender of personal genetic fitness for the enhancement of personal genetic fitness in others" (1975, 106).[8] At first glance, an altruistic act would appear to be harmful to an individual's genes, and therefore should be avoided. For example, a man endangers the future propagation of his genes when he risks his life to save another man. Obviously, however, human beings do take such altruistic risks, and so do other organisms, such as the bird that emits an alarm call at the sight of a predator or (less dramatically) the worker bee that does not reproduce. Sociobiologists who have dealt with these topics find that most cases of systematic altruism[9] can still be explained in terms of the enhanced reproductive success of altruists. The explanations are varied, and can be quite sophisticated mathematically. One type of explanation is the so-called kin-selection hypothesis (first put forward by Darwin in *The Origin of Species* [1859] and thoroughly developed in a series of papers by Hamilton [e.g., 1964]; see also Bowlby 1969, 131; Eibl-Eibesfeldt 1971, 59; Clutton-Brock and Harvey 1976, 200-202; Wilson 1975, 117-120; Alexander 1975; 1979b, 48 ff.; Dawkins 1979; Van den Berghe and Barash 1977; Ridley and Dawkins 1981; Boorman and Levitt 1980). An organism may risk its life for another

---

8. See Krebs (1970) for a survey of other, specifically psychological conceptions of altruism. Rushton and Sorrentino (1981) give an informative historical survey. Several scholars have noted the historical provenance of the sociobiological notion of altruism in Kropotkin's *Mutual Aid* (1902).

9. It should be kept in mind that the way sociobiologists claim to use the term "altruism" does not imply that an organism which is being altruistic is necessarily conscious of what it is doing or that it has any intentions or motives (conscious or unconscious) which may be altruistic in the sense used outside of sociobiology. As Symons remarks, "'altruism' [in the sociobiological sense] has *only* to do with the survival of genes" (1979, 51). However, as will become clear below, I do not agree with Symons when he says that "altruism in the ordinary sense has *nothing* to do with the survival of genes" (*ibid.*, 51). Nor do I feel it is necessary to restrict the ambiguity of the English language, so I will (along with Wilson 1978, Ch. VII) sometimes use "altruism" to refer to the emotions as well as to the acts benefitting others (see Midgley's [1978, 125 ff.] critique of Wilson's terminological ambiguities).

organism, but it is contributing to the survival of its own genes if it *shares* genes with the organism it is altruistic to. That is, selection should favor altruistic behavior directed specifically toward kin. A survey of the cross-cultural anthropological data (Essock-Vitale and McGuire 1980) shows that kin are in fact more likely than non-kin to receive assistance with no reciprocation (see also Alexander 1979b).

Sociobiologists like to tell the story of how J. B. S. Haldane replied to the question of whether he would give up his life for his brother. The famous evolutionist replied in the negative, but said he would be willing to die for *three* brothers, or perhaps *nine* cousins. The reasoning is clear: a human being shares half its genes with any given sibling, and therefore a net benefit would accrue to its genes only if its death resulted in saving the lives of more than two siblings. Or, in the case of cousins, which share only one-eighth of a given individual's genes, more than eight cousins would have to be saved to make such a suicide genetically worthwhile.[10] Sociobiologists do not of course imply that organisms (including humans) make conscious, intentional calculations in these matters (see note 9), or that real evolutionary situations are as starkly simple as Haldane's whimsical example. The arguments of sociobiologists deal with frequencies, percentages, and tendencies in sizable populations of organisms. Sociobiologists suggest that genes may program organisms to perform certain kinds of altruistic acts toward organisms that are likely to share genes. Such genetic programming would contribute to what Hamilton called the *inclusive fitness* of an individual, that is, " a sum of the consequences for one's own reproduction, plus the consequences for the reproduction of kin multiplied by the degree of relatedness of those kin" (Daly and Wilson 1978, 30). Altruistic behavior can enhance inclusive fitness not only by being directed toward immediate kin, but also by being directed toward members of a population who are more likely to share genes than others, or even by being directed toward individuals relatively unlikely to share genes but likely to provide favors in return. The latter kind of behavior is called "reciprocal altruism" (Trivers 1971), and is distinguished from symbiosis by the fact that it involves a time lag between the altruistic act and the reward (see Boorman and Levitt 1980 for an extensive mathematical/genetic treatise on the varieties of altruism).

---

10. Actually this explanation is an oversimplification. In fact a given human individual probably shares more than 99% of its genes with *all* other humans (see Essock-Vitale and McGuire 1980, 234; Dawkins 1979, 190-92). Dawkins explains: "siblings may share 99% of their genes altogether, but only 50% of their genes are identical by descent, that is, are descended from the same copy of the gene in their most recent common ancestor" (191).

Trivers calls human reciprocal altruism "the best documented case of reciprocal altruism known" (1971, 39). Wilson (1978) refers to systems of reciprocal altruism in humans as "soft-core altruism," as opposed to the "hard-core altruism" which operates in kin selection:

... in human beings soft-core altruism has been carried to elaborate extremes. Reciprocation among distantly related or unrelated individuals is the key to human society. The perfection of the social contract has broken the ancient vertebrate constraints imposed by rigid kin selection. Through the convention of reciprocation, combined with a flexible, endlessly productive language and a genius for verbal classification, human beings fashion long-remembered agreements upon which cultures and civilizations can be built. (156).

The price, however, of shifting from rigid, hard-core altruism to soft-core altruism is "a melange of ambivalence, deceit, and guilt that continuously troubles the individual mind" (159). Perhaps, then, whatever genes enable the human organism to have an unconscious (see above discussion of self-deceit) are contributing also to the human ability to engage in altruistic acts.

It may be noted in passing that the opposite of altruism, i.e., disruptive or maleficient behavior (including various forms of aggression, harassment, spite, selfishness, punishment, competitiveness, or anything else that might conceivably decrease the inclusive fitness of the recipient) has also been studied extensively by sociobiologists (e.g., Wilson 1975, 117-120; Hamilton 1970; 1975; Trivers 1974; Stamps and Metcalf 1980; Clutton-Brock and Harvey 1976; Symons 1979, 144-165; Freedman 1979; Hrdy 1977). I suspect that such studies will eventually throw much light on some important areas studied by psychoanalysts, such as the father-son competition within the Oedipal triangle (see Freedman 1979, 70), the child's notion of the primal scene, the common childhood fear of being killed by the parents, the competition of siblings for parental attention, etc.

It seems to me that the psychoanalytic notion of *identification* has much to do with the kinds of human altruism discussed by sociobiologists. The very identity of the growing child is, according to psychoanalysis, formed of a composite of identifications primarily with kin, that is, *with individuals likely to share genes*. The young child does not normally identify with adults who are genetically unrelated (step-parenting and adoption appear to be the exception, not the rule). As the child grows, its circle of contacts of course widens and identifications with genetically less related individuals become more and more likely. "Group identifications" (D. Campbell 1972, 33) develop, and these facilitate conformity to the values of various groups (see Campbell 1975, 1107; Barkow 1978b). But these new identifications often involve reciprocity. When an individual joins a group, for example, both the individual and the other members of the group stand to benefit. Genetically, the inclusive fitness of both the "joiner" and the other members of the group is enhanced by the various acts of altruism constituted by the activities of the group (however, not all the benefits of being in a group are necessarily reciprocal [Trivers 1971, 471]). The individual joining the group may be selfish in the genetic sense, i.e., may be oriented toward replicating its genes, but even this selfishness necessarily entails acts which appear to be "for the good of the group."

Using a remarkably parallel terminology, psychoanalysts say that the individual's "narcissism" has to be overcome and replaced at least for some purposes by "identification" with the group. Thus Freud contends that the individual effects "a reversal of what was first a hostile feeling into a positively toned tie in the nature of an identification" (*SE* XIX, 121); "social feelings rest on identifications with other people" (*ibid.*, 37).

To show how direct the connection between altruism and identification can be in humans, I will cite a clinical example from Anna Freud's revealing essay "A Form of Altruism." The patient in question recalls a childhood of always wanting to be *like* her older playmates: "her everlasting cry of 'Me too!' was a nuisance to her elders" (1966, 124). As an adult, she seemed to have no interests of her own. She was unmarried, dressed shabbily, and seemed to be primarily interested in helping other people. For example, she constantly gave advice to her friends about their love lives. She was devoted to her friends' children. She was ambitious for the men she loved. In Anna Freud's words, "she lived in the lives of other people, instead of having any experience of her own" (125). A particularly striking example, from a sociobiological viewpoint, is how her jealousy of her *sister* was transformed into altruism:

On one occasion it happened, as it had often happened before, that she found herself slighted. [A] young man called unexpectedly one evening to take her sister for a walk. In analysis the patient remembered perfectly distinctly how, from having been at first paralyzed with disappointment, she suddenly began to bustle about, fetching things to make her sister "pretty" for her outing and eagerly helping her to get ready. While doing this, the patient was bliss-fully happy and quite forgot that it was not she, but her sister, who was going out to enjoy herself. She had projected her own desire for love and her craving for admiration onto her rival and, having identified herself with the object of her envy, she enjoyed the fulfillment of her desire. (127).

Anna Freud says that such "altruistic surrender" (*altruistische Abtretung*) is not necessarily pathological, but is quite common in the everyday life of normally interacting individuals. What is interesting from the evolutionary viewpoint is that, when it occurs, the two individuals involved are likely to be related to each other.

But what precisely do psychoanalysts mean by "identification"? What specific components are involved, and to what class of proximate mechanisms do they belong?

F. Identification and Other Similarity Processes

Let's say that little Johnnie is picking up many of his father's behavioral quirks and wants to be "just like Daddy" when he grows up. At first glance at least two components of Johnnie's behavior can be discerned: 1) some of Johnnie's actions are imitations[11] of (or are at least intended as imitations of) his father's actions, and 2) Johnnie has a strong affective attachment to (dependency on, empathy with, love of) his father. The second of these components is as important as, and not the same thing as the first. In Freud's writings on identification "an emotional tie with an object" is always involved (Bronfenbrenner 1960, 22; cf. Yando *et al.* 1978, 23; 63-4). Imitation is a necessary but not sufficient condition for identification (cf. Kohlberg 1966; Parsons and Shils 1951, 129). Or rather, in view of what will be said below (section 16), the *intention* to imitate or to be objectively similar, even if objective similarity itself is absent, is a necessary condition for identification.

Freud himself never produced a definitive study of identification, though it repeatedly comes up in his works (e.g., *SE*, IV, 149-51; VI, 85-6; XIV, 240-58; XVIII, 105-10). Two particularly lucid surveys are Bronfenbrenner 1960 and Yando *et al.* 1978 (22-6, 63-4). The following passage from Bronfenbrenner's article indicates how various may be the entities with which the child "identifies":

At times, as in the example of the boy who identifies with a kitten by crawling about on all fours, refusing to eat at the table, etc., it is the overt behavior of the model which is being adopted. In other instances, as when Freud speaks of moulding "one's ego after the fashion of one that has been taken as a model," identification would appear to include internalization of the motives as well as the overt behavior of another. Finally, ... in his later writings it is not the parent's ego with which the child identifies but his superego, his idealized standards for feeling and action. In short, there are three aspects of the parent after which the child may pattern himself, the

---

11. Often the term "observational learning," rather than "imitation" is used in the literature (e.g., Kohlberg). I prefer the old-fashioned "imitation," since it seems to me that all learning involves observation, but not all learning involves the performance of actions on the basis of similarity. The other old-fashioned term, "identification," is a little harder to defend, since its meaning in the psychoanalytic literature has often been elusive, to say that least (see the critique by Bandura and Walters 1963, 91ff.). But I have retained this term too because what psychoanalysts describe cannot be reduced to imitation/observational learning only, and no one has offered an alternative designation for what psychoanalysts at least think exists (but see below, section 15).

parent's *overt behavior,* his *motives,* or his *aspirations* for the child. Which aspect of the model is in fact identified with becomes, from our point of view, an empirical question. (Bronfenbrenner 1960, 22).

Most psychoanalysts and psychologists would now agree that the very first identification (sometimes called "primary identification" − though this term has varying meanings) is with the child's principal caregiver, i.e., usually with the mother (see, for example: Mowrer 1950; Bronfenbrenner 1960; Lynn 1969, 21-3; Fairbairn 1954; Stoller 1968; 1976; Mahler *et al.* 1975; Sears *et al.* 1965, 156; Dinnerstein 1976; LaPlanche and Pontalis 1973, 192; Fisher and Greenberg 1977, 187ff.; Parsons and Bales 1955, 65-7; Chodorow 1978; Brunswick 1940; Balint 1954 [1931], ch. IV; Klein 1977 [1945], 417).[12] The first identification, moreover, is the foundation upon which the child builds an identity or sense of self: "insofar as the relationship with its mother has continuity, the infant comes to define aspects of its self (affectively and structurally) in relation to internalized representations of aspects of its mother and the perceived quality of her care" (Chodorow 1978, 78). Elsewhere (Rancour-Laferriere 1981) I have analyzed this sense of self as a "person organ" which has arisen by natural selection in the course of hominid evolution.

The core component of identification is *imitation* (even if the imitation may at times be incomplete or only intended). A variety of experimental studies shows that imitation in the broad sense − i.e., "motoric or verbal performance of specific acts or sounds that are like those previously performed by a model" (Yando *et al.* 1978, 4) − begins even at the stage of infancy. Meltzoff and Moore (1977) found that infants between 12 and 21 days of age can imitate such adult facial gestures as tongue protrusion, mouth opening, and lip protrusion. That is, without even seeing what they are doing, and therefore relying exclusively on proprioceptive feedback, infants can

---

12. For a review of the psychoanalytic literature on attachment to the mother, see: Bowlby 1969, 361-78. Bowlby tends to avoid the terms "identification" or "primary identification," preferring instead "attachment." In the semantics of associationist psychology, he focuses on the contiguity rather than the similarity component of the mother-child bond. Mahler too (e.g., Mahler *et al.* 1975) tends to emphasize the contiguity rather than the similarity process with her notions of "psychological birth" and "separation-individuation," which follow the "symbiotic" union with the mother (cf. Loewald 1980, 207-18). From a sociobiological perspective, incidentally, the reason for the infant's attachment to the mother should be obvious: "an infant who fails to attach to its mother dies; its genes get no second chance for evolutionary survival" (Gibson 1978, 446; cf. Weiss 1982, 181). But there are less obvious adaptive advantages to the infant's attachment, such as facilitation of later sexual and parental behavior (see Konner 1981, 9ff. for a clear discussion). Much of this book will in fact be concerned with ways in which the mother-child relationship is reflected in later, adult relationships.

reproduce something going on in the environment. Field *et al.* (1982) found an ability to imitate the three facial expressions "happy," "sad," and "surprised" in their sample of neonates averaging only 36 hours old. Another example is the four-month-old's known ability to follow its mother's line of regard to an object (Scaife and Bruner 1975). The latter behavior grows out of the infant's crucial eye-to-eye contact which helps bond it to its mother (see: Robson 1967; Stern 1974) and can later assist in primitive referential behavior, as when the mother names the object looked at and the child attempts to imitate her.

The great forerunner of current studies of imitation is of course Piaget's *Play, Dreams, and Imitation in Childhood* (1962 [1945]; Piaget's own forerunners in this area include James Mark Baldwin [see Broughton 1981] and Paul Guillaume 1971 [1926]). Piaget was apparently unaware that imitation begins very soon after birth. But his detailed work on imitation later in infancy (eight to twelve months and beyond) is still quite valuable and interesting. He discusses the transition from purely "sensorimotor" imitation to imitation that can be construed as semiotic, that is, as involving a fixed connection between one thing (a signifier) and the thing it represents (a signified). For Piaget, imitation is at the origin of semiotic (including linguistic) representation. The ability of the child to defer an imitation of something or somebody indicates that a permanent semiotic entity, the union of a signifier and a signified, is at work:

In a behavior pattern of sensorimotor imitation the child begins by imitating in the presence of the model (for example, a movement of the hand), after which he may continue in the absence of the model, though this does not imply any representation in thought. But in the case of a little girl of sixteen months who sees a playmate become angry, scream, and stamp her foot (new sights for her) and who, an hour or two after the playmate's departure, imitates the scene, laughing, the deferred imitation constitutes the beginning of representation, and the imitative gesture the beginning of a differentiated signifier. (Piaget 1977, 490; see ch. III of Piaget 1962).

One of the most striking manifestations of the child's ability to imitate, and one which Piaget did not study very extensively, is the acquisition of language. A child growing up in an environment of Russian-speakers does not speak Chinese. A child born and bred in Maine does not end up with a Texas twang. There is very likely a genetic basis to the ability to learn *a* language, as Jakobson, Lenneberg, Chomsky, and others have recently argued (cf. Rancour-Laferriere 1980, section II; for a readable and entertaining survey of research on language acquisition, see Aitchison 1976). But it is obvious that genes cannot program *which* language or dialect will be learned. It seems to me that the child's motivation and ability to learn *any* language that its parents happen to speak indicates the workings of genes other than those that might possibly be responsible for linguistic universals.

Anyone who has ever observed a relaxed mother-infant interchange (after the infant has attained the ability for eye-contact) will know how actively the mother engages the infant's attention. She directs a whole array of gazing, smiling, gesturing, and vocalization behaviors toward the infant — behaviors that would be perceived as quite bizarre if directed toward an adult, behaviors which often have the effect of encouraging the infant to repeat and intensify its own behaviors. And of all the behaviors which the mother directs at her child, it is vocalization which will eventually give the child its own most complex instrument for dealing with her and with other adults, i.e., the "mother tongue."

Well before the child speaks it is capable of making microscopic body movements that are synchronized with ('imitate') the rhythm of adult speech (Condon and Sander 1974). Beyond that, the child utters sounds (called "holophrases," or "primitive speech acts") that mimic the intonation patterns of adult sentences (Dore 1979; Ferrier 1978; Jakobson and Waugh 1979, 165; Crystal 1979). Bruner (1975, 10) speaks of this as the child's ". . . learning phonological patterns almost as place-holders, imitatively." The phonetic properties of the sounds produced by the child may in the beginning be very wide-ranging. But there eventually develops a "babbling drift" toward the parental language. The little babbler may by chance produce, for example, a consonant that occurs in Polish, but if the environment is Spanish-speaking, and if that consonant does not occur in Spanish, then it will soon disappear in the child's systematic efforts to imitate the sounds of Spanish. There will also be sounds that the child cannot physically reproduce until some later stage of language acquisition, so the child may often have to be satisfied with an imperfect imitation;

Recently a three year old child told me her name was Litha. I answered "Litha?" "No, *Litha.*" "Oh, Lisa." "Yes, Litha." (Miller 1964, 864; cf. Jakobson and Waugh 1979, 159).

For this child, the "th" sound is the closest approximation to an "s" sound that she is capable of producing, even though she is capable of hearing the difference between the sounds. That the "th" sound is here an *imitation* of the "s" sound ought to be clear not only from the behavioral context (where the child tries to repeat the adult word), but also from the close phonetic relationship of the two sounds. Lisa would not be expected to mistakenly say "Liba," for example, because "b" is separated from "s" by a larger number of what some linguists call acoustic distinctive features (see: Jakobson and Halle 1956, 20-36; Jakobson, Fant, and Halle 1955, 43) than "th" is (see Leonard *et al*. 1978 for more on the phonology of imitation). I assume that, as with other children, Lisa's imitation of "s" was eventually perfected, and that she developed an active store of systematically related consonants and vowels characteristic of something linguists call the English phonemic system (for more on the crucial role of imitation in language acquisition, see: Clark 1975; Rancour-Laferriere 1981, section 4).

Children are not, of course, the only imitators of other people's utterances. That adults imitate language is obvious from the existence of proverbs, TV jingles, political slogans, dead metaphors, frozen polite expressions, cliches, prayers, nursery rhymes, memorized poems and songs, etc. Our speech is full of fragments of the speech of others (what Baxtin [1971, 187] calls "alien words" ["chuzhaia rech"]).

One of the things implicit in the ability to imitate is the ability to perceive similarity. Little Johnnie cannot pick up (or intend to pick up) his father's behavioral quirks or plan to be "just like Daddy" when he grows up unless he possesses some notion of what "like" means. Such a notion is what I have elsewhere (Laferrière 1978, Ch. IV) termed a mental *similarity process*. Interest in similarity processes has existed in philosophical thought at least since Plato and Aristotle. It was renewed by some of the associationist psychologists (Hartley, Mill, Spencer) and was given a linguistic turn in the work of Jakobson (Jakobson and Halle 1956). As the two-week old infant's ability to imitate facial gestures indicates, there must be a "primitive awareness of similarity" (Restak 1979, 104) operating from the very earliest period of infant development.

The operation of similarity processes is prerequisite (or in sociobiological terms, *preadaptive*) not only to imitation, but to a whole host of other human behaviors. An example is the ability to make a metaphor:

> An aged man is but a paltry thing,
> A tattered coat upon a stick...

When William Butler Yeats made this famous metaphor (in "Sailing to Byzantium"), he was implicitly putting a similarity process into effect, a similarity process that can be more explicitly stated in the form of a simile: "an aged man is *like* a tattered coat upon a stick." Less sophisticated metaphors occur in everyday life (see various articles in Levin 1977; Ortony 1979; Lakoff and Johnson 1980), and are an essential ingredient of even the young child's language abilities, as when a child calls a river "a snake" (see Winner 1979). But whether metaphor appears in high literary art or in the primitive misnomers of a four-year-old, a similarity process is necessarily in operation (see Winner 1979, 486).

Some other areas of human existence where one may infer the workings of internal similarity processes are: perception of representational paintings, drawings, photographs, etc.; echolalia (and echopraxia in general); "sympathetic" or "contagion" reactions (e.g., crying, coughing, yawning, tongue-protruding, etc., upon observing someone else doing these things); empathy; agreement with one's interlocutor; postural echo (which often accompanies agreement with the interlocutor); utilization of tropes in everyday language or in literature (hyperbole, syllepsis, synecdoche, etc., in addition to metaphor); parody; acting; mockery; mime; dream symbolism; identifications; personification; homeopathic magic; trading, selling, buying, and other kinds of reciprocation; various obsessive behaviors, especially those which repeat ("perseverate") former (similar) behaviors or which represent (by similarity) repressed fantasy material. To be sure, this is only a partial list. The scope, the variety of similarity processes in human behavior is awesome, and has led the poets – i.e., those specialists in linguistic similarity processes – to proclaim that the entire world is but a "forest of symbols" (Baudelaire), or that "everything passing is but a likeness" (Goethe; see Laferrière 1978, Ch. IV).

What a mental similarity process offers to imitation is a necessary but not always sufficient condition for imitation to take place. The other necessary condition is (with some exceptions) an actualization at some motor level of the internal similarity process. For example, a mother may find that she cannot induce her child to open its mouth by placing a spoon in front of the child's mouth, but that when she opens *her* mouth at the crucial moment the child will obligingly follow suit. Not only has some process internal to the child registered the external similarity between the mother's opening her mouth and the child's opening its mouth, but that internal process is translated into the motor impulses necessary to perform the actual imitation. The internal similarity process (which may be thought of as a "plan" of action) and the motor act itself are typically both necessary. The exceptions are those instances in which the motor act is not quite complete (e.g., tongue movements without vocalizations in imitative "inner speech" [see the work of Vygotsky]) or is totally absent because of some inhibiting factor or defect. Unfortunately, it is not always easy to tell whether the imitative motor act is absent because of the curtailing factor or simply because there was never a mental similarity process or a "plan" to imitate in the first place.

Much more needs to be known about the brain mechanisms on which internal similarity processes and imitation in general are based. A very interesting first step is Paul MacLean's study of "imitative-creative interplay" of brain areas (1976). Evidently, very archaic ("reptilian"), evolutionarily more recent ("paleomammalian"), and very recent ("neomammalian") areas are all involved, depending on the kind of imitation. Elsewhere (1973a) MacLean discusses the possible implication of a portion of the limbic system in both the phenomenon of empathy (a similarity process related to identification) and visual aspects of socio-sexual behavior.

One more type of similarity process should be mentioned here, namely, *iconicity*. The action of icons is essential in human sexual relations, as will be argued below (sections 14-19).

As stated earlier in these preliminaries an icon is a type of sign in which there is some perceived similarity between what is doing the work of signification and what is being signified. The degree to which the perceived similarity is due to cultural conditioning (cf. Eco 1976, 191-217), other perceptual conditioning, or objective similarity varies from icon to icon, but the point is that in every icon an internal similarity process dominates (for general treatments of iconicity, see: Jakobson 1971, 347 ff.; Lyons 1977, vol. I, 102-5; Sebeok 1976a; Laferrière 1978, 44-64).

Here is an example of a sexual icon at work in a literary context:

> My love is like a red, red rose
> That's newly sprung in June....

Just how "red, red rose" manages to be similar to "my love" in this famous poem by Robert Burns is not immediately obvious, but the word "like" nonetheless asserts that there must be a similarity process of some sort in the beholder. That is, the force of the simile is to temporarily make "red, red rose" an iconic sign for a person called "my love." The simile tells us that the "red, red rose" is not related to "my love" merely by convention, i.e., that it is not a Peircean symbol, but an icon.

But what are the natural, non-conventional similarities between a rose and a woman ("my love")? Consider the usual color of the rose − red − as Burns emphasizes with two tokens of the same type in "*red, red* rose." What bodily parts of a woman are red? The only part of a woman's body that is even remotely suggested within the poem itself is the "oral" metaphor of music in the second couplet:

> My love is like the melody
> That's *sweetly* played in tune.

But let us take this hint more seriously. The mouth and lips, after all, are red. There is also the commonplace "rosy, red lips." The lips, of which there are two, have indeed an icon in the doubling of the token "red:" "*red, red* rose." But there are lips and there are lips. A woman has, and a man does not, something which Pauline Réage in *The Story of O* calls "the lips between the legs." By now it is clear that I am moving inexorably toward a "Freudian" reading of the rose in Burns' poem. For years the Freudians have been interpreting flowers in dreams, poetry, schizophrenic discourse, etc. as "symbols" (unintentional icons, if we adhere to semiotic terminology — Jakobson 1971, 702) of the external female genitalia (*SE* Vol. V, 374-7; Laferrière 1977a, 112). This proposed iconicity is even grounded, to a certain extent, in what biologists call analogy, for flowers are, as Freud pointed out, the genitalia of the plant. Furthermore, a related sexual icon seems to be at work here as well. Desmond Morris, in his writings on body self-mimicry says that the eversion of human (facial) lips is the clue that lips are functioning as an iconic sign:

It is this eversion, the turning inside-out of our human lips, that makes them unusual and renders them permanently visible. It has ... been suggested that our lips evolved as kissing organs, but ... apes can kiss well enough without permanently everted lips. The special design in the human case does appear to be a visual signal, rather than a tactile one, and it is worth recording that, like labia, the lips become redder and more swollen during sexual arousal and, like them, they surround a centrally placed orifice. (Morris 1977, 239).

Sexual iconicity can work at a higher level than this as well. If one body part can iconically represent another body part, so too an entire person can be an icon of another person in human sexual relations. More will be said about this, and about the interesting overlap of iconicity with Freudian identification (section 15).

G. Some Current Ideas on Hominid Evolution

Yet another thing that has to be done before offering more detailed speculations on the evolution of sexual signs is to briefly review how the hominid line is now believed (by some at least) to have evolved. This summary is based primarily on recent work by Lovejoy (1981), Johanson and Edey (1981), Johanson and White (1979), White (1980), Zihlman and Brunker (1979), and others.

Contrary to a belief long held by some anthropologists, even the Pliocene ancestors of the human race were already walking upright. There are two crucial finds to substantiate this claim. One is the remarkable 3.5[13] million year old "Lucy," discovered in Ethiopia by Donald Johanson in 1974, and officially taxonomized as *Australopithecus afarensis*. The shape and design of Lucy's knee joint in particular suggests to Johanson that she strode in a posture just as upright as in modern humans, though some specialists disagree, saying that her upright gait was somewhat of a shuffle due to bent knees and hips (see Stern and Susman 1983; Lewin 1983b). The second piece of evidence is a 3.6 to 3.8 million year old trail of hominid footprints unearthed in Laetoli, Northern Tanzania. These footprints (of two, perhaps three individuals) show a pronounced heel strike, with toes positioned directly ahead of the ball of the foot[14] — exactly as in modern adult humans.

Since it is traditional among anthropologists to classify a habitually bipedal ape as hominid, then the individuals who left these fossils had to be early representatives of the hominid line. Yet they were remarkably small-brained. Australopithecine cranial capacities have been measured at 430-550 cubic centimeters, less than half the normal range of 1,200 to 1,800 cubic centimeters in modern humans (cf. Holloway 1979 [1974]). Early hominids also had not yet invented stone tools. The earliest stone tools known are about 2.5 million years old, and are, according to some of the specialists at least, an invention of *Homo,* not *Australopithecus* (this does not mean the earliest hominids did not use such other tools as twigs, leaves, unmodified stones, etc., much as some of the great apes occasionally do today — see Goodall 1976; Parker and Gibson 1979).

The ecological conditions under which the first hominids lived is a subject of some dispute. Many theorists have regarded hominization as starting in

---

13. Or possibly 2.9 million years old, according to more recent studies (see Lewin 1983a).
14. This is an example of *neoteny* in the hominid line (see below, section 11).

savannahs and open woodlands (see Wilson 1975, 565-9 for an overview). But, although grassy savannahs have probably been the prime habitat for many representatives of the hominid family, there is now evidence indicating that hominids first appeared "in forest or mosaic conditions, or both" (Lovejoy 1981, 343). Mann (1981) believes that early hominids ranged (perhaps seasonally) over a variety of ecological zones. Isaac and Crader state their impression that the Plio-Pleistocene hominids ". . . ranged widely over varied environments, favoring terrain with a mosaic of swamps, grassland and woods rather than homogeneous expanses of forest or steppe" (1981, 89). The most distant primate ancestors of the hominids were themselves of course arboreal, forest creatures. There is some debate as to whether and to what extent emerging hominids were also still spending time in the trees (e.g.: Tuttle 1980; Stern and Susman 1983; Lewin 1983b; McHenry and Rodman 1980; Prost 1980). Parker and Gibson (1979, 371) believe the immediate ancestors of the hominids were "locomotor generalists, equally capable of movement on the ground or in the trees."

Judging from their dentition (molar dominance with somewhat reduced anterior dentition), as well as from their evidently diverse ecological surroundings, early hominids were probably omnivorous (as are in fact most primates today – Harding 1981). According to Lovejoy, among others, our ancestors were dietary "generalists" who spent much time on the move from one environment to another in search of a variety of foods.

The first hominids, then, were terrestrially-adapted, upright, small-brained, omnivorous creatures who probably were moving out of the African (and Asian? – cf. Lanpo 1980) forests and onto savannahs and diversified mosaics.

Not until well after these 'root' characteristics of hominids are established in the geological record do we observe the emergence of the two other key hominid features, namely, explosive expansion of the brain (see Gabow 1977 for an overview) and development of a complex material culture built largely around the semiotic system of language.

H. Some Sexual Consequences of Bipedalism

What does it mean, from the viewpoint of sexual signs, for a primate to have been walking upright for several million years? Conceivably, one could argue that everything that characterizes *Homo sapiens* depends, however indirectly, on the prior achievement of upright posture. Here, however, I want to consider only a few of the more direct and significant sexual consequences of bipedalism.

For one thing, bipedalism means a dramatic new potential for sexual signalling, or what is often in the biological literature called *epigamic display*. As Desmond Morris says, "because of his vertical posture it is impossible for a naked ape to approach another member of his species without performing a genital display" (1967, 85; see also Hewes 1961, 696 and Freud, *SE* XXI, 99 on the importance of epigamic signs in newly upright hominids). It should be noted, though, that it was primarily the male genitalia which were exposed by upright posture. Female genitalia went from being completely exposed (from posterior view) to being only partially exposed (from frontal view). But for both males and females the new upright posture exposed the whole frontal (ventral) area, making it a potential new source for epigamic signalling. Whereas a habitually quadrupedal organism does not, while standing, expose the ventral portion of its body to members of the opposite sex, an upright, bipedal organism potentially displays *both* ventral and dorsal portions of its body.[15] Thus, for example, a female biped can display both the hind quarters and, in the case of humans, a relatively enlarged mammary apparatus (more on this below, note 70). Also, in view of the fact that signs of aggression (threat, bluff) are enhanced by upright posture (see: Livingstone 1962; Hewes 1961, 696) then a new tie between aggression and sexuality has also been fostered by erect posture in the history of the hominids.

An interesting ontogenetic similarity to the phylogenetic enhancement of male genital display through upright posture is the fact that little boys start to take a great interest in their penises at about the same time (around the 12th-14th month) that they learn to walk upright. Mahler, Pine, and Bergman (1975, 104) say: ". . . the discovery of the penis, and particularly

---

15. Frequent upright sitting would also provide an opportunity for 'frontal' signalling. This is just what happens in mandrills and gelada baboons (see: Morris 1967, 71-2; Wickler 1967).

the important experience of its involuntary erection and detumescence, parallel the acquisition of voluntary free locomotion of the body." Ontogeny seems to be recapitulating phylogeny here, not in the classic sense of Haeckel (1866), i.e., not necessarily because of a genetically fixed propensity to repeat a phylogenetic event, but only because of a similarity of situations: how could an organism, early hominid or human child, *not* notice its newly conspicuous genitalia once it finally stood up?

I would like to emphasize that these consequences of upright posture (and they are not the only consequences) are specifically semiotic in nature. What, after all, is an epigamic display, if not the operation of a *sign*? E. O. Wilson defines "epigamic" as follows: "any trait related to courtship and sex *other* than the essential organs and behavior of copulation" (1975, 583, italics added). It is this very 'otherness' of epigamic display that describes its semiotic character. A signifier always has to be something other than what it signifies, even as it is doing the work of signification. An epigamic display is a signifier which refers to a signified defined by Wilson as "the essential organs and behavior of copulation." The manner of signification is not quite as remote as that in, say, the word "tree," where a certain monosyllabic sound tells the speaker of English about a certain object in the environment. Rather, an epigamic display is more like a threat, a promise, an imperative, a vocative, or other such complexes of signifiers called "performatives" by linguists (see: Austin 1975; Rancour-Laferriere 1980, 201-8). An erect penis, for example, or a wiggle of the pelvis is a signifier of something that may be about to occur, that is, a promise or an enticement. The penis in its function as a signal is *not* the same thing as the penis in copulatory action.

Even more abstracted from the realm of action is the *word* "penis." Or, to state the matter from a neurological perspective, the epigamic display of an actual, erect penis probably involves fronto-limbic or "core-brain" processing in both the addresser and addressee of this sign (cf. Pribram 1971; MacLean 1965; Rancour-Laferriere 1980, 213-15; and below, section 38), while the mere word "penis" entails only the usual left-hemispheric involvement characteristic of language (except in some of my more prudish academic colleagues, who cannot bear to hear even theoretical discussion of sexuality). Certain areas of language, it should be noted, do have an ability to elicit limbic response, even in the non-prudish. Thus the various slang words for a penis – such as "cock," "prick," etc. (see below, section 32) seem to have the unusual semiotic property of being both epigamic and linguistic in nature.

Another anatomical consequence of bipedalism in female hominids, i.e., forward rotation of the vagina,[16] made ventro-ventral copulation the rule. Ellis (1927-8, VI, 554) says: "the primary and essential characteristic of the specifically human method of coitus is the fact that it takes place face to face." Ford and Beach (1951) report that some variant of the face to face sexual position predominates in the 190 societies they surveyed. Frontal copulation makes it much easier for females to experience orgasm.[17] Perhaps this is why frontal copulation is sometimes practiced by certain other primates, such as the pygmy chimpanzee (see Savage-Rumbaugh and Wilkerson 1978). The zoologist Desmond Morris (1967, 72-4) believes that frontal copulation with, among other things, its enhanced potential for female orgasm (especially clitoral orgasm) facilitates personal bonding between male and female (see also Etkin 1954, 138; Endleman 1981, 83-5; King 1980, 191; Burton 1971; Campbell 1966, 258-60). I will argue later on that frontal copulation essentially repeats the face to face situation of mother and child, and that the adult pair bond in humans is basically a remodelled infant-mother bond.

One of the less obvious ways in which upright posture relates to sexuality has to do with hormones. Androgens, produced by the testes in males and by the adrenal cortex in both males and females, have a special relevance to bipedalism. It is known that humans excrete higher levels of androgens in the urine than rhesus monkeys and chimpanzees (Spuhler 1979, 458; Fish *et al.* 1941).[18] It is also known that androgens promote muscle growth, facilitate uptake of the sugar glucose in muscle, and increase sweat secretion rates. These effects naturally would make bipedal exertion more feasible (the ability of humans to sweat has been cited especially often as a factor promoting spurts of upright running in our ancestors). But androgens are also "libido hormones" (Spuhler) in both male and female humans.[19] Erotic imagery, erotic sensations, and sexual activity are enhanced in both males

---

16. The forward rotation is not entirely due to upright posture, but is also partially the result of neotenous retardation (see DeBeer 1962, 70).

17. Sherfey (1972, 125) disagrees, for rather complicated anatomical reasons. I do not think most women would agree that " ... the female prefers this [dorsal-ventral] position as much as, if not more than, the male ... " (*ibid.*)

18. Perhaps also humans have higher blood plasma levels of androgens than other primates. Wright *et al.* (1981, 165) say that plasma levels of testosterone are similar for humans, chimpanzees, and rhesus monkeys at comparable stages of maturity. I am not convinced that their charts show this for reproductively mature individuals, however.

19. It is curious that, before sex hormones were discovered, Freud had characterized libido as " ... of a masculine nature, whether it occurs in men or in women ..." (*SE* VII, 219). As it turns out androgens are now regarded both as "libido hormones" and as "male hormones."

and females by androgens. When women are injected with the androgen testosterone or with progestin (which has androgen-like properties), they experience increased libido (Money 1961; Bakke 1965; Hamburg 1978, 183; but see also Green 1979). In one experiment women's scores for self-rated sexual gratification correlated significantly with their own plasma testosterone levels (Persky *et al.* 1978). It has also been found that olfactory exposure to androstenol, an androgen derivative present in the urine and in the axillary sweat of men has an enhancing effect on female evaluation of male attractiveness (Cowley *et al.* 1977; Kirk-Smith and Booth 1977; but cf. Black and Biron 1982). Thus there seem to be some grounds at least for Spuhler's argument that, as hominids secreted higher levels of androgens and became endurance walkers and runners, "a side effect was the higher degree of continual sexual receptivity in hominid females" (*ibid.*, 461).

Another consequence of bipedalism is an effective separation of the sense of smell from the ano-genital area and its products. Quadruped primates, as a rule, sniff one another's genitalia during sexual encounters (the male is especially likely to make a prolonged olfactory examination of the vagina before mounting). Olfactory stimulation, like stimulation of the other senses, can take on a semiotic function. A male rhesus monkey can be 'informed' of whether a female is likely to be ovulating, for example, by a secretion of certain volatile fatty acids in the female's vagina (see Daly and Wilson 1978, 204-6). There are such substances in the human vagina (called "copulins" by Michael *et al.* 1975) which are probably the vestigial result of sexual chemistry in our olfactorily more sensitive ancestors.

It is of course easy for a male to make an olfactory examination of the female genitalia when his head is approximately at the same level with her pelvis. But with the attainment of habitually upright posture it would become necessary to lie down or get down on all fours to get a good whiff of what the female pelvic area has to offer (see Tanner 1981, 154), or to make a close visual inspection of the female genitalia. Also, upright posture makes it more difficult to examine odoriferous deposits of urine or feces left on the ground.

Given that upright posture has made it difficult for the olfactory sense to be as effectively utilized in a sexual or territorial context as it used to be, and given that hominids have never been the kind of carnivore that would use olfaction in other contexts, such as in the chase, then it is not surprising that the sense of smell does not have a highly developed physiological basis in today's hominids. Darwin spoke of olfaction as "enfeebled" and "rudimentary" (1885 [1871], 18) in humans. Nonetheless, the weakened olfactory sense does play a surprisingly large role in human sexuality. How can this be?

I. Upright Posture and Repression

> . . . and down they forgot as up they grew.
> — *e. e. cummings*

There are some exceptional individuals who are highly sensitive to odors. Ellis speaks of certain ". . . Asiatic princes [who] have sometimes caused a number of the ladies to race in the seraglio garden until they were heated; their garments have then been brought to the prince, who has selected one of them solely by the odor" (1927-8, IV, 66). The poet Goethe once confessed that, on a two-day trip away from his lady friend, he took her bodice with him in order to have available the scent of her body (*ibid.*, 74). Professionals in the perfume industry are known to be highly discriminating in their sense of smell, and the psychoanalyst A. A. Brill (1932) describes one perfumer who was formerly a *renifleur*, or olfactory pervert.

Perfume itself, which is made from oils extracted from plant genitalia, is used primarily by women. This is probably a cultural result of the biological fact that, in our olfactorily more sensitive ancestors, it was males who sniffed female genitalia rather than vice-versa.

Moncrieff (1966) has found that, although men and women generally agree on which odors are very good (rose, strawberry, sweet pea, etc.) and which are very bad (ethyl mercaptan with its sulphidy, fecal odor, trimethylamine with its fishy, ammoniacal odor, etc.), there are nonetheless differences in some areas. Men rank the musks higher than women do, and like the more complex floral scents. Women rank nutty smells and culinary odors such as bay leaf and onion higher than men do.

It is curious that today's human male seems to be generally less attentive to odors than the human female (Ellis, 86ff.). Part of this is probably due to a lower physiological sensitivity to odors in the male than in the postpubertal female (LeMagnen 1952; Doty 1976, 296-301; Hopson 1979, 114ff). But part of it may also be due to the fact that the male is typically less able to admit his sensitivity to smell than is the female. The occasional olfactorily-sensitive prince, poet, or male *renifleur* is the exception, not the rule. Males, for example, often find it difficult to comprehend that females can be 'turned on' by the odor of a sweating male. It may be that males prefer their females perfumed because they are disturbed by natural feminine odors. The male sexual ideal seems to be that she who smells least smells best, as in the ancient adage "*Mulier tum bene olet, ubi nihil olet.*"

In other words, the preference would seem to be for a woman who is not menstruating, not lactating, not sweating, and not careless about removing excretory odors (perhaps there are even some selective advantages in the preference for odorlessness — e.g., menstruating and lactating women are not likely to conceive).

Knowing how adverse a male can be to female odors, a female who wants to copulate may go to great lengths to remove or disguise these odors (or occasionally it is the reverse: Marshall [1971, 118-19] reports the case of a Polynesian girl who tested the devotion of her would-be lover by not washing her private parts for several days and then requiring that he perform cunnilingus on her before granting normal intercourse).

When I suggested to my lawyer that men are generally more repulsed by smells than women are, she ventured that women may be less squeamish in this area because they have no choice, not because they initially like smells better. For example, the mature woman who once upon a time was a fastidious little girl — probably more fastidious than her brother was — has *had* to learn to tolerate: cooking smells, her own vaginal and menstrual odors, the odor of childbirth, the odor of lactation, and especially the odors of continuously excretory babies and little children. It is women, not men who have constantly put up with those smelly creatures called "little shits" in a variety of languages (e.g., French "merdeux," Russian "kakashki"). Basically, every woman who becomes a mother goes through an olfactory hazing that a man seldom has to experience. Women learn to endure, and perhaps even to like odors, just as men learn to endure and to sometimes enjoy violence.

Of all the odors that can be produced by the body, the odor of feces (or, more specifically, a fecal component called *skatole*) evokes the strongest immediate reaction. This reaction is usually negative, and would appear to be an avoidance reaction that helps the organism keep out of contact with matter that is potentially harmful to health. Yet, Moncrieff says ". . . children up to the age of four will tolerate faecal odors without apparent distress, and the very young will even play with their own droppings. The same children, when they have reached the age of five or six will intensely dislike such smells" (Moncrieff 1970, 30; cf. Moncrieff 1966, 73). There are also adult humans who (often in the context of genital activities) practice the handling, smelling, and even eating of feces (the general terms *coprolagnia* or *coprophilia* refer to these practices — see Ellis 1927-8,V, 62ff. for some examples). Similar activities have been observed in captive non-human primates:

Chimpanzees often smear themselves with excrement, either their own or their comrades'. Here a curious point of contrast must be recorded. I have only observed one of this species who did not take to coprophagy during captivity (Koko, to wit). Nevertheless, if one of them steps in excrement, the foot cannot as a rule tread properly after — as would also be the case with us. The creature limps off till it finds an opportunity of cleansing itself, and that by preference *not with its hands* (though it may, a few minutes 'before, have lifted similar filth to its mouth, and refused to leave go, even when it was given sharp blows on the hand), but with twigs, rags, or pieces of paper. As the ape's behaviour and expression are plainly indicative of discomfort, there is no doubt that filth *on the surface of its body* is disagreeable to it. (Köhler 1959 [1917], 73-4).

Note the apparently ambivalent attitude toward feces displayed here. Psychoanalysts say that humans too have contradictory feelings about excrement: "anal eroticism makes the child treat an object, namely feces, in a contradictory manner: he expels the matter from the body and retains it as if it were a loved object; this it the physiological root of 'anal ambivalence'" (Fenichel 1945, 67).

In Captain Bourke's *Scatologic Rites of All Nations* (1891 — subtitled "Not for General Perusal") there are numerous descriptions which indicate a positive and not only a negative olfactory attitude toward feces. It is said, for example, that the Mongol Tartars mixed the ashes of yak manure with their snuff. Devotees of the Grand Lama of Tibet inhaled his dried feces as snuff. In many cultures there is an association of one kind or another of excrement with tobacco. I have explored some of the fecal implications of literary olfactory motifs in an earlier work (Rancour-Laferriere 1982, 80ff.).

In *Civilization and Its Discontents* Freud attached much importance to the separation of the emerging hominid's olfactory apparatus from the ano-genital region and its products:

... with the assumption of an erect posture by man and with the depreciation of his sense of smell, it was not only his anal erotism which threatened to fall a victim to organic repression, but the whole of his sexuality; so that since this, the sexual function has been accompanied by a repugnance which cannot further be accounted for, and which prevents its complete satisfaction and forces it away from the sexual aim into sublimations and libidinal displacements. I know that Bleuler ... once pointed to the existence of a primary repelling attitude like this towards sexual life. All neurotics, and many others besides, take exception to the fact that [as St. Augustine said] '*inter urinas et faeces nascimur* [we are born between urine and faeces]'. The genitals, too, give rise to strong sensations of smell which many people cannot tolerate and which spoil sexual intercourse for them. Thus we should find that the deepest root of the sexual repression which advances along with civilization is the organic defence of the new form of life achieved with man's erect gait against his earlier animal existence. (*SE* XXI, 106; cf. *ibid.*, X, 247; cf. Sulloway 1979, 369).

Freud, a Haeckelian recapitulationist (as we have seen), notes that in ontogeny the individual acquires a disgust for matters ano-genital, just as in phylogeny human ancestors at some point developed this disgust (*SE* XXI, 100; whether or not the recapitulationism is right or not, it is a fact that once upon a time, both in ontogeny and phylogeny, we did move about on all fours before switching to bipedal locomotion). Throughout the psychoanalytic literature it is easy to see that the notions of *sublimation* and *displacement* depend on the idea of a movement of attention up a vertical axis away from 'low,' ano-genital matters to substitute 'higher' matters (Freud's typical expression is "*Verlegung von Unten nach Oben*", i.e., "shift from below to above").

Norman O. Brown, in his famous analysis of "the excremental vision" in the works of Jonathan Swift, quotes the following passage in Swift's *A Tale of a Tub*:

For the *upper Region* of Man, is furnished like the *middle Region* of the Air; The Materials are formed from Causes of the widest Difference, yet produce at last the same Substance and Effect. Mists arise from the Earth, Steams from Dunghils, Exhalations from the Sea, and Smoak from Fire; yet all Clouds are the same in Composition, as well as Consequences: and the Fumes issuing from a Jakes, will furnish as comely and useful a Vapour, as Incense from an Altar. Thus far, I suppose, will easily be granted me; and then it will follow, that as the Face of Nature never produces Rain, but when it is over-cast and disturbed, so Human Understanding, seated in the Brain, must be troubled and overspread by vapours, ascending from the lower Faculties, to water the Invention, and render it fruitful. (quoted by Brown 1959, 196).

Swift's specifically olfactory formulation is what gives the 'vertical' orientation here. Whether it is "Mists," "Steams," "Exhalations," "Smoak," "clouds," "Fumes," "vapours," "Incense," or whatever — they all rise, making it unavoidable that what is 'below' contaminate what is 'above'. Even as sublime a word as "spirit" does not, in a Swiftian context, rise 'high' enough to escape its other meaning, i.e., flatus (*ibid.*, 197).[20]

Though the metaphorically vertical orientation is clear in Freud and in some of his 'Freudian' precursors and followers, the reasons for the repressive break in the vertical axis are not so clear. That is, *why* does vertical separation of the nostrils from the ground and from the ano-genital area of a conspecific necessarily lead to an attitude of disgust toward (or repression of) sexuality in general?

As I understand it, Freud at least hints at three possible olfactorily-related

---

20. In Nikolai Gogol's story *The Overcoat* the death of the hero is described in Russian as "ispustil dukh," which may be translated either as "he gave up the ghost" or "he passed gas" (see Rancour-Laferriere 1982, 68).

routes toward the repression of ano-genital matters in humans. The first is mere disuse of the olfactory channel. Since we (as adults) now walk around with our noses elevated well above the pelvic regions of our fellow-humans, and even further above the ground where excreta are deposited, then we are not as likely to be stimulated by the odors emanating from those low areas as our quadrupedal ancestors were. But if we are not receiving as much olfactory stimulation, it becomes easier to keep excretory and sexual matters below the threshold of consciousness (or, to modify an old proverb, it may be a case of 'out of smell, out of mind').

The second possible route toward repression is a neurological matter. Freud barely hints at this, though had he been younger he might have been more explicit, since once upon a time he had in fact been a neurologist (see Rancour-Laferriere 1980, section V). But more recently the neurologist Paul MacLean, who knows his Freud, has been successful in finding neuroanatomical correlates to the decreased importance of olfaction and the increased importance of vision in human sexual behavior. Much of MacLean's work has been concerned with the limbic system, which is known to play a role both in olfaction and in the expression of emotions. One area of the limbic system, known as the septum, is implicated in both olfaction and in "expressive and feeling states that are conducive to sociability and the procreation and preservation of the species . . ." (MacLean 1970, 340). It is known, for example, that stimulation of the septum in humans can produce sexual arousal (Blumer and Walker 1975, 205). Another part of the limbic system, called the third pathway by MacLean (and including the anterior thalamic nuclei), unlike the septum, by-passes the olfactory apparatus:

In the phylogeny of the primate brain, it is notable that the septal region remains relatively undeveloped, whereas the structures connected by the third pathway increase in size and become most prominent in man. Our brain and behavioral studies suggest that this condition reflects a shifting of emphasis from olfactory to visual influences in sociosexual behavior.... (*ibid.*).

In the squirrel monkey, electrical stimulation of *either* the septum or the third pathway results in sexual excitation.

Putting neuroanatomical and evolutionary considerations together, we might say that the existence of the third limbic pathway in our newly-erect hominid ancestors was a preadaptation that permitted sexual behavior to take place despite the decreased olfactory stimulation. Those neuroanatomical areas that did link sexual excitation to olfaction such as the septum thus became less necessary and did not need to develop as long as hominids stood upright. On the other hand, those areas which linked sexual excitation to vision, such as the third pathway, would have been under selective pressure to develop and become more elaborate.

In any case, such a clearly dichotomous neuroevolutionary development might easily be understood in Freudian terms as a 'repression' of specifically olfactory (and perhaps gustatory) information about excreta and the ano-genital area. Of course there exist other neurological models of repression or sexual inhibition (see: Gray and Buffery 1971; Blumer and Walker 1975), but the one I am suggesting is tied to specifically olfactory matters.

A third olfactorily-related route to repression involves the close anatomical association of the anal and genital areas. An already existing negative attitude of disgust toward what is anal or fecal is used to reinforce or even create a negative attitude toward what is genital.[21] All sexual matters become "dirty" or "filthy." As Dundes (1966, 103) says, "dirty jokes . . . are largely genital, not anal in content. Yet jokes about sex are called 'dirty jokes'." Animated reference to sexual organs and copulation is said to be "talking dirty" (cf. "foul mouth," "*copro*lalia"). Pornography is referred to as "filth" by those who disapprove of it. Conversely, leading the life of a saint, that is, leading a life of sexual (and other forms of) abstinence was once said to result in an aromatic and sweet "odor of sanctity," both during life and after death instead of the usual *odor mortis* upon death (Evans 1970, 774; Ellis 1927-8, IV, 62). Jesus Christ, customarily regarded as the epitome of sexlessness, was said to have a fragrant odor, while the devil, the personification of everything libidinal, was said to give off a hellish, sulphurous stink (Jones 1951, 184-5).

In sociobiological terms, if it is adaptive in some contexts to have a negative attitude toward genital sexuality, then the already existing negative attitude toward feces can serve as a preadaptation which promotes the negative attitude toward genitality. However, given that the negative attitude toward feces is apparently only one half of the overall attitude (the other half being a contradictory, positive attitude), then a positive attitude toward genitality is also reinforced (if covertly) by this process. For example, the more "filthy" a stag flim, the more the fraternity boys will like it. In any case, this kind of overlap makes it clear that, as psychoanalysts have always understood, a theory of human sexuality can never be *merely* a theory of genitality.

Freud postulated other routes to repression in hominids (cf. below, section 32) besides the withering and exploitation of olfaction (see Sulloway 1979, 368 ff., for a review; see also Foulkes 1978, 164 and Rancour-Laferriere 1980, 224 on the difficulties of defining repression). But the olfactory route to repression is, for Freud and for psychoanalysts generally, the one most closely associated with bipedalism.

---

21. Ellis (1927-8, I, 51ff.) and others have had similar ideas about the evolution of *modesty*, which is really only one aspect of what Freudians mean by *repression*.

Yet another connection of repression with bipedalism — and one which Freud does not seem to have noticed — involves considerations of energy expenditure. To stand upright, as opposed to sitting or lying down, requires a sustained effort. But it is a commonplace of psychoanalysis that repression itself requires an effort of some kind (called *Gegenbesetzung* or countercathexis by Freud — see LaPlanche and Pontalis 1973, 101-2). This similarity makes it possible for repression to be represented through analogy to upright posture. Thus in English a person whose erotic impulses appear to be repressed is said to be "upright" or even "uptight." Moral standards are "high" in the "upstanding" citizen, and an individual may be so "highly" principled as to appear "high and mighty." The very word "repress" (and the related "suppress") connotes an effort of pushing *downward*, which in turn suggests a forceful irruption of something unpleasant from *below*. Conversely, when the effort at repression is not made, moral standards are said to be "lowered," one is said to "fall," to "sink" to the depths of depravity, etc. In his essay on "The Upright Posture" the phenomenologist Erwin Strauss nicely captures this parallel between the cessation of the effort of repression and effortless, downward movement:

Because getting up and standing are so demanding, we enjoy resting, relaxing, yielding, lying down, and sinking back. There is the voluptuous gratification of succumbing. Sex remains a form of lying down or, as language says, of lying or sleeping with. Addicts, in their experience, behavior, and intention, reveal the double aspect of sinking back and its contrast to being upright. A *symposium* found the ancient Greeks, a *convivium* the Romans, stretched on their couches until, after many libations to Dionysus and Bacchus, they finally sank to the ground. *Symposium* means "drinking together," or "a drinking party." (Strauss 1966, 144).

The transition which Strauss makes from "lying down" to such unrepressed activities as "sex" and "a drinking party" is implicitly mediated by the notion of a decrease in effort or energy expenditure.

Perhaps the most important form of repression ought to be mentioned here: optimism. One temporarily becomes a pessimist just thinking about it. Ever since hominids have, as a by-product of their increased intelligence, known that death is inevitable, they have nonetheless given every indication of repressing this fact. That is, they have gone on living. This is remarkable. From the ancients onward, poets and philosophers have repeatedly said it is best never to have been born, and second best to die as soon as possible. Yet we are not typically suicidal. We know, intellectually, what will happen, and we are reminded regularly of what will happen by (among other things) the odor of our excreta. In releasing the odoriferous stool to the earth, our increasingly intelligent hominid ancestor must have understood that some part of the *self* was being lost. Something once one's own suddenly became "dead." Death must then have become associated with excreta, and the association remains to this day. ". . . All life comes from shit and returns to shit," says the coprophilic hero of Vladimir Voinovich's *Chonkin* (Voinovich 1979, 102). "For dust thou art, and unto dust shalt thou return" says the Lord in *Genesis* (3:19). ". . . The peculiar human fascination with excrement is the peculiar human fascination with death," says the classicist-become-psychoanalyst Norman O. Brown in his psychoanalytic study of history (1959, 295). Excreta constitute "the dead matter produced by the body . . . which incorporate the body's daily dying" (*ibid.*, 294).

To continue living in the face of constant (including olfactory) reminders of death must require some physiological process or processes that cancel or neutralize death awareness. Lionel Tiger (1979) has cogently argued that there is some brain location for and some neuro-physiological basis to "good feelings about the present and the future." How could there *not* be some adaptive optimism mechanism (facilitated, no doubt, by a loving mother in one's past) which cancels out the most appalling effect of foresight? Magic, religion, art, and other cultural illusions must all be manifestations of this mechanism (which is not to exclude their manifesting other mechanisms as well). As long as we sense the stench of death and putrefaction below us, we will also need something to *boost* our spirits, to keep our hopes *high*,[22] to put us into *seventh heaven* or on *cloud nine*, to give us *lofty* or *uplifting* thoughts, to keep us *on top* of the world, etc. etc. However, I do not wish to rub the reader's *nose* in this particularly morbid matter any further.

In quite a number of cultural structures a semiotic effect of bipedalism is the well known *above/below* opposition (cf.: Ivanov 1976a, 336; Bakhtin 1965; Needham 1973; Lévi-Strauss 1967, 149ff; Baumann 1955, 138ff., 320ff.; Rancour-Laferriere 1982b; Cohen 1980). Alfred Adler (1980, 45, 302-5) believed the opposition to be significant in the lives of neurotics. Numerous interesting examples of the *above/below* opposition from our own culture are given by Lakoff and Johnson (1980). Among speakers of English there are some definite emotional and evaluative associations with the up/down axis (some of which have already been hinted at). Here are some of the metaphors Lakoff and Johnson cite:

Happy is up/Sad is down
I'm feeling up. My spirits rose. I'm feeling down. My spirits sank.
Conscious is up/Unconscious is down

---

22. But the unconscious meaning breaks through in another meaning of "high": "That meat smells a little high," i.e., a little putrid.

Get up. Wake up. He fell asleep. He sank into a coma.
Having control is up/Being subject to control is down
I have power over her. I am on top of the situation. He fell from power.
He's in an inferior position.
Good is up/Bad is down
Things are looking up. The quality of life is high. We hit a peak last year,
but it's been going downhill ever since.
Virtue is up/Depravity is down
She has high standards. She is upright. That was a low trick. I wouldn't
stoop to that.

(see Lakoff and Johnson 1980, 14ff.)

Lakoff and Johnson propose a physical basis for each of these oppositions —
which is to say that they grant that the oppositions must have more than
just linguistic or culture-specific determination. For example, for the
conscious/unconscious pair they state: "humans and most other mammals
sleep lying down and stand up when they awaken" (*ibid.*, 15). Or, for the
happy is up/sad is down opposition they suggest: "drooping posture typically
goes along with sadness and depression, erect posture with a positive
emotional state" (*ibid.*).

Curiously, however, none of the proposed physical bases for the various
subsets of the up/down opposition contains a reference to the odoriferous
ano-genital region or to the feelings of disgust towards bodily excreta. This
Freud would certainly have called repression. The virtue is up/depravity
is down opposition seems especially relevant to what Freud was saying in
Civilization and Its Discontents. When, for example, we hear "I wouldn't
stoop to that," or "that was a low down trick," all kinds of unpleasant and
unavoidably sexual ideas come to mind. What is "below the waist" in our
culture is not just unfair, it has sexual connotations. To "go *down*" on
someone might seem like a harmlessly topographical phrase in English, if
we did not know that it indicated a willingness to perform fellatio or
cunnilingus (the latter being very much like what many non-human,
non-upright primate males habitually do before mounting).

The Irish poet William Butler Yeats made a striking contrast of an image
of uprightness (both literal and metaphorical) against an image of anal-genital
sexuality in some lines from *Crazy Jane Talks With the Bishop* (1959, 255):

> A woman can be proud and stiff
> When on love intent;
> But love has pitched his mansion in
> The place of excrement....

We know that a woman who has "fallen," who has lost her metaphorically
upright stance, has done something of a specifically sexual nature. In Russian

a number of abusive terms meaning "fallen one" ("padlo," "padla," "padal'") all connote a (male or female) person who is particularly disgusting, smelly, slimy, treacherous, or otherwise repellent. In most cultures high social rank is regarded as clean, low rank as dirty (Cohen 1980). One could go on citing examples of the general human tendency to make the following equations:

Up = good = clean = asexual = repressive
$Down$ = bad = dirty = sexual = unrepressed
(modified from Hamilton 1966, 11)

One of the important things that an upright posture in hominids eventually accomplished, then, was to provide the vertical *physical* opposition from which a number of other *semiotic* and *evaluative* oppositions could be built.

J. Upright Posture and the Origin of the Family

Perhaps the most interesting sexual consequence of bipedalism has to do with the formation of sexual (and associated familial) bonds. I have already said something about the relationship of upright posture to pair bonding, and will say more, but there is another, different scenario that also relates the two.

According to the anthropologist C. Owen Lovejoy (1981), upright posture permitted early hominids to carry things, including food and equipment, over considerable distances (cf. Tanner 1981, 143; Zihlman and Tanner 1976; Campbell 1966, 203; Hewes 1961; Fisher 1982; Spuhler 1979, 457; Isaac 1976b). Now, a number of hypotheses have at various times been put forth as to what newly released 'hands' could accomplish. Included are: making tools, making and brandishing weapons, gathering certain kinds of food, carrying children (whose parents may no longer have had enough hair to cling to), making and carrying containers, and, possibly, communicating by some kind of manual 'sign language.' But some of these, at least, had to have been relatively late developments. For example, the invention of the sling for carrying infants may have occurred less than one million years ago (Konner 1981, 24-5). Lovejoy (and Hewes before him) concentrates on what freed hands could have accomplished at a fairly early stage of hominid evolution. Lovejoy suggests that early hominids were probably benefitting copies of their own genes by carrying food to those individuals who were caring for offspring. Given that the early hominids probably had to travel considerable distances over diverse ecological surroundings in search of food, but were bipedal and therefore capable of carrying food, then it would have made sense for the larger, stronger males to do the carrying (eventually with the aid of primitive carrying devices), and for the females to remain and feed in a more circumscribed area while caring for offspring. Initially the males and females would have become separated because of the advantages of differential feeding areas, but this separation would have had sexual implications:

... the range of the female-offspring group could be... reduced by progressive elimination of male competition for local resources. This separation would be under strong positive selection. Lowered mobility of females would reduce accident rate during travel, maximize familiarity with the core area, reduce exposure to predators, and allow intensification of parenting behavior, thus elevating survivorship. Such a division of feeding areas, however, would not genetically favor males unless it specifically reduced competition with their own biological offspring and did not reduce their opportunities for consort relationships. Polygynous mating would not be favored by this adaptive strategy because the advantage of feeding divergence is reduced as the number of males is reduced. Conversely, a sex ratio close to parity would select for the proposed feeding strategy. Such a ratio would obtain if the mating pattern were monogamous pair bonding. In this case, males would avoid competition with their bonded mates and biological offspring (by using alternative feeding sites) and not be disadvantaged by physical separation, that is, there would be no loss of consort opportunity. In short, monogamous pair bonding would favor feeding divergence by "assuring" males of biological paternity and by reducing feeding competition with their own offspring and mates. (*ibid.*, 345).

What Lovejoy is saying, then, is that the early hominids were not like today's hamadryas baboons, which live in harem centered groups on arid grasslands, but more like today's gibbons, which form pair bonds involving extensive paternal care and live in tropical forests. Note that Lovejoy does not propose a specific proximate mechanism for the development of monogamy in the emerging hominids, but only argues that polygamously-inclined individuals would have been selected against. Later on I will suggest that the mechanism which promoted monogamy in the early hominids (to the extent that there was any monogamy at all) was an increasingly intensified mother-child relationship.

K. Terminological Problems

Lovejoy's theory sharply differs from some theories which assume that evolving male hominids were initially polygynous (e.g., Fox 1972; Campbell 1966, 276-81; Crook 1972, 272; Mellen 1981; Zuckerman 1933, 159; Strassmann 1981; Melotti 1981). Certainly it is the case *today* that polygyny characterizes more human societies than monogamy and polyandry combined. Here are Murdock's (1957, 686) rough figures, given as percentages of the 554 societies surveyed:

monogamous	24%
polygynous	75%
polyandrous	1%[23]

It is generally accepted that human males "incline to polygyny" (Symons 1979, 27; cf. Stephens 1963; Goody 1976, 51; Van den Berghe and Barash 1977; Daly and Wilson 1978; Alexánder *et al.* 1979). But it is also the case that most human societies — including the hunter-gatherer societies that are thought to be in many respects similar to early hominid societies — are based on the nuclear family of husband, wife, and offspring. The predominance of the nuclear family was recognized long ago by such authorities as Darwin, Tylor, Freud, and others, and continues to be recognized today (e.g., Reynolds 1974; Wilson 1975, 553; Murdock 1949, 219; Fairbanks 1977, 100; Beals *et al.* 1977, 378; Stephens 1963; Lancaster 1975; Beach 1978; Gough 1975; Campbell 1966, 276ff.).

But today's nuclear family, with its socially recognized bonds of husband to wife, and child to parent, hardly precludes extramarital or premarital copulation, or marital copulation with more than one wife.

Part of the problem is terminological confusion. Consult a biologist and you will find one definition of polygamy:

Polygamy — The acquisition, as part of the normal life cycle, of more than one mate.

(Wilson 1975, 592)

---

23. Note that, as is usually the case in cross-cultural research, the figures refer to number of societies, not number of human beings. Conclusions about reproductive success based on the cross-cultural studies therefore have to be made with great care. Incidentally, the more recent cross-cultural figures on monogamy, polygyny, and polyandry are approximately 16%, 83%, and less than 1%, respectively (Konner 1982, 273, based on Daly and Wilson 1978, 265 and Murdock 1967).

Consult an anthropologist and you will receive a quite different definition:
   Polygamy — A recognized system of multiple spouses.

(Beals, Hoijer, and Beals 1977, 711)

Whereas the second of these definitions has to do with kinship systems, the first does not. Someone could conceivably be polygamous by the second definition but not by the first, e.g., have many spouses but mate with only one of them. The first definition emphasizes actual sexual behavior and therefore speaks of multiple *mates*, while the second speaks of multiple *spouses*.

Consider also the anthropologist's definition of monogamy:
   Monogamy — Marriage to a single spouse.

(Beals, Hoijer, and Beals 1977, 710)

The biologist's definition is:
   Monogamy — The condition in which one male and one .female join to rear at least a single brood.

(Wilson 1975, 589)

Yet it is possible to be "monogamous" by the first of these definitions, but "polygamous" by a biologist's definition of "polygamous". That is, it is possible to be married to one *spouse* but have several *mates*, serially or simultaneously.

Most students of human nature would, I think, agree that in societies which allow only what anthropologists mean by "monogamy," there is in fact much of what biologists mean by "polygamy" going on. Conversely, in societies which officially permit males to marry more than one woman, there is undoubtedly much of what biologists mean by "monogamy" going on.

Consider yet another anthropological definition:
   Nuclear family — a married couple and their children.

(Beals *et al.*, *ibid.*)

Does this mean than an *un*married couple and their children do not constitute a nuclear family? Did the earliest hominids get married? Do gibbons marry?

Clearly, a terminological clarification of some kind is necessary here. In this book I will lean toward the biologist's definitions, that is, I will use the terms "polygamy," "monogamy," and "nuclear family"[24] to refer to what organisms (including people) *actually do*. Thus a person who is

---

24. I am aware that anthropologists used these terms long before zoologists and sociobiologists did (cf. Symons 1979, 128). See also Fedigan 1982, 41-2 on the problem.

in fact sexually faithful to his/her mate over an extended period of time (sometimes long enough for them to raise their offspring — Wilson 1975, 589 — but not necessarily always that long) will be called *monogamous*, while a person who has sexual relations with individuals other than the mate, even in the context of what an anthropologist might call a "monogamous" marriage, will be called polygamous (specifically, polygynous[25] if the person is male, polyandrous if female). When a man and a woman actually cooperate to raise offspring, the resulting social unit will be called a *bifocal* (cf. Lovejoy 1981, 348) or a *nuclear family*, regardless of the marital status of the parents, and regardless of their respective sexual behaviors. If the biological father is absent or his role is negligible, the remaining unit of mother and offspring will be termed a *matrifocal family*. If the male and female have a relationship that is officially sanctioned or formalized in some way, the two will be termed *spouses* (*husband* and *wife*), regardless of whether or not they are actually *mates*, that is, regardless of whether or not they are bonded by mutual sexual attraction and instances of copulation. The failure to distinguish between marriage and sexuality, like the common fallacy of confusing marriage proscriptions with the incest taboo, can only mislead. However, the failure to consider whether and how sexuality might be systematically related to marriage can be equally pernicious (below, section 20).

---

25. Looked at from the viewpoint of the species rather than the individual, a species may be said to be polygynous if males compete more for matings than females, with the consequence that fewer males contribute genetically to following generations than females, though harems are not necessarily involved (Alexander *et al.* 1979).

L. The Absence of an Ovulation Signal

Lovejoy's theory has to do with mating, not marriage. He is not saying, therefore, whether early hominids had anything like marriage and kinship systems. He argues against polygynous mating, not polygynous marriage, i.e., he favors monogamous pair-bonding as one (indirect) result of upright stance in early hominids.

To strengthen his argument, Lovejoy brings in the matter of human ovulation. As is well known, the human female does not show obvious external (behavioral, morphological, pheromonal) signs of ovulation to those around her, nor is she normally aware of her ovulation herself. Such "concealment" of ovulation is not typical of primates. Recent research does suggest that such animals as rhesus monkeys and chimpanzees copulate throughout the menstrual cycle, although most frequently near midcycle (Michael and Bonsall 1979; Savage-Rumbaugh and Wilkerson 1978; Lancaster 1979; Hrdy 1981; but cf. Symons 1982). Also, there is some (disputed) evidence that the human female has a peak of sexual activity or arousal (though perhaps not the only peak) at midcycle, around the time of ovulation (Udry and Morris 1968; Strassmann 1981, 37-8; Adams *et al.* 1978; Hrdy 1981, 138-9; Burley 1979, 849-53; James 1971; Steklis 1980). Nevertheless, human females are *relatively* much less cyclical in their sexual activities than are other primate females. This state of affairs has been variously described as continuous sexual receptivity, continuous estrus, 'sham' estrus, lack of estrus, continuous nonreceptivity, selective receptivity, etc. (see Alexander and Noonan 1979). Semiotically speaking, human females do not distinctly *signal* when they ovulate, and such a failure to signal ovulation must have appeared, gradually or suddenly, in the course of hominid evolution (Sade 1980 suggests it could be one of the effects of neoteny – cf. section 11 below). More than one scenario has been proposed for loss of the ovulation signal (cf.: Symons 1979, 96-141; Daniels 1983; Beach 1978; Benshoof and Thornhill 1979; Turke 1984; Alexander and Noonan 1979; Strassmann 1982; Burley 1979). I am most inclined to believe that the trigger for the loss of this signal was a combination of the new unavailability of female genitalia to close male inspection, and the enhanced possibility for clitoral stimulation – both ultimately due to upright posture (see below, section 2). This eventually led to a female hominid who seemed to a male hominid to be inviting sexual intercourse most of the time (and in effect therefore not signalling ovulation at all). I should emphasize that the female hominid *seemed* to be always signalling sexual availability, which is not to say that she was necessarily available in all circumstances. A similar problem crops up in the frequent but mistaken assertion that present-day female hominids are continuously sexually receptive. As Beach (1974, 354-5) says, "no human female is 'constantly receptive.' (Any male who entertains this illusion must be a very old man with a short memory or a very young man due for a bitter disappointment)." One of the reasons a female refuses may be her fear of the possibly resulting burdens of gestation, childbirth, and childrearing. Burley (1979) suggests that this fear played a crucial role in the concealment of ovulation. Her hypothesis is that ". . . natural selection concealed hominid ovulation to counter a human or prehuman conscious tendency among females to avoid conception through abstinence from intercourse near ovulation" (*ibid.*, 835). Of course a female may refuse a given male intercourse for other reasons too, such as homosexual preference, or the fact that the male is not the male of her choice (see below, section 5).

The effect of a failure to signal ovulation made it impossible for a male hominid to 'know' just when it would be profitable, genetically, to copulate. On the other hand, if hominid females seemed continuously available to hominid males, then the latter would not have needed an ovulation signal anyway (in order to take steps necessary to replicate genes).

Now, the evolving male hominid could have achieved "copulatory vigilance" (Lovejoy) by frequent copulation either with a number of females, or regularly with one female. Loss of the ovulation signal does not in itself predict one or the other. But according to Lovejoy (following a suggestion by Lancaster; cf. also Alexander and Noonan 1979; Strassmann 1981), the female strategy of non-signalled ovulation would have been dealt with more successfully by monogamous than by polygynous males:

... any sequestration of ovulation would seem to directly imply both regular copulatory behavior and monogamous mating structure. It establishes mathematical parity between males restricted to a single mate and those practicing complete promiscuity, and the balance of selection falls to the offspring of pair-bonded males, since their energetic capacity for provisioning (and improved survivorship and reproductive rate) is maximized. (Lovejoy 1981, 346).

I do not think, however, that a mathematician would agree that there is a "mathematical parity between males restricted to a single mate and those practicing complete promiscuity" (it depends on what numerical assumptions are made). In addition, the possibility of *female* sexual "vigilance" is not included in Lovejoy's scenario.

M. The Diversity of Human Sexuality

A number of factors may have tipped the balance away from monogamy (if originally there was monogamy) in the course of hominid evolution. For example, if there were significant deviations from a 1:1 male-female sex ratio caused by male-male competition or warfare, female infanticide, changing birth rates, etc., then changes in sexual behavior might have occurred. Guttentag and Secord (1983) have found demographic evidence that a relative overabundance of females tends to encourage (at least male) polygamy in today's hominids. Also, it may have been selectionally advantageous for the male hominid to become temporarily promiscuous when his mate was pregnant (see Lynn 1974, 229, and Offit 1981, 100-5 on the sexual adventuresomeness of expectant fathers). It may well also have been selectively advantageous for males to avoid their mates for a time after childbirth, since spacing of children promotes better early child care. But such avoidance is an incentive for males to behave polygamously. Thus Stephens (1962) finds that today *long* post partum sex taboo correlates with *high* percentage of polygynous marriages in the large sample of societies he surveyed (cf. also Symons 1979, 122; Mellen 1981, 151-2; Saucier 1972).

Furthermore, if the evolving hominid male invented a weapon with which he could both bring in more animal protein for his mate and offspring as well as eliminate some of his male conspecifics, he would have found polygyny more feasible than would otherwise have been the case. The early male hominids may not have had very large or dangerous canine teeth (strong canine dimorphism is missing as long ago as *Australopithecus afarensis*, as well as in the gibbon and siamang, both of which are monogamous — Lovejoy, n. 90), but the invention of increasingly more dangerous *artificial* weapons made it possible for males to hunt and to compete for females in new and intelligent ways (cf. Campbell 1966, 261; Darwin 1885, 51; but see Jungers 1978; Fedigan 1982, 62). That they did compete for females seems to be indicated by the fact that they were still larger and stronger than females.

It is an old chestnut of evolutionary biology, ever since Darwin (1885, 561-3), that sexual size dimorphism in mammals tends to characterize polygynous species, monomorphism monogamous species (e.g., Alexander *et al.* 1979; Kleiman 1977; Maynard Smith 1978, 184; Baer and McEachron 1982, 85; Leutenegger 1978; Short 1981; Daly and Wilson 1978, 100; Hrdy 1981, 206, 34-58; Crook 1972; Clutton-Brock and Harvey 1978, 370-2).

Harcourt (1981) found that among the great apes (chimpanzees, orangutangs, gorillas), who are our closest living relatives, sexual dimorphism is explained primarily by male competition for access to females. There is evidence, though, that size dimorphism can mean other things besides polygyny, such as large overall body size for the species (larger species tending to be dimorphic, smaller species monomorphic), differential niche exploitation by the sexes, and bioenergetic advantages for pregnant and lactating females of large species to be smaller than males (see: Fedigan 1982, 51-66; Maynard Smith 1978, 184-7; Clutton-Brock and Harvey 1978, 370-2 for reviews). Lovejoy (n. 85) in fact prefers to interpret the dimorphism of *A. afarensis* as indicating not a differential competition for mates, but differential competition for resources. Krantz (1982) suggests that the decreasing size dimorphism in more recent hominid evolution is explained in part by the selection pressure for increased female pelvic size to facilitate the birth of increasingly large-brained infants.

As early hominids occupied habitats which demanded greater ranging for food and increased protection against predators, there had to have been selection pressure to form sizeable, probably multi-male social groups. Large groups of animals are more efficient at feeding in an open habitat with only patchy food resources (Horn 1968; Wilson 1975, 52-3; 525) and are better able to defend themselves against predators (Wilson 1975, 52; Crook and Gartlan 1966; Clutton-Brock and Harvey 1978, 356) than are small, family-size groups. Among today's non-human primates the tendency to form large groups correlates with forest fringe, tree savanna, grassland, and arid savanna habitats (Crook and Gartlan 1966, 1200).

But in our primate relatives large social groups tend to be associated with polygyny (e.g., hamadryas baboons), or with promiscuity and occasional consortships (e.g., chimpanzees), while small groups tend to consist of monogamously pair-bonded individuals with offspring (e.g. – gibbons). Certainly, it would be difficult to imagine how the later hominids managed to hunt and butcher large prey unless they at least temporarily formed highly coordinated, multi-male cooperative groups of an effective size (see Washburn and Lancaster 1973, 60).

The geologic record does in several places indicate sizeable groups of hominids together. The (tendentiously named) "First Family" of *Australopithecus afarensis* at the Hadar site in Ethiopia, for example, consists of an absolute minimum of 13 individuals, including juveniles (Johanson and White 1979, 321; Johanson and Edey 1981, 217). The vast cave of Choukoutien, dating from the middle Pleistocene, contains nearly 50 representatives of *Homo erectus pekinensis* (Pilbeam 1975, 830). Generally speaking, the sites (often called "home bases") found in Plio-

Pleistocene Africa indicate groups ranging in size from 12-50 individual hominids (Mellen 1981, 99). These facts do not support the argument for hominid monogamy, if one is arguing by analogy with nonhuman primates.

On the other hand, it is well known that in both non-human primates and in human societies polygyny is associated with low paternal investment (e.g., Mitchell 1981, 86). But it is also well known that young hominids were requiring more and more parental investment. For example, the hominid brain was getting bigger, and therefore selective pressure favored both increase in the size of the birth canal and premature delivery of fetuses.[26] Also, young hominids were taking progressively longer to mature, overall. This prolongation of childhood was part of the general trend toward neoteny, i.e., retardation of aspects of ontogenetic development (see section 11). As young hominids became increasingly helpless and required increasing time and energy from adult hominids, there must have been increasing selective pressure on biological *fathers* to assist with childrearing, as many evolutionists have observed. Gould (1977, 403) has noted the historical tendency for delayed childhood development to be associated with theories of the origin of the human (nuclear) family. For example: "the heavy task of rearing and training the slowly developing young demanded a cohesive family unit" (Morris 1967, 38). Natural selection would not push males toward indiscriminate aid with child rearing, but toward assistance in the rearing of only those young who were most likely to be their own. But the cheapest way to insure such confidence of paternity is for the male to be monogamous. And the cheapest way to obtain continuing male assistance is for the female to be monogamous.

To conclude, then, whether the pre-human hominids were polygynous, monogamous, or perhaps some combination of both (e.g., serially monogamous) seems at this point an impossibility. The evidence is just not adequate. Besides, if the hominid line is at the very least four million years old, then there was plenty of time for reproductive strategies in both males and females to change. Perhaps, for example, the very earliest hominids were monogamous, as Lovejoy suggests, but then changing ecological pressures working together with increasing intelligence and the invention of weapons led to an increase in the strategy of polygamy in the males of

---

26. Some have argued that there was a conflict between selection for bipedalism, which favors narrow pelvic opening, and increasing brain size, which favors wide pelvic opening (e.g.: Ellis 1914, 86; Montagu 1971, 41; Fisher 1982, 82; Crook 1980, 108; Strassmann 1981, 33; Fox 1972). However, Leutenegger (1974; 1977) shows that the birth canal of the *already* fully bipedal *Australopithecus* was plenty large enough to accomodate delivery, and that selective pressure to enlarge the birth canal was absent or minor in *early* hominids.

some populations. Or perhaps the sequence was just the reverse, with an initial polygyny giving way to increased monogamy under the increasing advantageousness of extended parental care (e.g., Benshoof and Thornhill 1979).

Perhaps also the increasing intelligence of the hominids (facilitated by increasing cortical development) permitted a greater flexibility and variety of reproductive strategies — monogamous under some conditions, polygamous under others (cf. Wilson 1980). It is known that today's hominid societies, for example, are more likely to have some form of polygynous marriage if hunting/gathering is a major or important means of subsistence than if it is not (Mellen 1981, 153; cf. Coult 1965, 260). If hunting plays a particularly important role in exclusively foraging societies (and there is not female infanticide), then polygyny is quite likely because meat can be exchanged by men for women (Friedl 1975, 25). If in an agricultural society women do most of the farming, polygyny is more likely than if men do the farming (J. Whiting and B. Whiting 1975; Goody 1976, 34, 50).

There must have been variation from one individual to another, though perhaps not as much as there is in today's hominids. It is well known (e.g., Shepher 1978) that many ˙ (if not most) male individuals in societies classified by anthropologists as "polygynous" are in fact behaving monogamously. Polygamous behavior tends, in other words, to be the prerogative of high-status, and often older males. Females, particularly younger ones who can elicit altruism on the basis of 'looks' alone can profit genetically from union with such males, since the offspring are likely to have more access to resources than the offspring of union with inferior males in the social hierarchy. This is ultimately why hypergyny (the practice of women "marrying up") characterizes stratified societies in which polygyny grows in proportion to social status. Van den Berghe and Mesher (1980, 303) put it this way: ". . . women . . . tend to be 'sucked up' in the social structure, creating polygyny at the top, monogamy in the middle, and male celibacy or polyandry at the bottom" (cf. also Dickemann 1979).

The situation in *Homo sapiens* is complex and enormously varied. A prostitute is professionally polygamous, while a nineteenth century Mormon male was religiously so. A "good" Catholic is religiously monogamous, while an overburdened mother may be monogamous purely for lack of opportunity. And then of course there is "this thing called love," which can have all kinds of reproductive consequences, as we will see.

The variety and complexity of human reproductive behavior is one of the subjects of this book, and it has to have an evolutionary history. At some point flexibility of reproductive behavior within hominid populations has to have developed, and this flexibility gives modern hominids more variable and heterogeneous sexual behavior than can be observed in any other primate in the wild. This flexibility is in turn just part of what Konner (1982) termed the overall "lability" and "adaptability" that characterizes the human primate.

The potential for mental conflict over reproductive behavior *within* individuals also has to be taken into consideration: "man is the only organism in which conflict is normal and habitual . . ." (Waddington 1960, 172). Does the monogamous male *want* to be monogamous? Does the monogamous female *want* to be monogamous? A prostitute is capable of having a fantasy of settling down to a monogamous marriage. A tired Don Juan is too. These contradictions and conflicts constitute another topic of this book. They too must have an evolutionary history. At some point multiplicity of reproductive fantasies and desires, not only variability of actual reproductive behavior has to have appeared in hominids. Emotions, not only surface behaviors, must have come under the sway of natural selection. Sexual fantasies and feelings, as Symons is fond of pointing out, are "close" to genes: ". . . a great deal of the variability in human behavior results from the diversity of compromises among universally experienced emotions, and . . . these emotions can be considered to be 'closer to' the genes than behavior is" (Symons 1979, 72-3).

The complex Western society that we live in seems exceptionally able to generate occasions for conflict about whether to behave monogamously or polygamously. For example, our system of marriage seems, on its face, to require (at least serial) monogamy. But, in other monogamous species, there is relatively little dimorphism of parental investment in offspring, while in our society sexual dimorphism in roles and behavior is the rule:

The female's role is to rear the children, while the male "works" for food and shelter. Thus, paternal investment (although greater than in polygamous societies) is often indirect and may not involve continuous responsiveness to the needs of the young. Moreover, the legal, legislative, and executive branches of governments, as well as religious establishments, have generally supported this sexual dimorphism. Since both politics and religion are dominated by men in Western society, the result is an *apparently* monogamous system, with behavioral correlates, however, that are more appropriate to polygyny. In fact, polygyny commonly occurs. (Kleiman 1977, 61, emphasis added).

Certainly the most common context for conflict about whether to behave monogamously or polygamously concerns differences between the sexual inclinations of men vs. women. Sociobiology has made it abundantly clear that the reproductive interests of males and females are never completely identical. For Alexander *et al.* (1979) to classify humans as "mildly polygynous" may be a way of saying that there tends to be a compromise between the typically monogamous interests of women and the typically polygamous interests of men (cf. Dawkins 1976, 177).

Psychoanalysts, who as I have already mentioned, share remarkably many views with and anticipated many of the theories of sociobiologists, also see human males as tending to polygamy, females to monogamy. I will quote just two examples. First, a male psychoanalyst speaking about males:

Experience shows that they [married men] very frequently avail themselves of the degree of sexual freedom which is allowed them — although only with reluctance and under the veil of silence — by even the strictest sexual code. The 'double' sexual morality which is valid for men in our society is the plainest admission that society itself does not believe in the possibility of enforcing the precepts which it itself has laid down. (Freud, *SE* IX, 195).

Second, a female psychoanalyst speaking about females:

We know women who have grown up in social conditions that freed them from monogamy, women who freed themselves from its requirements individually, and women who, as a result of their passivity, have discarded it under the influence of others. Thus we have rich material at our disposal. Our impression is that the feminine woman in an overwhelming majority of cases is fundamentally monogamous. This monogamy does not necessarily require the exclusiveness of marriage or confine sexuality to one object for life. A woman may even change her love objects quite frequently; but during each relation she is absolutely monogamous and has a conservative need to continue the given relation as long as possible. (Deutsch 1977, 204).

None of this is to deny the considerable variation away from the mean which is possible within each sex. Alongside the domestically blissful housewife there is also the prostitute. The philandering middle-aged man may be a commonplace, but so is the faithful family man.

Variety, including variety of sexual behaviors, is at the heart of the human condition. To illustrate just how great is the diversity of (actual or fantasized) heterosexual interaction in humans, I offer the following limited list of slang words and idiomatic expressions, in merely alphabetical order, from just one of the languages that humans speak:

Bluebeard	confirmed bachelor
bride of Christ	damaged goods
campfollower	dirty old man
carry a torch	dominatrix
Casanova	Don Juan
Caspar Milquetoast	double standard
cat house	easy lay
child bride	eternal triangle
commonlaw wife/husband	faithful provider

fallen woman
fast worker
footloose and fancy free
free love
gay blade
gigolo
give away the bride
gold digger
grass widow
groupie
hooker
hustle
jail bait
john
ladykiller
Lothario
love child
love 'em and leave 'em
love match
lovebirds
man-hater
marriage of convenience
Mata Hari
May and December
midnight creeping
misogynist
mistress
old maid
on the make
one night stand
Platonic love

play around
play the field
Penelope
puppy/calf love
rob the cradle
a roll in the hay
Romeo
scarlet woman
shack up
shotgun wedding
slam bam thank you ma'am
slave of love
sleep around
Sodom and Gomorrah
sow one's oats
streetwalker
stud
sugar daddy
swinging (singles)
the other woman
to be pinned
to cruise
to go steady
tread the primrose path
trick
white slavery
white meat
wife-swapping
wolf
woman of pleasure/of the night
zipless fuck

It is as if the hominid primate had attempted to occupy every single heterosexual niche that any other primate has ever occupied (cf. McGuinness 1980b, 312), and then, still unsatisfied, and driven by enormously expanded semiotic (especially linguistic) capabilities, decided to invent whole new modes and nuances of heterosexual interaction which would be utterly inconceivable for the non-hominid primates. I am not saying there is no unity in this diversity, or that naturally selected genes had nothing to do with creating it. Rather, I am emphasizing what others have said before: somehow in the course of hominid evolution enormously complex systems of signs — semiotic complexes such as spoken language, gesture, religious rituals, courtship rituals, residence patterns, dreams, day-dreams, poetry, music, games, myths, kinship systems, avoidance rules, exchange systems, marriage rules, etc. — have managed to make the space between genes and behavior much larger than in any other creature on the planet. To discern just some of the specifically sexual structures lurking in this vast space is the purpose of the following pages.

Signs of the Flesh

1. Is the Female Orgasm Adaptive?

In Gershon Legman's book *Rationale of the Dirty Joke* is the following anecdote:

A woman in North Dakota complains to a lawyer that her husband has his orgasm too quickly and does not satisfy her. Can she get a divorce? The lawyer looks up the law on the subject and reports to her: "Madam there isn't a damned thing you can do about it. According to the laws of this state, when the man is through, the woman is fucked." (Legman 1968, 357).

I think this bit of folklore graphically illustrates three important facts about the female orgasm:

1) Heterosexual intercourse and resulting conception can take place without female orgasm, but not without male orgasm.
2) If it takes place without female orgasm too often, the female may get fed up and be inclined to break a monogamous bond.
3) If the society is repressive enough, it makes little difference whether she gets fed up.

Of these points, 1) is a statement of the obvious Darwinian adaptiveness of the *male* orgasm, 2) would appear to be a statement of the adaptiveness of the female orgasm, and 3) looks like a statement of one way whereby males combat the adaptiveness of the female orgasm. It is 2) that I will be primarily concerned with here: is the female orgasm adaptive in the Darwinian sense?

In attempting to answer this question I will assume that there is such a thing as female orgasm, that is, that the female orgasm is a phenomenon capable of functioning as a relatively discrete entity subject or not subject to natural selection. This is not to say that the physiology of the female orgasm is very well understood (see Levin 1981, for an overview). It is also not to say that female orgasm does not exist in more than one variety. There have been persistent reports that subjective experience of orgasm differs from one individual to another or within an individual at different times. A variety of orgasmic dichotomies has been established: uterine vs. vulval or clitoral (Singer 1974, ch. 3); vaginal vs. clitoral (for various viewpoints, see: Singer 1974, chs. 3-4; Koedt 1973; Bonaparte 1953; Masters and Johnson 1980

[1966], 65-7; Shulman 1972; Clark 1970; Sherfey 1972; Moore 1977; Kaplan and Sucher 1982, 9-12; various articles in vol. 16, no. 3 of *Journal of the American Psychoanalytic Association*; Goldberg *et al.* 1983; Money 1980, 118; Rohrbaugh 1979, 273-7; Freud, *SE*, VII, 220-1; XXI, 228; Fisher 1973; Eissler 1977; Robinson 1976, 132); Gräfenberg spot type (originating from a locus on the anterior wall of the vagina) vs. clitoral type (Gräfenberg 1950; Ladas *et al.* 1982; Goldberg *et al.* 1983; but see Hoch 1983); masturbatory vs. coital; short and intense vs. long, deep, and subtle; orgasm with much body movement vs. orgasm with non-movement myotonia (see Bentler and Peeler 1979 and Ladas *et al.* 1982 for reviews); and others. However, I doubt that the variety of ways in which the female orgasm can be experienced is any greater than the subjective variety of other, unitary and obviously adaptive phenomena such as the male orgasm (Hite 1981), defecation, drinking, eating, childbirth, nursing at the breast, and others.

The male orgasm, says Donald Symons (1979, 86), "for the most part is interesting only to people directly involved in one . . . ." It occurs with "monotonous regularity." It does not distinguish the human male from other mammalian males. No mammalian species can in fact last for long without orgasmic males. What is evidently unusual for mammals is the orgasm of human females. Beach (1978, 148) goes so far as to say: " . . . the weight of available evidence favors the theory that female orgasm is a characteristic essentially restricted to our own species," though this may be an exaggeration in light of the evidence for female orgasm in some non-human primates (see Lancaster 1979, 53-6, and Hrdy 1981, 166-72 for reviews, and especially Goldfoot *et al.* 1980). For example, Hrdy (1979, 312) suggests that female orgasm is "plausible" in those species, such as Barbary macaques and chimpanzees, where an estrous female may solicit and be mounted many times in close succession by a number of males. But such behavior has little to do with the conditions under which today's *human* female will achieve orgasm. Here, for example, is one of the main conclusions of a study of 100,000 readers of *Redbook* magazine:

For most women, orgasm depends on being in love and feeling comfortable with their lovers. The *Redbook* women who had had premarital sex on a casual basis — once or a few times with several partners — were apparently not doing so for pure sexual pleasure, as they were the *least* likely to be reaching orgasm. The women who were *most* likely to be orgasmic in their premarital experience were having sex in a regular, stable relationship. Among the women who had had a series of one night stands, for example, fully 77 percent said they never reached orgasm, compared to 23 percent of the women who had sex frequently with their partners. What matters in premarital responsiveness is not the number of lovers, actually, but the number of times with each one. As it ever was in this society, the great majority of young women need a sustained sense of intimacy, security, and trust from a relationship before they shake off inhibitions and respond sexually. (Tavris and Sadd 1977, 53-4; also quoted by Symons 1979, 219).

This tendency for human female orgasm to occur in a context of trust and intimacy is also a finding of such major studies as Fisher 1973 (sample size: 285 women) and Hite 1976 (sample size: 1844 women). Certainly any orgy of successive mountings of an "insatiable" (Sherfey 1972) female by different males is not going to encourage any atmosphere of intimacy — which is not to suggest that female licentiousness is completely nonexistent in today's hominid (below, section 13). Also, orgiastic behavior will hardly suggest that any of the males plan to stay around and help the females with raising offspring. At best the males would be confused about paternity, and natural selection would only tend to inhibit them from committing indiscriminate infanticide rather than foster pair bonding and associated paternal child care.

Given that the human female is capable of having orgasm(s) in heterosexual[27] intercourse, it is only natural to ask what purpose(s) orgasm(s) may serve. The customary answer to this question has been that a woman's orgasmic experience helps motivate her to engage in sexual relations in the first place:

... if women were never to experience the pleasure of an orgasm and the feeling of complete and utter contentment which follows, they might be less motivated to engage in sex. Nature, in her wisdom, has arranged it so that the female has a slower and less reliable orgasm. She seldom in the normal course of events has her orgasm before that of her male partner, so at least one ejaculation has usually taken place before she is contented. In terms of B. F. Skinner's learning theory, she is on an 'intermittent reinforcement schedule'. Being rewarded on some occasions and not others makes for a habit that is particularly persistent. Also, if a woman is sometimes left frustrated because she does not obtain orgasm on a particular occasion she might be able to make up for it by having multiple orgasms on another. (Eysenck and Wilson 1979, 180; the intermittent reinforcement theory of female orgasm has also been independently proposed by Hrdy 1979, 312, and Diamond 1980).

Other scholars (from a notable diversity of disciplines) have also viewed female orgasm as adaptive because it enhances male-female attachment and consequently encourages the various evolutionary benefits to be gained from

---

27. It may also motivate her to engage in homosexual relations or masturbation. Both of these activities may well be adaptive, but here I will be concerned only with female orgasm in the context of heterosexual relations. Female orgasm may also have a role to play in childbirth and lactation (Newton 1973; Ladas *et al*. 1982, 48-9; Offit 1981, 108; Ellis 1927-8, IV, 26-30).

the attachment (Newton 1973; Alcock 1980; Morris 1967; Masters and Johnson 1980 [1966]; Diamond 1980; Crook 1972, 254; Barash 1977; Etkin 1954; Short 1979; King 1980; Burton 1971; Eibl-Eibesfeldt 1971; Hamburg 1978; Alexander and Noonan 1979; Campbell 1966; Beach 1978). Many of these studies refer to the orgasmically facilitated attachment as a "pair bond."[28]

An entirely different view is presented by Symons in his recent important treatise, *The Evolution of Human Sexuality* (1979). For one thing, Symons is not very enthusiastic about the notion of a "pair bond." He speaks derogatorily about a "cozy Masters-and-Johnsonian 'marital unit'" (104), and declares: "Talk of why (or whether) humans pair-bond like gibbons strikes me as belonging to the same realm of discourse as talk of why the sea is boiling hot and whether pigs have wings" (108; see Fox 1980, 140 for similarly hostile comments on pair bonding ["dreary monogamy"] in hominids). Furthermore, Symons questions whether female orgasm has any adaptive value in humans, and suggests that " . . . the potential for female orgasm can be understood as a byproduct of selection for male orgasm" (94).

To support this latter thesis, Symons cites the literature on the numerous anatomical and physiological similarities between male and female orgasm (1979, 92-3: see also the evidence that gynecologists and psychologists are unable to reliably distinguish descriptions of orgasm written by males from those written by females – Vance and Wagner 1976 – as well as the evidence for similarities in size between such penile structures as the penile bulbs and corpora spongiosum and such homologous "cryptic clitoral structures" as the vestibular bulbs and anterior commissure – Sherfey 1972[29]). Symons (cf. Robinson 1976, 172) notes the dubious claim of Masters and Johnson (1980 [1966], 84) that conception is more likely if the female does *not* orgasm (an orgasm is said to reduce the stopperlike effect of vasocongestion in the outer third of the vagina, thereby allowing semen to flow out more rapidly). Symons refers to the anthropological evidence (e.g., Mead 1975; Davenport 1977) that in some societies women do not orgasm at all, and points to surveys (e.g., Hite 1976; Tavris and Sadd 1977; Fisher 1973) on women in our own culture who are more likely to give emotional intimacy than orgasm as the main reason why they enjoy sexual intercourse. The general conclusion

---

28. Hrdy (1979) claims she rejects the idea " ... that the female orgasm evolved in human females to enhance the pair bond" (312), but then inconsistently defends "... the view that female sexuality evolved as a set of adaptations for choosing and confusing potential mates (and not *just* as a means to promote bonds with consorts)" (313, emphasis added).

29. Sherfey's description of what structures in the clitoris and penis are homologous does not jibe completely with Stilwell's (1976) description.

that Symons reaches is that there is insufficient evidence for an interpretation of female orgasm as adaptive in humans.

But just what does "adaptive" mean? Here is what Symons says:

... "adaptation" is an aspect of structure, behavior, or psyche that has been produced by the operation of natural selection. Female orgasm is an adaptation only if in ancestral populations orgasmic females enjoyed greater average reproductive success than nonorgasmic females. (Symons, 89).

This is the sense of adaptation the sociobiologists and evolutionists (e.g., Wilson 1975, 577; Williams 1966) would endorse (cf. above, 7). I am going to argue that female orgasm is adaptive at least in this sense, if not in other senses. And I assume that *both* physiological potential for orgasm *and* learning experience (Jayne 1981, 22) have a role to play in the argument.

But first I would like to indicate one passage in Symons' own presentation which should, I think, have led him to suspect that female orgasm is adaptive. Symons observes (along with Kleiman 1977) that pair-bonded, monogamous mammals are characteristically "hyposexual" (e.g. — gibbons mate only at estrus, not throughout the cycle as humans do). Symons says this means there is a "special pleading implicit in the view that the human 'pair-bond' is associated with *hyper*sexuality" (*ibid.*, emphasis added). But such a "special pleading" is precisely what would normally alert a biologist to the possible presence of an adaptation. For example, one would not argue that the *rarity* of monogamy in mammals (Kleiman 1977) shows that monogamy is maladaptive. On the contrary, it is customarily argued that monogamy has some specific adaptive advantages under certain ecological circumstances. Similarly, it could be argued that the *unusual* association of "hypersexuality" with the "pair bond" in humans indicates that a specific adaptive mechanism must be at work — perhaps the female orgasm, for example. In any case, to say that humans do not pair-bond the way gibbons do is not to say that humans do not pair-bond.

I am not going to argue that other pair bonding primate females *necessarily* have orgasms. There is certainly no a priori reason to think that an organism as different from the human female as the gibbon female is — is going to use the very same proximate mechanism(s) for behaving monogamously as the human female uses (see Alexander and Noonan 1979, 444, on why the human kind of sexuality is not to be expected in monogamous primates such as gibbons). On the other hand, the presence of female orgasm in non-human primates does not necessarily indicate monogamy either (as I already mentioned), nor does it show that female orgasm is *not* adaptive in humans. I make this latter point because of the occasionally encountered misconception that a feature has to be *unique* to a species or other taxonomic group to be adaptive. The human eye and the eye of the octopus, for example, are obviously adaptive, even though they are nonhomologous structures in highly unrelated organisms (at some point in the remote ancestries of both organisms the presence of the eye has to have conferred enhanced reproductive success). Or, to take an example a little closer to home: infanticide is widespread among the primates, yet Hrdy (1977, 287-90) has argued convincingly that it is an adaptive strategy. And what about *male* orgasm? Surely it is adaptive, even if it is present in every single mammalian species.

2. Bringing the Males Around

It is important that female orgasm be seen specifically from the perspective of the female. At some point in the evolution of hominids (perhaps even before the appearance of hominids?) females had to have made the transition from being periodically estrous in the fashion of most mammals to not being periodically estrous. That is, they had to have shifted away from the mammalian norm of being sexually receptive only because ovulation was triggering certain morphologies and behaviors that invited males to copulate. In this shift, no matter whether it was gradual or sudden, they *still* had to be inviting interested males to copulate at least some of the time, otherwise they would have left no offspring (I assume they did not copulate only because males raped them, though rape does seem to have become a facultative minor alternative for males ever since females ceased signalling ovulation – see: Alexander and Noonan 1979; Shields and Shields 1983; Thornhill and Thornhill 1983). But if females had to have been open to the advances of males, or at least of a selected male, then there has to have been a mechanism motivating them to such openness. The mechanism by definition could *not* have been the one operating to make them *periodically* estrous. It must have been something else already operating before estrus was lost and available as a preadaptation for fertilization when the signalling of ovulation by behavioral estrus was lost. Furthermore, it must have been something that would operate throughout the female cycle in order to 'cover' for the new failure to signal ovulation. As Beach (1978, 149) says, " . . . the loss of behavioral estrus and consequent disappearance of synchronization between mating and feminine fertility necessitated an increase in copulatory frequency so that intercourse would occur by chance at the time when it could result in fertilization."

I would like to suggest that the specific preadaptive mechanism that assured adequate copulatory frequency was the female orgasm, and that it went into full operation after upright posture and accompanying ventro-ventral copulation began to enhance it (cf. also Beach, *ibid.*).

Seen in this way, the new failure of females to signal ovulation meant not *only* that males had to be sexually "vigilant" (Lovejoy 1981), but that females had to be "vigilant" too. In other words, it has taken "two to tango" at least ever since the loss of the ovulation signal, and the tangoing has to have occurred rather often, round the menstrual clock in order to cover for the absence of the signal.

From this theory of *dual* sexual vigilance it would be predicted that the less attractive to men a woman is, the more vigilant she has to be sexually in order to conceive. I am not aware of any data indicating that ugly women are sex-fiends. But it is known that the older (and presumably less attractive) a woman becomes, the greater her orgasmic ability becomes (Kinsey *et al.* 1965, 512; Kaplan and Sucher 1982, 13).

A striking demonstration of just how important sexual vigilance is in modern-day hominid females comes from a study of eleven married couples by Persky *et al.* (1978). Plasma testosterone levels in both the husbands and the wives were measured over a three menstrual cycle interval. Intercourse frequency was found to correlate significantly with *wives'* testosterone levels at their ovulatory peaks. Furthermore, "the wives' self-rated [sexual] gratification scores correlated significantly with their own plasma testosterone levels" (*ibid.*, 157), and wives with a high baseline testosterone level were more likely to rate their sexual gratification as high than wives with low baseline testosterone level. Here it should be recalled that testosterone is an androgen and that, according to Spuhler 1979 (see above, 37), androgens had a role to play both in the achievement of upright posture and in the consequent frontal sexual signalling and enhancement of frontal copulation. It should be cautioned, however, that the androgen and other hormone studies are not always consistent with one another, and that there is still much debate in this area.

It is possible that female sexual vigilance developed precisely to compensate for loss of the ovulation signal. Burley (1979) believes "continuous receptivity" evolved simultaneously with loss of ovulation cues. Strassmann argues that " . . . ovulation was probably concealed through the direct dampening of its visual signs and the masking of its hormonal signs" (1981, 36; cf. Cann and Wilson 1982, and Burley *ibid.*). Such a situation, argues Strassmann, would have squeezed polygynously inclined males out of the action because they by definition would have been interested only in females showing vigorous estrus (in baboons, macaques, and chimpanzees dominant males are attracted most to those females showing most pronounced estrus — Strassmann 1981, 35). More indulgent, paternally inclined males would have succeeded in copulating with females in dampened estrus — provided, I would like to add, that the females themselves had something (such as orgasm) to keep them interested in having sex despite waning estrus.

However, there is more than one way to lose an ovulation signal. From a semiotic viewpoint, a signal ceases to be a signal when 1) it is no longer given, or 2) it is given *all* the time. The Strassmann, Daniels, and Burley scenarios, which do not take the female orgasm into consideration, exemplify No. 1). The scenario of Alexander and Noonan (1979), which does take female orgasm into consideration, is an example of No. 2). According to Alexander and Noonan there developed in female hominids a kind of false or "sham" estrus, that is, what the semiotician would recognize as an *icon* of estrus: ". . . we postulate that sham estrus evolved for a time to mimic true estrus, and subsequently the elaborateness of both true and sham estrus was reduced" (Alexander and Noonan 1979, 448; cf. Endleman 1981, 79-80).

I will not attempt to resolve here the question of whether the ovulation signal was lost through dampening of estrus or through sham estrus (or some combination of both — see Turke 1984). What is clear is that upright posture must have played a role. From the viewpoint of a habitually bipedal male visual and olfactory inspection of female genitalia was not as easy as it had once been. There must therefore have been selection for males who required less olfactory stimulation and who were aroused by visual stimuli (e.g., enlarged breasts and buttocks) different from those presented by their quadrupedal female ancestors. From the viewpoint of a habitually bipedal female, on the other hand, there was now reason to copulate from the front, since neotenous forward rotation of the vagina accompanies bipedalism (as we saw earlier), and frontal copulation enhances stimulation of the clitoris (without necessarily decreasing stimulation of the vagina's sensitive anterior wall). Recall that frontal copulation is the rule in most human societies today (Ford and Beach 1951). I assume that at least part of the reason why this is so is because female orgasm (clitoral or vaginal) at some point became more likely, overall, with frontal copulation than with *coitus a tergo more ferarum.*

If the newly upright hominid female were slightly more intelligent than her ancestors, she would have understood that frontal copulation would be likely to give her pleasure, including orgasm. She would thus have been motivated to engage in sexual activity regardless of whether she was ovulating or not. Her orgasmic ability had what might be termed a *hedonic function.*[30]

If the female's partner were also slightly more intelligent than his ancestors, he would have understood that he could just as well have had *his* orgasm from the front as from the back — and probably more often to boot. His more basic impulse would have been to copulate from the rear, but in a state of sexual excitement he would have been persuaded to come around front. The intelligence required for such a negotiation to take place between male and female would not have to have been great. It would in fact have been at about the level of another familiar primate that spends much of its time on two feet, namely, the pygmy chimpanzee (see the photographs of a female chimp

---

30. The general sense of the word "function" is given in *Webster's Third New International Dictionary* as follows: "one of a group of related actions contributing to a larger action."

inducing a male to copulate from the front in Savage-Rumbaugh *et al.* 1977). Neither vocal language nor tools are necessary to bring the male around. Gesturing and facial signalling seem to be quite sufficient.

It seems reasonable to suppose that frontal copulation is a very archaic feature of the hominid line. It certainly must have appeared before *Homo sapiens*, and may go back to the Australopithecines or earlier. Savage-Rumbaugh *et al.* in fact make a comparison of the pygmy chimpanzees they studied with *Australopithecus:*

The gestural propensity and capability of the pygmy chimpanzee far exceed that yet reported for any other ape. This communicatory skill, coupled with the gracile, large brained skeletal structure reminiscent of early Australopithecines, suggests that *Pan paniscus* is, perhaps, the best living animal model to which we may look in the reconstruction of the history of our own species. (Savage-Rumbaugh *et al.* 1977, 113; for a contrary opinion, see Latimer *et al.* 1981).

Female gestural (and eventually vocal) persuasiveness was probably not the only thing that brought males around. Males would also have been eventually encouraged by the presentation of such other frontal enticements as enlarged, hairless mammaries, frontally visible genital slit, and everted facial lips (Morris 1967) — even as olfactory enticements were receding in accessibility and importance (Tanner 1981, 154).

I do not think, incidentally, that the transition to frequent and frontal copulation, with consequent increase in the probability of female orgasm should be credited to either exclusively male or exclusively female initiative. The general trend in hominid evolution has apparently been in the direction of increased sexual interaction, but both males and females have contributed to making what Morris (1967) calls "the sexiest primate alive." I doubt, however, that the increased (genital) "sexiness" of hominids, including female orgasm, is the *only* reason why today's hominids tend to form (at least temporary) pair bonds. Much else is involved, such as the ability to make a parental icon out of one's sexual partner, as we will see later.

Also, I do not want to give the impression that the hypothesized anatomical and behavioral changes did not occur without concommitant or pre-adaptive changes in brain structure and function. It is true that cranial capacity was not very large and was not changing very much in the Australopithecines. But there is evidence that changes in the limbic system were taking place (Vilensky *et al.* 1982; above, 43-44). These limbic changes were probably as significant for early hominid evolution as the expansion of the neocortex was for the later hominids.

3. In Search of the Female Orgasm

To say that frontal copulation increased the likelihood of female orgasm is not to say that it insured female orgasm. But even it orgasm was only achieved some of the time the females might have found copulation (frontal or otherwise) rewarding — perhaps on the theory of intermittent reinforcement mentioned above, though there are other rewarding aspects of intercourse for a woman besides orgasm. Certainly it is the case with human females today that orgasmic reinforcement does not have to be constant for there to be enjoyment of or satisfaction with intercourse (see, for example: Fisher 1973; Chesser 1957; Hite 1976; Tavris and Sadd 1977; Jayne 1981). All that the early hominid female (constant or intermittent, clitoral or vaginal) orgasm needed, *in order to qualify* as an ordinary Darwinian adaptation, was to result in greater average reproductive success than the complete absence of female orgasm did, as Symons has granted (above, 67).

Unfortunately the sex surveys do not appear to give any data specifically on whether women who orgasm at least some of the time have intercourse (or want to have intercourse) significantly more frequently than women who never orgasm. Nor are there, to my knowledge, any hard data indicating that mated women who orgasm at least some of the time have more offspring that reach reproductive age than mated women who never orgasm.

There are data indicating that women of all age groups who are unmarried (and therefore not likely to have offspring) are less likely to be having orgasms than married or previously married females (Kinsey *et al.* 1965, 549). There are also data indicating that women who *never* have orgasm are more likely to believe that men want intercourse more often than women do than women who *always* orgasm (Chesser 1957, 450). Ferguson (1938) found that a significantly higher percentage of orgasmically adequate women copulated more than four times weekly during the first year of marriage than the percentage of orgasmically inadequate women. Fisher (1973, 217) reported that ". . . orgasm consistency [measured on a scale from 1 = always to 6 = never] is not correlated with either intercourse rate or preferred intercourse rate." However, this lack of correlation does not necessarily mean that there was no significant difference in intercourse rates (or preferred intercourse rates) between exclusively those women who never orgasm and those who orgasm at least some of the time. It is a curious statistical fact, incidentally, that although orgasm consistency correlated with self-scored rating of sexual responsiveness (*ibid.*, 216), and although the latter correlated with (actual and preferred) intercourse frequency (217), nonetheless orgasm consistency itself still did not correlate with (actual or preferred) intercourse frequency.

The most serious possible objection to the theory being presented here is the possible existence of societies in which female orgasm is completely absent. Ellis (1927-8, VI, 550) believed that "among most uncivilized races there appear to be few or no 'sexually frigid' women." But more recent scholars think differently. Symons (1979, 85) says, for example: ". . . among many peoples, women do not experience orgasm . . . ." This important claim is based on statements of native informants and field workers culled by such scholars as Mead (1975), Davenport (1977), and Messenger (1971). But let us consider carefully what these scholars say. Symons quotes, for example, the following passage from Davenport (1977, 149; Symons 1979, 86):

> In most of the societies for which there are data, it is reported that men take the initiative and, without extended foreplay, proceed vigorously toward climax without much regard for achieving synchrony with the woman's orgasm. Again and again, there are reports that coitus is primarily completed in terms of the man's passions and pleasures, with scant attention paid to the woman's response. If women do experience orgasm, they do so passively.

What does it mean for a woman to experience orgasm "passively"? Is a "passive" orgasm any less of an orgasm? Does a woman have to make her orgasm obvious to her partner? Bunzl and Mullen's (1974) study of self-reports of orgasmic reactions revealed that one type of orgasmic myotonia involves a locking of the body ("body rigidification") during genital spasms. Here is one description of an orgasm gathered in *The Hite Report*:

> I move some, especially my hips, but I do not writhe or twist. I think my face must remain fairly expressionless. What's happening goes on primarily inside. *I'm told that I give few indications of what's happening.* (Hite 1976, 153, emphasis added).

Hite comments: "For women who don't move their whole bodies against the point of stimulation, this stillness at orgasm can be misinterpreted by a partner to mean lack of interest!" (*ibid.*).

If a man in Western society can miss his own sexual partner's orgasm, then it would appear to be even more likely that an anthropologist in a non-Western society would miss the presence of female orgasm there.

To continue with the quotation from Davenport (1977, 149) at the point where Symons left off:

> In the Ojibwa, a North American Indian group, it is reported that women are passive during intercourse and orgasm; however, they may take the lead in initiating coitus. In the Guinea survey of young single adults from several African ethnic groups, the women overwhelmingly reported passivity during

coitus, embarrassment at expressing satisfaction during intercourse, distaste for caressing and many admitted an inability to achieve orgasm.

If a woman experiences "embarrassment at expressing satisfaction during intercourse," is she likely to ever admit to an anthropologist-stranger that she has orgasms? And if many women "admitted" an inability to have orgasms, were they possibly encouraged to make such 'admissions' by their questioners?

The anthropologist Margaret Mead is also cited by Symons to support his hypothesis that the female orgasm is only a *potential* that goes unrealized in many cultures:

"Copulation is revolting," say Manus women. "The only bearable husband is one whose advances one can hardly feel." (Mead 1975, 206).

But is such a statement to be taken at face value? What about the husband whose advances one *can* feel? Mead adds: "Each culture *stylizes* the preferences of men and women in wives, husbands, and lovers . . ." (*ibid.*, emphasis added). Is the Manus declaration about intercourse being "revolting" perhaps just a *stylization*, a formulaic definition of the Manus culture, tailor-made for inquisitive anthropologists and not really representative of the true state of affairs between men and women?

Consider, for example, the well-known characterization of middle and late nineteenth century sexual mores in the English-speaking world as "Victorian," that is, as prudish in the extreme. Elements of this characterization include the allegation that "the full force of sexual desire is seldom known to a virtuous woman" (quoted from a nineteenth century treatise on prostitution by Tannahill 1980, 352). One woman visiting a doctor in 1885 declared she "would rather die than be examined," and that "no nice woman has any anatomy between her neck and her ankles" (Dickinson and Beam 1932, 12). Perhaps the most notorious of the nineteenth century treatises is Dr. William Acton's *Functions and Disorders of the Reproductive Organs* (1871[1857]), which makes the oft-quoted claim that ". . . the majority of women (happily for society) are not very much troubled with sexual feeling of any kind. What men are habitually, women are only exceptionally" (115).

But evidence unearthed by the historian Carl Degler (1974; see also Cott 1978; Bullough 1976, 549ff.; Ellis 1927-8, III, 192-227, and most recently and impressively Gay 1984) shows that urban middle class women of the nineteenth century, even "virtuous" ones, were in fact "troubled with sexual feelings." It turns out that Dr. Acton's book stated only one extreme of the then popular medical literature on human sexuality. Degler quotes extensively from a variety of medical texts which all assert that enjoyment of sex by the female is important. An example: "It is a false notion and contrary to nature that this passion in a woman is a derogation to her sex. The science of physiology indicates most clearly its propriety and dignity" (quoted from Dr. George Napheys's popular 1869 treatise *The Physical Life of Woman: Advice to the Maiden, Wife, and Mother* by Degler, 1470). A certain P. Henry Chervasse, in his *Physical Life of Man and Woman: or, Advice to Both Sexes* (1866) wrote: "Whatever may be the object of sexual intercourse, whether intended as a love embrace merely, or as a generative act, it is very clear that it should be as pleasurable as possible to both parties" (Degler, *ibid.*).

The most important aspect of Degler's study is the revelation of a survey of female sexual behavior undertaken by Dr. Clelia Duel Mosher (1863-1940). Most of the forty-five women included in the important Mosher survey were born before 1870. In response to the question "Do you always have a venereal orgasm?," 20% replied "always," 15.5% reported "usually," and 40% replied "sometimes," "not always" or "no" with   instances. These results are very roughly comparable with those of the modern sex surveys by Kinsey, Fisher, Hite, and others (see below, 78ff.), though it is difficult to make valid statistical comparisons because Mosher's sample is relatively small and because of other peculiarities of Mosher's questionnaire. Yet it is clear that most of the women questioned by Mosher truly enjoyed sexual intercourse:

Sexual intercourse "makes more normal people," said a woman born in 1857. She was not even sure that children were necessary to justify sexual relations within marriage. "Even if there are no children, men love their wives more if they continue this relation, and the highest devotion is based upon it, a very beautiful thing, and I am glad nature gave it to us." Since marriage should bring two people close together, said one woman born in 1855, sexual intercourse is the means that achieves that end. "Living relations have a right to exist between married people and these cannot exist in perfection without sexual intercourse to a moderate degree. This is the result of my experience," she added. A woman born in 1864 described sexual relations as "the gratification of a normal healthy appetite." (Degler, 1486-7).

Living in the Victorian age appears not to have made these women very "Victorian" at all.

Let us return now to the cross-cultural studies. Even the Victorian stereotypes pale in comparison to the sexual restraints which pervade the lives of the people of the Irish community of Inis Baeg. According to Messenger (1971), nearly 30 percent of marriageable persons there are single (most of these are apparently celibate). Both before and after marriage men associate primarily with men and women primarily with women. Breast feeding is uncommon because of its sexual overtones. Sex (and even pregnancy) cannot be mentioned in the presence of children. Fear of nudity prevents adequate medical examination in times of illness. Sexual intercourse is regarded as a "duty" of the wife, and is felt to be debilitating by the men. Supposedly the underclothes are not even removed for intercourse. The man quickly achieves orgasm and promptly falls asleep. Messenger states: "there is much evidence to indicate that the female orgasm is unknown — or at least doubted, or considered a deviant response" (16).

Messenger has to admit that it was "extremely difficult" for him to get information about sex on Inis Baeg. Secrecy and fear of gossip are rampant. There is no indication Messenger actually talked to the *women* of Inis Baeg about their sex lives. The most parsimonious conclusion that can be drawn from Messenger's research is that we simply do not know whether and how often women in Inis Baeg have orgasms.

Symons quotes Margaret Mead's conclusions about the potential for female orgasm in the numerous cultures she has studied:

There are many primitive societies in which women's receptivity is all that is required or expected, in which little girls learn from their mothers, and from the way their fathers pat their heads or hold them, unworriedly, close to their bodies, that women are expected to be receptive, not actively or assertively sexed. That whole societies can ignore climax as an aspect of female sexuality must be related to a very much lesser biological basis for such climax. (Mead 1975, 214; Symons 1979, 90).

But what does it mean for a society to "ignore" female orgasm? Does this mean it may in fact be present? Symons says: ". . . among some peoples female orgasm is unknown . . ." (89). What does it mean for female orgasm to be "unknown"? If it were actually there, might it still be "unknown"?

I would like to suggest that both Mead and Symons are (perhaps unintentionally) hedging in their assertion that the female orgasm does not exist in some cultures. They cannot be quite certain about their assertion because there never has been a physiological study (à la Masters and Johnson) of substantial numbers of copulating women in any non-Western society. The anthropologists have had to take women at their word (or the women's partners, an even less reliable source). Furthermore, they have not taken a precaution which would seem elementary to most (at least female) psychoanalysts: in a situation where feminine sexuality is of no importance, or is disdained, or is repressed outright, one has to *expect* that a woman will be embarrassed about or deny outright her sexuality, including possible orgasms.

When a culture is *not* dominated by sexual repression, anthropologists have little or no trouble getting reports about the female orgasm (though not always directly from females). This is not to suggest that some cultures are totally lacking in sexual repression, but that they are relatively less repressed than others. All human cultures share, as a minimum, a need for some form of privacy for most instances of sexual intercourse (Davenport 1977, 150). The apparent universality of this need indicates that it is adaptive, though no one has as yet developed a comprehensive theory of the adaptive value of sexual privacy.

The Mangaians provide a striking example of how easy it is to find out about the presence of the female orgasm in a culture that is relatively unrepressed. On Mangaia (an island in central Polynesia), a male who has recently gone through a superincision ceremony under supervision of a male expert has to go through "practice copulation" in order to learn how to promote orgasm in his partner:

The intercourse, often arranged by the expert, must be with an experienced woman; formerly she was an appropriately related kinswoman, but now she may be any mature and experienced female, including the village trollop. There is said to be a special thrill involved for the woman, although there are also some indications that many women object to the role. Of significance to the youth is the coaching he receives in the techniques that he has learned about from the expert. The woman teaches him to hold back until he can achieve orgasm in unison with his partner; she teaches him the techniques involved in carrying out various acts and positions about which the expert has advised him — especially the matter of timing (*kite i te tā'ei*). A touch of the old ceremony is often preserved in that the woman may insist upon carrying out this practical instruction on the beach, at a place where water seeps through the sands. Here the mistress and the pupil, these Polynesian "children of the sea," are in contact with the mother waters. (Marshall 1971, 115).

The Mangaian male aims for two or three orgasms in his partner to his every one. The female orgasm is essential both to his sexual reputation and to the maintenance of the sexual bond:

Men say that they are always careful of "women's talk," in order that the female will "pass on the good name" of the male. For the Mangaian believes that once he gives his girl the climactic pleasure, she "cannot keep away from him" — unless someone else deliberately "holds her back" by bettering the other male's performance. But it was generally agreed among my several informants that the really important aspect of sexual intercourse for either the married man or the more experienced unwed male is to give pleasure to his wife or woman or girl — the pleasure of the orgasm; supposedly this is what gives the male partner his own pleasure and a special thrill that itself is set apart from his own orgasm. In this connection, it appears to be an accepted cultural fact that following an argument between the couple, Mangaian (and central Polynesian) women in general must have intercourse with their partners before they can "make up." For, the women say, this copulation is proof that the male is still "in love" (desires her). (*ibid.*, 123).

The need to use copulation for purposes of "making up" testifies to its role in maintaining the pair bond, despite Marshall's belief that "there is no cultural connection between a willingness to copulate with a person and any feeling of affection or liking or admiration between copulating partners" (*ibid.*, 159).

Marshall's study of the sexual life of the Mangaians is one of four ethnographic studies selected by Symons (1979, 110) for their general reliability and their illustrativeness of the sexual diversity of cultures. The other three are Bronislaw Malinowski's classic work *The Sexual Life of Savages* (1929), I. Schapera's *Married Life in an African Tribe* (1940), and Verrier Elwin's *The Kingdom of the Young* (1968). Despite the diversity of sexual, affective, and marital practices described in these studies, however, the existence of the female orgasm is granted implicitly or explicitly in all four of them. We have already seen how important it is for women to orgasm on Mangaia. Among the Trobriand Islanders studied by Malinowski, the considerate male partner waits for the female to orgasm (1929, 339; cf. 477). Among the Kgalta (a Bantu tribe in South Africa) the male sometimes recognizes when his partner experiences an orgasm, and sometimes does not. One informant complained: "We never know whether a woman is satisfied or not because she never tells us!" (Schapera 1940, 189; cf. 181-2). The Muria of central India cultivate their sexuality while young, before marriage. Here is how one of Elwin's informants describes a sexual bout:

> When he is on her, she puts his organ in its place with her hand. She says nothing, nor does he. They are very quiet. He must do it hard: unless you sweat, unless your rut leaves you, you are not satisfied. She says, "Push on, push on". *She won't let him go till she is satisfied.* (Elwin 1968, 131, emphasis added).

.I think anyone would agree that this describes a female orgasm. Further evidence is the knowledge of the function of the clitoris among the Muria. One young man said: "When it sees the penis coming, the clitoris smiles" (*ibid.*).

It has to be admitted that obtaining information on the existence of the female orgasm has not been a high priority among ethnographers. Furthermore, ethnographers are usually men, and they tend to receive their information regarding sexuality from male informants. It is no surprise, then, that ". . . references to orgasm in the female in societies other than our own are relatively rare" (Ford and Beach 1951, 33). But it is also still the case, over thirty years later, that ". . . no statements [can] be found which indicate that the women of any society fail to experience a sexual climax" (*ibid.*).

4. Sex Surveys

Unlike most of the anthropological and ethnographic literature on the female orgasm, the surveys of female sexuality in our own, Western culture have several advantages: 1) the women are questioned by members of their own culture; 2) they are guaranteed confidentiality of their responses; 3) large samples are taken and the results are tabulated in a systematic way.[31] A chart from Fisher (1973, 179) gives a reasonably good idea of the proportions of women in carefully designed studies in our culture who do and do not attain orgasm:

Percentages of Women Attaining Orgasm with High Consistency and Never

Sample	Always or Nearly Always	Never
1 (N = 42)	50	14
2 (N = 46)	39	13
3 (N = 44)	41	5
4 (N = 40)	31	0
5 (N = 30)	37	0
6 (N = 48)	37	8
7 (N = 36)	38	0

As can be seen, among the seven samples studied by Fisher there were 31-50% of the women reporting they experienced orgasm "always" or "nearly always" in intercourse (with clitoral stimulation by hand included – cf. Hite 1976, 232), while there were 0-14% reporting they "never" experienced orgasm at all in intercourse. The remaining women experienced orgasm in a middle range of categories designated by Fisher as "frequently," "occasionally," or "rarely." These results are "not grossly different" (*ibid*, 179) from the results of Kinsey *et al.* (1965 [1953]) and Terman (1951), and are roughly comparable with the British findings of Eysenck (1976), the German findings of Sigusch and Schmidt (1971), the contemporary American findings of Hunt (1974), Hite (1976), and Tavris and Sadd (1977),

---

31. Sometimes the surveys are very sophisticated, statistically, and sometimes they are not. There is also the potential problem that the sex surveys may tap non-representative segments of the general population. Tavris and Sadd (1977, 12-15) give a readable summary of this problem and how it is dealt with.

and the earlier findings of Terman (1938), Chesser (1957, 423), and Dickinson and Beam (1932, 62). It is clear from these studies of women of various ages and various social backgrounds that only "a substantial minority" — to quote Kinsey — do not experience orgasm at all during intercourse. The great majority experience at least the intermittent reinforcement of orgasm.

This is not to say that the minority might not make an interesting subject of study in its own right. It is just that absence of orgasm in a minority of women does not necessarily testify to the non-adaptiveness of female orgasm — any more than impotence or premature ejaculation in a minority of males testifies to the non-adaptiveness of the male orgasm.

There is in fact a surprisingly frequent failure rate in the performance of the obviously adaptive male genitalia. Here are the results of a questionnaire administered to 745 American husbands by Terman (1938, 307):

In sexual intercourse with your wife do you have an ejaculation?

Never	9	1.2 %
Sometimes	44	5.9 %
Usually	125	16.8 %
Always	567	76.1%
	745	100.0 %

In other words, nearly 24% of the men questioned were *not* having an orgasm *every* time they had marital sexual intercourse (one could say, indeed, that they were by definition not having intercourse in these cases at all — see Moulton 1975). Compare these questions addressed to a group of British students:

Have you ever suffered from impotence?
  a) Never   } 164 subjects
  b) Once or twice
  c) Several times
  d) Often   } 120 subjects
  e) More often than not
  f) Always

Have you ever suffered from *ejaculatio praecox* (premature ejaculation)?
  a) Very often
  b) Often   } 132 subjects
  c) Middling
  d) Not very often
  e) Hardly ever   } 152 subjects
  f) Never

Compare Eysenck's figures for *female* orgasm:
  Do you usually have an orgasm during intercourse?

    a) Very often
    b) Often } 83 subjects
    c) Middling
    d) Not very often
    e) Hardly ever } 86 subjects
    f) Never

(all based on Eysenck 1976, 67)

To judge from these figures, men seem to be having nearly as much trouble with their orgasms as women with theirs. The two Hite studies reveal a similar comparability. While in Hite (1976, 603) it is reported that 11.6% of a sample of 1,844 women do not orgasm at all, in Hite (1981, 1117) it is recorded that 18% of a sample of 7,239 men "sometimes" to "often" have sex *without* having an orgasm. Hunt (1974, 213) found that, in his American sample, 15% of the husbands under age 25 failed to have orgasm a quarter of the time or more.

Hite's latest study shows that "faking" an orgasm during intercourse is not just a female prerogative, but occurs sometimes in men as well (1981, 459-62). Ruth Stotter reports that sexually active older men are particularly likely to simulate orgasm (personal communication).

Perhaps we do not need to go so far as to propose an intermittent reinforcement theory of *male* orgasm. Perhaps also the quoted figures on male anorgasmia are not altogether representative. But hopefully these figures will at least prevent further citation of the figures on female anorgasmia as evidence for the non-adaptiveness of female orgasm.

5. Female Orgasm and Female Choice

Full sexual sensation binds
the woman to the man. . .
Karl Abraham, 1922

John Alcock, in his critique of Symons' theories, says: "if female orgasm were automatic, a woman could not use its occurrence or absence to help assess the emotional quality of a sexual relationship" (Alcock 1980, 182). Similarly, Richard Alexander says: ". . . perhaps females are more likely to have orgasms with males they prefer . . ." (1979a, 87). What this suggests is that the female orgasm may function as a semiotic entity (specifically, an *index*) which enables a female to choose between copulating regularly with one male as opposed to copulating regularly with another.[32] I will term this potentially adaptive aspect of female orgasm the *domestic bliss function*.[33] The ultimate benefit of copulating regularly with a male is assistance with care of offspring, and a woman's experience or non-experience of orgasm may therefore be a proximate device of sexual selection: ". . . female orgasms would perhaps be more likely in females trying to obtain or keep a 'good' male, identified as a male with much parental investment to offer" (Alexander and Noonan 1979, 451).

Implicit in the domestic bliss function of female orgasm is the notion that females have some *choice* of possible mates. It is true that female choice may be restricted to varying degrees in various human cultures today, depending on how much economic control males have and to what extent marriages are arranged for the benefit of the families of the marrying parties. In the so-called "stateless" or "preindustrial" societies it is particularly likely to be the case that "the behavior of women is much more constrained by reproductive rituals and beliefs than is the behavior of men . . ." (Paige and Paige 1981, 2). In the literature on such societies women are often described as a "reproductive resource" to be exchanged by males and their kin.

More will be said about the exchange of women by men below (sections 19-22). For now it is important to indicate the existence of at least three

---

32. Musaph's and Abraham's (1977) "signal function of hypogyneismus" would appear to be related to the theory being proposed here, but Musaph and Abraham do not say exactly what it is that "hypogyneismus" consistently signals.

33. Cf. the genetic "domestic bliss strategy" of Dawkins (1976). See also below, section 9.

kinds of evidence for female sexual choice in ancestral hominids.

First, there are many human societies today in which females have a say in sexual matters. Whyte (1978a, 222) found that bride and groom had equal ability to initiate or refuse a match in 57.5% of the societies he sampled.[34] When men refrain from controlling the choice of sexual partners/ mates for their daughters and sisters, female choice readily becomes apparent. For example, the Trobriand women described in Malinowski's classic *The Sexual Life of Savages in North-Western Melanesia* (1929) experience little interference with sexual choice from their male kin, they exercise their own judgement in picking a lover, and they decide for themselves whether they want to marry him or not. But a behavior such as this which surfaces in the absence of a restriction against it is likely to be one that was previously present and adaptive under different circumstances.

Second, consider the high intelligence required for men to exercise sexual choice on behalf of their daughters/sisters. Here is Napoleon Chagnon's description of how Yąnomamö men traffic in women:

In generation I, x_1 married the sister of y_1 and, in exchange, gave his own sister to y_1 as wife. This marriage practice is called *brother-sister* exchange and characterizes Yąnomamö marriage behavior. A man is under considerable obligation to *reciprocate* a woman to the kinship group from which he has taken one. [....] Because of this obligation of reciprocity, kinship groups become interdependent socially and form pairs of woman-exchanging kin groups. (Chagnon 1977, 55).

Marriages are arranged by the male members of the local descent group. It cannot be supposed, for example, that the marriage rules automatically dictate the manner in which a woman is disposed in marriage; there are always some negotiations brought about by the situation. For example, a small village may require alliances with larger villages for purposes of defense, and the men of the small village may promise to give daughters to men in the larger village; or there may be a number of men within the village that stand in wife-receiving relationship to the girl, and a decision must be made regarding her ultimate disposition. In some cases a woman's daughters are promised to young men even before they are born. Generally, the girls are near puberty age by the time they are definitely given to a specific male, and they begin cohabiting with the man shortly after the puberty ceremony is over. In some situations a woman must be reassigned to an appropriate mate because her first husband died or abandoned her; or she might run away from a cruel husband and seek refuge among her brothers, bringing about a situation in which they must decide what to do with her. (*ibid.*, 69).

No anthropologist would seriously contend that an early hominid such as

---

34. 93 societies were sampled. In 33.8% the groom has more ability than the bride to initiate or refuse a match. In 3.8% the bride has more ability than the groom.

Australopithecus africanus was capable of such complex negotiations. At the very least a kinship classification system, language abilities (e.g., the ability to make a promise), and sophisticated bargaining abilities would have been necessary for early hominids to carry out the restrictions on female sexual choice which Chagnon describes, and there is no evidence that early hominids had these abilities. Some scholars believe that as complex a semiotic system as language in particular came relatively late in hominid evolution (below, section 34). It is therefore safest to conclude that *early* hominid females at least exercised their own sexual choice, and that limitations on their choosiness came later, perhaps much later.

Third, when males do restrict the sexual choice of their daughters and sisters, they nonetheless do so with female interests in mind. That is, they behave "as if" they were themselves female. Even the Yąnomamö male is capable of sympathizing with a female, especially if that female is his sister and her husband is treating her too cruelly (Yąnomamö brothers will intervene if their sister's husband beats her too often or too violently).

It is not trivial that, whenever a man in any society chooses a mate for his sister or daughter, he at least bothers to choose a male, that is, an individual with whom there is a prospect of offspring. Ask any father even in our relatively egalitarian society how he feels when his teen-age daughter goes out for an evening with a girl friend as opposed to how he feels when she goes out with a boy. In psychoanalytic terms a father is capable of identifying with his daughter at least to the extent that he finds a person of the opposite sex for his daughter, even if that person may not be initially sexually attractive to the daughter (I cannot imagine either a chimpanzee or an australopithecine performing such a maneuver). The father also attempts to find a male who will render her and her offspring the maximum possible altruism: "best to pick a young prime male of a wealthy, powerful lineage, with a guaranteed inheritance" (Daly and Wilson 1978, 275). In doing these things for his daughter a father is of course enhancing the fitness of half his *own* genes. The curious result is that female choice, in effect, remains, only it is exercised by a male. Perhaps the disturbing homosexual overtones of this process have prevented its recognition in the past (cf. Devereux 1978, 185ff., and below, section 47).

On a priori sociobiological grounds female choice is to be expected. Trivers (1978[1972], 83-91) shows that the female (i.e., the sex that usually has to make the greater initial investment in offspring) should theoretically be expected to choose among males on the basis of: 1) ability to fertilize eggs, 2) quality of genes, including ability of genes to survive and reproductive ability of genes, and 3) quality of paternal care, including both willingness and ability of the male to invest in care of offspring. Dawkins subsequently argued (1976, 161ff.) that it is an "evolutionarily stable strategy" for the female to be "coy" for some time before consenting to copulation with a male. By the time copulation occurs, says Dawkins, the male will be so "committed" to the female that "there will be little temptation for him to desert her, if he knows that any future female he approaches will also procrastinate in the same manner before she will get down to business" (*ibid.*, 162). Or more precisely, if we make the same numerical assumptions Dawkins does, it will turn out that a population in which 5/6 of the females behave "coyly" and 5/8 of the males are faithful, is evolutionarily stable.

Lancaster's survey of the available primate data (Japanese macaques, chacma baboons, chimpanzees, rhesus monkeys) reveals a clear pattern of female choice (Lancaster 1979, 68-70; cf. Fedigan 1982, 282-5). Even in a dominance-oriented species such as the rhesus, ". . . the higher-than-expected, observed success of alpha males in mating was related to female preference and not to the male's ability to dominate other males and limit their access to females" (*ibid.* 69). Tutin and McGinnis (1981) conclude that, among chimpanzees, females prefer males who are willing to spend much time with them during estrus peak and who show much affiliative behavior such as grooming and foodsharing. Consortships are also observed in orangutangs, with females exercising considerable prerogative in their formation (Galdikas 1981).

Influenced in part by the work of Trivers and other evolutionary biologists, Zihlman and Tanner (1976) come up with a scenario of early hominid sexual behavior in which the female is very choosey indeed:

Mothers chose to copulate most frequently with ... comparatively sociable, less disruptive, sharing males – with males more like themselves.

A male could attract a female's attention by disruptive displays or through friendly interaction, including greetings, grooming, playing with her offspring, food sharing, protecting, or simple social proximity. Females preferred to associate and have sex with males exhibiting friendly behavior, rather than those who were comparatively disruptive, a danger to themselves or offspring. The picture then is one of bipedal, tool-using, food-sharing, and sociable mothers choosing to copulate with males also possessing these traits. (1976, 606; cf. Fisher 1982, 144; McGuiness 1980a; Zihlman 1981; Tanner 1981, 164; Pfeiffer 1978, 128).

Yet, influenced by the very same sociobiological school of thought, Symons nonetheless comes to the opposite conclusion. Basically, Symons believes that men have had too much control over females for there to have been female choice:

Although copulation is, and presumably always has been, in some sense a female service or favor ..., hominid females evolved in a milieu in which physical and political power was wielded by adult males, and the substantial evidence, documented in the ethnographic record, that men will use their power to control women should not be underestimated. A particularly brutal example is provided by Chagnon (in press) from his studies of the Yąnomamö: "the wife of one of the village headmen began having a sexual affair with another man. She came from the other large lineage in the village, and her brother, also one of the village headmen, attempted to persuade her to stop the affair. The two headmen were brothers-in-law and had exchanged sisters in marriage. The woman in question refused to follow her brother's advice, so he killed her with an ax." (Symons 1979, 203-4).

Symons grants that modern Western societies are not like this, but still seems to believe that our Pleistocene progenitors were. Symons knows perfectly well that his view does not accord with that of most evolutionists, including Darwin himself who in *The Descent of Man* argued that ancestral females were "selecters" of males (1885, 597)[35]. Yet Symons seems eager to convince the reader that he is merely the bearer of unbiased evolutionary tidings to currently fashionable feminists:

... the natural desire to have one's views accepted may – given current standards of acceptability – lead evolutionary theorists to exaggerate the importance of female choice: perhaps it is felt that the often unwelcome messages of an evolutionary view of life – an amoral universe and a creative process that is founded on reproductive competition – can be to some extent ameliorated by the welcome news that in the battle of the sexes nature has given females the upper hand. (*ibid.* 203).

Or perhaps it is just an old tendency among his fellow-anthropologists that Symons is resisting: "anthropologists for some reason seem particularly inclined to indulge in reverse sexism. They perhaps overreact to the fact that the female has always been the under-bitch in the battle between the sexes among primates" (Ghiselin 1980, 188). What Symons does not see, according to Ghiselin, is that ". . . female choice is a kind of male-male competition" (Ghiselin, 188) – and Symons as well as most other specialists in hominid evolution agree that males have competed with one another for access to females in our Pleistocene past.

The fact that females (or their surrogates, male and/or female kin) exercise sexual choice does not at all imply that males (or their surrogates)

---

35. Darwin does not seem to have been consistent on this topic. Tanner points to another passage in *Descent* where Darwin says that men have gained the power of selection over women (cf. Westermarck [1922, I, 493], who complains that Darwin underestimated the importance of "female coyness"). Apparently Darwin was trying to suggest that female choice has decreased in the course of hominid evolution.

do not exercise sexual choice. It is just that the criteria are different. One sentence from Daly and Wilson (1978, 275) neatly summarizes a sociobiological view of the ideal male choice: "Take a woman at puberty and all her reproductive years are yours." Even as non-sociobiological and utterly un-Darwinian a study as *The Politics of Reproductive Ritual* identifies this basis of male choice: ". . . a woman's lifetime fertility is an important capital asset" (Paige and Paige 1981, 44).

But to return to female choice, and its relationship to female orgasm. Is there evidence that the presence of orgasm is related to paternal investment and to a woman's choosing to stay with a man she has copulated with? Does the absence of orgasm indicate a lack of paternal investment and a potential for separation? In other words, does the female orgasm have a domestic bliss function?

Rainwater's (1966b) study of lower class sexual behavior supports the notion that a woman's sexual satisfaction is an index of her receiving other forms of cooperative assistance from her mate. Rainwater found that 64% of white wives who participate in joint non-sexual activities with their husbands rate their sexual satisfaction as high, while only 18% of the wives who do not participate in cooperative activities give a high rating to their sex lives (for negro couples the figures are 64% and 8%, respectively). Speaking of the wives who find little satisfaction in sexual intercourse, Rainwater states: "Since the wife's interest in sex tends to be more heavily dependent upon a sense of interpersonal closeness and gratification in her total relationship with her husband, it is very difficult for her to find gratification in sex in the context of a highly segregated role relationship" (*ibid.*, 101).

One of the important findings of Kinsey and his associates (Kinsey *et al.* 1948; 1965[1953]; cf. Lewis 1976, 127-30) was that sexual enjoyment between spouses decreases with socioeconomic class level. This is particularly true for females. Here, for example, are Kinsey's results (in percent of females) for a sample of 1,448 females in their fifth year of marriage:

Percent of Marital Coitus with Orgasm	Educational Level in Years			
	0-8	9-12	13-16	17+
0	28	17	15	15
1-29	17	15	13	13
30-59	17	15	15	14
60-89	6	18	15	13
90-100	32	35	42	45

(after Kinsey *et al.* 1965, 401, Table 102)

The authors state that ". . . a distinctly smaller number of the females of the lower educational levels and a distinctly larger number of the better educated females had responded nearly 100 per cent of the time in their marital coitus . . ." (*ibid.*, 378). As Lewis (1976, 129) says: "The poorest, least educated women have the least fun in sex, and many of them have no fun at all" (cf. also Bell 1974). Now, assuming a wife's own socioeconomic level is roughly the same as her husband's (i.e., there is homogamy — see section 18), then the poorer, lower class woman is by definition likely to be getting less parental assistance from her husband than the richer middle or upper class woman (and from a *male* viewpoint it makes sociobiological sense to be very cautious about rendering such assistance when income is unpredictable, as it typically is at the bottom of the economic ladder in America — see Weinrich 1977). But the poorer woman is also less likely to be having coital orgasms than the richer woman. Ergo, the likelihood of female orgasm in marital coitus is an index of receiving paternal assistance.

A fairly strong correlation has been found between women's perception of their marital happiness and the extent to which they are orgasmic. Fisher (1973, 32) states: "Generally, the happier a woman's marriage, and therefore presumably the better her relationship with her husband, the higher is her orgasm consistency." A similar conclusion is reached by: Newton 1973, 92; Terman 1938; 1951; Kinsey *et al.* 1953; Chesser 1957; Gebhard 1966; and others. It should be emphasized that the *woman's* satisfaction with the marriage is what correlates with her orgasmic consistency. Terman (1938; 1951; cf. Fisher 1973, 33) found that the woman's orgasmic consistency does *not* correlate (i.e., shows only a chance correlation) with how satisfied the *husband* reports he is with the marriage.

The absence of female orgasm, on the other hand, has been associated with the rupture of a monogamous bond (and by implication a decrease of paternal investment arising out of that bond). In the numerous available sexual surveys, anorgasmic women who are married often say that they are considering adultery and/or divorce. Gebhard (1966, 90), reporting on his work at the Institute for Sex Research, states that ". . . our clinical impression has always been that separation and divorce is frequently presaged by a decline in female orgasm rate." Levine (1982, 322) says that "many newly-divorced women notice enormous increases in their sexual appetites." Gebhard (1970) found that indeed coital-orgasm rate in divorcees tends to be higher than it was before they were divorced.

The survey of over 6,000 English women by Chesser (1957; see also Symons 1979, 232-3) is revealing. Of the women who rarely or never had orgasms, 10% stated they often felt they would like to have intercourse with a man other than their husband, while just 3% of the women who frequently or always had orgasms were interested in extramarital sex (144). Among the former group 52% did not desire extramarital intercourse, while 72% of the regularly orgasmic women did not want intercourse with a man other than their husband. Chesser also found (445) that 94% of the regularly orgasmic women felt they loved their husbands as much as they did during the first year of marriage, while only 61% of the women who rarely or never orgasmed felt this way. As for Kinsey's sample of 6,927 women who had had extramarital intercourse, 42% reported that orgasm occurred more often in extramarital than in marital intercourse (34% reported a roughly equal frequency, and only 24% reported greater frequency in marital than in extramarital intercourse — Kinsey *et al.* 1965 [1953], 432). Assuming that what women *say* on the questionnaires reflects how they actually feel, then the general drift of these figures is to substantially implicate the female orgasm (or lack thereof) in female sexual infidelity.

I believe these data support the notion that presence or absence of female orgasm can be used by the female as a *sign* of whether she should continue to copulate with a given male on a regular basis, and of whether the altruism he renders is adequate enough. In other words, female orgasm has a domestic bliss function, and is one more component in the complex of mechanisms that make females "selecters" (Darwin) of males.

It should be emphasized that the domestic bliss function implies communication of the female *with herself*. Furthermore, the information communicated by definition has to be unknown before the orgasm does or does not take place, and may still not be consciously known even after the orgasm does or does not take place. Richard Alexander (personal communication) says: ". . . [females] do not always know when it [orgasm] is going to happen easily or only with difficulty, and they are not entirely (at least) aware of the contexts in which ease or difficulty will be the case. Nor are they always aware of the significance of success or failure as a part of their overall interaction with a mate." The unconscious nature of this internal communication by means of the orgasm-sign is part of the overall complex of unconscious processes that both psychoanalysts and sociobiologists have been concerned with (see Preliminaries, section D). I will attempt to describe the unconscious psychoanalytic structure of the communication later on (section 23).

6. The Specter of Infidelity

Pater semper incertus
Roman saying

While a woman who feels happy about her relationship with her mate is likely to be having orgasms, the woman who is miserable in this respect is much less likely to be having them. From an evolutionary viewpoint, the important thing about lack of orgasm in a married woman is that it may tempt her into infidelity, and thus endanger her mate's confidence in paternity[36] of her offspring. The man may end up helping to care for children who do not carry any immediate replicas of his genes, and he may fail to produce as many replicas of his genes as he might otherwise have produced, while a woman whose mate is unfaithful can go on caring for children who, she can be sure, carry replicas of her own genes.

The problem of confidence of paternity is really just part of a larger picture that is now seen by sociobiologists as the basic opposition between the sexes in most animal species, that is, the opposition between what Daly and Wilson (1978) call "the reluctant female" and "the ardent male":

The female's greater investment in each offspring means that her maximal reproductive potential is lower than the male's[37]. Males therefore compete

---

36. The "confidence" I am speaking of here has to do with genes, not necessarily with psychology. I doubt that the husband is as concerned about whether the children he cares for are biologically his own as about the *attachments* he has to his wife and to her children. An anonymous reader says: " a woman's faithlessness disturbs not only knowledge of paternity, but a secure base in a home environment as well." I would go further and say that the psychologically "secure base in a home environment" is the overall *proximate mechanism* whereby one ultimate genetic effect, "confidence in paternity," is accomplished. The proximate mechanism in question is, I think, quite complex, involving other behaviors besides the fostering of female orgasm. It probably has an ontogenetic background involving at least: 1) male indentification with the mother (including language acquisition from the mother), 2) male envy of the mother's ability to give birth to children, 3) male identification with an adult male during childhood, 4) an ability of the male to recapture his earlier relationship with his mother in his relationship with his mate, and 5) an ability to be possessive/jealous of his mate, just as he was once possessive/jealous of his mother. These ideas are developed in greater detail below.

37. *The Guiness Book of World Records* reports 69 live births (including twins, triplets, and quadruplets) from 27 pregnancies in a nineteenth century Russian woman *vs.* 888 children sired by the Moroccan emperor Moulay Ismail (Daly and Wilson, 59).

among themselves for fertilization opportunities. Investing little in each off-spring, males are selected to sow their seed wherever opportunity arises. Investing considerably in each offspring, females are selected to exhibit greater selectivity in their choice of mates. One feature on which females may exercise selectivity is the male's willingness or ability to make an effective parental contribution. But wherever males do in fact invest parentally, they are under selective pressure to protect themselves against cuckoldry, and therefore males have a greater concern than females over the fidelity of their mates. (Daly and Wilson 1978, 298; for general discussions, see: Trivers 1972; Barash 1977; Symons 1979; Dawkins 1976; Williams 1975; Ghiselin 1974; Van den Berghe 1979; Ruse 1979; Jensen 1980).

Long before sociobiology was invented — but also well after Darwin had promulgated his theory of sexual selection in *The Descent of Man* (1871) — the geneticist A. J. Bateman discerned the underlying evolutionary reason why the males tend to be aggressively indiscriminate or promiscuous and females passive and choosey:

The primary feature of sexual reproduction is ... the fusion of gametes irrespective of their relative size, but the specialisation into large immobile gametes [eggs] and small mobile gametes [sperm] produced in great excess (the primary sex difference), was a very early evolutionary step. One would therefore expect to find in all but a few very primitive organisms, and those in which monogamy combined with a sex ratio of unity eliminated all intra-sexual selection, that males would show greater intra-sexual selection than females. This would explain why in unisexual organisms *there is nearly always a combination of an undiscriminating eagerness in the males and a discriminating passivity in the females. Even in derived monogamous species (e.g. man) this sex difference might be expected to persist as a relic.* (Bateman 1948, 365, italics added; see Fedigan 1982, 296ff. for a dissenting view, and Bonaparte 1953, 78, for the psychoanalytic version).

Most of the evidence does indeed indicate that the difference persists in humans. There are examples galore in the literature on human sociobiology (Symons 1979, Van den Berghe 1979, and Daly and Wilson 1978 are especially readable), in the older anthropological and sexological treatises (e.g., Westermarck 1922, vol. I, chs. 13-15; Ellis 1927-8, vol. III), in such pioneering modern sexological studies as Kinsey *et al.* (1948; 1953) and Ford and Beach (1951), in the current sexological journals, and elsewhere.

     Just one randomly chosen example is from a survey of 150 male and female German workers:

Of 20-year-old virgin women (as compared to men) the significantly more frequent opinion is that "they're waiting for true love," "they're decent," or "they're living properly." As opposed to that, it is significantly more often assumed of abstinent males that "they're afraid," "they can't find a girl," "they're not a real man." Women who have many coital partners are significantly more often criticized than promiscuous men as follows: "they'll get a bad reputation," "no one will want to marry them," and "they should be ashamed." Of promiscuous men, the opinion is significantly more often: "they're doing it right," "they're enjoying life," "those are real men." It follows from this that abstinence is more proper and characteristic of the female role while in the male role it is partner mobility. (Sigusch and Schmidt 1971, 37-8; cf. Daly and Wilson 1978, 301-2).

Compare the earlier, cross-cultural findings of Ford and Beach:

Sixty-one percent of the 139 societies in our sample for whom evidence is available forbid a mated woman to engage in extramateship liaisons. In some societies the mated man is similarly restricted, although the great majority of these peoples are much more concerned with the behavior of the mated woman than with that of the mated man. (Ford and Beach 1951, 115; cf. Whyte 1978a, 220; Daly and Wilson 1978, 309).

In many nonindustrial societies concern with the extramarital behavior of mated women is so extreme that wars are fought (by men of course) when adultery occurs (Chagnon 1977; Symons 1979, 151-3; Paige and Paige 1981, 177).

At the psychological level, males and females appear to be equally capable of experiencing the complex emotion of jealousy when a mate is (or is imagined to be) unfaithful (White 1981, 135). But when a male experiences jealousy he is more likely to feel angry and to do things which threaten the relationship, while a jealous female is more likely to do things to maintain the relationship, such as make herself more attractive to her partner (Shettel-Neuber *et al.* 1978). This makes sense, sociobiologically, because, as Daly *et al.* (1982, 17) say, ". . . the reproductive threat in a wife's infidelity lies in the risk of alien insemination, whereas the reproductive threat in a husband's infidelity lies more in the risk of lost resources."

Kinsey *et al.* (1948, 592) summarize their American findings: "wives, at every social level, more often accept the non-marital activities of their husbands. Husbands are much less inclined to accept the non-marital activities of their wives. It has been so since the dawn of history." Such a broad statement is in fact not broad enough: it has been so since *before* the dawn of history, i.e., at least since male hominids started making significant paternal investment in offspring.

In any case, more often than not there is a double standard. Broude and Greene (1976) report that in 66% of the societies in their sample of 116 societies there is a double standard for extramarital sex. And I suspect that, even where women do indulge in some extramarital sex, they do so much less often than the men do, and for more serious emotional reasons.

Daly and Wilson go to the heart of the matter:

Maternity defines parenthood: A man can be cuckolded, whereas a woman cannot. An adulterous wife places her husband at risk of misdirecting his parental investment altogether. An adulterous husband puts his wife at no such risk, though she may fear the lesser danger of his diverting his investment from her and her offspring. (Daly and Wilson 1978, 281).

There is nothing about proximate mechanisms here (e.g., female orgasms or male dominance), but the ultimate causal logic is impeccable. There is also no accounting for the exceptions, though, such as the apparent decline of the double standard in some modern technological cultures. A recent American survey by *Psychology Today* (November, 1981) indicates that 49% of males and 44% of females responding said they had extramarital affairs (with males, I suspect, having more of their affairs with unmarried partners). These are remarkably close percentages. But, "modern people do not live in the social and technocultural circumstances to which natural selection has adapted them, and the strategic goal of fitness maximization has apparently been derailed" (Daly and Wilson 1978, 311). How the derailment has taken place would be an interesting topic in itself. One may ask, for example, whether the apparent increase in female sexual infidelity in some modern societies reflects an underlying female interest in polygamy, or is just a reaction of revenge against promiscuous male mates and an envious desire to be *just like* what is perceived as the male norm. One might also speculate that increased female polygamy is a " fashion," a cultural trait with its own replicative impetus or cultural fitness, and which spreads in a population despite its negative Darwinian fitness, as some cultural features do (see below, section 36). Also, the availability of reliable contraceptives and/or safe abortions has made it much easier for women to be polygamous.

Symons (1979, 226-46) gives a wide ranging review of the literature on the double standard, adding spice with pertinent quotations from the world's most insightful students of adultery, i.e., literary artists.

Symons (cf. also Scarf 1980b) notes that the epithet "promiscuous" is pejorative (in English and in a number of other languages) when applied to a woman, but not necessarily so when applied to a man. There are many more derogatory terms in English for promiscuous women than for promiscuous men, as can be established by looking at any thesaurus (cf. Stanley 1977). I might add that, while there is in many languages a special term denoting a woman's act of infidelity, namely, "cuckoldry" (related to "cuckoo," a bird which may lay eggs in the nests of other species), I know of no language in which there is a special term for infidelity committed by a *man*. Also, the term "cuckold" (cf. Russian "*rogonosets*," German "*Hahnrei*," French "*cocu*" or "*cornard*," Polish "*rogacz*") applies specifically to the man who is victimized by the infidelity, but there is no such term for a woman who is sexually betrayed by her husband (cf. Stanley 1977, 316). There is even a special gesture, the so-called vertical horn-sign (hand held up with forefinger and little finger extended vertically, the *manus cornuta* of antiquity) which designates a cuckold, but no corresponding sign for a deceived wife.

The controversy surrounding the origin of the horn-sign is, incidentally, quite remarkable. Morris *et al.* (1979, 120-134) have turned up at least fourteen different theories of its origin. I am inclined to believe that the theory that the two "horns" represent the two penises in the love-life of the adulteress (theory No. 10, 120-5) is the unconscious idea which has most strongly sustained the cuckold gesture over the centuries, though one of the other theories might better explain the actual etymology of the gesture. The fact that the gesture nowadays is dying out in such northern European countries as England, Holland, and Germany, but is still common in some other parts of Europe testifies to differing attitudes toward female infidelity: "[the horn-sign] has only survived as a commonly used insult in those regions where divorce remains illegal or is strongly condemned — in other words, in strongly Catholic countries such as Portugal, Spain and Italy" (*ibid.*, 131). I might add that the Catholic church hierarchy is an exclusively male institution, and it is therefore no surprise that the strict Catholic prohibitions against divorce are a kind of 'sympathetic' reflection of precisely male genetic interests.

From a female viewpoint the male's greater vulnerability to sexual infidelity means the female can *use* the threat of it in an effective way. As Symons (1979, 241) observes, ". . . having an affair is a more effective female than male tactic in marital skirmishing . . ." White (1980) found that, in his sample of 150 heterosexual romantic relationships, females were more likely to report attempts to induce jealousy in the partner than males were. If the male's desire for sexual variety (typically stronger than the female's desire for variety, as amply demonstrated in chapter 7 of Symons' book) leads the male to neglect his mate sexually or emotionally, then she may retaliate with her own infidelity (Symons, 251). Or, if he is sexually or emotionally inadequate for reasons other than his own infidelity — a possibility that is much more distasteful to the male ego because it does not include a sexual compliment — then she may also look elsewhere for satisfaction. Yet a third possibility is that the female partner is herself incapable of responding sexually, no matter how faithful, solicitous, or sexually talented the male may be, and as a result she may move on to another sexual relationship. In all of these cases there is a good chance that the female's infidelity is preceded by a lack of or decrease in her orgasms in intercourse with her mate, and this may be read as a signal by her mate that infidelity may occur.

If lack of orgasm signals potential infidelity to the male, then presence of orgasm can of course signal fidelity. Alexander and Noonan (1979, 449) have already proposed the idea that female orgasm can be "... a communicative device which tends to raise [the] male's confidence that the female is disinclined to seek sexual satisfaction with other males" (cf. Alexander 1979a, 86-7). The potential for presence/absence of female orgasm to signal fidelity/infidelity to the male will here be termed the *paternal confidence function*. As with the domestic bliss function, the paternal confidence function is semiotic (specifically, indexical) in nature. However, where the domestic bliss function involves communication of the female with herself, the paternal confidence function involves the communication of information from the female to the male.

7. Fake Orgasms and the Male Ego

Given the communicative or semiotic potential of the female orgasm for the male, it becomes possible, as Alexander and Noonan observe, for females to use the orgasm signal for *deceptive* purposes. Indeed this is one of the properties that makes it clear that female orgasm is a semiotic entity: ". . . semiotics is in principle the discipline studying everything which can be used in order to lie" (Eco 1976, 7). It is well known that women "fake" orgasm, or conversely, deny having orgasm when they do orgasm. Hite's statistics (1976, 257) are as follows:

Do you fake orgasms?	
Yes	567
No	775
Used to	318
It's no use, it's not convincing	4
	1664

Rainwater (1966b) found in his study of lower-class sexual behavior that there was much deception going on as regards sexual pleasure. In one group half the men indicated that their wives enjoyed intercourse more than the wives themselves indicated. Perhaps some of these men were kidding themselves, or the interviewers, but I suspect that a substantial number of fake female orgasms contributed to the results.

Hite gives ten continuous pages of quotations from women who explain why they do or do not simulate orgasm in sexual intercourse. Throughout it is clear that, when women do simulate orgasm, it is primarily to please the male ("to protect the man's ego," "I should build up his ego," "you'll emasculate the man," "to save his pride," "why be rude?," "to avoid confrontation," "to please men," "I know it would hurt the guy I live with if he knew otherwise," etc.; cf. Koedt 1973, 203-4). Some of the women were quite explicit about the role of deception in "holding on" to a man and in competing with other women:

A few times, to keep a man. Never again. (262)
I used to fake them to keep my husband from straying. (260)
I used to, because my partner was comparing me to another woman he was sleeping with. He made me feel terrible with descriptions of how she went into a screaming orgasm before he even entered her. (258)

I never fake orgasm. I am angry with other women who do, because then men can tell me that I am incapable sexually .... (257)

Evidently, then, if a woman can "please" a man with her orgasm, she believes she stands a better chance of keeping him attached to her.

It is remarkable how sensitive a woman in a society that encourages female orgasm can be to the male's sensitivity to whether she is having an orgasm or not. If she cares about her partner at all, she is very concerned about *his* sense of failure when *she* fails to orgasm. In the long run, he may "stray" if there is a sign that *she* may "stray," that is, if she does not demonstrate an orgasm. In other words, evolutionarily speaking, she may lose his parental assistance. But in the short run her failure to (at least pretend to[38]) orgasm seems to damage his sense of masculinity, his 'delicate male ego', which is ultimately rooted in his castration anxiety.[39] For him the female orgasm has what might be called a *male potency function*. When she is having orgasms, this function provides him with essentially libidinal satisfaction (above and beyond the libidinal satisfaction of his own orgasm, and quite apart from the female's libidinal satisfaction from her own orgasm), and he is likely to remain interested in staying with her. When she is not

---

38. Writing about "impotency in women" in 1878, Van de Warker said that the husband " ... not only demands pleasure and satisfaction for himself, but he requires something much more difficult to give – the appearance, if not the real existence, of satisfaction and pleasure in the object of his attentions" (quoted by Degler 1974, 1473).

39. Evidence for male castration anxiety will be detailed below, sections 38ff. For now it is sufficient to indicate that, from a male viewpoint, when a female has an orgasm, she is doing something *similar* to what a man does when *he* has an orgasm, that is, when he *ejaculates*. At a deep psychological level the male's feeling is that, although a woman does not have a penis, she can at least have an orgasm (or many orgasms). His old childhood anxiety about humans who do not possess penises is thus somewhat assuaged when he sees his partner enjoying the same orgasmic spasms he enjoys. In some cultures male are relieved of castration anxiety not only by their encouragement of female orgasm, but by other practices that seem to make a female "phallic." A Ponapese man, for example, may stimulate his wife to urinate before having intercourse with her. Apparently, one way he does this is to tug at her labia minora with his teeth, thereby simulating fellatio (Devereux 1958, 282-3). Also, various manipulations are made on Ponapese women to increase the size of the clitoris and labia (*ibid.* 279; stretching of the labia is performed by other peoples as well, such as the Dahomeans and the Nama – Ford and Beach 1951, 51, 86). The men of Ponape themselves sometimes undergo removal of one testicle ("unilateral castration" or "hemicastration"). On the islands of Truk a woman whose genital area is "full of things," such as a prominent clitoris and labia minora, is said to achieve orgasm rapidly and is very desirable from a male viewpoint (Gladwin and Sarason 1953, 109-10). Among many peoples, such as the Mohave Indians (Devereux *ibid.*) and the Trobriand Islanders (Malinowski 1929, 167-8),

having orgasms this libidinal source of pleasure in the male may be blocked, and he may feel inadequate, guilty, or defensively unconcerned:

"It's something I have done wrong."
"I have not done enough or the 'right' thing."
"I let her down."
"I failed her."
"I must be inadequate." (Hite 1981, 644)

"Guilty and selfish. My fault."
"Sometimes I feel I am taking advantage of her, or that she is 'putting up' with me." (*ibid.*, 646)

"It's her business. She is responsible for her own orgasms."
"I offer everything. If she doesn't accept, I'm clean."
"It's her decision." (*ibid.*, 651)

Even the usually anti-Freudian Hite detects the defensive hostility in the last set of answers quoted here. Hite is of course unconcerned with the underlying sociobiological implication that all of these answers have, namely, the danger that the sexual partners of the men who responded have been or are about to be unfaithful.

When a woman (other than a paid prostitute) goes out of her way to demonstrate to her sexual partner that she has orgasms with him on a regular basis, he can probably count on her being faithful. Whether she has genuine orgasms or simulated ones should make little difference to him from a long-term viewpoint, even if he can detect the difference. Both types can be understood by him as an indication of her commitment. It is only when she neither has genuine orgasms *nor* cares enough to simulate them that he should be truly alarmed.

Or rather, in societies where there is a real possibility of female infidelity, he should be alarmed. It has to be granted that (high status) males in some societies exercise such extensive control over their women — e.g., claustration in guarded harems, clitoral excision, infibulation, long postpartum taboo, and other practices that repress female sexuality (see: Paige and Paige 1981; Hrdy 1981, 177ff.; Huelsman 1976; Hosken 1979) — that the question of the Darwinian adaptiveness of female orgasm in such societies becomes somewhat academic (so also, by the way, does

---

there is a belief that "female ejaculation" takes place. It should be cautioned, however, that in some women there may be an actual forceful release of fluid in intercourse (Gräfenberg 1950; Ellis 1927-8, V, 145; Devereux *ibid.*, 284; Ladas *et al.* 1982; Heath 1984; Goldberg *et al.* 1983), so that the idea of "female ejaculation" may not be *only* the product of the anxious male imagination.

the question of the adaptiveness of orgasm in those *males* who are excluded from breeding by their polygynous brethren). However, the very lengths to which some Rajput, Kikuyu, Somali, Sudanese, Galla, Harrari, and other males (and their female kin) will go in order to repress the eroticism (including orgasm) of their women should make us suspect that such eroticism, if left unchecked, would be a formidable adaptation indeed (cf. Hrdy, *ibid*.).[40] Also, we should suspect that a specifically male adaptation is at work (or overworked) in such situations. Even in societies in which female eroticism is not so obviously repressed, males may still feel threatened if females express *too much* interest in having intercourse. That is, what is perceived as a desire to have too many orgasms (and too often) can be as threatening to the 'delicate male ego' as no orgasms at all, and it is possible that this feeling is itself adaptive for males (see section 45 on the adaptiveness of castration anxiety).

---

40. Hosken (1979) estimates that 74 million females living in continental Africa have been subjected to genital mutilation. In Bonaparte's words (1953, 207), the "enemies of the clitoris" in Africa are legion. The success of genital mutilation in repressing female enjoyment of intercourse may be easily judged from Khattab's study of 106 Egyptian women who had suffered complete or partial loss of the clitoris, together with infibulation in some of the cases (the number is not specified). Of these women, only 36% enjoyed coitus, and 71% did it *only* to get pregnant. See: Khattab 1981, 63. For a detailed anthropological survey of female genital mutilation, see Huelsman 1976. According to Huelsman infibulation is typically accompanied by clitoral excision. Huelsman cites a report that 80% of a sample of infibulated Sudanese women never had orgasm.

8. The Misery Factor

It is probably safe to say that neither Western societies nor the stateless, tribal societies studied by anthropologists and ethnographers provide the kind of social environment in which the female orgasm originally evolved. All societies today have kinship systems and rules of marriage which guarantee that most females of reproductive age will periodically be inseminated whether or not they like the experience or the particular man who inseminates them. But at some point there had to have been no such thing as the kind of complicated social arrangements by which women now get inseminated. They had to have been motivated to be inseminated (preferably by a 'good' male), and when they were not being inseminated (by same) they must have been taking measures to insure they would be — much as any hungry or thirsty organism takes measures to obtain food and water. As argued above, the possibility of having orgasm was probably a motivating factor, and the consistent lack of orgasm must have been experienced as unpleasant or upsetting — again, much as hunger or thirst is disturbing. The cure would have been to find a sexual partner (or a *new* sexual partner), and obviously there would have been genetic consequences.

Female sexual misery, in other words, should not be underestimated as a factor in hominid evolution. I believe the following statements by completely anorgasmic women testify not only to psychological damage, but also to the potential genetic consequences of the damage:

I've tried everything, but I've never had one. I feel that having an orgasm would leave me more satisfied and satiated. Now I never feel contented when we are finished. *I feel very frustrated and insecure* without them. It causes me *more unhappiness than anything else in my life. I'm not sure that I want to stay married* to my husband because of such an unfulfilled sex life.

The questionnaire is okay except it is oriented to the orgasmic woman and *I have become very depressed* since beginning it. *I feel cheated and envious* of women to whom all questions apply!

I have never yet come, so having sex usually ends up a little sour. I have been very excited and feeling very good when the man I'm with comes — which is the end of really active exciting lovemaking — but still *I feel very depressed,* unloved, and I feel like crying — sometimes I have cried (though I usually tried not to, so I wouldn't upset my lover). *It's hard to describe how bad and totally alone and ignored this makes me feel.* (Hite 1976, 205-7, emphasis added).

These are women speaking about their own anorgasmia. It is interesting to compare what a well known male sexologist has to say about the same subject. After declaring that single females without orgasm pose "a problem of some social importance," Kinsey goes on to say:

When such frustrated or sexually unresponsive, unmarried females attempt to direct the behavior of other persons, they may do considerable damage. There were grade school, high school, and college teachers among these unresponsive or unresponding females. Some of them had been directors of organizations for youth, some of them had been directors of institutions for girls or older women, many of them had been active in women's clubs and service organizations, and not a few of them had had a part in establishing public policies. Some of them had been responsible for some of the more extreme sex laws which state legislatures had passed. Not a few of them were active in religious work, directing the sexual education and trying to direct the sexual behavior of other persons. Some of them were medically trained, but as physicians they were still shocked to learn of the sexual activities of even their average patients. If it were realized that something between a third and a half of the unmarried females over twenty years of age have never had a completed sexual experience . . , parents and particularly the males in the population might debate the wisdom of making such women responsible for the guidance of youth. (Kinsey *et al.* 1965 [1953]).

My lawyer says this is sexist poppycock. However, I wanted to cite it, just in case it is true (or was true in Kinsey's day) as another example of the potentially deleterious effects of female anorgasmia. Whereas Hite's anorgasmic women are just plain miserable, Kinsey's anorgasmic spinsters seem to want other people to be as unhappy as they are.

Married women who do not have orgasms are also quite capable of communicating their misery. According to sex therapist Avodah Offit, "fear of disturbing maternal dominance" can interfere with a daughter's orgasmic ability. The mother seems to be whispering into her daughter's ear: "Don't be foolish . . . You will not have it better than I did. Love is not true, and sex is the messenger of deception. I failed, and so must you" (Offit 1977, 160). Not all, perhaps not even most cases of female anorgasmia can be explained this way, for the prior relationship with the *father* has been found to play the major role (below, section 12). But Uddenberg (1974) did find that mothers of women with orgasmic problems expressed a negative or ambivalent attitude toward their daughters more often than did other mothers, even though the daughters themselves were not necessarily reporting this attitude (psychoanalysts would spot denial or repression at work here). Below (128) I report a specific case in which a daughter's sexual unhappiness derives from her mother's sexual unhappiness.

Now, I am aware that, as Symons (1979, 127) says, ". . . natural selection is for reproductive success, not happiness . . ." (cf. Wilson 1975, 255).

However, this cannot mean that the happiness/unhappiness category is, a priori, completely irrelevant to natural selection. For example, a person who is starving is both less likely to be happy and less likely to leave offspring than a person who is well fed. That person's state of unhappiness has something to do with genes. Also, the person who is starving is more likely than not to search for measures that reduce the unhappiness he is enduring. People may not actively strive for happiness, but they at least work to *avoid unhappiness*. Symons says that ". . . many features of human sexuality suggest that it is ill-adapted to ensure marital happiness" (126). But it may well be correct to say that human marital arrangements are adapted to ensure the *least* amount of *un*happiness, because unhappiness is associated with conditions that can exterminate genes.

There would undoubtedly be much more unhappiness, including a much lesser incidence of female orgasm, if there were no marital arrangements at all, for example. As has already been indicated, the female orgasm is most likely to occur in the context of a stable relationship — and what better way is there to promote the existence of such a relationship than marriage? This is far from saying that all marriages are successful, or that marriage is exclusively in the service of female orgasm. But from a female viewpoint marriage is more often than not going to be the best context in which a woman can count on having orgasms (cf. Kinsey *et al.* 1965, 514). Female orgasm and marriage — to slightly change the words of an old song — appear to go together like a horse and carriage.

9.   Four Functions of Female Orgasm

Shere Hite grudgingly admits that one of the major reasons why some women do not like sexual intercourse is because "Mr. Right" is lacking. Here are a couple of her respondents:

In order to have orgasms with a man, I would have to have a deep trust in him. He should be a really sensuous and intensely sexual man with a lot of patience and very perceptive, but easy-going. I think once I *knew* someone could satisfy me, I'd be able to come.
I don't know what would help but I think I have to know beyond a doubt that I'm the only piece of pussy he's interested in at the moment, the past ones were substandard, and that he'll be damned lucky to find another like me if he lives to be a hundred. (Hite 1976, 252-3).

I say Hite *grudgingly* accepts the "Mr. Right" explanation because, after quoting sixteen different women on the crucial importance of having a caring, sensitive male partner in sexual intercourse, she makes the following ideological statement to her (presumably female) readers: "... don't wait for the Right Man to be dependent on, but create your own good situation— which can include yourself as being the Princess Charming, who knows pleasurable things to do and who finds another person to do them with" (*ibid.*, 255). In other words, the committed feminist really ought to behave like the committed Don Juan of yore — search for pleasure, not for love and the dependency that goes with it. Such advice reveals a need to fight male chauvinism essentially by imitating it. It is like many a little girl's belief that she cannot possibly be as worthy as her brother unless she too were to possess a penis.

The four functions of the human female orgasm may now be summarized. The *hedonic function* helps insure that a female will be interested in having sexual intercourse with a male throughout her cycle. The *domestic bliss function*, which is semiotic (specifically, indexical) in nature, helps the female choose the male most likely to stay around and benefit her offspring in the long run. Both the hedonic and the domestic bliss functions exist from the viewpoint of the individual female who is or is not having orgasms. From the viewpoint of her male partner her orgasms (or absence thereof) appear to have two functions: a *potency function* which helps to keep his 'delicate male ego' intact and thereby keeps him interested in being with the female, and another semiotic function (also indexical) which I have designated the *paternal confidence function*, which helps keep him informed about how confident he can be of his paternity of the offspring he is helping to care for. This latter semiotic function seems to be accomplished by both the simulated and the genuine orgasms of his mate. The four functions may be schematized as follows:

	Semiotic	*Libidinal*
Male Viewpoint	paternal confidence function	potency function
Female Viewpoint	domestic bliss function	hedonic function

Very generally speaking, all four of these functions may be seen as "... part of the female's continual effort to obtain resources from males" (Richard Alexander, personal communication). More strictly speaking, only the hedonic and domestic bliss functions are adaptive in the evolutionist's sense, since only these two functions exist from the female viewpoint. As Symons stated in the passage quoted earlier (67), it is "orgasmic females" who have to have enjoyed a greater reproductive success than "nonorgasmic females" in order for female orgasm to qualify as a Darwinian adaptation.

However, males do benefit genetically from what I have termed the potency and paternal confidence functions. The female is the one who is or is not having female orgasms, but the male possesses a perceptual-cognitive apparatus capable of detecting her orgasms, and he is therefore in a position to behave adaptively in response to her, i.e., to do whatever maximizes his inclusive fitness. Again, strictly speaking, it is his perceptual-cognitive apparatus which is being adaptive (or perhaps preadaptive), not *her* orgasms.

But it is probably quite artificial to separate female orgasm from male response to it, both in terms of proximate functioning and in terms of ultimate genetic benefits. Indeed, it is difficult to imagine how the hominid female orgasm could have evolved in isolation from male response to it, just as it is quite impossible for the mammalian breast to have evolved separately from the mammalian infant's sucking apparatus.

Furthermore, it is not only females who cash in on the genetic benefits of female orgasms. Every human individual, male or female, possesses genes derived from both males and females in its ancestry. A woman who is doing things that are adaptive for her genes is by definition doing things that are adaptive for roughly half of her father's genes and half her future son's genes. A father who is altruistic to his daughter is benefitting roughly half his own genes. Particularly relevant here is Fisher's (1973) finding that a female is more likely to be orgasmic if her father was dependably present and actively involved in her childhood life than if he was not (more will be said about this). If *her* orgasms are adaptive, as I have been arguing, then *his* earlier altruism has paid off. Males and females simply do not evolve in genetic isolation from each other the way, say, humans have evolved in genetic isolation from gorillas. In adopting different evolutionary strategies, the sexes may appear to be engaged in a "battle of the sexes." But neither side can "win" as long as genes are shuffled back and forth between the two sides (while in a "battle of the species" one side may in fact "win," i.e., extinguish the other).

It should be emphasized that the semiotic half of the above four-fold schema would not exist if the female orgasm could either *always* or *never*[41] be counted on to take place during intercourse ("female orgasm is unpredictable, unreliable" – Hrdy 1981, 165). No entity can function as a sign, and no information can be transmitted if the potentially signifying entity is completely predictable.

For example, in languages such as French, Polish, and Armenian stress always falls on a predictable syllable in a word, and therefore stress is not capable of signifying anything in these languages (= is nonphonemic). But in languages such as English, Russian, or German stress can conceivably fall on any syllable in a word, and therefore can be used to distinguish meanings (= is phonemic). Thus, for example, English "behind" conveys a different meaning (adjective or adverb) than "béhind" (noun only). In linguistic jargon, we might say that the female orgasm is *emic*.

The fact that a woman does have an orgasm in a given instance of sexual intercourse conveys meaning to the participants because they know that female orgasm could also be absent. If female orgasm were *infallibly present*, however, its function would only be libidinal at best. Furthermore, it is difficult to imagine why females would be as inclined to monogamy as they are if they could always count on an orgasm, and males would therefore lose confidence of paternity and abandon monogamy too. Promiscuity would reign, kinship systems and marriage rules would be irrelevant or unnecessary, and the entire structure of human society – if such could be called a human society – might be radically different. Conversely, if female orgasm were *predictably absent*, then there would also not be the two semiotic functions discussed above, but it is hard to imagine why females

---

41. The digital quality of female orgasm ("all or none") does not exclude its having analogue qualities as well when it occurs. Thus "there are orgasms and orgasms" (Richard Alexander, personal communication; cf. Money 1980, 119). In his book *The Goals of Human Sexuality* Irving Singer (1974) eloquently argues that at least three types of female orgasm exist.

would then be nearly as interested in intercourse as they are now. Either males would have to rape them much more often than they do now, or they would have to be periodically estrous as their ancestors were at some point. Either of these alternatives might also result in societal structures fundamentally different from what we find in our species today. It therefore is safest to conclude that the phenomenon of intermittent, unpredictable female orgasm in heterosexual intercourse was essential to forming basic human social structures as we know them, and that the female orgasm was most likely, then, another of the many Darwinian adaptations contributing to the development of the hominid line.

10. An Ontogenetic Precursor of Mr. Right: I

I know it's real love because I liked
him even *BEFORE* I met him!
Bobby Sox

Those who have read Richard Dawkins' brilliant yet readable book *The Selfish Gene* (1976) will recognize that the domestic bliss function of the female orgasm owes its name to what Dawkins calls the "domestic-bliss strategy" of female reproductive behavior. Here is Dawkins' description of the strategy, with my interpolated modifications pertinent to a woman who may have copulated but not yet made a long-term commitment:

The simplest version of the domestic-bliss strategy is this. The female looks the males over, and tries to spot *signs* of fidelity and domesticity [e.g., her own orgasms] in advance. There is bound to be variation in the population of males in their predisposition to be faithful husbands. If females could recognize such qualities [such as the ability to give them orgasms] in advance, they could benefit themselves by choosing males possessing them. One way for a female to do this is to play hard to get [permanently] for a long time, to be coy. Any male who is not patient enough to wait until the female eventually consents to copulate [or 'consents' to orgasm] is not likely to be a good bet as a faithful husband. By insisting on a long engagement period [or long pre-orgasmic period], a female weeds out casual suitors, and only finally copulates [has an orgasm] with a male who has proved his qualities of fidelity and perseverance in advance. (Dawkins 1976, emphasis added).

Dawkins later (p. 177) states his belief that the domestic-bliss strategy is indeed utilized by human females. Being a sociobiologist he is not, of course, arguing that women consciously calculate about possible future genetic benefits of withholding copulation from a male suitor. Genetic "strategies" are not necessarily conscious the way military strategies are. Nor have I suggested in my interpolations that a woman who withholds or permits herself to have orgasms has any conscious control over what she is doing, or that a male who reacts to the absence or presence of orgasms in her knows anything about what he is doing either. All that is required is for the partners to behave *as if* they knew what they were doing.

What has been said thus far about female orgasm relates to *phylogeny*. Over many generations the female orgasm has become established as one proximate mechanism which keeps the female behaving as if she were interested in doing what is necessary to reproduce, and doing it with a male who is likely to support her psychologically and materially (Hite's "Mr. Right"). But what about the *ontogeny* of her orgasms? How did she develop the ability to orgasm, and to orgasm discriminatingly, in her own personal development? No adaptation exists in an ontogenetic vacuum, but requires certain specific environmental conditions in order to develop.

As we have seen, female orgasm usually occurs in a context of intimacy and trust. But how does a grown woman know what intimacy is, and under what conditions did she first learn to be intimate and trusting with another male? If her orgasmic ability indicates she is going to depend on her heterosexual partner for both emotional support and assistance with offspring, then where and when did she learn to have such feelings of dependency?

Any psychoanalyst will guess that I am now going to say something about the father (or primary male caretaker) of the child who eventually becomes an orgasmic woman in heterosexual intercourse. However, first I would like to give some (not particularly psychoanalytic) reasons for why childhood should be so important for understanding adult human sexuality, including adult female orgasm. Adult hominids, as it turns out, acquired a very special relationship to the personal past, and this relationship made human sexuality different from that of any other primate.

11. Blast From the Past

> If I wished to express the basic principle of my ideas in a somewhat strongly worded sentence, I would say that man, in his bodily development, is a primate fetus that has become sexually mature.
>
> *Luis Bolk,* 1926
> (as translated by S. J. Gould)

> It seems, therefore, that we only grow up in order to remain children.
>
> *Géza Róheim,* 1943

> Mankind is moving more and more in the direction of infancy, and childhood is the image of the future.
>
> *Milan Kundera,* 1978

One of the most striking features of the immature human primate is its enormously intensified and prolonged dependency upon adults. The development of the hominid line over the last several million years is a story of new-born infants becoming more and more helpless, and young taking longer and longer to reach sexual maturity.

Biologists speak of the *neoteny* of today's hominid. Ashley Montagu defines this term as follows: "the process whereby the organism's own ancestral fetal and/or juvenile traits are retained in the development of the adult descendants of a group" (1962, 335).[42] Some anatomical examples of neoteny in *Homo sapiens* are:

> Absence of brow ridges
> Thinness of skull bones
> Flatness of face (orthognathy)
> Late eruption of teeth
> Prolonged growth period
> [Relative] hairlessness of body

---

42. S. J. Gould (1977, 483) makes neoteny synonymous with paedomorphosis, i.e., the retention of formerly juvenile, but not fetal characters by adult descendants. I prefer Montagu's more general definition, which will simplify some of the discussions later in this book.

Large volume of brain [relative to body size]
Non-rotation [to opposable position] of big toe
Thin nails
Long neck

(*ibid.*, 326-7)

There is a considerable heterogeneity to the items on this list, as Gould (1977, 357ff.) has shown. Quite a variety of evolutionary adaptations is also involved. For example, non-rotation of the big toe contributes to habitually upright posture. Prolonged growth contributes to educability (acquisition of culture). Woman's slightly more neotenous head and facial features help her to elicit altruistic attention from men (see below, section 36). But all neotenous features of humans share a "common efficient cause" (Gould), namely, retarded ontogenetic development: "we are not neotenous only because we possess an impressive set of paedomorphic characters; we are neotenous because these characters develop within a matrix of retarded development that coordinates their common appearance in human adults" (*ibid.*, 397). Gould directly links our neotenous "retardation" to our advanced intellectual and social abilities: "this retardation has reacted synergistically with other hallmarks of hominization — with intelligence (by enlarging the brain through prolongation of fetal growth tendencies [i.e., extension of fetal growth rates into the postpartum period] and by providing a longer period of childhood learning) and with socialization (by cementing family units through increased parental care [including paternal care] of slowly developing offspring)" (400). Gould concludes that "it is hard to imagine how the distinctive suite of human characters could have emerged outside the context of delayed development" (*ibid.*).

Human neoteny, then, is not only an anatomical phenomenon. Desmond Morris, in his marvelous picture book *Manwatching* (1977) describes the neotenous behavior of the human species as follows:

It is the 'Peter Pan' syndrome — the case of a species that never grows up, but starts to reproduce while still in the juvenile condition. In many ways, man is a neotenous ape. An adult man is more like a young ape than like an adult ape. He has the curiosity and playfulness of a young ape. When the ape becomes mature, he loses his infantile playfulness; but man never loses it. (151; cf. Lorenz 1971, 180; Gould 1977, 402; Róheim 1934, 255).

Morris singles out religious behavior in humans as another example of behavioral neoteny:

[He] becomes sexually mature and yet he still needs a parent — a super-parent, one as impressive to him as a man must be to a dog. The answer was to invent a god — either a female superparent in the shape of a Mother Goddess, or a male god in the shape of God the Father, or perhaps even a whole family of gods. Like real parents they would both protect, punish and be obeyed.

It is a fair question to ask why a man's real parents could not play this role themselves. The answer is that, biologically speaking, parents must be bigger than their offspring if they are to remain truly parental. A child must physically look up to its parents. They must have superior strength to be biologically protective. Once the children have grown up and become the same size as their parents, and started to breed like their parents, the true parent-image has gone.

But the gods and goddesses are immense. Like parents, they are 'up there' — we must look up to them in the heavens. And they are all-powerful, like good parents should be. No matter how old we become, we can still call them 'Holy Mother' or 'Father' and put a child-like trust in them (or their agents, who often adopt similar titles for themselves). (152; cf. Lorenz 1971, 180-81).

Being somewhat partial to psychoanalysis, I cannot resist mentioning *The Future of an Illusion*, where Freud, as Konrad Lorenz has already observed (1971, 181), gives essentially the same explanation for the origin of basic religious ideas:

These [ideas] which are given out as teachings, are not precipitates of experience or end-results of thinking: they are illusions, fulfilments of the oldest, strongest and most urgent wishes of mankind. The secret of their strength lies in the strength of those wishes. As we already know, the terrifying impression of helplessness in childhood aroused the need for protection — for protection through love — which was provided by the father; and the recognition that this helplessness lasts throughout life made it necessary to cling to the existence of a father, but this time a more powerful one. Thus the benevolent rule of a divine Providence allays our fear of the dangers of life; the establishment of a moral world-order ensures the fulfilment of the demands of justice, which have so often remained unfulfilled in human civilization; and the prolongation of earthly existence in a future life provides the local and temporal framework in which these wish-fulfilments shall take place. (*SE* XXI, 30).

Freud does not have the fancy biological term "neoteny" to describe what he means. He is also quite a bit more male-oriented than Morris in the kinds of gods he chooses. But the principle is the same for both thinkers: well into adulthood the child's need for a loving, protecting parent survives, and the religious concepts of god and goddess are manifestations of this neotenous need.[43]

Psychoanalysts have also described other psychological processes which have a relationship of some kind to neoteny. What psychoanalysts mean by *regression*, for example, is a type of neotenous process, but with the

---

43. See Spiro and D'Andrade 1967 for a statistical cross-cultural study of the relations between child training practices and supernatural nurturance and punitiveness.

perspective reversed from that of biologists. Whereas a biologist (A) sees a structure or process as *retained* into adulthood, the psychoanalyst (B) sees a structure or process as *reverted to* in adulthood. Such complementarity might be diagrammed as follows:

(A) Feature of (ancestral)[44] juvenile form $\xrightarrow{\text{neoteny}}$ Adulthood

(B) Feature of juvenile form $\xleftarrow{\text{regression}}$ Adulthood

Perhaps even the very existence of what psychoanalysts call "the unconscious" in adults is a manifestation of neotenous retardation, since infants and little children appear to be unconscious of many of the things they do in social interaction, while consciousness only develops in later ontogenetic stages.[45] Other psychoanalytic processes that might be studied in the light of neoteny include transference, acting out, the repetition compulsion, return of the repressed, certain defense mechanisms (denial, projection, etc.), and the phenomenon of free association.

There is ample psychoanalytic grist for the biological mill here, though these various processes will probably be seen to have rather complex relations to neoteny and will involve linguistic and other semiotic capabilities of the human species which, like language itself, are phylogenetically new and therefore definitely not neotenous. That is, the development of neotenous features in hominids did not by any means exclude "terminal additions of new abilities" (Parker and Gibson 1979, 380), as Gould (1979) and Jolly (1979) have recognized.

One psychoanalyst who has taken quite seriously the biological notion of neoteny is Géza Róheim (cf. Robinson 1969, 112ff.). First in *The Riddle of the Sphinx* (1934), then more extensively in *The Origin and Function of Culture* (1943) and in *Psychoanalysis and Anthropology* (1950) Róheim argued that the varieties of human culture, with all the miseries and repressions Freud attributed to it in *Civilization and Its Discontents,* can be explained as the result of neotenous retardation of individual human beings:

Humanity has emerged, as the human being emerges today, by the growth of defence mechanisms against the infantile situation, by the development of the unconscious. (1934, 210).

---

44. The theoreticians of human neoteny generally assume that today's juvenile forms are similar to ancestral juvenile forms. For example: "What juvenile among living primates is most similar in form to the young stages of our forebears? The answer must be: our own juvenile form itself" (Gould 1977, 387).

45. I suspect, however, that some aspects of "the unconscious" are not neotenous, but appear as completely *new* adaptations resulting from a selective pressure to *repress* awareness (in a highly sincere way) of certain actions that benefit one's own genes (see above, section D).

The prolongation of the period of infancy is the cause of a trauma that is common to all mankind. Differentiation in the erotic play activities in different hordes has modified it and so produced the typical traumata and the specific cultures of different groups. (*ibid.*, 235).

Although Róheim does ."... not claim that *our prolonged infancy* is the only biological factor behind the cultural process" (1943, v), he does claim (citing Bolk, Zuckerman, Huxley, and other biologists) that many aspects of humanity, such as the Oedipus complex, the latency period of development, the ability to delay and substitute gratification, the tendency toward sublimation, the desire to exchange gifts, the domestication of animals, and some other human features are due to neoteny. Particularly interesting is Róheim's idea that adult neurosis is basically a form of neotenous retardation:

According to the consensus of various analysts and to my own clinical experience neurosis is also due to retardation. Instead of cathecting the present the neurotic is fixated to the past. His real opponents in life are merely dummies of the father of his infancy and the women he is in love with stand for the beloved mother. Present situations are distorted because they appear as mere replicas of the past and the whole disease is an anachronism. (1943, 21-2).

Later in this book I will suggest that such "dummies" of people from the personal past characterize not only neurotic individuals, but also those who participate in normal adult love relationships.

Róheim's work is extremely suggestive, though it is full of sweeping generalizations ("Civilization originates in delayed infancy . . ." — *ibid.*, 100; "Our sexual ethics are based on our juvenilization" — 1950, 413) that are not always supported as extensively as their breadth would require. Róheim also tends to jump from one pronouncement to another without developing a coherent thread of argumentation, and often relies on psychoanalytic concepts that are now irrelevant. But his insights, particularly those concerning the neotenous retardation of humanity, have a startling intuitive appeal and have been an impetus for several of the lines of thought in this book.[46] Most importantly, Róheim's work provides a major vantage point from which the originally biological concerns of psychoanalysis (Sulloway 1979) can be viewed.

---

46. For further discussion of the importance of neoteny in human evolution see, in addition to sources already mentioned: Alexander 1979b, 135, 214; Keith 1948, 192-201; Morris 1967, 32ff.; de Beer 1962, 68-76; Jonas and Jonas 1970; Langer 1972, II, 217ff; Crook 1980, 106ff.; Guthrie 1976, 156-65; Konner 1981, 19-21; Endleman 1981; Muensterberger 1969.

12. An Ontogenetic Precursor of Mr. Right: II

Tell me, daddy, can't you see
How much you mean to me?
Mae West ("If I could Be with You")

Father, bridegroom, in this Easter egg
Under the coronal of sugar roses
The queen bee marries
the winter of your year.
Sylvia Plath
("The Beekeeper's Daughter")

Armed with the general notion of neoteny as a principled and potentially fruitful way of relating adult to childhood behavior, we may now proceed to further aspects of the evolution of female sexuality.

One of the major findings reported in Fisher's study of 207 married American women is that previous childhood relationship with the father is important:

One of the primary findings was that the greater the woman's feeling that love objects are not dependable (that they are easily lost or will disappear) the less likely she is to attain orgasm. Women with orgasm difficulties were found to produce an elevated number of projective test themes referring to death and separation. Also, there was actual evidence that such women are likely to have suffered the literal loss (through death) or functional loss (because of long periods of absence from home) of their fathers during childhood. (Fisher 1973, 398).

Conversely, if the father was dependably present during childhood, there was a greater orgasm consistency. This paternal presence has to be psychological, not just physical. For example, Fisher found ". . . a trend for a woman's orgasm consistency to be positively correlated with her recall of how demanding and definite (as contrasted to casual and permissive) her father's expectations of her had been" (405). A woman with low orgasm consistency would tend to agree with the following statements about her father, while a woman with high orgasm consistency would tend to disagree:

He let me spend my money any way I liked.
He let me stay up as late as I liked.
He let me do pretty much what I wanted to do.
He did not tell me what time to be home when I went out.
He did not bother much about making rules stick. (Fisher, 236).

Here is a typical statement from one of Fisher's "low orgasm" subjects:

Subject 2
My father, like I say, was in the Army .... I don't know whether he enjoyed his Army life or not. I suspect that in the beginning he did but he grumbled a lot about it. But then that doesn't always necessarily mean that a person doesn't like it. I think sometimes grumbling with him was just a habit because he grumbled about everything. As far as beliefs, he talked a lot about being honest and about not stealing or lying or cheating people, although he was never honest — as I got older I realized that he wasn't even honest with himself. Maybe he didn't even know it, I don't know. He was very dictatorial. He was usually kind to me. I only remember one spanking I ever got. The things that he did were all emotional. He was so strict and sometimes unreasonable and sometimes he would tell you that you could do something and then five minutes before you got ready to go he'd change his mind, and you never got an explanation for it, but his only explanation for it was, "I said so, therefore that's the way it is...." He drank quite heavily and life was really pretty miserable when he was around .... (259).

Contrast this with a statement from a "high orgasm" subject:

Subject 4
My father was ... a very loving man and he had a pretty tough childhood, as I can understand, although he's never said it outright.... My dad has many interests but most of them are involved in the outdoors. He loves to fish and loves to hunt. He's the type of person who could be perfectly happy in a one-room shack in the middle of a forest ... because he's a real true woodsman. His work — he works in an automobile factory. He's been doing this for a number of years.... His beliefs: he's quite a devoted Christian, I feel. Politically he's definitely a conservative, not an extremist. His problems: my dad's the sort of guy who doesn't look like he's got any problems but I'm sure he does and I never realized this about him until I was quite grown. But he appears to be a very happy person and he enjoys life and he enjoys people. And concerning his relationship with me, I guess I almost feel as if he has a better relationship with me than he does with my two brothers. I was his only daughter, his pride and joy. He sang to me, he rocked me, he played with me. He did all kinds of things. (262).

Fisher also found that a woman's orgasm consistency does *not* statistically correlate with the perceived degree of dependability of the *mother*.[47] This makes sense, according to Fisher, because a woman's ". . . orgasm potential does, after all, express itself in her interactions with a male sex partner, and so it would be logical that her feelings about the dependability of the prime male figure in her early life should be the specific ones to carry over

---

47. A daughter may not *perceive* or *remember* her mother's attitude toward her, however, and if that attitude is negative in some way, it may be a factor in the daughter's orgasmic problems (see above).

to her later sexual relationship with men" (405). Or, viewed biologically, there is a neotenous persistence of childhood experience with the father into adult sexual interaction.

A Swedish study of father-daughter relations renders conclusions similar to Fisher's. Uddenberg (1974) questioned 101 nulliparous, pregnant women and found that reported high orgasmic consistency correlates with a reported good childhood relationship with the father, while low orgasmic consistency correlates significantly with a poor father relationship. A correlation was also found between unsatisfactory sex life in adulthood and reported poor contact with the father in adolescence. Uddenberg suggests the psychoanalytic notion of transference as a possible interpretation of the way his subjects were responding. Again, to speak biologically, what the subjects were doing was behaving neotenously. Aspects of a juvenile interpersonal relationship — good or bad — were being retained in specific adult interpersonal relationships.

The noted sex therapist Avodah Offit sums up her clinical impressions on female anorgasmia: "The fathers of nonorgasmic women in my practice were mostly alcoholic, or travelling businessmen, or deserters, or they died when the girl was young. They left their daughters alone, one way or another" (Offit 1981, 32). Curiously, Offit finds that it is easier to treat anorgasmia in women who perceived their fathers as cruel and tyrannical than in women whose fathers were absent.

13. "Matriarchy" and the Hand that Rocks the Cradle

> It is not necessary to believe myths of a feminist Golden Age in order to plan for parity in the future.
>
> *Kathleen Gough*

One of the old theories of human origins that many scholars still find difficult to discard is the so-called "matriarchy" theory. According to this theory our ancestors at some point lived in societies in which females both lorded it over males and enjoyed promiscuous sexuality.

But if high father salience is crucial to the development of female sexuality, as we have just seen, then how could "matriarchies" ever have existed? To judge from today's females at least, female orgasm and female (hetero-)sexuality in general could *not* have flourished in the hypothetical milieu of female dominance, orgiastic license, and indeterminate paternity suggested by the "matriarchal" theory of human origins. As has already been discussed (above, section 6), it is primarily males who are inclined to promiscuity, not females. There is a growing recognition, moreover, that female promiscuity (including what is often called "nymphomania," but not necessarily including prostitution and episodic promiscuity sanctioned by sociocultural mores) tends to be associated with manic-depressive illness, temporal lobe disease, an overdeveloped "need to be held," compulsive acting-out, drug abuse, and other disorders (Scarf 1980a; 1980b; Levine 1982; Oliven 1974, 425-7; Offit 1981, 147-50; Hollender *et al.* 1969). Add to this the size dimorphism that has always been present to a greater or lesser degree in hominids, as well as the cross-cultural tendency for today's adult male hominids to dominate adult female hominids (below, section 40), and it becomes difficult to believe that anyone ever took the idea of "matriarchal" human origins seriously.

But the "matriarchal" theory has nonetheless been remarkably persistent in various segments of the psychoanalytic, anthropological, and feminist literature, and the theory's persistence offers an instructive lesson in both male and female sexuality that cannot be passed up.

Proponents of the "matriarchy" theory say that female sexuality languishes in a context where females are dominated or subjugated by males, but flourishes in a context of female dominion. "Matriarchy," it is said, implies a sexual freedom and sexual enjoyment which women can never have in "patriarchal" societies. Bronislaw Malinowski's imaginary crowd of flappers and other avant-gardists expressed this theory as well as Bachofen (1943-67 [1861]), McLennan (1865), Morgan (1877), Briffault (1952[1927]), Hartland (1909-10), Reich (1969 [1930), and other scholars of past generations ever did:

At the beginning of things love was satisfied to the full measure in primeval promiscuity, and law did not interfere, since there was no institution of marriage at all. Under matriarchal conditions, women chose their lovers but were not submitted to their husbands. This we can and should imitate. Law became only necessary when under patriarchal tyranny women were made into chattels and were traded into the possession of the male. What made everything wrong was the influence of religion − above all, of Christianity. (Malinowski 1962, 99).

The problem is that no evidence of "matriarchy," that is, of matrilineal kinship and strong matrifocality accompanied by pervasive female dominance of *adult* males has ever been found.[48] The notion of a primeval "matriarchy" therefore has now largely been abandoned by anthropologists (for historical reviews, see: Martin and Voorhies 1975, 146ff.; Webster 1975; Fluehr-Lobban 1979). Sherry Ortner (1974, 70) says: "The search for a genuinely egalitarian, let alone matriarchal, culture has proved fruitless." The term "matriarchy" does not appear in the glossary of the standard anthropology textbook of Beals *et al.* (1977), nor can it be found in the glossaries or indexes of leading texts of ethology (Eibl-Eibesfeldt 1975), sociobiology (Wilson 1975; Alexander 1979b), human evolution (Campbell 1966), human sexuality (Symons 1979), and various other texts. The term does still get credence from time to time in feminist tracts (e.g., Reed 1975; Davis 1971) and elsewhere (Hawkes and Woolley 1963; Thompson 1981, 149; Lederer 1968; Fisher 1982). Whyte (1978b, 7-8) confronts the feminists who argue for ancestral "matriarchies":

... there is no available evidence to suggest that matrilineal descent, or myths dealing with powerful women, or female gods indicate a present or past period of female supremacy. Nonetheless, some uncritical contemporary writers continue to build theories of original female supremacy on fragmentary information about selected aspects of the role of women in some early societies. For instance, Davis (1971) posits female dominance in the recently

---

48. Nor has any real historical evidence for the existence of "Amazons" been found. Kleinbaum (1983) shows that the mythical tradition of the "Amazon," which extends from the ancient Greeks up to modern feminism is essentially a way for males to express their ambivalence − now admiration, now hostility − toward women. Zilboorg (1944, 490-2) psychoanalyzes the Amazon myth as "one gigantic projection" made by males who both envy and hate women.

excavated Anatolian city of Catal Huyuk ... on the basis of a few such traits: the importance of women in agriculture, the existence of female goddesses, and the larger number of female than male skeletons found in gravesites. She goes on to construct a revived version of Bachofen's "gynocracy" (i.e., matriarchy) based on such evidence, without stopping to ask about the importance of men in hunting and warfare, the nature of sexual regulations, the division of household authority, and the type of political structure that governed the ancient city. By being very selective in the indicators used for the status of women almost any point can be proved, but we do not move any closer to real understanding.

Many feminists reject the theory of primal "matriarchy" (e.g., de Beauvoir 1961; Montagu 1974; Leacock 1981, 20; Rich 1977; Hrdy 1981; Bamberger 1974). Even the Soviet Marxist anthropologists now reject the notion of a "matriarchate" (Semenov 1979).

As I hope to establish later on (section 45), male (hetero-)sexuality tends to be reduced to zero in a situation of female dominance. If this is so, then it is difficult to see how a truly "matriarchal" society, even if some quirky historical circumstances had allowed for its development, could ever have survived. There may be some reasons why a "matriarchy" would promote genetic fitness, but castration anxiety leading to impotence is absolutely fatal to genes.

A number of scholars (Rich 1977; Dinnerstein 1976; Rancour-Laferriere 1981) explain the "myth of matriarchy" as a psychological construct built simply upon the universal personal experience of having had a mother. As Steven Goldberg (1977, 31) says, ". . . every infant does indeed live in a matriarchy . . ." (cf. Slater 1968, 72; May 1980, 119). Chasseguet-Smirgel (1976, 284) says: ". . . Bachofen's work . . . touches upon a profound psychological truth, because we can thus observe projected on to the history of civilizations the individual adventure of development in men and women."

In semiotic terms, the idea of a "matriarch" is inadvertently an *iconic sign* of the mother one was once subjugated by. Mothers seem to have ruled the ancient world because mother was once the sensuously overwhelming and almighty ruler of the child:

Woman is the will's first, overwhelming adversary. She teaches us that our intentions can be thwarted not only by the inconvenient properties of objects but also by the opposed intentions of other living creatures. In our first real contests of will, we find ourselves, more often than not, defeated: The defeat is always intimately carnal; and the victor is always female. Through woman's jurisdiction over child's passionate body, through her control over what goes into it and what comes out of it, through her right to restrict its movements and invade its orifices, to withhold pleasure or inflict pain until it obeys her wishes, each human being first discovers the peculiarly angry, bittersweet experience of conscious surrender to conscious, determined outside rule. It is against this background that child's occasional victories over woman are experienced, and its future attitude toward contact with her formed. (Dinnerstein 1976, 166).[49]

In poetry, myth, religion, and literature the misty, transformed memory of this all powerful, sensuous mother takes many forms. She is the Great Mother or *Magna Mater* (cf. Neumann 1955; Roellenbleck 1974), the White Goddess (cf. Graves 1966), the Other (de Beauvoir 1961), the Great Goddess of Life, Death and Regeneration (Gimbutas 1974), the Eternal Muse, the Eternal Feminine, the archetypal or transcendent anima (Jung 1958), the Mother of All Living, the Divine Sophia, Mother Earth, the Glorified Madonna, Mother of God — to quote just some of the grandiose epithets that appear in the literature on her.

Even Freud — despite the strong male bias in his reconstruction of late hominid evolution in *Totem and Taboo* and in *Moses and Monotheism* — accepted Bachofen's theory of a primordial "matriarchy" (*SE* XIII, 144; XXIII, 82-3, 131-2; cf. also the psychoanalysts Chadwick 1925; Rank 1973 [1924], 36; Horney 1967, 115; Fromm 1951, 205ff.; Eissler 1977, 52ff.; Adler 1980, 5-6). Freud could not seem to make up his mind, however, as to whether "matriarchy" came before patriarchy, after it, or sandwiched in between two patriarchal phases. This indecision is curiously similar to the way Freud waffled on the ontogenetic question of whether a child establishes its primary identification with the mother, with the father, or with some combination of both (see below, section 28).

As for Sherfey, she is careful (1972, 138-9) to separate the "matriarchy" controversy from her contention that there was a long period in human prehistory when women were not sexually subjugated: ". . . the biological data presented support only the thesis on the intense, insatiable eroticism in women. Such eroticism could be contained within one or possibly several types of social structures which would have prevailed throughout most of the Pleistocene period."

It should be emphasized that to reject "matriarchy" as an ancestral social

---

49. It is interesting and revealing that Friedrich Engels (1972[1884], 87) metaphorically described Morgan's alleged matriarchal stage of "savagery" as the "*childhood of the human race.*" Joan Bamberger interprets a series of South American Indian myths about the demise of female power also in specifically ontogenetic terms: "The myth of the Rule of Women in its many variants may be regarded as a replay of ... crucial transitional stages in the life cycle of an individual male. In both sets of South American myths, for example, final accession to the adult male role is gained by capturing the symbols of power (masks and sacred trumpets) from the women. In this battle of the sexes women are consistently portrayed as the perennial losers of their male children to the men's lodges" (1974, 277).

structure is *not* to reject the important role of female fertility cults, goddess cults, and mother rites in our recent ancestry and in a variety of cultures today (see: Preston 1982a; Friedrich 1978; Gimbutas 1974; Lederer 1968, 8-24; James 1959). Also, the idea of *occasional* sexual promiscuity in ancestral hominids is not ruled out, though the rampant and prolonged promiscuity imagined by some of the theorists of "matriarchy" seems unlikely.[50]

I also do not want to throw out the useful historical idea of "matrism" proposed by G. Rattray Taylor (1954). Basically, according to Taylor, in "matristic" periods of Western history there has been a relative emphasis on permissive attitudes to sex, enhancement of female status, promotion of democratic principles of government, minimization of sex differences, etc. In contrast, "patrist" periods of history have been characterized by a restrictive attitude to sex, limitation of freedom for women, promotion of political authoritarianism, maximization of sex differences, etc. In Taylor's strictly historical scheme, for example, the Italian Renaissance was a matrist phenomenon, while the English Reformation was patrist.

---

50. Various forms of promiscuity are well-documented in the history of Western civilization and in other cultures (see: Partridge 1960; Knight and Wright 1957; Olearius 1967; Stern and Stern 1980; Jones 1971, 202ff.; Hurwood 1975, chs. 3,8; Frazer 1935, II, 98-104; IX, 127, 148; 251; 177; numerous entries under "license" and "promiscuity" in Goodland 1931, 707-8; Crawley 1965, 21-25, 209; Robbins 1959; Stoehr 1979; Constantine and Constantine 1973; Brecher 1969, ch. 9; Bartell 1971; Davenport 1977, 160; Taylor 1954, 266ff.; Hartland 1951; Ellis 1927-8, IV, 218ff.; Symons 1979, 246ff.; Rancour-Laferriere 1982b; issue No.2, vol. 6 of *Journal of Sex Research*, 1970; Kakar 1978, 142-4; Ford and Beach 1951, 114-115; Eliade 1976, 85 ff.; 1965, 125ff.). In the literature we find, for example: the Greek rites of Dionysia; the Roman Saturnalia, Bacchanalia, Liberalia, Floralia, and Priapeia; the ancient Egyptian festival of Osiris; the Krishna-cult festivals of India; various Medieval and Renaissance Carnivals, Witches' Sabbaths, Feasts of Fools, May Day festivities, and Whitsunday revelries; the eighteenth-century English Medmenhamite debaucheries; the eighteenth-century Scottish Beggar's Benison; medieval Russian peasant festivals (such as Christmas, St. John's Eve, and Shrovetide) assisted by the lascivious *skomorokhi* or buffoons; the German tradition of *Fasching*; licentious festivities among such non-industrial peoples as the Iroquois and Pueblo Indians, the old Hawaiians, the Australian Dieri, the Ngadju Dyaks, the Hovas of Madagascar, the African Ibo, and others; group marriage, open marriage and "swinging" in modern America; spouse exchange in such nonindustrial societies as the Alaskan Eskimo and the Qolla of Peru; American "free love" communes such as the Oneida Community, Modern Times, and Berlin Heights; premarital promiscuity among such peoples as the Muria of India or the Polynesian Mangaia. Several observations may be made on these phenomena. First, many of them seem to be an expression of a desire for multiple heterosexual coupling. Second, the fact that institutionalized promiscuity has existed and does exist in today's hominids does not mean that it is the norm, or that it is a major source of offspring. As Van den Berghe says in his very clear

Finally, the fact of varying degrees of *matrifocality* in some societies and in our hominid ancestors is also not rejected here.[51] Matrifocal organization, though it has never been very clearly defined (Smith 1973, 142), usually refers to some form of emphasis on the mother-child relationship, at the expense of the father-child and mother-father relationships. Matrifocality can exist in a variety of social contexts — matrilineal (e.g., the Minankabau of Sumatra) or patrilineal (e.g., the Igbo of eastern Nigeria), Western (e.g., American ghetto blacks) or non-Western, polygynous (e.g., the Igbo), or nominally monogamous (see Tanner 1974).

From an evolutionary viewpoint, the interesting thing about matrifocality is that it tends to be accompanied by a rather weak level of pair-bonding. Either divorce is fairly easy to come by, or "visiting unions" tend to supplement "conjugal unions" (these terms are used by Smith to describe the West Indian lower class). Tanner says: "In none of these [matrifocal]

---

sociobiological analysis of human promiscuity (1979, 51-60): "We are *capable* of being promiscuous on occasions, and we might even temporarily enjoy it for a change, especially if we are male, but we dare not produce offspring and organize a society on random, indiscriminate mating" (*ibid.*,60).

Also it is not reasonable to conclude from the marginal promiscuous practices that ancestral hominids were promiscuous. As we saw earlier (sect. M) the bulk of recent research has focused on the question of whether our hominid ancestors were monogamous or polygynous, and the old notion of an ancestral "horde living in promiscuity" (Morgan 1877, 508) has for the most part been abandoned (an exception is Cucchiari 1981, who argues for a "pre-gender society" or "bisexual horde" in which there was "unrestricted sexuality").

The so-called "oldest profession" should also be mentioned here, since it is essentially an asymmetrical form of promiscuity in which relatively small numbers of women have promiscuous relations with relatively large numbers of men on a commercial or religious basis, with relatively few offspring being produced. Curiously, even the polygamous prostitute will often retain the vestiges of mono-gamy in her apparently gratuitous relationship with her pimp (see Van den Berghe *ibid.*, 60-62).

If we go back *far enough* in hominid (perhaps even prehominid) ancestry, then it is possible that we would reach a point where promiscuity prevailed (with chimpanzee-like consortships as occasional as human promiscuity is today). But I suspect that such ancestral promiscuity dates back at least to before the loss of the ovulation signal (cf. Fisher 1982, 87ff.), and possibly before the development of upright posture. Whitten (1982) argues that *Australopithecus* was as promiscuous as chimpanzees are today (cf. Livingstone 1969, 48; Campbell 1974, 318; Tanner 1981, 164).

51. Sanday (1981, 117) tries to rescue the term "matriarchy" by redefining it as "female economic and ritual centrality and not female rule" — in other words, strong *matrifocality*. Leghorn and Parker (1981, 20) also redefine the term "matriarchal" to mean essentially *egalitarian*.

societies are women socialized to find their identity in intimate dependence on men. Instead, they are socialized to become relatively independent, active women and mothers" (*ibid.*, 155); ". . . what we find is priority of emphasis placed upon the mother-child and sibling relationship, while the conjugal relationship is expected to be less solidary, and less affectively intense" (Smith 1973, 140-41). This shift to an investment in maternally-determined (as opposed to paternally-determined) relations is of course just what the sociobiologist would predict, given the relative unreliability of paternity for each individual in a matrifocal society.

Fathers in matrifocal societies tend to be quite segregated from the domestic world, including from children. Thus children tend to have not only little 'certainty' of their paternity, but also relatively little fathering. From the mother's viewpoint, there is relatively little assistance in rearing offspring. All of these facts, despite the greater overall importance of mothering over fathering in childhood anyway, are undoubtedly connected with the scarcity of matrifocal societies.

Van den Berghe (1979, 75-6) speaks of matrifocal societies as resulting from "social disorganization:" "the more unstable social conditions are (in terms of likelihood of migration, anonymity of large cities, family disruption through chattel slavery and the like), the more likely men are to desert their mates." And of course a man is more likely than a woman to abandon a mate and children because a man has more to gain reproductively (or at least less to lose) by it than a woman does (*ibid.*, 76).

Given that the father has been found to play such an important role in the development of female sexuality, it would be interesting to find out whether women in relatively matrifocal societies are less orgasmic than women in the less matrifocal societies that have been analyzed in greater detail. Fisher studied the orgasm consistency of American black women (1980), and found that it did not significantly differ from that of his earlier white sample (1973). But the 35 black women studied were middle class (just as the white women were), not lower class ghetto blacks who live in relatively matrifocal surroundings (cf. Rainwater 1966a). Stern and Stern (1980) devote some pages (97-101) of their informal study to the apparently rampant "frigidity" in the Soviet Union. They estimate, on the basis of clinical experience, that about 30% of Soviet women suffer from "primary, or absolute frigidity" (compare Fisher's figure of only 0-14% of American subjects not achieving orgasm). It could be argued that, since the Bolshevik revolution, Russia has been a relatively matrifocal society. This is especially true of the Stalin years, when so many fathers were absent because of war, imprisonment, or execution.

14. The Sign of the Father

The crucial importance of the father for healthy female development (not just orgasmic ability) is well known to psychologists, psychoanalysts, anthropologists, and other scholars (see: Lynn 1974; 1979; Scarf 1980a; Forrest 1966; Freud, *SE XXII*, 112-35; Dinnerstein 1976, ch.8; Klein 1977, 309-17; Biller and Weiss 1970; Leonard 1966; Johnson 1975; Whiting and Whiting 1975; Biller 1982; and the numerous references cited in these works). This literature variously describes the father as necessarily contributing to the "character," "sex role development," "psychosexual development," "identification," "object choice," etc. of the daughter. Daughters from so-called "father-absent" home situations are almost always adversely affected in their psychological development, as are daughters whose fathers were aloof from them or otherwise inadequate in dealing with them. At the risk, perhaps, of some degree of reductionism, I would like to translate some fundamental insights of these studies into a semiotic model of female selection of male mates.

For a man to be Mr. Right is to be a sign of the father.[52] By "sign" I mean what is usually meant in the more scrutable writings on semiotic theory: ". . . besides the direct awareness of the identity between sign and object (A is A_1), there is a necessity for the direct awareness of the inadequacy of that identity (A is not A_1)" (Jakobson 1976, 175). In other words, a sign both *is* and *is not* what it represents. Mr. Right is a woman's father and is not a woman's father, just as, say, a portrait both is and is not the person portrayed. All signs have this dual nature of appearing to violate the Aristotelian principle of contradiction. A sign is always a sign *of* that which it is *not*. A woman can have her father as a mate and still not really be committing incest. I will express this substitutive signification by referring to Mr. Right as an icon of the father, or more simply, a father-icon (for the woman).

I am not saying that, in searching for the man of her choice, a woman is necessarily conscious of this ontogenetic background to her behavior. On the contrary, she is likely to be unconscious of the fact that she wants to have a man who is in some sense the "spitting image" of her Dad, and would most likely be quite disturbed to hear anyone tell her just what she

---

52. By "father" in the present discussion I mean perceived principal male caretaker in childhood — not necessarily, but in fact usually the biological father ("genitor").

is up to. But there are women – e.g., writers, patients on the couch, literary characters, dream narrators, etc. – who for some reason or other overcome the usual inhibitions and unambiguously state that Mr. Right is, for them, their father in disguise.

A striking example is quoted from the diary of the writer Anaïs Nin by Lynn (1974, 115):

> I thought that the *image* of my father had become blurred with time; yet at thirteen I describe in the diary the man I am going to marry:
>
> "A very pale and mysterious face, with very white teeth, a slow noble walk, an aloof smile. He will have a sweet and clear voice. He will tell me about his life filled with tragic adventures. I would like him proud and haughty, that he should love to read and write, and to play some instrument."
>
> This is a portrait of my father. An *image* engraved indelibly in mysterious regions of my being, sunk in sand, yet reappearing persistently, in fragments, in other men. (emphasis added).

A psychiatric patient declares that the man she loves is "in *his* image," that is, is her father all over again (Scarf 1980a, 446). This term "image" comes up again and again, and is particularly appropriate in the present, semiotic context, for an "image" was for Peirce precisely a subspecies of icon in which the similarity between signifier and signified was especially complete (cf. Jakobson 1971, 350). In the psychoanalytic literature the term "image" (or "imago") is also very often encountered in writings about the father. Thus Leonard (1966, 326), in her psychoanalytic study of father-daughter relations, says: ". . . the father often remains more of an *image* than a real person" (emphasis added). The title of one of Simon O. Lesser's best known papers is "The Image of the Father" (1963). Freud used the term "imago" in his early works, and the common psychoanalytic term "Vater-imago" comes specifically from Jung (*SE*, XI, 181; XII, 100; XIX, 168). Róheim (1950, 7) cautions that the "paternal imago" is a fantasy object, and does not have to be *just like* the person of the real father. Systematic distortions can, according to psychoanalysts often affect the father-imago: ". . . c'est ainsi que l'imago d'un père terrible peut fort bien correspondre à un père réel effacé" (Laplanche and Pontalis 1973, 196). But women who have actually had incestuous relations with their fathers may be obsessed with the quite literal memory or "vision" of the father during sexual intercourse (Meiselman 1978, 243).

Empirical evidence of the mate's iconicity of the father comes from a study which shows that adult women prefer lovers who are either *like* their fathers, or in some cases as *unlike* their fathers as possible. Miller (1969) reports that "when 32 female s[ubject]s chose a photo of a physique which they would desire as a 'lover,' s[ubject]s tended to choose a physique which either received a rank of 1 or 7 (most or least like father) on a scale of perceived likenesses to 'father'." We might say that women who prefer a man as *un*like their father as possible have a 'negative' father-icon – rather in the manner of a photographic negative, where all features are reversed but nonetheless bear a systematically contrastive (i.e., still iconic) relationship to the original.[53]

Further evidence is presented by the numerous studies of the sexual and marital relationships of women from father-absent homes (see Biller 1982, 706-20, for a review). Absence of the father, especially in the early stages of development, is typically associated with later difficulties in interacting with males. For example, Hetherington (1972) found in her sample of 72 adolescent girls that the daughters of divorcees and widows, unlike the daughters of married women, regularly had problems in their interactions with males: "In the daughters of divorcees this took the form of proximity seeking and attention seeking from males, early heterosexual behavior, and various forms of nonverbal communication associated with openness and responsiveness. In contrast, in the daughters of widows it was manifested in inhibition, rigidity, avoidance, and restraint around males" (*ibid.*, 313). The daughters of divorcees, although they aggressively sought out males and were often sexually promiscuous, nonetheless were very insecure and anxious in interactions with them. Also, they seemed to have a need for males to constantly bolster their (measurably low) self-esteem. Hetherington proposes that ". . . for both groups of father-absent girls the lack of opportunity for constructive interaction with a loving, attentive father has resulted in apprehension and inadequate skills in relating to males" (*ibid.*, 234).

I have been assuming, incidentally, that *non*-human primate fathers (genitors) do not have a special relationship of any kind with their daughters, and that grown daughters do not therefore interact with males on the basis of their prior interaction with their fathers. These assumptions could be proven wrong, which is to say that non-human primates may have more neotenous tendencies and greater semiotic capabilities than we have given them credit for in the past. In any case, it is a question that I would think evolutionarily oriented primatologists would want to look into.

---

53. Strauss (1946) administered a questionnaire on marital choice to 373 engaged, informally engaged, or recently-married persons. Statistical analysis revealed a pattern of parent-mate resemblances that could not have been expected on the basis of chance alone, but that the sex of the parents did not seem to make much difference (except with regard to physical resemblances, which held between mate and opposite sex parent). Below (section 23) I will adduce evidence that a husband is a *mother*-icon as well as a father-icon.

15. The Ontogenesis of Mrs. Right

Though I have said that the ontogenetic precursor of Mr. Right is the father, a closer look at the ontogenetic background requires that something be said about the mother as well.

As I see it, the mother is involved in three ways. First, the developing female, like the developing male, acquires most of her social (including linguistic) abilities from interaction with her mother. Given that mothers are the most altruistic creatures known, and given that a young woman needs assistance with rearing offspring, it would only make sense for the woman to choose a husband on the basis of her experience of her mother's altruism, i.e., on the basis of his similarity to her mother. This is not to say that his similarity to her father as well is excluded. Rather, Mr. Right can be both a father-icon and a mother-icon. I will say more about this below, in section 23.

Second, a daughter's mother has a relationship with the father which is sexual, and the daughter knows it. If the daughter perceives that this relationship is good and positive, she is better prepared to enjoy good sexual relations with a man. If not, her sexual future may be handicapped. Uddenberg (1974) found, for example, that a mother's report of unsatisfactory sexual relations with the father was associated with low orgasmic consistency and sexual dissatisfaction in the daughter. According to Clausen (1966; cf. Lynn 1974, 113; Biller 1982, 718-19), a mother's derogatory comments or otherwise negatively expressed attitude toward her husband and other males can cause a daughter to distrust all males. I can illustrate this theoretical point with a concrete example. A good friend of mine was for several weeks seeing a young woman who appeared to be very fond of him, and who on several occasions invited sexual intercourse. Each time, however, the sexual encounter ended in fiasco. No sooner did entry take place than she would suddenly become rigid and push him away. He was, needless to say, frustrated and puzzled, especially since she always at first appeared to be very desirous of intercourse. After one of these bouts, the two of them had a conversation about her mother, who had died when she was an adolescent. It turned out that the mother had, on her deathbed, given her daughter a lecture about how evil men are, and had warned her never under any conditions to trust a man. The daughter did not have an opportunity to discuss this subject with the mother again before the mother's death, and even came to feel that the mother would not have died if it were not for men. Thus did a mother forever destroy the possibility that her daughter would ever be able to find Mr. Right.

Finally, the mother contributes to the development of a notion of Mr. Right by being a *third party* that exerts special influence on the father-daughter dyad. The young girl does not interact with her father in a vacuum, but in the context of a larger triadic relationship: "if the daughter senses that her mother loves and respects her father, she is freed to develop a close relationship with her father without guilt and without resentment toward her mother. Later she can transfer these warm feelings held toward her father to a young man and give herself freely to him" (Lynn 1974, 112). As with Fisher's discussion of how a girl's feelings about her father ". . . carry over to her later sexual relationship with men" (1973, 405), so too Lynn's notion of how a girl can "transfer" her warm feeling about her father to a young man necessarily implies that the young man is functioning as an iconic replacement of the father in her development.

But there is more than just choice of male object. In psychoanalytic terms, the girl does not develop "object choice" without also going through "identification" with the mother as well (*SE* XVIII, 105-10; cf. Mowrer 1950, 605-13). This identification is not the same kind of mother-identification which takes place earlier, at a pre-Oedipal stage, and which is essentially synonymous with the acquisition of language and other basic social skills (see below, sect. 28ff.). Rather, Oedipal identification with the mother assumes that basic skills of social interaction are already present, and is a side-effect of the daughter's wish to possess her father *just as mother does*.

This last phrase states, in fact, yet another iconicity process in female sexuality. If Mr. Right is an icon of the girl's father, then 'Mrs. Right' is herself (to herself) an icon of her mother. That is, a woman in interaction with a man who is perceived as an icon of the father herself tends to become transformed into an icon of her own mother (or of his mother — but that is a different story, as we shall see).

I would like to illustrate this specifically Oedipal mother-iconicity with two literary examples. The first is from a monologue of one of the women narrators of Virginia Woolf's *The Waves*:

... soon in the hot midday when the bees hum round the hollyhocks my lover will come. He will stand under the cedar tree. To his one word I shall answer my one word. What has formed in me I shall give him. I shall have children; I shall have maids in aprons; men with pitchforks; a kitchen where they bring the ailing lambs to warm in baskets, where the hams hang and the onions glisten. *I shall be like my mother*, silent in a blue apron locking up the cupboards. (Woolf 1978 [1931], 98-9, emphasis added).

"What has formed" in this woman is specifically an internal representation of an icon of her mother ("like my mother").

The second example is from Boris Pasternak's *Childhood of Luvers*. Zhenia Luvers is an adolescent girl who is quite upset about her mother's recent miscarriage, and is also infatuated with a young man. She is standing alone, crying:

A sudden thought occurred to her. She suddenly felt that she was terribly like her mother. This feeling was combined with a sensation of vivid certainty, sufficiently powerful to contrive that the idea should become reality, if it was not already reality, and make her similar to her mother only by the force of a sweetly obliterating state of mind. This feeling entered into her so sharply that she began to groan. *It was the feeling of a woman perceiving from within herself, inwardly, her outward charm.* Zhenia herself could not render an account of what had happened. She felt this for the first time. (Pasternak 1958, 249: emphasis Pasternak's).[54]

The "outward charm" is the clue here, like the "lover" in the Woolf passage, to the Oedipal nature of the identification. But again, this kind of identification is above and beyond the ontogenetically more archaic and more pervasive identification with a mother that often gives rise to great difficulty in separation from her. Such clever feminist titles as *My Mother My Self* (Nancy Friday), *The Autobiography of My Mother* (Rosellen Brown), and *My Mother's Daughter Is My Daughter's Mother* (recent lecture delivered by Merline Williams at University of California, Davis) all suggest that most fundamental, originally pre-Oedipal type of identification in women, rather than the Oedipal kind of identification seen in the two literary examples. But pre-Oedipal identification can, nevertheless, support and be intertwined with the more superficial identification the girl makes within the Oedipal triangle, or the grown woman makes in relating to Mr. Right.

The reader may have noticed by now that I have waffled a bit on terminology. Is it "identification" or is it "iconicity" that describes the way a woman is behaving and feeling when, on the model of her mother, she interacts with Mr. Right?

It is both. The identification in question is just a special case of iconicity in which 1) the interpreter is herself a signifier (to herself or to others) of the signified, and 2) a particular emotional intensity reinforces the otherwise purely semiotic bond between daughter and mother, i.e., between signifier and signified. In the technical treatises on iconicity one does not find any suggestion that an interpreter him/herself is any less capable of being an iconic signifier than anything or anyone else. Also, unfortunately, one does

---

54. Williams (1977, 183) quotes a remarkably similar passage from a story by Jessamyn West.

not find much discussion of the affective bonds which can accompany semiotic bonds. But affect is not the proper concern of semiotics anyway – unless it somehow turns out to be 'semiotizable,' as might be the case if affects are reduced to certain *messages* conveyed between different parts of the central nervous system.

It might be noted in passing that no terminological confusion arises when Mr. Right is dealt with (from the woman's viewpoint). He is an *icon* of the father. Psychoanalysts would not speak of "identification" here, except from *his* viewpoint (i.e., with respect to his own father, which is another matter). Thus "iconicity" is a more general term than "identification." Or: *identification is a type of iconicity in which the interpreter is also the signifier, and a special affective intensity colors the equation of the signifier with the signified.*

The reader may also by now have objected to the idea that a woman's identification with/iconicity of her mother suggests an objective similarity between mother and daughter. But the notion of iconicity does not, as mentioned earlier, necessarily mean a real similarity at all, but minimally just a perceived similarity between signifier and signified. There are varying degrees of 'reality' to the similarity of an iconic process. A silhouette of a person, for example, can be an icon of the person, but the degree of perceived similarity will obviously be greater in a full-color, detailed photograph of that person.

Daughters can thus be iconic of their mothers with varying degrees of objective similarity. The extent of perceived similarity can vary too, without necessarily (as long as *some* similarity is focused upon) nullifying the iconicity of the relationship or without necessarily having an effect on the strength of the affective bond with the mother.

Psychologists have in fact measured both the perceived and objective similarities between daughters and mothers:

It studies of perceived similarity the daughter fills out a questionnaire or takes a test first by giving her own responses, then by giving the responses she thinks her mother would. The similarity between her two ways of responding is then noted. Studies of tested [i.e., objective] similarity require both the daughter and the mother to fill out the same questionnaire or to take the same test. In this way, the degree of resemblance of genuine mother and daughter responses is ascertained. (Lynn 1979, 120).

As it turns out, on tests of both perceived and objective similarity, daughters are more similar to their mothers than to their fathers, and curiously enough, they are more similar to their mothers than sons are to their fathers (see Lynn *ibid.* for a bibliography of the research in this field). Thus the commonly accepted statement of iconicity "Like father, like son," has a less solid foundation in both objective and perceived reality than does the formulation of Lynn, "Like mother, like daughter" (*ibid.* – these also happen to be the very words of Ezechiel 16:44). But all this makes good sense when we consider that a boy's identification with his father is typically merely Oedipal (or post-Oedipal), while a girl's identification with her mother is pre-Oedipal, Oedipal, and post-Oedipal.

I would like to mention just one more piece of evidence that indicates that daughters act as icons of their mothers in relating sexually to men. In her cross-cultural surveys of premarital sex norms for females, Broude (1975; 1981) finds that one of the best predictors of whether there are permissive or restrictive attitudes on female premarital sexuality in a given culture is the kind of *mothering* that exists in that culture. Where mothers are relatively emotionally accessible to their children (as measured by the amount of time infants are carried by their mothers) there is more likely to be a permissive attitude about female premarital sex. Where mothers are relatively inaccessible, the premarital sex norms are likely to be restrictive. Assuming that females internalize these social attitudes and norms,[55] their premarital relationships with men are replicating their earlier relationships with their mothers. An emotionally distant mother is likely to produce a daughter who is sexually distant from a man before marriage, while an emotionally accessible mother is more likely to produce a daughter who is sexually accessible to a man. In either case the daughter is the spitting image, that is, an icon, of her mother at a level where emotional and sexual availability are equated.

Of course, the man with whom the daughter is interacting premaritally may himself be a mother-icon for her as well, that is, her sexual permissiveness or non-permissiveness with him may iconically reflect her mother's earlier emotional availability or non-availability to her. This latter type of iconicity is dealt with below (section 23).

---

55. Hart *et al.* (1982, 4) report that, in their sample of 161 women between the ages of 17 and 20, "sexually inactive subjects came from families who were more conservative in their attitudes about premarital sex ...."

16. Oedipal Facts and Fictions

What we are primarily interested in here is not overall iconicity of the mother by the daughter, but the daughter's iconicity of the mother in situations that are sexual for the daughter. The first instance where this iconicity has a chance to develop is obviously the "triangle" involving the little girl with her two parents. Psychoanalysts and others have, on the model of what Freud discovered about boys in *The Interpretation of Dreams* called this triangle "Oedipal" — though some scholars with a more feminist orientation have objected to both Freud and the universal cultural tendency to use the masculine designation as the unmarked form, and have spoken instead of a daughter's "Electral" triangle with the parents (e.g., Jung, Malinowski, Firestone). For simplicity's sake, however, I shall retain the traditional term "Oedipal" to describe triangular situations involving a child of either sex.

It is precisely in the Oedipal phase, which is roughly from about two to six years of age, that a girl is most likely to build the foundations of an icon of her mother. Both parents (or adequate surrogates thereof, such as step-parents, a mother's brother, etc.) have to be present for this icon to form in a maximally effective way. The daughter cannot eventually become Mrs. Right in interaction with Mr. Right if either the mother or the father is absent for a significantly long time during the Oedipal period. For example, one reason why women in matrifocal societies tend to do what their mothers did, i.e., emphasize the bond with children over a bond with a mate is that in childhood they were not given adequate opportunity to construct a Mr. Right icon (their fathers having been absent for the most part).

To follow psychoanalytic convention in labelling the child's triangle with its parents as Oedipal is not the same thing as accepting all aspects of Freud's view of the Oedipal situation. A particularly large grain of salt has to be taken with what Freud says about *female* Oedipal and post-Oedipal development: ". . . most of [Freud's] formulations concerning the Oedipal process in the female are either uselessly vague or empirically contradicted and therefore need complete rethinking" (Fisher and Greenberg 1977, 224). I think this statement is an exaggeration, but the serious problems in Freud's account do need to be indicated. Specifically: 1) Freud was never clear about whether the growing girl develops conscience ("superego") through interaction with the mother or with the father; 2) Freud was erroneous in implying that women who perceive their orgasms as clitoral have not resolved their Oedipal complex or are psychologically less adapted and less mature than women who perceive their orgasms as vaginal (*SE* VII, 220-21, and XXI, 225ff. vs. Fisher 1973); 3) there is no evidence to support Freud's suggestion that a woman experiences her body as inferior to that of men (which is not to rule out penis-envy in women [Fisher and Greenberg 1977, 220], any more than the way a man experiences his body rules out pregnancy-envy in men — see below, section 50); 4) Freud erred in proposing that the female's early sexual development is more complex and difficult than the male's because it involves a shift from same-sex to opposite-sex love object (*SE* XXI, 225ff.) — when in fact very young girls at least seem to have an easier time than little boys in achieving sex role definition because they, unlike boys, do not have to break away from the initial identification with the mother that all children experience (Lynn 1969, 34ff; Mowrer 1950; Chodorow 1972; Stoller 1976, 35; Fisher and Greenberg 1977, 187ff.), though later they may experience problems with sex role definition as they discover they are second-class citizens in a world dominated by men (Kagan and Lemkin 1960).

Freud does seem to have been right about some crucial aspects of the so-called Oedipus theory as it relates to female development. I have already cited above the evidence for the mate's/lover's iconicity of a woman's father. A particularly impressive confirmation of (both male and female) Oedipal conflict in children is Friedman (1952), here summarized by Fisher and Greenberg (1977, 179):

... in order to involve more unconscious response levels, [Friedman] used two ... procedures. One called for the child to complete two "Oedipal fables" that had to do with engaging in a pleasurable activity alone with a parent and then meeting the other parent. The second procedure called upon the child to make up stories about two pictures, one portraying a child and a "father-surrogate" and the other a child and a "mother-surrogate." It was predicted and significantly affirmed that the children would give more negative endings to the "Oedipal fables" in which they were initially alone with the opposite-sex parent and subsequently met the same-sex parent. It was also predicted and significantly affirmed that when making up stories about interactions with mother and father surrogates, the boys would produce a greater proportion of conflict themes than girls when the stimulus was a father-figure, and girls would produce a greater proportion of conflict themes than boys when the stimulus was a mother-figure.

When confronted with a picture of an adult male (father surrogate) and a child standing next to a stairway, girls significantly more frequently than boys concocted a story in which the father surrogate climbs the stairs (here Friedman assumes the well known psychoanalytic icon, climbing stairs = sexual intercourse [*SE* V, 369-72]).

Part of the Oedipal picture painted by Freud includes of course the notion that the child tends to identify with the *same*-sex parent. Fisher and Greenberg (*ibid.*, 182) survey a number of fairly sophisticated experimental studies which show, by and large, and in ways sometimes more complicated than Freud imagined, that children do tend to identify with the same-sex parent. Generally, when a child is asked the question "Who would you like to grow up to be?," the same-sex parent is named significantly more often than the opposite-sex parent (Kagan and Lemkin 1960; cf. Maccoby and Jacklin 1974, 279). This is not to say that at some fixed age the child knows once and for all which gender role it is going to assume. Kohlberg (1966) stresses that it takes time for the "stabilization of gender-identity concepts" to occur.

Although doubts have been expressed about the extent to which actual imitation of or objective similarity with a same-sex parent are involved in the child's sex-typing (Maccoby and Jacklin, chap. 8), these doubts do not nullify the existence of identification with the same-sex parent, because affective attachment need combine only with intended or conceptualized similarity to make an identification. Certainly the match of the child's actual sexual identity with the same-sex parent's sexual identity must be an important trigger for the whole Oedipal (as opposed to pre-Oedipal) identification process.

Identification with the same-sex parent is not necessarily the basis of *knowing* what one's sex is. It has been found that the child perceives its own sexual identity at a very early stage (regardless of whether or not there is knowledge of differences in *genitalia*). Two-year-olds are quite opinionated (and usually correct) as to what sex they and other children are (Thompson 1975). As Daly and Wilson (1978, 254) say, "there can hardly be a surer way to provoke an outburst of childish indignation than to teasingly suggest the wrong gender identity." If a child for whatever reason already knows at an early stage that people come in two kinds as well as which kind he or she belongs to, then little else is needed other than an internal similarity process linking the child to the same-sex parent, plus a strong affective bond to that parent. Any later imitation of the same-sex parent is, as it were, just frosting on the cake of identification.

Primal knowledge of sexual identity, a knowledge which is a basic component of later Oedipal identifications, must be very close to genes. Not only do little children have this knowledge (see Green 1979, Stoller 1968, and Luria 1979 for more evidence), but adults find it nearly impossible to conceive of a person *without* a sexual identity. Imagine how absurd it would be to forget the sex of a person one has met. My lawyer has pointed out that we may fail to remember how a person dresses, how tall the person is, what color the eyes, the name of the person, etc., but we never forget the sex.

17. Males Too

We tell neurotics to give up their infantile
objects. But the normal man loves that
woman most who most reminds him of
his mother.

Otto Fenichel

If identification with the same-sex parent is characteristic of development in *both* sexes, then it would seem reasonable that adult males should be under the influence of icons analogous to the icons which determine female sexuality. That is, if a female consciously or unconsciously sees a father-icon in Mr. Right and is a mother-icon herself, then it would make sense that a male consciously or unconsciously perceives Mrs. Right as an icon of his mother and is himself acting as a father-icon.

Such a notion is of course one of the implicit cornerstones of psychoanalytic theory, for ever since *The Interpretation of Dreams* psychoanalysts have been saying that a son identifies with his father and seeks specifically his mother in the woman of his destiny. For example, Melanie Klein says (1977, 315) that a husband's "... early wish to be capable of doing what his father did for his mother, sexually and otherwise, can be fulfilled in relation to his wife." Sandor Ferenczi (1938, 18) believes that the act of sexual intercourse, from a male viewpoint, is itself a reunion with the mother:

... the purpose ... of the sex act, can be none other than an attempt on the part of the ego — an attempt at the beginning clumsy and fumbling, then more consciously purposive, and finally in part successful — to return to the mother's womb, where there is no such painful disharmony between ego and environment as characterizes existence in the external world. The sex act achieves this transitory regression in a threefold manner: the whole organism attains this goal by purely hallucinatory means, somewhat as in sleep; the penis, with which the organism as a whole has identified itself, attains it partially or symbolically; while only the sexual secretion possesses the prerogative, as representative of the ego and its narcissistic double, the genital, of attaining *in reality* to the womb of the mother. (cf. Alexander 1923, 40-41; Brown 1966, 47).

This is not to exclude, incidentally, the possibility that for a *female* sexual intercourse also represents reunion with the mother (see section 23).

If a male experiences his mate as his mother, it is to be expected that he will experience himself as his father. Here is a literary example of how intensely a son can feel about being the icon of his father. The passage is from Andrey Biely's great novel *Saint Petersburg*:

Nikolai Apollonovich cursed his own mortal self, and, insofar as he was the image and the likeness of his father, he also cursed his father; his spiritual self hated his father. Nikolai Apollonovich intuitively knew his father, his least sinuosities and his most inarticulate tremors. In his physical perceptions, he was absolutely like his father. He was unsure where he himself ended or where the Senator, that bearer of many sparkling Orders, began in him. He actually experienced rather than saw himself in that splendid uniform.... (Biely 1959 [1913], 80).

Elsewhere in the novel Nikolai Apollonovich, whose feelings toward his mother are explicitly described by the narrator as "unnatural," falls in love with a woman who bears many resemblances to his mother: both women are estranged from their husbands, both are described as flighty and irresponsible, they both have the same patronymic (the mother is Anna Petrovna, the beloved Sophia Petrovna), their husbands both nearly perish because of Nikolai Apollonovich, etc. In other words, Nikolai Apollonovich's iconicity of his father is intimately tied to his beloved's iconicity of his mother.

One of the problems with the traditional psychoanalytic conception of a son's iconicity of his father is that paternal threat and filial anxiety, contrary to what Freud originally implied, are not the only things involved. Rather, " ... most [experimental] studies have shown that friendly and nurturant attitudes on the part of the father are most likely to cause his son to become like him." Such studies measure " ... how similar a father and his son are (or how similar a son perceives himself to be to his father.)" For example, one study disclosed that " ... the more boys responded to a personality inventory in the same fashion as their fathers, the more they described them as rewarding and affectionate on a story completion task" (Fisher and Greenberg 1977, 204-5).

But even if the son's identification with the father involves more paternal affection than Freud realized, the identification (iconicity of the father) is nonetheless still there. I will not repeat Fisher and Greenberg's survey of the enormous experimentally-oriented literature on male identification with the father. It is curious, though, that no comparable *scientific* literature exists on the related topic of whether the woman in a man's love life is a mother-icon. It is as if the threat of castration postulated by psychoanalysis as the fantasized price for incestuous union with the mother (e.g., *SE* XIII, 130; Laplanche & Pontalis 1973, 78; Fisher and Greenberg 1977, 192ff.) has prevented scientists (who tend to be male) from investigating experimentally whether the women they married are maternal icons. Perhaps, also, the dearth of experimental studies in this area reflects the fact that it is easier for a man to believe he replaces his mate's father (at least a man gets the credit) than to comprehend that his mate replaces his mother.

Some cultures strictly avoid anything that might suggest an equation of mother and wife, while other cultures treat the equation in an open and relaxed manner. Thus Devereux (1978, 183) reports that " ... among the Mojave a man may not kiss the breasts of his partner, for this would make their coitus resemble incest." But, as an epigraph to his book, Stephens (1962) quotes (from DuBois 1969) the following simple declaration by an Alor native:

... Wives are like our mothers. When we were small, our mothers fed us. When we are grown, our wives cook for us. If there is something good, they keep it in the pot until we come home. When we were small, we slept with our mothers. When we are grown, we sleep with our wives. Sometimes when we are grown, we wake in the night and call our wives 'mother' ... (quoted also by Róheim 1950, 254).

In Indian mythology the wife-mother equation often surfaces, as in this passage from one of the Upanishads: "The breast that he sucked before he presses and finds joy; the vagina from which he was born before — he takes pleasure in that. She who was his mother before is now his wife, and she who is his wife is indeed his mother" (as quoted by O'Flaherty 1980, 105; cf. Kakar 1978, 95). Half-way around the world, in our own culture, we have the popular lyrics,

> I want a girl
> Just like [i.e., an icon of] the girl
> That married dear ole' Dad ....

Psychoanalysts know that any male patient on the couch will produce very specific memories of his mother that carry over into current sex life. But one does not have to be mentally ill to free associate, and any male who is willing to honestly think about his mate for just five minutes cannot also avoid thinking about his mother.

The compilers of *The Book of Sex Lists* came up with some examples that are perhaps a little more curious and perverse than most of us are capable of:

"My first experience with a woman was my mother taking me to the live poultry market. I felt jealous sitting in my little baby buggy while the chickens were getting all the attention. Now, whenever I have sex, I fantasize being one of those chickens."

"Whenever we are going to have sex, my wife and I put a raw fish in bed with us. I was brought up in a fish store and whenever I was feeling insecure, I would hide under my mother's skirts and breathe the smell of fish on her body." (Gerber 1981, 174).

The classic example in the psychoanalytic literature is of course Sophocles' King Oedipus, whose wife literally *was* his mother (*SE* IV, 261ff.). Curiously, however, the incest committed by Oedipus was merely literal, for he had not known his mother in childhood (having been abandoned as an infant). His wife could not, in other words, have been a mother-icon, even if she was his mother. But this is generally the case with incest, that is, incest is usually for one reason or another sex with defective iconicity (see below, section 21).

In the matrilineal Trobriand Islanders, who Malinowski (1955[1927]; 1929) believed had no such thing as an Oedipus complex, there are very obvious mother-icons in male sexual life. Melford Spiro's refutation of Malinowski, *Oedipus in the Trobriands*, provides the following example:

Almost all marriages in the Trobriands are monogamous, polygyny – a mark of wealth, power, and prestige – being practiced only by the chiefs. That the sons of chiefs are as adulterous as the sons of commoners is not surprising. What is surprising, however, is that they typically seek (and find) their paramours from among their fathers' wives (excepting, of course, their own mothers). This, surely, is a most extreme example of a son's fulfillment of his Oedipal wishes. To be sure, since his lover is only his stepmother, their affair does not, in the literal sense, constitute mother-son incest. Since, however, she is his father's wife, and therefore *the structural equivalent of his mother, she is certainly, psychologically viewed, her symbolic [i.e., iconic] representation.* (Spiro 1982, 103-4, emphasis added).

If father and son compete in this particular 'grown-up' triangle, they had also competed in an earlier triangle, that is, when the son was nursing at the breast and sleeping with his mother to the exclusion of his father. In other words, the Trobriand Islanders had a long postpartum sex taboo.

Stephens (1962) found a high correlation in his cross-cultural sample (which included the Trobriand Islanders) between long postpartum taboo, which allows a child to become very close to the lactating mother *at the expense of the father*, and strict menstrual taboo, which supposedly indicates a carrying over into male adulthood of anxiety about the possibly bloody consequences of being close to the mother (the psychological reality of castration anxiety will be discussed below, section 44).

As for the postpartum taboo itself, which exists in many nonindustrial societies, it has been interpreted psychoanalytically as a husband's defensive reaction against recognition of the maternal aspects of his wife: " ... the woman must be wife or mother, but never both simultaneously" (Devereux 1978, 183). The polygyny known to be associated with long postpartum taboo (e.g. Saucier 1972; Whiting 1964) supports this view because polygyny is an ideal way for a man to avoid having a sustained, exclusive relationship with a woman, i.e., a relationship just like the one he had once upon a time with his mother. The fragility of the pair bond in matrifocal societies is also a good example (above, sect. 13). In semiotic terms, the more mothering (beyond a necessary minimum) that a male gets early in childhood, the less capable he seems to be of dealing with a mother-icon in his reproductive years (see below, section 26).

18. The Complementary Iconicities of Human Mating

Melanie Klein, in her collection *Love, Guilt and Reparation* nicely summarizes the psychoanalytic view of the complementary processes needed for a stable monogamous relationship:

... In both partners a relationship of mutual sexual gratification and love will be felt as a happy re-creation of their early family lives. Many wishes and phantasies can never be satisfied in childhood, not only because they are impracticable, but also because there are simultaneously contradictory wishes in the unconscious mind. It seems a paradoxical fact that, in a way, fulfilment of many infantile wishes is possible only when the individual has grown up. In the happy relationship of grown-up people the early wish to have one's mother or father all to oneself is still unconsciously active. Of course, reality does not allow one to be one's mother's husband or one's father's wife; and had it been possible, feelings of guilt towards others would have interfered with the gratification. But only if one has been able to develop such relationships with the parents in unconscious phantasy, and has been able to overcome to some extent one's feelings of guilt connected with these phantasies, and gradually to detach oneself from as well as remain attached to the parents, is one capable of transferring these wishes to other people, who then stand for desired objects of the past, though they are not identical with them. That is to say, only if the individual has grown up in the real sense of the word can his infantile phantasies be fulfilled in the adult state. (Klein 1977 [1937], 316-17).

In other words, from a psychoanalytic viewpoint, intimate marital relations permit a *regression* to psychological processes that characterized earlier stages of individual development (or, a psychoanalyst might say there is a *transference* of perceptions of and attitudes about the parent onto the mate).[56]

---

56. *Regression* is the term I prefer here because 1) it is amenable to use by non-psychoanalysts (such as the ethologist Wickler 1972), and 2) because *transference* (*Übertragung*), as it is used in most of the psychoanalytic literature today, refers specifically to the therapeutic patient-analyst relationship. The psychotherapeutic situation is often said to involve a "transference neurosis" (e.g., Loewald 1980; Racker 1968), though the kinds of transference observed in narcissistic personality disturbances seem to be different from the classical "transference neurosis" (see Kohut 1971). Some psychoanalysts even go so far as to equate transference with "the patient's experience of the relationship [with the therapist]" (Gill and Hoffman 1982, 4, cf. Gill 1982). Leites (1979) raises some serious questions about the idea that most of what goes on in the patient is part of the patient's trans-

In more biological terms, what Klein and other psychoanalysts are saying is this: the preadaptive and proximate mechanism for establishing the adult human pair bond appears to be the child's earlier bond with ("attachment" to − Bowlby) the opposite sex parent. That is, the adult pair bond in humans (as opposed to, or at least more so than other pair-bonding creatures such as gibbons) is a specifically *neotenous* carry-over of an immature feature into sexual maturity.

Or finally, to use semiotic terms, one's mate is an *iconic sign* of the way the opposite sex parent was experienced in the past.

To summarize these three views:

	Human long-term mating requires
Psychoanalytically	regression (transference)
Biologically	neoteny
Semiotically	iconicity

---

ference onto the analyst. Fisher and Greenberg (1977, 383-6) observe that not much experimental work has been done on transference. A question that has not been seriously discussed (except by a few analysts, such as LaPlanche and Pontalis 1973, 492-3, and Meerloo and Coleman 1951) is whether and to what extent nonpathological everyday (including sexual) experiences of transference are qualitatively different from what goes on in the psychoanalyst's office. Could it be that, in all of our ordinary emotional entanglements in adult life we are just undergoing transferences and countertransferences? Much of the evidence adduced in this book suggests (though in non-psychoanalytic parlance) that the answer to this question is affirmative. And certainly Freud would have approved. In *The Interpretation of Dreams*, for example, Freud speaks of " ... how my warm friendships as well as my emnities with contemporaries went back to my relations in childhood with a nephew who was a year my senior ...;" "all my friends have been in a certain sense reincarnations of this first figure who 'Früh sich einst dem trüben Blick gezeigt' [Goethe]: they have been *revenants" (SE* V, 483; cf. *ibid.*, 562; X, 51).

It ought to be mentioned that the Bowlby-Ainsworth term "attachment" could be used to describe some of the phenomena being discussed in the present section. Weiss (1982) has shown a continuity between a child's attachment to its parents and its later attachments in adulthood.

I would also like to mention in passing the so-called "sleeper effect" found by Kagan and Moss (1962) in their statistical longitudinal study of 89 subjects. By "sleeper effect" Kagan and Moss mean " ... a stronger relation between a variable measured early and one measured late in development than between similar variables measured contemporaneously or more contiguously in time" (*ibid.*, 278). For example, "... selected maternal practices during the first three years of life were more sensitive indexes of the child's preadolescent and adult behavior than

What is common to all three views is the postulation of a *principled onto-genetic connection between two distant points in time, one anchored in childhood, the other in adulthood.* There has to be a systematic way, as Leites (1979, 102ff.) says, of getting "from there and then to here and now." To ignore the connection with the ontogenetic past is to miss the adaptive essence of human sexuality, namely: individuals whose behavior is regulated by this ontogenetic connection are likely to leave more replicas of their genes in subsequent generations than are individuals whose behavior is not so regulated. In particular, the connection makes it more likely that females will get long-term assistance in rearing offspring to reproductive maturity, and that the males will be investing in offspring who are in fact their own.

The specifically semiotic portion of the above scheme can be further broken down into its component icons:

From Viewpoint of	Self Is	Spouse Is
husband	father-icon	mother-icon
wife	mother-icon	father-icon

These are not the only four possibilities, however. When, for example, the spouse is acting as a parental icon (either mother or father), the self may be acting as a child. Conversely, when the self is acting parentally (either maternally or paternally), the spouse may be a child icon. This particular set of iconicities is recognized even outside of the psychoanalytic arena. For example, Havelock Ellis (1927-8, VI, 572) says: "Everyone from his first years retains something of the child which cannot be revealed to all the world; everyone acquires something of the guardian paternal or maternal spirit. Husband and wife are each child to the other, and are indeed parent and child by turn" (cf. Parsons and Bales 1955, 151ff.). Many specific examples will be adduced in the remainder of this book. For now it is suffi-cient to diagram these additional possibilities:

From Viewpoint of	Self Is	Spouse Is
either spouse	child-icon	parent-icon
either spouse	parent-icon	child-icon

---

evaluations of 'similar' parental practices in later childhood" (*ibid.*). It seems to me that any evidence of a "sleeper effect" in human psychological development also constitutes evidence for the regression/transference/neoteny/iconicity that I have been discussing.

The possible relationships summed up by this and the previous diagram I term the *complementary iconicities* of long-term mating in today's hominids. I believe that some or all of these iconicites are at work in human heterosexual mating relationships cross-culturally (whether marital or nonmarital, monogamous or polygamous).

Other iconicities are not precluded, however. For example, in societies where the avunculate is established, a woman's husband could conceivably be the icon of her mother's brother rather than of her father. Or, non-iconic signs might very well be at work simultaneously with iconic ones. For example, the wife that a husband has sexual intercourse with may be an *index* for him of the male(s) he 'obtained' her from, and thus she may be a substitute outlet for his homosexual interests (see below, section 47).

The foregoing discussion, though it identifies those multiple semiotic, psychoanalytic and biological factors in human long-term mating that will figure importantly in the remainder of this book, by no means covers all of the factors. In passing I would like to at least mention two other items that must play a role:

1) *Homogamy ([Positive] Assortative Mating)*, which is the tendency for people to pair off on the basis of similarity in such traits as race, size, intelligence, age, socioeconomic status, religion, general physical attractiveness, etc. (Thiessen and Gregg 1980; Wilson 1975, 80; Feldman and MacCulloch 1980, 77-9; Kerckhoff 1974; Eckland 1982; Burgess and Wallin 1953, 204-14; Garrison *et al.* 1982). To some extent homogamy can be explained by mere physical availability of potential mates − e.g., people of the same race or socioeconomic level tend to live near one another and thereby are more likely to interact in courtship situations. But this is probably not the whole story. For example, part of the reason why a woman is likely to marry a man close to her in size is that she has chosen a father-icon, and the reason why a father-icon would be close to her in size is the fact that her own size is in part genetically determined by her father's size (thanks to my lawyer for this one). Or, to take an example that involves cultural rather than genetic transmission: part of the reason why a woman in Western cultures is likely to marry a man of the same religion or political persuasion is that he is a father-icon for her, i.e., is someone who is likely to have the same religion or political persuasion as she has by virtue of the fact that she is likely to have the same religion or political persuasion her father has.

As Thiessen and Gregg (1980) and others point out, assortative mating tends for some traits to be correlated with marital stability, fecundity, and fertility. These facts not only "... point to a strong natural selection pressure for assortative mating" (*ibid.*, 121), but also indicate a selection pressure for whatever proximate mechanisms are producing the positive assortment in the first place including the tendency to search for a mate who is an icon of the parent.

2) *Exchange or Equity Processes.* Some psychologists have developed theories about what one partner can offer the other in the psychological "economics" of choosing a mate. Both partners are said to have certain "assets" and "liabilities" which figure in their relationship. For example, physical attractiveness and willingness to render altruism are "assets." Murstein states that, although an attractive woman may pair with an unattractive man, "he might render services to his partner far above what she gives him, waiting on her hand and foot" (1982, 660). Murstein shows that individuals "... seek a partner who represents a fusion of their ideal self and ideal spouse[57], although ... they may be prepared to lower their aspirations somewhat if they perceive themselves as not possessing high marital assets in their own right" (*ibid.*, 664). Also, "... men occupy a higher status than do women in contemporary American society; consequently, the confirmation of the man's self and ideal-self concepts by his partner should be more important to progress in courtship than is confirmation of the woman's concepts" (*ibid.*).

I think that an "economic" conception of what goes on between the sexes in courtship is indeed valid. But I prefer to treat the "economics" of such relationships in terms of the differential rendition of altruism implicit in the overall biological and semiotic differences between the sexes (see especially section 36, below). I feel the same way about social learning theories of intimacy, which often conceptualize intimate interaction in terms of balanced reciprocal exchange, reward/cost ratios, equity vs. inequity, etc. (see: Margolin 1982, Hatfield 1982, Walster *et al.* 1978 and Walster and Walster 1978, 134-46 for recent discussions of this fascinating topic).

---

57. Translating back into semiotic/psychoanalytic terms, the "ideal self" appears to be a parent-icon (cf. Freud's notion of the parentally-derived superego as an "ego ideal" [*Ichideal*]), while the "ideal spouse" appears to be an icon specifically of the opposite sex parent.

19. Avoiding Incest and Exchanging Icons

Substandard English is a rich source of evidence about the relations of the sexes. A familiar way for a man to refer to his wife or lover, for example, is "my momma," while a woman will often refer to her husband or lover as "my daddy" (compare also "old lady," which refers ambiguously to either mother or wife, as in "How's the old lady?"; "old man," likewise, can refer to either father or husband, as in "How's your old man?"). There is also the affectionate expression "baby," which places the speaker in a quasi-parental relationship with the lover/spouse. The geneticist should find it interesting here that all of these expressions attach the name of a person with whom the speaker *does* share genes (father, mother, child) to a person with whom the speaker *does not* share (as many) genes (lover/spouse). To my knowledge the converse never happens in any language, i.e., a father, a mother, or a child is never customarily referred to by the term which originally refers to a lover/ spouse. What is even more interesting, from a linguistic as well as a genetic viewpoint, is that the terms specifically *suggest* inbreeding of the incestuous sort even though they are *applied* to persons with whom the speaker is in fact outbreeding.

Scholars of the human phenomenon are generally agreed that the avoidance of sexual relations with one's own parents, siblings, or children is now and always has been a characteristic of the great majority of human societies (Murdock 1949; see Van den Berghe 1983 and the attached commentaries for the latest on this popular subject; other valuable works are: Shepher 1983; Fox 1980; Lumsden and Wilson 1981, 147-58; Bischof 1972; Meiselman 1978; Stephens 1963, 259-65; Murray 1980; Bixler 1981). The few societies in which brother-sister incest is or was encouraged — such as the ancient Egyptians, Hawaiians, the Incas of pre-Columbian Peru, the Bunyuro of Uganda, the Dahomeans, and some others — are or were all predominantly non-incestuous, hypergynous societies, with the brother-sister marriages limited to royalty or to high-status groups, and with the incestuous males tending to be polygamous and therefore also exogamous anyway (see Van den Berghe and Mesher 1980 for a very clear sociobiological analysis of royal incest). It should be noted that among many of the non-human primates there is also avoidance of copulation with close relatives (see: Sade 1968; Packer 1979; Alexander 1979a, 94-6; Van den Berghe 1983, 92; Maynard Smith 1978, 141ff.; Shepher 1983, 105-7 for examples and discussions).

All too often the studies of incest avoidance focus on its negative aspect: one should *not* have sexual relations with such and such close relatives for such and such reasons. But a semiotic perspective affords us the opportunity to see the taboo in a more positive way: 1) for the young boy the incest taboo is a way of telling him he must find an icon of his mother (or his sister) to have sexual relations with; 2) for the young girl the taboo tells her to find an icon of her father (or brother) for sexual purposes; 3) for the parent, the taboo requires an icon of the child as a sexual object.

An iconic sign, as has already been observed, is not identical with what it signifies. Indeed, one of the basic criteria of signification is that a sign can never *be* what it signifies. Thus a wife, insofar as she is by definition an iconic sign *of* the mother, cannot also *be* the mother. The genetic effect of such necessary non-identity in the icons of human mating is therefore to discourage inbreeding and encourage outbreeding. The fitness reducing consequences of inbreeding (e.g. – homozygosity of harmful recessive genes) are avoided, and the fitness enhancing effects of outbreeding (e.g., genetic variability) are promoted.

Van den Berghe (1983) points out, however, that it is not outbreeding which humans 'try' to maximize, but fitness. Too much outbreeding can, in fact, be a bad thing (e.g., breeding across species boundaries usually lowers fitness in animals). Because of the advantages of rendering altruism to and receiving altruism from relatives, a certain degree of inbreeding is advantageous because it increases the relatedness of individuals in a population. For example, in many human societies cousin marriage is preferred and results in fairly high inbreeding coefficients. But an individual who enters into such a marriage will, in caring for offspring, for example, be rendering altruism to a carrier of slightly more replicas of his own genes than an individual who marries someone totally unrelated. Preferential cousin marriage might thus be seen as one way of attaining "an optimum balance between outbreeding and inbreeding" (*ibid.*, 93).[58]

Mating iconicities probably accomplish a breeding optimum too. A young man does not literally mate with his mother (or sister), but if he mates with someone who reminds him of her at some conscious or unconscious level (is an icon of her), then he is likely to be mating with someone who shares more genes with him than if he mates with someone who does not remind him of his mother. The phenotypic configuration, after all, is a reflection of genotype. Of course, the technical genetic term here would be positive assortative mating, not inbreeding. But the genetic effect would still

---

58. There may be some technical problems with Van den Berghe's argument, but still other grounds for moderate inbreeding can be adduced (Dawkins 1983).

be very much like the "optimum" discussed by Van den Berghe and some other sociobiologists. In mating with an icon of his mother a man is most definitely not committing incest, yet he is at the same time mating with someone more likely to share genes and therefore he (his genes) will be in a better position to take advantage of kin selection or any other benefits associated with inbreeding. I suspect, moreover, that hominids were cashing in on the advantages of such mating iconicities long before the invention of formal rules of exogamy (Van den Berghe speculates that the latter arose only 10,000 years ago — *ibid.*, 93).

But to return to incest avoidance. There appear to be several mechanisms, in addition to mating iconicity (and the ubiquitous psychoanalytic defenses — above, 17), which reduce the likelihood of incest:

1) A conditioned sexual distaste for, "surfeit" of (Bischof), or "negative imprinting" on (Shepher 1971) persons one has grown up with (this is originally Westermarck's idea, and is supported by Van den Berghe 1983, Fox 1980, Shepher 1970, Wolf 1970, Shepher 1983, etc.). Especially persuasive is Shepher's finding that unrelated (and therefore marriageable) children who are socialized together on Israeli kibbutzim between birth and age six nonetheless do not have affairs or marry one another later in life.

2) An avoidance reaction based on infantile fantasies of parental punishment such as castration by the father or engulfment and/or castration by the maternal vulva (see, for example: Freud, *SE* XIII, 121ff.; LaPlanche and Pontalis 1973, 74-8; Jones 1961, 452-84; Loewald 1980, 13-19; Horney 1967, 133-46; Lederer 1968; below, sections 44ff.).

3) A universal human inclination to practice reciprocal altruism (cf. Mauss 1967; Lévi-Strauss 1969, 62-8; Trivers 1971; above, section E), including the formation of alliances by exchange of daughters and sisters between the men of different clans, lineages, or families or the exchange of women for money, goods, or services (Lévi-Strauss 1967, 54-65; 1969; below, section 22).

4) The male child's subordination to his hierarchically dominant mother (Sade 1968; Abernethy 1974; Jonas and Jonas 1975b; Meiselman 1978, 24).

5) Possibly clothing: there is some evidence to indicate that the incidence of incest is higher among nudists than in the general population (Smith *et al.* 1981, 96-7).

It has always been a mystery to me why these various theories of incest avoidance have so often been seen as mutually exclusive. In some of the literature ultimate genetic strategies and proximate mechanisms are confused. Often the different types of incest are just lumped together, when in fact different avoidance mechanisms may be working for different types of incest (thus Shepher 1971 recognizes that his "negative imprinting" theory may be more appropriate to sibling-sibling than to father-daughter relations).

But I suspect that intellectual territorialism has played the largest role. For some reason the topic of incest avoidance seems always to be a heated issue, with strident claims being made on the various sides. The psychoanalytic position in particular has come in for a heavy beating. Kowalski *et al.* (1980, 239) speak of the psychoanalytic explanation as "the major countertheory to the sociological explanation." It is not in fact a "countertheory." It is a theory of its own, and the commonplace observation that little children at one point or another openly declare their intention to marry their opposite sex parent should lend some credence to the theory, without at all jeopardizing other theories. Certainly a little child's incestuous desires are not going to result in progeny (cf. Bischof 1972, 27-8). But Freud too was rather intolerant of theories of incest avoidance that were not his own, and attacked Westermarck's aversion hypothesis with particular vehemence (*SE* XIII, 122ff.).

One of the most controversial theories of incest avoidance, and one that has wider ramifications for the study of human mating than most of the other theories do, is the exchange theory of Claude Lévi-Strauss. Like the notion of human mating as a complex of related iconicities, the notion of marriage as reciprocal exchange offers a positive way of viewing a phenomenon that all too often is characterized in a limited, negative way, that is, as the taboo on incest. Also, the Lévi-Straussian (and ultimately, Freudian) idea of exchanging women deserves close scrutiny because it is so obviously offensive to feminists.

First, for men to exchange women in marriage is not to exclude the possibility of iconicity. The future spouses are at least potential opposite-sex parental icons for each other. Indeed, to define marriage as *only* exchange, without iconicity, is to leave out an important fact: *the marriage partner must be a member of the opposite sex.* What is intrinsic to the exchange hypothesis that could possibly require this fact? If marriage rules were a random and merely 'cultural' thing, then why would they not result in homosexual marriages in approximately 50% of known cultures?[59] The obvious long-range, biological answer to this last question is that such cultures would be at a considerable disadvantage in terms of genetic fitness. Therefore a proximate mechanism must at some point have been programmed into our species to guarantee that, when marriage rules did originate, they would result in offspring, i.e., they would be primarily heterosexual in orientation. The hypothesis that the marriage partner is matched to an iconic remnant of the opposite-sex parent includes just such a mechanism.

---

59. Cf. Rubin 1975, 180: "Lévi-Strauss comes dangerously close to saying that heterosexuality is an instituted process."

20. Marriage and Economics

Of course it could be claimed that we, like all other sexually reproducing organisms, are programmed to be attracted (in numbers sufficient to maximize inclusive fitness) to members of the opposite sex anyway. Thus, *whenever* marriage rules were invented, no special 'heterosexual instruction' had to have been programmed in.

However, anthropologists like to claim that attraction to members of the opposite sex is not necessarily a basis for marriage at all: "In most preliterate societies marriage is 'not erotic, but economic'" (Symons 1979, 122 is quoting Lévi-Strauss 1969, 38). In his book on the evolution of human sexuality Symons goes to some lengths to show that the basis of marriage is not necessarily a "sexual tie," "pair bond," or "sexual imprinting." Rather, Symons argues, marriage is an economic investment made by two groups of individuals:

For the great majority of humanity – and possibly for all of it before modern times – marriage is not so much an alliance of two people but rather an alliance of families and larger networks of people; among most non-modern peoples marriages are negotiated and arranged by elders, not by the principals, although the latter may have a say in the matter; in some cases a girl is betrothed before she is born. Marriage begins with a public announcement – and usually a ceremony – and can be said to exist only insofar as it is recognized by the community at large. Obligations and rights entailed by marriage vary among societies, but marriage is fundamentally a political, economic, and child-raising institution, based on a division of labor by sex and on economic cooperation between the spouses and among larger networks of kin. (Symons 1979, 121).

It is difficult to disagree with this, yet something important seems to be missing. After all, what relationship between two people (or two groups) is ever *not* political or *not* economic? In other words, how does a purely politico-economic conception of marriage distinguish marriage from all other human relationships? Even if we are still left with marriage as a "child-raising institution," how does it differ from other such institutions, such as baby-minding, teaching children (not necessarily one's own) how to hunt and to cook, putting adolescents through puberty rites, etc.?

Part of the answer is iconicity. The two who cooperate economically and politically are also likely to be in one or more of the relationships of complementary iconicity discussed above (section 18). Politico-economic cooperation outside the marital sphere does not involve the delicately balanced iconic interactions of husband and wife. For example a baby-sitter from outside of a family cooperates with the parents of that family in a simple reciprocal exchange of money for parent-surrogation. Iconicity is not involved (except in unusual cases, which may lead to marriage!).

Another part of the answer is *affection* or *love*. If one was emotionally attached to one's parent(s), one should similarly be attached to whoever happens to be a parental icon. Even in societies in which marriage is arranged by kin, one may come to love one's spouse, and there usually is some element of choice of spouse anyway in such societies. Rosenblatt (1974, 91) says that "complete lack of freedom of choice seems rare, and its rarity may well stem from the need for at least token commitment." Alexander (1979b, 123-4) questions the assertion often made by anthropologists that "falling in love" is an ethnocentric notion, and adduces evidence from several societies that romantic love occurs despite strict arrangements of marriages in these societies. John and Beatrice Whiting (1975, 199) observe that " ... it is seldom customary for husbands and wives to room apart." This would make sense if it were assumed that husband and wife got some kind of emotional gratification from spending time with each other. Tennov (1979, 182) points out that the existence of "love magic" in many nonindustrial societies ought to be taken as evidence for the existence of romantic love (or what she calls "limerence") in those societies. Mellen (1981) argues at length that the ability of the male and the female to love one another is a universal characteristic of humans, and may go back as far as two million years ago in the hominid line.

And finally, *sexual intercourse* is a major consideration. There are numerous ways in which people can get together to cooperate politically and economically, but the one and only way in which the individuals involved are supposed to have regular[60] sexual intercourse into the bargain is something called "marriage." Sex may not be sufficient, but it is necessary for the marital tie (see Van den Berghe 1979, 47).

Economics combines with most anything, but when it combines at least with sex we have the uniquely marital institution: " ... marriage exists only when the economic and the sexual are untied into one relationship, *and this*

---

60. Postpartum, pregnancy, and menstrual taboos may of course interfere, not to mention prolonged male absence in hunter-gatherer societies. Stephens even speculates that " ... in the 'average' primitive society (if there is such a thing), sexual intercourse between husband and wife is socially legitimate *less than half the time*" (1963, 10-11). But when there is intercourse in marriage, it is usually expected to be regular for a period of time.

combination occurs only in marriage" (Murdock 1949, 8, emphasis added).[61]

A good non-Western example of how sex and economics combine may be seen in the marriage customs of the Alorese, who live on an island north of Timor. In her detailed study, Cora Du Bois (1969, 84ff.) describes the elaborate "marriage finances" that are involved in establishing a long term heterosexual relationship. Often the principals reach a financial arrangement, and then call on their elders to assist with negotiations. First a *wamana* or "option on the girl" has to be given by the boy or his kin. Then both a bride-price (*kafuk*) and dowry (*moling*) have to be established. On the average, bride-prices are about three times the value of dowries, but this varies considerably and depends on the bargaining powers of each side. The payments are made in the local currency, or in pigs, piglets, corn, or rice. Payments are made by both sides on a complicated installment plan that essentially extends throughout the life-times of the two who have gotten married.

The perpetual haggling over payments is closely tied to the sexuality of the marital relationship. Often a woman will refuse her husband sexual favors because she feels he owes more bride-price to her kinsmen. Of particular interest is the Alorese divorce proceeding, during which tallies of sticks or pebbles are laid down in separate rows to represent accumulated bride-price versus dowry payments:

> As each tally is named in connection with the occasion of payment, witnesses may be called upon to substantiate the correctness of the claim. These witnesses are usually people who have some financial interest in the settlement. However, since such financial exchanges are invariably public affairs and so much a matter of common knowledge, skill in divorce reckonings depends more on memory than on chicanery. The objective is to balance bride-price payments against dowry payments.
>
> Since such reckonings are the favorite way for husbands, wives, and affinal kin to air their grievances, these encounters are frequent. I should hazard the guess that there averaged one a week in the Five Villages. Naturally not all led to divorce. Usually after bluffs had been called and grievances aired, the couple settled down again. (Du Bois 1969, 87).

If the complaints of both parties are successfully resolved, the whole proceedings is likely to end with the tribal chief reading the couple a moral

---

61. It is interesting (and many feminists would agree) that prostitution could conceivably be subsumed within Murdock's definition of marriage. Everyone has heard of the kind of husband who insists on paying off his wife for sexual favors. Among the Trobriand Islanders the husband is said to pay a kind of sexual salary (*mapula*) to the wife or her kin (Mauss 1967, 71). Symons (1979, 260) points out, however, that marriage, unlike prostitution, usually entails a reduction of the man's sexual opportunities.

lecture " ... in which the wife is urged to be a mother to the man and the husband is urged to be a father to the woman" (*ibid.*, 96). In other words: re-establish complementary iconicity.

Divorce is a particularly strong argument for the inseparability of sexual and economic factors. In most societies a divorce proceeding, which always results in a financial rearrangement, includes past sexual favors and/or offenses among the items that potentially figure into the divorce. Murdock's (1950) sample of 40 non-European societies contains 35 in which divorce is permitted to the man for "repeated or exaggerated infidelity," and 33 in which divorce is permitted to the woman for the same reason. In 33 of the societies divorce is permitted to the man for "sexual impotence or unwilling-ness," and in the same number of societies divorce is permitted to the woman for this reason. In the United States divorce can involve any one of a great variety of new economic arrangements, such as alimony, child support, dividing up of previously shared property, etc. But "adultery is either grounds for divorce or evidence of irreconcilable differences and a breakdown of the marriage *in all states*" (Lane 1980, 150, emphasis added). In 20 of the 50 states impotence is also grounds for divorce (*ibid.*). In Canada not only adultery, but other sexual infidelities or abuses such as sodomy, bestiality, rape, and homosexual acts constitute grounds for divorce (*ibid.*).

21. Incest and Defective Iconicity

The economic or exchange basis of marriage may be so important to the members of a given culture that the specifically erotic basis recedes from view. But perhaps the erotic stays out of view precisely because the incestuous iconic basis of marriage is so unpleasant to deal with at a conscious level. Thus, can it be surprising that, when Margaret Mead probed her Arapesh natives with indelicate questions[62] about the possibility of brother-sister incest, they replied with a vigorous defense of their *economic* system? "What, you would like to marry your sister! What is the matter with you anyway? Don't you want a brother-in-law? Don't you realize that if you marry another man's sister and another man marries your sister, you will have at least two brothers-in-law, while if you marry your own sister you will have none? With whom will you hunt, with whom will you garden, whom will you go to visit?" (1963[1935], 84). Lévi-Strauss himself grants that this oft-quoted passage " ... is a little suspect, because it was provoked ... " (1969, 485). Yet in the end he does accept it at face value: "There is nothing in [a man's] sister, mother, or daughter which disqualifies them as such. Incest is socially absurd before it is morally culpable" (*ibid.*).

Imagine Lévi-Strauss trying to tell this to poor Oedipus. Can there be nothing which disqualified Jocasta "as such"? Is what Oedipus did "socially absurd" *before* it was "morally culpable?" What can this "before" mean? Did Oedipus tear his eyes out because he committed a "social absurdity" rather than a "morally culpable" act? And what about people who have *actually* participated in incestuous unions? The available literature indicates that they perceive incest as more than merely "socially absurd."

For example, in cases where the mother initiates sexual relations with her son, the son is later likely to suffer such problems as impotence, phobias, depression, alcoholism, suicidal tendencies, etc. (Meiselman 1978, 302-11). The behavior of both the mother and the son is likely to be quite "absurd" by any society's standards, but it is more than that. The pathology is psychological as well as social. One incestuous son was a borderline mental defective and a hairbrush fetishist who eventually murdered his mother when she found his collection of stolen hairbrushes. Another son who had since childhood had sexual relations with his mother (at her insistence) was

---

62. I am not the first to suggest that Mead embarrassed her informants with overly direct questions about sex. See: Marshall 1983, 1044.

repeatedly rehospitalized in a catatonic stupor after hospital authorities would release him to her care. When the home visits were finally stopped, the mother wrote irate letters to her congressman and to the American Legion complaining about interference with "mother love" (these cases are described by Meiselman 1978). Lévi-Strauss would no doubt speak of the "social absurdity" of these situations, but I suspect the participants were much too wrapped up in their psychological problems to be thinking of the "absurdity" of what they were doing.

The most likely victim of parent-child (heterosexual) incest is of course not the son, but the daughter (see Van den Berghe 1983, 97-8 for a statistical overview). This is because the male dominance usually necessary for heterosexual intercourse to take place (see below, sections 38ff.) is present in an exaggerated way in the father-daughter relationship, but is absent in the mother-son relationship. Sociobiologically, the father who is incestuous also has less to lose in terms of inclusive fitness than the incestuous mother – though ultimately all parties of incest have something to lose genetically (see Barash and Waterhouse 1981 and Van den Berghe 1983 for genetic discussion). As Van den Berghe (*ibid.*) shows, the daughter's typical defense against further incestuous relations with her father at the time she reaches puberty (i.e., at the time when offspring are likely to result) is to avoid the father in some way – e.g., run away from home, find a boy friend (or husband) to protect her, or become sexually promiscuous.

Besides the danger of getting pregnant by one's father and possibly giving birth to genetically defective offspring, there are many psychological dangers for the victim of father-daughter incest. Maisch (1972, 167) found that 70% of a sample of daughters who had sexual intercourse with their fathers suffered personality disturbances. Lynn (1979, 129) describes the psychological state of the daughter who has had sexual relations with her father: "Typical is a devastating sense of guilt because of her own participation (incest seldom involves force). She blames herself for having failed to realize it was wrong and having failed to resist." The "overwhelming guilt and depression" (*ibid.*) can lead to drugs, nightmares, phobias, running away from home, truancy and other delinquent behavior, and sometimes suicide. Long term aftereffects include persistent conflict with husbands or sex partners, conflict with parents or in-laws, and such "sexual problems" (Meiselman 1978, 234) as promiscuity, frigidity (often tied to promiscuity), prostitution, and Lesbianism.[63] There is quite a variety of outcomes in the victim of

---

63. Meiselman grants that not all of these phenomena are "problems" in all contexts. By "frigidity" she means "orgasmic dysfunction," and she defines promiscuity as "a level of sexual activity that is unacceptable in a certain culture at a certain point in time" (1978, 121).

father-daughter incest (see Lynn 1979, 128-30 for a concise summary; Meiselman 1978 and Maisch 1972 for detailed treatises; Devereux 1939 for a non-Western sample). From an evolutionary viewpoint these outcomes are more likely than not to be maladaptive — above and beyond the simple maladaptiveness in inbreeding depression. [64]

From a proximate viewpoint that is specifically semiotic, the damage may be thought of as a defective internal schema of the father in the abused daughter. Her Oedipal fantasy of intercourse with the father has been literally fulfilled. He has proven himself an imperfect protector of his daughter. There is no neotenous delay of gratification which is essential to forming a positive internal paternal schema and to promoting complementary iconicity in later adult relationships.

How could a female build a positive internal schema of a man who was unfaithful to his wife in this very special way? And how could there be any loving and protecting aspects of the internal schema of the father if the father has by definition failed to love the child enough to protect her from himself?

It is interesting in this connection that one can say in English that a father who has seduced his daughter has "betrayed" her (Lynn 1979, 129), or has even been "unfaithful" to her — as if the father-daughter relation were itself a marriage. It is also curious that, according to the *Oxford English Dictionary*, the word "incestuous" used to have as one of its meanings "adulterous."

In an important sense the typical father and daughter are "married" to one another. So also are mother and son, though perhaps to a lesser extent (see Johnson 1975, 18). To use such a marital metaphor for parent-child relations is just the reverse of saying that husband and wife "parent" one another (as in complementary iconicity). The fact that these two metaphors— "marriage" and "parenting" — are so systematically related is further indication that marriage and parenting are themselves systematically related.

Whereas a child is *not* supposed to have sex with its parent (incest avoidance), a grown-up is *supposed* to have sex with a parent-substitute (complementary iconicity of marriage). If a child does in fact have sex with a parent, the iconic signs discussed above are (from the child's viewpoint) excluded, or they are working very defectively at best. For example, a father who has sexual intercourse with his daughter is not a father-icon for her because he already *is* her father. Parent-child incest is (from the child's

---

64. In very small endogamous bands some forms of incest may have been necessary to prevent extinction, and therefore may have been adaptive. See: Hammel *et al.* 1979.

viewpoint) sex without iconicity, or with defective iconicity at best. Later on, when the child grows up and has sex with a mate, the iconicity will continue to be defective for her at best.

The difference between being parented and being married may be stated another way: in the relation with the parent there is supposed to be no sex, while in the relation with the spouse there is supposed to be no parent. Incest between parent and child shares one aspect of each of the other two relations. Schematically:

	Being Parented	*Being Incestuous*	*Being Married*
± Sex	−	+	+
± Parent	+	+	−

Semiotics comes in when individuals attempt (consciously or unconsciously) to represent iconically to themselves and to the world that the lower right corner of this diagram should be "+" instead of "−", just as in the lower left corner. But then the constellation looks more like the middle column. Thus, as a result of the semiotic work, marriage is a kind of "incest."

Lévi-Strauss also views marriage as semiotic, but he focuses instead on the exchange or circulation of the signs rather than on their structures. It is not specified who the marital partners are signs *of* − except possibly in one curious passage where the metaphorical *chassé-croisé* of parental and marital bonds is mentioned: ". . . marriage is an arbitration between two loves, parental and conjugal;" "their meeting is doubtless merely a prelude to their substitution for one another . . .," and at the time of their meeting ". . . all marriage verges on incest" (1969, 489). Yet the semiotic consequences of this metaphorical crossing are not pursued, and indeed they are quickly blocked by what the psychoanalyst would recognize as a defensive new formulation of the notion of incest: "At this moment, all marriage verges on incest. More than that, it is incest, at least social incest, if it is true that incest, in the broadest sense of the word, consists in obtaining by oneself, and for oneself, instead of by another, and for another" (*ibid.*). To follow *this* train of thought to its logical conclusion would be to simply re-define incest as the exercise of sexual choice on one's own behalf. We would then be left without a name for that unspeakable, iconically defective thing that is not supposed to take place between father and daughter, mother and son, brother and sister.

22. Why Men Pay for Sex

My Cunt is My Fortune
anonymous title

Perhaps the most controversial aspect of Lévi-Strauss' marriage scheme is that the objects of semiotic exchange can only be of one sex, namely, female:

The emergence of symbolic thought must have required that women, like words, should be things that were exchanged. In this new case, indeed, this was the only means of overcoming the contradiction by which the same woman was seen under two incompatible aspects: on the one hand, as the object of personal desire, thus exciting sexual and proprietorial instincts; and, on the other, as the subject of the desire of others, and seen as such, i.e., as the means of binding others through alliance with them. But woman could never become just a sign and nothing more, since even in a man's world she is still a person, and since in so far as she is defined as a sign she must be recognized as a generator of signs. In the matrimonial dialogue of men, woman is never purely what is spoken about; for if women in general represent a certain category of signs, destined to a certain kind of communication, each woman preserves a particular value arising from her talent, before and after marriage, for taking her part in a duet. In contrast to words, which have wholly become signs, woman has remained at once a sign and a value. This explains why the relations between the sexes have preserved that affective richness, ardour and mystery which doubtless originally permeated the entire universe of human communications. (1969, 496).

This is of course the sort of thing that makes feminists see red. To allude to the "mystery" of relations between the sexes is at best an "ineffectual sentimental appeal" (Wilden 1972, 292) thinly disguising Lévi-Strauss' "well-meant guilt" (*ibid.*). Janssen-Jurreit (1982, 93) says: "how this affective richness and the ardor of love can be explained in the exchange he describes remains a mystery that Lévi-Strauss invented but did not solve." Eleanor Leacock (1981, 241) comments: "the terminology of woman exchange distorts the structure of egalitarian societies, where it is a gross contradiction of reality to talk of women as in any sense 'things' that are exchanged." Basically, Lévi-Strauss is presenting "one of the greatest rip-offs of all time as the root of romance" (Rubin 1975, 201).

Most significant, I think, is Lévi-Strauss' admission that woman is herself a "generator of signs," which I take to mean a generator of other women/ signs. Such an admission is very close to but also very much beside the more significant point that women, but not men, can have babies, can generate living signs of themselves in that infuriatingly literal and unmatchable process known as childbirth (see below, sections 50ff.). A man can "give" a daughter or sister in marriage only if a woman has "given" him a child first.

Even many feminist critics of Lévi-Strauss will agree, though, that exchange of women by men is a fact of many human societies (e.g., Rubin 1975; Leacock 1981, 222-41; Wilden 1972, 289), and may have been a fact of our hominid ancestry. It is just that ". . . men do more than exchange women, and . . . a focus on authority, in the traditional anthropological sense, disguises and distorts the full dimension of male pursuits as it also allows us to ignore women" (Weiner 1979, 330).

Robin Fox has taken the Lévi-Straussian scheme of exchange and has in an interesting way defused it of some of its condescending male bias. Fox grants that, from a male point of view, women are exchanged. But originally, in phylogeny, "the women aided and abetted . . . in a program that was entirely to their selective advantage and probably their idea in the first place" (1980, 150). But what was the advantage? And why does Fox think it was women's idea that they allow themselves to be exchanged by men?

Fox's answer has to do with the well-known *tendency* in most hunter-gatherer societies today for men to be the suppliers of animal protein and women the suppliers of vegetable food. Murdock 1937 is one of the pioneering studies in this area. Murdock found, for example, that in 166 of the societies he surveyed hunting was an exclusively male occupation, while in none of the societies sampled was hunting an exclusively female occupation. But the gathering of fruits, berries and nuts was an exclusively female occupation in 63 societies vs. an exclusively male occupation in 12 societies.

It has been pointed out time and again in the paleoanthropological literature that 1) male hominids were developing a musculature adapted for running and throwing, 2) they were not impeded by the increasingly enlarged pelvic structure which only the females needed for giving birth to increasingly large-brained infants, 3) they were not impeded by the weight of the fetus or by the requirements of nursing, and 4) it therefore must have been primarily male hominids who did long-distance scavenging and/or hunting for large carrion and/or prey. Assuming that the relatively less mobile females and their dependent offspring had something to gain from the nutriments in large game and/or carrion, and assuming that the females themselves continued to gather vegetable foods and perhaps killed small game, then the way was paved for "active food-sharing" (as opposed to the "tolerated scrounging" sometimes observed in chimpanzees — these terms are from Isaac and Crader 1981). A number of scholars (e.g., Endleman 1981, 83; McGrew 1981; Morris 1967; Campbell 1979; Lancaster 1975; Passingham 1982, 257, 292-5; Washburn and Lancaster 1968; Reynolds 1974; Isaac 1978; 1976b; Zihlman 1978; Zihlman and Tanner 1976; Fox 1972; Fisher 1982; Shepher 1978; Daniels 1983; Parker and Gibson 1979; Galdikas and Teleki 1981; Mellen 1981) believe that males and females at some point had to start sharing/exchanging food,[65] and most of these scholars would agree that male and female hominids were already exploiting food resources in slightly different ways before they started actually exchanging food. The exchanges probably took place, moreover, at the "home base" (Morris, Isaac, Crader, Mellen)[66] of a group, where males rejoined females and young after an expedition.

What Fox seems to suggest is that the ever increasing period of infant dependency put females at a disadvantage in the exchange, that is, left them more in need of meat than males were in need of plant food. Fox then directly states that females began to offer *themselves* as part of the exchange:

The impulse was more likely to have come from the female kin-coalitions. The need of the female coalitions for male provisioning – meat for the children – was undoubtedly the push. The females could easily trade on the male's tendency to want to monopolize (or at least think he was mono-polizing) the females for mating purposes, and say, in effect, "Okay, you get the monopoly – or the appearance of it anyway – and we get the meat." Insofar as the male was successful in turn, he would have females to trade .... (Fox 1980, 147; cf. Symons 1979, 139; Shepher 1978, 260; Rancour-Laferriere 1981, 500-1; Fisher 1982, 100; Riencourt 1974, 11; Mead 1975 [1949], 189).

Fox's scenario does not necessarily rule out the idea that the eventual exchanging of females by males served also to buffer agonistic relations between males (see the discussion of a postulated "intergroup prestational exchange among adult males using lower-ranking, non-mated attachment figures as tokens" in Reynolds 1981, 247-8). From a male viewpoint, the advantages of using females to forge alliances are obvious. It is just that Fox would rather see the whole process as having been initiated by female coalitions, while others (such as Reynolds) prefer to believe that male coalitions started the ball of exchange rolling. I will not try to resolve this

---

65. Lovejoy (1981) and some others such as Konner 1981, 33 do not speak of exchange, but focus instead on male "provisioning" of females.

66. More recently Isaac has been using the term "central place" instead, in order to avoid some of the connotations of the term "home" (lecture delivered at the University of California, Davis, 8 Feb. 1983).

particular dispute, but will focus instead on how sexuality is now involved in exchange.

I have already argued that female hominids at some fairly remote time must have been interested in having sex round the menstrual clock. That is, they had something to gain from sexual intercourse besides male provisioning. Males, too, clearly must have been interested in having sex regularly.

But what is curious about the involvement of sex in exchange today is that sex has come to be seen as something that females have to offer to males rather than the other way around. As de Beauvoir says, "from primitive times to our own, intercourse has always been considered a 'service' for which the male thanks the woman by giving her presents or assuring her maintenance" (1961 [1949], 350; cf. Murphy 1977). For example, in prostitution, it is primarily women who sell their sexual services to men, not men who service women (the gigolo is an uncommon phenomenon).

Symons (1979, 253-85) has documented this asymmetry cross-culturally. When, for example, Symons surveyed the Human Relations Area Files for accounts of gifts given in sexual situations (other than in prostitution, where there is payment, and in marriage, where gifts tend to be exchanged between families rather than individuals), he found that in the great majority of instances men rather than women give gifts.

Even when it is families which give the gifts, the family of the bridegroom is much more likely to be the giver or the purchaser. Considerations by the bridegroom's family (bride-price, bride-service), are much more common, cross-culturally, than considerations by the bride's family (dowry). Besides, dowry is not symmetrical with bride-price, for it is not so much a gift to the groom but rather to the bride or to the bride and groom jointly. Dowry payments are particularly likely in highly stratified, hypergynous societies where the bride's family is in effect paying for a high status, sexually restrictive but wealthy male who can render considerable altruism to his wives/concubines and their offspring (see Dickeman 1979; 1981, for cogent analyses of such societies). Since hominid societies probably did not become stratified in any meaningful sense until only recently, it is probably the case that 'proto-bride-price' is older than 'proto-dowry.' For further discussions of exchange of goods and services at marriage, see: Goody and Tambiah 1973, 6, 61-2; Alexander 1979b, 163; Daly and Wilson 1978, 270-1; Whyte 1978b, 75; Konner 1982, 174.

If at the individual level copulation is usually a female service, so also at the level of kin groups marriage is usually a service rendered by the bride's kin in return for payment by the groom's kin. At both levels women are a reproductive resource. In many societies, moreover, this resource is itself a unit of exchange. In the extreme structuralist view of Lévi-Strauss, as we have seen, woman *is* a "gift": "the woman herself is nothing other than . . . the supreme gift among those that can only be obtained in the form of reciprocal gifts" (Lévi-Strauss 1969, 65; cf. Symons 1979, 140).

Thus, whenever (hetero-)sex is involved in exchange, it is the female or her sexuality that is most commonly the object of exchange, and it is males who do the exchanging. The ultimate evolutionary cause for this situation is as follows: ". . . since the minimum male parental investment is almost zero, males stand to benefit from copulating with any fertile female (if the risk is low enough), whereas females do not stand to benefit reproductively from copulating with many males no matter what the risk is" (Symons 1979, 261). Consequently, female rather than male sexuality ends up being the scarce reproductive resource in the long run. Once this is understood, the interesting questions are those of "proximate sexual economics" (Symons).

One of the problems with the notion of the female (or her sexuality) as a gift is the fact that the female herself is capable of enjoying sex. Even the most enlightened male mind can have difficulty in recognizing this — so much difficulty, in fact, that perhaps we should suspect the hand of natural selection at work.

Consider the old story about how Tiresias the Theban seer was blinded:

He one day saw snakes coupling and struck them with his stick, whereat he became a woman; later the same thing happened again and he turned into a man. Being asked by Zeus and Hera to settle a dispute as to which sex had more pleasure of love, he decided for the female; Hera was angry and blinded him, but Zeus recompensed him by giving him long life and power of prophecy. (Hammond and Scullard 1970, 1078; see O'Flaherty [1980, 305] for the similar tale of Bhaṅgāśvana in the *Mahābhārata*).

Symons, after quoting this same passage from *The Oxford Classical Dictionary*, comments as follows: ". . . were Tiresias's decision to become generally known [read: known to males], it would give males added leverage in sexual transactions with women and very likely in nonsexual transactions with women as well" (1979, 262).

Presumably Tiresias was aware, during the period when he was a woman, of the multiple orgasms women can have. Thus Symons rightly suggests that ". . . an economic analysis based solely on orgasm scarcity might predict copulation to be a male service" (263). Yet just the opposite is the case, as Symons recognizes. Men are paying women for something women 'ought,' at the hedonistic level, to be paying men for. The proximate level of sexual pleasure appears to contradict the ultimate-causal analysis. We have to ask, therefore: what *other* proximate device(s) could be operating to make men give both sexual pleasure *and* gifts/money/assistance to women?

When I posed this paradox to my lawyer, she instantly replied that women are more clever than men. Perhaps, at some level, my lawyer is right here. Harry Belafonte, I might add, once sang the same thing in a song about his Carribean experiences: "De woman is smarter!"

Feminine wiles are not, of course, something the intelligence tests measure. But a woman may in fact be very adept at making a man feel guilty in sexual interaction, and a man may in fact be inclined to guilt feelings in such interaction — with the result that he pays for the interaction in order to assuage his guilt. Furthermore, if psychoanalysts are to be believed, women are adept guilt-inducers because they feel that men *owe* them something, namely, a penis. And men readily feel guilty and anxious because they, but not women, possess this wonderful organ:

> If this interpretation is correct, we can understand certain traits of the relationship between man and woman; on his part the inclination to make sacrifices for her, on her part, even on the part of very independent women, the demand for sacrifices coupled with a deep feeling that all the man does and gives to her is not enough, which may be due to her resentment over the lack of a penis. (Nunberg 1947, 175).

I leave it for later to discuss whether men actually have guilt-inducing castration anxiety, and whether women in fact have penis-envy. For now it can probably be agreed that both male and female children, insofar as they initially develop a willingness to render altruism and a capacity to feel guilty specifically in interaction with their principal caretaker (their mother — see below, sections 27-8), will later feel especially inclined to render altruism to or feel guilty toward anyone who is a mother-icon. Consequently, if the women in a man's life are mother-icons, he will feel obliged to them. If his mother taught him to be "nice," he will at least render a "thank you ma'am" after the "slam bam." If his mother taught him to *earn* her favors, he will later pay for the sexual favors of the women who represent her.

I do not think, however, that male guilt and anxiety are the only proximate factors that make sex a primarily female service. Many other mechanisms are apparently also at work:

> 1) Adult females, cross-culturally, appear to emit more altruism-eliciting verbal and non-verbal signals overall than adult males do (for details, see below, section 36).
> 2) Females in our society are more likely to have fantasies or daydreams about receiving presents, clothes, etc. from members of the opposite sex than males are (G. Wilson 1978, 39, 42).
> 3) In courtship interaction in our society females are less "romantic" (or more in control of their "romantic" feelings) and more "practical" or "rational" than males are in such interaction, as measured by a variety of psychological tests (Coombs and Kenkel 1966; Rubin 1974, 398; Kephart 1967; Walster and Walster 1978, 45-51; Rubin *et al.* 1981).

4) Adult males, who are physically stronger than adult females and wield greater political power are more likely than females in most societies to control the money and other resources necessary for buying and giving.

5) Males are more easily sexually aroused by the sight of unclad females than females are by the sight of unclad males, as is obvious from a thriving pornography industry directed primarily at males (Symons 1979, 170-84; Kinsey *et al.* 1965, 651-64), [67] from the fact that concealment of female genitals is more common, cross-culturally, than covering of male genitals (Davenport 1977, 127), and from the fact that the facial veil tends to be used more by females than males, cross-culturally (Gregersen 1982, 125-26).

6) Females tend to be more repressed, sexually, than males (Murphy 1977; Bonaparte 1953, 70; Masters and Johnson 1970, 275; Freud, *SE* VII, 219), or more modest than males (Westermarck 1922, I, 433). That is, females are better able than males to conceal their sexual desire and avoid stimulating it in others. This is because females are typically trained to be inhibited in potentially sexual situations (e.g., they learn to avert their gaze at a member of the opposite sex more than men do, cross their legs while sitting, speak less than men in mixed company, swear less often than men do, etc. − see Henley 1977; below, section 36), and possibly because the neural equipment necessary for delayed and inhibited reactions is more highly developed in females than in males (Gray and Buffery 1971).[68]

7) Females have a greater tolerance for lack of orgasm over prolonged periods of time than males do (Kinsey *et al.* 1965, 526-7; 537ff.; Hite 1976, 536ff.; Symons 1979, 265).

8) Males generally have a greater desire for sexual variety than females (Symons 1979, ch. 7).

9) At the level of sexual attraction, man does and woman is.[69] Male sexual attractiveness depends as much, if not more on skill or prowess (Ford and Beach 1951, 86), status or power (Symons 1979, 191ff.; Van den Berghe and Barash 1977; Sontag 1972, 129; Daly and Wilson 1978, 299), and emotional sensitivity − all of which indicate ability to render altruism − than on physical handsomeness. But female sexual attractiveness tends to depend on youthful, healthy appearance (Symons 1979, 187-91; Sontag 1972, 132; Williams 1975, 128; Mellen 1981, 199ff.) and specific physical features such as enlarged, hairless mammaries[70] and

---

67. There are some indications of increased female interest in pornography in the more recent surveys (e.g., Lowe *et al.* 1983).
68. It is possible that some of the differences in item 6) account for the differences in item 5). That is, females may only *appear* to be less arousable by unclad members of the opposite sex because they repress or fail to report their arousal.
69. Cf. the *being/doing* dichotomy introduced by Horney (1967[1932] and de Beauvoir (1961[1949]), and followed up by Chodorow (1972). The asymmetry being discussed here, however, only has to do specifically with sexual attraction, while Horney, de Beauvoir and Chodorow are concerned with overall sex differences.
70. I am aware that anthropologists have not found evidence that breasts are sexual stimuli in all cultures. For example, the sample of 20 cultures surveyed by Stephens

curvaceous, fleshy hindquarters (Morris 1967, ch. 2; Short 1979. 151; Lancaster 1975, 82; Guthrie 1976, 104-7; Wickler 1972, chs. 30, 33; the enlarged breasts and buttocks of hominid females may be interpreted as epigamic signs compensating for the concealment of ovulation and advertising a female's ability to make high parental investment — see: Shepher 1978; Cant 1981; Gallup 1982). This attractiveness asymmetry between the sexes is quite marked. As Symons says, "... women inspire male sexual desire simply by existing" (1979, 284). Or, as Ellis put it long before the invention of sociobiology: "beauty in the human species is, above all, a feminine attribute ...;" "... the normal woman experiences no corresponding cult for the beauty of man" (1927-8, IV, 189; cf. Bernard 1981, 475-9).

Each item on this list is of course a complicated and interesting matter in itself. Some of the items will be discussed in more detail later. For now it is sufficient to observe that the *collective effect* of the listed proximate mechanisms is to make female rather than male sexuality a service that members of the opposite sex would want to exchange for payment of some kind.

Incidentally, the fact that a male may lose sexual interest in his mate with time does not always mean he will "stray" or stop rendering altruism

---

(1962, 229) contains six in which "breasts are not considered sexual stimuli." However, I am as suspicious of this as I am of the allegation that some cultures do not know female orgasm. A much touted example is furnished by the Mangaians, who supposedly are flabbergasted by the importance Western men attach to a woman's breasts (Marshall 1971). Yet stimulation of the woman's breasts is in fact a part of sexual intercourse in Mangaia (*ibid.*). A Mangaian woman may desire that her lover stimulate her breasts, but I doubt that the Mangaian man cooperates only for her benefit, and I am sure that he would be somewhat reluctant to repeatedly suck on, say, her elbow, her left index finger, or on the top of her head.

In any case, if breasts were not a sexual attraction for the human male, it would be difficult to explain why they are so large and prominent by comparison with the mammary apparatus of other primate females (Morris 1967, 70), and it would also be difficult to explain why human breasts reach full development *before* they are needed for lactation, i.e., in adolescence before the first pregnancy and remain fully developed in the absence of lactation (Morris 1977, 240; Morris 1973, 52; Short 1979, 151). As for the somewhat controversial thesis that "the protuberant, hemispherical breasts of the female must surely be copies of the fleshy buttocks ... " (Morris 1967, 75; cf. Morris 1973, 49ff.; Morris 1977, 239ff.), I would like to add some observations. First, as has so often happened in evolutionary speculation in the second half of the twentieth century, the Freudian wheel is reinvented. Thus, in *The Interpretation of Dreams* we read that " ... often — both in *doubles entendres* and in dreams — the lesser hemispheres of a woman's body are used, whether as contrasts or as substitutes, for the larger ones" (*SE* IV, 186; cf. XV, 156; Stärcke 1921, 197; Spector 1972, 218, n. 67). Second, Eibl-Eibesfeldt's to her and to offspring. That is, even if copulation eventually becomes a *male* service in what Symons calls the "micromarketplace of marriage," the male may still be motivated to stay around and continue copulating with his mate, proximately because he has by then probably made a large emotional investment both in his mate/mother-icon and in his children, and ultimately because maintaining this investment may contribute more to his inclusive fitness than desertion and attempted re-mating would.

The female too may get sick of copulating with her mate, particularly if she is not having orgasms or has to fake them. In other words, her mate may fail as a father-icon, just as she may fail as a mother-icon. Marital sex can lose its 'romance' for wife as well as husband. But there are good ultimate-causal or sociobiological reasons (reviewed above, section 6) why she should still be somewhat less inclined to desert than he. What we need to consider is the proximate basis for her greater sluggishness in abandoning her mate or in being unfaithful.

Some of the items listed above, such as greater physiological tolerance for lack of orgasms and higher ability to conceal sexual desire must contribute. Her children too (including the infant who regularly stimulates her breasts) divert her attention and make the need for a new lover less pressing. They may in fact drive potential lovers away.

But there is still another factor that, I think, makes a woman more likely than her mate to remain monogamous and tolerate unfaithfulness. This factor has to do with her mother. Even when her mate fails as a father-icon,

---

objection that " ... the woman's breast acquired its signalling function in connection with parental care" (1971, 147) does not really contradict Morris's thesis at all, but simply describes an *additional* reason why men tend to be very interested in a woman's breasts during, if not before sexual intercourse (see the quotation from Morris below, p. 198). Finally, the breast-buttock equation is made suspiciously often in a variety of linguistic contexts. Legman reports the following anecdote: "Abraham Lincoln ... attended a charity bazaar, and tendered a twenty dollar bill in payment for a bunch of violets. Receiving no change, he reached over the counter to pat the girl's breasts. 'What are these, my dear?' he asked. 'Why they're my breasts, Mr. Lincoln.' 'I see,' he said; 'everything is so high around here, I thought they might be your buttocks'" (1968, 245). Gerber (1981, 58) gives "forebuttocks" as one slang term for breasts, and Rawson (1981, 21) provides "bosom of the pants" as one euphemism for buttocks. Often the terms for breasts and buttocks are paired together, as in *Buttocks and Breasts* (a paperback porno title—Webb 1975, 408) and "tits and ass" (a Lenny Bruce expression). Some of the terms suggest an opposite. If breasts are "headlights" (Gerber 1981, 58), then what are *tail*-lights? If breasts are "topsides" or "upper deck" (*ibid.*), then what are *bottom*sides or *lower* deck? Conversely, if buttocks are the "southside," "rumble seat," or "fundament" (Rawson, *ibid.*), then what would be the *north*side, the *front* seat, or the *super*structure?

he may still exert some influence as a mother-icon. The same cannot be said for her mate, that is, if she fails in some way as a mother-icon for him, he has nothing else to resort to (I am not aware of any evidence that she could possibly be a father-icon for him). The evidence that he eventually becomes a mother-icon for her is quite abundant, and leads to some interesting insights about human long-term mating.

23. The Husband as Mother-Icon

"Daddy, You've Been a Mother to Me"
Fred Fisher

"Behind every successful man stands a
surprised mother-in-law."
Hubert Humphrey

A husband could not possibly be *only* a father-icon, given that a father
is so much more likely to be absent from a female's childhood experience
than a mother is, or to enter her childhood experience well after the
mother is already established as her primary socializing influence.

The husband's iconicity of his wife's mother is particularly obvious in
certain kinds of psychopathology. David Klimek illustrates this in his
nontechnical but insightful book *Beneath Mate Selection and Marriage*:

An attractive woman in her early fifties came to my office ostensibly to
"straighten out her thoughts" about her pending divorce. Actually, she
came to allay her guilt about divorcing her husband — her fifth — and to
complain about his badness. As she became less defensive, I asked, "Would
you please take a moment to think about how husband number five was
similar to husband number four?" She immediately responded, "Oh, they
were nothing alike. Dale had red hair, was tall and well-built, and was self-
employed. Charley was shorter, had blonde hair, a pot gut, and a college
degree." Before she went on, I interrupted with, "I don't mean the outside
stuff. I was wondering how similar your *relationship* was with each of them."
A long silence accompanied her contemplation. Quietly, she murmured,
"There really wasn't much difference, I guess." "How then," I inquired, "was
husband number four different from number three?" Impulsively she said,
"They were much different! I told you about Charley. Well, Jim was the best
looking guy I ever had. He was tall, dark, and handsome. He had a college
degree too, but liked working with his hands, so he became a carpenter."
"Yes," I said, "but how was the quality of your relationship different?" Her
mood thickened with a silent depression, and she finally whispered, "I think
it was pretty much the same." We repeated the interaction down to the first
husband. Quietly and slowly, I said, "Strange, isn't it, how similar these
relationships were for you? Prior to your first husband, do you recall ever
having a similar relationship?" She sank into the chair with a moan. After a
few minutes of noiseless tears, she firmly gripped the armrest, sat up angrily,
and shouted, "Yes, dammit! I had exactly the same kind of relationship with
my mother, and I couldn't wait to dump that lying bitch either!" (Klimek
1979, 4).

The fact is that the developing female acquires most of her basic social abilities specifically from interaction with her mother. These include the one ability that most characterizes the human species, namely, language (the "mother tongue"). Also included are basic systems of gesture and facial expression, the ability to reciprocate objects and messages, and various other rudimentary social abilities (below, sections 28 and 33). If these abilities are prerequisite to perceiving and constituting *any* iconic representation of an important person in childhood, then the mother is consequently important in a woman's search for Mr. Right. If, for example, a girl learned from her mother that one good deed should in principle be rewarded by another good deed (primitive reciprocal altruism), then that girl's mother is necessarily involved in a later decision by the girl to reward Mr. Right's present of flowers and dinner with sexual intercourse.

Psychoanalysts have long recognized that a husband is an icon of the mother as well as of the father. In his 1931 essay on female sexuality Freud says the following:

... the phase of exclusive attachment to the mother, which may be called the *pre-Oedipus* phase, possesses a far greater importance in women than it can have in men. Many phenomena of female sexual life which were not properly understood before can be fully explained by reference to this phase. Long ago, for instance, we noticed that many women who have chosen their husband on the model of their father, or have put him in their father's place, nevertheless repeat towards him, in their married life, their bad relations with their mother. The husband of such a woman was meant to be the inheritor of her relation to her father, but in reality he became the inheritor of her relation to her mother. This is easily explained as an obvious case of re-gression. (*SE* XXI, 230-31; cf. Greenson 1950; Slater 1968, 108-11).

This is perhaps a rather left-handed way of giving the mother credit for the daughter's ability to discern Mr. Right. Presumably some positive aspects of the mother-daughter relation also influence the daughter's choice of a husband:

Because our mother first satisfied all our self-preservative needs and sensual desires and gave us security, the part she plays in our minds is a lasting one, although the various ways in which this influence is effected and the forms it takes may not be at all obvious in later life. For instance, a woman may apparently have estranged herself from her mother, yet still unconsciously seek some of the features of her early relation to her in her relation to her husband or to a man she loves. The very important part which the father plays in the child's emotional life also influences all later love relations, and all other human associations. But the baby's early relation to him, in so far as he is felt as a gratifying, friendly and protective figure, is partly modelled on the one to the mother. (Klein 1977, 307).

The obvious problem a woman will have in seeing her mother in a potential mate is that he is not of the same sex (cf. Dinnerstein 1976, 208). A man does not have this problem. His mother and his potential mate are both women, and as Freud originally suggested, it is all too easy for him to transfer the feelings he had about his mother onto his mate, or in semiotic terms, to make her into a mother-icon.

Not only does a woman have to use more imagination to see her mother in her mate, but that imagination is more laden with intense (and unresolved) feelings about the mother than in the case of the male (Dinnerstein 1976 writes especially well on this topic). According to psychoanalysis, the male child, encouraged by his mother and jealous father, breaks the all-engulfing involvement with her at an early (Oedipal) stage, while the female child tends to remain attached to the mother right into adolescence (e.g., Chodorow 1978). Nonpsychoanalytic psychologists too find this greater dependence in girls than in boys, and know that it is fostered by the different kinds of attention parents and siblings give to girls than to boys: ". . . girls are not encouraged to give up old techniques of relating to adults and using others to define their identity, to manipulate the physical world and to supply their emotional needs" (Bardwick and Douvan 1972, 227).

In any case, when a grown woman does finally manage to recreate the old relationship with the mother in the relationship with the mate, she is likely to have taken longer to do so than a man would have, and at the same time she is likely to end up more intensely and dependently attached to the mate than a man would be − all other things being equal. Here may lie one proximate mechanism for (and ontogenetic background behind) both greater female "coyness" and the greater tendency toward monogamous attachment in females.

Here also we may have one proximate explanation[71] for the observed lower incidence of homosexuality in females (Kinsey *et al.* 1965, 487; Money and Ehrhardt 1972, 147). A man can be a mother-icon, but a woman cannot be a father-icon. Therefore a woman has the possibility of acting out homosexual impulses either with a female or with a male mate,[72] but a man can act out his homosexual impulses only with a male.

Since a man does not, at first glance, look like a mother, it will also take some effort on *his* part to convince a woman that he is, or rather, that he is *just like* a mother, a pseudo-mother or a mother-icon. In evolutionary terms,

---

71. But not a distal one. See below, section 47.
72. In the recent American film *Tootsie*, the heroine continues her relationship with the hero, even though she has just learned that he is a man (previously he was in drag and she was convinced that he, like she, was a lesbian).

her scrutiny of his wooing her with speech, gestures, gifts, and other signs constitutes the set of proximate mechanisms whereby a woman can select a partner who will maximize her own inclusive fitness. Assuming courtship progresses successfully, she can begin to see a mother-icon in him and permit the more intense, emotionally charged interactions that she once experienced with her real mother.

Ultimately he will be able to insert an organ into an orifice of hers, just as her mother did when caring for her (the psychological equivalence of the penis and the nipple is analyzed in detail below, section 41). This copulatory 'insertion' will be experienced as pleasurable and will lead to orgasm if she feels that he, like her mother before him, will continue to make the 'insertion' on a regular and reliable basis. Sociobiologically, the consequence of his sexual reliability is a likelihood that he will assist her with the resulting offspring (domestic bliss function of orgasm, above, section 5). In other words, one ontogenetic strand leading to the semiotically functional adult female orgasm goes back to the experience of the mother. This is not at all to deny the other important strand that goes back to the father, and specifically to the little girl's anticipation of being able to take into herself a representative of her father's penis. At least one psychoanalyst has perceived the connection of this unconscious double anatomic background with female orgasm: "When the orgasm is inhibited, it is because of fear of losing this love (*breast, penis*, affection, etc.), and of being left alone, apart, and empty" (Lorand 1939, 435, my italics).

In our society it is commonly observed that, if a woman's relationship with her mate does not work out well, she can always run back to her mother. Semiotically speaking, if the icon turns out to be unsatisfactory, what the icon signifies may be reverted to. Evolutionarily speaking, if the mate appears to be bad for her genes (and their replicas in her offspring), she can return to the care of the individual who is the most certain to be related to her and therefore the most likely to render altruism to her (including finding her a better mate). In the long run, then, a husband is always under pressure from his mother-in-law to "prove" to her that he can take care of her daughter as well as she did, that he can in effect be the impossible male mother (more on this in section 50). He is under similar pressure from a father-in-law, but evolutionary theory would predict that the pressure is less, given that there is always less certainty that the father-in-law is the daughter's father than that the mother-in-law is the daughter's mother.

Mothers-in-law are known to play a special role in the folklore, taboo-restrictions, and witticisms of most human cultures. Fathers-in-law much less commonly have this role. Here is an example from the Yanomamö:

The avoidance taboo prohibits a man from saying his mother-in-law's name. My informants would be extremely embarrassed when I would say the name of their mother-in-law while collecting genealogies. Kąobawä, for example, would grin sheepishly and hide his head. Men must also avoid their mothers-in-law physically and should not look at them. If I took a group of people for a ride in my canoe, there would always be considerable shuffling of bodies so that the men could be situated in the canoe as far away from their mothers-in-law as possible. (Chagnon 1977, 64).

In *Totem and Taboo* Freud explained the mutual avoidance between mother-in-law and son-in-law as a reaction against 1) the mother's inclination to identify with her daughter so much that she becomes sexually attracted to the daughter's husband, and 2) the son-in-law's inclination to see his mother-in-law as the older, maternal figure (=mother-icon) he once loved and renounced during the Oedipal period of his life (*SE* XIII, 12-16). There is, no doubt, some truth to this double proximate explanation, as sexual attraction between mother-in-law and son-in-law does often surface:

The stingiest Scotsman is the one who slept with his mother-in-law, to save the "wear and tear" on his pretty wife. (Legman 1968, 471).

But a certain kind of hostility as much as eroticism characterizes the relationship of son-in-law and mother-in-law. To take another example from *Rationale of the Dirty Joke*:

The bride-to-be's worried mother asks the groom if, by any chance, the men of his family are "built large," because, on the bride's side of the family, the women all are "very small." "Well," asks the groom, "is hers as big as a duck's arse?" "Of course," says the mother, a bit testily. "Well then, don't you worry," replies the groom; "mine is no thicker than a good big duck's egg." (*Ibid.*, 449).

The subject matter is certainly sexual here, but there is hostility in the mother-in-law's implicit challenge to the son-in-law's virility. A typical sequence in mother-in-law jokes is for the mother-in-law's perverse curiosity in her daughter's sex life to be squelched by proof that the son-in-law is quite capable of 'taking care' of the daughter sexually.

In *Totem and Taboo* Freud quotes a Zulu woman who explains the mutual avoidance of son-in-law and mother-in-law as follows: "It is not right that he should see the breasts which suckled his wife" (*SE* XIII, 14). But *breasts* are as maternal as they are sexual, which is to say a Zulu man may find it as unsettling to be reminded that he competes with his mother-in-law in nurturing his wife as to be reminded that his mother-in-law is a potentially incestuous object of his sexuality. More generally, his mother-in-law simply reminds him of his mother, as Freud said, but as much in her capacity as the one who taught him to feel guilty about not rendering altruism as in her capacity to attract him sexually.

A striking example of the husband's parental role vis-a-vis the wife is the Tiwi custom of sending *pre*pubescent daughters out to be "fed" and "grown" by their future husbands. A woman will say of her husband, "He took me like a daughter," or "He grew me up" (Goodale 1971, 44). Even before a mother-in-law's daughters are born she may make a contract with a (usually older) man regarding marriage to the daughters. This contract obliges the man not only to care for the mother-in-law's daughters, but to care for her as well, supplying her with clothes, tobacco, money, etc. — until death do them part. It is as if a Tiwi man marries his mother-in-law rather than her daughters. Yet he is not allowed to have direct speech with her, or with other mothers-in-law with whom he may enter into contract for daughters.

There are sometimes interesting problems between *daughters*-in-law and mothers-in-law, as can be seen from the occasional ethnographic literature on this topic (e.g., Harding 1975, 293ff.). But a daughter-in-law, as opposed to a son-in-law is a woman, and therefore is inherently more able to 'mother' a spouse. In a sense the competition between daughter-in-law and mother-in-law is more 'fair' than the competition between son-in-law and mother-in-law (at least this is how my lawyer views it).

I would like to note that the iconic (or pseudo-) mothering that plays a role in in-law relations does just that, i.e., plays only a role, and is not by any means a complete explanation of what goes on between in-laws, cross-culturally. Many aspects of parent-in-law taboos, for example, have to be explained by correlations with residence pattern, as Lowie (1920, 84-97) emphasized in his critique of Freud. Cultural diffusion must also play a role.

Step-mothering is another interesting phenomenon which, like 'son-in-lawing', must have an iconic or pseudo-mother component. In fact the English word "mother-in-law" used to have the meaning "step-mother" (Goody 1976, 53). The French word "belle mère" can refer to either a step-mother or a mother-in-law (*ibid.*). But step-mothers are generally seen as even more pernicious than mothers-in-law (e.g., the so-called "evil stepmother"), and well they should because their genes stand to gain nothing from altruism toward children from a previous marriage, while a mother-in-law's genes benefit at least indirectly from altruism toward a son-in-law who is having offspring related to her.

The stereotypical competitor with a step-mother is of course the daughter by previous marriage. In most of the numerous variants of the *Cinderella* tale, for example, it is a young girl who is ill-treated by a step-mother (or step-sister or other female relative) (Cox 1892; Goody 1976, 54). As Bettelheim (1977, 236-77) has shown, many of the *Cinderella* variants are founded on a repressed Oedipal entanglement of father and daughter, as well as on the sexual and other envies siblings have toward each other. But this does not exclude the daughter's competition with the step-mother to 'mother' the father. The girl's original mother has in one way or another been removed before the step-mother arrives, and usually the girl fills in for the mother in taking care of the father (cooking, cleaning, and generally attending to home and hearth – where the "cinders" are). When the girl is accused of "not loving the father enough" (cf. Cordelia in *King Lear*), the meaning is not only denied Oedipal desire, but also, in effect, "not mothering the father enough."

If both mothers-in-law and step-mothers are substitute mothers, the individuals with whom they compete are also trying to be substitute mothers. But whereas a son-in-law or daughter-in-law competes with a mother-in-law to mother a spouse, a daughter competes with a step-mother to mother a parent.

All three – daughter-in-law, son-in-law, and step-daughter – have to overcome odds. But of the three, the daughter-in-law is best equipped to succeed, while the son-in-law has the problem of being the wrong *sex*, and the step-daughter has the problem of being in the wrong *generation*. The son-in-law 'wins' by staying with his mate and being a good father to resulting offspring. The step-daughter 'wins' by renouncing or by being driven away by her father and marrying a rich man. In other words, the persecuted son-in-law proves himself good at being a 'male mother', while the persecuted step-daughter *finds* herself a 'male mother.'

In sociobiological terms, the mother-in-law joke and the Cinderella motif are archetypal examples of what each sex is supposed to accomplish in life: for the male it is a question of knowing how to *render* altruism in a way that maximizes inclusive fitness, while for the female it is a question of being able to *elicit* altruism in a way that maximizes inclusive fitness.

This is not to say that there are not many circumstances under which males elicit altruism and females render it. But the altruism characteristic of the female tends to be seen as mere background because it is *obligatory*. Insofar as the female is equipped in such a fashion as to have no choice but to render altruism to (at least the early development of) offspring, then her relationship to the other sex is more likely to be one of eliciting rather than rendering altruism. The male, on the other hand, is free of the female apparatus that obliges altruism to offspring. His altruism is foregrounded because it is *facultative*. This fundamental difference between the sexes will be considered at greater length below (sections 24, 36, 37, 41).

24. Male Altruism as a Sign

A male has much to gain in the long run from impressing his potential mate (and her kin) with his altruistic powers. What he pays for the female or for her sexual services may be more than compensated for by the fact that she is obliged to at least gestate and nurse, if not rear the offspring that may result. She in turn gains the obvious evolutionary benefit of promoting the fitness of offspring she can be 'certain' are her own.

There are situations, though, where the adult male is very lax about rendering altruism, or even comes to depend on female altruism. The feminist literature (e.g., Leghorn and Parker 1981) abounds with evidence of male economic exploitation of females. Here, for example, is the response of an Upper Volta woman to the question of who — men or women — work the hardest:

Ha! Women of course. The men have only their field of millet to worry about. We must help the men in their fields and plant our own fields of peanuts, corn and condiments too. It's hard to get everything done, especially in the planting season. And then there are meals to prepare, flour to grind, and the house to clean, not to mention looking after the babies. How often do you see a woman wasting her time drinking in the dolohut (a bar selling millet beer) like the husbands? Why do you think I'm so skinny? I eat plenty, but I have too many worries. (as quoted from Claudia Fonesco by Leghorn and Parker, *ibid.*, 196).

If we are to believe some of the feminists, there are situations where the male not only shoulders little of the responsibility for offspring and behaves promiscuously, but also is actually parasitic on female labor. That is, the overall output of labor is preponderantly female, and males become essentially loafers who, in addition to periodically inseminating women, perform merely symbolic tasks and do little real, life-sustaining work. Such males would appear to be cashing in on the female tendency to render altruism to children, since the male who is always "out playing," or "playing around," or who is just self-absorbed generally is in essence acting like his mate's children.

The anthropological evidence does not indicate, however, that such extreme irresponsibility and exploitativeness is *typical* of the human male. It is true that the male has on balance a greater tendency to promiscuity and abandonment than the typical human female does, but he usually has some sense of responsibility too (which he no doubt acquired as a result of having experienced his mother's obligatory altruism). The economic contract of marriage is rarely viewed as trivial in any society, and necessarily encourages the male sense of responsibility toward wife and offspring. Also, there are significant psychological benefits, not merely economic benefits which both sons and daughters reap as a result of good fathering (e.g., Lynn 1974). "Usually the division of labor is an equitable one," said Lowie of nonindustrial societies in 1920 (202). More recently, Ember concluded that, ". . . unless warfare interferes, males may generally do more toward subsistence than females because women are universally occupied with the demands of child care and other domestic chores" (1981, 542). In the cross-cultural study made by Whyte (1978a, 218), men and women were found to expend roughly equal time and effort on subsistence activities in most (61.4%) societies sampled, though there was a larger percentage of societies in which women expend more time and effort (22.7%) than societies in which men spend more time and effort (15.9%).

A man may be willing to work hard in most societies, but he can be choosey about who is going to benefit from his labor. He can, for example, choose not to render altruism to the woman he has impregnated. He may sometimes be the proverbial Don Juan who "loves 'em and leaves 'em." A female already gestating a fetus or nursing an infant cannot make the Don Juan's kind of decision — unless she selects the extreme measures of abortion or infanticide.

To make an analogy, female altruism toward offspring is rather like male orgasm. It is background, something that can usually be taken for granted. Male gifts to females and/or their kin, on the other hand, are rather like female orgasms. They may or may not be given. They therefore are capable of *signifying* something, especially in the early stages of a relationship. In semiotic terms, they are *indexical* signs (see above discussion of the indexicality of female orgasm, section 5). Or, insofar as a man's gifts to a woman are perceived as 'similar' to the altruism he will later render to her and to offspring, we may say that they are also *iconic* signs of that altruism.

And, just as female orgasms can be used for deceptive purposes (fake orgasms), so too male gifts to the female can deceive. I have already mentioned Don Juanism (what Freud calls "male erotomania"). The Don Juan may *pay* a woman compliments of all kinds (cf. also the expression "pay attention"), not to mention give her gifts of a more material nature. As an anonymous reader suggested to me, "the typical Don Juan is a male who *signals* he cares, when he doesn't; that is he appears sensitive, caring, loving, and trustworthy, when he is not."

But just as fake female orgasms can be beneficial to males as well as females, perhaps Don Juanism can be beneficial to females as well as to males. That is, perhaps females stand to reap benefits from occasional clandestine, extramarital copulations with the Don Juan. Strassmann suggests that ". . . subconscious physiological and psychological correlates of ovulation in humans may have tempted females to exploit infrequent, low-risk opportunities to mate outside the pair-bond with males of superior genetic fitness" (1981, 31; cf. Benshoof and Thornhill 1979). Such females may not gain the Don Juan's parental assistance but may gain other benefits, including possibly a son who is like his father (cf. the "sexy son hypothesis" of Weatherhead and Robertson 1979).

But the Don Juan may not necessarily be genetically "superior," either. Perhaps instead the reason women sometimes copulate with a Don Juan (as opposed to just any extramarital male) is that he simply provides a new libidinal outlet while at the same time being 'safe', that is, does not stay around and endanger the otherwise monogamous and genetically profitable relationship the woman is having with her mate and wants to preserve. In other words, a woman's extramarital relations with a (perceived) Don Juan may be just a temporary and genetically inconsequential side effect of the hedonic function of female orgasm. But her extramarital relations with *other* males may be part of a systematic and genetically consequential search for sexual pleasure and happiness or for better parental assistance than she is currently getting. The new male she eventually finds may not be "genetically superior," but the altruism he renders will probably enhance her reproductive success.

25. The Semiotic Virgin

The first time is never the best.
ad for a bitter liqueur

Thus far we have encountered a number of semiotic phenomena that may be used for purposes of deception: estrus signs, female orgasm, male orgasm, and male altruism. To this list I would like to add another important sign, namely, female virginity.

As we saw above (section 6) a woman's sexual restraint is of much greater concern in most societies than a man's. This is often true even for the very beginning of a woman's heterosexual life. Broude and Greene (1976, 414-15) report that, in a little over 38% of the 141 societies of the Standard Sample for which the information was available, a woman's virginity is valued before marriage (information on premarital virginity of males is not even coded). If a woman's loss of virginity takes place outside of the proper marital context, she is in many societies considered "damaged," while in no societies that I am aware of is a man's premarital loss of virginity seriously considered harmful.

Goody reviews cross-cultural data that ". . . support the idea of a positive association between societies where women inherit 'family' property and those where pre-marital sex is prohibited" (1976, 14). Dickeman argues that "the most extreme forms of claustration, veiling, and incapacitation of women" occur in the highly stratified societies in which there is an abundance of impoverished males at the bottom and a few rich males with concubines or harems at the top (1981, 425). Broude (1981, 638-47) surveys the extensive literature on premarital sex norms for females and, using regression analysis, finds that class stratification, degree of cultural complexity, and especially inaccessibility to children of mothering are the best predictors of restrictive premarital sex norms (above I argued that this last factor offers support to the idea that a woman is acting as an icon of her mother in her sexual relations with men).

Paige and Paige (1981) find that societies with strong fraternal interest groups are especially likely to take drastic measures to insure that a woman is a virgin before she is given in marriage. For example, the Somali perform infibulation, in which the sides of the vulva are scarified and then held together until they fuse during healing. The Egyptian Nubians both excise the clitoris and fuse the labia so that only a tiny hole is left for urination.

Consummation of marriage is obviously traumatic for both parties, and sometimes a knife is resorted to (see Paige and Paige 1981, 88-9, Hosken 1979, and Huelsman 1976 for more on infibulation). When infibulation is not practiced outright, there may nonetheless be a "virginity test" in which it is necessary to prove rupture of that natural fibula known as the hymen or maidenhead:

Like infibulation, a virginity test gives the husband and his kin proof of the bride's virginity. Final compensation may be contingent on this proof, which usually takes the form of a public display of the bloody sheet upon which the couple consummated their marriage. If the daughter is not a virgin, the father may be forced to pay back some of the bridewealth or, if a husband insists, to take back his daughter and declare the marriage invalid. Failure of the test brings great shame on the father's family and may impair their ability to contract marriages for other daughters. (*ibid.*, 89).

Paige and Paige cite several societies where virginity tests are or have been important, such as the Basseri of southern Iran, the Kazak of central Asia, and the Hebrews described in the Old Testament.

Both the infibulated vagina and the loss of blood during coitus are *signs* of (previous) virginity. Semiotically, both are indexes of virginity. Also, the sexual abstinence implied by virginity may itself be a sign. Some men would like to believe, at least, that virginity is an icon of future abstinence with all men save the groom. Freud says, for example, that loss of virginity creates ". . . a state of bondage in the woman which guarantees that possession of her shall continue undisturbed and makes her able to resist new impressions and enticements from outside" (*SE* XI, 193; cf. Rosenblatt 1974, 90).

There has always been a great interest in the signs of (loss of) virginity in Western culture. Here are some of the alleged signs of recent defloration culled from ancient, medieval, and more recent sources by Havelock Ellis: increased circumference of the girl's neck, deepening of her voice, goaty smell from her armpits, "crisper" pubic hair, loss of ability to urinate in a high arc, and failure to blush (Ellis 1927, V, 203-4). I cite these examples not to consider their validity, but to emphasize that female virginity, or loss thereof, is a semiotic phenomenon.

As with any sign, such as female orgasm,[73] there is a large potential for deception. Simulated loss of blood during virginity tests is well known. Daly and Wilson (1978, 271) mention the thriving business in the surgical treatment of ruptured hymens in Japan. Paige and Paige (1981, 91) cite a report that Ashanti women may insert ants into the vagina just before

---

73. Legman (1968, 453) explicitly compares fake virginity and fake orgasm.

the marriage in order to irritate the tissue and thereby cause bleeding at consummation. In some societies there may be pressure to arrange for a virginity test to take place during menstruation. Legman (1968, 453) mentions the Gypsy practice of killing a bird to obtain blood. In his discussion of the "defloration mania" in eighteenth-century England, Taylor mentions ". . . a girl who had been stitched up four times pleading (in vain) to be excused further operations of the sort" (1954, 187). This last example concerns a prostitute, and shows that preoccupation with female virginity is not only a readiness to interpret signs, but also a libidinal outlet, an expression of male *Schadenfreude.*

Many societies that do not go so far as to practice infibulation or virginity tests nonetheless manifest some concern with whether the bride is a virgin or not. In a number of Western societies, for example, a bride wears white to signify 'purity.' Her bridal veil is commonly thought of as a signifier of the hymen. The Russian word for a bride is "nevesta," which means, etymologically, 'one who does not know' (in the sexual sense; cf. "ved'ma," 'witch,' i.e., 'one who *does* know' — Vasmer 1953-8, I, 178; II, 205-6). It is traditional for the groom at a Jewish wedding to smash a glass under his foot (=an icon of defloration). Legman's *Rationale of the Dirty Joke* includes a whole spate of anecdotes about the questionable virginity of the bride, such as:

A girl's former lover is pressed to say a few words of congratulation at her wedding dinner. He tries to beg off, but the bride herself insists. "Well," he says, "I don't know what to say, so I'll just offer a toast to the happy couple. — Here's to the bride: they say there's just as good fish left in the sea as were ever caught, but I doubt it! And here's to the groom: he's got her — us other fellows didn't. And here's to marriage: it's like going fishing — the fish you really want always gets away, and all you're left with is a little piece of tail." (Legman 1968, 455-6).

A woman's view of virginity (or the loss thereof) is quite different from a man's. A woman may take pride in being (or appearing to be) a virgin when the wedding night comes, just as her male and female kin do. But she has to look forward to some pain at the breaking of the hymen, which is apparently a neotenous and uniquely human organ. Desmond Morris believes in fact that the hymen has evolved precisely to produce the pain and anxiety necessary to put a "partial brake" on developing female sexuality: ". . . the hymen demands that she shall have already developed a deep emotional involvement before taking the final step, an involvement strong enough to take the initial physical discomfort in its stride" (1967, 82). Understandably, feminists are not always happy with such an interpretation (e.g. Janssen-Jurreit 1982, 200). A quite different view is offered by Havelock Ellis, who considers the hymen a kind of insurance against male incompetence: "it [the hymen] is an obstacle to the impregnation of the young female by immature, aged, or feeble males. The hymen is thus an anatomical expression of that admiration of force which marks the female in her choice of a mate" (Ellis 1927-8, V, 140). In either case, whether it is Morris or Ellis who is right (or both), the hymen may be said to be originally an organ of female sexual choice. Eventually males too fathomed its semiotic potential, and it became also an organ serving male choice.

Margaret Mead says virginity is a state of *being* for a woman. One *is* or *is not* a virgin. The loss of virginity is something very definite and irreversible (Mead 1975[1949], 174). It can never be regained, and for this reason alone can be thought of as something that is "lost." Or, to quote a collegiate graffito: "virginity is like a bubble on the ocean – one prick and it's gone forever" (Nilsen 1981, 86).

Yet, objectively speaking, can the anticipated slight discomfort and loss of blood really account for the often reported fear and trepidation, the reluctance, and the drawn out hesitation before defloration, as well as the variety of negative feelings a woman experiences afterwards?

Here are three literary descriptions of the loss of virginity:

Margaret Drabble:
I was guilty of a crime, all right, but it was a brand-new, twentieth-century crime, not the good old traditional one of lust and greed. My crime was my suspicion, my fear, my apprehensive terror of the very idea of sex. I liked men, and was forever in and out of love for years, but the thought of sex frightened the life out of me, and the more I didn't do it and the more I read and heard about how I ought to do it the more frightened I became. It must have been the physical thing itself that frightened me, for I did not at all object to its social implications, to my name on hotel registers, my name bandied about at parties, nor to the emotional upheavals which I imagined to be its companions: but the act itself I could neither make nor contemplate. I would go so far, and no farther.

* * *

So I shut my eyes, very tight, and waited. It was quite simple, as it was summer and I was wearing very few clothes, and he seemed to know quite well what he was doing: but then of course so did I *seem* to know, and I didn't. However, I managed to smile bravely, in order not to give offense, despite considerable pain, and I hoped that the true state of affairs would not become obvious. I remember that he stroked my hair, just before, and said in his oh so wonderfully polite and chivalrous way:
"Is this all right? Are you all right, will this be all right?"
I knew what he meant and, eyes shut, I smiled and nodded, and then that was it and it was over. Which proves that deception is indeed a tangled web.

And I had no one but myself to blame. But it was something that when I opened my eyes again, there was only George: I clutched his head to my bosom and I cried:

"Oh George, tell me about you, tell me about you," but now it was his turn to shut his eyes and, moaning softly, he buried his face against me while I stroked his hair and the thin brown hollow of his cheek. After a while he did say something which, though hardly distinguishable, I took to be "Oh God, how pointless this is." I was a little perturbed by this statement, though not so much then as later, and after a couple more minutes I got up, switched off the radio, and went off to the bathroom, leaving him enough time to straighten himself up or even, if he so wished, to disappear. I returned, some time later, in my dressing gown, and found him still there, sitting where I had left him, but now upright and with his eyes open.

"Hello," I said, stopping in the doorway and smiling brightly, willing to show anything rather than the perplexing mass of uncertainties which possessed me. (*Thank You All Very Much,* 1969, 17, 27-8).

Doris Lessing:

He sat on the edge of the bed, pulled off his shoes, laying them neatly side by side, and began unbuttoning his clothes. Martha lay as if her limbs had been struck by a nervous paralysis, conquering the impulse to avert her eyes, which might have been interpreted by herself, if not by him, as prudishness. There was something dismaying about these methodical preparations. Like getting ready for an operation, she thought involuntarily.

* * *

... Afterwards she lay coiled meekly beside him like a woman in love, for her mind had swallowed the moment of disappointment whole, like a python, so that he, the man, and the mirage were able once again to fuse together, in the future. (*Martha Quest,* 1970, 183, 184).

Sylvia Plath:

When I was nineteen, pureness was the great issue.

Instead of the world being divided up into Catholics and Protestants or Republicans and Democrats or white men and black men or even men and women, I saw the world divided into people who had slept with somebody and people who hadn't, and this seemed the only really significant difference between one person and another.

I thought a spectacular change would come over me the day I crossed the boundary line.

* * *

I woke to the sound of rain.

It was pitch dark. After a while I deciphered the faint outlines of an unfamiliar window. Every so often a beam of light appeared out of thin air, traversed the wall like a ghostly, exploratory finger, and slid off into nothing again.

Then I heard the sound of somebody breathing.

At first I thought it was only myself, and that I was lying in the dark in my hotel room after being poisoned. I held my breath, but the breathing kept on.

A green eye glowed on the bed beside me. It was divided into quarters like a compass. I reached out slowly and closed my hand on it. I lifted it up. With it came an arm, heavy as a dead man's, but warm with sleep. (*The Bell Jar,* 1971, 90, 92).

The intense anger or feeling of revenge that is sometimes described in the clinical literature (e.g., Abraham 1922, 6; Horney 1967, 52) does not come through here because these women are healthy, enlightened, and have made their own choice. Yet there is an obvious apprehension before the fact, and a depressing disappointment after the fact. Drabble's heroine is so hypocritical and upset at the same time that she doesn't even know what she feels. Lessing's Martha is just plain disappointed. Plath's Esther feels she has been poisoned (death and sexuality walk hand in hand throughout Plath's fascinating life and work). In all three novels the man who takes away the heroine's virginity is definitely not God's gift to woman, but more like an experimental sex object. Above all, the women depicted have been *hurt* by what has happened, though they are reluctant to admit a humiliation that is of their own choosing. Plath's metaphor for both the physical and mental injury of defloration is particularly interesting:

An hour later I lay in my hotel bed, listening to the rain. It didn't even sound like rain, it sounded like a tap running. The ache in the middle of my left shin bone came to life, and I abandoned any hope of sleep before seven, when my radio-alarm clock would rouse me with its hearty renderings of Sousa.
Every time it rained the old leg-break seemed to remember itself, and what it remembered was a dull hurt.
Then I thought, "Buddy Willard made me break that leg."
Then I thought, "No I broke it myself. I broke it on purpose to pay myself back for being such a heel." (*ibid.,* 95).

As if a broken leg were not enough, there is also an image of a new bride as trampled upon (recall the Jewish wedding ceremony):

And I knew that in spite of all the roses and kisses and restaurant dinners a man showered on a woman before he married her, what he secretly wanted when the wedding service ended was for her to flatten out underneath his feet like Mrs. Willard's kitchen mat. (*ibid.,* 93-4).

But if a husband is a father-icon, as I have attempted to show, then ultimately it is the father who tramples the bride:

> Every woman adores a Fascist,
> The boot in the face, the brute
> Brute heart of a brute like you.
> You stand at the blackboard, daddy,
> In the picture I have of you,

> A cleft in your chin instead of your foot
> But no less a devil for that, no not
> Any less the black man who
> Bit my pretty red heart in two.
> (from "Daddy," in *The Collected Poems*, 1981, 223-4).

Sylvia Plath is not Everywoman, but she is (or was) a literary artist, and presumably had some sensitivity about the relations between the sexes. The aura of violence surrounding her depiction of defloration is perfectly in keeping with what Karl Abraham said in his psychoanalytic classic on "the female castration complex:"

I know several cases in which women after defloration produced an outburst of affect and hit or throttled their husband. One of my patients went to sleep with her husband after the first intercourse, then woke up, seized him violently and only gradually came to her senses. There is no mistaking the significance of such conduct: the woman revenges herself for the injury to her physical integrity. (Abraham 1922, 8).

The violent injury of defloration can be generalized to other forms of violence, as is shown by the following entries under "tselka" ('cherry,' 'virgin') in a current dictionary of Russian obscenities:

sidet' za tselku to do time (in prison) for rape [lit., for the hymen].
slomat' tselku 1. to break the hymen 2. to tame, harness *smb*.
raskolot'sia kak tselochka to crack/break down (under interrogation) [lit., to break apart like a hymen]. (Drummond and Perkins 1980, 72).

Until the violence of defloration has been committed, a woman may be proud of her virginal state, even if she is looking forward to the pleasure of sexual intercourse. Anthropologists know that a woman's virginity is a matter of pride in many cultures (Russian "stroit' tselku," i.e., 'to build a hymen' is a slang term meaning 'to be pretentious'). But after defloration may come feelings of humiliation. The deflowered woman may be perceived by herself and others as "fallen". In the Plath example she has descended so low as to be flat as a kitchen mat.

If defloration wounds a woman's (and her kin's) pride, it can build a man's (provided the man is not related to her). For example, shortly after Adolph takes away Martha's virginity in *Martha Quest*, we read:

They went down to the Knave of Clubs. Martha wondered why it was that before he had always hastily left when the crowd came in; now he remained, dancing every dance, smiling his uncertain smile, in which there was more than a hint of triumph. It annoyed Martha. Every time she lifted her face and saw that small gleaming smile, she had to smother anger. (Lessing, 184).

Not only is the heroine's anger finally coming to the surface (three paragraphs earlier it was only disappointment), but the momentary hero's pride is clearly showing as well.

From a psychoanalytic perspective, a man's pride in his sexual prowess is a specifically phallic matter. He is the proud possessor of a penis, and entry of that penis, erect, into previously unoccupied territory is felt as no mean conquest. Conversely, failure to enter that territory or, worse yet, failure to even become erect, is a defeat — for the man identifies with the penis, and its defeat is *his* defeat (see below, section 43, on the synecdochal function of the penis). As far as he is concerned, a penis that does not work is no penis at all, i.e., impotence is the psychological equivalent of castration (an article on impotence in *Psychology Today* [July, 1980, 42] is illustrated with a drawing of the traditional male symbol, the sword and shield of Mars, in which the sword is *broken*).

I will have much more to say on castration anxiety below (sections 44-49). For now it should be observed that, from a male viewpoint, a virgin female is an implicit challenge to a man's penis (i.e., to him). In deflowering a woman a man by definition has to do damage, that is, he has to draw blood. But the idea of such damage inspires a fear of retaliatory damage being done to him. And since it is specifically the penis which breaks the hymen, the man imagines that his penis will be the object of revenge, that is, his fear of revenge takes the form of a fear of castration. Legman cites, for example, a fantasy in which "an ignorant bride castrates her newlywed husband when *jokingly* told to do so" (1975, 614). This fear of castration is heightened by the man's perception that the woman envies him (and all men) his penis in the first place (below, sect. 53), and his perception that defloration will only aggravate in her an archaic hostility toward men (see Freud's paper on "the taboo of virginity," *SE* XI, 193-208; Legman 1968, 525-34; Abraham 1922; Yates 1930; Flügel 1924, 175). Some scholars, though, believe that the male fears castration by a punitive father figure who 'owns' the virgin, rather than by the virgin herself (see, for example, Gough's [1955] analysis of Nayar and Tiyyar female initiation rites).

Perhaps the best folkloric evidence for this male fear of castration is the widespread idea of a "vagina dentata," which very often is the attribute of a virgin (see below, section 44). In the famous fourteenth century *Voiage of Sir John Maundeville* is a tale of virgins who had serpents in their vaginas which "stongen men upon hire Zerdes, that thei dyeden anon," i.e., stung men's penises and caused them to die (Penzer 1952, 37; cf. Yates 1930, 178). A form of guillotine used in 16th and 17th century Scotland was called a "Maiden" (Evans 1970, 675; cf. the old terms "iron maiden," "the duke of Exeter's daughter," and "the scavenger's daughter" — all of which referred to instruments of torture according to Rawson 1981, 173; cf. also the Russian slang term "devka" ['virgin'], which refers to a noose — Flegon 1973, 82). In the various recensions of "poison-damsel" lore (Thompson motif no. F.582) a beautiful young maiden is capable of killing a man by her embrace and her perspiration, by her kiss, by her breath, by her evil glance, and even by her poisonous words (Penzer 1952; Lederer 1968, ch.7).

Apart from folklore, there is a widespread reproductive ritual which suggests great fear of virgins: "It is well known that in many countries the first intercourse after marriage is looked upon with such dread, and as an act of so inauspicious a nature, that the husband either appoints a proxy for the first night, or else takes care that if the girl is a virgin the hymen be broken by artificial means" (Penzer 1952, 36). Among the Arunta of central Australia a newly menarcheal woman was subjected to insemination by not only one but by three different men from three different kinship groups before her husband was allowed sexual intercourse with her (Spencer and Gillen 1927, II, 472ff.; cf. Paige and Paige 1981, 105). In contexts as various as ancient Cambodia, Medieval Europe, the Arawaks of South America, the Marshallese, the Tamil Non-Brahmans of Tanjore, the Circassians of the Caucasus, the Sakais of Celebes, the Ballante of Senegal, and many others some form of the *droit du seigneur* (also called *jus primae noctis* or *jus cunni*) is or was observed (see: Schmidt 1881; Baumann 1955, 78ff.; Crawley 1965, 66ff.; Westermarck 1922, I, 166-206; Gough 1955; Taylor 1954, 31; Penzer *ibid*.; Goodland 1931, 686 for an extensive bibliography on ritual defloration; and Thompson's Motif-Index T161 for the folklore on *jus primae noctis*). Metaphorical forms of the practice are noted by Slater: "High officials are required to cut tapes, lay cornerstones, and break earth, and it is even necessary for the president of the United States to throw the first pitch of the baseball season" (1968, 69).

The psychoanalytic interpretation of *droit du seigneur* is that in some cultural contexts a man who plans to be attached to a woman for the rest of his life would rather avoid the possibility of castration anxiety than claim the privilege of deflowering her. This hypothesis has not been falsified, and is not at all incompatible with other hypotheses, such as that of Paige and Paige (1981, 105) who interpret the Arunta example as a strengthening of the rights of the fraternal interest groups from which the three men come.

Another, perhaps lesser known wedding rite, is nuptial transvestism. Plutarch (see Delcourt 1961, 2; Eliade 1965, 112) reports that in ancient Sparta a bride's head was shaved, she was dressed in a *man's* clothes, and in that state she waited for the bridegroom. At Argos she wore a false *beard* on the wedding night. At Cos (Kos) the *bridegroom* wore a *woman's* attire to receive the bride. This last example seems to be more a couvade-like rite designed to impress the bride with the bridegroom's willingness to take part in the production and care of offspring (see Bachofen 1943-67 [1861], 631-2).

For a man, it is as if a virgin were another *man* (note that, in English, "*vir*gin," "*vir*ile," and "*vir*ago" are etymologically related). Not until he has deflowered her has he 'made a woman out of her.'

Among the Gimi of Papua New Guinea, for example, a virgin bride arrives at her husband's village carrying two phallic bamboo objects as offerings, and Gillison infers from this that ". . . when a woman is sexually penetrated, she loses something (a penis) which she *already possesses* — something which she brought with her in marriage as a virgin" (Gillison 1980, 156). Recall also that the legendary *Virgin* of Orleans ("La Pucelle d'Orleans," i.e., Joan of Arc) dressed up as a *man* to accomplish her exploits. Delcourt (1961, 91ff.) reviews the cult of the *bearded* virgin saint which spread in Europe after the advent of Christianity. An example is Wilgeforte (=*virgo fortis*) who was threatened with the loss of her virginity when her father wanted to marry her off to the king of Sicily. She prayed to Christ, who caused her to grow a beard, whereupon her father had her crucified. From that time, she was called Saint Liberata.

The young sharpshooting virgin Annie Oakley in the film *Annie Get Your* [arguably phallic] *Gun* is simply unable to miss the targets she shoots at in a contest with the man she loves. But then her Indian father comes forward to save the day, as Gershon Legman describes:

Out from under his capacious blanket he takes surreptitiously the biggest, ugliest goddam triple-action barbed-wire cutting pliers you have ever in your born days seen; grabs aholt with his perfidious Red Injun paw of Annie Oakley's superb *red-gold* rifle, presented to her by the Biggest Daddy of them all, the Emperor of Austria-Hungary, and SNIPS the frontsighting sticker-upper dooflicker off the end of her championship rifle with those ugly blue-steel pliers! Annie then cannot hit the side of a barndoor with a cannon, loses the competition, marries the guy, and they all live happily ever after. (1968, 529).

The Russian writer Nikolai Gogol, a homosexual and a misogynist, wrote a tale about a certain Ivan Fedorovich Shponka, who was terrified of getting married. Ivan says he would not know what to do with a wife because he "has never had a wife before." In a nightmare a whole flock of wives with goose-faces persecute him: he is forced to hop on one leg, he is dragged up a tower by his aunt, and he finally buys a 'wife' in the form of a piece of cloth that has to be cut to fit him. Ivan's aunt, the woman who wants him to get married, is an extremely masculine virgin:

Aunt Vasilisa Kashporovna was at this time about fifty. She had never married, and commonly declared that she valued her maiden state above everything. Though, indeed, to the best of my memory, no one ever courted her. This was due to the fact that all men were rather timid in her presence, and never had the courage to make her an offer. "A girl of great character, Vasilisa Kashporovna!" all the young men used to say, and they were quite right, too, for there was no one Vasilisa Kashporovna could not get the better of. With her own manly hand, tugging every day at his forelock, she could, unaided, turn the drunken miller, a worthless fellow, into a perfect treasure. She was of almost gigantic stature and her breadth and strength were fully in proportion. It seemed as though nature had made an unpardonable mistake in condemning her to wear a dark brown gown with little flounces on weekdays and a red cashmere shawl on Sunday and on her name day, though a dragoon's mustaches and high topboots would have suited her better than anything. (Gogol 1964 [1832], 183).

Factually of course, a female virgin is not phallic at all. But, if we are to believe the psychoanalytic literature on this subject, the fact that females do not possess a penis is not something males find easy to accept, for it makes them wonder whether or not *they* will be able to keep their own penis. And, if the theory of penis-envy is to be believed (below, section 53), even females may in some cases have difficulty accepting the lack of a penis, and may perceive defloration the same way males do, namely, as a kind of mutilation, or even as a castration. Not until she is deflowered is a woman penetrated by precisely the organ she can never (permanently) possess, and therefore not since she first learned of the anatomical distinctions between the sexes is she so directly confronted with her penisless state.

At the fantasy level, a woman may *be* a phallus, or she may *possess* a phallus. Otto Fenichel, in his famous paper "Die symbolische Gleichung Maedchen-Phallus" (1954[1936]) described examples of the former type. Thus a woman patient had fantasies of herself as a child hanging from her father's abdomen in place of a penis. Another woman patient identified with the talisman her father carried around the world with him in his pocket. Géza Róheim, in another well known psychoanalytic paper entitled "Aphrodite, or the Woman with a Penis" (1945a), reminds us that, according to Hesiod, the virgin Aphrodite sprang from the foam (*afros* in Greek) formed by the remains of the *penis* of her father, Ouranos, who had been castrated by Kronos. Aphrodite was not only the Greek goddess of feminine beauty, but was an aggressively sexual figure (some of whose variants or descendants threatened men with castration — Friedrich 1978, 68), was a lover of the penis (i.e., was *philommeidēs* — ibid., 202-4), and wore an irresistible cestus or girdle under which was supposedly hidden her own penis (Róheim). Eventually she fused with a phallic Hermes (or with the figure of an ithyphallic herm) to form the unquestionably phallic figure *Hermaphrodite*, the protector of sexual intercourse (Róheim, 352; cf. Laferrière 1977a, 72; Friedrich, *ibid.*, 205-6; see Howard 1979, on the hermaphroditic aspects of the portrayal of Venus in the history of painting; Delcourt 1961 for a general treatment of the widespread cult of the "bisexual figure" of Hermaphrodite in classical antiquity; O'Flaherty 1980 for an extensive comparative study of the mythology of "androgynes," i.e., what she defines as those creatures "simultaneously male and female in physical form"; Baumann 1955 for an ethnological study of "das doppelte Geschlecht" or "Bisexualität" in ritual and myth; and the extensive bibliographies given in these works).

Real phallic women do exist, incidentally. They constitute one of the types of possible biological hermaphrodites or pseudohermaphrodites (see Money and Ehrhardt 1972; Stoller 1968) and are occasionally depicted in lewd poses in the pornographic literature. For example, the November 1980 issue of a slick magazine called *Club International* features a series of photographs of "the Boston bat-wanger," a long-haired, ample breasted, lipstick-wearing individual who appears to possess both a fully-developed vulva and a penis. The editors of the magazine claim to have paid $50,000 to induce him/her to pose. Evidently they thought this phallic woman would appeal to readers. In any case the resemblance between the hermaphrodites studied by medical doctors and exploited in pornography and the representations of Hermaphrodite in ancient myth and art (see the plates in Delcourt 1961 and Zolla 1981) suggests that the ancients may have been concocting their images from more than fantasy alone.

There are contexts, then, where the human female may be thought of as "phallic" (more examples below, section 44). Defloration is one of these contexts. Given a society that is sexist and phallocentric (and most societies are), defloration inevitably becomes an important matter. For the male it is an affirmation of his phallic prowess, while for the female it is a temporary phallic defeat.

But it is a defeat that is at least somewhat mitigated by the new possibilities for future orgasms and future offspring. In the evolutionary long run a woman is willing to be deflowered because defloration is an obviously necessary step on the way to reproductive success. And a man is ultimately very concerned with the bride's virginity because of his need to be confident of paternity.

As was pointed out above (91), however, the male's need for confidence in paternity is something that has to do with genes, and is not something that anyone other than sociobiologists and other evolutionary biologists are normally aware of. Even in societies where great care is taken to define who the social father of a given child is, there still may exist practices which make biological paternity ambiguous, which is to say that proximate mechanisms do not work 100% "in sync" with ultimate strategies. I have already mentioned the practice whereby someone other than the bridegroom deflowers the bride. Among the Massai, the Kipsigis, and the Shilluk a child whose biological father is not the mother's husband is nonetheless cheerfully taken on by the husband, who claims exclusive paternal rights (Paige and Paige 1981, 93-4). Obviously this behavior would not be predicted by a sociobiologist, but there must be some proximate mechanism(s) causing it to happen that would be adaptive in other circumstances, and not maladaptive enough in this circumstance to preclude the bridegroom's investment in the marital tie. For example, the practice of joint defloration of a bride by several males could be a side-effect of otherwise adaptive homosexual tendencies which help to bind fraternal interest groups (see below, section 47). Or perhaps, as Freud suggested, surrogate defloration helps ward off the bridegroom's fears of the bride's revenge — fear of revenge being quite adaptive in most situations where violence has been committed. And male generosity in claiming paternity to biologically unrelated children may be the result of an otherwise adaptive inclination of males to imitate mothering (below, section 50) and thereby be convinced that paternal investment is worthwhile.

I want to emphasize that the interest which males have in a bride's virginity is rarely a conscious concern with biological paternity. No males in nonindustrial societies know about genes. They only behave *as if* they knew about them. Their great concern about whether a woman is a virgin or not (or about whether she is promiscuous or not) *cannot* be a concern about the fate of their own genes. It must, rather, be something else, some other process which is merely a proximate mechanism operating in the service of genes.

That something else, if we follow a psychoanalytic line of thought (regression), or a biological line of thought (neoteny), has to go back to childhood experience, and specifically to the relationship with the mother. Given that a mate is a mother-icon, as argued above, then concern with the virginity of a future mate reflects past concern with the virginity of the mother. According to psychoanalysts, when a male child realizes that his mother *has* to have had sexual intercourse with his father, the child is upset: "when . . . he can no longer maintain the doubt which makes his parents an exception to the universal and odious norms of sexual activity, he tells himself with cynical logic that the difference between his mother and a whore is not after all so very great, since basically they do the same thing" (*SE* XI, 171). But the fantasy that the mother was a virgin is never quite given up, and manifests itself in a variety of individual and cultural practices, ranging from the simple tendency to put certain women 'on a pedestal,' to the widespread primitive Western practice of worshipping a man whose mother was supposedly a virgin (the man is Jesus, the mother is Mary, a woman who would have been the perfect bride in any one of a number of nonindustrial societies that practice virginity tests). Jesus is not the only mythical hero, incidentally, whose mother is characterized as a virgin (see: Rank 1952[1909], 78; Frazer 1935, vol. 5, 264; Dundes 1980, 239; see Preston 1982b, 334ff. and Lederer 1968, 119, 173-9 on mother deities who are also virgins). Thompson's *Motif-Index* lists 18 different bibliographic references under "miraculous conception" (T510; see also nos. A1234.1, V211.1.4, T547 and V312).

Dundes summarizes the psychoanalytic view of the idea of a Blessed Virgin Mary: "a son who is born of a virgin can deny that his father ever had sexual access to his mother" (*ibid.*). Translating this into the requirement by fraternal interest groups that a bride be intact, we obtain: a son who wishes his *real mother* were a virgin will prefer that other males never have had sexual access to his future *mother-icon*.

26. The Female Bodyguard

Let us now backtrack to the matter of male return discussed above in section 22. It was stated that ancestral male hominids established a pattern of returning to the home base, and that ancestral female hominids welcomed them with open arms. Eventually what each male was returning to on a regular basis was not merely a female, though, but a female who represented for him the mother in his past, i.e., a mother-icon. But if she was a mother-icon, then the fact of his return (or failure to return, or the pattern of his returning) must have had something to do with his prior mothering. But what?

A hint is offered by today's hominid societies in which contact between mother and child is emphasized, while contact between father and mother is minimal (matrifocal societies would be an example). By definition the male in such societies does *not* return on a very regular basis, and does not like to stay. Having himself experienced a more intense relationship with his mother than a man in a different kind of society has, he may (however irrationally) wish to avoid repeating the experience in the future, especially if his memory of his mother is primarily one of having been dominated or 'engulfed' by her — and having been insufficiently fathered into the bargain. His mother, herself lacking a dependable mate, may in fact have had to channel all her feelings, both tender and hostile, onto him (and onto her children generally), overwhelming him emotionally. The result would be that as an adult he would never be able to form a very close attachment to a woman, and would thus (if he did not become homosexual) move endlessly from one woman to another, never quite finding an icon of the mother because an icon of the threatening mother is precisely what for him has to be avoided.

This is of course a merely intuitive account. But it is not original, and there is evidence for it. It is known, for example, that postpartum sex taboo and separate sleeping arrangements for mother and child tend to be associated, cross-culturally, with polygyny (e.g., J. Whiting 1964; Saucier 1972). In Ember's (1978) cross-cultural sample, long postpartum sex taboo combined with arrangements whereby the mother sleeps closer to the baby than the father predicts male fear of sex with women (as measured by beliefs that women are polluting, etc.). Apparently a male who has experienced intimate sleeping arrangements with his mother and the concommitantly minimal interactions with his father at an early age is later more inclined to associate with males and behave in an exaggeratedly masculine way ("masculine protest" or "defensive masculinity" — see Munroe *et al.* 1981, 621-3; B. Whiting 1965) than to cultivate a monogamous relationship with a female.

Among the matrifocal Black Carib of Belize studied by Munroe *et al.* (1973), the absence of an adult male in the household in the early years is associated with "hypermasculine" behavior (cursing, gambling, drinking) later in adulthood — even though covert feminine identity is detectable in the form of intensive couvade (see below, section 50). Munroe *et al.* report that more than 40% of the Carib children in their sample area live in households without any adult males, and that only about 25% of the households are nuclear families (*ibid.*, 46). Often the "partners" living in a household do not even bother with a marriage ceremony, and their relationship is not likely to last. Clearly the males are not very monogamous in this society, or are not monogamous for long. Neither are the females, of course, but I suspect that their polygamy is less of their own choosing and more the consequence of male wandering.

In our own society father-absence in a boy's early years has been found to have a deleterious effect on later sexual and marriage relationships (sexual and marital problems are of course not conducive to monogamy). In his review of the psychological literature on this subject, Biller (1982, 713) says: "Difficulty in forming *lasting* heterosexual relationships often appears to be linked to paternal deprivation" (emphasis mine). I would add that such sexual difficulty is, at least by implication, linked also to the relative overdose of mothering that goes with paternal deprivation. Biller notes that "maternal overprotection" is especially likely when the father departs early rather than late in child development (*ibid.*, 719).

The specifically psychoanalytic approach to males in our own and other societies also ties resistance to monogamy with past experience of the mother. Melanie Klein believes, for example, that the Don Juan intensely fears being dependent on a woman because he so loved the first woman in his life — his mother — that he feared she would die from the greediness and destructiveness of his love and consequently now fears that deep attachment to a woman would kill her (1977, 323).[74] A number of psychoanalytic studies link male homosexuality — something which obviously can hinder heterosexual monogamy — with faulty fathering and concomitant overemphasis on mothering (see below, section 47). Male transsexualism, a rare phenomenon in which an anatomically normal male very much wants to be female, has been linked to intense and prolonged intimacy with the

74. The Don Juan may be secretly more interested in males than in females, as Freud suggests (*SE* XII, 63), but I think this is only part of the story.

mother in early childhood (Stoller 1976). Abernethy interprets the findings on male homosexuality and transsexualism (as well as findings on some societies with high mother salience) in terms of her thesis that ". . . male dominance facilitates male-female copulatory behavior while female dominance inhibits it" (1974, 813). Kakar (1978) traces the male's "mildly phobic attitude towards sexually mature women in many parts of India" back to the overwhelming mother-infant relationship, and offers a striking example in his paraphrase of the myth of Skanda, son of Shiva and Parvati:

When Skanda killed Taraka (a demon who had been terrorizing the gods), his mother, Parvati, wished to reward him, so she told him to amuse himself as he pleased. Skanda made love to the wives of the gods, and the gods could not prevent it. They complained to Parvati, and so she decided she would take the form of whatever woman Skanda was about to seduce. Skanda summoned the wife of Indra (the king of gods), and then the wife of Varuna (the wind-god), but when he looked at each one he saw his mother's form, and so he would let her go and summon another. She too became the image of his mother, and then Skanda was ashamed and thought, "the universe is filled with my mother," and he became passionless. (*ibid*, 94-5; cf. O'Flaherty 1980, 106).

Slater (1968) believes that the male narcissism and male derogation of females in ancient Greece resulted at least in part from male fears of an envious and devouring mother. Both Kakar and Slater see the vicious circle that connects an overdose of mothering with negative male attitudes toward women. Kakar puts it this way:

... mature women are sexually threatening to men, which contributes to 'avoidance behaviour' in sexual relations, which in turn causes the women to extend a provocative sexual presence towards their sons, which eventually produces adult men who fear the sexuality of mature women. (Kakar, 195; cf. O'Flaherty 1980, 108-9).

Below (section 45) I will interpret male sexual avoidance of women specifically in terms of male castration anxiety, and will suggest that in some situations this avoidance has (Darwinian) adaptive value for males.

Sex therapist Avodah Offit suggests that a male in our own society may *want* a maternal figure to limit his Don Juanish tendencies:

In my experience, when a man does not — for whatever reason — seek to control his own sexuality, female jealousy and sensitivity take over the task. They are major deterrents, major forces that keep society more orderly than it might otherwise be. It seems to me that the male requirement for a dominant female mother figure is the most powerful, the most resented, and, paradoxically, the most sought-after control of male sexuality in our society.

Not that it works 100 percent of the time, or even 50 percent of the time. But it does seem to serve to keep males oriented to a home base [cf. the anthropologists' frequent use of this term]. Though it forces many to lie and to conceal, they do have less sex, with less pleasure, than they might if they were free of concern about their dreadful gatekeeper, or, while single, if they weren't always searching for a woman to play the role.

Without his female bodyguard, a man might be totally subject to the wild excesses of his desire. Though he may wish to control the forces that seem to control him, often he cannot. Society does not help him to keep his life in order. And so he must invent or create a warden, a battle-ax, an infirm "old lady," a sexless, unattractive keeper of the morals, a sensitive creature whose life would be ruined if she knew, who watches for him from the window, wonders with whom he has lunch, awaits him at night, and runs his life. (Offit 1981, 82).

Even more provocative is Offit's idea that the sexually wayward male is underdeveloped and in need of therapy:

The major therapy for waywardness when the reins wear thin may be for a wife to refuse the role if the husband can be made to feel no shame at needing a controlling "mother." If a wife is able to overcome her own need to maintain the marriage through maternal watchfulness — if she is able to establish independence — the man will either try to seduce her into returning to the role, invent her, or train someone else to play jailer. Occasionally, he will grow up. (*ibid.*, 83).

The last sentence is of course the kicker. It could not have been written by a man, any more than "You've come a long way, baby" could have been said by a woman. To coin a term, what Offit says is somewhat matronizing, just as what some male anthropologists and psychologists say today is patronizing.

This does not mean Offit is wrong. I think she is in fact correct in believing that a man who curbs his sexual waywardness "grows up," given that the norm for most "grown up" men is (at least prolonged periods of) monogamy. But, paradoxically, the norm itself depends on a man not being very "grown up," i.e., requires that a man be neotenous, be immature enough to resurrect and accept his old exclusive relationship with his mother in the relationship with the mate. It is just that if the old relationship was very threatening, the new relationship will be so threatening as to repeatedly drive the male to abandonment. But, barring special psychological problems, and if there was only mild maternal dominance and some accompanying paternal presence — the experience of children in most human societies — then the adult male will be able to settle into prolonged periods of faithfulness and provision of offspring.

27. The Maternal Origins of Love

Readers who are disgusted by Offit's idea of a "female bodyguard" might prefer the approach taken in Sydney Mellen's interesting recent book, *The Evolution of Love* (1981). Mellen says that ". . . when proto-human hunters at the end of a chase carried heavy loads of meat back to their home bases, often kilometers away . . . they did this fundamentally because they *wanted* to do it" (1981, 107, emphasis Mellen's). And the males wanted to do it because they already were capable of *loving* a female (or females) back at the home base, and were consequently glad to share or exchange their supply of "red meat."

Mellen at first seems a little reluctant to grant that females had a role to play in the phylogenetic origin of love. Did not the females *want* the males to bring back the meat and *want* to provide other kinds of food in exchange? And did not the females too have the ability to love their mates? Why would a loving male bring food back to an *un*loving female? In a section entitled "the beginnings of love" Mellen goes so far as to propose a specific date: ". . . an adult *male's* tendency to love a female existed already in some degree in the earliest days of big-game exploitation − 2,000,000 years ago and perhaps earlier" (*ibid.*, 108, emphasis added). He says that "inborn tendencies" to bring food home ". . . would have been transmitted genetically *from adult males* to some of their own children . . ." (*ibid.*, emphasis added).

But then Mellen does grant that the hominid female ". . . was already profoundly adapted for emotional tenderness" (110; cf. Darwin's assertion that women are capable of "greater tenderness" than men − 1885, 563). Just, then, as it took two ancestral hominids to copulate (above, section 2), so also it probably took two of them to love. Indeed, this is not just an analogy. It seems unlikely that love[75] would have attained such

---

75. I confess to an inability to define "love," but in the present context it is intended as a broad term including what others have meant by "love," "romantic love," "passionate love," "falling (or being) in love," "tenderness," "devotion," "limerence" (Tennov 1979), "lovesickness" (Money 1980), "romance," "boinng" (Older 1981), "infatuation," "ardor," etc. There are some resemblances between love and what ethologists call "imprinting" or "pair-bonding," as many scholars have noted. I would say, however, that the ethological terms are merely descriptions of what organisms *do* − two animals stay with each other physically and participate in certain activities jointly for prolonged periods of time. The notion

importance in hominid evolution had it not been useful specifically to repeated sexual interaction. The strongest feelings of love in the adult human are typically associated with sexual interaction (and with subsequent childrearing, if offspring result). Love is not tied to just any random activity such as, say, walking, running, sleeping, eating, defecating, urinating, etc. Love and sex go together.

The ultimate reason why males were coming back and females were welcoming them back was that repeated copulation and offspring resulted. But the copulation had to be arranged in the ultimate reproductive interests of each sex, and love facilitated the arrangement. Thus, the male who was capable of loving was more likely (than an unloving male) to copulate with a female regularly, to be the father of her offspring, and to be rendering altruism to both the female and the offspring. Correspondingly, the female who was capable of loving was more likely to copulate with a male regularly and to receive parental assistance from him. Love, in short, was selected for (cf. Wilson 1978, 141; Alexander 1979b, 122-4; Russell 1957, 122-3; Rizley 1980, 108-13; Tennov 1979, ch. 7; Morris 1967, 64).

This is not to say that something as complicated as love arose out of thin air at some point in hominid evolution. It would be silly to suggest a single-gene "mutation" which suddenly induced hominids to pair-bond on the basis of love.

But pair-bond they did, and it is as important to specify the proximate mechanism(s) as to state the ultimate cause for the pair-bonding. Above I proposed that human long-term mating involves regression/neoteny/iconicity — depending on how you look at it. When an adult male and an adult female make a long term commitment to each other (and to resulting offspring) they are essentially re-using and elaborating upon prior relationships in their respective ontogenetic pasts. In particular, the love for the adult

---

of love, on the other hand, is not so much a description of what organisms do as a designation for one of the proximate psychoneuroendocrine mechanisms that makes them do what they do. Thus we know that one of the reasons humans pair-bond is love. Whether other organisms, such as gibbons or eagles pair-bond for the same reason is unknown, and will probably remain unknown until it is determined just what the biochemical and neural basis of love is and whether these other organisms are capable of the regression/neoteny/iconicity that typically characterizes love in humans. As for the commonplace that love fades with time, I would say that appearances are deceiving. It is true that initial stages of love are often characterized by euphoria (an endorphin rush facilitating the establishment of iconicities?), and that this euphoria decreases or becomes less frequent. But psychotherapists know that *something* special is lost when a person loses or abandons a relationship, and that something is not *only* the "boinng" that may have started the relationship.

sexual partner is linked with the feelings once felt toward the parent(s). The adult sexual partner is not merely an adult sexual partner once the relationship is established, but is a parental icon as well. Specifically, the wife tends to be a mother-icon for the husband, and the husband tends to be both a father-icon and a mother-icon for the wife.

But note that maternal iconicity is what is common to both. The maternal background to both the male and female adult's aptitude for heterosexual love is much more basic than anything that has to do with the father. Scholars from remarkably diverse fields have noted the similarity of heterosexual intimacy to the intimacy of mother and child.

1) a zoologist:

The young lovers, like the baby, say "hold me tight." Occasionally they will even call one another "baby" as they say it. For the first time since babyhood, intimacies are once again extensive. As before, the body-contact signals begin to weave their magic and a powerful bond of attachment starts to form. To emphasize the strength of this attachment, the message "hold me tight" becomes amplified by the words "and never let me go." (Morris 1973, 27; cf. Morris 1967, 65).

This return to intimacy, so beautiful to those who are experiencing it, is often belittled by those who are not. The epigrams tell the story: "The first sigh of love is the last of wisdom"; "Love is a sickness full of woes"; "Love is blind"; "We are easily duped by what we love"; "Love's a malady without a cure"; "'Tis impossible to love and to be wise"; "Lovers are fools, but nature makes them so." Even in the scientific literature, the term "regressive behaviour" takes on the flavour of an insult, instead of an impartial, objective description of what is taking place. Of course, to behave in an infantile manner in certain adult contexts is an inefficient way of coping with a situation, but here, in the case of young lovers forming a deep bond of personal attachment, it is exactly the opposite. Extensive, intimate body contacts are the very best way of developing such a bond, and those who resist them because they are "babyish" or infantile will be the [reproductive!] losers.

When courtship advances to the stage of pre-copulatory behavior, the infantile patterns do not fade. Instead they grow still younger, and the clock ticks backwards to the sucking at the mother's breast. The simple kiss, in which lips are gently pressed to the lover's mouth or cheek, becomes a vigorous, moving pressure. With muscular actions of their lips and tongues, the partners work on one another's mouths as if to draw milk from them. They suck and squeeze rhythmically with their lips, explore and lick with their tongues, like hungry babies. This active kissing is no longer confined to the partner's mouth. It seeks other sites, as if searching for the long-lost mother's nipple. In its quest it travels everywhere, discovering the pseudo-nipples of the ear-lobes, the toes, the clitoris and the penis, and, of course, the lover's nipples themselves. (Morris 1973, 103-4).

2) another biologist: Guthrie 1976, 96-7.
3) a linguist and an anthropologist: Hockett and Ascher 1964, 142.
4) more anthropologists: Malinowski 1955 [1927], 213-14; Mellen 1981, 140; Stephens 1962; Spiro 1982.
5) an ethologist: Eibl-Eibesfeldt 1971, 143, 147.
6) a philologist/literary scholar: Friedrich 1978, 184.
7) a sexologist: Ellis 1927-8, VI, 572.
8) psychologists: Dinnerstein 1976, 61 *et passim;* Lewis 1976, 46.
9) various psychotherapists: Hamburg 1978, 163, 196; Klimek 1979, 126; Jonas and Jonas 1970, 121, 124.
10) and of course numerous psychoanalysts, such as: Ferenczi 1938, 18; Balint 1949, 256-7; Freud *SE* XXIII, 188; Klein 1977 (1937), 306-43; Kakar 1978, 52-112; Endleman 1981, 113; Devereux 1978, 183; Rank 1973 (1924), 43.

I do not want to give the impression that the specialists listed in nos. 2)-10) all say exactly what Morris says in no. 1). I quote Morris at length only because he is such a good writer, but the others are conveying essentially the same message: there is some kind of basic connection between what goes on between mother and infant and what goes on between lovers/mates (even though these scholars may conceptualize the connection in quite different ways).

I should add that for some nonhuman primates too the past experience of the mother can also be essential to competent heterosexual behavior (see the discussion of chimpanzee and rhesus sexuality in Nadler 1981, 193-201). Also, there is a good neurological reason why *genital* excitation often occurs in the nursing child and why *oral* manipulations such as kissing, nibbling, fellatio, cunnilingus, etc. occur during sexual intercourse in adults, namely, the close association of limbic areas governing genital and oral response (MacLean 1962; 1973b; 1975).

28. The Maternal Origins of Altruism

Love is not love without accompanying altruistic behavior, and if human love is originally maternal in nature, so too is the human inclination to altruism.

Mellen quotes Zihlman's statement (1978, 18) that "the sharing of gathered foods, developed initially between mothers and offspring, was probably the source for expanding sharing patterns to include adult males . . ." (Mellen, 101; cf. McGrew 1981, 61; Slocum 1975, 45; Parker and Gibson 1979, 373; Martin and Voorhies 1975, 174-5). In Darwinian terms, maternal altruism seems to have been one preadaptive basis upon which males developed an inclination to return home with their "red meat."

Mothers were indeed the focus of early hominid social life:

Mothers, as primary socializers, were important carriers of group tradition. Social and technical inventions by females passed to their offspring and eventually became part of the group's behavioral repertoire. The stable basic social unit for the transitional hominids was that of mother-offspring, as it is for other primates.[76] Among contemporary human groups this unit remains important: it is incorporated in all known social organizations; in some societies it is elaborated in such a way that the mother-offspring dyad is both the fundamental building block of kinship organization and ideologically central. And in every society it is the basic organizational form that is relied upon when other more complex or extended structures become ineffective. (Zihlman and Tanner 1976, 604).

This is *not* a description of "matriarchy," nor is it a description of the kind of pathological matrifocality that exists among, say, the Black Carib proletariat. Rather, it is a specifically prehistoric type of matrifocality that can tell us much about the origins of human altruism, including the exchange of women by men. Fox may well be right to say that the exchange of women is women's idea.

To put it bluntly, any man who exchanges women is himself born of and raised by a woman. Every macho was once Momma's boy. Whatever notions a man may have about reciprocal and other kinds of altruism cannot be seen in isolation from the mother who inculcated in him the essentials of generosity and of give-and-take which characterize most adult relationships.

Some students of human nature, though, have given mothers surprisingly

---

76. This particular matrifocal concept of early hominid social life is often encountered in the Soviet literature on human origins (e.g., Tikh 1970).

short shrift in this area. Freud (père!) is a good example from the psychoanalytic literature. As argued in the Preliminaries (above, 20-24), identification is one psychoanalytic reflex of what sociobiologists mean by altruism, and the child's first identification is with the mother. Freud was very reluctant to grant the mother her due even in pre-Oedipal matters. Rather than being categorical and explicit about pre-Oedipal identification with the mother, he tended to speak synecdochally about attachment to the breast, i.e., to what Klein, Fairbairn, and some others would call a "part-object," something which supposedly is cathected before the "whole object" of the mother can be. Freud also speaks of an individual's "most important identification, his identification *with the father* in his own personal prehistory" (*SE* XIX, 31; my italics) — only to grudgingly add: "perhaps it would be safer to say 'with the parents'; for before a child has arrived at a definite knowledge of the difference between the sexes, the lack of a penis, it does not distinguish in value between its father and its mother" (*ibid.*, n.1). Perhaps the male-chauvinist bias evident in these statements by Freud is mitigated by his reluctance to even distinguish identification from object attachment in the very early, pre-Oedipal stage: "at the very beginning, in the individual's primitive oral phase, object-cathexis and identification are no doubt indistinguishable from each other" (*ibid*, 29; cf. *SE* XVIII, 105). But if by this Freud means that there is no way to distinguish the pre-Oedipal child's emotional attachment to its mother from its ability to form and exteriorize internal representations of (imitate) its mother's behavior, then he is wrong. It is one thing for the child to be affectively attached to its mother — as manifested, for example, in the wailing which takes place when it is deprived of its mother. It is yet another thing for the child to exhibit that wide range of imitations of the mother (necessarily based on internal similarity processes) discussed earlier in this book. The two things — affective attachment and imitation, i.e., the two components most basic to identification — are not the same thing just because they occur simultaneously. Thus Freud's reluctance to bestow the term "identification" on the way the pre-Oedipal child relates to its mother is really unjustified, and is a part, I think, of his more general reluctance to see the complexity and importance of pre-Oedipal matters.

Freud seems to have a general aversion to considering how much the child owes to the mother, as opposed to the father. Such an aversion has already been detected by various scholars of Freud's theory of the origin of the superego (see Fisher and Greenberg 1977, 210). Whereas, on the one hand, Freud is certain that the boy's superego derives primarily from an early identification with the father (and supposedly the more severe and threatening the father, the more repressive the superego), on the other hand, he really is not very clear about where the little girl could possibly get *her* superego, probably because making the father responsible for the origin of her superego would make us all wonder why most girls don't then become homosexual. The idea that identification with the mother might play an important role in both male and female superego formation was simply never pursued by Freud.

The British psychoanalyst D. W. Winnicott claims that Freud "paid full tribute to the function of maternal care," and cites the following passage from Freud as evidence:

It will rightly be objected that an organization which was a slave to the pleasure principle and neglected the reality of the external world could not maintain itself alive for the shortest time, so that it could not have come into existence at all. The employment of a fiction like this is, however, justified when one considers that the infant — provided one includes with it the care it receives from its mother — does almost realize a psychical system of this kind. (quoted in Winnicott 1960, 586).

This seems, however, to be a rather parenthetical and off-handed way of recognizing the mother's importance to the child. Winnicott adds that "it must be assumed that he [Freud] left this subject alone only because he was not ready to discuss its implications" (*ibid.*, 586). As far as I can see, Freud never really discussed its implications. He did, however, make a very interesting declaration about the importance of the pre-Oedipal mother-child bond in one of his last papers:

This first object [the breast] is later completed into the person of the child's mother, who not only nourishes it but also looks after it and thus arouses in it a number of other physical sensations, pleasurable and unpleasurable. By her care of the child's body she becomes its first seducer. In these two relations lies the root of a mother's importance, unique, without parallel, established unalterably for a whole lifetime as the first and strongest love-object and as *the prototype of all later love-relations* — for both sexes. In all this *the phylogenetic foundation* has so much the upper hand over personal accidental experience that it makes no difference whether a child has really sucked at the breast or has been brought up on the bottle and never enjoyed the tenderness of a mother's care. (*SE* XXIII, 188, my italics; cf. Bowlby, 1969, p. 363).

Feminists will probably approve of this, but are unlikely to consider it enough penance to make up for Freud's neglect of pre-Oedipal maternal care in the bulk of his writings. From a sociobiological viewpoint, as we will see below, this passage contains the kernel of a non-male-chauvinist hypothesis about the genetic origin of certain forms of human altruism.

The French psychoanalyst Jacques Lacan, even more than Freud, is reluctant to mention the role of the mother in the child's first identification.

Lacan prefers to claim that the self originates when the child first comprehends its mirror-image during the so-called *stade du miroir*:

We have only to understand the mirror stage *as an identification*, in the full sense that analysis gives to the term: namely, the transformation that takes place in the subject when he assumes an image — whose predestination to this phase-effect is sufficiently indicated by the use, in analytic theory, of the ancient term *imago*.

This jubilant assumption of his specular image by the child at the *infans* stage, still sunk in his motor incapacity and nursling dependence, would seem to exhibit in an exemplary situation the symbolic matrix in which the *I* is precipitated in a primordial form, before it is objectified in the dialectic of identification with the other, and before language restores to it, in the universal, its function as subject. (1977, 2).

The mother is simply deleted here (but note how she irrupts into the discourse in *"nursling* dependence" [*dépendance du nourisage*] and "symbolic *matrix*" [*matrice symbolique*]). What makes Lacan's notion of a *stade du miroir* unlikely is the absurd assumption that every infant (up to the age of 18 months, says Lacan) has the opportunity to look into a mirror (the whole process is of course impossible for the congenitally blind). What makes the notion of a *stade du miroir* possible in some other sense, however, is the extent to which a "reflective" neural event in the infant is triggered by the interaction of the mother (or mother-surrogate) with the infant at some crucial stage. Lacan, in a rare concession to biology, even mentions an "intraorganic mirror" (*miroir intraorganique*) of some kind. Perhaps this "mirror" is the genetically programmed proclivity to imitate discussed above, taken in combination with the ability to use deictics. I have noticed, incidentally, that the image of a *mirror* appears quite often in theoretical writings about early infancy (especially in the work of such feminists as Juliet Mitchell [1974] and Dorothy Dinnerstein [1976]).

If in the psychoanalytic literature there has been some difficulty in recognizing the importance of the mother for the child's first identification, in the sociobiological literature there has been an even greater reluctance to mention the role of the mother in the acquisition of altruistic behavior. The discussions of human altruism in Wilson's *Sociobiology* (1975; see also Wilson 1976), for example, pay no attention to the most totalistic form of human altruism, the care lavished on an infant by its mother (of course such altruism is itself explained in ultimate terms by Hamilton's [1964] model, and the proximate mechanism for it, in mammals generally, appears to be under the control of a portion of the limbic cortex — MacLean [1982]).[77] Trivers's classic paper "The Evolution of Reciprocal Altruism"

---

77. Curiously, Wilson (1976) keeps his discussion of human altruism separate from his

(1971) makes passing mention of the effect of "nurturant models" on the development of altruism (p. 53), but does not pursue the subject. Another important paper of his (1974) pays considerable attention to human mothers, but primarily in their role of conflicting with their offspring (see also Stamps and Metcalf 1980). Dawkins (1976) and Barash (1977), though they both have some important things to say about altruism, basically ignore mothering in humans. Van den Berghe devotes a section of his interesting sociobiological ("evolutionary") study *Human Family Systems* (1979, 34-35) to the topic of infant dependency, but does not relate this topic to altruism. Even Freedman, who has studied both human infancy and human sociobiology extensively (1974; 1979), does not explore the relationship of maternal care to human altruism.

Although there has been some reluctance to mention the mother in this context, a more abstract "parent" has been discussed. Alexander, for example, sees the preadaptive significance of parenting for general kin altruism and reciprocal altruism in humans:

Parental behavior is the primary evolutionary source (or preadaptive basis) of nepotism within the family, and ... nepotism within the family is similarly the primary source of extrafamilial nepotism. Nepotism in turn is a likely source of systems of reciprocity. (1979b, 150).[78]

---

assertion that human "societies are largely organized around prolonged maternal care and extended relationships between mothers and children" (p. 345). Perhaps he is being influenced by the technical definition of altruism that excludes self-sacrifice for the benefit of offspring (1975, 117). But other sociobiologists use the term "altruism" as including maternal care (e.g., Dawkins 1976, 6-7; Alexander 1979b, 36-58).

Sahlins, later noted as an enemy of sociobiology, mentions suckling of children as an example of "generalized altruism" (1965, 147). For Sahlins, food-giving is tied to the mother: "food is life-giving, urgent, ordinarily symbolic of hearth and home, if not of mother" (p. 170).

78. See also Alexander (1978) and Alexander and Borgia (1978). Barkow (1978b), who may or may not mind being called a sociobiologist, clearly sees the altruistic significance of acquisition of *behavioral norms* from the parents. The behavioral norms are established by "internalization of significant others," i.e., by a process which is essentially the same as Freudian identification (but with emphasis on the contiguity rather than the similarity process). Dawkins (1979, 189-190) makes it clear that altruism toward siblings can derive, with little genetic change, from altruism toward offspring. Danielli (1980) makes the very interesting suggestion that the proximate mechanism for human altruism may be an internal reward system involving release of endogenous opiates upon completion of an altruistic act. A natural question that arises is: what might parenting (and mothering in particular) have to do with setting up this system in the child? Another question is: where might this system be? MacLean points to portions of the limbic system and the

Compare Midgley (who might, rather, be characterized as an anti-socio-biologist):

All the creatures that it makes sense to suppose could develop positive altruism are already caring for their young. And the first element of parental care which develops is defense and rescue from danger. (Even some fish and reptiles do this, as well as the social insects.) All that is needed is to extend the patterns to adults. Now the development of sociability proceeds in any case largely by this extension to other adults of behavior first developed between parents and young — grooming, mouth contact, embracing, pro-tective and submissive gestures, giving food. In fact, wider sociality in its original essence simply *is* the power of adults to treat one another, mutually, as honorary parents and children. (1978, 136).

I don't know whether most sociobiologists missed this because of their generally male-centered orientation, their tendency to neglect or postpone analysis of ontogenies (Alexander 1979b, 96; King 1980, 97-98), or both.

There are some interesting psychological tests which demonstrate kin bias in subjects who are asked to imagine performing altruistic acts for another person. For example, Freedman reports that "some 70% of respondents presented with a choice of throwing a life preserver to a brother or to a best friend (equally good swimmers being pulled out to sea by the tide) answer immediately that they would toss the preserver to the brother" (1979, 114). But consider what the respondents must have been thinking when asked this excruciating question: *Who* is my brother, and who is my best friend? The experimenter's question depends on the subject's *knowing* real people in personal history (and knowledge of who one's brother is depends in turn on knowledge of who one's parents are). But assume for a moment that a child has been tricked into believing that another, unrelated child whom it grows up with is its brother. A close relationship between the two would no doubt develop nonetheless, with all the attendant "kin" altruism, and one of them would perhaps even save the other rather than a best friend. Thus the *fact* of kinship and the *awareness* of kinship are theoretically two different entities (cf. Alexander, 1979b, 110), and if genes are operating to promote kin altruism, they are doing so remotely, via the cognitive properties of the brain, not directly through some magical sense that can sniff out kin from non-kin, or degrees of kin. But the cognitive mechanism in question is precisely the one developed

---

associated prefrontal cortex, and asks: "Is it possible that the misting of the eyes so commonly experienced upon observing an altruistic act is in any way owing to a reciprocal innervation of mechanisms for parental rescue and for crying represented in the cingulate gyrus?" (1984).

principally by reciprocal interaction with the dominating mother, and later (under the guidance and at the insistence of the mother) by altruistic interaction with siblings and other kin, including the brother one may later save from drowning. Indeed, most of the respondents in Freedman's study may have favored the brother over a friend simply out of guilt. They may have preferred the friend, but, since their mothers had long ago trained them to be "nice" to their siblings, they may have behaved accordingly (in Barkow's [1976] terminology, an "internalized representation" of the mother — what I would call an internalized mother-icon — may have induced guilt). Evidently, the feelings of guilt which so often lead to altruism in adult human relationships (cf. the common finding that public transgression leads to reparative altruism [Krebs 1970, 265; Trivers 1971, 50]) derive in a large measure from childhood interactions with the mother.

Nothing but interaction with the mother can remotely compare in intensity with interaction with siblings close in age, except possibly interaction with the father, depending on how interested in parenting the father is (see below, section 50). Mother is the first and most "significant other." Friendships, though they may be intense, come later, *after* one has already learned, usually from the mother, and often with the involvement of a sibling, the basics of altruism. Friendships may be important for fostering and regulating reciprocal altruism, as several biologists have noted (see Trivers 1971, 48-49). But ontogenetically they appear to be derived from or modeled on relations with parents and siblings, as Freud argued in *The Interpretation of Dreams.*

The kin altruism which the "Who would you save?" tests do demonstrate is thus inseparable from the basic altruism which individuals acquire on the mother's lap. To extend a metaphor, blood is thicker than water in humans because mother's milk is thicker than both. Incidentally, the fact that the basics of altruism are acquired from the mother makes it more likely that mother's relatives will benefit from this altruism than father's relatives. This makes good evolutionary sense because one can usually be more certain anyway about who one's mother is than about who one's father is.

It is interesting to note how often in the history of the study of human behavior the connection between altruism and mothering has surfaced. Midgley (1978, 136), for example, refers to the ethologist Irenäus Eibl-Eibesfeldt, who devotes much of *Love and Hate* (1971) to the essentially maternal basis of "the development of the personal bond and of basic trust":

In human beings, in order that trust should develop out of ... attachment, certain social experiences are necessary, which normally every child has with its *mother.* They are to some extent events 'provided for' in advance, experiences to which the developmental programme is open at this point. If the child is not able to evolve the personal relationship with its mother (or mother-substitute) which is 'anticipated', then a disturbance in its development occurs – the abandonment syndrome (Verlassenheitssyndrome). Normally the child learns in the *dialogue with its mother* that there is always someone there who will look after it in a friendly way and fulfill its social as well as its material needs. He acquires as a fundamental attitude the positive notion that one can rely on one's fellow men, an attitude that Erikson has described as 'basic trust' (Urvertrauen). This basic trust is the foundation of a healthy personality. We give evidence of this fundamental attitude in countless everyday situations, whether we are entrusting ourselves to a means of public transport or asking someone for information in the street. Basically we expect good of our fellow men and nothing embitters us more than misplaced trust. *This basic trust is the prerequisite for all positive attitudes towards society, for all ability to identify with a collective, for all social commitment.* (Eibl-Eibesfeldt 1971, 215-216; my italics).

A number of altruism-eliciting and altruism-rendering behaviors in adult *Homo sapiens* are treated by Eibl-Eibesfeldt (126 ff.) as forms of regression to mother-infant interaction: kissing, nibbling, sucking ear lobes, passing food from mouth to mouth, embracing, burying the head in another person's chest, and pleasant, perfunctory conversations. Most of these behaviors are specifically *tactile* in nature, as Ashley Montagu would no doubt observe (Montagu's marvelous book *Touching* [1971] is a storehouse of evidence on how much of adult mental health depends on a satisfying tactile relationship with the mother during childhood).

As is obvious from the passage just quoted, Eibl-Eibesfeldt owes his basic idea to the psychoanalyst Erik Erikson, who, in *Childhood and Society* (1950) and other works, clearly saw the origin of human trust and individual identity in mothering behavior:

Mothers create a sense of trust in their children by that kind of administration which in its quality combines sensitive care of the baby's individual needs and a firm sense of personal trustworthiness within the trusted framework of their culture's life style. This forms the basis in the child for a sense of identity which will later combine a sense of being "all right," of being oneself, and of becoming what other people trust one will become. (1950, 249; cf. Crook 1980, 259 ff.).

It is worth noting that many statistical studies show that altruism is more likely when there is an altruistic model, or when the recipient is dependent in some way on the potential altruist (see Krebs 1970, for an overview). But a mother, as we have repeatedly seen above, is certainly treated by the child as a model at various stages, and a child is certainly "dependent" on its mother. Thus such studies at least indirectly tie the acquisition of basic altruistic behavior to mothering.

I will not resort to any more citations or quotations on this topic. By now it is clear that a number of scholars — male as well as female, psychoanalysts as well as nonpsychoanalysts (but evidently not many sociobiologists) — have noticed that human altruism can be related to maternal care. There are of course great differences in approaches among these scholars. Eibl-Eibesfeldt, for example, goes out of his way to deny that sexuality is involved in the ontogenetic origin of altruistic love, while the early Freud, who underestimated the role of maternal care, as well as the later Freud, who recognized it as the basis of altruistic love, insists on the sexual element.[79] Erikson (following in Freud's footsteps) emphasizes the role of orality in the development of love, while Eibl-Eibesfeldt (1971, 206) argues that much more than oral gratification (e.g., caressing, being spoken to, picked up, etc.) is needed by the child, and cites the example of the Kibbutz children, who are more attached to their parents than to the nurse who feeds and washes them.

To say that the mother is the first and most important personal contact for the development of altruistic behavior in the child is not to deny the influence of other figures, such as fathers, maternal uncles, peers, and others. There is considerable cross-cultural and within-cultural variation in patterns of altruistic behavior acquired by the child (see, for example: B. Whiting and J. Whiting 1975; Mussen and Eisenberg-Berg 1977), and both mothers and non-mothers seem to have something to do with these patterns. But when it comes to learning how to perform an altruistic act per se, the mother is the first and most important teacher.

---

79. Part of the problem is just semantic. By "sexual" Eibl-Eibesfeldt seems to mean only what Freud meant by "genital," while Freud regarded a number of nongenital concerns (anal, oral, urethral) as by definition "sexual" or "erotic." Generally speaking, the ethological and sociobiological literature on human sexuality (cf. also Symons 1979) focuses exclusively on genital relations between the sexes.

29. Reciprocation and the Breast

After being around an altruistic mother for a sufficiently long period of time, the child itself begins to be altruistic. It is well known to psychologists, ethologists, and psychoanalysts that a young child will imitate its mother's altruistic behavior (among many of her other behaviors). A nine-month-old, for example, is capable of holding a cup to its mother's mouth (Trevarthen and Hubley 1978, 222). The child may also offer food to its siblings or to other people in the environment (cf. Eibl-Eibesfeldt 1971, 209; Eibl-Eibesfeldt 1979; Parker and Gibson 1979, 373; Rheingold and Hay 1980). Even the battered child may be remarkably responsive to the parent's needs (deMause 1982, 21). Various caregiving behaviors were observed in a group of two girls and three boys about twenty-four months of age: "The boys as well as the girls held the dolls and toy animals, patted them, fed, bathed, groomed, and put them to bed. They instructed the dolls in how to behave, one boy spanking a doll for behavior for which his parents had disciplined him" (Rheingold and Hay 1980, 95; see Grusec 1981 for an overview of the ways in which parents, especially mothers, facilitate the development of altruism in children). In many cultures children reliably care for younger siblings (see B. Whiting and J. Whiting 1975, 95ff. for examples of the "child nurse").

When the child's imitation of an altruistic act is directed toward another altruist, the child is by definition engaging in *reciprocal altruism* of a rudimentary kind. Given, then, an *altruistic* mother hominid and an *imitative*, intelligent baby hominid, the way was paved for the evolution of helping behavior, food sharing, and more complex forms of exchange in adults of the hominid line.

This is not to say of course that the way was completely paved. For example, differing adult male and female foraging areas and strategies was probably another prerequisite to the development of hominid reciprocal altruism, as observed above (section 22). It has been established that the rudimentary food sharing that goes on between mother and infant chimpanzee facilitates the transition from nursing to independent foraging. Quite possibly the prolongation of parental care further and further beyond weaning contributed to the elaboration of hominid food sharing: "The energetic savings from a behavioral food-sharing strategy, as compared to a physiological lactation strategy, would have been even greater in a species requiring five or six years' apprenticeship for efficient independent foraging" (Parker and Gibson 1979, 373; cf. Silk 1978).

Other things would also have been necessary for the development of the forms of altruism known in today's hominids. Empathy is often mentioned, for example, though it should be noted that empathy can just as well play a role in agonistic as in altruistic interaction (e.g., the sadist empathizes as much with the person he is whipping as the mother empathizes with her crying baby). There is evidence of involuntary empathic arousal in infants which occurs independently of past experience with the mother. A newborn child's crying at the sound of another child's crying is probably not acquired by imitation of the mother. The most rudimentary forms of empathy, which are more obvious but less complex than identification, may be directly (neurally) programmed (see: MacLean 1973a; Hoffman 1981). They are also probably involved with other known rudimentary systematicities of interaction such as the Condon effect (see section 35 below on interactional synchrony), and may be, in part, remnants of earlier forms of social grooming behavior, which is universal among the primates. In humans, stroking, patting, and other varieties of empathic tactile contact are well known. In nonhuman primates grooming commonly accompanies (or is) a care-giving behavior rendered by mother to offspring, subordinate to dominant animal, and between individuals who just have, or are about to copulate. Peter Reynolds argues that grooming behavior is ". . . not a trivial antecedent to louse picking in man . . .," but that ". . . the grooming networks of nonhuman primates are ancestral to the object-exchange networks of modern man" (Reynolds 1981, 172, 193).

In his *Essai sur le don*, Marcel Mauss explains human exchange, that is, "the obligation to give and the obligation to receive" as follows:

Whatever it is, food, possessions, women, children or ritual, it retains a magical and religious hold over the recipient. The thing given is not inert. *It is alive and often personified* ....
The pattern of symmetrical and reciprocal rights is not difficult to understand if we realize that it is first and foremost a pattern of spiritual bonds between things which are to some extent *parts of persons* .... (Mauss 1967 [1925], 10, 11, emphasis added).

My question is: what is there in the ontogeny of every adult exchanger that would lead him or her to regard the things exchanged as *persons or parts of persons*? The answer I would like to suggest has to do with the exchanger's mother and with a part of her, i.e., her breast.

The first object altruistically rendered to the child by the mother after birth is the breast. The earliest lessons in sharing/reciprocation/exchange revolve around this organ. Much of course has been said in the psychoanalytic literature about the oral phase of infant development and about the child's very special attachment to the breast. The work of Melanie Klein is especially relevant here. According to Klein, the child directs both positive and negative feelings toward the breast, and eventually toward the mother whom the breast metonymizes. Thus, in her book *Love, Guilt and Reparation*, we read:

In the very beginning [the child] loves his mother at the time that she is satisfying his needs for nourishment, alleviating his feelings of hunger, and giving him the sensual pleasure which he experiences when his mouth is stimulated by sucking at her breast. This gratification is an essential part of the child's sexuality, and is indeed its initial expression. But when the baby is hungry and his desires are not gratified, or when he is feeling bodily pain or discomfort, then the whole situation suddenly alters. Hatred and aggressive feelings are aroused and he becomes dominated by the impulses to destroy the very person who is the object of all his desires and who in his mind is linked up with everything he experiences – good and bad alike. (Klein 1977 [1937], 306-7).

From the child's viewpoint there is thus both a "good breast," and a "bad breast." According to Klein, what is crucial to the development of reciprocating abilities in personal relationships is the fact that the oral sadism directed toward the breast produces guilt and a fear of loss, which in turn serve as a basis for altruistic *reparation*: "if the baby has, in his aggressive phantasies, injured his mother by biting and tearing her up, he may soon build up phantasies that he is putting the bits together again and repairing her" (*ibid.*, 308). Such reparation is at the core of altruistic/identificatory attachment to the mother, and of later personal attachments. The child "sacrifices" its own hostilities toward the mother and tries to become as loving and non-frustrating with other people as it wishes the mother had been. Klein says: ". . . making reparation – which is such an essential part of the ability to love – widens in scope, and the child's capacity to accept love and, by various means, to take into himself goodness from the outer world steadily increases. This satisfactory balance between 'give' and 'take' is the primary condition for further happiness" (*ibid.*, 342).

Not all psychoanalysts look at the origin of reciprocalism quite the same way as Klein does. But the association of the *oral* phase with the acquisition of a sense of 'give-and-take' is remarkably widespread in the analytic literature. Erik Erikson says: ". . . in thus *getting what is given* and in learning to *get somebody to do* for him what he wishes to have done, the baby also develops the necessary ego groundwork to *get to be* a giver" (1963, 76). Ernest Jones discusses in terms of the oral phase ". . . why so many men feel unable to put something into a woman unless they have first gotten something out of her" (1961, 462).

The association of oral matters with reciprocalism can crop up again in adulthood. For example, the "series of rather esoteric aphorisms" gathered

by Margaret Mead (1935, 83) on the subject of Arapesh exchange is headed
by a reference to the *mother* and revolves around whether something should
or should not be *eaten*:

> Your own mother,
> Your own sister,
> Your own pigs,
> Your own yams that you have piled up,
> You may not eat.
> Other people's mothers,
> Other people's sisters,
> Other people's pigs,
> Other people's yams that they have piled up,
> You may eat.

The English language is full of "oral" expressions that relate to exchange or
reciprocation. Money, which is the medium of financial exchange, is colloqui-
ally referred to as "bread" or "dough." A person is required to "cough up" the
money for a financial transaction, or has to "put his money where his *mouth*
is" in order to substantiate a claim. A "sugar daddy" gives money to a female
who may herself be referred to as a "money grubber." Conversely, a woman
who subsidizes a man is a "nipple mom" (cf. Klimek 1979, 172-5).[80]

Speech too is a method of reciprocalism, namely, exchange of messages,
as Lévi-Strauss has repeatedly told us. What is curious is that the anatomical
apparatus once used to obtain nourishment from the mother is very roughly
the same one used to convey linguistic messages.

Anyone in American culture who has ever had a teenage daughter knows
how much she likes to *talk* to her *female* friends over the telephone. A
telephone is of course a device for the exchange of messages. Here are the
words on the front cover of my daughter's phone number/address book:

Baby, I've got your number.

On the back cover:

EMERGENCY
NUMBERS

Police _____
Fire _____
Ambulance _____
Pizza _____
Mom _____

---

80. There also exist well known *anal* associations with money ("filthy lucre"), which
have been dealt with extensively in the analytic literature (e.g., *SE* IX, 174; XII,
187; Fenichel 1945, 281 ff; Dundes 1966; 1979). In other words, *both* ends of the
alimentary canal have come to be associated with financial reciprocation.

Read in sequence, this little book of exchange begins with the word *baby* and ends with the word *Mom*. Everything in between consists of codes for reciprocal exchange of messages, i.e., telephone numbers (including one number for receiving oral gratification — *pizza*, right beside *Mom*). Whoever designed this little book must have known a lot (consciously or unconsciously) about a very specific psychoanalytic commonplace, namely, about how adolescent girls are in the process of shifting their (primarily oral) attachment away from their mothers and onto other people.

While screaming in the mother's arms both the future exchanger of women and the obsessive talker on telephones emit the prototypical form of their later vocalizations. And the prototypical vocalizations may well be reciprocated in the form of either comforting sounds from the mother or by the breast itself. Babies are known to respond to sounds by sucking on a teat, even if it gives no milk (Young 1978, 179). Repeated time and again in the numerous feedings necessary in infancy, the mother's altruistic reciprocation must become established eventually for the child (or must have become established for the increasingly intelligent hominid infant) as a kind of semiotic equation of two items:

utterance (scream) = object (breast)

(cf. Róheim 1950, 441).

Or, to judge from the fantasies of some poets and religious writers,

words = milk

(Wormhoudt 1949),

as when the apostle Peter declares that the word of the Lord nourishes like "pure milk" (I *Peter* 2:3), or when the poet produces metrical rhythms to substitute for rhythmic sucking at the breast (Brill 1931, 376). This equation of words with mother's milk is about as primitive as signification gets, ontogenetically. It is a semiotic union of signifier and signified that is charged with the intense affects that accompany separation from the mother. It *is* the first step toward separation from her, because it is the *first* time a substitute for her is accepted. Greenson's paper on "The Mother Tongue and the Mother" nicely captures this paradox of primal signification:

... it appears that the auditory incorporation of words is a critical factor in the maturation of the child. Speech is on the one hand a means of *retaining a connection* with the mother as well as a means of becoming *separated from* her. The child who suckled at the mother's breast now replaces this by introjecting a new liquid of the mother — sounds. (1950, 22, emphasis added).

Greenson adds that ". . . the earliest relationship between child and mother's breast will have a decisive influence on the relationship of the child to its mother tongue" (*ibid.*).

But not only the breast should be considered. While at the breast the child gazes at its mother. Conversely, the mother looks at her child. An infant is more attracted to a pair of eyes than to any other visual stimulus (cf. Freedman 1979, 95-6). As we saw earlier, there is an ability in infants to imitate facial gestures. Thus, while gazing at one another, mother and child are in a position to exchange or reciprocate facial gestures. Face-to-face contact of mother and child (see, for ex.: Robson 1967; Mahler *et al.* 1975, 46; Papousek and Papousek 1979, 467; Trevarthen 1979, 541 ff.) seems to be the most important kind of contact for setting up an exchange of messages between the two, that is, for semiotizing the relationship of mother and child. It is face-to-face contact which prepares for the child's acquisition of language. Speech may not be visual, but it emanates from the face. It is not really mother who speaks at first, it is mother's face. Indeed, as Robson (1967, 18) asserts, mother's face *is* mother for the four- to six-month-old infant. If the face-tie with the mother (or principal caregiver) is not established and maintained, future personal relationships of the child are deleteriously affected. It is worth remembering in this connection that, in the child's first representative drawings of people, the limbs are usually attached directly to the face, and only later are the torso and limbs correctly represented.

Eventually the give-and-take between mother/face and child comes to revolve around the exchange of vocalizations. The two make sounds back and forth at each other. The child does not always have to have a nipple inserted into its mouth after it makes a sound (with its mouth). It will sometimes accept instead a reassuring sound or touch from its mother. Vocalizations and food are very closely associated at this stage. Eventually, through joint action of the child's inclination to imitate and its internal "universal grammar," the vocalizations become words and phrases, and these are exchanged with the mother in increasingly complex contexts. In other words, the child acquires language.

30. The Origin of Linguistic Reciprocation

Language, said Freud, was "one of the most important stages on the path to hominization" (*SE* XXIII, 113). Language not only opens up vast new possibilities for reciprocation in non-linguistic areas, but is itself a highly complex form of reciprocation. The complexity of facial, gestural, financial, kinship and other kinds of exchanges that can take place between two individuals is nothing in comparison to the complexity of the grammar of whatever language the two individuals happen to share and to utilize for the exchange of messages. Most linguists would agree that a descriptively adequate and comprehensive grammar has never been produced for any human language. Only fragments of grammars exist. There of course also exist various characterizations of the "universals," the "design features," the "functions," or the "essence" of language (see: Greenberg 1963; 1966; Hockett 1960; Jakobson 1960; Jakobson 1971, 345-59). But even these are rather complex. It is difficult to imagine how even the simplest and most reduced "universal grammar" (Chomsky) could have appeared on the hominid scene. I am inclined to believe that language would never have appeared in hominid evolution at all were it not for the existence of some already rather complex and overlapping preadaptive entities, such as: hominid vision (Gregory 1970); a "rhythmic motor" of some kind (Lenneberg 1967, 119), such as the "universally observed rhythmicity of the vertebrate brain" (*ibid.*) which underlies a variety of motor processes; various structural asymmetries of the hominid brain (LeMay 1976); "sensorimotor intellectual capacities that arose as adaptations for extractive foraging with tools" (Parker and Gibson 1979, 374); a "transformational grammar" of late hominid tool use (Lieberman 1975); an ability to convey complex gestural messages (Hewes 1976; 1977a; Steklis and Harnad 1976 [vs. Steklis and Raleigh 1979]; Ivanov 1976b; Parker and Gibson 1979; Kimura 1979); a supralaryngeal vocal tract with certain specific acoustic characteristics (Lieberman 1976); cortical structures and functions that would not be isolated from, but be coordinated with limbic influences (Robinson 1976; Pribram 1971); possible new (yet still unknown) developments at the neuromolecular level (Lenneberg 1966); and perhaps even some sort of utilization of the genetic code itself (Jakobson 1974, 50-3; Edelheit 1978).

Phylogenetically, language must have begun as dialogue of some sort. As Richman (1980, 234), following the tradition of Vygotsky, says: ". . . speech must at all times and everywhere be regarded as a social act." Ontogenetically, the first dyad in which dialogue is likely to take place is mother (principal caretaker) and child. In sexual interaction the dyad is typically male and female. More than once in this book I suggest that mother-child linguistic interaction is the primary proximate basis for later adult-adult sexual interaction.

In recent years there has been increasing emphasis on the role mother-child interaction might have played in the phylogenetic development of language (Carini 1970; Marshack 1976; Jonas and Jonas 1975a; Mellen 1981; Dinnerstein 1976; Zihlman 1978; Rancour-Laferriere 1981; Jaynes 1976; Konner 1982, 166; Goodall 1981; Anderson and Jaffe 1979; Parker and Gibson 1979). The old idea that language might have *originated* with hunting males has foundered for the simple reason that talking and hunting do not mix (cf. Marshack 1976, 281; Jonas and Jonas 1975a, 628; Wind 1976, 747). Anyone who has ever hunted game knows the problem. I can still remember how difficult it was for me, as an extremely verbal six-year-old, to hold my tongue while stalking white-tailed deer with my father. In fact, I gave up hunting at the tender age of thirteen, while my much less talkative brothers remain big game hunters to this day. Gordon Hewes points out, however, that an original *gestural* communication would not have been incompatible with hunting (personal communication).

31. Some Adaptive Values of Language

The linguist Noam Chomsky (1979, 36) believes that language must have conferred "extraordinary selectional advantages" upon evolving hominids. Similarly, the anthropologist Gordon Hewes says ". . . even a rudimentary language capacity would have improved early hominid survival" (1974, 23). Indeed, *vocal* language has been so advantageous as to persist *despite* the fact that the specialized anatomy necessary for language is itself "less suited for breathing, swallowing and chewing than the vocal tract anatomy of Neanderthal and Australopithecine hominids and non-human primates" (Lieberman 1977, 16).

What might some of the selective advantages of language have been? The following is just a partial list of items that strike me as necessarily adaptive aspects of language:

1) *Enhancement of memory and foresight* (cf. Hewes 1974; Konner 1982, 166; Crook 1980, 134ff.; Haldane 1955, 399-400; Isaac and Crader 1981, 94; Campbell 1979, 305-6; Lancaster 1975, 73). It is easier for an individual to codify past experiences (including experiences in multiple sensory modes) and to plan future adaptive activities (tool making, childcare, gathering, hunting, mating, etc.) if there is speech — either speech with other members of a collective, or "internal speech" (Vygotsky) with one's self.

2) *Classification of kin, non-kin, or degrees of kin.* All languages classify ego's relatives in one fashion or another, usually in a way that facilitates the ability of ego to distinguish degrees of genetic relatedness to him/her. Such an ability, which may be assisted by non-linguistic mechanisms as well, is essential if ego is going to be altruistic toward kin (or compete with non-kin) and thereby maximize his/her own genetic fitness (on the genetic advantages of altruism toward kin ["nepotism"], see: Hamilton 1964; Wilson 1975; Alexander 1979b; above, section D). The ability to distinguish varieties of kin and non-kin is also necessary for avoiding incest and practicing exogamy. Livingstone (1969, 48) goes so far as to argue that "... the origins of incest and exogamy depend upon the existence of language" (cf. Meiselman 1978, 19), though this idea has many critics (see the discussion attached to Livingstone 1969; Maynard Smith 1980, 29-30).

3) *Facilitation of reciprocal altruism.* A number of scholars have remarked on the important role which hominid language (or proto-language) must have played in early food sharing and eventually in the division of subsistence labor (e.g.: Roe 1963; Campbell 1966, 203; Mellen 1981, 126; Leakey 1981, 141; Lancaster 1975, 73; Parker and Gibson 1979; Isaac 1976b; Isaac and Crader 1981, 91). Primitive forms of coopera-

tion, such as cooperative butchering of large carcasses, keeping watch for predators, and joint lifting of heavy objects (cf. the old "Yo-heave-ho" theory of Noiré and Engels) were undoubtedly facilitated by language (Savage-Rumbaugh *et al.* 1979). Later more complex forms of reciprocal altruism, such as "enduring alliances" (Livingstone 1969, 48) between groups of various types were made possible by language. Alliances between both individuals and groups involved exchange, and it is difficult to imagine exchange without naming of the items exchanged. Generally speaking, whether it is exchange of food, gifts, money, women, ritual objects, or whatever — langauge is almost always involved for today's hominids.

4) *Elicitation of altruism.* One of the most effective ways to induce another individual to render altruism is to *ask* for it (see Heeschen *et al.* 1980 for an interesting ethological study of requesting behavior). The appearance of the verbal request on the hominid scene (as opposed to nonverbal begging behavior) must have had considerable adaptive value — especially for female and immature hominids. Besides requesting, there are other linguistic means of eliciting altruism (below, section 36).

5) *Strengthening of bonds between individual hominids.* The linguist Edward Sapir called language "a great force of socialization, probably the greatest that exists" (quoted by Jakobson, n.d., 102), and Jespersen (1925, 25) says language is an important component of the "instinctive fellow feeling" in humans. Insofar as the personal bonds ("attachment behavior" — Bowlby) between siblings, mates, friends, mother and child, father and child, etc. are genetically advantageous, then the initiation and strengthening of these bonds by linguistic means are also adaptive.

The earliest ontogenetic stage of language, i.e., infant crying, has an especially important role to play in this context. Lester (1984, 240) says: "Because human infants, unlike some other species, are not locomotor at birth, the potential for exclusive dependency on vocal communication to signal distress and maintain proximity is heightened."

Goodall (1967) observes that falling from the mother's body is a high cause of infant mortality in chimpanzees, and that infant vocalizations are important in keeping the mother chimp attentive to the infant (cf. MacLean 1982, 15). Since loss of body pelt greatly diminished one channel of socially facilitative grooming activities and simultaneously made it more difficult for the infant hominid to cling to its mother, then there may have been particularly strong pressures toward linguistic strengthening of personal bonds in hominid evolution (see: Etkin 1954, 139; Goodall 1981). It is interesting in this connection that Eric Berne's term for what goes on between friendly interlocutors is *stroking* (see Berne 1977). Van Hoof's term is *grooming talk* (Morris 1967, 245), and Goffman's metaphor is *supportive* interchange (1971, 62-94) — as if the conversing parties were physically holding on to one another.

Jaffe and Anderson (1979, 17-18) suggest that "... skill in interpersonal matching of communication rhythms (variously designated as congruence, convergence, synchrony, conversational coupling, etc.)

... was an important principle in the evolution of language ...." Richman (1980, 241) has a very specific theory about this: "... human speech developed in the social context of many-voiced singing: very early people produced many-voiced vocal displays with complex rhythmical and tonal patterns as an expression of group cohesion, which resulted in the development of speech." Whatever the nature of hominid vocal matching was, it must have contributed significantly toward the bonding of individual hominids to one another. Edelheit (1978, 60) believes that "the *close fitting* of one's own voice to that of another, *the striving for vocal congruence in the ontogenesis of speech, provides ... a meaningful model for empathy* ..." (emphasis Edelheit's). I have argued (Rancour-Laferriere 1981) that acquisition of a "mother tongue" is basically one form of identification with the mother, and that childhood identification with the mother is in turn the ontogenetic basis for most of the altruism that characterizes the bonds between adult humans.

6) *Transmission of complex factual and cultural information across generations ("Lamarckian" inheritance) and between groups.* Adaptive methods of hunting, cooking, building shelters, constructing tools, etc. do not disappear as soon as they are invented, but are passed on to genetically related and unrelated individuals with the help of language (cf. Campbell 1979, 306). Arguably adaptive cultural entities such as religious rituals, folklore, magic, clothing styles, etc. are also transmitted with the help of language (some of the recent burgeoning literature on the relationships of cultural to biological evolution includes: Wilson 1978; Alexander 1979b; Wilson and Lumsden 1981; Boyd and Richerson 1976; Mundinger 1980).

7) *Facilitation of genetic isolation and systematization of outbreeding.* Language does not only enhance communication between linguistically related individuals, but also *blocks* communication between individuals who do not speak the same language, or marks those individuals who have acquired a given language too late in life as speaking with an "accent." Thus reciprocal altruism, interbreeding, and other social intercourse between linguistically unrelated individuals may be blocked, limited, or systematized in very specific ways. Insofar as temporary isolation of small populations (demes) has for a number of reasons speeded up evolutionary rates, promoted genetic variability, and been generally adaptive in hominid evolution (see: Neel 1970, 816; Gabow 1977; Mellen 1981, 112-29; Boorman and Levitt 1980, 362), language differences have therefore also been adaptive (Hill 1972, 313). But it has also been argued that linguistic differences between populations have worked to systematize outbreeding between the populations (Hill 1972; Steklis and Raleigh 1979, 306-7).

8) *Replacement of aggression.* In many animal species outright violence can be avoided by means of ritualized aggression (e.g., Lorenz 1977 [1963]; Maynard-Smith and Parker 1976). In humans language sometimes serves this function. Freud has made the often-quoted statement that "the man who first flung a word of abuse at his enemy instead of

a spear was the founder of civilization" (*SE* III, 36).[81] When real, physical violence might be genetically maladaptive (e.g., a father killing his own son), linguistic violence can come to the rescue. The analogy to weapons can be strongly felt. Montagu (1967, 8) speaks of "... certain Arabs who, when cursed, ducked their heads or fell flat on the ground in order to avoid a direct hit." In *The Gulag Archipelago* Solzhenitsyn (1973, 104) reports that foul language was effectively used to break some prisoners during the Stalin period.

9) *Selection and solicitation of a sexual partner.* In any mammalian species copulation with a fit partner under the right circumstances is a behavior that can result in the replication of genes. In humans the exchange of linguistic messages often initiates a copulatory bout, or prevents it from taking place. Ford and Beach (1951, 99) say: "for human beings speech is undoubtedly the most important single medium of sexual solicitation;" "spoken invitations serve in many societies as the primary means of initiating the customary precoital acitivities and may even be directly followed by copulation" (*ibid.;* cf. Konner 1982, 165). When sexual solicitation is made by the male, the female's evaluation of the male's linguistic performance is an important part of female sexual choice.

10) *Replacement of sexual intercourse.* In situations where there is an inclination to copulate, but copulation itself would be maladaptive or impossible, or should be delayed, language can be of help. Thus tales of sexual exploits, love lyrics, love letters, love songs, verbal promises, sexual taunts, sexual gossip, and other ways of speaking about sex without actually doing it can have considerable adaptive potential.

11) *Deception.* Long ago Leonardo da Vinci said: "Man has great power of speech, but the greater part thereof is empty and deceitful" (quoted by Key 1977, 20; cf. Konner 1982, 169). Key (1980, 9-12) discusses some of the many social advantages of lying. One of the core human features, according to various Darwinian theorists (Alexander 1979b; Ghiselin 1974; Barash 1977; Hamilton 1975; Rancour-Laferriere 1981) is the ability to deceive. Deception in many cases enables one to cheat other individuals out of potential genetic benefits and obtain them for one's self. *Self*-deception, which is the basis of the psycho-analytic notion of the unconscious, can be particularly advantageous from a genetic viewpoint, since it can protect an individual from the potentially harmful psychological consequences of genetically selfish acts (above, section D). Lying, including lying to one's self, is the most complex and advanced form of deception, and is a specifically linguistic achievement.

This is not meant to be a complete list of the adaptive advantages language might have conferred, nor are the individual items on the list always easy to separate from one another. It is hard to imagine, for example, how any

---

81. In fact the statement is not Freud's. He attributes it to an unnamed "English writer."

of the items 2)-11) could be separable from item 1), the enhancement of memory and foresight provided by language, since so many hominid activities have required dealing with the future on the basis of complex lessons learned in the past. Items 9) and 10) are difficult to separate, given that it is not always easy to decide when courtship behavior is a prelude to sexual intercourse and when it is a substitute for it. Item 11), deception, is intertwined with many other adaptive aspects of language, as in facilitation of bonding between individuals by means of lies. Another overlap is between items 5) and 9), since sexual intercourse in hominids has taken place (at least according to the theoreticians of monogamy) in the context of a personal bond of some kind. Yet another example of overlapping is items 8) and 10), given that verbal abuse ("maledicta") is often of a specifically sexual nature.

32. The Role of Obscenities

In a number of the above categories language functions as "a substitute for action" (to use Freud's expression, *SE* II, 8). For example, a verbal insult can replace an act of aggression, a salacious phrase could defuse an impulse to copulate, a request might substitute for a begging gesture, a promise will do until an altruistic act is performed, a person who is absent can be mentioned, etc. In all of these language is acting in a kind of magical way. Even what is utterly impossible can at least be signified by the possessor of language. It is no accident that Freud links what he calls the "omnipotence of thoughts" in children, neurotics, and nonindustrial peoples to the origin of language (*SE* XXIII, 113).

In addition to substituting for an action, language may be seen (from a psychoanalytic viewpoint) as repressing various intentions and thoughts associated with that action. Reynolds (1981, 236) paraphrases Freud well on this point: "For Freud, repression was a failure to attend to certain stored events associated with a word." Gray and Buffery (1971) also propose an "inhibitory" function for language, and Endleman (1981, 98-9) ties negation/denial to the origin of language.

A man aroused by an attractive young woman may at least temporarily be unable to actually think of or intend to make contact with her genitalia, and as a result may produce an *utterance* about *flowers* instead (see above, 31). The "stored events" not attended to in this case would be the mental image of female genitalia and affects associated with this image, and the substituting linguistic event might be something like "red, red rose." When language started to replace other mental constructs in this fashion, it was probably in part because activation of such constructs was leading to inappropriate or dangerous emotive arousal. In effect, not only substitution for an action, but also deletion (or at least conversion) of potentially nonadaptive affect associated with that action was accomplished by language (cf. Hewes [1974, 12], who speaks of "unloading of affect from messages," or Whitney [1878, 283], who stated that "it is where expression quits its emotional natural basis, and turns to intellectual uses, that the history of language begins"). In evolutionary terms, the potential fitness-decreasing consequences of intense emotional arousal probably constituted one of the selective pressures for the development of language.

But there are ways of referring to female genitalia (or other potentially disturbing matters) that do involve considerable affective arousal in both the speaker and hearer. I am referring to such obscene exclamations as

> What a piece of ass!
> You cunt!
> Fuck off!
> You motherfucker!
> etc.

If non-obscene language is a form of repression, these utterances clearly accomplish a lifting of repression. Affective arousal is definitely present in the speaker. Whether the utterances also provide *relief* from that very arousal is a matter of some dispute (Montagu 1967, 85 reviews the literature which shows that swearing reduces psychological and physiological stress, while Tavris 1982, 129-30, adduces evidence that verbal aggression offers relief only in very limited circumstances). But it is clear that an obscenity provides a very graphic, perhaps even hallucinatory (Greenson 1950, 20) *substitute* for action, whether or not it relieves the emotive arousal, and in some cases there is definitely relief as well. For example, the man who exclaims to another man,

> Take a look at those tits!

feels at least partially relieved of the need to copulate with the woman in question (he is probably expressing a homosexual solidarity with his interlocutor as well — see below, section 47). Or, a man inclined to commit a violent act against another man may instead engage in ritualized aggression, exclaiming

> You cocksucker!

or

> Suck my cock!

and may thus feel satisfied at having attained a relationship of dominance to the other man (as long as the other man does not retaliate — cf. Tavris *ibid.*, 130 — or as long as the retaliation is no more than another verbal insult, as in the practice among ghetto blacks of "playing the dozens" — *ibid.*, 56, 258). A nonspeaking hominid ancestor, however, may have required a literal performance of fellatio in order to defuse a homologous affective state. Similarly, while today's hominid might be satisfied with shouting

> Shove it up your ass!

an ancestral hominid might have tried to perform an actual pedication (see section 38, below, on dominance mounting in non-human primates).

It is remarkable how highly developed obscenity and abuse are in the languages of the world today. An entire journal is now devoted to this subject. It is entitled *Maledicta: The International Journal of Verbal Aggression*, edited by Reinhold Aman. Perusing the seven volumes of *Maledicta* published so far reveals a wealth of obscene and abusive expressions from such various sources as Cuban Spanish, north-central Macedonian, Canadian French, Australian English, the speech of Menomini Indians, Cantonese dialect, the Bono language of Central Ghana, United States Army speech, lesbian slang, Persian insult poetry, pre-adolescent teasing and jokes, Chaucer's English, prison slang, hospital staff slang, Russian folklore, backwards sex talk in Thai, ancient Roman graffiti, etc., etc.

A standard source for Slavists, *Dictionary of Russian Obscenities*, compiled by D. A. Drummond and G. Perkins (2nd edition, 1980) contains 61 terms for the penis and 36 for the vagina — though these are modest totals, to judge from the much larger and more comprehensive dictionary of Flegon (1973). *The Book of Sex Lists*, compiled by Albert B. Gerber (1981, 50-58) lists 147 English synonyms for the penis, 98 for the vagina, and 46 for the female breasts. Gerber has evidently missed many English items, however. Tim Healey reports he has found approximately 1,000 English terms for the penis, 1,200 for the vulva, and 800 or so for the sexual act (Healey 1980, 181). Farmer and Henley (1890-1904) reported roughly 1,200 English terms for sexual intercourse. The German totals found by Ernest Borneman are: approximately 860 for the penis, 600 for the vagina, and 250 for the female breasts (as reported by Aman in *Maledicta* II, 286).

Obviously these grand totals do not represent the knowledge of typical individual speakers, but of populations artificially thrown together over space and time.

Walsh and Leonard (1974) found that, although their synchronic sample of 248 American students yielded totals of 130 (females) and 162 (males) terms for sexual intercourse, on the average each female reported only six, and each male only nine terms for sexual intercourse. These latter figures may seem small, but there are not all that many linguistic terms for *most* commonplace actions (it would be difficult to think of more than six or eight words, for example, which refer to eating, walking, talking, etc.). What is interesting is that so many terms have come into existence over time and across population boundaries. Perhaps this is a result of avoidance. That is, perhaps speakers wish to avoid the strictly taboo words, such as "fuck," and therefore constantly invent euphemisms such as "have," "make," "lay," etc. Small pockets of speakers using specific euphemisms thus develop (in some cases, such as "genital pet names," the terms are limited to two or even one speaker — see Cornog 1981). Otherwise perfectly innocent items of the lexicon are easily pressed into sexual service. Nouns such as "tool," "root," "hog," "banana," "rod," "pole," and "pickle," or "sheath," "slit," "purse," "box," "hole," and "jelly" are readily given sexual significance. Even the apparently sexless pronoun "it" takes on a sexual meaning, given a suggestive context. Here, for example, are some potentially lascivious song titles collected by Laurence Urdang:

"it" = sexual intercourse
Do It Again
Do It, Baby
I Got To Have It, Daddy
Mama Like To Do It
Woncha Do It For me
That's The Way She Likes It
He wouldn't Stop Doing It
Do It If You Wanna

"it" = genital organ
Ease It To Me
Give It To Me Good
It Must Be Hard
Put It Where I can Get It
Take Your Hands Off It
You Got To Wet it
Who'll Get It When I'm Gone?
Wobble It a Little, Daddy

(Urdang 1981, 70-2)

But the inventiveness of speakers does not lead to the extinction of the truly obscene terms. Nor does the censoriousness of parents, clergymen, publishers, and other authority figures. Every adult speaker knows the word "fuck." It does not matter that this word could not (except in scholarly and official publications) be printed in full anywhere in the British Commonwealth until 1961 (Partridge 1966, 239). Nor has "fuck" lost currency because many major publications, such as *The New York Times*, still refuse to print it. Incidentally, the Russian equivalent, which is the verb *ebat'*, is not to be found in any Soviet publications, but every Russian understands it perfectly well.

The syntax of obscenities can be very peculiar. Take the common English curse, such as

Fuck you!

A speaker could conceivably interpret this as

I fuck you! (deleted subject added),

or

Fuck yourself (deleted reflexive added),

or a number of other rough paraphrases. Historically, the phrase may even go back to an utterance

(may) the Devil fuck you!

(Gregersen 1977)

But there are factors which render these other expressions linguistically irrelevant to what goes on in the speaker and hearer of "Fuck you!" If, for example, the phrase were really an imperative, like

Wash the dishes!,

then one could say

Please fuck you,

just as one can say

Please wash the dishes.

But obviously one cannot (see Quàng Phúc Dòng [1971a]). Or, if the phrase

were a true reflexive, then "you" should be "yourself," as in
> Wash yourself!,

but it is not (Gregersen *ibid.*, 262). What Quàng shows is that the word "fuck" in "Fuck you!" (as opposed to the same word in a non-expletive such as "he fucked her") is not even a verb in the transformationalist-generative sense (he calls it a "quasi-verb"). Nor is "Fuck you" even a sentence, properly speaking (Quàng calls it an "epithet" which can be analyzed as "quasi-verb + N[oun] P[hrase] ").

The best known of Russian curses,
> Eb tvoiu mat'!

is also very peculiar grammatically (see Dreizin and Priestly 1982, 42-3). Without going into the linguistic details, it can be said that this curse has been variously interpreted as "I fucked your mother" (and therefore "I could be your father"), "Fuck your mother!," "a dog fucked your mother," and "the devil fucked your mother" (see the note by Reinhold Aman in *Maledicta* I, 267). Professor Simon Karlinsky has pointed out to me a passage from Nabokov's *Bend Sinister* which illustrates some of the quasi-subjunctive possibilities of the curse. The novel's hero encounters two soldiers on a bridge, who demand that he show his pass:

> While he was fumbling for the pass they bade him hurry and mentioned a brief love affair they had had, or would have, or invited him to have with his mother.

This rendition of the obscenity is rather like a linguistic analysis of it. Affect slips almost entirely away, leaving behind just an intellectual tickle.

Obscenities, like many other affective matters, probably involve the limbic or what MacLean (1970) would call "paleomammalian" areas of the brain (cf. Hewes 1976, 490; Robinson 1976, 767). Other areas are also involved, including the ("reptilian" — MacLean) corpus striatum and the thalamus (Martindale 1977).

Martindale discusses in detail the neurolinguistic basis of the interesting pathological phenomenon known as Tourette syndrome (named after the Paris physician Georges Gilles de la Tourette who lived from 1857 to 1904). Individuals suffering from this disease uncontrollably interject "coprolalic tics" into their speech:

> See, FUCK MY FUCKING FUCKING FUCKING CUNT, FUCK, FUCK, FUCK, FUCK FUCK, I finished tenth year of high school FUCK MY FUCKING CUNT and the new year started, the eleventh, and I went to school, and I was in school 10 minutes when one of the teachers that knew me FUCK MY FUCKING CUNT and was teaching at the school when I was there before, I'd never had him for a teacher, he knew about me. He was wise thought he'd be having a little fun or something. So I ended up leaving school

and making a ... Kinda though it'd be funny anyway FUCK FUCK FUCK. I was in school 10 minutes the first day and then I ended up not going the year. (quoted from a patient by Martindale 1977, 233).

Facial grimaces and obscene gestures may accompany such speech. The young child suffering from Tourette syndrome, and who has not yet learned such obscenities, makes peculiar coughing and grunting noises. Eventually the obscenities substitute for the noises. Martindale observes that Tourette symptoms abate during sexual arousal (cf. Shapiro *et al.* 1973). 'Obscene action' thus appears to substitute for obscene language, and vice-versa. Freud's idea of language substituting for action is supported by these findings. At another level there appears to be another kind of substitution as well. Martindale found that when one patient talked about oral, anal, or genital matters fewer actual obscenities were uttered. Martindale concludes that "references to drives and tics seem to form a substitution class" (*ibid.*, 240).

Most people at one time or another use obscenities. Also, there is evidence that Tourette syndrome is genetically transmitted (e.g., Kidd *et al.* 1980). These facts suggest that the human penchant for using obscenities (without of course any specification about which language the obscenities are in) is built into the human genome.

33. The Child's Brain and the Mother Tongue

Viewed in evolutionary perspective, today's obscenities appear to be just one of the phylogenetic remnants of the affect-laden cries emitted in less encoded form by our hominid ancestors. Neurologically, the transition from these cries to propositional speech meant decreasing limbic control and increased (lateralized) neocortical involvement (MacLean 1982, 15).

More generally, the transition — however slow or sudden it may have been in hominid phylogeny — must have involved a special kind of interaction between the brain of the immature hominid and that hominid's principal caretaker (most likely its mother). Today we can see this interaction as constituting the two principal proximate mechanisms necessary for the acquisition of language by the child:

1) Chomsky believes that language is an evolved "organ" and that the "universal grammar" shared by all languages is "genetically determined" (see: Chomsky 1976; 1978; Pribram 1978; Lenneberg 1967; Alexander 1973 [a critique of Chomsky]; other speculations on a possible genetic basis for language have been made by numerous scholars ever since Wilhelm von Humboldt — see Rancour Laferriere 1980, n. 6 for some of the literature). In addition to a uniquely-shaped vocal apparatus, the other components of the linguistic "organ" include — to greatly simplify — certain brain areas, in most individuals on the left side, such as Broca's area (anterior speech cortex), Wernicke's area (posterior speech cortex), the supplementary motor cortex, and frontolimbic areas. Beyond this, certain cross-modal associative abilities are involved, which require the presence of specific cortico-cortical connections (perhaps located in Brodmann's areas 39 and 40 within Wernicke's area) as well as cortico-subcortical connections (see: Geschwind 1970; Popper and Eccles 1977, 305ff.; Hewes 1977a, 129ff.; Corballis and Morgan 1978; Pribram 1971; Lieberman 1975; Reynolds 1981, 209-42; and the numerous sources cited in these works). It should be cautioned that "localization" aspects of linguistic functioning no more imply a knowledge of the physiological basis of language than knowledge of the sun's location implies knowledge of how sunlight is produced. Indeed, the "capacity for language ... may be due to structural innovations on a molecular level" (Lenneberg 1967, 72). But whatever the neuro-physiological bases for the linguistic "organ" may be, they are evidently already operating in the very young infant. Otherwise it would be difficult, for example, to account for the fact that "the responses of 4-week-old infants to the phonetic feature *phonation onset* ... show that they recognize the acoustic cues that differentiate sounds like [b] and [p] in the same manner that adults do" (Lieberman 1975,

161). Or, to take another example of the infant's adult-like linguistic abilities, it has been found that even before speech appears, the child is capable of making microscopic body movements that are synchronized with the rhythm of adult speech (Condon and Sander 1974; Kempton 1980, 72-4).

Another component of the language acquisition "organ" is the child's (doubtless neurophysiologically based) ability to *imitate* the language spoken by its mother and by others in its environment. "Without imitation, there can be no civilized life, at any rate no linguistic life" – said Otto Jespersen (1925, 24). The child not only possesses a "universal grammar," but is capable while still young (and only rarely as an adult) of mastering a *particular* grammar. A child growing up in Lithuania does not acquire the grammar of Hindi. A child raised in Maine does not speak with an Oklahoma accent. As an American who spent many years learning Russian as an adult, I never cease to be amazed at how the little urchins playing on the back streets of Moscow shout and sing in perfect Muscovite dialect. Not only the level of sound, but many aspects of the syntactic level as well are acquired by imitation (cf. Clark 1975; Ferrier 1978). Yando *et al.* (1978, 4) have argued that "... imitation might profitably be regarded as a capacity that is built into the human species much as language appears to be built in." I would only qualify this by saying that imitation is (among other things) a *part of* language ability (Rancour-Laferriere 1981). It is probably not an accident that both sign language and spoken language aphasics have difficulty imitating meaningless movements of the arms and mouth (Kimura 1979).

2) A committed principal caretaker (usually the mother) is just as essential to the ontogenesis of language as are the other proximate mechanisms. As Jerome Bruner whimsically puts it, for every LAD (language acquisition device) in the child there is a LASS (language acquisition support system) provided by the mother (see Bruner 1982, 5). So-called "feral children" are always speechless (see Malson/Itard 1972).[82] The fact that most children acquire their 'mother tongue' from a female teacher may explain the persistent reports (summarized by Buffery and Gray 1972; Maccoby and Jacklin 1974, 75-85) of greater language ability in females than in males (Gray and Buffery 1971; Harnad 1976), though it seems just as likely that females are linguistically the more talented either because their typically subordinate social position requires them to use "verbal finesse and subterfuge" to elicit male altruism (Harding 1975, 293; cf. Kramer 1977, 160; Kramarae 1981, 122-3), or because they have a greater interest in reducing agonistic encounters and social tension than males do and can accomplish this linguistically (Mitchell 1981, 138-9; cf. Kramarae 1981, 30). In communicating with her small child the mother modifies her own normal speech, producing what has been termed "baby talk" or "motherese,"

---

82. Some of the cases of "feral children" may of course have been mentally retarded or autistic.

that is, a speech variety which would be perceived as highly bizarre if directed toward an adult (except perhaps during lovemaking), and which has such specific structural characteristics as exaggerated intonation, small lexicon, slow tempo, simple syntax, etc. (see: Snow 1979). The mother also incessantly addresses questions to the child, which further encourage it to speak. The mother's speech is of course just one of a whole array that includes gazing, smiling, gestural, and tactile behaviors which all initiate the child into the complexities of social interaction (cf. Bruner 1975; Rancour-Laferriere 1981).

These two classes of proximate mechanisms probably did not appear all at once at some point on the hominid scene, but must have come into existence over a long period of time, with some of the components perhaps appearing suddenly and flourishing due to great adaptive value.

Whatever the timing was for the origin and evolution of vocal language, it is clear that components in both categories 1) and 2) must have been involved. To treat the evolving hominid child and its mother in isolation from one another may sometimes be necessary for specialized research purposes, but the two are inseparable in a realistic reconstruction of language phylogeny.

However, theories that proclaim that enhanced mother-child interaction was the only original adaptive advantage (as opposed to proximate mechanism) of language strike me as erroneous. The rudimentary language "organ" *may* have evolved initially only for reasons having to do with the increasing need for prolonged and elaborate maternal care of neotenous offspring. The linguistic interaction of mother and child *might* then have been a *preadaptation* for language use in other contexts, i.e., uses which would themselves have been selected for. But this does not have to have been the case. There are plenty of organs and processes which are adaptive specifically for results they produce in adulthood rather than in childhood (the uterus, for example, or the male orgasm). Thus it is no more reasonable to suppose that language initially evolved because of enhancement of the mother-child bond than to suppose it evolved because of the adaptive value of, say, linguistically facilitated planning for the future (others who have cast doubt on the mother-child interaction hypothesis of initial selection for language include: Steklis 1976; Glick and Raleigh 1976; Smith 1976; Wind 1976 — all of whom are reacting to Jonas and Jonas 1975a). It is probably closer to the truth to say that possessors of genes for language acquisition and language teaching abilities cashed in on many of language's adaptive benefits, not just one. The tendency for some to identify the mother-child bond as the first adaptive context for language in *phylogeny* probably reflects the fact that language first appears in the context of the mother-

The Child's Brain and the Mother Tongue

child bond *in ontogeny*. Like the myth of matriarchy, the mother-child interaction hypothesis of initial selection for language is most readily explained as the product of a very human tendency to project vaguely remembered ontogenetic events into phylogenetic reconstructions.

34. Dating the Origin of Language

As for the specific period in hominid phylogeny when children developed language learning abilities and mothers developed language teaching abilities – the evidence is spotty at best. With the comparative linguistic method of historical reconstruction we can only move back 10-20,000 years (Kiparsky 1976). It is not known just when in the course of hominid evolution language appeared. It is also not known whether language appeared suddenly or developed gradually. There are proponents of both saltationist and gradualist theories. An example of the former is E. O. Wilson's statement that "the development of human speech represents a quantum jump in evolution comparable to the assembly of the eucaryotic cell" (1975, 556). An example of the latter is Hill's belief that ". . . the view of the origin of language which would seem most appropriate is that language evolved rather gradually and in conjunction with developing socio-cultural complexity in humans" (1972, 315). Given the complexity of proximate mechanisms necessary for language, I am more inclined to accept the gradualist position (though there may well have been "punctuations" in language evolution due to the appearance of specific, adaptive subcomponents of language, or a series of genetic "cascades," as Boorman and Levitt 1980, 362 suggest).

One of the more solid kinds of evidence we have concerning the origin of language is the hominid supralaryngeal vocal tract. When the tract becomes a bent, two-tube structure, it is capable of producing fully encoded language as it is known today. But such a structure apparently did not develop until modern *Homo sapiens sapiens*. According to Lieberman (1974; 1977), the vowels [i], [u], and [a], which are universally present in today's human languages, could not have been produced by the vocal tract of *Australopithecus africanus*, nor even by the vocal apparatus of *Homo sapiens neanderthalensis*.[83] Yet Lieberman believes that "speech communication must have existed in late hominid forms like Neanderthal man" (1977, 17). It is just that Neanderthal man's ". . . language was encoded but not nearly so much as that of modern *Homo sapiens* . . ." (1975, 170).

Further evidence relating to the origin of fully encoded vocal communication in hominids is the "cultural spurt" (Isaac 1976a, 286) which took place about 30,000-40,000 years ago in the Upper Pleistocene: ". . .

---

83. For a review of some of the evidence that seems to contradict Lieberman's conclusions, see Steklis and Raleigh 1979, 292-3.

the record gives the appearance that a threshold was crossed with the emergence of much more complex and more style-ridden systems of material culture. From this . . . period . . . come the first surviving manifestations of art and of bodily adornment" (*ibid.*). This cultural "threshold" has been associated with the origin of vocal language (or with crucial developments in the origin of vocal language) by a number of scholars (Pumphrey 1953; Haldane 1955; Jakobson 1974; Dart 1959; Oakley 1962; Clark 1975; Hewes 1977a; and others).

A time-table constructed by Isaac graphically shows just how recent and sudden was the appearance of many classes of human cultural artifacts:

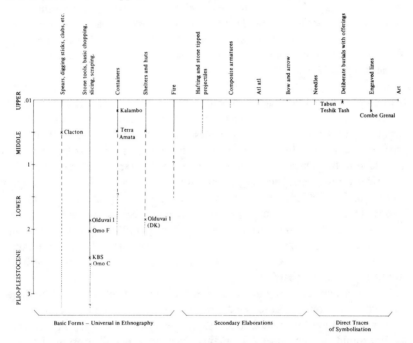

Fig. 1. Time-table indicating the oldest evidence for various major classes of artifacts. Dotted lines show conjectured time ranges. Isaac 1976a, 278.

What makes the period from about two million years to about 100,000 years ago so monotonous, archaeologically, is that practically no new kinds of artifacts were invented.[84] But in just the last 100,000 years at least seven

---

84. Compare Washburn: "If you look at the general record, you find something on the order of two million years, according to the potassium-argon dates, where you find the use of only very crude pebble tools. This is incredibly slow evolution, if we think of it in relation to the Middle Pleistocene. Then, in turn, if we think of

new classes of artifacts appear, several of which have "direct traces of symbolisation" (Isaac), that is, which involve brand new semiotic systems that are not needed for mere subsistence activities. Included are animal statuettes, crude anthropomorphic figures, engraved bones, bored pendants, and other items. These prehistoric objects have repeatedly engendered speculations about the origin of language. For example: "figurative art seems to imply the presence of language and thus the earliest vestiges of representative art provide glottogony with a plausible *terminus ante quem*" (Jakobson 1974, 58); "the development of visual art was probably accompanied by storytelling . . ." (Alland 1977, 112). Leakey and Lewin go so far as to say that ". . . it is *impossible* that abstract symbolism, such as we see elaborated during the past thirty thousand years, could arise in a speechless animal. Without words with which to name them, a statuette of a horse, a rock painting, or a nation's flag, could never exist; they would be meaningless" (1978, 220).

The most explicit and daring (some would say reckless) attempt to date the origin of verbal language is Julian Jaynes' contribution to the New York Academy of Sciences conference on language origins (Jaynes 1976a). According to Jaynes, not until the mesolithic period (10,000-12,000 years ago) did reasonably full-blown linguistic powers develop in *Homo sapiens*. This is not the place to detail the evidence utilized by Jaynes, but the rhetorical center of Jaynes' argument should be mentioned: ". . . I simply cannot imagine a species with words for actions, qualities, and things leaving so few and only such primitive artifacts around for us to pick up now" (*ibid.*, 327). Contrast this with Holloway (1976, 33), who on the basis of paleoneurological evidence regards language as a "uniquely human activity" which ". . . came relatively early in hominid evolution, perhaps two to three million years ago."

Halloway may be erring in the opposite direction from Jaynes. But there are some scattered pieces of evidence that should make supporters of the late-language hypothesis have doubts. There is, for example, an engraved ox rib found in Pech de l'Azé, France, in a level dated at approximately 300,000 years old (Bordes 1972, 61-2; Marshack 1976, 278; 1977, 291-2). According to Marshack the serpentine style of engraving on the rib (there are lines called "meanders") is just like that found on the nonutilitarian objects and cave walls of the later paleolithic. i.e., of a recent period (40-15,000 years ago) when even most late-language theorists believe

---

the rate of tool evolution in the next few hundred thousand years – Acheulian and the like – it is also incredibly slow by comparison with the rate for *Homo sapiens*" (1969, 94).

hominids were speaking. According to Marshack, ". . . the ability to initiate and maintain an image system, such as the meander or macaroni, requires naming and language" (1977, 300). Marshack also reports (1981) on findings of red, brown, and yellow ochre (for painting?) from a 300,000 year old *Homo erectus* site in Terra Amata, France. Other nonutilitarian items of interest are nearly perfect stone spheroids that appear with Acheulean tools and large Acheulean handaxes that seem to be "unnecessarily" symmetrical and pleasing to the eye. A review of some of these apparently "aesthetic" findings from pre-Neanderthal times is given by Edwards (1978). But we must keep in mind that many non-speaking creatures are able to produce and/or perceive things that are arguably "aesthetic." There are, for example, the highly structured "songs" of some birds, mammals, reptiles, and insects, the elaborate and colorful nests of bowerbirds, the finger paintings of chimpanzees, the architectural edifices of beavers, etc. (see Sebeok 1981, 210-59 for a survey of some of the "prefigurements of art"). As Darwin said in *The Descent of Man* (1885 [1871], 86), ". . . an instinctive tendency to acquire an art is not peculiar to man."

It seems to me that if "aesthetic" clues to language origin are going to be sought for, they would be most relevant if they were either in the acoustic realm (poetry, vocal and instrumental music) or in the related visual-proprioceptive realm (dance). Language, like poetry (Laferrière 1980), music (Cooper and Meyer 1960), and dance (Sachs 1937) is a *rhythmic* activity. This is true of both vocal language and gestural language. Timing is of the essence in conveying meaning-laden sequences. Lenneberg (1967, 109-19) adduces several kinds of evidence to show that there is a basic periodicity of approximately six cycles per second underlying speech. The tempo of speech can be increased or decreased with electrical stimulation to the thalamic area of the brain (*ibid.*, 117). The linguist Ilse Lehiste has found evidence for both subjective perception of isochrony (= "rhythmic organization of speech into more or less equal intervals" – Lehiste 1977) as well as objective isochrony of certain syntactic units.

Unfortunately, poetry, music and dance do not fossilize, and we have to rely therefore on indirect indications of these phenomena. Poetry, for example, can be written down, but systems of writing are only six or seven thousand years old and therefore younger than language even according to the late language theorists (and in any case written language itself implies that spoken language already exists).

Dart (1959) believes there are parallels between "song that is melodious" and "speech that is articulate," and Darwin (1885 [1871], 572) believed that ". . . musical sounds afforded one of the bases for the development of language." But written records of music, like written poetry, are geologically recent. There are musical instruments which have survived the ravages of time. The oldest appear to be a collection of eight fragmentary bone pipes from a 20,000 year old level in the Isturitz cave in the Basses-Pyrénées (Megaw 1968a, b). A 17,000 year old rock painting in Les Trois Frères depicts a skin cloaked figure playing what has been interpreted as either a pipe or a musical bow (*ibid.*; cf. Sadie 1980, vol. 6, 312-315). Quite a few prehistoric musical instruments have been unearthed in Europe and the Near East, such as pottery drums, rattles, pan-pipes, reed pipes, horns, and lyres. But practically all of the finds date back only to the mesolithic at the earliest, i.e., 12,000 years ago or later.

As for dance, which Sachs calls "the mother of the arts" because it exists in time *and* in space (1937, 3), the geologic record is sparse indeed. Some paleolithic rock figures may possibly be dancers (*ibid.*, 207ff.; Hanna 1979, 51). Most scholars would probably agree, though, that there was no music until there was dance (e.g., Bowra 1962, 263), and that both were prerequisites for the appearance of articulate language.

35. Rhythms and Synchronies in Sexual Interaction

If we are to believe Wolfgang Köhler, non-speaking chimpanzees are capable of a primitive "round dance":

... two would wrestle and tumble about playing near some post; soon their movements would become more regular and tend to describe a circle round the post as a centre. One after another, the rest of the group approach, join the two, and finally they march in an orderly fashion and in single file round and round the post. The character of their movements changes; they no longer walk, they trot, and as a rule with special emphasis on one foot, while the other steps lightly; thus a rough approximate rhythm develops, and they tend to "keep time" with one another. They wag their heads in time to the steps of their "dance" and appear full of eager enjoyment of their primitive game. (Köhler 1959 [1917], 280; cf. Sebeok 1981, 220; Sachs 1937, 10-11).

On occasion Köhler himself would join in the festivities:

A trusted human friend is allowed to share in these games with pleasure, as well as in other diversions, and sometimes I only needed to stamp rhythmically, as described, round and round a post, for a couple of black figures to form my train. If I had enough of it and left them, the game generally came to an abrupt end. The animals squatted down with an air of disappointment, like children who "won't play any more," when their big brother turns away. (*Ibid.*, 280-1).

Perhaps what these chimpanzees were doing fits the definition of dance given by Curt Sachs: "all rhythmical motion not related to the work motif" (1937, 6). Certainly what Köhler describes is *play*ful, and is arguably rhythmic.[85] But it does not appear to *signify* anything, and this fact may be related to the lack of language in chimpanzees. Human dancing often represents action other than itself. It can be more than merely ecstatic. For example, belly dancing ("abdominal dance" with "pelvic roll" — Sachs) can signify

---

85. Williams (1967, 64ff.) believes that what chimpanzees do is not properly rhythmic, or is only accidentally rhythmic: " ... it would be very difficult to perform any repeated action without some semblance of rhythm ... " (*ibid.*, 66). Williams says chimps do not have a *sense* of rhythm, even if what they do looks objectively like rhythm. Admittedly, rhythm is a difficult thing to define (see Laferrière 1980). But how does one distinguish a "semblance" of rhythm from true rhythm? This strikes me as a legitimate question for neurophysiologists to investigate. In the meantime I am inclined to believe chimpanzees have the rudiments of rhythm.

copulatory movements. Squat dancing may represent the act of sitting. War dances, rain dances, animal dances, and others involve a variety of complex (largely iconic) representations. In her information-packed *To Dance Is Human*, Hanna (1979,26) says: "Dance is a whole complex of communication symbols, a vehicle for conceptualization. It may be a paralanguage, a semiotic system, like articulate speech, made up of signifiers that refer to things other than themselves." Specifically linguistic analogies are made again and again for the semiotic system of dance. For example: "Choreography involves knowledge of a grammar, relational rules for using a motor lexicon or corpus of movements and semantics" (*ibid.*, 35).

In her philosophical study of dance, Susanne Langer (1953, 169ff.) emphasizes the close relationships of dance with *gesture* on the one hand, and with *music* on the other: "the rhythm that is to turn every movement into gesture, and the dancer himself into a creature liberated from the usual bonds of gravity and muscular inertia, is most readily established by music" (203).

Viewed narrowly, dancing is just rhythmically gesturing with the hind legs. But whether it is the front legs, hind legs, torso, head, fingers, eyebrows, shoulders, or whatever that are in motion, the motions are highly coordinated and are rhythmic. Rhythm is a common element in many human motor activities, and is therefore in a position to serve as a preadaptive entity for newly evolving activities.

To return to language as a specific example: the rhythms of locomoting, dancing, gesturing, and vocalizing very likely all contributed in some way or other to the rhythmic organization of primitive language. Gestural rhythm, which itself may derive from upper-trunk locomotor rhythm, strikes me as a particularly strong candidate for a preadaptation to linguistic rhythm (see the abundant evidence gathered by G. W. Hewes for gestural precursors to language as we know it today). The vocal rhythms of prehominids and early hominids must also have been an important preadaptation, especially since no shift in modality and probably only little change in neuromuscular basis was needed to go from the rhythm of non-articulate vocalization to the rhythm of articulate language. It has even been argued, on the basis of observations on the complex vocal displays of gelada baboons, that the rhythm of prelinguistic vocalization might have been the forerunner of linguistic *syntax*:

If human speech developed in a social context similar to that of gelada many-voiced vocal displays and human choral singing, this could explain why such an extremely complex syntax actually did develop. A complex syntax of rhythm (necessary for controlling the production of vocal displays) could have developed *solely* under pressures to produce more and more elaborate and complex coordinated vocal displays. (Richman 1980, 242). As more and more complex vocal displays developed, the syntax of rhythm that was used in the production of these displays had to become ever more elaborate. The *semantic use* of this complex rhythmical syntax could have come later, much later. In short, a complex rhythmical syntax developed first, and then this rhythmical syntax could have been put to semantic use. (*ibid.*).

In other words the "syntax" of vocal rhythm may have been, in evolutionary terms, a preadaptation for linguistic syntax (the "syntactical component" of language "originally was the syntax of rhythm" – *ibid.*, 243). This theory is quite interesting, but still needs substantiation in at least two areas: 1) a detailed comparison of the formal properties of the "syntax" of musical/vocal rhythm (cf. Cooper and Meyer 1960) with the formal properties of linguistic syntax (as described, for example, by Chomsky's *Syntactic Structures* or in post-transformationalist treatises); and 2) a comparison of the neuroanatomical basis of musical/vocal rhythm with that of linguistic syntax.

The second of these areas offers curious difficulties, since it is generally agreed that syntax is primarily a function of areas in the *left* cerebral cortex (see above, 228), while musical ability and some of the prosodic features of language are associated with the *right* cerebral hemisphere (see Popper and Eccles 1977, 307, 336-41; Kolb and Whishaw 1980, 201-2; Kent and Rosenbek 1982 for reviews of the literature). For example, ". . . left hemisphere lesions and left carotid injections of sodium amytal can produce aphasia while leaving singing ability relatively intact" (Kolb and Whishaw, 201). Conversely, "lesions resulting in amusias usually have been located in the right middle temporal regions . . ." (*ibid.*, 202). Also, " . . . the right hemisphere appears to process the intonational component of speech" (Kent and Rosenbek 1982, 277).

However, it does not follow from these findings that the specifically rhythmic component of musical vocalization (or of all vocalization, including ordinary speech) is programmed by (or only by) the right cerebral hemisphere. The neuroanatomical basis for vocal rhythm appears in fact to involve both right and left cerebral hemispheres as well as subcortical areas. Gates and Bradshaw (1977, 411) review the literature on the production of vocal rhythm, and conclude that both hemispheres are involved, though the left seems to be slightly superior in processing rhythmic information. It is known that stimulation of portions of either the left cortex or the thalamus can slow down or speed up speech *rate* (Lenneberg 1967, 117-18; Ojemann and Mateer 1979). Kent and Rosenbek (1982) report a slowed, halting rhythm of pronunciation in some apractic patients with left-hemisphere lesions. Luria has found evidence for cortical components to vocal rhythm (1966,

73-127; cf. Laferrière 1980, 442ff.). Also, Lenneberg (1967, 116-7) has noted that an electroencephalographic rhythm of about 7 cycles per second has been identified over the temporo-parietal region.

It would be interesting to know whether gestural rhythms share neuroanatomical substrates with vocal rhythms. It is known that body parts do tend to change movements simultaneously, and that body motions tend to be coordinated precisely with aspects of speech pattern (the term for this is "self-synchrony" — see Condon and Ogston 1967; Kendon 1970; Jaffe and Anderson 1979; Key 1980, 16; Condon 1980). It cannot be an accident that there exist what Jaffe and Anderson (1979, 17) call ". . . startling similarities between the immediate time patterns of gestural events studied by kinesics and the temporal course of articulatory actions and hesitations that occur during speech."

Conjoined speech and body rhythms are not only produced, but are also perceived and are 'infectious.' That is, they elicit specifically synchronizing reactions from the perceiver. Painstaking, frame-by-frame analysis of films of conversation reveal striking synchronies between participants. For example, in describing one point in a filmed dinner table conversation between a mother, father, and four-year old son, Condon and Ogston note that "the father moves his fork to and from his plate in precise cadence with the syllabic segments of the mother's speech." The researchers have the impression that "metaphorically, the three interactants looked like puppets being moved by the same set of strings" (1967, 229). Paraphrasing another of Condon's experiments, Montagu and Matson say:

... two persons were hooked up to an electroencephalograph while engaged in conversation, with one camera filming the principals while another focused on the machine. During the entire period of conversation, the two EEG recording pens moved in such perfect unison as to appear "driven" by a single force; only when the talk was interrupted by a third person did the readings diverge. (1979, 153).

A remarkable film made by a student of Edward T. Hall shows a playground full of children playing and skipping about in apparently random fashion. Upon closer examination, however, it turns out that all of the children are moving 'in sync' with one particularly active little girl who is moving over the entire playground and 'orchestrating' the other children's movements. The group rhythm, once discerned, was so regular that a rock musician was able to find a tune to go with it, and the tune stayed 'in sync' with the visual rhythm for the entire 4 1/2 minutes of the film (Hall 1976, 66).

The various levels of rhythmic matching between interactants is termed *interactional synchrony* (or sometimes the *Condon effect*):

... while the speaker is speaking and moving the listener is moving as well. He may be sitting relatively still, not making any specifically gestural movements, but yet moving his hands or head, moving his eyes, or blinking. Where *interactional synchrony* is occurring it is found that the boundaries of the movement waves of the listener coincide with boundaries of the movement waves in the speaker. For synchrony to occur, in this sense, it is only this coincidence of boundaries that must obtain. The listener may otherwise be moving in quite a different fashion, and he usually is. (Kendon 1970, 103-4).

This 'interactional synchrony' is most pronounced at the syllabic level, but occurs from the phone up through the word level, and in certain social settings characterized by 'heightened synchrony' it will occur at the phrase level as well. Interactional synchrony has been observed in *all* normal human interaction, including that of nonliterate peoples from diverse cultures ..., and in group interaction, where several listeners move in synchrony with one speaker .... (Kempton 1980, 69; cf. Lomax 1968, 171ff.; von Raffler-Engel 1980, 108; Condon and Ogston 1967; Condon 1980; various papers in the conference edited by Davis 1982).

Kempton reviews several kinds of evidence which indicate that the responses in interactional synchrony are too fast (no more than 20 milliseconds) to be mere reactions or reflexes. It must therefore be the case that ". . . synchronization occurs as a result of both interactants sharing *mutually known rhythmic patterns*" (*ibid.*, 71; cf. Delcomyn 1980 on the widespread presence of rhythmic behavior not determined by sensory feedback in animals).

Kempton says that "we move together in all everyday interaction by using the same ability that allows us to dance with someone, or sing in time with another person's song" (*ibid.*). Such obviously rhythmic activities as dancing, marching, singing, chanting, playing a musical instrument, and reciting poetry may all be thought of as (among other things) ways of facilitating or heightening the interactional synchrony with a partner or with a group of people.

This facilitation seems in turn to have a disinhibiting effect that permits normally repressed feelings to be expressed. In neurobiological terms, a rhythmically heightened Condon effect apparently activates limbic areas of the brain. Just why this should be so is unknown, but many scholars of rhythm have recognized that powerful feelings and desires (typically controlled by the limbic system) can accompany the production and/or perception of highly rhythmic activities. Dance in particular is known for the way it facilitates specifically erotic feelings, feelings which in most contexts cannot be expressed:

What is disturbing to orthodoxy is not merely that the rhythmic movement of dance has its analogue, if not its origin, in the act of sexual embrace. It is rather that dancing, like loving, affirms and celebrates an untamed spontaneity in the human, a free spirit, which is intuitively recognized as the enemy of society. Official authority has traditionally held the dance in suspicion; in the Western world the authority of the church, in particular, was marshaled against nearly all forms of dance for more than a millennium. (Montagu and Matson 1979, 162-3).

My lawyer pointed out a literary example of this phenomenon. The passage is from Alice Walker's recent novel *The Color Purple*:

I tell you something else, Shug say to Mary Agnes, listening to you sing, folks git to thinking bout a good screw.
     Aw, *Miss Shug,* say Mary Agnes, changing color.
     Shug say, What, too shamefaced to put singing and dancing and fucking together? She laugh. That's the reason they call what us sing the devil's music. Devils love to fuck. (Walker 1982, 99).

Lomax's discussion of the very precise and complex interactional synchronies of the Mbuti pygmies leads directly to considerations of dance and sexual intercourse:

Among the Mbuti ... support comes unbidden to everyone present in the form of tuned-in, interlocked synchrony of voice, of hand outstretched with food, and with naked, dancing, frolicsome, bodily synchrony. In the Pygmy culture we find social solidarity in its earliest and purest form in playful, affect-filled, mirror behavior. When we reflect that the peak in mirror inter- action is sexual intercourse, the act of love itself, we may surmise that social solidarity is a generalization of the act of generation. (Lomax 1968, 203).

The consciously or unconsciously perceived analogy of copulatory rhythm to dance (many more examples in Ellis 1927-8, VI, 515-16; III, 41-58; Partridge 1960, 99-102; and Rancour-Laferriere 1982b) and to other types of interactional synchrony may be at least one key to understanding the disinhibiting effect of rhythm. To my knowledge this analogy has not been seriously investigated, though it is often mentioned, and sometimes vigorously and prudishly rejected (e.g., Vygotsky 1968, 104). Another possibility is that the effort saved by the rhythmical automatization of any motor act somehow interferes with the energy necessary to maintain repression (see Laferrière 1978, 32-43, for some speculations). But much more will need to be known about the neurophysiology of the Condon effect (and its rhythmically exaggerated forms) before the emotive consequences of the effect (and thus the overall proximate mechanism) can be explained.

     The Condon effect must be at least a minimal requirement for "empathy" to occur (cf. Edelheit, above 219), and is probably a necessary step on the way to most cases of psychological identification. It may *not* take place if the interactants are from different cultures, or if there is hostility or some other attitudinal block. It is also thought that some forms of autism, schizophrenia, and dyslexia are due to self asynchrony and interactional asynchrony.

Speech and body synchronies, then, can profoundly affect the way individuals relate to one another. In sociobiological terms, the altruistic and/or maleficient relationships which determine the fate of genes are affected by interactional synchronies. This includes relationships which lead directly to the replication of genes, i.e., mating relationships: "the capacity for rhythmic entrainment in social communication, both verbal and nonverbal, may have been and may still be an important principle in human assortative mating . . ." (Jaffe and Anderson 1979, 20).[86] Or, to speak in terms of the semiotic characterization of human heterosexuality given above, interactional synchronies (especially singing, dancing, and copulating) facilitate the formation of complementary icons. A fullgrown hominid has an easier time of making a *parent* out of a member of the opposite sex if things 'click' on the level of interactional rhythms and synchronies. Indeed the ontogenetic background to adult interactional speech and body rhythms, like the ontogenetic background to language generally, resides largely in the interaction of a parent — the mother — with the child:

For both vocal and kinesic modalities, (a) coaction [simultaneous action] between mother and infant is the dominant pattern; and (b) the mother contributes to the coactive pattern by prolonging the duration of her behavior. Furthermore, the less frequent, noncoactive kinesic pattern revealed a rhythmic matching that presages the matching found in adult vocal conversation. (Beebe, Stern, and Jaffe 1979, 33; cf. Condon and Sander 1974; Kempton 1980, 72-74).

Beebe *et al.* suggest that the synchronous mother-child coactions in particular are the basis for the more "emotional" exchanges later in adulthood, such as choral speaking, cheering, and lovemaking. Again, it should not necessarily be concluded that enhancement of the mother-child bond was the (only) reason that such coactions and rhythmic interactions developed in hominid *phylogeny*. They were probably selected for just as much on the basis of adult benefits as childhood benefits. I have already mentioned facilitation of sexual interaction. There is also facilitation of adult altruism. In cultures where interactional synchronies are very precise and highly developed, individuals are more inclined to engage in helping and sharing

---

86. An interesting but neglected precursor of current research on speech and body rhythms, including the effect of such rhythms on assortative mating, was the work undertaken by Sievers and Becking on the so-called "Beckingkurven" during the first third of our century. For an overview, see Jakobson 1975, 53-5.

behaviors (Lomax 1968, 203). It is known that interactional synchronies (including "Yo-heave-ho" singing) greatly facilitate cooperative forms of labor (Bücher 1924; Ellis 1927-8, IV, 114; Hall 1976, 67-8), and that the precision and sophistication of interactional synchronies (in dancing, singing, and everyday activities) of a culture are a measure of the social stability and extent of female participation in subsistence activity in that culture (Lomax 1968, 201). Also, the already enumerated selectional advantages of language, which act at various age levels, presuppose a basis in interactional synchrony.

Indeed, the reason I have dwelt upon the remarkable recent findings in the area of interactional synchrony is to make a point about the evolution of language: since interactional synchrony and/or rhythmicity characterizes all linguistic interaction as we know it today, and since there are some indications of it in non-human apes (cf. Köhler's dancing chimps), then it is reasonable to assume that language itself must have originated and evolved in the context of such interactional synchrony and/or rhythmicity.

Further refinement of this hypothesis can be made in the light of the cross-cultural studies of rhythmic interation (dancing, story-telling, conversation, and especially singing) which have been made over the years by Alan Lomax and his colleagues (e.g.: Lomax 1968; 1982). Lomax has found that "a patterned approach to speaking where tempo is steadily maintained, where vocal stance varies little, and speech bursts are similar in length is found low on the scale of economic productivity, while varied styles are found at higher levels:" ". . . conversational style tends to become steadily less rhythmic and more varied, as societies grow larger and more complex" (Lomax 1982, 168, 169). Presumably the societies of ancestral hominids were less complex and less productive, economically, than those of today's hominids. Therefore it is likely that vocal interaction was more uniform, temporally, or more rhythmic in ancestral hominids than in today's hominids.

If rudimentarily rhythmic vocal interaction was one basis for the origin of language, then what would have been the social context for such interaction? Was it mother and child? Male and male on the hunt? Male and female in courtship? Group activities of various kinds?

Eventually, of course, all of these contexts would involve rhythmic vocal interaction. But for some reason the most popular idea has been that *sexual* interaction was the first and most important context for the rhythmic vocalizing that may have given rise to language. For example, the linguist Otto Jespersen declares:

... the genesis of language is not to be sought in the prosaic, but in the poetic side of life; the source of speech is not gloomy seriousness, but merry play and youthful hilarity. And among the emotions which were most powerful in eliciting outbursts of music and of song, love must be placed in the front rank. To the feeling of love, which has left traces of its vast influence on countless points in the evolution of organic nature, are due not only, as Darwin has shown, the magnificent colours of birds and flowers, but also many of the things that fill us with joy in human life; it inspired many of the first songs, and through them was instrumental in bringing about human language. In primitive speech I hear the laughing cries of exultation when lads and lasses vied with one another to attract the attention of the other sex, when everybody sang his merriest and danced his bravest to lure a pair of eyes to throw admiring glances in his direction. Language was born in the courting days of mankind; the first utterances of speech I fancy to myself like something between the nightly love-lyrics of puss upon the tiles and the melodious love-songs of the nightingale. (Jespersen 1950 [1922], 433-4).[87]

The reference to Darwin suggests that Jespersen had read the following, somewhat less romantic and less fanciful passage in *The Descent of Man*:

... Primeval man, or rather some early progenitor of man, probably first used his voice in producing true musical cadences, that is in singing, as do some of the gibbon-apes at the present day; and we may conclude from a widely-spread analogy, that this power would have been especially exerted during the courtship of the sexes, — would have expressed various emotions, such as love, jealousy, triumph, — and would have served as a challenge to rivals. It is, therefore, probable that the imitation of musical cries by articulate sounds may have given rise to words expressive of various complex emotions. (1885 [1871], 87; cf. *ibid.*, 566 ff.).

In other words, ". . . musical sounds afforded one of the bases for the development of language" (*ibid.*, 572). Darwin seems to neglect the rhythmic aspect of music in his speculations (Williams 1967, 12). But the essential idea about a musical origin to language was nonetheless quite explicit and recurrent in his writing on hominid evolution.

Perhaps some support for Darwin's idea is offered by the arguably 'musical' calls uttered in a sexual context by some non-human primates. In the Mentawei langur, the siamang, and various species of titis and gibbons, a sort of complex musical 'duetting' between mates is said to occur (Sebeok 1981, 227-9; Hrdy 1981, 46-8; Marler and Tenaza 1977, 1007-9). But such vocalizing also occurs in other contexts which are not necessarily (hetero-) sexual (for example, in several species of gibbon there is all-male chorusing). Also, it is very difficult to decide when vocalizing is 'musical' and when it

---

87. For a much more globally sexual theory of the origin of language, see: Sperber 1912.

is not. The highly rhythmical, multi-voiced coordinated vocalizing of gelada baboons, for example, is termed "musical" by Richman (1980, 241), and is compared with human choral singing. But geladas are a polygynous species, unlike the monogamous 'duetters,' such as titis and gibbons. Also, gelada chorusing does not seem to be especially associated with sexual interaction. Darwin may well be right about musical vocalization being one basis for the origin of language, but the evidence from our primate relatives does not indicate that such vocalization occurs only (or even primarily) in "courtship of the sexes." Indeed our own species employs music in contexts that are not necessarily sexual. To be sure, there are many cultures in which singing and playing of musical instruments are a part of courtship (see Ford and Beach 1951, 96-7, for some examples). In our own culture one can be reduced to tears upon hearing a melody that is associated with a recent lover ("They're playing our song"), or a man can be sexually excited by the combined presence of "wine, women, and *song*." But there can also be a great surge of emotion when one's national anthem is heard, or a military march is played. Personally, I find Slavic folk music more emotionally stimulating than any other kind of music because it is the most capable of evoking childhood memories and longings, that is, feelings that do not necessarily lead to sexual arousal. Perhaps all music operates by resurrecting emotionally colored (= limbically stored) memories, and is therefore one of the mechanisms of human neoteny discussed earlier in this book.

A survey of the known social functions of non-human primate vocalization ('musical' or otherwise) reveals many possibilities: group coherence, intergroup spacing, sexual relations, threat, call for assistance, mobbing, predator alert, etc. (see the reviews of primate communication by: Klopfer 1977; Oppenheimer 1977; Gautier and Gautier 1977; Marler and Tenaza 1977). At this point it would be foolhardy to guess at which (if any one in particular) of these might have furnished the earliest *linguistic* vocalizations with a selective or adaptive advantage. Similarly, when I listed some of the potential adaptive functions of language above (section 31), I was reluctant to speculate on which of the functions came first. Indeed I am not sure that it even makes sense to conceive of the "first" selective advantage that language possessed because 1) *several* advantages can theoretically be derived from a new organ/function, and 2) the precise structural point at which hominid vocalizations would have qualified as "language" has never been determined, and may in fact be arbitrary and therefore trivial.

36. Sex Differences and the Differential Rendering of Altruism

> . . . The duties and expenses of a master
> are part of his dominion, and define it,
> prove it, fully as much as his rights.
> *Marcel Proust*

One of the things about human vocalization that has unquestionable sexual significance is pitch. Ellis (1927-8, IV, 124), Mellen (1981, 142) and others have observed that the great difference in musical pitch between human males and females develops precisely at the onset of reproductive age. This difference is due to a supralaryngeal vocal tract that is longer in males than in females, to the longer and thicker vocal cords in males, and to the efforts of males to speak as though their supralaryngeal tracts were longer and larger than they actually are (Lieberman 1975, 178; Eakins and Eakins 1978, 90-92). More remotely, the difference is due to a surge of testosterone production and consequent pituitary changes in the adolescent male. It is well known that removal of the male gonads before puberty produces a *castrato*, that is, a male with a singing voice in the contralto or soprano range of female or prepubescent singers.

In the popular imagination voice pitch is closely associated with sexual matters. Eakins and Eakins (1978, 98) report a joke that fallaciously exploits the connection of high pitch with castration:

[There is] the old joke about the male swimmer being chased by several sharks. "Help! Help! Help!" he shouted in a deep, low-pitched voice. As the sharks streaked by and bit him, he squeaked in a falsetto voice, "Too late! Too late!" (cf. Legman 1975, 465).

Darwin says that "women are generally thought to possess sweeter voices than men, and as far as this serves as any guide, we may infer that they first acquired musical powers in order to attract the other sex" (1885 [1871], 573). Ellis, on the other hand, focuses on the sexual attractiveness of the male voice, and observes that "in novels written by women there is a very frequent attentiveness to the qualities of the hero's voice and to its emotional effects on the heroine" (1927-8, IV, 130 — the influence of Stephen Guest's voice on Maggie Tulliver in *Mill on the Floss* is cited).

It is no doubt true that the voice of the opposite sex exerts some attraction on heterosexual individuals. One can argue that the selective value of this attraction at least partially explains why the voice difference between the sexes appears precisely at reproductive maturity (it would not make sense for the difference to appear before, because no extra offspring would result, and if the difference appeared well afterward, one would be inclined to look at some area other than sexuality for a selectional advantage).

I say, however, that sexual attractiveness "partially" explains the vocal difference because initially, in a non-human ancestor, the deeper male voice would have been only a side effect of selection for bigger and more competitive males, and would also have appeared at the onset of reproductive ability. In other words, the voice of the opposite sex probably became attractive as much because of changes in the perceiver as because of changes in the voice perceived.

It is essential to recognize that the voice which changes at puberty is male, not female. The effect of this change is for the adult female voice to be more like a child's voice than the adult male voice is. In biological terms, the adult female voice is more neotenous than the adult male voice is.[88]

But this difference is not an isolated one. Darwin was perhaps the first biologist to observe that the mature human female more closely resembles a child than does the mature male (1885 [1871], 557). The relatively high-pitched, melodious female voice is just part of a complex of female features, some of them sexual releasers, and some of them neotenous, that owe their existence in part to what Alexander and Noonan (1979, 459) have called "the selective value of being a juvenile, or of giving that impression" (cf. Guthrie 1976, 161-2; Baer and McEachron 1982, 83-4). These features include, in addition to the pitch difference already mentioned, the following:

1) The more globular shape of the head in the female than in the male (Montagu 1974, 70), which is due to less pronounced brow ridges, relatively shorter mandible, generally more delicate and smooth structure of skull bones, and more adipose tissue in the cheek area. This shape is more "infantile" (Ellis 1914, 88ff.) than the shape of the male skull, and has more in common with the altruism-releasing "Kindchen-schema" ("baby face" – Lorenz 1943; Eibl-Eibesfeldt 1975, 490ff.; Eibl-Eibesfeldt 1971, 149; cf. Reynolds 1981, 246; Guthrie 1976, 165; Wickler 1972, 255-65; Sternglanz et al. 1977) than does the shape of the male head.

2) The greater degree of anatomical 'roundness' in females generally – rounded shoulders and knees, large, hemispherical breasts, and larger buttocks than in men. This 'roundness' may suggest the chubbiness of a child, and is in part due to

---

88. I am aware that the adult supralaryngeal vocal tract (male or female) could *not* be *so* neotenous as to resemble that of an infant. If it were, then adults would be incapable of producing language (Lieberman 1975, 179).

3) The greater amount of subcutaneous body fat in females than in males (Reynolds *ibid.*).

4) The greater hairlessness of females than males (see Alexander and Noonan 1979, 451-2; Ellis 1914, 519; Reynolds *ibid.*; Guthrie 1976, 162).

5) The smaller size of females relative to males (Reynolds *ibid.*; Wickler 1972, 264).

6) The slightly greater behavioral neoteny of females (cf. Keith 1948, 198, who says that women are more likely to retain "youthful mentality"). Women on the average smile more, cry more, scream more, permit themselves to be touched more, disclose more about themselves, are more compliant, more likely to be agoraphobic, and generally more affiliative than men are (see: Thorne and Henley 1975a, 290-305; Lynn 1974, 141-2; Maccoby 1966; Maccoby and Jacklin 1974[89]; Henley 1975; 1977; Eakins and Eakins 1978; Morris 1977, 137-8, 230-38; Bardwick and Douvan 1972; Bardwick 1976, 114-34; Rohrbaugh 1979, 218-40; Dowling 1981; Seidenberg and DeCrow 1983; Lewis 1976, ch. 14; Deaux 1976, ch. 6; Lombardo *et al.* 1983).

Quite a few of the features listed here are utilized in exaggerated form in the depictions of females by magazine and newspaper advertisements (Umiker-Sebeok 1981; Goffman 1979).

Janssen-Jurreit (1982, 192-3) makes the interesting observation that the greater degree of female neoteny[90] has been used to support arguments

---

89. Most of the studies cited in the Maccoby and Jacklin survey are of sex differences in *children*. An evolutionary biologist would not be surprised, therefore, at how few unambiguous sex differences Maccoby and Jacklin were able to dredge up. Sex differences in sexually mature, reproducing organisms are much more likely to be the products of selection, and therefore more likely to exist, than sex differences in sexually immature organisms. It is revealing that, of the following four sex differences that Maccoby and Jacklin believe are "fairly well established," three are most prominent after the onset of adolescence:

   1) Girls have greater verbal ability than boys. This difference first appears in early adolescence and increases in magnitude through adolescence. The tests involved measure both language production and perception.

   2) Boys have greater visual-spatial ability. The male advantage in this area is most pronounced in adolescence and adulthood.

   3) Boys have greater mathematical ability. Again the difference between boys and girls appears and increases during adolescence.

   4) Males are more aggressive. This is true of both children and adults in all of the cultures which have been studied by experimental psychologists.

   (*Ibid.*, 351-352).
   An interesting problem for future researchers is to determine which of these distinctions might involve neoteny and which involve terminal addition.

90. She does not use the technical term.

both for inherent female inferiority and for female superiority. Thus the philosopher Arthur Schopenhauer concluded that "women are suited to be nurses and educators by virtue of the fact that they themselves are childish and shortsighted — in a word, big children all their life: a kind of intermediate stage between the child and the man, who is the actual human being" (as quoted by Janssen-Jurreit, 193; see Hays 1964, 205-10 for an account of Schopenhauer's misogyny). On the other side we have the noted feminist Ashley Montagu who, in his book *The Natural Superiority of Women* (1974) says: "the female, in most respects, is a more highly fetalized type than man, and adheres more closely to the line of evolutionary development indicated by the child than does the male" (72); "in this trend woman, as compared with man, stands in the vanguard of the evolutionary process" (73; cf. Ellis 1914, 519).

Both of these opposed positions strike me as unwarranted. In an evolutionary context neither sex can be said to be more or less "human" than the other, nor can one sex be said to be more or less "progressive" than the other. Such judgments have no place in biology. But judgments about neoteny and the elicitation of altruism do. The adult human female appears to possess more neotenous and/or care-eliciting features than the human male does. This makes sense because, on balance, adult females are more in need of altruism from the opposite sex than adult males are. Such a contrast does not make it any less true that *both* male and female humans are more neotenous than the *other* primates (see section 11 above). Room is also left for the human male to be more neotenous than the human female in some particular contexts. For example, the soldier recently wounded on the battlefield will probably behave more neotenously than the female nurse who cares for him.[91]

---

91. It is reasonable to assume that various signs of poor health are care-eliciting stimuli (cf. Morris 1973, ch. 5), and thus one consequence of war (usually fought by men) is for males to elicit altruism. Apart from the war situation, females apparently emit more health-related care-eliciting signals. According to a recent survey published in *Psychology Today* (October, 1982), women are more likely to report symptoms of ill health (especially symptoms of depression, irritability, tiring easily, headaches, crying spells, and nightmares) than men are (cf. Rohrbaugh 1979, 385-422; Lewis 1976, 228ff.). Married women in particular are likely to manifest signs of depression, phobic tendencies, and passivity, as Bernard (1972) establishes in an article which ends with the sentence: "Could it be that marriage itself is 'sick'?" (*ibid.*, 158). Yet it is generally known that women, including married women, have a greater life expectancy than men. If the typically feminine "sicknesses" are not fatal, and do not curtail reproductive success, then we have to consider the possibility that they were selected for because of their altruism-eliciting properties, and that they are more highly developed in women because of the facultative nature of male altruism.

The sexual asymmetry of neoteny does not at all preclude the operation of neoteny in *both* sexes when they are interacting. For example, a logical consequence of the complementary iconicities in the monogamous bond discussed above (section 18) is *complementary neoteny*: because both male and female see a parental icon in a mate, both are behaving neotenously vis-a-vis that mate. The psychologist Dorothy Dinnerstein expresses this quite clearly: ". . . both the things women say about the childishness of men and the things men say about the childishness of women have a basis in fact . . ." (1976, 86-7). But Dinnerstein also sees the sexual asymmetry of altruistic inclinations: "what female talent tends to be deprived of, starved for, is the quasi-parental nurturant support that most of us, male and female, still need in adult life from other adults" (*ibid.*, 194); ". . . female enterprise is malnourished" (195).

In other words, on balance males are judged to be less nurturant, less altruistic by nature. Feminists perceive this quite clearly when they speak of the "emotional invalidism" (Firestone) of males, or when they say "Women failed because they did not have husbands who devoted their lives to bolstering their egos and who freed them from the petty details of daily life" (Stannard 1977, 224, paraphrasing Lorine Pruette).

My lawyer is convinced that men are much more self-centered and narcissistic than women are. Men find it more difficult to "give" emotionally than women do. I think my lawyer is right (if we exclude adolescent girls, whose narcissism is extreme). In fact, the great self-centeredness of men is precisely a neotenous trait, one of the areas where the man is more like a child than a woman is, and an aspect of male behavior that should be expected from the facultativeness of male altruism (above, sect. 23). And it is curious that this neotenous trait in males must in the course of hominid evolution have been a selective pressure on females to develop altruism-eliciting mechanisms, including neotenous ones.

I have not yet mentioned the specifically linguistic aspects of female elicitation of altruism. The most complex and semiotically most interesting of all the sex differences are in fact the linguistic differences. An enormous literature on this subject has recently sprung up. Some specialists go so far as to speak of two distinct "genderlects." Related to the sex differences are the gender differences within the grammar of language itself. Some of the sex and gender differences have been found to be cross-culturally valid. The following is a compilation of those sex and gender differences which strike me as interesting from an evolutionary viewpoint. Some of the differences are admittedly still under dispute by the specialists, but the overall asymmetry conveyed by these differences is striking:

1) The volume or loudness of voice tends to be greater in men than in

women. This difference contributes to the perception of the male voice as authoritarian and the female voice as timid.

2) There is a greater overall linguistic ability and linguistic sensitivity in women which, as indicated above, may help the socially subordinate sex gain various kinds of altruism from the inferior altruists of the species (women also score higher than men on both sending and receiving *non*verbal signals).

3) In interaction between intimates (as opposed to public, mixed company interaction) it appears that the female takes more conversational initiative and generally speaks more than the male, though the male's silence or indifference on topics raised by the female can control the direction of the conversation.

4) There is some evidence that women make more (accomodating) adjustments in speech style when conversing with men than men do when conversing with women.

5) Women permit interruptions of their speech and tolerate changes of topic more than men do.[92]

6) Women are more likely than men to put an interrogative intonation on their declarative statements, or to attach tag questions to declaratives (aren't they?).

7) Women make more frequent use of hedging modifiers such as "I guess," "kind of," "rather," "about," "around," or modals such as "may," "must," etc.

8) A woman is more likely to make a request where a man would use an imperative ("Won't you please water the dog?" vs. "Water the dog!").

9) Women cross-culturally do not curse and use obscenities as much as men do, but prefer euphemisms. Also, the person most frequently mentioned in verbal abuse is a woman, i.e., the opponent's mother.

10) Women's speech is more polite and grammatically "correct" than men's speech (this entails the use of more prestige forms — a clear indicator of desire for upward social mobility).[93]

11) Women are more likely to be addressed by their first names, or be subjected to other familiar forms of address than men are.

12) Women use and tolerate hearing terms for themselves which are much more likely to be derogatory or trivializing than are terms for men — e.g., "spinster" vs. "bachelor," "witch" vs. "devil," "whore" vs. "whoremonger," "authoress" vs. "author," etc. There are many more sexually derogatory terms for women than for men in English and probably in other languages as well.

13) A female is more likely to take a male's name than vice-versa; her name is also more likely to proclaim her marital status than is a man's ('Miss' and 'Mrs.' vs. 'Mr.').

---

93. This particular topic is hotly debated by the linguists — see Philips 1980, 537-8 for overview. There is probably an interesting sociobiological paper lurking here. It should be entitled: "Hypergamy and Hypercorrection in the Human Female."

14) In languages which have grammatical gender at any level the masculine gender is usually unmarked, the feminine marked. For example, "he," "his," "man," "guy," "poet," "aviator," etc. are the general terms in English, while "she," "her," "woman," "gal," "poetess," "aviatrix," etc. are specific and could not be substituted in for such generalizations as *"Man* is mortal," *"Poets* are liars," "To each *his* own," etc. The result of such markedness asymmetry, according to some scholars, is the suggestion that women are or ought to be excluded from many areas of life, or that women are second-class citizens in a man's world. (See the following: Ayim 1981; Thorne and Henley 1975b; Fishman 1978; Lakoff 1977; 1975; Parlee 1979; Jespersen 1950 [1922]; Miller and Swift 1976; Kramer 1975; 1977; Schulz 1975; Swacker 1975; Philips 1980; Zimmerman and West 1975; Eakins and Eakins 1978; Key 1975, 147-57; Henley 1977; Weitz 1977, 189-93; Gregersen 1979; Kramarae 1981; Stanley 1977; Stannard 1977; Rosenthal *et al.* 1979; Knapp 1978, 416ff.; Wilson 1981; Rancour-Laferriere 1979b, 73-6; Bendix 1979; Waugh 1982; McConnell-Ginet 1980; Brown 1980; Martyna 1980; Bernard 1981, ch. 16; Maccoby and Jacklin 1974; Dundes 1980, 160-75; Deaux 1976, ch. 6; McMillan *et al.* 1977; Frances 1979).

Most of the listed items are of course manifestations of male dominance, as has been made clear in the literature of feminist linguistics. I take it as obvious that adult males, cross-culturally, tend to dominate or control adult females (more on this below, section 40).

But male dominance is itself a rather male-centered notion. There is no male dominance without *female* subordination or even deference, and there is no female deference without some kind of reward. When a woman behaves in a subordinate fashion, she does not usually do so because she is being held at gunpoint. She does so because she has something to gain from her subordinate behavior. In allowing herself to be dominated (however reluctantly) on various verbal and nonverbal levels, a woman is increasing the likelihood of receiving altruism. Conversely, in occupying a dominant position, a male is more likely to have to render altruism. This asymmetry of the sexes would appear to illustrate the general sociological principle put forth by Homans: authority over others is gained at the cost of having to reward others (Homans 1961, ch. 14; cf. also the "equity theory" of love relations put forth by Walster *et al.* [1978]; Dickeman's [1981] analysis of male rendition of altruism to females in purdah; and Blumstein's and Schwartz's [1983] finding that, in a large sample of American couples, belief in the male provider philosophy tends to be associated with greater perceived power of husbands).

For example, not only is a certain authority attached to the louder male voice, but the softer female voice requires the listener to pay careful attention, and such attention can be a prelude to helping behavior. When a

254 Signs of the Flesh

woman accomodates to the style of speech of the men around her, she is more likely to elicit their approval (cf. Kramarae 1981, 105), and social approval is a form of altruism. Men do not only tend to call women by their first names; women *tolerate* being called by their first names because the men who do so are more likely to be at a higher level than they are on the social hierarchy, and therefore more likely to be in a position to render altruism. Women typically tolerate being known by their husband's name ("Mrs. John Jones") because this makes them less responsible and more *dependent* in legal and financial matters. Grown women are *willing* to be called "girls" (i.e., be *icons* of girls — Ayim 1981) because girls are literally children who still require the altruism of parental investment. Women are more likely to ask questions and make requests (of men) because they are more in need of male altruism, which tends to be optional (while men give orders because they can take female altruism for granted, though the women who obey men's orders may be doing so out of a condescending attitude toward men who, like cantankerous children, have to be humored). Women are more likely than men to be labeled with sexually derogatory epithets not only because men typically have a derogatory attitude toward women, but also because most of these epithets refer specifically to a transaction in which the male renders financial altruism (e.g. — "whore," "floozy," "hooker," "hussy," "honey pot," "slut," "tart," "wench," etc.[94]). The prostitute is the "paradigmatic woman" (to quote Julia Stanley 1977) because she is the one who is most honest and forthright about the fact that she is eliciting male altruism. The typical housewife/mother, on the other hand, lives off the male in a more covert fashion. Here is now Stanley, in part reinventing the wheel of early twentieth-century feminism, puts it:

The state of marriage, signified by the application of the term *wife,* is one in which the man pays and pays, sometimes for life, for his use, and exclusive property rights, of one woman. What we can see ... is a movement from general terms, applicable to any woman in the world, to the specific term *wife.* The more time and money that a man is willing to invest in a woman, the more he legitimizes her existence in our society. But it all comes down to the same thing. (*ibid.*, 315; cf. Leghorn and Parker 1981, 126; Ehrenreich and English 1979, 25, 304, 320).

This "same thing," as I see it, is male altruism, not merely male sexual pleasure. Whether the female is a "streetwalker" or is "barefoot, pregnant, and in the kitchen" — she is being *paid* for what she does.

The feminist Signe Toksvig declared in 1921 that women essentially

---

94. Healey (1980, 181) has found nearly 2,000 terms for "prostitute" in English.

exchange their maiden names for "bed and board for life" (Stannard 1977, 193). In 1902 another feminist, Olive Schreiner, castigated her fellow-females for allowing themselves to be dependent on male wealth (Ellis 1927-8, VI, 408; cf. Ehrenreich and English 1979, 105-6). The anarchist feminist Emma Goldman characterized marriage in 1917 as an institution that ". . . makes a parasite of woman, an absolute dependent" (Goldman 1972[1917], 230). There is, Goldman says, "no need for the woman to know anything of the man, save his income." What distinguishes marriage from love, according to Goldman, is the emphasis on the husband's ability to render financial altruism to the wife, or on the wife's ability to exploit that altruism:

> The moral lesson instilled in the girl is not whether the man has aroused her love, but rather is it, "How much?" The important and only God of practical American life: Can the man make a living? Can he support a wife? That is the only thing that justifies marriage. Gradually this saturates every thought of the girl; her dreams are not of moonlight and kisses, of laughter and tears; she dreams of shopping tours and bargain counters. This soul-poverty and sordidness are the elements inherent in the marriage institution. (*ibid.*, 228).

One does not have to agree with Goldman's politics, or with her idea that love and marriage have nothing common, to understand what she is saying about the advantages of receiving male altruism. Such advantages must at least partially explain the common finding that in industrialized societies not only men, but women too are only moderately interested in having women take more responsibility outside the domestic sphere (see: Goode 1963, 16-17, 54-66, 373; Bernard 1968, 10-11). Such advantages may also explain the finding that ". . . census data from 1977 indicate that although approximately one-half of the wives in the United States work, their income on the average is less than one-third that of their husbands.[95] In fact, another way of looking at these figures is that approximately four in five wives are financially dependent on the husband for an adequate standard of living" (Guttentag and Secord 1983, 31). Finally, the advantages of receiving altruism from males may also have something to do with the fact that even women who have demonstrated a superior ability to function outside the domestic sphere may nonetheless suffer from a "cinderella complex" or a "fear of success" syndrome (see: Dowling 1981; Horner 1972; Deaux 1976, chs. 4,5). Apparently, the mechanisms that keep adult females on the

---

95. Ivan Illich (1982, 22-66) reviews some of the abundant evidence for economic discrimination against women in industrialized countries. Illich's hostility to sociobiology (*ibid.*, 75ff.) as well as his refusal to take female reproduction seriously (*ibid.*, 35-6) hamper his effort to further understand sexual economics, however.

receiving end of adult male altruism are rather difficult to dislodge.

Earlier in this book I made the point that in cross-cultural perspective, a woman's altruism toward offspring tends to be taken for granted (from a sociobiological viewpoint, this follows from a woman's initial obligatory investment in offspring.) But the man's altruism is not to be taken for granted. It is something optional and special, and tends therefore to be perceived by male and female alike as justifying male dominance. Or at least the female resentment against male dominance can be curbed or hidden when attention is focused instead on the male breadwinning role. When female resentment does surface, and males are reminded that females can be as (or more) altruistic than they are, then they may react by feeling betrayed, hurt, and angry (Goode 1982, 139-40). As with the absence of female orgasm, the 'delicate male ego' is damaged (above, section 7). If a woman is willing to fake her orgasms in order to hold on to a male, so too she will probably treat his altruism as more significant than it really is in order to keep him. In fact the woman who does not exploit the various avenues for building the male ego may lose both male altruism and opportunities for insemination, and may thus not be as successful, reproductively, as her less feminist sister. But in building his ego she is of course putting herself down, lowering herself to the level of a child. Feminine wiles may capitalize on a man's infantile tendencies, but they infantilize the woman even more.

I would not want to claim that all the linguistic differences between the sexes make women more like children than men are. Not much research has been done on male vs. female linguistic similarities to children. But most linguists would probably provisionally agree that both women and children, as opposed to men, are interrupted more in their speech (see Kramarae 1981, 93), use fewer obscenities, ask more questions, make more requests (as opposed to using imperatives), allow the more familiar forms of address to be directed at them, and are more likely to be referred to by derogatory terms.

I also do not wish to claim that all the listed linguistic characteristics involve female mechanisms for eliciting altruism. The lesser use of obscenities by females, for example, cannot be viewed as a mechanism *per se*. Rather, it is probably just a logical consequence of the fact that other emotional outlets than swearing exist for women. Where a woman would be permitted a tearful tantrum, for example, a man might have to resort to a stream of obscenities (cf. Montagu 1967, 87).

The child-like aspect of woman's subordinate social position has been repeatedly discussed in the feminist literature. Shulamith Firestone's feisty chapter "Down with Childhood" is a good example. Firestone acknowledges that "women and children are always mentioned in the same breath" (1970, 81), as in the expressions "Women and children first!," "Women and children to the forts!" Any sociobiologist would agree with Firestone's statement that "the heart of woman's oppression is her childbearing and childrearing roles" (*ibid.*). According to Firestone, the "myth of femininity" is closely paralleled by the "myth of childhood":

Both women and children were considered asexual and thus "purer" than man. Their inferior status was ill-concealed under an elaborate "respect." One didn't discuss serious matters nor did one curse in front of women and children; one didn't *openly* degrade them, one did it behind their backs. (As for the double standard about cursing: A man is allowed to blaspheme the world because it belongs to him to damn — but the same curse out of the mouth of a woman or a minor, i.e., an incomplete "man" to whom the world does not yet belong, is considered presumptuous, and thus an impropriety or worse.) Both were set apart by fancy and nonfunctional clothing and were given special tasks (housework and homework respectively); both were considered mentally retarded ("What can you expect from a woman?" "He's too little to understand."). The pedestal of adoration on which both were set made it hard for them to breathe. Every interaction with the adult world became for children a tap dance. They learned how to use their childhood to get what they wanted indirectly ("He's throwing another tantrum!"), just as women learned how to use their femininity ("There she goes, crying again!"). All excursions into the adult world became terrifying survival expeditions. The difference between the natural behavior of children in their peer group as opposed to their stilted and/or coy behavior with adults bears this out — just as women act differently among themselves than when they are around men. In each case a physical difference had been enlarged culturally with the help of special dress, education, manners, and activity until this cultural reinforcement itself began to appear "natural," even instinctive, an exaggeration process that enables easy stereotyping: the individual eventually appears to be a different kind of human animal with its own peculiar set of laws and behavior ("I'll never understand women!" ... "You don't know a thing about child psychology!"). (*ibid.*, 99-100).

The tie between women and children is so strong, according to Firestone, that women's liberation cannot be separated from children's liberation: "we must include the oppression of children in any program for feminist revolution . . ." (*ibid.*, 118). Historically, this programmatic tie has in fact always existed: "the feminist movement emerged as a defense community for the interests of women and children" (Janssen-Jurreit 1982, 191).

The tendency of many feminists to want to include children's liberation with women's liberation only underlines the traditional connection of women and their burdensome children, and can paradoxically have a rather unliberating effect. Fighting for two political causes rather than one can decrease the potential success of each. Just as Lenin and his colleagues eventually shed their feminism in the process of increasing their political power in Russia (the Soviet Union to this day remains a sexist nation), so too feminists may find it easier to attain their political-cultural goals by not being concerned with children's liberation.

However, it is conceivable that some of the means for achieving children's liberation are identical to those for attaining feminist goals, and thus there may not be a debilitating diversion of energy. For example, it could be argued that

1) use of contraceptives,
2) access to abortions,
3) greater involvement of men in the domestic sphere,
4) greater involvement of women outside the domestic sphere,

would enhance the lives of children *and* promote feminist interests. But of these items, 1), 2), and 4) could also very well decrease the *reproductive success* of feminists. Contraceptives and abortions clearly reduce the number of births. It is known also that, for the societies studied, the public status of women (as measured by education, income, and occupation) tends to be inversely related to birth rate (Bernard 1968, 8; Westoff 1978, 55). Birth rate, though, is not necessarily a fair index of the rate at which offspring reach reproductive age (cf. Shepher 1983, 20-21). But it seems obvious, a priori, that a feminist who chooses to space children in order to enhance child care *and* spaces them because she wants to be heavily involved in non-domestic pursuits will probably bring fewer offspring to reproductive age than a woman who is motivated by only one (or neither) of these reasons. To this extent, then, women who try to live in accordance with the goals of both feminism and children's liberation are probably reducing their own reproductive success. I would go one step further and say that feminists generally, whether or not they have any particular interest in improving the lot of children, have less reproductive success than non-feminists. Insofar as some elements of feminist ideology delete potential offspring or consistently withhold potential altruism from offspring (which is not to say that *all* elements of feminism entail these things), then feminists always run a greater risk of lowering reproductive success than non-feminists.

What may be an ideological gain could thus become a loss in the evolutionary long run. In the past female hominids have profited genetically from giving birth to children, being devoted to them, and acting like them. It remains to be seen whether women who become as unattached to and unlike children as men are will leave as many offspring reaching reproductive age as their downtrodden sisters. If they do not, though, it would not be the first time that a trait has managed to spread in a population despite its negative Darwinian fitness (see Cavalli-Sforza and Feldman 1981, 345). Feminist ideology, like religious celibacy or smoking can have a strong appeal to both males and females in certain cultural contexts, which is to say that it could be another example of a trait that spreads "under the force of cultural fitness, in opposition to Darwinian fitness" (*ibid.*).

I want to emphasize that, in pointing out the potential reproductive disadvantages of feminism, I am not polemicizing against feminism. In fact, as the product of an impoverished and devoutly Roman Catholic family of twelve children, I can personally testify to the horrors of reproductive success, and I would never wish such success on any woman. Nonetheless, I have to observe that eleven of my mother's children have since produced offspring themselves, and that this enormous reproductive multiplication would never have occurred if she had gotten some feminist sense into her head.

37. The Supreme Parent is the Supreme Scapegoat

One of the things Freud is most famous (or infamous) for among feminists is the question he once addressed to Marie Bonaparte: "What does a woman want?" ("Was will das Weib?" — Jones 1953-7, II, 421). To ask this question was to reveal not only that Freud had some difficulties understanding women (even the founder of psychoanalysis was supposedly bamboozled by the "feminine mystique"), but was also to reveal an insight: a woman *wants* something.

It would not have been interesting for Freud to ask: "What does a *man* want?" Men do want things from women, but the fact that women want things from men is of much more consequence because, historically women have had much more trouble getting things from men than men have had getting things from women.

In her book *What Women Want*, Yates (1975) answers Freud's question by reviewing the many explicit goals of the women's movement, such as: rights and opportunities equal to those available to men, cessation of discrimination against women, access to abortions and contraceptives, more male involvement with childcare, maternity leave benefits, more opportunities for forming solidary relationships with other women, abandonment of the sexual double standard, etc.

But of these (and the many others proposed by feminists) there is one which, from an evolutionary viewpoint, stands out: what women primarily "want" is more long-term male assistance in their lives. All of their altruism-eliciting signals, including the neotenous ones, are ways of expressing this "want," and have been selected for essentially because they end up benefitting the offspring of the females emitting them. Even when immature females direct altruism-eliciting signals at their fathers (and mothers), they are benefitting future offspring because they are getting some training and practice in how to elicit altruism from a future mate.

I put the word "want" in quotation marks here because it refers to ultimate matters, something that maximizes the fitness of the genes which happen to be originally housed in a female body. At a more proximate level, that is, at a level perceived as need or desire, long-term male assistance with offspring may not be the most important thing a woman wants from a man at all. Rather, she is more likely to want from him the sort of things that will make her feel good. For example, she will typically want to have orgasms with him (above, sections 1-9). She may not know consciously what it takes on his part for her to have orgasms, but she does know what feels good and what does not feel good. Typically she will do neotenous or childlike things as part of her work on the relationship with him. If she succeeds in this project she has not only learned that he is a safe bet for a long-term involvement with her, but she has in effect learned that he is also a good candidate for long-term care of her offspring. What could be a better semiotic index of his future willingness to care for *children*, after all, if not his present willingness to respond to the *child-like* signals she emits? Conversely, his own childlike behaviors, which add up to the "vulnerability" she is looking for in a man, serve to indicate future compatibility with and attachment to children (but he should not be *too* "vulnerable" if he is going to be a competent altruist – a contradictory requirement that, again, may leave him wondering: "*What* does a woman want?").

Among the many feminists who have addressed Freud's famous question, there is one whose answer is unique: "*what women want is to stop serving as scapegoats* (their own scapegoats as well as men's and children's scapegoats) *for human resentment of the human condition*" (Dinnerstein 1976, 234, her italics). But in what sense is woman the "scapegoat" of humankind?

Consider some of the better known hostile practices and attitudes relating to women (I refer to a variety of cultures and societies). Their clitorises are removed. Their feet are bound. Their faces are veiled. They are claustrated in harems. They are to be avoided before the hunt, when they menstruate, or after they give birth. They smell like fish. Their vaginas are lined with teeth ("vagina dentata"). They "henpeck" and "pussywhip" their men. They envy men their penises. They are intellectually inferior to men. They cause mental disease in their children ("schizophrenogenic mothers"). They either "reject" or "overprotect" their children. When they are stepmothers they are by definition "evil." They are synonymous with death ("mother earth," "the womb is the tomb," "femme fatale," "Mater genuit – mater recepit," etc.). They are witches who cast evil spells on men, women, and children. They are demonic seductresses with unspeakable power over men. They are sexually insatiable. They sap a man's sexual strength. They are sirens who lure men to their deaths. They are medusae who turn men to stone. They are cannibals who kill and devour their children. They are "Jewish mothers" who specialize in making their children feel guilty. They are incompetent drivers. They spoil male friendship. They are an alien and inferior "Other" incapable of existing as a "Subject" of their own. They have no sense of justice or morality. They are blood-thirsty Amazons. They are shrews to be tamed.

The list seems endless (whether or not specific attitudes listed have any validity is another question). There are, of course, some beliefs and practices which some *women* advocate which are openly hostile toward *men*. For example, Valerie Solanas, in her castratory *SCUM (Society for Cutting Up Men) Manifesto* (1970), declares that "to be male is to be deficient, emotionally limited; maleness is a deficiency disease and males are emotional cripples" (3-4); "Every man, deep down, knows he's a worthless piece of shit" (7); "The male is, by his very nature, a leech, an emotional parasite and, therefore, not ethically entitled to live . . ." (36). Whether any of these highly charged assertions are in any sense valid is, again, another matter. But by and large, it is much easier to find manifestations of male antipathy toward women than female antipathy toward men. The widespread misogynistic trend has been documented by Mill (*The Subjection of Women*, 1869), Horney ("The Dread of Woman" – 1967[1932]), Lederer (*The Fear of Women*, 1968), Dworkin (*Pornography: Men Possessing Women*, 1981), Slater (*The Glory of Hera*, 1968), de Beauvoir (*The Second Sex*, 1961[1949]), Penzer (*Poison-Damsels*, 1952), Hays (*The Dangerous Sex*, 1964), Ehrenreich and English (*For Her Own Good*, 1979), Millet (*Sexual Politics*, 1970), Pomeroy (*Goddesses, Whores, Wives, and Slaves: Women In Classical Antiquity*, 1975), and many others. Feminists and nonfeminists alike have recognized the existence of male hostility toward women. Freud asserted that there is a "need on the part of men to debase their sexual object" (*SE*, XI, 187). Klein (e.g., 1977, 290-305) identified the mother's breast as the first object of *every* child's aggression. Slater tied the misogyny of men in ancient Greece to "penis envy in the mother;" "a society which derogates women produces envious mothers who produce narcissistic males who are prone to derogate women" (1968, 45).

Dorothy Dinnerstein's contribution to this topic is more interesting than most. In her book *The Mermaid and the Minotaur* (1976) Dinnerstein makes a correlation between universal misogyny and the universal experience of having been mothered:

What we learn, when we finally manage to escape the enforced obedience of childhood, is that we are still not our own bosses. And we feel in this shocking lesson an echo of the related lesson that we learned at the beginning under female auspices: that our powers to manipulate the environment are limited, and that there exist other human wills strong enough to prevail over our own. The echo adds depth to the mother-raised human's fear and resentment of female authority. That we are never, after all, wholly our own bosses means that the early mother has after all won. We have not escaped helplessness as well as we thought we would when we left her; the proof is that we must still submit to unconquerable forces: to the indignity of bodily illness, and the inexorability of bodily aging; to the thwarting of ambition; to unwelcome orders from more powerful adults; to the pressure of social custom and economic need and the ravages of natural disasters. Every such proof of our weakness and fragility silently activates a rage that goes far back to our first encounters with the angry pain of defeat. *If these first encounters had not taken place under all-female auspices, if women were not available to bear the whole brunt of the unexamined infantile rage at defeat that permeates adult life, the rage could not so easily remain unexamined: the infantilism could more easily be outgrown.* Under present conditions, what happens is that each setback imprisons us more firmly than ever in the patriarchal trap: inside it, safe under the control of a new boss, we can go on raging at the old one.

On an inarticulate level, then, *both men and women use the unresolved early threat of female dominion to justify keeping the infantilism in themselves alive under male dominion. (ibid.,* 190-1).

To use semiotic terms, males make scapegoats out of their mates (and often other women) because their mates are icons of their formerly resented mothers. Females too resent the power their mothers once held over them and, escaping from the dominion of their mothers, settle for the male dominion which the male-imposed iconicity entails. According to Dinnerstein, this sexist situation will cease, or at least will be modified when the necessarily tyrannical relationship between parent and (male or female) child becomes de-stereotyped, sexually. That is, although control over the child cannot be relinquished if the child is to survive, the controller can at least be made to be male for half of the time. Thus, the idea goes, when the child grows up it would not take revenge specifically on women, i.e., women would stop taking it out, "masochistic" fashion, on themselves, and men would stop taking it out, "sadistic" fashion, on women. Or at least men and women would be equally victimized by this new kind of child rearing, rather than unequally, as in the past. Neotenous or regressive aspects of relations between the sexes would not disappear, but a certain androgynous flexibility would now be possible:

There is no reason to suppose that our need for games of the now-you-be-the-baby-and-I'll-be-the-grownup-for-a-change variety will disappear when early parental care is as much male as female. It is a legitimate need. The emotional repercussions of our long infancy, and the multilayered nature of our sentience, will inevitably still color and flavor adult life. But under those conditions the rigid male-female complementarity of emotional opportunity offered by sex should disappear. The game should become flexible, its make-believe roles more straightforwardly exchangeable and far more open to innovation. The feelings on which it bears should be available to be taken out and played with, so to speak, in a freer way, and in this unstereotyped play (unstereotyped not only in adult lovemaking but throughout the many years of childhood make-believe that precede it) more genuinely reworked, so that they both modify and are modified by what we now think of as adult awareness, with consequences for the deepening of this awareness which we can now only schematically imagine. (*ibid.*, 244).

If the androgynous future that Dinnerstein envisages were to actually come true, then the following joke would no longer be funny, or even in bad taste:

Why won't [name some plain-spoken, forthright female head of state, or congressperson, or controversial author] wear a miniskirt? Because she's afraid her balls will show! (ibid., 270).

Dinnerstein reports that even the most laid-back, flower-wearing long-haired males in her classroom "laughed explosively" at this riddle. Our society is a long way, in other words, from a future non-sexist structure. The reason for her students' laughter, to use the psychoanalytic terms implicit in Dinnerstein's work, is that even these males were not free of repressed hostility toward the mothers who once dominated them, and they therefore gave momentary expression to that hostility when opportunity came along in the form of a tendency-witticism (cf. *SE*, vol. VIII; Rancour-Laferriere 1982, 26-7).

Dinnerstein seems to undermine her own argument about the possibility of future egalitarian *cooperation* between the sexes when she declares that women at the leading edge of feminism are now more likely than ever to *hate* men: "It seems possible that now, for the first time in history, women in substantial numbers hate, fear, and loathe men as profoundly as men have all along hated, feared, and loathed women" (*ibid.*, 276). In fact, the "substantial numbers" of women who are discovering that they hate men are probably rather insubstantial on a world scale, limited as they are to a primarily American upper-middle class intellectual and political elite.

But granting that substantial enough numbers of both women and men eventually arrive at a point where hatred can be overcome and the lopsidedness of parental care evened out, would there be any less emotional ambivalence in adult relationships? According to Dinnerstein, the child in every grown-up resents as much as loves the old parental authority and blames that authority for everything that is evil. But there is no reason to believe the ambivalence would automatically disappear if the authority were no longer stereotypically female. Male and female grown-ups would continue to make mates into the old authority figures who are hated as much as loved. People who would be no more "mother-raised" than "father-raised" should be just as capable of this emotional intensity as their "mother-raised" ancestors.

There is also the question of whether it is even possible to have people who are other than "mother-raised." Presently the possibility is only theoretical: "there is no human society in which males have primary responsibility for care of offspring or even share this responsibility equally with females" (Konner 1981, 33). In her book *The Reproduction of Mothering*, Nancy Chodorow says:

> Women mother. In our society, as in most societies, women not only bear children. They also take primary responsibility for infant care, spend more time with infants and children than do men, and sustain primary emotional ties with infants. When biological mothers do not parent, other women, rather than men, virtually always take their place. Though fathers and other men spend varying amounts of time with infants and children, the father is rarely a child's primary parent. (Chodorow 1978, 3).

Chodorow believes that the female propensity to maternalness in not due to genes or hormones. Rather, mothering is "reproduced across generations" by means of "social structurally induced psychological processes." In Chodorow's psychoanalytic ('object relations') scheme, these are primarily two. On the one hand, mothers are closer to daughters than to sons: "Because they are the same gender as their daughters and have been girls, mothers of daughters tend not to experience these infant daughters as separate from them in the same way as do mothers of infant sons" (*ibid.*, 109). On the other hand, daughters are close to mothers for a much longer time than sons are: ". . . girls tend to remain part of the dyadic primary mother-child relationship itself. This means that a girl continues to experience herself as involved in issues of merging and separation, and in an attachment characterized by primary identification and the fusion of identification and object choice" (166). Or, in the psychoanalytic terms used above (section 15), the daughter's pre-Oedipal identification with the mother carries over into and is reinforced by the Oedipal identification with her. As a result, daughters tend to be both objectively more similar to, and perceive themselves as more similar to their mothers than sons to their fathers (also section 15). According to Chodorow, it is the fact that a woman never quite 'gets over' her complex, archaic relationship with her mother that makes her more likely to mother than a man:

> As a result of having been parented by a woman, women are more likely then men to seek to be mothers, that is, to relocate themselves in a primary mother-child relationship, to get gratification from the mothering relationship, and to have psychological and relational capacities for mothering. (*ibid.*, 206).

Compare Helen Deutsch: "in her relation to her own child, woman repeats her own mother-child history" (1944, 205).

 While a mother can regress to her old relationship with her mother in relating to her infant, the father of that infant cannot: ". . . having a child recreates the desired mother-child exclusivity for a woman and interrupts it for a man, *just as the man's father intruded into his relation to his mother"* (*ibid.*, 201, emphasis added). Thus, not only is the woman attracted to mothering for reasons which lie in her past, the man is pushed away from mothering for reasons which lie in his past.

Chodorow's psychoanalytic explanation of why mothers tend to be more inclined to mother than fathers are strikes me as reasonable, but highly incomplete. Other conceivable (and perhaps overlapping) reasons why mothers tend to be more "prepared" or "primed" (as sociobiologists would say) than fathers for the caring of offspring (especially in the early stages) include: 1) babies are gestated and born out of mothers' bodies, not fathers' bodies (some psychoanalysts believe [e.g., Winnicott 1960, 594] that a mother even identifies with the fetus she carries); 2) mothers are given unquestionably pleasurable stimulation of the nipples (and consequent uterine contractions) while nursing (Ellis 1927-8, IV, 26-30; Newton 1973; Rossi 1974, 17, 29), a stimulation which fathers obviously cannot have; 3) the act of nursing, which fathers cannot perform without a bottle, is accompanied by visual, tactile, olfactory, and acoustic stimulation of both parent and infant, and such stimulation probably contributes to building an emotional attachment in both parent and infant; 4) adult females are more likely to carry young infants against the left side of the body than adult males are, and thereby are more likely to provide the soothing stimulation of the rhythmic heartbeat (Lockard 1980b); 5) females are more likely to respond to the sight of an infant than males are (Lockard 1980c, 312-15); 6) mothers in all societies are expected to be maternal, and have in their formative years learned a maternal "role," while fathers typically have not.

It is remarkable how much of the mother-infant bond depends on what happens during the first few hours or days after birth. A number of studies have shown that enhancement of mother-infant contact right after birth results in mothers who later have more en face contact with, stand closer to, more frequently fondle, are less likely to abuse, and are more successful at breast feeding their infants than control mothers. Also, mothers are able to recognize the cries of their own babies shortly after birth, and the infant shows a preference for a nipple that is accompanied by a tape recording of its mother's rather than another woman's voice (for reviews, see: Kennell and Klaus 1979; Wilson and Lumsden 1981, 79-82; Lockard 1980b, 21-2).

Chodorow's notion that "bioevolutionary" or "evolutionary-functional" factors are irrelevant or contradictory to her proposed psychoanalytic factors is misguided. Her theory may simply describe one (of perhaps many) proximate mechanisms that have induced later hominid mothers to mother. All the proximate mechanisms, in turn, have to have been in the service of the ultimate selective reasons why mammalian females generally tend to be more devoted to their offspring than males, namely: females, by virtue of their obligatorily gestating and nursing offspring, make a greater initial energetic investment than males do, and are more likely to bring offspring to reproductive age by continuing that investment than by lowering it, since males cannot be counted on to take up much of the slack if it is slightly more to *their* reproductive advantage to be competing with other males for access to resources or to females. Note that this sociobiological account does not name specific proximate mechanisms, such as possible hormonal systems or a possible "maternal instinct." But it does not exclude these either. Chodorow's strong objections to hormonal and instinctual theories (the latter developed by such psychoanalysts as Alice and Michael Balint, and Therese Benedek) are simply irrelevant to what her evolutionist contemporaries (e.g., Daly and Wilson 1978, 56-79) are saying.

Whatever the proximate mechanisms are that make females more interested in mothering than males, they would have to be eliminated or neutralized in some fashion before Dinnerstein's ideal of truly equal parenting could ever be achieved (cf. May 1980, 109). For example, males would have to get some kind of sensuous and psychical pleasure from nursing, or both males and females would have to bottle-feed so as to eliminate the net libidinal difference. Males and females would have to become equally susceptible to/resistant to the cries of the child. Fathers would have to spend as much time cleaning the child, fondling the child, etc. as mothers do (in Sweden paid paternity leaves encourage this behavior, but even when Swedish fathers get very involved in childcare, children still prefer their mothers — Lamb 1982). If it turns out that the nine-month sojourn of the fetus in the mother predisposes the mother to later maternal behavior, either this sojourn would have to be eliminated (babies would be totally "test-tube produced"), or a corresponding mechanism predisposing males to mother would have to be invented. If hormones are involved, there would be injections of some kind, or pills. If parental role-modeling and identification with parents are involved, many substantial social changes would have to be made, changes that could make us unrecognizable to ourselves as we are now.

There is truly a brave new world of possibilities for parenting, a future world I will speculate on no further because past and present are already difficult enough. In the meantime, what Havelock Ellis said half a century ago still holds: "It is the mother who is the child's supreme parent" (1927-8, VI, 2). Unfortunately, as Dinnerstein has established, she remains the supreme scapegoat as well.

38. Male Dominance and the Male Organ

> I was the phallus that subjugated
> the woman ... .
>
> *Gregory Zilboorg*
>
> We tame our women with the banana.
> *Mundurucú informant,* quoted by
> Robert Murphy

As we have seen, female altruism toward offspring tends to be obligatory. Male altruism toward offspring, by comparison, tends to be facultative or optional. As a result, what typically goes on between the (adult) sexes is an exchange of altruism for power. That is, women gain care, provisioning, protection, etc. from men, and men gain some degree of dominance and control over women, who are their reproductive resources. On the early hominid scene this exchange probably took the primitive form characterized by Fox as: "Okay, you [males] get the monopoly – or the appearance of it anyway – and we [females] get the meat" (see above, 160). On any hypothetical future hominid scene where egalitarianism of the sexes might arise, the exchange would have to be at least partially reversed, as Gloria Steinem makes clear in her essay "What It Would be Like if Women Win": "Men will have to give up ruling-class privileges, but in return they will no longer be the only ones to support the family, get drafted, bear the strain of power and responsibility" (Steinam 1972, 184).

Given that adult males typically exercise some control or dominance over adult females, we may ask: what is the proximate mechanism (or mechanisms) whereby this control is exercised? Mechanisms for eliciting and rendering altruism are only half the story.

Conceivably, one could argue that the male's greater physical strength and fighting ability are his best weapons in the "war of the sexes." It would seem that, when all else fails, he can resort to physical coercion. There is ample cross-cultural evidence of physical abuse of women, particularly in the feminist literature (e.g., Leghorn and Parker 1981). But I am inclined to believe that such abuse is not the norm in today's hominid. Even the most gruesome statistics on wife-abuse do not indicate that *most* men beat their mates (see below, 281). Rape is not something males *typically* do, except perhaps in endemic warfare. The father who has sexual relations with his daughter usually does not use force. Furthermore, males fight wars primarily against each other, not against women per se. Extensive warfare does not even appear to correlate with male domination, cross-culturally (Whyte 1978b). Males in some societies often fight over females, but not against them. And when boys fight, it is with each other: "... boys are more dominant than girls, in the sense that they more frequently attempt to dominate others, but their dominance attempts are *primarily directed toward one another*" (Maccoby and Jacklin 1974, 273).

I would like to suggest (though I am not the first) that there is a far more effective weapon than brute strength for accomplishing male domination over females. This weapon is a mere signifier, the penis.

More than any other bodily organ, the erect penis (or a representation of it, often called the "phallus" or a "phallic symbol") traditionally signifies male dominance. As feminists and others have been arguing for some time now, phallocentrism and patriarchal power are inseparable.

Not that the penis does not have other physiological and semiotic functions as well. It eliminates urine, and it transmits genetic information in copulation. But when it comes to the signification of power, dominance, aggression, control, and related notions in human culture, the penis is, as Lacan (1966, 642) would say, "le signifiant sans pair."

Even non-human primates sometimes utilize the penis for aggressive purposes. For example, when male vervet monkeys (*Cercopithecus aethiops*) sit "on watch" in trees with their backs toward their own troop, their thighs are spread and their brightly colored genitalia – blue scrotum and extended or erect red penis – are exposed to any possible intruder from another troop (Wickler 1966, 424-25; see also Wickler 1972, 52-3). In squirrel monkeys (*Saimiri sciureus*) a male will thrust its erect penis at the face of another male. This behavior "... may be followed by vicious assault by the displaying male if the recipient does not remain passive and quiet during the act" (Ploog and MacLean 1963, 34; cf. Pruscha and Maurus 1976). More extreme are instances of "dominance mounting" by males on either males or females of the same species, as well as so-called "rage-induced copulations" of males with females that may or may not be in estrus (Wickler 1967, 110ff.; cf. Koford 1963; but see below, note 98). In all of these examples the originally sexual activity has apparently taken on a non-sexual, aggressive significance (cf. Strage 1980, 36ff.; Gajdusek 1970, 60; Chance 1961, 25; Morris 1977, 198). From a semiotic perspective, what was originally a behavior adapted exclusively for the transfer of genetic information (in the spermatozoa) from male to female has become a sign of the dominance of one individual over another individual. MacLean (1973a, 49) observes, for example, that the male squirrel monkey spreads its thighs and thrusts its erect penis at the head of another animal in courtship behavior *and* in aggressive behavior. In evolutionary terms, penile erection in a sexual context turned out to be a preadaptation for aggressive penile display — though at a more proximate level it was probably penile display in a territorial context that was the preadaptation (Wickler [1972], 51-2 postulates that penile display originally evolved from territorial urine-marking activities in which the urine is ejaculated by an erect penis; MacLean [1973a], 47-8 also believes the penile display is olfactory in origin, and that it has become visual in the higher monkeys).

A major breakthrough in the study of primate sexuality is MacLean's discovery of a neurological basis for penile erection. He reports the following results of experimentation on the squirrel monkey:

... the positive loci for erection in the forebrain and diencephalon are found distributed along parts of three corticosubcortical subdivisions of the limbic system.... First, there is evidence that they coincide with the distribution of known hippocampal projections to parts of the septum, anterior thalamus and hypothalamus. Second, they have been located in parts of the so-called Papez circuit, comprising the mammillary bodies, the mammillothalamic tract, the anterior thalamic nuclei and anterior cingulate gyrus. Finally, they have been found in parts of the medial orbital gyrus, the medial part of the medial dorsal nucleus of the thalamus and regions of their known connections. (1965, 205-6; cf. MacLean 1962).

No less important are MacLean's findings on the neurological connection between penile erection and aggression:

Within the space of a millimeter, one may pass from a point at which stimulation results in erection and an apparent state of placidity to one at which the electrical current elicits erection in conjunction with an angry or fearful type of vocalization and showing of fangs. As one lowers the electrode a little deeper, one may obtain only fearful or angry-appearing manifestations during stimulation, yet see erection appear as a rebound phenomenon after stimulation is terminated. (1965, 209-210).

One could hardly ask for a more substantive connection between the penis and male aggression.

The neurological evidence is not as detailed for humans, but there are some interesting facts. MacLean notes that frontal lobotomy patients (in whom the connections between the medial dorsal nucleus and the orbito-frontal and prefrontal cortex are severed) sometimes demonstrate bizarre, uninhibited sexual behavior (1962, 294). "Hypersexuality" can result also from deep fronto-temporal tumors (Blumer and Walker 1975, 206). Temporal lobe epilepsy has in a number of studies been associated with erectile failure (see Wagner and Green 1981, 45-6, for a review). It has been found that electrically produced lesions in parts of the hypothalamus, as well as hypothalotomy, obliterate or partially obliterate sexual behavior in male sex offenders (Money and Ehrhardt 1972, 240; Kelley and Stinus 1984, 20). It is also known that electrical stimulation of the septal region in human males can produce penile erection (Wagner and Green 1981, 44; Blumer and Walker 1975, 205).

MacLean draws parallels between his neurological findings on squirrel monkeys and Freud's earlier work on the relationship of sexuality and aggression (e.g., MacLean 1965, 210).[96] There is some evidence (summarized by Rohrbaugh 1979, 48-50; and Dixon 1980) that the male sex hormones or androgens are linked to male aggression, but we have already seen that some scientists regard androgens as "libido hormones" as well (above, 37). Glenn Wilson (1978, 65ff.) reviews the abundant psychological evidence for the connection between sexuality and aggression. It has been found, for example, that (especially male) subjects who are insulted and humiliated before writing T.A.T. stories produce more aggressive *and* sexual imagery than subjects who are not so treated.

Perhaps one of the preadaptive routes whereby some primates (including humans) came to respond to penile display as if it were an act of aggression is the phobia of snakes, lizards, worms and other elongate vermin typically occupying primate habitats (see Mundkur 1983, 218-42, for an overview of ophidiophobia in primates). A hominid ancestor who displayed his erect, hairless penis to conspecifics may have, in part, been taking advantage of their ophidiophobia via the same iconic route that, say, today's speaker of Yiddish-English slang follows when using the word for a snake, "schlang," to refer to the penis (cf. Wentworth and Flexner 1975, 738).

But with a directional difference. If indeed the anxiety we feel about a displayed penis is due in part to its similarity to a snake, then this would be an interesting reversal of the iconicity which occurs in dreams, slang, myths, ritual, etc., where, according to Freud (*SE*, V, 357; cf. Róheim 1945b, 264; Jones 1971, 94; LaBarre 1962, 53ff.) a snake is supposed to represent a penis, not vice-versa.

That snakes *can* be penile icons is easy to show, even without the help of the psychoanalysts. Once a year in ancient Lanuvium and Epirus a virgin priestess would remove her clothing and offer food to a snake in order to ascertain by the snake's acceptance or refusal whether the year's harvest would be good or not (Crooke 1896, II, 144). Among the Greeks it was believed that a woman could have intercourse with and conceive by a serpent (Welsford 1951, 421; Mundkur 1983, 251; MacCulloch 1951, 406). The Ewe of the old Slave Coast had a fertility cult in which women were "married"

---

96. Among today's Freudians, it is Robert J. Stoller (e.g., 1979) who has explored the relationship between sexuality and aggression/hostility in greatest depth.

272 Signs of the Flesh

to a snake (*ibid.;* the idea of a woman "marrying" a snake is known among the Zuñi, the Kafirs, ancient Greeks and Romans, and sundry other peoples — see MacCulloch 1951, 409-10). In India snake-worship is often associated with marriage ceremonies, and women may pray to snake images to conceive children (Crooke 1951, 416). Scott (1966, 72) quotes a certain J.H. Rivett-Carnac as saying of some Nagpur paintings that "the positions of the women with the snakes were of the most indecent description and left no doubt that . . . the cobra was regarded as the phallus." Many in India of course worship the explicitly phallic *lingam,* which may be entwined with snakes, or sometimes take the form of a snake (Ferro-Luzzi 1980; Mundkur 1983, 264). Among the Dahomeans "girls and women attacked by hysteria were supposed to have been touched by the serpent and thus inspired or possessed" (MacCulloch 1951, 400). A description of a snake-handling cult in southeastern United States focuses primarily on the ecstasies of the *female* practitioners:

A plump girl in a dark dress, her eyes closed, her face twisted into a moaning scream that somehow seems a pleasurable agony to her, is almost shaking herself out of the preacher's grasp on her arms as she jerks massively forward and backward. One young woman in a dark suit-dress lies slightly twisted on her back on the floor, the thumb of her half-opened right hand at her mouth, the left hand clasped at her turned-aside neck. The preacher places his left hand on her forehead, his right hand on her pubic region. (La Barre 1964, 320).

After a brief snake-handling episode, Bunn [the snake-handling preacher] turned the meeting to "healing of the sick, laying on of hands, and speaking in other tongues." The latter was perhaps the most spectacular event of the evening. Bunn lined up about twenty-five female followers all chattering simultaneously, and as he embraced them one by one they toppled over like tenpins. (*ibid.,* 326; see photographs in La Barre 1962).

La Barre regards the snakes as phallic objects eroticizing the relationship of the preacher and congregation (1962, 135, 157). Freud's method of healing here would not have been snake-handling, of course, but a few simple sessions of introspection on the couch. The religious ecstasy of these women bears an uncanny similarity to the *arc de cercle* and other phenomena of female hysteria. Freud's colleague, the Viennese gynecologist Rudolf Chrobak, might have given his whimsical prescription, "Rx *Penis normalis dosim repetatur"* (*SE* XIV, 15).

None of this is to suggest that snakes cannot have other, non-phallic meanings, depending on culture and circumstance (see Mundkur 1983 for an encyclopedic study of serpent cults, and below, section 45). But the phallic meaning does extend well beyond the confines of turn-of-the-century Vienna, as for example in the New Guinea Arapesh story in which a demon called a *Marsalai* takes the form of a snake and enters a woman's vulva (Róheim 1950, 436).

39. The Other Side

Many nonhuman primates have an interesting method of *countering* aggressive behavior with what appears to be a sexual sign. In at least fourteen species (including the hamadryas baboon, the chimpanzee, and various macaques), males as well as females "present" their hind quarters toward other individuals (Wickler 1967, 79-80). A given "presentation" greatly reduces the likelihood of being attacked, and is therefore believed by some ethologists to be a gesture of submission or appeasement. Wickler (*ibid.*, 84ff.) finds that there often exist resemblances between the color patterns of the hind quarters of males and females within the same species of primate, and concludes that these resemblances help the subdominant males utilize what was originally a female gesture (or, more proximately, anogenital scent-marking? – see Andrew 1964, 268-70). Insofar as the submissive or appeasing behavior of younger and weaker males prevents actual combat, the overall degree of agonistic interaction in the group is lower.

It is noteworthy that hind quarters presentation can be performed by either males or females, and sexual arousal is not necessarily involved. Solly Zuckerman, who did pioneering observations on hamadryas baboons, speaks of hind quarters presentation in this species as a "liberation of sexual responses from the function of reproduction" (1932, 232). From a semiotic viewpoint, there is an ability to use the hind quarters not only as an epigamic sign, but as a sign of submission as well. The Soviet semiotician Viacheslav Ivanov views the latter as a "figurative use" ("perenosnoe ispol'zovanie") of the originally sexual sign (1974, 85).

Wickler cites the following example for the human primate: "On very stormy nights the men and women of ancient Germany would stick their bared bottom outside the front door in order to appease [the deity] Wotan" (1972, 272). In Goodland's annotated bibliography of sexual customs there is mention of the Ait Yusi belief that fog can be dispelled by exposure of a boy's buttocks (1931, 348, 644). Among the Iatmul of New Guinea there are various ceremonial contexts in which a man shames himself or expresses mock submission toward another person by turning his buttocks toward and/or rubbing them against that person (Bateson 1958).

As many children in many cultures know, a parent sometimes cannot resist the urge to slap the child on its bottom. Such "discipline" can later turn up as an adult sexual preference. Consider the behavior of an (unnamed) New York City municipal official:

He wanted a girl to punish him, and it had to be a different girl every time, so Valerie told me to go see him. 'All you have to do is spank him, that keeps him happy,' she said, so I said 'Fine,' and I met George at his apartment. Right away he took me into the bathroom, and I thought, 'Boy, do I have a nut job.' He pulled down his pants and whimpered, 'I'm sorry, mommy,' and I said, 'You know you were a bad boy, you were using bad language and I know you went out with another woman who was telling you bad things and you were very naughty, you listened to her.' 'Oh, mommy, I'm sorry, I'm so sorry,' he said, whining and standing sort of scrunched over, jerking himself off.

I grabbed his belt and beat his buttocks very calmly, until they were a bright beet-red. (Janus *et al.* 1977, 167).

Not only does this man try to appease the hired mother-icon with his hind-quarters display, but he throws in verbal appeasement as well ("Oh mommy, I'm sorry, I'm so sorry"). Of course there is more happening here than appeasing display of hind quarters. The man is a masochist, that is, an individual who needs to suffer a certain specific kind of pain in order to be adequately aroused.[97] But as so often is the case in masochistic practices, it is the buttocks (*nates* in the old sexological literature) which are exposed to and stimulated by the 'dominating' partner (for clinical examples, see: Krafft-Ebing 1929, 131ff.; Reik 1941, *passim;* de River 1958, 60-8; Glasser 1979, 295). Other frequent masochistic fantasies and practices include being stepped or trampled upon, being ridden, and being constrained from bodily movement — all of which are reminiscent of aspects of dominance/submission behaviors observed in non-human primates.

---

97. Leopold von Sacher-*Masoch* (1836-1895) was a German author of Ukrainian origin who wrote novels, such as *Venus in Furs,* which depicted men who enjoyed being whipped or otherwise humiliated by women. The term "masochism" was coined by the pioneering sexologist Richard von Krafft-Ebing (1840-1902) in his *Psychopathia Sexualis* (1886; English edition 1929, 132).

40. The Power Asymmetry of the Sexes

Just as hind quarters display is not necessarily performed only by females, so too penile display is not only the prerogative of males. For example, females of the genus *Saimiri,* which have a very large clitoris and pseudoscrotal enlargement, display their genitalia as a dominance gesture (Wickler 1967, 112; cf. also MacLean 1973a, 50). A surprisingly large and prominent clitoris is present in many primate genera (Lowry and Lowry 1976, 29-32). In a way, female usage of the penile display is a 'lie' (just as male usage of the hind quarters presentation gesture is a 'lie'). The study of primate dominance relationships would thus definitely have to overlap with semiotics even in Eco's narrow "intensional" sense, for "... semiotics is in principle the discipline studying everything which can be used in order to lie" (1976, 7).

These two great 'lies' in the sexual life of some primates — hind quarters presentation by *males,* and penile display by *females* — suggest a distinct 'male chauvinist' orientation even outside of the human species. However equal the mimicry of one sex by another may be, the net effect is to connect dominance even more firmly to maleness. A specifically male gesture is what enhances dominance in females, while a specifically female gesture is what enhances submissiveness in males. There is no evidence that it is the other way around, i.e., that males mimic a female aggressive gesture or that females mimic a male submissive gesture.[98]

A similar asymmetry can be discerned in human language use. A very strong signifier of male aggression in English, for example, is the word "fuck," as in

> He fucked her.

But there is also

> She fucked him.

Both of these utterances can refer to copulation, *or* they can refer to aggression/maltreatment of some kind. In either case, though, the idea of what

---

98. It is probably not true that noncopulatory mounting always expresses dominance/ aggression, or that hind-quarters presentation always expresses submission/appeasement in non-human primates. Fedigan (1982, 100-101) points out several studies showing that there is no relationship between rank on a dominance hierarchy and the direction or frequency of male-male mounting (eg., Hanby 1974). She states that hindquarters presentation is more likely to be motivated by a "desire for affiliation" than by "either submissive feelings or a desire to appease." She does not state, however, what the difference between affiliativeness and appeasement/

276 Signs of the Flesh

the *male* does in the copulatory act seems to be primary. Quàng (1971b) reports that many English speakers even require a male subject of the transitive verb "fuck," so that the second of the above sentences would be downright ungrammatical for such speakers.[99] In any case, even for run-of-the-mill speakers, the second of the two utterances is more metaphorical than the first in that it suggests that a female is perpetrating a properly male, sexual-aggressive act. Similarly, of the two utterances

He acted demurely with her

and

She acted demurely with him,

one is more metaphorical than the other, namely, the first is more metaphorical than the second because the adjective "demure" is thought of as a quality of passivity proper to the human *female* (cf. also "coy").

Thus in English it is possible to use what is perceived as a properly female quality or act to refer metaphorically to a male's passivity and it is also possible to use what is perceived as a properly male quality to refer to a female's aggression. But it does not appear that the converse is true, that is, there seem to be no cases where 1) a properly female act or quality is used metaphorically to describe male aggression, or 2) a properly male act or quality is used metaphorically to describe female passivity or submission. Thus the following attempts at metaphor would probably require somewhat contrived contexts in order to make any sense:

---

submission could be. Also, it is conceivable that hindquarters presentation could mean different (though nonsexual) things in different contexts, as Wickler himself realized (1972, 212). Finally, the lack of correlation with rank in a dominance hierarchy| could mean that rank is being measured in an irrelevant way. In fact the primatologists are not at all in agreement on just how to measure dominance (for reviews, see Fedigan *ibid.*, 91-120; Hinde 1978; Mitchell 1981, 97-107). But even if the interpretation of penile/clitoral display and mounting as assertions of dominance, and the interpretation of hindquarters presentation as an expression of submission – were in some sense or in part wrong for *non*human primates, nonetheless the very anthropomorphism of the error would be more evidence that *hominids* did at some point come to interpret penile display/mounting as assertions of dominance, and hindquarters display as an expression of submission.

99. Compare French "foutre." The utterance "Jean fout Marie" is grammatical, whereas "Marie fout Jean" is ungrammatical (Gouet 1971). In Russian the equivalent verb is "ebat'," and it too does not normally have a female subject (DeArmond 1971, 103). Quite a few sexual verbs in English (besides "fuck") can have only male subjects (unless there is a passive construction). Thus it is possible to have "Dick bangs Jane," "Dick did it to Jane," and "Dick humps Jane," but speakers would reject "Jane bangs Dick," "Jane did it to Dick," and "Jane humps Dick" (see Baker 1975 for an illuminating discussion).

1) Bill henpecks his wife
   Sam is a real shrew
2) Jane is a momma's boy
   Sally is behaving like a sissy.

Other languages would of course have to be examined to determine whether this asymmetry is a general tendency.[100]

The associations 'dominance-male' and 'subordination-female' have of course existed in human cultures for millenia — e.g., the 'active-male' vs. 'passive-female' dichotomy proposed by Aristotle, the *yang* vs. *yin* of ancient Chinese philosophy, the *lingam* vs. *yoni* in Indian mythology, etc. As Havelock Ellis put it, "the more energetic part in physical love belongs to the man, the more passive part to the woman..." (1927-8, IV, 192).

The best known work on this topic in the psychoanalytic literature is by Helene Deutsch: "The anatomy of the sex organs leaves no doubt as to the character of their aims: the masculine organ is made for active penetration, the feminine for passive reception" (1944-5, I, 224); "... activity is the share of a man, passivity that of woman" (*ibid.*, 280; cf. Freud, *SE* VII, 219; Benedek 1968, 445; Bonaparte 1953; Forrest 1966, 23). But Deutsch adds an important caveat: "... it must be emphasized [that] passivity does not mean apathy or lack of sexual energy" (*ibid.*). Female sexual energy may in fact be very high in Deutsch's scheme. Similarly, the psychoanalyst Imre Hermann says: "... the man cannot penetrate the woman's body unless she actively presents it — i.e. actively makes herself accessible to him" (1935, 220; cf. Ellis 1927-8, III, 229; de Beauvoir 1961, 354-5). One is reminded of some of the primatological findings: "... females [among Japanese macaques] not only make genital presentations to males, they also initiate sexual interactions, and stimulate the continuation of series mounts, through particular vocalizations (estrus calls), facial expressions (an intense stare and lip quiver), body movements (hand slaps, head bobs, reaching back), mounting of the partner, and in some cases where the male fails to respond or to begin copulating, by literally pulling him up onto their backs" (Fedigan 1982, 145). But still, no matter how actively the (human or nonhuman) female works, there can be no copulation if the male is not responding enough to have an erection. For humans specifically, we may say that the female's sexual 'activity' is not necessary (she can even be raped), while the male's 'activity' of having an erection is necessary for copulation to take place (see: Horney 1967, 145; Mead 1975, 216-17; Lewis, 1976, 47; Murphy 1977, 20). It is in

---

100. A possible exception in English is the verb "bitch" which may be construed as a properly female act of aggression, and which can be used metaphorically in reference to males (e.g., "He bitched to his boss").

this sense that the dichotomy of 'active-male' *vs.* 'passive-female' has some logical validity.

In the anthropological literature there is Robert Hertz's famous essay "The Pre-eminence of the Right Hand" (1909), where Hertz speaks of a universal "law of polarity" that includes "a male side, strong and active, and another, female, weak and passive" (in Needham 1973, 10). Hertz gives this exotic example:

Among the Wulwanga tribe of Australia two sticks are used to mark the beat during ceremonies: one is called the man and is held in the right hand, while the other, the woman, is held in the left. Naturally, it is always the "man" which strikes and the "woman" which receives the blows; the right which acts, the left which submits. (*ibid.*, 14).

Compare the following militantly feminist characterization of heterosexual copulation in our own culture:

"The sex act" means penile intromission followed by penile thrusting, or fucking. The woman is acted on; the man acts and through action expresses sexual power, the power of masculinity. Fucking requires that the male act on one who has less power and this valuation is so deep, so completely implicit in the act, that the one who is fucked is stigmatized as feminine during the act even when not anatomically female. In the male system, sex is the penis, the penis is sexual power, its use in fucking is manhood. (Dworkin 1981, 23).

The remark about homosexuality is quite accurate, cross-culturally. Dundes (1980, 194) finds that "In almost any all-male society or male subsection of society, one finds a distinction between so-called active and passive homosexuality. Typically, the active homosexual has high status and prestige whereas the passive homosexual — who is often considered to be playing the part of a female — has low status and little prestige." An example is the ancient Greek distinction between the *erastēs*, who was the older, dominant male, and the *erōmenos,* the subordinate young male who played the passive role in a homosexual relationship (see Dover 1978, one of the best of the available treatises on Greek homosexuality). Wickler (1972, 228-9) discusses a practice of French youth gangs in which the "chief" sodomizes his subordinates. Bateson, in his classic theoretical study of ritual behavior among the New Guinea Iatmul, says that "during the early period of initiation [of boys] when the novices are being mercilessly bullied and hazed, they are spoken of as the 'wives' of the initiators, whose penes they are made to handle" (1958, 131). Vanggaard (1972, 105) reports that when T.E. Lawrence ("of Arabia") was captured by the Turks he was brought to the governor Hajim Bey and forcibly sodomized. This experience of "phallic aggression" left Lawrence's psyche permanently damaged.

Because the 'active-passive' opposition carries over into the homosexual realm Millet is able to cite both the heterosexual anal rape of a servant-woman in Mailer's *An American Dream* and the homosexual ravishment of a 'feminine' male by a 'masculine' male in Genet's *The Thief's Journal* as examples of the very same kind of "sexual politics" (Millet 1970).

However oversimplifying, vague, and undesirable the power polarity of the sexes may seem, there are some empirically established male-female contrasts in adult humans that tend to support it:

1) In 66.7% of the societies sampled, Whyte (1978a, 225) found that there is "an explicit view that men should and do dominate their wives."

2) Males are generally larger and more muscular than females, and are better fighters (Short 1979, 149; Symons 1979, 140).

3) Males tend to be more aggressive, more dominance-oriented, and more Machiavellian than females (Rohner 1976; Maccoby and Jacklin 1974, 227-74; Goldberg 1977). Most of the psychological and cross-cultural studies measure aggression in children, not adults. But just in case it is not obvious that adult males are more aggressive than adult females, I should mention war, which is fought almost exclusively by males (though the victims are often females). In the Second World War alone, a total of 14,943,062 human beings were killed by (mostly male) combatants, according to the 1982 edition of the *Information Please Almanac* (401). Lewis (1976, xiii) estimates that 100 million people have been killed in wars since the year 1900.

4) Males are less likely to be phobic or fearful (or are at least less likely to admit being afraid) than females (Gray and Buffery 1971; Maccoby and Jacklin 1974, 182-90; Dowling 1981).

5) Rape and other forms of sexual violence such as marriage-by-capture and Polynesian "sleep crawling" is perpetrated primarily by males, not females.

6) Husbands tend to beat wives, rather than vice-versa (cf. Rohrbaugh 1979, 350-68).

7) Males, though they tend to be slightly inferior to females in linguistic ability, use language in ways that subjugate women; also, the structure of language in many ways reflects or even facilitates the subordinate status of women (above, section 36).

8) The father (or in some situations the mother's brother) tends to have more authority in the family, cross-culturally, than the mother does, though in many domestic areas the mother is clearly in charge (Stephens 1963; Lynn 1974; Murdock 1967; Whyte 1978a, b; Goldberg 1977). Matrilineal societies in which neither a woman's husband nor her brother dominate her provide the greatest opportunities for female domestic and extradomestic authority (Schlegel 1972).

9) In a given society positions of leadership both within and outside kin groups are most likely to be occupied by males, and roles given highest status are attained primarily by males (though what is considered high status will vary from society to society – e.g. – medicine is a high status profession in the U.S., and most American doctors are males,

and although most doctors in the Soviet Union are women, medicine is a low status profession in that country: see Goldberg 1977; Mead 1975, 159; Whyte 1978a, 217; 1978b, 56-9; Rosaldo and Lamphere 1974; Friedl 1975, 7; Lowie 1920, ch. 8; Stephens 1963, ch. 6; Tiger 1969, ch. 4; Ember 1981, 545-6; Guttentag and Secord 1983; de Beauvoir 1961 [1949]; Lewis 1976, 56; Mill 1906; Stockard and Johnson 1979; Bullough 1973).

10) Even if a woman attempts to break out of her low status position she may have to struggle against obstacles that a male is less likely to have to deal with, such as the so-called "fear-of-success" syndrome and related fear of independence (the "Cinderella complex"), various kinds of discrimination against women, sexual harassment, etc. (see Rohrbaugh 1979, 218-40; Williams 1977, 185-7; Dowling 1981; Horner 1972).

11) Males are more inclined to (or less inhibited about) promiscuity than females are, cross-culturally (above, section 6).

12) Males are expected to take the sexual initiative (to "court" and to "proposition") in most contexts (see: Murphy 1977; Davenport 1977, 149; Ellis 1927-8, VI, 530; Maccoby and Jacklin 1974, 329; above, section 6; Ford and Beach 1951, 101-2).[101]

13) Males are more likely than females to suffer from castration anxiety. As argued below (section 45), such anxiety can serve as an index of the power asymmetry in the relationship between a male and a female, and can terminate the relationship, reproductively, if the female is perceived by the genitally anxious male as having too much power.

14) Females, assert some psychoanalysts either implicitly or explicitly (*SE XIX*, 161-2; Deutsch 1930; 1944-5; Endleman 1981, 199; Rado 1933; Bonaparte 1953; Horney 1967, 214-33) are more likely to be masochistic than males.[102] Psychoanalysts and nonpsychoanalysts alike have questioned this claim (e.g.: Blum 1977; Reik 1941; Millet 1970, 195-6; de Beauvoir 1961, 373ff; Rohrbaugh 1979, 327-8; Greer

---

101. This is a statement about social *expectations*, and women have many ways of initiating sexual activity covertly. Friedl (1975, 91) suggests that females may openly initiate sexual activity as much or more than men do in parts of Polynesia and West Africa. Broude and Greene (1976, 415) report that, in 18% of the 34 societies of the Standard Sample for which information was available, women always or usually take the initiative in premarital sex, but in 50% of these societies men always or usually take the initiative. Hite (1981, 1119) reports that 80% of the men in her anonymous general sample of American men say that they usually make the initial sexual advance. Blumstein and Schwartz (1983, 206-8) found, in their sampling of American couples, that the male is the initiator in more than twice as many couples as the female is.

102. Outside of psychoanalysis we find Krafft-Ebing (1929, 196) saying: "...it is easy to regard masochism in general as a pathological growth of specific feminine mental elements, — as an abnormal intensification of certain features of the psycho-sexual character of woman, — and to seek its primary origin in that sex." Feminist Betsy Belote (1976, 335) argues that "the dynamics of masochism are crucial to an understanding of woman's psychological, social and sexual relationship to man in this culture."

1972, 94ff.; Ehrenreich and English 1979, 270-74; Leghorn and Parker 1981, 114ff.). One of the problems with the Freudian notion of "feminine masochism" is that it is not always clear whether psychoanalysts mean women are more masochistic in the original erotic sense of Krafft-Ebing (1929, 131ff.), i.e., are more likely to be sexually aroused in connection with the experience of physical pain/punishment, or mean "masochistic" in some more generic sense, i.e., women are more likely to simply accept or even welcome pain/punishment, regardless of whether the context is erotic or not. Kinsey's results do not support the erotic sense of the psychoanalytic theory. Roughly equal numbers of males and females reported an erotic response to being bitten or having other pain inflicted upon them (Kinsey *et al.* 1965 [1953], 677-8). But Hunt (1974, 333) found that nearly twice as many females as males in his sample obtained sexual pleasure from receiving pain. *Fantasies* of being sexually assaulted or of some form of sexual slavery appear to be quite common in women (Offit 1981, 133; Coles and Shamp 1984; G. Wilson 1978, 28, 30, 33, 42, 52, 142; Lee 1973; Hunt 1974, 92; Friday 1975; Benedek 1968, 442; Hariton and Singer 1974; Hazen 1983). It is curious that, although a woman may enjoy masochistic fantasies during intercourse, she in most cases would find it absolutely unacceptable to put these fantasies into practice.

As for the more generic "masochism," there is the phenomenon of wife-abuse. One of the highest estimates has it that 10% of the wives in the U.S. are battered (Langley and Levy 1977, 3). What is relevant here is that most wives who are beaten by their mates continue to live with them and 'take it.' In some cultural contexts wives are even proud of being beaten (Ellis 1927-8, III, 79ff.). Many argue, though, that tolerance of being beaten does not imply female "masochism" (or masochism), but other factors such as general societal approval of family violence, negligence by clinicians and legal authorities, sex-discriminatory laws, a history of violence in families of both the wife-beater and the wife-beater's wife, alcohol use by the wife-beater, economic dependency of the wife, etc. (Hilberman 1980; Rohrbaugh 1979, ch. 16; Langley and Levy 1977; Roy 1982). The numerous factors involved in wife-abuse do not completely rule out the wife's "masochism," however, and Hilberman's statement that "aggression was most consistently directed against themselves [the abused wives], in the form of suicidal behavior, depression, grotesque self-imagery, alcoholism, or self-mutilation" (1980, 1342) sounds very much like one of Freud's definitions of "masochism" as sadism "turned inwards" (*SE XIX*, 164).

Then there are the oft-mentioned physical and emotional sufferings that tend to accompany defloration, menstruation, childbirth, and childcare. To the extent that women welcome the painful aspects of these female activities they may be said to be more "masochistic" than men. But I doubt that women any more enjoy the pain of their essential female functions than men enjoy, say, the pain of being killed, wounded, or tortured in warfare, or welcome the tortures that often accompany male initiation. Even the self-sacrificial "masochism" in such female stereotypes as the "Jewish mother," "Our Lady of Sorrows" (or the *Mater dolorosa*), "Mother Russia," etc. is not so much an affirmation of pain as a mechanism for inducing guilt and eliciting altruism.

15) Males are more likely to be sadistic, i.e., derive sexual pleasure from inflicting pain, than females. Kinsey and his colleagues found that "... one-third of the females as against one-half of the males reported pleasant thrills at some time from inflicting pain on a person or animal" (Kinsey *et al.* 1965 [1953], 677), and a higher percentage of males than females had responded to sado-masochistic stories (*ibid.*). While masturbating males are more likely than females to have a fantasy of forcing someone to have sex (Hunt 1974, 93), and more than twice as many males as females in Hunt's sample reported obtaining pleasure from inflicting pain (*ibid.*, 333). I have already mentioned that wife-beating is much more common than husband-beating and that men do most of the killing and maiming in warfare, though I am not aware of any detailed studies of the role male *sexual* arousal plays in wife-beating or in warfare. Insofar as rape by definition involves sexual arousal in connection with the infliction of pain, then the fact that rape is committed primarily by men also indicates that men are more likely to be sadistic, in the erotic sense, than women.

It is obvious that many of the items in this overall set of contrasts work against female sexual choice in today's hominids. Rape is the clearest example, for it reduces female choice (at least momentarily) to absolute zero. But despite the typically asymmetrical power relationship between the sexes, there are still reasons (already enumerated above, section 5) to believe female choice existed (alongside male choice) in ancestral hominids, and exists in varying degrees in various hominid societies today.

The 'male-dominant-active' *vs.* 'female-subordinate-passive' opposition is of course only one aspect of the relationship of the sexes. Also, in some societies it is stronger than in others, as Sanday (1981, 210) has established in her cross-cultural study: "Generally, male dominance evolves as resources diminish and as group survival depends increasingly on the aggressive acts of men."[103]

It should be noted that the dominance asymmetry of the sexes applies specifically at an adult level. That is, it is relevant to reproductively mature individuals who have the potential for sexual interaction. This would make sense if the asymmetry had something to do with reproductive success. In the evolutionary long run, adult males have more to gain by competing with one another for sexual access to members of the opposite sex than adult females do, as the sociobiologists have shown (see Daly and Wilson 1978,

---

103. Sanday cautions that male dominance is not the only response to stress, and she probably would not agree that adult male dominance is as pervasive as I have depicted it here.

ch. 4, for a particularly clear discussion). Also, males have more to lose if they do not attempt to control the behavior of their mates than females do because only males can be cuckolded and because males are under more pressure to render care and protection (which entail control) to adult members of the opposite sex than females are. These ultimate asymmetries between the sexes probably account for most of the more proximate power asymmetries listed above. That is, they tend to result in the proximate associations 'male-active-dominant' *vs.* 'female-passive-subordinate'.

The tendency for adult males to control adult females does not necessarily mean, as I argued earlier, that the males are using physical force. True, for someone who does not live in an abusive family the statistics on wife-abuse may seem quite remarkable. But from the larger, sociobiological viewpoint, the human male does not *typically* resort to violence to control the behavior of the human female. The male mink (and other male mustelids) *typically* forces copulation with the female, and it is therefore reasonable for the biologist to assume that such violence is a key element in mink reproductive behavior. But physical force is not the normal way for the human male to control the human female, and therefore it makes more biological sense to regard it as, at most, only one of several means of control which the male has at his disposal.

For example, force pales in comparison with the numerous forms of altruism that a male can render in order to gain the upper hand in the relations between the sexes. But the *logical equivalence* of altruism and violence as alternative forms of maintaining dominance can be seen in those situations where, instead of altruism being rendered, violence erupts. For example, a young woman invites her date into her apartment, he offers to make love (= an offer of gametes, a form of altruism), but then rapes her when she resists (= annihilation of female choice). Or, a wife confronts a husband who has just received his paycheck, he refuses to give her as much money (= a form of altruism) as she wants, and beats her up into the bargain (= violence substitutes for the rendition of altruism). Or, a wife gets a new hairdo, her husband imagines that she must have taken a lover (= his altruism is possibly being wasted on offspring that are not his), so he beats her (= violence as an attempt to correct the misdirection of altruism).

There are some interesting ambiguities in the English language which also suggest how intimately related are altruism and force (and not only as applied to male-female relations):

> She is at his mercy
> You're asking for it
> He knows how to dish it out
> I'll take care of him
> She had it coming to her

He received his just deserts
Take your medicine!
etc.

In each of these utterances (as in the polemical feminist title *For Her Own Good* by Ehrenreich and English [1979]), the meaning at a superficial, lexical level is altruistic. When one "asks" one expects altruism, when one "takes care" of someone one renders altruism, when one administers medicine one is being altruistic, etc. But for the native speaker of English most of these sentences suggest just the opposite, i.e., force or violence. And the reason this can happen is the same as what makes an abusive parent alternate between cuddling and beating a child, or what makes an audience pay for and laugh gleefully at the comic who commits mock violence upon himself.[104] For the human primate, altruism and aggression are alternative and equivalent modes of dominance.

Just as altruism can shade over into force in extreme cases, so too altruism eliciting behavior can in extreme circumstances become instead an attempt to induce guilt and remorse. Many an abused wife is deriving some satisfaction from knowing how guilty her partner must feel (here I assume that guilt is essentially a form of violence against one's self). The abused wife is in many cases not so much deriving pleasure from the pain she experiences ("feminine masochism") as from inducing psychological pain in the abuser. This pain can lead in time to more abuse, and a vicious cycle is thereby perpetuated.

I do not want to suggest that there are not exceptions to the general tendency for adult males to dominate adult females. There are some henpecked husbands in every society (though the very term "henpecked" is derogatory to women, and has to have been invented because it refers to a departure from the norm, while "cockpecked" has not been invented precisely because it would refer to something so typical as to go unnoticed). I also do not want to deny the possibility that there are some few entire societies in which a nearly egalitarian relationship between the sexes obtains. The interesting thing about such exceptional societies is that, in addition to the relative absence of male dominance over females, there is little male-male competition and apparently little concern on the part of males with whether children are their own or not:

As they have neither political organization, nor office, nor dignities, nor any authority, for they only obey their Chief through good will toward him, therefore they never kill each other to acquire these honors. Also, as they are

---

104. I have used the psychoanalytic notion of pity as sadism transformed in my analysis of Gogol's pathetically funny Akakii Akakievich Bashmachkin (Rancour-Laferriere 1982a, 195-7).

contented with a mere living, not one of them gives himself to the Devil to acquire wealth.

I told him that it was not honorable for a woman to love any one else except her husband, and that this evil being among them, he himself was not sure that his son, who was there present, was his son. He replied, "Thou hast no sense. You French people love only your own children; but we love all the children of our tribe." I began to laugh, seeing that he philosophized in horse and mule fashion.

These passages are quoted by Eleanor Leacock (1981, 49, 50) from letters written by the Jesuit priest Paul Le Jeune in the 1630's. They describe the Montagnais-Naskapi of the eastern Labrador peninsula, as they lived before missionaries and traders changed them. According to Leacock, "... egalitarian relations have existed until recently in many foraging and horticultural societies" (*ibid.*, 279). The evidence for such an assertion is scarce by definition, since reliable ethnographic studies tend to postdate the influence of colonization by the male-dominant societies which produced the very ethnographers. But even if Leacock and the few others in her camp (cf. Strage 1980, 23ff.) are right about an earlier abundance of egalitarian societies, members of such societies were nonetheless behaving in ways that a sociobiologist would have predicted. Males who did not control the sexual behavior of the *females* they were attached to as mates would have ill served their genes by competing with other *males* over females. And the male whose mate copulated with other males would have been inefficiently altruistic to love and care for only the child technically designated as his 'own'. In societies where biological paternity was not clear, the child of the next man's wife may just as well have shared a man's genes as his wife's child. Indeed, the most efficient altruism of the putative egalitarian societies generally would have been relatively indiscriminate, because there would have been a greater likelihood that people outside of one's family were in fact biological kin than in a non-egalitarian society. In a passing nod toward the possibility of prehistoric egalitarian societies, Alexander says: "... the unstratified or egalitarian bands presumed to represent the ancestral kind of human sociality can almost be defined by saying that in them the major resource by which reproductive competition could be maximized is kinsmen" (1979b, 216).

Crook (1977, 31) has argued that "... among primates collective care is especially pronounced where paternity is in question." As for the human primate, there is statistical cross-cultural evidence that "... males tend to aim investment at their wives' children when paternal confidence is high and away from these children when it is low" (Gaulin and Schlegel 1980, 301; cf. Flinn 1981). An example of an investment "away" from the wife's children would be inheritance of real property by the sister's son rather than the wife's son (matrilineal inheritance). This and other altruism patterns characteristic of the avunculate have repeatedly been associated with low confidence of paternity (e.g., Flinn 1981; Alexander, *ibid.*, 169ff.). As Daly *et al.* (1982, 23) point out, the very same Father Le Jeune cited by Leacock was the first ethnographer ever to note the connection between avuncular inheritance and low confidence of paternity.

Most anthropologists would agree that, although some truly egalitarian societies with rampant uncertain paternity may have existed, there have never been many of them, just as there have never been many societies like the Yąnomamö, in which male-male competition and male control and exploitation of females is extreme. Whenever the relatively egalitarian peoples have come into contact with societies in which male dominance and control was the rule, their egalitarianism has disappeared. An evolutionist would conclude from this that some degree of male dominance is the more stable social situation, and that egalitarianism is an odd behavior that has only occasionally appeared as a result of unusual circumstances (as yet to be elucidated by anthropologists and/or ecologists). The Montagnais-Naskapi may not have been behaving maladaptively as long as they were isolated, but as soon as they came into contact with the French colonizers they reverted to the mild male dominance which is more typically adaptive for adult humans. Similarly, the recent increase in egalitarianism in twentieth-century West European and American society may continue as long as it is supported by an economy of technology and abundance,[105] but a severe economic crisis could cause a reversion to the male dominance that characterizes most non-industrial human societies, as well as most primates in which there is a sexual dimorphism in size.

---

105. This is not to say that an affluent economy is the only thing that supports the relative egalitarianism of advanced Western societies. Other factors are considered by Whyte (1978b, 181-4).

41. From the Nipple of the Dominatrix
to the Penis of the Dominator

> ... This enormous, long, thick penis (with a giant knob on the end) is entering me. When we are just starting, I imagine this huge organ is rubbing my enormous breasts, and especially is more or less duelling with them, trying to slide up between them and poking at first one and then the other, and that I am holding it off from me by sticking my huge breasts in the way.
>
> Clarissa, in *Friday's* My Secret Garden

The notion of male dominance applies, as I said, to adults. But for the child, especially for the very young child still closely managed by its mother, the situation is quite the opposite of what has been discussed here. That is, the child's view is 'female-active-dominant'. In growing up in most cultures, children of both sexes are therefore faced with the task of *realigning* their experience of power and dominance with the males instead of with females. I have already mentioned this phenomenon in the above discussions of "matriarchy" and of altruism's maternal origins. What I would like to do here is to focus on the anatomical specifics of the realignment.

The most obvious and tangible form of altruism that the mother renders to the infant is milk. The organ from which the infant obtains this precious fluid is the nipple. If, as I argued earlier, a husband is an icon of the mother, then where on that mother-icon's body will a woman find the most likely analogue of her real mother's nipple? Or, to look at it from his viewpoint, what part of his body must he exercise in order to act altruistically, that is, maternally, toward his wife?

The penis is of course what I have in mind. From a strictly sociobiological perspective the nipple and the penis are similar because they both dispense important *resources* from one individual to another. The nipple provides the only food the young infant is capable of efficiently metabolizing (or did so before the advent of bottle feeding). Without the nipple the infant would not survive. The penis, on the other hand, is the only dispenser of another kind of resource, i.e., male gametes (or it was before artificial insemination came along). Since there is no verified parthenogenesis in humans, the penis is absolutely essential to a woman's reproductive success.

Of course *female* gametes are essential to *male* reproductive success too.

But they, unlike women's bodies as a whole, or their babies, or their milk, are not dispensed in any obvious way. The ovary, egg, fallopian tubes, etc., are all out of sight, and therefore not nearly as subject to the kind of rampant semiotization that takes place with such observable entities as penises, nipples, hind quarters, vulvas, feces, babies, adult bodies, etc. Also, the production of female gametes is not signalled by estrous morphologies and behaviors the way it is in most other primates. Ovulation has for the most part lost its status as a semiotic entity. As a result, a male has to copulate with a given (nonpregnant) female on a regular basis in order to score reproductively. But, just as a male must regularly dispense semen to a female to insure the replication of his genes, so too a mother must regularly dispense milk to her infant to insure the survival of replicas of her genes. Or, from the viewpoint of the resource recipient, the female should regularly desire intercourse just as the infant regularly demands to be fed.

I confess that I would not have looked for these semiotic and socio-biological parallels between the nipple and the penis if it were not for the already extensive psychoanalytic literature on the equations 'nipple = penis' and 'milk = semen'.

Here, for example, is Géza Róheim's treatment of the subject in his classic paper "Aphrodite, or the Woman with a Penis:"

The male child first reacts to the separation trauma (withdrawal of breast) by identifying his own genital with the maternal source of pleasure, and thus having obtained a magical guaranty against deprivation goes through the same process again in the opposite direction. First, 'It is not true that I am deprived of pleasure (mamma), since I have my penis'; second, 'It is not true that something is missing there (at sight of maternal vagina). My mother has the same pleasure organ that I have (phallus; originally nipple).' (1945a, 372; cf. 1945b, 177).

Somewhat less male-oriented is Melanie Klein's treatment of the same equation:

In the relation of the suckling to his mother, sensual feelings are already present and express themselves in the pleasurable mouth sensations connected with the sucking process. Soon genital feelings come to the fore and the craving for the mother's nipples diminishes. It does not altogether vanish, however, but remains active in the unconscious and partly also in the cons-cious mind. Now in the case of the little girl the concern with the nipple passes over to an interest, which is for the most part unconscious, in the father's genital, and this becomes the object of her libidinal wishes and phantasies. As development proceeds, the little girl desires her father more than her mother, and has conscious and unconscious phantasies of taking her mother's place, winning her father for herself and becoming his wife. (1977 [1937], 309-10).

Even phallocentric Freud grants that adult phantasies of fellatio *might* indicate that the penis has substituted for the nipple in psychical development (*SE* XIX, 251; cf. VII, 51-2). But Freud really skirts this issue and moves on instead to the matter of penis-envy: "They [little girls] notice the penis of a brother or playmate, strikingly visible and of large proportions, at once recognize it as the superior counterpart of their own small and inconspicuous organ, and from that time forward fall a victim to envy for the penis" (*SE* XIX, 252). I do not want to berate Freud for his penis-envy theory, because I think it is a valid theory (below, sect. 53). It is just that his considerations on infantile orality do not rule out, or might just as well have led to a theory of male nipple-envy or breast-envy. Other psychoanalysts have recognized this. Felix Boehm, for example, reports the following statement by one of his patients:

I had a brother nearly eight years younger than myself, and one day his nurse took him on her knee to feed him. In order to remove the drops of milk which had dried on her breast, she took it in her hand and squeezed it so that a fine but forcible spurt of milk came out of the nipple and sprayed my face. This unexpected happening filled me with amazement and terror, and the thought took root in my mind: You will never be able to do that; women have the advantage of you there. (Boehm 1930, 457).

According to Boehm a woman's breasts represent a "tremendous penis" in the little boy's egocentric unconscious. A boy will eventually have a large penis that he can take pride in, but early in his development his mother seems to have the superior anatomical equipment.

For more on the psychoanalytic and psychiatric evidence of an equivalence between the breast/nipple and the penis, the reader may wish to consult such works (in addition to those already mentioned) as: Abraham 1968, 269; Stärcke 1921; Klein 1975, 78, 199-200; Nunberg 1947, 174-5; Bergler and Eidelberg 1933; Bergler 1935; Offit 1981, 68-9; Greenson 1950, 20; Jones 1961, 461-2; Brunswick 1940; Moore 1977; Chasseguet-Smirgel 1976; Jaffe 1977. Here, however, I would like to consider some of the *non*-clinical aspects of the matter.

Ellis, for example, focuses on the outright anatomical similarities between nursing and copulation: "... the erect nipple corresponds to the erectile penis, the eager watery mouth of the infant to the moist and throbbing vagina, the vitally albuminous milk to the vitally albuminous semen" (1927-8, III, 18). Ellis even believes that absorption of semen by the vaginal wall may have a mildly invigorating and intoxicating effect on the woman (V, 171-81; the idea may sound preposterous, but I have not seen it falsified by today's sexologists).

Dinnerstein says that a man's penis, "... taken into a yearning orifice of the body as the nipple once was taken, can provide a comparably miraculous joy" (1976, 42). Dinnerstein's definition of female coital satiety is "to be fucked as the baby would like to be fed: on demand and at the rate one chooses and as long as one wants" (*ibid.*, 63).

Ellis quotes a passage from John Cleland's eighteenth century erotic novel *Fanny Hill; or, Memoirs of a Woman of Pleasure* which dwells on "... the compressive exsuction with which the sensitive mechanism of that part [the vagina] thirstily draws and drains the nipple of Love" (*ibid.*, 19). In some fantasies and in some folkloric contexts the vagina that drains the "nipple of love" may, however, also cut it off. Hence the widespread notion of a "vagina dentata," which I will discuss as evidence for male castration anxiety (below, section 44).

In India, where Hindus have for centuries worshipped the explicitly phallic *lingam,* equation of this object with the breast sometimes occurs, as in the so-called *chantilingam* or *"lingam* of the breast" (Ferro-Luzzi 1980, 52). Kakar (1978, 94) says that among Hindu males there is a fantasy of "vaginal suction, *'milking* the penis'" (my italics). As is well known, the Hindus also consider cows to be sacred, regarding them as maternal entities (mother of India, mother of man, and mother of the gods – *ibid.*, 51). But there are Hindu legends in which a cow changes into a clearly phallic *lingam,* or vice-versa (*ibid.*). Róheim speaks of "the 'phallic nipple' significance of the udder" (1945a, 376) in India (cf. *SE* VII, 52), and argues that "... the udder's anatomical position makes it easier for the boy to identify this symbol of the mother's nipples with his scrotum" (*ibid.*, 375). In her study of sexual fluids in Vedic and post-Vedic India O'Flaherty (1980, 18) says that "... when the term *payas* occurs in the sentence 'The bull sprinkles his *payas* in the cow,' we may confidently say that at least one meaning of *payas* is 'semen'; and when we read '*Payas* streams from the udder of the cow,' we may say that at least one other meaning of *payas* is 'Milk'." Of course, judging from the fact that the same term describes what comes from both the penis and the udder, we also have to suspect a psychological equivalence of semen with milk, or of the bull's penis with a cow's nipple (O'Flaherty gives many other examples). Incidentally, I doubt that cows would be as important as they are in India if their udders were not in roughly the same position as a *bull's* genitalia are, therefore suggesting equations of nipple and penis, milk and semen. On the other hand, I have no idea why Hindus in particular – as opposed to, say, peoples who slaughter cows for food – should be so impressed with the apparently male qualities of cow udders.

Baker cites some Polynesian languages in which terms for the penis and the breast are related:

Maori: *u,* breast; *ure,* penis.
Hawaiian: *u,* breast; *ule,* penis.
Mangarevan: *u,* breast; *ua,* penis.

(1950, 177)

DeMause argues that the Jewish infant's freshly circumcised penis is *sucked* by the mohel because "... the penis, and more particularly the glans, is the mother's nipple returned, and the blood is her milk" (1982, 26; there are also homosexual overtones to this practice — below, section 47). In his discussion of the folklore of the evil eye, Dundes (1980, 100) quotes a modern Greek formula which associates breasts with male genitalia: "If it is a woman who has cast the eye, then destroy her breasts. If it is a man who has cast the eye, then crush his genitals." Tannahill (1980, 69) quotes an ancient Assyrian law which stated: "If a woman has crushed a man's testicle in an affray, one of her fingers shall be cut off; and if ... the second testicle is affected with it and becomes inflamed or if she has crushed the second testicle in the affray, both of her [breasts or nipples] shall be torn off." Legman (1975, 137-40) provides a number of jokes about "semen as food," including: "Did you hear how they found [a woman aviator] and her companion alive on a desert island? All this time they kept alive by him sucking her *tit* and her sucking his *cock.* A vicious circle, you know. They just kept the food in circulation" (italics mine). One of the current tabooed English terms for masturbation, according to the Wentworth and Flexner dictionary (1975, 723) is "to milk." According to Morris (1973, 104) this expression is also an old slang term for fellatio. In Spain the term *leche* can refer to semen as well as to milk (Brandes 1981, 224). Devereux (1969) reports that fellatio is regarded as a form of 'nursing' among the Mohave Indians. My colleague Jim Gallant informs me that the English term "cocksucker" has, in addition to its obvious homosexual meaning, the metaphorical meaning of a *motherless* child that has been raised by its father.

When I was in graduate school I had a friend who, when peeved at someone, would shout: "You nipple!" I recall thinking he was *about* to say "You prick!" — which is in fact the more common American expression.

A perusal of lists of slang terms for the penis reveals many terms which suggest specifically *oral* gratification of one sort or another:

almond rock	dead meat
banana	drumstick
black pudding	fig
bone	gristle
candy bar	groceries
carrot	haricot/bean
cookie	honey stick
cream-horn	hot dog

cream-stick	loaf
dark meat	lollipop
meat	rhubarb
meat with two vegetables	sausage
mutton	sugar-stick
(as in "jerk one's mutton")	white meat
pork sword	wiener/weenie

(see: Healey 1980; Gerber 1981, 50-52; Rancour-Laferriere 1979b).

The combination of penis and ejaculate can be referred to as "rhubarb and custard" or "bananas and cream" (Healey 1980, 192). Some food-items also refer to ejaculate: "cream," "melted butter," "honey" (*ibid.*, 196).

The abundance of these terms suggests that the act of fellatio is thought to offer as much oral gratification to the fellator as it offers genital gratification to the fellatee. However, it seems to be primarily males who think this. Male homosexuals in particular place a high value on the penis, focusing on it almost as an object of worship. The oversized penises exhibited in the "gay" magazines thrive on such phallicism. As for heterosexual males, they will often resort to prostitutes if their mates refuse to perform fellatio (cf. Kinsey 1948, 578).

Sex researcher C.A. Tripp says: "Women are bored out of their heads by fellatio, and that goes for the best practitioner you will ever meet. She's learned to do a marvelous job, but she's really adding up the grocery list during the act" (Nobile 1977, 274). In other words, she is doing it for the man, and her pleasure is mainly vicarious. As Nobile observes, fellatio did not get very high ratings from the women questioned in the Hite report (Hite 1976, 630).

I think that "bored out of their heads" is probably not what women really feel, however. Offit's view seems more convincing: "Perhaps the most common interpretation of fellatio has been as an expression of male dominance and female submission. For some, to conquer a woman has been to spray semen onto her face or into her throat, to violate her dignity, like spitting or urinating on her. In consequence, for at least a century, many normal and self-respecting women have declined to perform fellatio" (Offit 1981, 65; cf. Strage 1980, 96; Gagnon and Simon 1973, 87). In extreme cases the element of domination can be so strong that fellatio becomes irrumation, which is basically a kind of rape of the mouth. It differs from fellatio in that the penis is forced into the mouth of a person who is not in control, and who thereby has to endure pain or humiliation. In newspaper parlance irrumation is "forced oral copulation." Webster's dictionary once again reveals its ignorance (or omission) of sexual matters by equating irrumation with fellatio (Gove 1971, 1197; see below, 308). The etymology of the term is, incidentally, a perfect example of the penis-nipple equivalence:

Latin *irrumāre*, 'to give suck' derives from *rumis/ruma*, 'breast'/'nipple'.

As both predecessors and followers of Freud (*SE* XIII, 154-5) have argued, the Christian sacrament of the Holy Eucharist is a distorted form of cannibalism. The eleventh-century Roman Catholic doctrine of "transsubstantiation" insists that the Eucharistic wafer eaten by the faithful *is* the body and blood of Christ, even if its "accidents" of color, taste, shape, etc. are those of bread.

However, I think there is something else to Holy Communion besides a cannibalistic metaphor. Consider the sexual sense of "eating." Norman O. Brown says that Jesus Christ "... gives himself to his bride [the communicant] with the bread. Eat your fill, lovers ..." (Brown 1966, 167). Crawley cites reports that the heretical Manicheans and Albigenses sprinkled their Eucharistic bread with human semen (1965, 142; cf. Ellis 1927-8, V, 173). Eliade quotes a very explicit description by Saint Epiphanius of sexual rites practiced by the Gnostic sect of the Phibionites:

... they serve rich food, meat and wine even if they are poor. When they thus ate together and so to speak filled up their veins, from the surplus of their strength they turn to excitements. The man, leaving his wife, says to his own wife: "Stand up and make love with the brother" ("Perform the *agapē* with the brother"). Then the unfortunates unite with each other, and as I am truly ashamed to say the shameful things that are being done by them . . . , nevertheless I will not be ashamed to say those things which they are not ashamed to do, in order that I may cause in every way a horror in those who hear about their shameful practices. After they have intercourse in the passion of fornication they raise their own blasphemy toward heaven. The woman and the man take the fluid of the emission of the man into their hands, they stand, turn toward heaven, their hands besmeared with the uncleanness, and pray as the people called *Stratiotikoi* and *Gnostikoi*, bringing to the Father of the Nature of All, that which they have on their hands, and they say: "We offer to thee this gift, the body of Christ." And then they eat it, their own ignominy, and say: "This is the body of Christ and this is the Passover for the sake of which our bodies suffer and are forced to confess the suffering of Christ." Similarly also with the woman: when she happens to be in the flowing of the blood they gather the blood of menstruation of her uncleanness and eat it together and say: "This is the blood of Christ." (quoted from the *Panarion* of Epiphanius by Eliade 1976, 110).

For Christ to be represented by both semen and menstrual blood makes him a decidedly hermaphroditic figure for the Phibionites.

The failure of Christ to marry or to have heterosexual relations (in the non-apocrypha at least) certainly sets his life apart from the more typical folk heroes such as Moses, Oedipus, Cyrus, Lohengrin, and others (cf. Dundes 1980, 238; 255). Christ, after leaving his mother at a rather late age, seems to have spent most of his time with his male companions, the apostles.

If taking the Eucharist can be an act of metaphorical fellatio, then taking in the *word* of Christ is an even more far fetched metaphor of suckling at the breast:

> Believe me, unless you become like little children again, you shall not enter the kingdom of heaven. He is greatest in the kingdom of heaven who will abase himself like this little child. (Matthew 18: 3-4; cf. Thass-Thienemann 1973, II, 129).
>
> ... a woman in the multitude said to him aloud, Blessed is the womb that bore thee, the breast which thou hast sucked. And he answered, Shall we not say, Blessed are those who hear the word of God, and keep it? (Luke 11: 27-8; cf. Dundes 1980, 259).
>
> ... You are children newborn, and all your craving must be for the soul's pure milk, that will nurture you into salvation, once you have tasted, as you have surely tasted, the goodness of the Lord. (I Peter 2: 2-3; Stannard 1977, 294).
>
> Jesus saw children being suckled. He said to his disciples, 'These children who are being suckled are like those who enter the Kingdom'. (Coptic Gospel of Thomas, as quoted by Dundes, *ibid.*, 244).
>
> My own breasts I prepared for them, that they might drink my holy milk and live thereby. (God speaking in the anonymous early Christian *Ode of Solomon*, as quoted by Stannard 1977, 294).

The God of the Old Testament also occasionally represented himself in a maternal role:

> Thus says the Lord, Peace shall flow through her [Jerusalem] like a river, the wealth of the nations shall pour into her like a torrent in flood; this shall be the milk you drain, like children carried at the breast, fondled on a mother's lap. I will console you then, like a mother caressing her son, and all your consolation shall be in Jerusalem .... (Isaias 66: 12-13).

Dundes interprets the passage from Luke as follows: "In other words, father's word is more important than mother's womb and breasts" (259). To this I would add: father's word is a *substitute* for mother's womb and breasts because he does not have such organs himself, and he envies them (note how Isaias too slips from the image of a *female* [Jerusalem] giving suckle, to the image of a *male* mother ["I," i.e., God himself], and back again). The best that God-the-father as a mere male can offer is his word (*logos*) which in the gospel parables is repeatedly compared to seed (*sperma*) that is planted in the ground, but which of course also suggests the "seed" implanted by the male organ (cf. Thass-Thienemann 1973, I, 92-3; Eliade 1976, 111-12). As the First Epistle of John (3: 9) says, "No one born of God commits sin; for the sperm of God abides in him, and he cannot sin because he is born of God" (Eliade translation [*ibid.*, 111-12], as opposed to Monsignor Knox's euphemistic rendering as "... if a man is born of God, he does not live sinfully, he is true to his parentage; he cannot be a sinner if he is born of God"). I will pursue this topic of male envy of female reproductive functions later (section 50).

The richest ethnographic material on the penis-nipple association that I am aware of is to be found in Gilbert Herdt's *Guardians of the Flutes* (1981), which is a study of the Sambia of Papua New Guinea (see also Herdt 1982). All Sambian boys go through a phase in which they are obliged to fellate older males, and later on they are fellated themselves by younger males and by females. Much of the lore surrounding this practice associates the fellated penis with the breast/nipple(or more specifically, milk with semen). The males believe, for example, that orally ingested semen furnishes a girl with breast milk (1981, 178-9). Vaginal intercourse is said to "feed" semen to the developing fetus (192-5), and homosexual fellation is a nutritive act that "grows" the boy-initiate (234). The initiates refer to semen as "our breast milk," and their elders state outright that "if you try it [semen] it is just like the milk of your mother's breast" (235). Husbands during postpartum taboo must not watch their wives nurse, for this might stimulate in them a desire to be fellated (210-11). The ritual flutes used to teach fellatio to the initiates are paired in such a way that the smaller "female" flute (the tip of which is called a "female breast nipple") is contained within the larger "male" flute or "penis" (283). Within the Sambian male collective there thus exists "... some kind of primary-process association linking the child's experience of suckling at his mother's breast with the novice's act of sucking the bachelor's penis" (Herdt 1982, 79).

Roger Keesing (1982, 29) says of Sambian initiation that "... the boys become *dependent* on the initiators the way infants are dependent on their mothers." This analogy seems quite justifiable in view of the boys' great longing for their mothers, from whom they are traumatically separated at the onset of the initiation rites ("I felt sorry to lose my mother," say the old men, recalling their own initiations: Herdt 1982, 68). Herdt hypothesizes that the older bachelors who impersonate female spirits for the novices and want to be fellated by them are "thinly disguised surrogates for the mothers of [the] boys" (*ibid.*, 78).

The switch from dependency on females to dependency on males entails a switch in subordination as well. Whereas the boys were formerly subordinate to their nipple-possessing mothers, they now must submit to the penis-possessing men: "Men ... place boys in an invidious state of subordination which the boys may sense as being like that of a woman and wife ... " (*ibid.*, 70). Keesing (1982, 29) says that the relationship of succorance-dependence disguises a relationship of dominance-submission, but one could just as well assert that the obvious dominance-submission of the initiating process disguises an envious succorance-dependence.

The typical human male — be he a temporarily homosexual Sambian or a red-blooded American homophobe — eventually does get around to inserting his penis into a female. But when he does, he is virtually trapped into the kind of dominance his mother once held over him.

I doubt that anyone would disagree that the idea of inserting something into someone has a distinct suggestion of power and domination to it. Many obscene expressions of domination involve insertion (explicit or implicit) of the male organ:

> Shove it up your ass!
> Stuff it!
> Stick it in your ear/your rear!
> Eat me!
> Suck my cock!

But even non-obscene ways of expressing domination often involve the idea of insertion or penetration:

Take your medicine!
He will balk if you try to force it down his throat [literally or metaphorically].
She is so gullible as to swallow anything that is said to her.
You can't feed me those ideas.
etc.

Under the entry "submission" *Roget's Thesaurus* lists the following distinctly oral expressions for humbling oneself:

> eat dirt
> eat crow
> eat the leek
> eat humble pie
> bite the dust
> lick the dust
> swallow the leek
> swallow the pill
> kiss the rod
> gulp down
>
> (Mawson 1963, 311)

The thesaurus gives a wealth of "ingressive" verbs which have distinct overtones of power and domination:

invade	horn in	ram in
intrude	interject	drive in
penetrate	inject	whip in
insinuate	thrust in	impact
butt in	obtrude	pierce

(*ibid.*, 111, 115)

Many of these verbs could be used to describe *either* a mother's force-feeding a child *or* a man's sexual entry into a woman.

The male's transition from being the infantile 'insertee' to being the adult 'inserter' thus seems to be inseparable from his transition from being dominated to being dominating. What happens in female erotic development is of course different. And the need to view dominance as interchangeable with succorance or rendition of altruism is something I have already discussed. What I woud like to do now is look more closely at what the male's organ of 'insertion' means to him.

42. Penile Possibilities

What the adult human male inserts into the female is extraordinarily large, by primate standards. Of all 200 or so living species of primates,[106] *Homo sapiens* possesses the largest penis, larger even than that of a male gorilla, an animal that may weigh more than 500 pounds. What is more, the human penis becomes erect and ready for insertion without the help of the penile bone or cartilage (*os penis* or baculum) which aids erection in the Great Apes and most monkeys (see Short 1977, 15; Mellen 1981, 143). Also, the flaccid penis protrudes from the body wall in humans while in the Great Apes it is flush with the body wall and its shaft therefore is invisible (Short, *ibid.*).

Why such a large human penis? Scholars have suggested a number of answers. For one thing, the vagina has grown larger in the course of hominid evolution. Perhaps the hominid penis grew larger (and in particular, wider) to keep up with the enlarging vaginal passage, especially in late hominid evolution when there was considerable selective pressure for the birth canal to accomodate the passage of large-brained infants (cf. Gregersen 1982, 52). A penis that did not itself accomodate may not have deposited semen as efficiently as the penis that did.

Other factors might well have been operating too, however. Hockett and Ascher 1964 (142) say that the "dorsal [sexual] approach" must have been made awkward by the "expansion of the gluteus maximus." Morgan (1973, 54) suggests that the hominid penis could have lengthened because, as the vagina rotated forward with the development of upright posture, a longer penis was necessary in order to still gain access from the rear (cf. Lewis 1976, 6; Mellen 1981, 143). Short (1977, 15; 1979, 152; 1981, 339) hypothesizes that the penis may have gotten larger to make males more attractive to females (cf. Tanner 1981, 272; it is known that penile display in chimpanzees serves to attract estrous females [e.g., Short 1981, 333], though to judge from both psychoanalytic findings [below, sect. 53] and women's erotica [e.g., Friday 1975, 214ff.], women are as much vicariously pleased with, honored by, or envious of the erect human penis as they are "turned on" by it). Short also suggests that the larger penis has enhanced the ability of the female to experience sexual pleasure, including orgasm (cf. Morris 1967, 80; Fisher 1982, 96), and he points out that the larger penis has made possible a variety of copulatory positions. Guthrie (1976, 86-8; cf. Baer and Mc-

---

106. The figure varies from 176 to 250 living species of primates, depending on which expert is cited (Fedigan 1982, 9).

Eachron 1982, 86) believes the size increase evolved to enhance threatening penile display (Short rejects this theory, though there is an enormous literature [see below] on aggressive/threatening penile display in humans).

I suspect at least a grain of truth in most of these theories. One theory might be more appropriate to one period of hominid evolution, another to a different period. All of them imply the operation of *female choice*. That is, those males who had penises that, from a female viewpoint best fitted, best reached, most attracted, most stimulated, and yielded the most orgasms were the males who left the most offspring. Even the idea that large penis size evolved as a result of male-male competition depends, in a sense, on female choice, for "female choice is a kind of male-male competition" (Ghiselin 1980, 188; cf. above, p. 87).

Though the erect penis is large and extremely obvious in today's upright hominids, it is nonetheless rarely displayed in public. When it is, the displayer is considered deviant, an exhibitionist (or, to use the proper legal term, a wiennie wagger). If the authorities manage to catch him, he is incarcerated, or placed in a mental facility.

What the male exhibitionist does is considered a threat, an act of aggression or hostility:

... you will find, if you get to talk with an exhibitionist, that his purpose in displaying his genitals is not to seduce a woman into making love with him but rather to shock her. If she is upset — is embarrassed, becomes angry, runs away — and especially if she calls the police, he has, he feels, absolute proof that his genitals are important. When you learn that he is likely to exhibit himself following a humiliation earlier in the day, you will be alert to the hostile components he experiences in his excitement. For him, this sexual act serves as a kind of rape — a forced intrusion (at least, that is how he fantasizes it) into the woman's sensibilities and delicacy. If he cannot believe that he has harmed her, the act has failed for him. (He is mortified by the woman who is amused, not shocked, at his show.) Therefore, we find that the exhibitionist displays himself to strange women, not to his wife, who could hardly feel assaulted by a view so ordinary. To show his wife his genitals would be to risk further humiliation, for he knows she would never respond dramatically to the sight, with outrage or a sense of being invaded. (Stoller 1979, xiii).

When a *woman* uncovers herself, as in a strip-tease, she is not thought to be committing an act of aggression. There is a fundamental difference between male and female exhibitionism: "if females tended to be sexually aroused by the sight of male genitals, men would be able to obtain sexual intercourse via genital display; but the deliberate male display of genitals to unfamiliar women is understood to be a kind of threat, whereas a similar female display is understood to be a sexual invitation" (Symons 1979, 181).

Much more common than overt, public penile display are substitutions for such display or private display (or a combination of both). Elsewhere (Rancour-Laferriere 1979b, profusely illustrated, and stolen from most libraries) I have detailed the involvement of penile display in a wide variety of human activities such as: pornographic literature and film (appealing primarily to the gay community); ornamentation and clothing of the penis (phallocrypts, codpieces, etc.); phallic trophies; rape; fellatio; the phallic hand (*manus obscena*), phallic finger (*digitus impudicus*), and other gestures that substitute for penile display; verbal phallicism, which includes those obscenities which have the same intimidating effect that penile display has (e.g., "Fuck you!") or those verbal expressions which suggest a penile act of aggression (e.g., "she fucked him over"); vocal phallicism, which refers to fantasies of the singing voice as an erect penis (cf. also Legman 1968, 336-40); lingual phallicism, where the protruded tongue does penile service, as in cunnilingus, or is displayed in erotic or hostile contexts; fetishism, in which the fetish, such as a foot or a braid, is often a substitute for the penis the fetishist once imagined his mother to possess; some forms of transvestitism in which the orientation of the transvestite is strongly exhibitionistic; apotropaic phallicism, whereby the evil eye or some other evil influence is warded off by means of phallic amulets, medals, sculptures, etc.; territorial phallicism, including ithyphallic herms and other phallic objects used at borders, gates, doorways, etc.; phallic worship, an ancient practice in many cultures that is often associated with orgies and ritual promiscuity; phallic synecdoche, in which the male genital is a part used to represent the person as a whole.

There is a substantial literature on each one of these topics (see, for example, the extensive bibliographic lists under "phallus," "penis," "Priapus," "Phallicism," etc. in Goodland 1931). I cannot hope to review the literature here, nor do I wish to repeat all that I said in the earlier paper. What I will do instead is focus on the last of the above-named items, i.e., phallic synecdoche, because it illustrates better than any of the other items how much a man's penis means to him, and leads naturally to considerations of castration anxiety, which I believe has been a major force in hominid evolution.

43. The Personified Penis

The penis is the man...
Andrea Dworkin

As is well known, body *parts* are capable of representing the *whole* human body (*pars pro toto*, a type of synecdoche). For example, a tall person may be referred to as "legs." A character in a Gogol story is "the nose." A weak, effeminate man may be called a "pussy" (slang for female genitalia) as may any woman (Russian *pizda* works the same way). A particularly obnoxious person, male or female, may be called a "prick" (slang for penis — compare Russian *khui*). However, of all the parts of the male or female body which may be equated with the whole body, the penis seems to be the most commonly used and is the most elaborately developed as a sign. Moreover, the equation 'penis=body' is not only a one-directional sign, i.e., the synecdoche can just as well be *totum pro parte* as *pars pro toto* (see Lausberg's *Handbuch der literarischen Rhetorik*, pars. 573, 581, on these two kinds of synecdoche). Penile synecdoche is, as it were, commutative. Thus, for example, not only might the penis stand for the whole person in male fantasies of uterine regression (what Ferenczi refers to as "Identifizierung des ganzen Organismus mit dem Exekutivorgan," 1972, II, 351), but conversely the whole person can be represented as accomplishing what the penis normally accomplishes, as in the kinds of pornographic art which portray a man inside a huge vagina (this is what Ferenczi would call "Genitalisierung des ganzen Organismus" — *ibid*.; see Rancour-Laferriere 1979b, and *The Village Voice*, 21 Sept. 1967, for some pictures).

Early in his psychoanalytic writings Freud recognized the synecdochal powers of the genitalia, without however designating these powers with the rhetorical term:

The progressive concealment of the body which goes along with civilization keeps sexual curiosity awake. This curiosity seeks to complete the sexual object by revealing its hidden parts. It can, however, be diverted ('sublimated') in the direction of art, if its interest can be shifted *away from the genitals to the shape of the body as a whole*. (*SE*, VII, 156; emphasis added).

Freud's theory of beauty in the visual arts makes the whole a sublimated synecdoche of the part. In *The Interpretation of Dreams* Freud also suggested that in the manifest content the penis may be represented by one's own body or the body of another. In the famous study of the "Wolf Man," on the other hand, the penis was said to represent the whole body (*SE*, XVII, 102). Later studies by other psychoanalysts focused on how the male organ functions synecdochally in a wide variety of human activities. Fenichel (1954, 11) found, for example, that the comic figure of the slapstick clown or Punchinello is a personified penis (the word 'Punchinello' derives ultimately from Neapolitan 'polecenella', i.e., the young of the turkey-cock, as Jones had earlier observed in his own remarks on the phallic Punchinello figure – 1961 [1916], 99-100; cf. the phallic "Hanswurst" figure of Viennese folk comedy). Bertram Lewin, in his study of "The Body as Phallus" (1933), described a male patient who referred to his penis as his body (31). Another patient compared being sponged and bathed while ill to masturbation (*ibid.*, 41). An "improper story" is paraphrased by Lewin as follows: "How, it is asked, can that little man sexually satisfy that big woman? The answer is: he puts his head and shoulders up her vagina, wiggles his ears, and vomits" (*ibid.*, 26). After discussing a wealth of examples, Lewin classifies the four different varieties of the equation 'penis=body' as follows:

> a) One's own body is one's own penis.
> b) One's own body is another's penis.
> c) Another's body is one's own penis.
> d) Another's body is another's penis.

(*ibid.*, 43)

From a semiotic perspective, all four of these equations are the *totum pro parte* type of synecdoche.

The penis can even be identified with one's *person*. In effect, not only 'penis=body', but also 'penis=person'. This new equation represents the superimposition of the rhetorical process of *personification* (προσωποποιία) upon the basic phallic synecdoche. Examples abound, and in fact some given above, such as the Punchinello character as the personification of a penis, already represent personified phallic synecdoche. Melanie Klein, in her discusion of children's fantasies of an imaginary penis within the mother, is clearly aware that both synecdoche and personification are operating: "... at this early stage of development the principle of *pars pro toto* holds good and the penis represents the father *in person*" (1949, 189, emphasis added). The *names* of persons (usually male) are particularly common phallic synecdoches. Litewka (1977, 25) says: "We can ... give our penis a name, like John Thomas or Peter, which states positively to the world that our penis is its own man" (Litewka's essay, which is entitled "The Socialized Penis," is essentially based on the rhetorical synecdoche-cum-personification device).

"I have punished the head...by a literal decapitation, killing *Myron* so that Myra might be born," says Myron of his castration in Gore Vidal's novel. "I for such a Gill have a fit *Jack*," says friar John of his phallic powers in the

Urquhart/Motteux translation of Rabelais (cf. the English expression "to *jack* off," i.e., to masturbate). In English the names "Peter" or "Dick" ("Willie" in England) are the most common .proper names for the penis. In her article on "genital pet names" Cornog (1981) reports such proper names for the penis as "Casey," "Chuck," "George," "Hank," "Jason," "Lazarus," "Mortimer," "Winston," and others – most of them limited to private language between lovers. Cornog points out that it is specifically the genital organ (most of her examples name the male genital), and not other bodily organs and parts that receive a "pet name": "After all, no one names feet, hands, or elbows" (*ibid.*, 34). Aman and Friends (1981) add more English examples to Cornog's list, and give Hebrew ("Moishe") and Serbo-Croatian ("Draganović," i.e., "little Dragan") examples. In Amenian the diminutive of a man's name can refer to his penis (A. Dedekian, pers. comm.). Even personal pronouns are known to refer to the penis (e.g. – in English, "him" or "himself" – Healey 1980, 189-90).

In ancient Greece (particularly Lampascus) the famous fertility god Πρίαπος (Priapus) was invented specifically as the personification of a penis. Other ancient gods who personified the penis were Phales (a daimon), Mutunus (or Tutunus), Liber (the Latin name of Bacchus), and Fascinus (see Hartland 1951, 822; *Oxford Classical Dictionary*, 802, 876). Of particular relevance to the personified phallic synecdoche is the Latin distinction "fascinum" or "fascinus" *vs.* "Fascinus": the former (grammatically neuter or masculine) referred to the penis itself or to an apotropaic image of the penis which was worn suspended around the necks of women and children (cf. Wright in Knight and Wright 1957, 28), while the latter (grammatically masculine only) referred to the personification of the penis, i.e., to the deity.

Perhaps the most striking visual examples of the personified penis are the obscene blendings of penis and person often found in erotic art (for illustrations see: Kronhausen and Kronhausen 1968; Rancour-Laferriere 1979b, fig. 17; Webb 1975, figs. 36, 39, 40). Almost every erotic art collection features at least one depiction of a man with such a large penis that the man seems to be an appendage of the penis rather than vice-versa. My earlier study of penile display includes a seven-year-old boy's self-portrait in which the boy has (spontaneously) signed his name where the penis should be (Rancour-Laferriere 1979b, figure 16).

The personified penis is to be found in the folklore of a variety of cultures. The Muria of central India furnish this example (which also illustrates, incidentally, the castration motif):

Once the penis was so long that as a man lay in bed it could get out of the house and penetrate a woman a hundred yards away. When he went abroad, a man would wind it round and round his waist and tuck in the end.

One day a penis broke through the wall of the house, entered a woman, came out of her mouth, dipped its head into a cooking-pot and ate all the supper, and in withdrawing killed the woman. Then all the women came to cut it off. The man grasped his penis with his hand, but that was all he could save. The women cut it off and it is now only a hand's breadth long. (Elwin 1968, 105).

Among the erotic Russian sayings gathered by the nineteenth century philologist Vladimir Dahl are many which personify the penis, such as:

Glup, kak arkhireiskii khui.
He is as stupid as a bishop's prick.
Kashei khuia ne nakormish'.
You can't feed a prick with kasha.
Tesh' moiu plesh', veseli moi mude.
Amuse (the head of) my prick, cheer my balls. (Carey 1972, 46, 49, 58)

In the second volume of his *Rationale of the Dirty Joke* Gershon Legman (1975, 605) quotes an American "speaking-penis story"; "A man, standing in the bathroom shaving in the nude, as was his custom [!] found his grip unsteadied by a bothersome hangover, and he dropped his straight-edge razor, amputating his penis, which fell to the floor. As he stooped to recover the razor [!!] the organ addressed him as follows: 'I know we've had lots of fist-fights in our time, but I never thought you'd pull a knife on me!'"[107] This so-called *Mentula loquens* motif (index no. D. 1610.6.2 in Thompson 1955-8, vol. II, 283) is present in the lore of a number of North American Indian tribes. Here is an example from the Crow (which also illustrates, incidentally, Freud's theory of the relationship between son-in-law and mother-in-law):

A man was hunting buffalo. He saw some and rejoiced. Jumping off his horse, he began to urinate, shook his penis at the buffalo and said, "My penis, do you see the buffalo?" "Yes." Then he asked again and received the same answer. He asked again. It replied, "Yes, I see, I see it, I see it, I see it," and never ceased to speak. He put his hands over it, but it continued repeating the same words. "I won't stop," it said, "unless you get your wife's mother to press me." So he walked to camp and stopped outside. His organ kept repeating, "I see it." His wife asked, "Why don't you come in?" "I have done something wrong. When I espied buffalo, I was glad and urinated and asked my penis till it said, 'I see,' and would not stop speaking. It told me I should have to get my mother-in-law. See your mother and find out what she thinks of it." "Well, my son is having a hard time, he had better come in." The mother-in-law sang a song, seized his penis, and that cured it. (Lowie 1922, 225-6).

---

107. Exclamation points Legman's. In the two volumes of *Rationale* Cornog finds "...nearly twenty jokes or tales dealing with genitals named, speaking, spoken to, or acting on their own" (1981, 37).

Several literary examples of conversations between characters and their genitalia are given by Cornog (1981, 37-8).

Cornog states that "... we have yet to understand fully why genitals are personified ..." (*ibid.*, 38). My general hypothesis is that the entities which humans personify are those which are most likely to be involved in the maximization of inclusive fitness, i.e., other humans, especially related humans. To personify an entity, i.e., to treat it as a person, is to attempt to parlay that entity into interactions which are good for genes. The personification of entities which can in fact interact with the personifier must have been the original adaptive process, that is, must have been the preadaptation from which arose other derivative personifying processes such as primitive animism, totemism, personification of group ties, etc. (Rancour-Laferriere 1981, 506-16) — not to mention personification of genitalia.

A dog is not a person. But there were evidently some benefits to be gained when our hominid ancestors treated certain canids as if they were persons — fed them, talked to them, stroked them, etc. Perhaps the canids helped the hominids with hunting, as retrievers do today. Perhaps they guarded hominid home-bases, as watchdogs do today.

A penis is not a person either. But if ancestral hominids started treating it as a person — talking to it, worshipping it, making special efforts to protect it, etc. — then the genes of penis possessors and their relatives may have benefitted. After all, how much 'closer' to genes can one get than the physical conduit which transfers genetic information from one individual to another?

But was the penis in some kind of danger that would make its possessor want to give it this special synecdochizing and personifying attention? Or, to be more precise: was the penis in any kind of *differential* danger such that it, and not some *other* part of the male body should get the privileged treatment of synecdoche and personification, i.e., should come to represent the very self of its possessor?

What I am suggesting, of course, is the threat of castration. Stoller (1976, 284) argues that "the danger in castration is not organ loss but the far more profound loss of one's sense of existing." Freud believed that the castration fears (among other fantasies) expressed by his patients reflected "real occurrences in the primaeval times of the human family" (*SE* XVI, 371; XVII, 86; cf. Daly 1957). The Lamarckian and biogenetic routes whereby Freud arrived at this conclusion may be questionable (see above, 12). But conditions may in fact have been conducive to castration behavior in our ancestors.

Given that aggressive forms of penile display exist both in today's hominids and in some other primates, it seems very likely that ancestral upright hominids gave penile displays. At some point, however, the thought must have entered the increasingly intelligent hominid brain that one way to overcome an aggressive penile display, besides also displaying, would be to eliminate the opponent's displayed penis. The elimination could have been accomplished by *biting* (or, in more recent hominid history, by sharp instruments).

It is known that grinding of the teeth (bruxism) occurs during nocturnal penile erection in today's hominids, i.e., during REM periods (see MacLean 1973a, 57). The teeth commonly chatter when a squirrel monkey engages in aggressive penile display (*ibid.*, 48). MacLean devotes some attention to the neurological connection of teeth grinding and penile display (*ibid.*, 58).

Psychiatrists are of course quite familiar with the connection between biting and castration because their patients produce fantasies about a *vagina dentata* or express anxieties about biting or being bitten during fellatio. Klein believes that a little boy's aggressive inclination to bite his mother's breast leads him to fear that his own penis will be bitten (1977, 411). Mothers do not, to my knowledge, bite their sons' penises very often, though in some societies, such as the Balinese, mothers are known to tease their sons by pulling on their penises (Mead 1975, 72; Freeman 1968, 388, witnessed an incident where a five-year-old Iban boy who, "... after being teased in public by his mother with repeated pullings of his penis, suddenly broke down and, flinging himself on her lap, impulsively bit at her skirt immediately over her genitals."

Biting is itself a typical form of aggression in primates, and in his chapter on human anger in *The Expression of Emotions* Darwin devotes some pages to the "retraction of the lips and uncovering of the teeth during paroxysms of rage" which signify that the angry person is inclined to "bite the offender" (1965[1872], 242).

From the viewpoint of current evolutionary theories there is a simple genetic consequence of castration: any male hominid that has been castrated cannot produce offspring, and its only hope for maximizing fitness is through kin altruism. Castration is *not* like most other forms of survivable body damage or mutilation. A man with a missing finger can reproduce, but a man with a missing penis cannot. The perpetrator of castration, on the other hand, may have enhanced his fitness because he has by definition eliminated a potential competitor for access to the reproductive resources of females.

Given that castration is practiced by some of today's hominids, and given the likelihood that it was practiced by our ancestors, then would it come as any surprise, a priori, that a predisposition to be anxious about castration developed in hominids? The answer is: no, but more has to be said about just what constitutes castration, and it remains to be shown that castration anxiety did in fact develop.

44. Forms of Evidence for Castration Anxiety

> As, without exception, all these stories
> are quite unsuitable for printing, in a
> book intended for general reading, I
> must ask the serious student to refer to
> the references given.
>
> *N. Penzer*, Poison-Damsels

The term "castration" (from Indoeuropean *çásati,* 'to cut') generally refers either to removal of the penis or to removal of the gonads, or to both.[108] In any of its meanings, castration destroys the ability to produce offspring. Among many veterinarians, endocrinologists, physiologists, etc. the term covers removal of either male or female gonads (i.e., either testes or ovaries). Among psychoanalysts removal of the penis is what is usually meant, and only the male can be castrated (though psychoanalysts often have to deal with fantasies of the female as a "castrated" male).

The reason why Freud and his followers concentrated on the penis as the organ which could be castrated was that the penis is obvious even early in ontogenetic development, while the testes do not descend and become externally visible or palpable until puberty, long after the Oedipal fireworks which interest psychoanalysts are over. Most psychoanalytically-inclined scholars of course link castration with the Oedipus complex and with the Oedipal stage of development (e.g., Freud, *SE*, X, 3-149; XIX, 172-9; Fenichel 1945, 91; LaPlanche and Pontalis 1973, 74-8; Spiro 1982, 109-13; Mitchell 1974, 74-91). But one can discuss whether or not castration anxiety fits into a scenario of hominid evolution without necessarily deciding just where it fits into any ontogenetic scenario.

It is a remarkable fact that, many decades after the founding of psychoanalysis, the commonly used psychoanalytic definition of the term "castration" has not found its way into many major dictionaries.[109] I have searched

---

108. Some rather fine distinctions have been made in the past. Ellis (1927-8, III, 9) reports that "the Romans recognized four different degrees: 1. True *castrati,* from whom both the testicles and the penis had been removed. 2. *Spadones,* from whom the testicles only had been removed; this was the most common practice. 3. *Thlibiae,* in whom the testicles had not been removed, but destroyed by crushing; this practice is referred to by Hippocrates. 4. *Thlasiae,* in whom the spermatic cord had simply been cut." For a detailed philological discussion on the various notions of castration, see Thass-Thienemann 1973, II, 99-117.

109. A definition of the psychoanalytic term "castration complex," however, usually is given in the better dictionaries.

in vain for the psychoanalytic meaning of the term "castration" (or its linguistic equivalent) in *Webster's Third New International Dictionary* (1971 edition), in the Soviet Academy's *Slovar' sovremennogo russkogo literaturnogo iazyka* (1950-65), and in Littré's *Dictionnaire de la langue française* (1958).[110] This omission is not only shameful to the lexicographic profession,[111] but is suspiciously like one of the very definitions of "castration" given in Webster: "the deletion of a part of (a text) esp. for purposes of expurgation." I am not saying that the omission of a major dictionary definition is intentional. Lexicographers cannot possibly be ignorant of the commonly accepted meaning of "castration" in both psychoanalytic and lay circles. But lexicographers are also human, and therefore can be unintentionally forgetful of unpleasant things. Their forgetfulness is no more astounding, really, than the amnesia of Freud's patient "Little Hans" who, upon returning to Freud's office as a strapping young man of age nineteen, reported (with a straight face) that he could remember none of the documented anxiety he had had about his "widdler" when he was just five years old (*SE* X, 148-9).

Largely disregarding what the psychoanalysts meant by castration, the sexological profession has since produced quite a few new terms: ablation of the penis ("ablatio penis"), penectomy, phallic amputation, penile loss, amputation of the penis (all these terms appearing in a recent issue of *Archives of Sexual Behavior*).

For present purposes, I will retain the old term "castration" and use it to refer to removal of any or all external male genitalia, specifying which genitalia only if the context is not clear (with "ovariectomy," "mastectomy," "clitoral excision," and "infibulation" covering the major types of female sexual mutilation). Thus, for example, the term "castration" will refer to any or all of the three surgical steps that used to be taken by male *Skoptsy* (a Russian religious sect): one testicle was removed in some cases ("poluoskoplenie," 'half castration'[112]), both testes were typically removed ("malaia

---

110. But at least one major dictionary of Freud's native language, the Brockhaus Wahrig *Deutsches Wörterbuch* (1980-) manages to include Freud's meaning of the word under the entry "entmannen," but not under "kastrieren".
111. Strage (1980, 54-5) thinks the continued use of "castration anxiety" by psychiatrists, when the dictionaries do not carry the psychiatric sense of "castration," is shameful to the *psychiatric* profession. But this is exactly backwards. People who make dictionaries are supposed to reflect usage, not legislate it.
112. Among the Ponapeans of the Caroline Islands in Micronesia one testicle is removed from a male undergoing initiation. Ford and Beach refer to the practice as "hemicastration" (1951, 177). Gregersen (1982, 104) says it is (or was) also performed among the Janjero of Ethiopia, the Hotentot of southern Africa, and another (unspecified) Micronesian people.

pechat'," 'minor seal'), and sometimes the penis was removed as well ("tsarskaia pechat'," 'the czar's seal' – see Shlezinger 1900).

It is easy to document the practice of castration (in the sense of removing the testes) in humans (see: Tannahill 1980, 246-54; Gray 1951[1917]; Kinsey *et al.* 1965, 738-45; Stürup 1972; Browe 1936 for general historical and medical discussions). The soldiers of defeated armies were castrated (Zaborowski 1896, 653-5, for examples). Religious fanatics, such as the young Origen, or the devotees (*Galloi*) of the goddess Cybele did castrate themselves. In imperial Rome infants and boys were castrated so they could later be used in brothels (de Mause 1982, 54). Eunuchs did attend to harems, and *castrati* did display their powerful contralto voices on European stages. In the United States castration has been used to "treat" epilepsy, masturbation, pedophilia, homosexuality, exhibitionism, and juvenile delinquency. Castration is still one treatment for cancer of the prostate (see Money 1972, 217ff.). "Therapeutic castration" is still performed on sex offenders today in such countries as West Germany, Czechoslovakia, Denmark, Sweden, Norway, Holland, and Switzerland (Stürup 1972). Usually it is voluntary, according to Stürup.

Castration (in the sense of loss of the penis) can result from an improperly performed circumcision (Money reports a case in which a seventeen-month-old boy was reassigned female gender – 1975). There are occasional reports of non-medical castration of the penis in the news media today. For example, United Press International recently issued an item about an angry father in Pasadena, California who cut off his eight-year-old son's penis with a butter knife and flushed it down a toilet (the penis was retrieved and reattached by doctors).[113]

What is much more difficult to do is to demonstrate the existence of *castration anxiety*, which psychoanalysts consider to be a key element of the Oedipal picture. Fisher and Greenberg (1977, 193-8) review the experimental evidence for such anxiety. Most of the literature, however, deals with the question of whether males have more castration anxiety than females, not with the question of whether there is such a thing as castration anxiety in the first place. This strikes me as peculiar. I doubt that it would have occurred to anyone to ask whether females have more anxiety about miscarriage or mastectomy than males do, or whether rich capitalists fear a stock market crash more than proletarians do. If anybody is going to have castration anxiety, it should, a priori at least, be males.

In particular, it should be immature males who, though they are still quite little and dependent on their relatively 'huge' mothers, nonetheless possess

---

113. As reported in *The Sacramento Bee*, 20 Nov. 1980, p. B4.

an externally visible organ which makes them different from their mothers. This difference should be most noticeable to children in societies where mother-infant contact is close and prolonged, and mothers are scantily clad when interacting with children. Immature females are not confronted with such an anatomical difference,[114] and it should not therefore be as likely for them to think they have something to *lose*.

The little boy learns that there are some people – including the person most precious to him and with whom he identifies totally at first – who do not have a penis. He quite naturally thinks that penisless people might have had penises before, might have them in the future, or might even want to expropriate penises from those who do possess them. After all, having a penis can be a pleasurable thing, as the boy knows from his own erotic experience and narcissistic/exhibitionistic activities, while deprivation of a penis must obviously be painful (the boy has experienced pain) and would leave him without one of the most erotic and self-aggrandizing joys of life.

Child psychiatrists (and parents who simply listen to their children) hear all kinds of bizarre theories about penises from little boys (though the more one hears about trans-sex operations and circumcision accidents the less bizarre these theories seem). One woman reported to me that her two-year-old son said to *her*: "You just have to wait till you grow up, and you'll have a penis too!" More examples:

The conversation took place in a locker room where both the father and son [about six years old] were changing from their swim suits to street clothes. The father asked: "Johnny, what's the difference between boys and girls?" The little boy replied with a long list of differences in clothing, hair style, etc. But the father (a university professor) pressed him, saying: "That's not what I mean. You know that the real difference is that boys have a penis and girls don't." To which the little boy emphatically replied: "Oh, I know that, but girls *used* to have a penis!" (Rancour-Laferriere 1982a, 234).

Henry E., 8;11, who had first noticed the difference at 6 years used to think that girls' genitals were cut off. Even after correction of this notion, he still spoke of the girl's genital as having "a cut in it." (Conn and Kanner 1947, 47).

James P., 10;6, had a unique idea, which he based on what he believed to be a well-remembered actual experience. He always believed and continued to believe that a girl's "pee-wee" was first like a boy's. "My sister used to have one like mine, and the dear Lord changed it. When I was a little boy about 4 years old, I saw my sister's. The next morning she woke up with one that was flat. The Lord changed it. The dear Lord can do anything." (*ibid*., 47-8).

... I [Hans' father] explained to him that his sister has not got a widdler [*Wiwimacher*] like him. Little girls and women, I said, have no widdlers:

---

114. *Both* little boys and little girls are of course confronted with the fact that their mothers have breasts, whereas they do not.

Mummy has none, Anna has none, and so on.
'*Hans*: "Have you got a widdler?"
'*I*: "Of course. Why, what do you suppose?"
'*Hans* (after a pause): "But how do little girls widdle, if they have no widdlers?" (*SE*, X, 31).

Obviously, Little Hans assumed that females *do* have "widdlers," else he would not have made such a famous fuss about it.

Grown up males (and females too) may imagine that females have (or once had) penises, though grown ups tend to disguise their beliefs about this much more than children do. Among the Gimi of Papua New Guinea the phallic flutes used in men's rituals are believed to have been "stolen" from women (Gillison 1980, 154-6). The Brazilian Mundurucú have a similar belief (Hays 1964, 75). Among the African Chaga the women have a tradition according to which women were deprived of their penises by mysterious horned beings (Raum 1939, 557). As we saw earlier (section 25), in some contexts males think of virgin females as phallic and regard defloration as a kind of castration. Many of the androgynes and hermaphrodites of folklore and mythology are essentially phallic women (see: O'Flaherty 1980; Baumann 1955; Kakar 1978, 158ff.; above, section 25). In India a common term of abuse is "Your mother's penis" (Kakar 1978, 94), and the commonly worshipped *linga-yoni* of the Hindus consists of a phallic icon fused with and projecting out of a vulval icon (*ibid.*, 185). In the clinical literature fantasies of phallic women abound. Devereux reports a case in which

A medical psychoanalyst had analyzed a gynecological surgeon (!) of exceptional ability, who firmly believed that women had a penis, though his professional training and experience should have taught him differently. He clung to this — at first unconscious — idea so tenaciously, that his analyst had to show to him periodically a text book of anatomy, so as to convince him, at least momentarily, that the female had no penis. The analysis revealed that the unconscious objective of this surgeon's gynecological operations was the discovery of the female phallus. (Devereux 1967, 184-5; for more on the "phallic woman" fantasy, see: Brunswick 1940; Spiro 1982, 118; Stärcke 1921; Hutchinson 1959; Bak 1968; Fenichel 1945, 330-46; Laferrière 1977a, 74-5; LaPlanche and Pontalis 1973, 310; Rancour-Laferriere 1982a, 132-40; Freud *SE* XXI, 154; Stoller 1968, ch. 16).

But to return to castration anxiety. Fisher and Greenberg conclude from their survey of the experimental data on castration anxiety that the findings "... may be sensibly interpreted as indicating that males are probably characterized by more anxiety about, and preoccupation with, *body damage* (*castration*) than are females" (*ibid.*, 195, my italics). Unfortunately, yet another definition of "castration" seems to have been introduced here, namely, "body damage."

As an example of this particular definition, we may cite the kind of fable
Friedman addressed to the children in his study:

Once there was a little monkey named Franky (Mary). He had a long curly
tail. He liked this tail so much that he looked at it every day and he had all
sorts of fun with it. One day, Frankie woke up and saw that something was
different. What do you think had happened? (Friedman 1952, 73; the monkey is male in telling the fable to male children, female for female children).

Friedman simply assumed that a "central projecting organ," in this case the
monkey's tail, represented a penis for the child (the same assumption is made
for the so-called Blacky Test, in which the subject is shown a picture of a
large knife about to descend on the tail of a blindfolded dog). The 141 (out
of 295) children who ended Friedman's fable by "cutting off" the monkey's
tail were supposedly removing a penis (in semiotic terms, a presumed icon of
a penis). The remaining 154 children who left the tail intact were said to be
dealing with their castration anxiety by denying that the tail could be lost.

I am inclined to agree that the monkey's tail as presented in Friedman's
fable had penile significance for the children tested. But this is just an intuition, the standard kind of intuition that is rife in the psychoanalytic literature.[115] One interesting finding was that "... a significantly greater number
of the children who ended the fable by not removing the projection were
blocked in their reaction times" (*ibid.*, 77). Obviously, if it takes a long time
to leave the tail on the monkey some mental events must be going on in
that period of time, and denial of the possibility of removing the tail could
be one of the events. But still it is not established that the tail has the meaning of a penis, as Rohrbaugh (1979, 99) has pointed out: "The children may
have reacted much as they would to the loss of any bodily extremity such
as an arm or a leg. With this research method it is impossible to differentiate
between a threat to general bodily integrity and a threat to the penis per se"
(cf. G. Wilson 1978, 16; Eysenck and Wilson 1973, 153).

Schwartz's (1955) experimental approach to castration anxiety was
different, and much more convincing. He showed a film of Australian Arunta
subincision rites to a group of college age males. The film was very explicit
and very gory, containing close-up shots of the penis being sliced down its
underside and blood dripping from it. Such graphic visual stimulation is
clearly much closer to what castration literally is than the fable about a
monkey's tail. Fourteen out of the fifteen psychiatrists, psychologists and
social workers who were asked to view the film agreed that the film elicited

---

115. Once little Hans pointed to a monkey depicted in a book and said of its curled-
up tail: "Daddy, look at its widdler!" (*SE*, X, 14).

a very powerful castration anxiety.[116] As for the experimental subjects, they registered "strong anxiety and revulsion" against the penile mutilation presented in the film (*ibid.*, 212). Their scores on a subsequent Thematic Apperception Test (which involves inventing stories to go with pictures) were significantly different (beyond .01 level) from the scores of subjects who had been exposed to two different films containing no suggestions of castration.[117] More specifically, their T.A.T. scores differed from those of the other two groups of experimental subjects in the categories of "intrapsychic threat," "extrapsychic threat," "loss of cathected objects," "general repetitive attempts at mastery," and "damage to or loss of extensions of the body image." What these abstract categories mean in concrete terms may be seen in the summary of stories invented by subjects exposed to the film of penile mutilation:

Stories scoring high in castration anxiety typically started with a description of the hero engaging in some sexual misbehavior, usually with a woman described as a prostitute or as otherwise immoral. The hero was generally described as an inadequate or undesirable individual. Often these unflattering descriptions of the characters of the story were repeated and elaborated in considerable detail, as was the description of the sexual activity. Following the sex act, the hero was described as tormented by remorse and guilt, and often as well by threats or punishment from external sources. The description of the hero as guilt-laden was often repeated. The threats from external sources were varied, stemming from wife or family, from the law, or from less specific societal sources. Following this, there was often a description of loss of loved individuals. The immoral sex partner was frequently described as abandoning the hero to seek "greener pastures," following the series of objective misfortunes he experiences. In many cases the hero committed suicide or was injured or killed to end the story. In general, death, debility, loss of status or possessions, or some other "bad" ending of the story occurred. (*ibid.*, 217-18).

This summary raises some interesting questions for the evolution of hominid sexual relations. Why should castration anxiety be associated with "sexual misbehavior?" If the castration anxiety generated by the bloody subincision scenes can lead the subjects to ideas of illicit sex, can the converse occur, i.e., can ideas of illicit sex lead to castration anxiety? If so, then castra-

---

116. Devereux (1967, 50-80) psychoanalyzes the reactions of anthropologists, psychoanalysts, and analytic candidates to the film, and finds much castration anxiety in the reactions (I assume Devereux and Schwartz are referring to the same film).

117. Farrell (1981, 156-8), who expresses considerable skepticism regarding Friedman's work on the castration complex, does not mention the Schwartz study. The same is true of Rohrbaugh (1979, 96-100). Eysenck and Wilson, however, do pay attention to Schwartz's work, and suggest that there is no way of knowing whether or not the film of subincision simply evoked more generalized anxiety (as opposed to castration anxiety) than the other films (1973, 137-8).

tion anxiety may have been one of the proximate mechanisms regulating or limiting male-male competition for females in the course of hominid evolution. Not only may castration anxiety have facilitated the avoidance of incest (above, section 19), but it may have helped males to focus their sexual attentions on just one (or a very limited number of) females, and thereby have permitted them to cash in on the advantages of monogamy. A male suffering from a constant low, subliminal level of castration anxiety would have been less likely to wastefully divert altruism from his mate/offspring to other females whose offspring might not even turn out to be his. At the same time he may have been more likely to be the genitor of his *own* mate's offspring if *other* males were equally susceptible to this same castration anxiety.

Among the Awa of New Guinea there is a mutilatory ritual called *ahpwi tari ege*, translated as "severe penis cutting" by Newman and Boyd (1982, 275). Part of the ritual involves cutting small wedges of flesh from either side of the glans penis of each initiate. To add insult to injury, the older men then strike the already lacerated penis with the knife and rub it vigorously with salt or nettles. They then proceed to bleed their own penises by puncturing them with small arrows. After both the older men and the initiates have rested, they retire to a secluded area and a lecture is given on the dangers of sexual intercourse with women: "Following this instruction, the initiates are taken into the men's house, where they are further lectured about the *social consequences of marital infidelity*. In the men's house they are shown a display of bows, arrows, axes, and fighting sticks. These, they are told, are the instruments of reprisal which will be used against them by enraged husbands *should they be discovered seducing other men's wives*" (*ibid.*, 277, italics added). Certainly the initiates must make a connection between the admonishment to monogamy and the near-castration they have just experienced. Just as the viewers of the subincision film produced fantasies of "sexual misbehavior" (Schwartz), similarly the participants in the penis cutting ritual turned their attention to "marital infidelity" (Newman and Boyd). Illegitimate sexual intercourse was associated with castration anxiety in two very different cultural contexts.

But why castration anxiety? Why not some other form of anxiety to accomplish the same thing? Why not some other bodily organ?

I would like to suggest the following hypothesis. The penis represents, more efficiently than any other organ, *both* a male's heterosexual behavior (he inserts it and not something else into a vagina that either does or does not belong to him) *and* his overall reproductive potential. The idea of a penis being removed for indulging in sexual variety – as opposed to an ear, a finger, etc. – manages to allude to the sexual misbehavior itself (the penis was the offender) and to the possibility of future reproductive failure (a man cannot reproduce without his penis).

The latter possibility accounts, I think, for the frequent association of castration with *death* (cf. Devereux 1973, 46). A castrated male might as well be dead, reproductively, compared with other, intact males. In terms of the logic of penile synecdoche, if the part is destroyed, the whole is destroyed (Rancour-Laferriere 1982a, 193). Suicide only makes sense. A scene in the film *El Topo* shows a man who, after being castrated by another man, shoots himself of his own accord. Or, the association of castration with death may be made in the reverse order. For example, it was a custom in the Ethiopian Galla tribes for a male to castrate his opponent after killing him (Wickler 1972, 54).

However, before getting further carried away with speculations on the adaptiveness of castration anxiety in ancestral hominids, I had better point out a problem in the study that precipitated this discussion. Although the subincision film plainly showed cutting of the penis, the control films presumably did not show cutting of some *other* body organ. It is possible the same stories of "sexual misbehavior" would have been elicited by a film sequence of a form of mutilation other than (near-) castration. The famous eye-slicing scene in Buñuel's *Un chien andalou* comes to mind. Likewise, I did not mention that the penile mutilation ritual of the Awa is accompanied by nosebleeding (instruments are pounded into the nostrils, and profuse bleeding results). Could the lecture about "marital infidelity" have resulted from anxiety about the nose instead of castration anxiety?

A psychoanalyst would retort that the eye in Buñuel or the nose bled by the Awa is itself a penile icon. Freud had interpreted Oedipus' self-blinding, for example, as castration (*SE*, V, 398; cf. Rancour-Laferriere 1982a, 165-71; Dundes 1980, 113-21; Devereux 1973), and the loss of a nose by one of Nikolai Gogol's literary characters has been repeatedly interpreted as castration (see Rancour-Laferriere 1982a, 81, for a bibliography).

The problem then becomes one of determining when the mutilated eye or nose is an iconic penis and when it is not, and the psychoanalysts offer no clear solution. An eye is obviously phallic in some contexts (e.g., the *phallus oculatus* – Dundes, 115), and a penis hanging where the nose should be (see Morris 1977, 244) clearly gives the nose a penile meaning. But more commonly it is difficult to decide when such iconicity is at work. Rather than struggle with this problem, then, I would rather simply look for other forms of evidence for castration anxiety.

One other problem for the theory of male castration anxiety should also be mentioned, namely, male transsexualism (see: Stoller 1968; 1976). This is a rare disorder in which anatomically normal males are convinced they are female, and usually insist on dressing and acting as females do from an early age. In our society they often desire to have a sex-change operation, which includes castration.

Unlike the male transvestite, who is very concerned about and attached to his penis, the male transsexual feels his penis is misplaced and in many cases he would just as soon be without it. The transsexual is permanently and truly feminine, while the transvestite is only periodically effeminate. Stoller (e.g., 1976) found a background of exaggerated and prolonged intimacy with the mother in transsexual males, and a marked physical and/or psychological absence of the father. Stoller's interpretation is that the transsexual male never had the opportunity to go through a masculine period of development, and hence never got around to placing a high value on his penis. His sense of merging with his mother was from earliest infancy encouraged by her own pathological need not to be separated from him, and his resulting feminine identity was complete before he had any significant contact with males.

The occasional transsexual who would just as soon have his penis removed is the exception that, in my opinion, proves the adaptive rule. *Most* men find literally unthinkable (for themselves) what the transsexual typically and firmly believes: 'I am a woman.' If all males thought that way, extinction would obviously soon result. Or, in genital terms, if all males wished they did not have penises, their reproductive success would be drastically lowered. Male transsexual behavior thus helps us realize what an important reproductive asset the penis is. What is more, its etiology suggests that, no matter how important prolonged and intensified maternal care has been in hominid evolution, there is an adaptive limit to it. The mother of the transsexual male is as exaggeratedly maternal as her son is inadequately masculine. Sociobiologically speaking, there is evidently a point beyond which more mothering has deleterious effects on reproductive success.

45. Has Castration Anxiety Been Selected For?

> A man who refuses to make love to a
> woman tortured by desire is a eunuch.
> —the *enchantress Mohini*, as translated
> by W. O'Flaherty

One unquestionable indication that males are capable of being anxious about the possibility of castration is the widespread myth of the "vagina dentata." The semantic basis for the myth is the overall similarity between the oral opening and the vaginal orifice. Perhaps also the fact that some individuals *bite* their partner's body during intercourse (see Ellis 1927-8, III, 84ff. on "love-bites") is a contributing factor.

Ford and Beach (1951, 99) report that "... the Tikopia speak of intercourse as the female genitals eating the male organ." Among the Umeda of Papua New Guinea the term for 'gullet' and the euphemistic term for 'vagina' are the same (Gell 1979, 140). Baker (1950, 173) reports that in such Polynesian languages as Maori, Samoan, Fiji, and Hawaiian, the words for vagina/labia and for mouth/lips are identical or are closely related. The folkloric/mythological motif of impregnation by mouth is not uncommon (see O'Flaherty 1980, 169-70, for some Irish examples).

In our own culture such slang terms for the vagina as "dog's mouth" and "one that bites" (Gerber 1981, 53) clearly equate the vaginal and the oral (cf. the nineteenth century terms "gape over the garter," "lower mouth," and "the upright grin" — Healey 1980, 185). Even the Latin technical terms labia majora and labia minora tell us that anatomists have oral imagery in mind when dealing with female genitalia (cf. Dundes 1980, 124). And, as we saw earlier (above, 32), the unique eversion and coloring of human facial lips suggests that they have evolved through 'mimicry' of genital lips.

The mouth has teeth, ergo the vagina must have teeth. One American joke on this subject (which I have never seen printed) goes as follows:

A shy young man has put off marriage for many years because he is convinced that every woman's vagina has teeth. When he finally does get up the courage to marry, he declares to his eager bride on the wedding night that he cannot make love with her because he is terrified of the teeth in her vagina. She laughs and tells him there is no such thing as a vagina with teeth. She then takes off her clothes and tells him to have a look for himself. After very carefully examining her genitalia with the help of a flashlight, he looks up and says: "You're absolutely right, there are no teeth. But with a gum problem like that, how *could* there be any teeth?"

On the opposite side of the globe, in central India, the Muria tell many tales about toothed vaginas, such as the following:

> In the old days there were teeth far back in the vagina. One day when the long penis went in, the teeth cut it and all that remained was a stump of its present length. Angry at this, the man brought a rice-husker and broke off the teeth. In those days the penis itself was covered with thorns; it stood up like a semur tree. But there were no thorns at the root. The thorny part was cut off, and the smooth part remains to this day. (Elwin 1968, 105-6).[118]

There is an entire chapter devoted to the motif of the vagina dentata in Lederer's *The Fear of Women* (1968, 44-52; see also: Legman 1975, 427-74; Penzer 1952, 41-4; Neuman 1955, 168-9; Strage 1980, 64ff; Gay 1984, 198-200; Kakar 1978, 92; O'Flaherty 1980, 81ff, 267; Murphy 1977, 22; Thompson's *Motif-Index*, entries K1222, A1313.3.1, and F547.1.1; Eliade 1958, 51-2, 63, 66; Paige and Paige 1981, 26; Fenichel 1945, 79-80). Kiell (1976, 85-93) cites several literary examples of vaginas that cut and bite. Such an "incredibly prevalent" idea (Lederer, 44) cannot be explained by cultural diffusion, or at least not by cultural diffusion alone. It is most probable that peoples as disparate and distant from one another as the Yąnomamö and Mundurucú of South America (Chagnon 1977, 47; Murphy 1960, 108), various North American Indian peoples (Thompson 1929, 309), the Kgalta of southern Africa (Schapera 1940, 185), the Muria of India, and many other peoples independently concocted their unlikely stories about vaginas lined with teeth. And the most obvious psychological motivation for such stories is the feeling that the object that typically gets inserted into the vagina, i.e., the penis, can be (might be, ought to be, must not be) severed from its owner.

Though the idea of a vagina with teeth is patently absurd, the idea that a hole, crevice, or hollow in the ground may contain an animal that bites is not absurd at all. Nor is it absurd that we should be phobic about the creatures that typically inhabit such places. Fear of snakes (ophidiophobia), for example, has been adaptive in hominid history. The fact that conditioned phobic responses to snakes are much more readily acquired and more difficult to extinguish than such responses to dangerous artificial objects (e.g., electric outlets) indicates a high degree of biological "preparedness" for the phobia (Seligman 1972; Hugdahl and Kärker 1981; Wilson 1977, 135).

What I want to suggest (in the spirit of Seligman 1972) is that it has been profitable in the past for hominids to avoid those chthonic places where snakes, lizards, scorpions, spiders, and other biting, stinging, and potentially

---

118. Note that, in addition to the vagina dentata, there is also a "penis aculeatus" in this particular tale, though the latter motif is generally much less common than the former, cross-culturally.

poisonous creatures live, and that whatever predisposition we have to be afraid of such places and their inhabitants has in some circumstances carried over into our sexual life. This may be seen not only in the idea of a vagina dentata, but also in the recurring folkloric motif of a vagina containing one or more serpents (Lederer 1968, 47-9). Among the Tembu of South Africa, for example, it was believed that the vagina of a lascivious woman contained serpents which bit the penis that entered and caused it to be diseased (Laubscher 1937, 21-2). Among the terms for the vagina listed by Gerber (1981, 53) are "snake pit" and "rattlesnake canyon."

We are "prepared" to associate dangerous terrestrial apertures with vaginal apertures specifically through the action of mental similarity processes. In semiotic terms, vaginal apertures easily function as *icons* of terrestrial apertures. Or, stated evolutionarily, the adaptive hominid tendency to be anxious and cautious in dealing with little hollow places in the earth may be the *preadaptation* which makes today's hominid male a lot more careful about inserting his penis into a vagina than he otherwise might have been.

Lederer hints at this preadaptive route to male castration anxiety when he says: "Earth-mother symbolism may underlie these myths [of sexually dangerous maidens], for snakes live in holes in the earth and in some countries make it decidedly unwholesome to investigate dark caverns" (1968, 49).

The relationship of terrestrial apertures to vaginal apertures is what a psychoanalyst might call "symbolic." For example, Róheim cites a report of a rite practiced by the natives of the Ooldea region of Australia:

Singing over a hole: the man who is to perform this rite goes out secretly into the bush where, in a clear space, he digs a hole that symbolizes the vulva. Sitting over it, he sings,
    "Labia vulva, labia vulva, labia vulva."

(1945b, 263)

Or, here is a statement made by a male Hua native of the New Guinea highlands:

The holes in trees, rocks, but, most particularly, the ground in which possums live are like women's vaginas/urethras.

(Meigs 1976, 396)

Baker (1950, 173) provides the following lexical items from some Polynesian languages:

Maori: *puta*, vagina: hole, cave. *hika*, vagina; *kohika*, a hole.
      waha, vagina; entrance of a hole.
Samoan: *pu*, vagina; hole.
Marquesan: *pokopoko*, vagina; *pokoa*, a hole. (cf. Latin: *cunnus*, vagina;
      cuniculum, hole, mine.)
Hawaiian: *pukapaa*, vagina; *puka*, crevice.

But note that the direction of Freudian "symbolism" in all these examples is, in a sense, opposite to that of the preadaptive iconicity I have been discussing. In *The Interpretation of Dreams* Freud said that pits, narrow spaces, subterranean channels, etc. in dreams represent female genitalia (*SE*, V, 397-401; cf. Róheim *ibid.*, 216, 263), while here it is being argued instead that female genitalia represent pits, narrow spaces, etc. (the same reversal of perspective obtains for my suggestion [above, p. 271] that fear of penile display is preadaptively based on snake phobia).

Combining this preadaptive iconicity of female genitalia with the properly Freudian iconicity (though Freudians call it "symbolism") of snakes yields a new kind of evidence for castration anxiety in males. If female genitalia iconize terrestrial apertures containing such vermin as snakes, and if snakes themselves can be penile icons, then female genitalia in effect can contain male genitalia — but of course severed from their owners!

Let us then consider now a potential indexical function (above and beyond the iconic function) of the snake(s) in the vaginal snake pit. Perhaps another reason why an ancestral hominid male exercised caution in copulation was that he took the imagined inhabitant of the desired vagina to indicate the presence of *another* male who 'owned' or 'possessed' this vagina. To extend a metaphor, his snake would have kept away if another snake was already there. This transfer of territorial behavior into the realm of sexual behavior would have helped promote monogamy insofar as it would have made males anxious about approaching females attached to other males (cf. above discussion of the monogamy-facilitating function of castration anxiety). The imagined 'other' male would, in effect, be giving a hostile penile display to would-be intruders (ancient ithyphallic herms were often used as *border*-stones or *entranceway*-guardians, and Wickler [1967, 132; 1972, 54-8] discerned the parallel between the human use of phallic herms and the territorial penile display behavior of certain Old World monkeys — see my discussion of territorial phallicism in Rancour-Laferriere 1979b, 63-6).

The idea that another man's penis would be present in or guarding a woman's vagina is familiar to psychoanalysts, but the analytic literature usually deals specifically with the child's viewpoint, i.e., with the child's feelings about the father's penis in the mother's vagina (e.g., Klein 1977, 190, 211, 213, 226-7; Lederer 1968, 49; Gough 1955, 64). The theory I am proposing deals instead with reproductively mature individuals and their reproductive success. But psychoanalysis is still obviously my chief guide and neoteny is my chief biological justification for applying the facts of child psychology to reproductively mature individuals. The *child* in the neotenous adult hominid imagines a threatening penis of a *potential father-icon* to be present in the threatening vagina of a *potential mother-icon*, and as a consequence great caution is exercised before entering that vagina — if it is entered at all.

Though a man may fear a castrating agent either inside of or apart from the woman's body, it is equally, if not more likely that male castration anxiety relates to the woman herself. The *Malleus maleficarum*, for example, which was a fifteenth century inquisitorial handbook on witchcraft, stated that witches were capable of causing impotence ("ligature") and could also "... truly and actually remove men's members" (see: Hays 1964, 152; Lea 1957, vol. I, 306-53). O'Flaherty (1980, ch. 4) cites some examples of females literally or figuratively castrating males in Indian mythology. The fantasy of the vagina dentata is of course an expression of the feeling that specifically a female, rather than a male, can castrate. Legman (1975, 434ff.) provides several jokes and anecdotes on the theme of "castration by women," such as:

A man is berated by the state-troopers for not having strapped on his girl friend's seat belt before the accident in which she was thrown through the windshield and killed, while he is still alive behind the steering-wheel. "So what?" he says bitterly, "go take a look at what she's got in her hand!" (*ibid.*, 438).

In the psychoanalytic literature the castrating agent is often female. Klein (1977[1926], 129) goes so far as to say that "... in both sexes it is the mother who in the deepest strata of the unconscious is specially dreaded as a castrator" (cf. Devereux 1967, 56; Roellenbleck 1974, 75; Horney 1967, 133-46). Freud originally postulated that "More or less plainly, more or less brutally, a threat is pronounced that this part of him which he values so highly will be taken away from him. Usually it is from women that the threat emanates ..." (*SE* XIX, 174). If circumcision is an icon of castration, as I will argue below, then the son of Moses was iconically castrated by his own mother, Zipporah, when she circumcised him (Exodus 4: 24-6; see Roellenbleck 1974, 71ff.; Nunberg 1947, 175). Also, more than one scholar has noted the passage in Deuteronomy (25: 11-12) where a woman is portrayed as a danger to male genitalia: "If two men fall out and come to blows, it may be that the wife of the weaker man will come up to his rescue, and lay hands upon the other, taking shameful hold of him [euphemistic Knox translation]. That hand of hers must be struck off, and no mercy be shewn to her."

Consider serpents again. I have already mentioned the idea that the (penile) snake occupying the folkloric vagina is by implication severed from its owner. In effect a "phallic woman" comes into existence at a man's expense (though there are other routes to this image in the psychoanalytic literature). It is difficult for a male to conceive of a "phallic woman" without also thinking of her as a "castrating female."

A dangerous serpent can *be* a female as well as be *inside* a female. One of the characteristics of snakes not often mentioned in the folkloric literature is their sinuous movement, which is reminiscent of the undulating, rhythmic motion of a slim woman who is dancing or simply walking.[119] Such motion is of course attractive to a male. Mundkur points to Hindu myths about men attracted by "beauteously seductive maidens, actually *nāginis* or female cobras masquerading as humans" (1983, 178). Snakes are also known to coil around their prey, and this property is possessed by the passionate Salmacis as she attempts to seduce the shy Hermaphroditus in Ovid's *Metamorphoses*: "... in spite of all his efforts to slip from her grasp, she twined around him, like a serpent when it is being carried off into the air by the king of birds: for, as it hangs from the eagle's beak, the snake coils round his head and talons and with its tail hampers his beating wings" (Naso 1955, 112). Ultimately, a snake may also swallow its victim. Echidna, the monster of Greek mythology who was half-snake, half-woman, ate raw meat and killed all the men who came to her (Lederer 1968, 57). Slater argues that the chief danger of the serpent in its feminine aspect is specifically oral: "... the serpent, whether viewed as genital or not, is orally defined, and the fear which it evokes is of being absorbed by the mother, or poisoned, or enveloped, or strangled – all common schizophrenic fantasies" (1968, 87).

Needless to say, if anyone construes these terrible feminine/ophidian deeds as castration, it is the males, the phallocentric sex. Otherwise, there is not much objective evidence in the lore of snake-women that they are castrators. The myths of vagina dentata, vaginal snake pit, and castrating witches are much stronger indicators that castration is what the male creaters of these myths were preoccupied with.

That a female may *actually* threaten castration is of course possible. Lederer furnishes an appalling example:

The most blatant castration threat I ever heard of was reported to me by a social worker who acted as consultant in an orphanage run by nuns: they had informed her quite blandly that they were dealing with masturbation successfully by threatening to cut off the boys' penises; and that they were reinforcing this threat by blindfolding each suspect and touching his penis with a lump of ice! (1968, 218).

From a strictly ethological perspective we would say that these nuns are engaging in "dominance behavior," and indeed the perception of being dominated must be one of the phylogenetic bases of castration anxiety. Jonas and Jonas say: "The evolutionary basis of castration anxiety ... may

---

119. Havelock Ellis quotes an anonymous woman correspondent to this same effect (1927-8, VII, 454).

... be seen as a loss of sexuality that the primate male experiences in the presence of a dominant animal" (1975b, 605). In his discussion of "female dominance" and "the 'castrating' female," Van den Berghe (1979, 197) says that "... female dominance is a sexual 'turn off' for most men," and that men "... can be threatened to the point of sexual dysfunction when women attempt to assume the dominant role...."

A man's perception of a woman as a "castrating female" is usually based on much more subtle signals of dominance than the ice-wielding nuns were giving off. All kinds of feminine hints and innuendos may "castrate" a man:

A boy, a man, on a date, is in competition against an unknown number of invisible competitors, and in an unpredictable number of different arenas. He can be deflated and cut down when he makes the date ("I really don't anticipate a free evening for several weeks..."); when he comes to fetch her ("I thought you had a convertible..."); at the restaurant ("Oh dear, my dress is too formal for this place; if you had told me..."); during dinner ("You *really* don't know how to eat an artichoke?"); in conversation ("*Everybody* today reads Kierkegaard, of course..."); or conversely, "You must think me very simple but I haven't understood a word you've said during the last five minutes..."); when paying ("My father always tips at least 15 per cent..."); after dinner ("Is there nothing more exciting you can suggest? I hate those stuffy little movie houses..."); on the way home ("You surely don't expect me to get that familiar on a first date?"); etc.... Whatever he does, and whichever way he does it, he risks the possibility that his penis may be just a little smaller, and just a little less adept, than someone else's. (*ibid.*, 219).

One may disagree as to whether the woman in every one of these instances is being a "castrating female" or not. Some feminists would in fact say that the tradition of kowtowing to the male ego, of bending over backwards to avoid "castrating" a man is precisely what has to stop if women are to be liberated from sexist bonds.

Yet the male ego really is a delicate thing, as we saw in the discussion of fake orgasm (above, section 7). There are circumstances where a man does find a woman's behavior *genitally* threatening, even if there is no overt reference to genitalia. Enough of such behavior will drive a man away, or will make him impotent, which is the same thing, from the viewpoint of their joint reproductive success.

Above (section 4) I have already noted the rather high incidence of impotence in American and British samples. Broude and Greene (1976, 417) report that fear of impotence is present in 80% of the 40 societies of the Standard Sample for which the information was available. The sexual lore from a great variety of societies reveals that men commonly believe that coitus weakens and debilitates them, or depletes their limited supply of precious semen (e.g., Dundes 1980, 121-4; Herdt 1982; O'Flaherty 1980; Brandes 1981). The fact that a male is always temporarily impotent after sexual intercourse probably has something to do with the typical male fantasy of success followed by destruction, "ascensionism" followed by an "Icarian" fall (see: May 1966; 1980, 150ff.; Murray 1955). We have already seen (above, section 7) that a man can in some contexts feel threatened if his partner does not appear to be having orgasms. But there are also contexts where he is threatened if she is having or wants to have too many orgasms, that is, where she appears to him to want more penile service than he can possibly provide. In such contexts he may feel that she wants his penis so badly that she wants to keep it. Folklore and mythology are full of images of genitally dangerous women who are at the same time very desirous of sex. O'Flaherty says that "... the woman whose vagina contains a tooth, or a poisonous snake, or a penis, or a devouring mouth is always the erotic woman — the woman who experiences pleasure in sex" (1980, 292). More accurately, I think, the woman with a dangerous vagina is the one who is perceived as *too* erotic, for any heterosexual male other than a necrophiliac is pleased with *some* sexual response in a woman.

If a woman perceived as a genital threat still does not discourage a man from attempting copulation, his penis may fail to perform anyway. There are of course many physiological reasons why a man becomes impotent, such as diabetes, low testosterone level, spinal cord damage, etc. In such "organogenic" impotence even the nocturnal erections of REM sleep are absent or weakened (see Wagner and Green 1981 for a comprehensive overview). But when the cause is "psychogenic," as the therapists say, then "the most common psychotherapy of impotence relates to solving conflict in men's power relations with women, as the name of the disorder suggests" (Offit 1981, 123). Speaking of "... the poor fellow attempting coitus with a partner who is always either a hostile victim or an aggressive opponent," Offit says: "... impotence is a healthy response...;" "the man needs to be potent enough only to rise from the bed and take his lady into the living room for a talk, or to the nearest therapist, or back to her apartment or mother" (*ibid.*, 124).

In extreme cases a male may experience something even more unpleasant, i.e., retraction of all or part of his penis into the abdominal wall or into the inguinial tissue. Masters and Johnson have observed this phenomenon in their laboratory: "Particularly does hyperinvolution become clinically obvious immediately following attempted and failed sexual encounter" (1980[1966], 181). They add that "clinical observations tend to support the possibility that penile hyperinvolution, like penile erection, although frequently developed on a reflex basis, may also respond directly to higher cortical centers" (*ibid.*). The occurrence of penile hyperinvolution is also documented cross-culturally (see Edwards 1984 for a survey). Perhaps the best known designation of this phenomenon by anthropologists is *Koro* (from a Malay word meaning 'to shrink'). *Koro* occurs not only in the context of sexual interaction with a female, but is also said to result variously from masturbation, excessive physical labor, exposure to cold, improper diet, sorcery, falling off a horse, etc. The cultural and biological strands of the phenomenon have not yet been disentangled. But it clearly renders a man incapable of sexual intercourse, that is, makes him impotent. For example, in one case reported from the Tagabawa Bagobo of Mindanao, the man's wife abandoned him because he was "not good sex" (*ibid.*, 8). In a case from Sulawesi a man developed *Koro* shortly after taking a second wife, apparently because he feared the jealousy of the first wife (*ibid.*, 5). Most kinds of *Koro* (or whatever it is called in the native culture) would qualify as psychosomatic illnesses. Sexologically, they constitute the most extreme form of psychogenic impotence.

Lewis (1969) views psychogenic impotence as an expression of sexual conflict. He discusses examples of impotence in which there is "... a passive, withdrawing expression of the husband's anger toward the wife's assertiveness. The wife's dominating, capable manner may awaken childhood feelings of helplessness and resentment toward the mother" (*ibid.*, 75 – note the wife's implicit iconicity of the mother in this statement). Derogatis *et al.* (1976) administered a questionnaire that distinguishes psychogenically impotent males as having "hypermasculine role definition." They believe that psychogenically impotent males have overly rigid expectations regarding how females should act (but see Segraves *et al.* 1981).

That the behavior of a potential or current female sexual partner should be measured specifically in terms of the feelings a man has about the length, performance, or presence/absence of his penis, that is, in terms of his own castration anxiety,[120] makes good evolutionary sense from his viewpoint. The penis is a very efficient, polysemous signifier because it is *both* an index

---

120. I realize that, with this definition of castration anxiety, I have not completely adhered to the definition of castration that I gave above (308), i.e., *removal* of any or all male genitalia. However, even if this semantic extension cannot be forgiven, it should be pointed out that psychoanalysts and non-psychoanalysts alike typically make it, and I take this as evidence that anxiety about *removal* of male genitalia is at least closely related to anxiety about their proper functioning. Stronger evidence, though, is the fact that the little boy appears to be unaware of erectile problems. What concerns *him* is simply the danger that the penis might be absent, i.e., that he might be castrated. Later on, in adulthood, it then becomes very easy for him to translate his potency problems into the old castration anxiety he used to have. A penis that does not function when called upon to function is like having no penis at all. Semiotically, the adult male's penis func-

of what he does (or may do) with her (his penis is what he does or does not insert into her) *and* an index of his reproductive potential (its regularly being erect for her roughly predicts his reproductive success with her). As already suggested in the previous section, no organ but the penis can serve this dual function for a man. What I have added here is an alternative specification of the dual function: it can be the woman with whom the penis comes into contact, and not necessarily (or necessarily only) a third male party, who is perceived as the threat to the penis. I have also added a claim about the woman: if she does something that makes the man feel threatened, she stands to lose in the reproductive long run (cf. Van den Berghe 1979, 197). If she cannot refrain from doing things that he perceives as a threat to his penis, then her only hope of future offspring is with another man (not to mention potential loss of paternal care).

But to return to the male perspective. What precisely could a perceived "castrating female" be doing to threaten a male's reproductive success? Wouldn't it be more profitable for him to just inseminate (or continue inseminating) her on the off chance that she would at least bear (more) offspring for him, rather than avoid her or be impotent with her? In other words, why does there seem to have been selection for male intuitions about "castrating females" and for situational impotence?

Offit says that (psychogenic) impotence is associated with a power problem in the relation of the sexes: "there may be a very direct relationship between male impotence and being weak with women " (*ibid.*, 123). A man who is psychogenically impotent needs to regain some control that he feels he has lost to his sexual partner: "He needs to do as he pleases with his partner, or to tell her what to do. The requests he may learn to make are occasionally as simple and physical as, 'Please move your elbow; it's in my ribs.' Sometimes they are more complex: 'I would like you to stop asking me to put the house in your name because I don't intend to'" (*ibid.*). The "more complex" of these requests is the one, I think, that answers the questions posed: if she cannot accept a certain degree of power asymmetry in his favor, then he is in the position of feeling obliged to render altruism *without the normal compensatory return in the form of power and control* (see above, sections 36-7). Even if he himself cannot consciously discern when he has relinquished too much power to her, his penis will do it for him. Just as a woman can

---

tions as an icon of the penis he worried about as a child. Psychoanalytically, the adult male who is suffering from psychogenic impotence is regressing. And biologically, he is the picture of neoteny. Clearly, this tripartite characterization of iconicity/regression/neoteny is parallel to the tripartite characterization of human long-term mating offered above, section 18.

unconsciously "use" absence of orgasm as an indicator that the man may not stay around to render altruism to her and her offspring, so too the man can "use" the extreme of castration anxiety, i.e., impotence as a signal to avoid rendering altruism when power is not given in exchange. The whole castration complex in males is as semiotic an entity as the female orgasm. Even the physiological basis is homologous for the two sexes, being founded in part on presence *vs.* absence of sexual orgasm.[121] But in the male the failure to orgasm puts a definite stop to further production of offspring, while in the female conception can still take place without orgasm (if she is tolerant enough or if she lives in a society that is repressive enough — which is probably also a society in which males suffer greater castration anxiety than males suffer in other societies).

At this point we can also see what is probably the major (though not the only — see note 123) adaptive advantage of castration anxiety: it is one male semiotic mechanism in most[122] human societies for measuring the "quality" of his interaction with a female (or females). *Too much* castration anxiety means altruism is being rendered out of proportion to control gained. The source of male gametes is blocked and attempts at sexual interaction come to naught until a less threatening partner can be found. *Some* castration anxiety, on the other hand, means that altruism is being profitably rendered. Sexual interaction with a woman (or women) remains a challenge, but it is a challenge successfully and regularly met when a man has the impression the woman is in some sense devoted to him or under his control. Finally, *no* castration anxiety in interaction with a woman means there is no point in even rendering altruism. As we saw earlier, the transsexual is probably the only kind of male who does not experience castration anxiety. He does not find women sexually interesting, much less challenging, and his reproductive success is nil.

The middle ground — *some* castration anxiety — is thus the norm for the human male because it typically leads to the greatest reproductive success.

---

121. That males and females should use specifically *sexual* organs and *sexual* responses to measure the quality of their *sexual* relationships should not really be surprising, though. After all, we use taste and smell sensations to determine what we put into our mouths, the feeling of a full bladder tells us when to urinate, temperature receptors determine our responses to heat and cold, etc. It is remarkable how easy it is to ignore the essential connection between the sexual apparatus and sexual interaction (cf. Murphy 1977, 16). The problem must be one of the side effects of the human tendency to self-deception.

122. I exclude, in addition to the societies which practice clitoral excision and infibulation, the extremely matrifocal societies where castration anxiety also appears to be so constantly high among most males as to no longer function as an efficient measuring device.

The extremes — too much or too little castration anxiety — drastically lower reproductive potential in the absence of compensatory measures such as clitoral excision or compulsive abandonment. In other words, some degree of castration anxiety appears to have been selected for in hominid evolution.[123]

No other primate, to my knowledge, suffers from castration anxiety. This in the long run is because no other primate engages in 'castration behavior'. True, some male monkeys may be so intimidated by their mothers as to be unable to accomplish incestuous copulation with them. Or they may be wary of dangerous critters in crevices. But I do not think they have castration anxiety per se. Non-hominid primates do not use tools to slice their genitalia, they do not have the semiotic ability to represent a vagina with teeth or a vagina with a snake in it, and they do not appear to have the intelligence to worry abouth the length of their penis or whether it will perform or not with a given female.

Above all, the nonhuman primate does not have a mate who is a semiotically complex mother-icon. The human male's relationship with his mother is so indelible, ontogenetically, that he needs some superadded mechanism to reverse (or keep reversed) the direction of dominance in his relationship with the mother-icon from what it was in his relationship with his mother. Castration anxiety provides just this mechanism, while at the same time leaving intact the fitness maximizing advantages of the maternal iconicity (e.g., the advantages of staying in the vicinity of offspring by being as attached to the mother-icon as one was once attached to the mother). The psychoanalysts are amply justified in linking castration anxiety to the mother because it makes good evolutionary sense for the performance of a male's penis to be linked to the behavior of his mother-icon.

It should be noted that, had neoteny and prolonged maternal care not developed in hominid evolution, then the castration anxiety mechanism would probably never have developed as much as it did either. As the Jonases

---

123. Some other more minor and more patchily distributed adaptive advantages of castration anxiety that I would not want to rule out are: 1. to avoid actual castration (perhaps this was the original adaptive function which developed when ancestral hominids first started castrating other hominids); 2. to help reduce the likelihood of incest (above, section 19); 3. to reduce (via postpartum taboo) the likelihood of pregnancy during early stages of an investment already made; 4. to deflect (via menstrual taboo) male energetic investment when it would be impossible for a female to conceive (below, section 48); 5. to encourage a male to exercise great caution and restraint in attempting extra-mateship copulations (above, section 44); 6. to facilitate male-male cooperation (below, section 47).

observe, "... the lengthening childhood of human beings has made it more difficult for adult males to be confident of their masculinity than for adult females to feel secure in their femininity, and this has led to an overreaction by the male" (Jonas and Jonas 1980, 73). Perhaps "overreaction" is too strong a term, though. I would say that male castration anxiety is, in part, simply an *adaptive* reaction. More specifically, it is a mechanism which was selected for in part because of the maladaptive side-effects of the otherwise highly adaptive phenomena of neoteny and prolonged maternal care of offspring.

But what specifically is maladaptive? As we saw earlier (section 26), when maternal care is exaggerated a son may later develop an aversion to sustained or even temporary intimacy with a woman. Psychoanalytically, he suffers an excess of castration anxiety (except in the most extreme case, where he simply becomes transsexual). In other words, high maternal salience leads to high castration anxiety. Correspondingly, moderate maternal salience leads to moderate castration anxiety, i.e., a level that is adaptive because it can be used as a measuring device. A male who does not have to live with a high level of castration anxiety (and assuming he is not homosexual or transsexual) is capable of successful interaction with a sexually challenging woman. If the interaction develops into a stable relationship the resulting male offspring will themselves acquire only moderate levels of castration anxiety because their mother is occupied by their father. The sexually secure father *prevents* the mother from overwhelming her sons, emotionally. Thus is an adaptively moderate level of castration anxiety passed on from one generation to the next.

A recent cross-cultural study of the relationship of female power to sexual behaviors and attitudes (Gray 1984) bears directly on this psychoanalytic theory of castration anxiety. It was found that, for the 122 societies in the Standard Cross-Cultural Sample, high female marital power is significantly associated with low male fear of impotence, greater tolerance of female-initiated sexual activity, greater likelihood of sexual foreplay, and several other indicators of male sexual function. I interpret this to mean that females are free to enjoy more power in their marital relations with males when males have less castration anxiety. Conversely, they are deprived of power when males have more castration anxiety. In either case the amount of power they have is of course less than that of males (*contra* Gray, 230), for in practically all societies males hold more power, absolutely speaking, than females (see section 40, above). But within the range of variation permitted by this overall power asymmetry, interesting things can still happen, as we have seen. Unfortunately, Gray did not study the influences of the power relationship between mother and son (as opposed to that between wife and husband) on male sexual functioning. But he is at least open to the possibility (in agreement with Abernethy 1974) that maternal dominance of young males might later inhibit their sexuality.

46. The Next Best Thing to Castration

> He [Elagabalus] toyed with the idea of
> castrating himself, but finally settled for
> circumcision.
>
> *Burgo Partridge*

Another form of evidence for concern about castration in males is offered by the widespread ritual practice of mutilating the penis, that is, of 'almost' castrating a male. Most anthropologists (apart from van Gennep 1960, 70-2, and a few others) would agree that genital mutilation practices in general have considerably more psychological and social significance attached to them than do non-genital forms of mutilation, such as tattooing, cicatrization, perforation of the ear lobes or nasal septum, nose bleeding, lip-plugging, tooth-pulling, etc.

The varieties of penile mutilation may be grouped into four categories: circumcision, in which all or part of the prepuce is removed; superincision, in which a longitudinal cut is made on the dorsal portion of the prepuce; subincision (cf. Roth's "introcision" — 1897, 177 ff.), in which the under-side of the penis is slit open with one or more cuts, exposing the urethra; miscellaneous forms of penile mutilation, such as the periodic "severe penis cutting" of the New Guinea Awa, in which wedges of flesh are cut from the glans, or small, stone-tipped arrows are driven into it (Newman and Boyd 1982, 275-6).

Circumcision, the most common form of penile mutilation, is encountered even in parts of enlightened, modern Western civilization. Many justifications have been advanced for the practice, such as: cleanliness, avoidance of phimosis (a very rare condition in which the prepuce is so tight it cannot be pulled back over the glans), avoidance of penile cancer, aesthetic reasons, enhancement of sexual pleausre, avoidance of venereal disease, discourage-ment of masturbation, etc. To judge from the Paiges' review of some of the enormous literature on this subject (1981, 263-7), the reasons given for circumcision are largely fallacious. The Paiges see circumcision in complex industrial societies as the result of a sexual ideology whose social, political, and economic bases have yet to be investigated.

Harrington's cross-cultural study (1968) established that circumcision in non-industrial societies is tied to socialization practices that emphasize the differences between the sexes. Adult males in such societies feel a solidarity in their differentiation from females, and are likely to form strong fraternal interest groups. As Paige and Paige (1981, 122-166) have shown, circumcision is a practice typical of nonindustrial societies with "powerful and sometimes massive fraternal interest groups, chronic internal warfare and feuds, and tight contractual control over women and marriage" (*ibid.*, 123). Examples are the Rwala of northern Arabia, the Somali, and the ancient Hebrews. Such societies, according to the Paiges, have an especially aggravated "dilemma of fission." The dilemma is "... that lineage elders must extend the right to ultimate political power and potential independence to descendents in order to win their loyalty but that by doing so they ultimately lose that loyalty through lineage fission" (*ibid.*, 257). The link of the dilemma of fission with the phenomenon of circumcision runs as follows:

Circumcision is a ritual attempt to solve this dilemma by ascertaining the continuing loyalty of kin-group members. By subjecting sons to a dangerous operation which could result in castration or death, the lineage elders gain evidence that the head of a family unit in their faction is willing to entrust them with his most valuable political asset – his son's penis. Circumcision offers public evidence that a father is sufficiently loyal to the fraternal interest group to risk publicly his future basis of power. (*ibid.*, 257-8).

This interpretation is just that – an interpretation. The sophisticated statistics behind the interpretation only show that it is more reasonable to assume that the practice of circumcision is conditioned by strong fraternal interest groups than by such other factors as polygyny, residence patterns, patrilocality, postpartum taboo, and economic resource base. But no *psychological* data about populations of individuals in these societies are examined by Paige and Paige, and therefore no psychological interpretations – such as the hypothesis of castration anxiety – are excluded by the study. Nor would a *sociobiological* interpretation in terms of fitness maximization be excluded. Indeed, it is possible that the Paiges' political interpretation, a psychoanalytic interpretation, and a sociobiological/evolutionary interpretation – are all correct. To envisage this possibility, we need only change a few words in the crucial sentence from the Paiges' statement just quoted. Thus, from a psychoanalytic viewpoint, we may say that

By subjecting sons to a dangerous operation which could result in castration or death, the lineage elders gain evidence that the head of an *Oedipal unit* in their faction is willing to entrust them with *that organ that he feels most ambivalent about* – his *Oedipal rival's* penis.

While from a sociobiological viewpoint,

By subjecting sons to a dangerous operation which could result in castration or death, the lineage elders gain evidence that the head of a *kin unit* in their faction is willing to entrust them with his most valuable *fitness maximizing asset* – his son's *gene conduit*.

The Paiges completely ignore sociobiology, and thus are not in a position to notice that their "dilemma of fission" is also a dilemma between reaping the genetic advantages of competing with (varying degrees of) kin and cashing in on the genetic advantages of kin altruism.

But the Paiges do not ignore psychoanalysis. They perceive a similarity between the dilemma of fission and what they call the "Oedipal dilemma," that is, the dilemma of competition *vs.* love between father and son. Yet they think the dissimilarities are more important: "The dilemma of fission, ... unlike the dilemma of Oedipus, is a problem for adults and is rooted in the social structure of adult society. If the dilemma of fission is the source of circumcision or any other ritual practice, it will not require a theoretical detour through infant personality, Oedipal rebellions against the primal father, or neurotic primitives" (*ibid.*, 125). The problem is that the Paiges' correlations do not *require* the dilemma of fission as the only source of circumcision, while all the evidence adduced above (sections 14-18) does suggest that neoteny/regression and parental iconicity are in fact typical "detours" that all human adults themselves make in their family relations.

As the Paiges are aware, not all psychoanalytic interpretations of circumcision are alike. One of the major psychoanalytic theories is that of Bruno Bettelheim who, in his book *Symbolic Wounds* (1954) argues that genital mutilation expresses male envy of female sexual functions (cf. Róheim 1945b, 155-77; Mead 1975 [1949], 180-81; Montagu 1937, 302-3). Among the aboriginal inhabitants of parts of Australia, for example, the linguistic term for the subincised penis is in some cases identical to the one for vulva or womb (e.g. Róheim 1932, 72; Roth 1897, 180). In the New Guinea Wogeo the penis is periodically slashed, producing what is natively called "men's menstruation" (Hogbin 1970; see Allen 1967, 17 for similar examples from other cultures). Sometimes it is not the penis which is slashed, but some other part of the body, as in the practice of letting blood from the abdomen, lower back, or buttocks in imitation of menstruation among the Hua of Papua New Guinea (Meigs 1976).[124] The identification of males with females in these rites is obvious and makes the rites quite different from more typical circumcision rites proper. But (contrary to Bettelheim, and in agreement with Allen 1967, 16-22), castration anxiety is not precluded by envy of female reproductive functions. Nor is male envy of female functions in the societies studied by Bettelheim at all precluded by the strong fraternal interests which Paige and Paige focus on.

---

124. Legman (1968, 591) reports the following anecdote from Fredericksburg, Virginia: "I once heard of a fellow who was so effeminate that he was afraid of the company of men, and that he was with women most of the time, so that his nose bled every 28 days."

The other major psychoanalytic theory of circumcision is that of John Whiting (see: Whiting, Kluckhohn, and Anthony 1958; Whiting 1964; Burton and Whiting 1961; cf. Shlegel and Barry 1980, 704). The basis for the Whiting theory was the observed cross-cultural correlation of circumcision with polygyny, prolonged postpartum sex taboo, and exclusive mother-son sleeping arrangements: "Children raised in polygynous households, or households where the men do not sleep with their wives, have little contact with their fathers during the first two years of life, perceive their mother as the controller of resources, and identify with her" (Whiting and Whiting 1975, 9). Circumcision (and the sometimes associated practices of hazing, endurance tests, and seclusion from females) supposedly helps to break the early cross-sex identification with and strong dependency on the mother in such societies, and helps the boy establish a strong masculine identity and respect for male authority (cf. Daly 1957).

Paige and Paige (1981), using a different sample and more sophisticated statistical techniques as well as re-examining Whiting's data, show that their fraternal interest group model is statistically more powerful than Whiting's psychoanalytic model. For example, their model accounts for a much larger percentage of the variance in circumcision than does the Whiting model. Also, Whiting's sample under-represents the Circum-Mediterranean area, where postpartum taboo tends to be short and circumcision tends to be present. In the end, Paige and Paige conclude that the major correlation posited by Whiting, i.e., circumcision and long postpartum sex taboo, is only "modest" at best.

On the surface, then, the study by the Paiges would appear to demolish a major psychoanalytic account of circumcision. But several objections have to be raised. First, strong fraternal interest groups do not at all preclude conflicted, cross-sex identification of males with their mothers in childhood. A strong adult fraternal interest group may in fact be an overcompensating reaction against the earlier childhood experience of extreme closeness to the mother. Munroe *et al.* (1981) have shown that circumcision (along with couvade, which I will discuss later) is strongly associated with *close* infant-mother contact in a sample of 96 societies. Rather than postpartum taboo, Munroe *et al.* used infant carrying devices as the index of closeness to the mother. Societies in which a carriage, cradleboard, or similar device is used for carrying the child permit only distal and verbal contact of the mother with the child, while societies in which the child is carried in the mother's arms, or in a sling or shawl, foster an intimate, tactile-motoric contact of mother and child.

More importantly, Munroe *et al.* found that close mother-infant contact is associated with circumcision specifically in societies with corporate patrilineages, that is, in societies which are very likely to have what the Paiges mean by fraternal interest groups (Munroe *et al.*, 627-8). Clearly, the solidarity of adult males must have something to do with their childhood identification with their mothers.

Another psychoanalytic notion that is not excluded by the Paige and Paige analysis of circumcision is castration anxiety. Indeed, since cutting the penis is by definition the datum of central interest in the study of circumcision, and since such cutting is so close to castration itself (i.e., is in certain respects like it, and therefore a potential icon of it), then an attitude of anxiety about castration is at least strongly hinted at.

Even the Paiges grant that circumcision must have *something* to do with castration, since they are aware that castration can and does sometimes result from a botched circumcision: "Circumcision may represent symbolic [again, a semiotician would say iconic] castration, but in some cases the castration is all too real" (155).

Freud is more direct of course, saying simply that circumcision is "another symbolic substitute for castration" (*SE* XIII, 190), and Legman declares that "The folk-mind has never been in any doubt that circumcision is a modified form of castration, or genital harm, enacted against the helpless (and perfectly innocent) child or adolescent" (1975, 536; cf. Róheim 1932, 72; Daly 1957; Nunberg 1947; Róheim 1945b, 68-79; Spiro 1982, 169; Roellenbleck 1974, 75ff.; Reik 1931, 105ff.; Allen 1967, 18). Allen notes that, amongst the Tiv of Nigeria, the word used for the castration of animals is the same as that for circumcision (*ibid.*).

Incidentally, well before the invention of psychoanalysis the relationship of circumcision to castration was recognized. In 1883 Frederic Baumann had stated that "la castration, l'eunuchisme et la circoncision ne sont que des modifications amoindries l'une de l'autre" (as quoted by Reik 1931, 118). Zaborowski (1896) doubts this idea, but grants that the Roman emperor Elagabalus "... sur l'autel du dieu (adoré sous la forme d'une pierre) duquel on jetait des phallus, s'était fait circoncire" (653; cf. Partridge 1960, 82-3).

Curiously, the chapter in which Paige and Paige reject the psychoanalytic theories of circumcision contains a long digression on the hypothetical and actual political advantages of castration. The chapter begins with an attempt to explain why castration is *not* encountered very often as a political tactic, since "... there is no logical reason why the father in a strong fraternal interest group society cannot use castration to solve the problem of fission" (141):

The reasons for the absence of this practice are instead political. One of the most important ties between a son and his father is the prospect that the son will be able to start an independent "long" lineage of his own. A father who deprived a son of this hope would be unable to prevent the son's immediate defection since without wives, children, or herds the son would have nothing to protect, nothing to lose, and no reason to remain in a military coalition with his father. The same reasoning applies to higher-order lineage segments, which remain together only so long as the gains in protection and military aid are not offset by costs in obedience and tribute to the clan or lineage elders. The absence of castration in strong fraternal interest group societies actually indicates the political weakness of these systems. Patriarchs must extend the right to ultimate power to their descendants and collaterals in order to win their loyalty even though this means sharing power and, if a lineage fission occurs, losing some. Thus, castration is never regularly employed as a political tactic by societies organized on the basis of kin-group armies. (143-4).

This statement strikes me as politically astute, but it does provoke a rhetorical question: why would any psychologically normal father in any culture consciously contemplate treating his children the way he treats his cattle? One of the things that makes fathers similar to mothers, cross-culturally, is that they feel some affection toward and attachment to their children. Any hostile impulses, including the impulse to castrate, must certainly be tempered by such feelings. Indeed, all the examples of actual circumcision ceremonies cited by the Paiges show the father to be either absent from the ceremony or present as the child's protector, comforter, and possible avenger, should the knife slip. No doubt some fathers may be held back from castrating their sons by political considerations such as those described by Paige and Paige. But political motivations do not exclude the psyche, and can in fact be reinforced by psychological motivations. And whatever motivations are at work to prevent fathers from actually castrating their sons (whether in strong or weak fraternal interest societies) are only proximate mechanisms anyway. There has to be a long-term, evolutionary advantage for such motivations, namely: fathers who, all other things being equal (including mean reproductive success of males and females), refrain from castrating their sons will be approximately twice as successful in replicating their genes as fathers who do not refrain from castrating their sons.

Paige and Paige do discuss many examples in which fathers castrate males *other* than their sons. Historically, "centralized agrarian bureaucracies supported by professional armies" (144) have often had high administrative and court positions filled by eunuchs. China under the Han and T'ang dynasties, Byzantium, Arabia, Mesopotamia, Assyria, Persia, and the Ottoman empire are given as examples. Typically a powerful male ruler would surround himself with eunuchs who had no hope of having families of their own, were personally dependent on the ruler, and assisted the ruler in preventing members of noble families from gaining too much power. Of the eunuchs in later Byzantium Paige and Paige say:

Much of the unfavorable commentary on the unreliable character, torpor, indulgence, sycophancy, gluttony, envy, and acquisitiveness of eunuchs seems to have come from the eloquent but frustrated aristocrats who found themselves reduced to political impotence by eunuchs who formed a solid wall around the emperor. The resiliency of the system was such that even if the nobles succeeded in retiring, exiling, or murdering one influential eunuch, his place was invariably taken by another. The attractiveness of eunuchs to the emperors was not their personal ties, not their willingness to subordinate themselves through mutilation, since emperors were quite willing to dispense with long-established personal ties and replace eunuchs with bewildering speed. Their attraction was simply their lack of issue and hence of dynastic ambitions. (146).

These insights in no way exclude what the sociobiologist would observe: 1) the emperor's genes no doubt replicated more successfully as a result of his political acumen; 2) the emperor only castrated individuals not related to him, and thereby did not prevent the replication of genes more likely to be his own than the genes of those he did castrate. Psychoanalytic considerations are also not excluded by the Paiges' political analysis: the emperor probably experienced less anxiety about castrating strangers than about castrating family members, such as his father, sons, or brothers, since these members would have been previously involved in anxiety-producing Oedipal triangles with him.

One of the most interesting findings made by the Paiges is that, although circumcision may take place at any age from infancy to young adulthood, it always takes place *before* marriage. The Paiges interpret this to mean that it does not make much difference when a father affirms his allegiance to his lineage group, as long as he does it before he finishes negotiating his son's marriage contract: "Since it is the loyalties of the father rather than those of the son which are the principal concern in the ceremony, the son's age is irrelevant" (151).

But there are no a priori psychoanalytic reasons why the son's age should be relevant either (though most of the psychoanalytic theorizing cited by the Paiges does focus on the child's rather than the adult's psyche and is therefore justly criticized by the Paiges as neglecting the interests of the actual perpetrators of circumcision). The Paiges themselves make a psychoanalytic statement that suggests another (but not necessarily contrary) reason why circumcision is functional at any time until the son marries, but is irrelevant afterwards: "... the son's marriage breaks the close Oedipal confines of the original domestic group and thus eliminates sexual conflict as a source of friction" (125). This statement necessarily implies that "sexual conflict as a source of friction" does in fact exist in the original domestic group *before* the son is married off, and that the conflict and friction are gone *afterwards*.

But if no circumcision occurs afterwards either, then circumcision might have something to do with the conflict and friction that the Paiges say comes before.

The association of circumcision with marriage is important. The Paiges observe that, among the Egyptian Nubians the word for circumcision ceremony translates as "big wedding" (150). They also point out that in Hebrew the words for bridegroom, son-in-law, and father-in-law all have the same root *hatan,* meaning 'to circumcise' in Arabic. Legman's chapter on circumcision mentions a letter from a physician published in the *Medical Tribune* calling for compulsory circumcision of all men *planning to get married* (1975, 529). Legman also quotes a letter to a popular writer on sexual matters, Dr. D.O. Cauldwell, who had approved of masturbation in one of his books:

My 12-year-old son found one of your books at a neighbor's and read that you condone masturbation. I personally circumcised him and I do not think he'll ever masturbate again. He probably will not be capable of having any sort of sex relations *until he is old enough to marry,* and I go to the expense of paying a high-priced plastic surgeon to straighten out his organ after the way I deliberately misshaped it to keep him sexually pure .... (*ibid.,* 536, italics added).

As shown earlier in this book, marriage is an institution in which two individuals get together for iconic purposes, among others. Man and wife are to each other father-icon and mother-icon. Before marriage (or at least before psychological bonding of some kind) has taken place there are just two individuals. Afterwards there are at least two icons as well. As long as individuals are unmarried there is a possibility for marriage, for complementary iconicity. But there is also the possibility of not bothering with the iconicity, that is, of sexual intercourse directly with the parent, with what the icon would otherwise have signified. Incest is always lurking in the wings of the family stage.

The father whose son is not circumcised may very well feel that circumcision will affirm allegiance to the lineage group. But if the father is human, he will also be capable of jealousy. He will not be able to ignore the especially close and intense relationship which Munroe *et al.* (1981) found is likely to exist between his wife and his son. He will not be able to avoid the "sexual conflict" which the Paiges mention (but do not explore).

The husband's own interaction with his wife would of course be impossible without his penis. His erect penis typically *means* that he desires an intense and important form of interaction with her. Might, then, his son's intense interaction with her have something to do with *his* penis? Would the father's son like to do with this woman what he himself does with her?

It is well known that male infants nursing at the breast may have an erection (e.g., Devereux 1967, 196; Guthrie 1976, 97), particularly if the breast is not yielding milk or access to the breast is hampered (Halverson 1938). This phenomenon makes sense in light of the close neurological relationship of limbic areas responsible for oral and genital excitation in both human and non-human primates (see the discussion of "orosexual functions" in MacLean 1973b and MacLean 1975). In some contexts the mother (or mother-surrogate) will even fondle or kiss the infant's penis (see: Glasser 1979, 292 for an example from clinical practice; Freeman 1968, 387, for an Iban example; deMause 1982, 56, for examples from Western history; Stephens 1962 for a Pilaga example; Hogbin 1943, 298, says the Wogeo mother repeatedly kisses her infant's genital region). An infant's mini-penile display must be especially hard on fathers in societies where a long postpartum sex taboo and exclusive mother-child sleeping arrangements obtain. The (apparently) sexually aroused child manages, in effect, to bar the father's sexual access to the mother for a prolonged period of time. The mother, herself frustrated by the taboo on relations with her husband, inevitably satisfies some of her libidinal needs in her relationship with her child (see Spiro 1982, 88-92; Stephens 1962, 34ff.; and Brown 1981, 600-1 for reviews of some of the evidence for the eroticism of the mother-and-child [especially mother-and-male-child] unit, an eroticism which psychoanalysts had of course suspected all along).

What I am suggesting is that the father's jealousy cannot but focus on the son's penis (whether the still unweaned son himself would like to insert his penis into his mother is another question, just as the existence of castration anxiety in males does not settle the question of whether there is penis-envy in females). But it is, after all, the son's penis that the father mutilates in societies that practice circumcision. Or rather, it is the son's penis that the father *or* a representative of the father — such as a rabbi, a barber, or some elder kinsman — circumcises. The Paiges belittle Róheim's psychoanalytic image of a "furious father" (Róheim 1945b, 74) iconically castrating a son, and observe that in penile mutilation ceremonies the father "... more often plays the role of the son's protector than that of his persecutor" (Paige and Paige, 153). This is literally true, and is to be expected of a father who *loves* his child, as I have already said. But Róheim (*ibid.*, 75) recognizes that the father is sympathetic in his feelings, not *only* "furious" (for more on the father's ambivalent feelings, see: Reik 1931, 118; Allen 1967, 15). Also, the Paiges offer no evidence against interpreting the circumciser as a father-figure (semiotically, an *icon* of the father). On the contrary, they thrice refer to the circumciser in their detailed description of an Ndembu circumcision as a "patriarch" (158). They also observe (5) that the circumciser in aboriginal Australian societies was the future *father*-in-law. There is a fairly abundant psychoanalytic literature on male authorities as father-icons (e.g., *SE* V, 353; Rank 1932, 71ff). There is also an interesting paper by Ferenczi (1927, 418ff.) on the paternal role often played in the lives of neurotics by butchers, tailors, barbers, etc. – all professional *cutters* of one kind or another.

The parallelism between the father's penis and the son's penis can surface in various ways. Paige and Paige report that "Among the Mongo it is the father's responsibility to wash and care for the circumcision wound of post-pubertal sons. It is believed that *if the father does not remain continent* until the wound heals, the wound may become seriously infected" (153, emphasis added). Among the Australian Pitjentara the parents of the mutilated boy are supposed to avoid intercourse until he has healed else the boy would become too desirous of intercourse himself (Róheim 1945b, 76). Legman tells a penile parallelism joke that explicitly deals with circumcision: "Mother: 'Should we have little Johnny circumcised?' Father: 'Hell, no! Let him *wear* it off the way I did!'" (1975, 541).

So, the father consciously or unconsciously contemplates that his son's penis may be inclined to go where his goes, and this dreadful thought cannot really be banished *until the son is married*. At any point in the meantime the son's penis may be mutilated as one way of dealing with this thought. When the son does marry he breaks, once and for all, the tie with his mother because his mate is by definition a mother-icon. As the proverb says, "A son is a son till he takes a wife."[125]

This way of accounting for the fact that circumcision invariably occurs before marriage complements, I think, rather than contradicts the Paiges' account. A father is as capable of being jealous of his son as of being concerned about demonstrating allegiance to his lineage group (sociobiologically, signifying altruism to kin). In having his son circumcised he manages to kill two birds with one stone.

Or perhaps even three. There is something else about old men handling the genitalia of young boys that needs to be discussed.

---

125.   "But a daughter is a daughter for the rest of her life."

47. The Homosexual Hominid

> Since I have become acquainted with
> the notion of bisexuality I have regarded
> it as the decisive factor, and without
> taking bisexuality into account I think it
> would scarcely be possible to arrive at
> an understanding of the sexual mani-
> festations that are actually to be
> observed in men and women.
>
> *S. Freud*

The Paiges say that circumcision affirms and strengthens a man's ties to his fraternal interest group. The Whitings (1975) found a correlation between the existence of fraternal interest groups and "aloofness" between husbands and wives. Schlegel and Barry (1980) find that same-sex social bonding is much more likely to characterize male than female initiation ceremonies. Young (1965) emphasizes the male solidarity fostered by male initiation ceremonies.

But where do "fraternity," "aloofness" from one's spouse, "same-sex bonding," and "male solidarity" leave off and homosexuality begin?

In some societies penile mutilation ceremonies are directly tied to homo-sexual practices. Among the Australian Nambutji an adolescent boy's future father-in-law has sexual relations with him for a period of time after circum-cising and subincising him (Róheim, 1945b, 72). With the Big Nambas on Malekula (New Hebrides) the boy's male guardian or *dubut* is his lover both before circumcision and after the circumcision wound has healed (Deacon 1934, 260-9; cf. Dundes 1980, 195; Allen 1967, 96-7). In various south Australian districts the foreskin is eaten by some male participant in the ceremony, such as the elder brother or brother-in-law of the novice (Róheim, 69). Citing Spencer and Gillen (1927), Reik says that "Among the Mara and Anula tribes, after circumcision some blood from the wound is allowed to drop on the man upon whom the youth lies during the operation; this is done in order to produce an especially intimate friendship" (1931, 142). In an Orthodox Jewish circumcision the father or a representative of the father (the mohel) is supposed to kiss the bleeding penis or even suck the blood from the penis and then spit it out (Zimmerman 1951; Legman 1975, 538; deMause 1982, 26; Gregersen 1982, 19-20). Nandi boys wear girl's clothing just before the circumcision ceremony and, after being circumcised, they have to wear women's garments (Hollis 1909, 53-5; Dundes 1980, 193).

How could homosexual fantasies *not* be activated when males handle the genitalia of other males? True, the older male does not actually fondle the younger male's penis, but instead attacks it, cuts it, damages it. But it is still a sexual organ that he handles. We might say that penile mutilation rituals give older males both an opportunity to affirm homosexual impulses and an opportunity to deny such impulses in the same aggressive act.[126]

But, given that homoerotic feeling is in some way being expressed in the act of circumcision, what more distal functions might this proximate feeling serve?

In Freud's *Group Psychology and the Analysis of the Ego* there is adumbrated a hypothesis about the function of homosexual feelings:

Even in a person who has in other respects become absorbed in a group, the directly sexual impulsions preserve a little of his individual activity. If they become too strong they disintegrate every group formation. The Catholic Church had the best of motives for recommending its followers to remain unmarried and for imposing celibacy upon its priests; but falling in love has often driven even priests to leave the Church. In the same way love for women breaks through the group ties of race, of national divisions, and of the social class system, and it thus produces important effects as a factor in civilization. It seems certain that homosexual love is far more compatible with group ties, even when it takes the shape of uninhibited sexual impulsions — a remarkable fact, the explanation of which might carry us far. (*SE* XVIII, 141; cf. Ellis's discussion of the family as an "anti-social influence" — 1927-8, VI, 570).

Elsewhere in the work Freud speaks of "desexualized, sublimated homosexual love for other men, which springs from work in common" (103). In *Totem and Taboo* there is also a passing reference to the possibility that homosexual feelings and acts helped unite the "brothers" who had been expelled from the primeval "horde" (*SE* XIII, 144). Freud apparently did not explore the topic any further, but other psychoanalysts and psychoanalytically inclined social theorists did.

For example, in his study of the unconscious meaning of male exchange of females, Devereux not only interprets marriage as a bond between two families rather than two individuals (in this he follows Lévi-Strauss), but also as a sublimated homosexual bond between the two male heads of families:

What society regulates is, thus, not the mere circulation of women; it is the *form* which it assumes and the *circumstances* and *conditions* in which it takes place; abduction, exchange, purchase, bride service, etc. Moreover, the

---

126. For further discussion of the homosexual overtones of male initiation ceremonies, see: Dundes 1980, 194-6; Dinnerstein 1976, 59; Reik 1931, 141ff; Nunberg 1947; Hays 1964, 63-78; Churchill 1967, 81-2.

principal regulations do not concern the relationship between men and women but the relations between the men themselves, since such transactions occur between men; women are simply their objects. The institution of marriage which stands with kinship, both consanguine and affinal, in a relationship of co-emergence has as its goal not the socially advantageous resolution of the heterosexual problem but the repelling of the threatening specter of latent homosexuality, product of the Oedipus complex. (Devereux 1978, 211).

In semiotic terms, the female sex object obtained from (or lost to) another male can function as an indexical sign of that other male. But the operation of such an index implies homosexuality.

The latent homosexuality that Devereux speaks of is characteristically anal in orientation. One of Devereux's examples (furnished by Melford Spiro) is a Burmese marriage proverb:

In Burma there exists "a stereotypic, culturally expected tension, allegedly motivated by the brother's resentment of his sister's (especially his younger sister's) husband. 'Until her marriage' as one villager put it 'she has been his.' Hence, he is jealous if she shows affection to anyone else' let alone marries him. His (putative) feeling is reflected in the proverb 'When the younger sister takes a husband, her brother develops a pain in his anus' (*huama lin nei/maun pin cein*). The expression 'pain in the anus' is intended as a *double entendre*, i.e., it pains the brother to lose her, and it arouses pangs of sexual longing for her." (*ibid.*, 214).

Another of Devereux's examples is clinical. A heterosexual patient whose best friend's sister became his mistress dreams that the friend wants to make love with his wife. In the dream the friend specifies that he desires the patient's wife because she possessses a special 'farting vagina.' But upon free association the patient realizes that it is not a vagina, but an anus that 'farts', and moreover he declares that "... I have the impression that it is not my wife's anus, nor that of my sister, nor even the anus of a woman – it is my anus" (187). Without going into further details of the patient's history, it seems obvious that he has equated his wife's vagina with his own anus in the dream, and that his friend's intercourse with his wife represents the idea of intercourse with him.

Early psychoanalysts had already dealt with the homosexual implication of sharing a woman with another man. Flügel, for example, discussed a case in which "... the original homosexual tendency had been converted into a heterosexual one, by a curious process ..., namely, the development of a special attraction toward prostitutes or other women of promiscuous habits, just because such women came into contact with other men" (Flügel 1924, 195-6; cf. *SE* XII, 63). Reik (1950) interpreted cases of syphilophobia along these lines. I analyzed an epistolary *ménage a trois* in the life of Alexander

Pushkin as an example of displaced homosexuality (Laferrière 1977a, 60-2).
The sex therapist Avodah Offit speaks of the "pseudohomosexual" fantasies
of men who are obsessed with the idea of a "second man" (1981, 128-30).
Psychologist Dorothy Dinnerstein says that woman-sharing ceremonies such
as "gang bangs" and "fraternal excursion to whorehouses" permit "male
homoerotic impulse some expression in a safe context of triumphant, harsh
masculinity" (1976, 59). The practice of "wife-swapping" (so named because
it is usually instigated by husbands, not wives) probably also serves to siphon
off threatening male homosexual impulses (Devereux 1978, 208; above, note
50) — which is not to say it does not answer the male need for sexual variety
as well (Symons 1979, 246-50). To do a little folk-etymologizing, we might
say that many "swingers" are "switch-hitters" in disguise.

Perhaps the most elaborate and formalized method of sharing women is
cicisbeism (from Italian "cicisbeo," the socially sanctioned gallant of a
married woman), in which a man permits his wife a lover of her choice, but
for a price. The practice is rather like pimping (note that in English a "pimp"
refers to *either* a procurer *or* a male homosexual prostitute — Wentworth and
Flexner 1975, 390). In some contexts multiple cicisbeism can result in a
fairly complex structure of male political-economic cooperation. Speaking of
the Birom of northern Nigeria, Daly and Wilson (1978, 272) say: "... a man
accumulates allies in the husbands of his mistresses and the lovers of his
wives. The most powerful Birom leader at the turn of the century had nine
wives and twelve married mistresses and consequently had a formidable group
of bondsmen."

At one point in his article Devereux paraphrases an anecdote from the
French writer Brantôme: "A certain aristocrat, in love with his wife's lover,
contrived to catch them in flagrante delicto. As a compensation, he demanded the right to sodomize the lover *while* the latter was cohabiting with
the aristocrat's wife" (*ibid.*, 207). Legman's chapter on adultery (cf. Devereux
1973, 45) provides more instances (going back to the ancient Romans) of this
type of anecdote in which the adulterer is punished with pedication by the
cuckold (1968, 725-7). Dover (1978, 105-6) reports that a male adulterer
among the ancient Athenians might have a (phallic) radish pushed into his
anus as one form of punishment.

A sizeable number of anecdotes devoted to "masking homosexuality"
are given in Legman's chapter on adultery, such as: "A man at the funeral of
a friend's wife, with whom he has been carrying on an affair, breaks into
tears and finally becomes hysterical, while the husband remains impassive.
'Calm yourself,' says the husband. 'I'll be marrying again.'" (1968, 771).
In Legman's interpretation of the enormous folkloric material he has unearthed, there is a "camaraderie between the husband and the adulterer"

which serves "... to devaluate the woman, as not really worth fighting about at all" (*ibid.*, 769).

Exchange of women, wife-sharing, tolerated adultery, etc. constitute only the tip of the iceberg of male social cooperation. There are many other ways in which men interact without necessarily using women as a crutch for the expression of homoerotic sociality.

One of these ways is the formation of *male dominance hierarchies.* Fenichel speaks of a homoerotic "apprentice complex" or "psychology of the pupil" that develops in a boy as he forms a relationship with his hierarchically superior father: "Every boy loves his father as a model whom he would like to resemble; he feels himself the 'pupil' who, by temporary passivity, can achieve the ability to be active later on. This type of love could be called the apprentice love; it is always ambivalent because its ultimate aim is to replace the master" (Fenichel 1945, 334). As we have already seen (above, 278), the ancient Greek pupil-apprentice or *erōmenos* was sometimes literally pedicated by his master or *erastēs*. In contexts of institutionalized male homosexuality among nonindustrial peoples today the male who sodomizes is usually of higher rank than the male who is sodomized (the Sambians are an exception only in that the higher ranking bachelor inserts his penis into the initiate's mouth rather than into his anus).

Kakar's analysis of "the ontogeny of *homo hierarchicus*" in India utilizes Fenichel's notion of quasi-homosexual apprenticeship: "[the] resolution of the Oedipal conflict by means of a submissive, apprenticelike stance toward elder men in the family leaves a psychosexual residue in the unconscious that influences the rest of a boy's life; in the identity development of Indian men, this has generated a passive-receptive attitude towards authority figures of all kinds" (1978, 134). Kakar interprets the prevalence of obscenities of the type "Fuck you in the anus" among young Indian males as "another index of the common masculine preoccupation with hierarchical status" (*ibid.*, 135). Such obscenities are of course not peculiarly Indian (e.g., see 223 above), but are a characteristic of competitive young bucks in many cultures and reveal the underlying homosexual meaning of hierarchical relations among today's hominid males. In essence, the hierarchical organization of interactions in a human male collective is a complex icon of males mounting and being mounted by one another (cf. Rancour-Laferriere 1982a, 214). Giving orders is an icon of anal penetration, taking orders is an icon of being anally penetrated. Insofar as male hierarchical organization has been at all adaptive in the course of hominid evolution, male homosexuality — whether overt, as in the ancient Greeks, or covert, as in the modern corporate hierarchy — has of necessity been preadaptive.

Politics, a primarily male occupation in all societies, is supported by underlying homosexual currents. In his *Psychopathology and Politics* Harold Lasswell says: "Political life seems to sublimate many homosexual trends. Politicians characteristically work together in little cliques and clubs, and many of them show marked difficulties in reaching stable heterosexual adjustment" (1960, 178 — the last of these assertions is supported by an array of case histories of political personages who had remarkably pathological heterosexual lives).

Lionel Tiger, in his *Men in Groups* cautiously agrees with Lasswell's statement and mentions the "very special male bond of senior Nazis" (1969, 79). Gays and bisexuals were in fact an important part of the Nazi movement, and a current joke had it that "Out of the Hitler Youth an SA [Storm Trooper] man will emerge!" But this tolerance lasted only until 1934, when Hitler decided that Ernst Röhm, homosexual head of the SA, was a political liability. Röhm was executed, and the extermination of male homosexuals in Germany — and later in all of Nazi-controlled Europe — got into full swing. The basically psychoanalytic insight of Richard Grunberger applies here: "... the Nazi movement itself was of course essentially an all-male collective, and the cult of comradeship fostered in its formations represented a pervasive, though naturally unacknowledged, form of homosexuality" (as quoted by Rector 1981, 67; see also Heger 1980).

Tiger describes the transparently homosexual iconicity of a fraternity initiation ceremony at a major American university:

Included are a five-inch nail and a bottle of Vaseline. Pledges are ranged in a circle facing in. Behind each pledge is a senior member of the fraternity. In a progression articulated with various vows and statements, the pledges remove all their clothes. They are handed their nails and Vaseline and told to grease the nails and pass the nails back to the seniors behind them. The room is now dark. Then they are told to bend over, in effect presenting their buttocks to the seniors. The right hand is placed on the right buttock and the left hand extended back to the senior, to receive the nail, but a can of beer is placed in the hand, the lights come on, the pledges dress, and a drinking party begins. It is difficult to avoid mentioning the superficial parallel between this ceremony and the pattern, among some primates, of dominant males briefly mounting subdominants; this appears to define or redefine status. (*ibid.*, 147).

Similarly homosexual fun and games go on in the American male workplace. John Lippert, describing his work in an auto plant, says that "... even though homosexuality is generally considered to be some kind of disease, most men are free to engage in what seems to be a pretty basic need for physical intimacy or reassurance. This can be expressed very simply, through putting arms around shoulders or squeezing knees, but it can also become much more intense and explicit, through stabbing between ass cheeks or pulling at nipples" (1979, 52). Jim Stodder's "Confessions of a Candy-Ass Roughneck" reveal the homosexual nature of male banter on oil-drilling rigs:

A: Hey, wasn't that you in my sack last night?
B: Naw, couldn't have been. I'm tied down in bed every night, asshole, for protection from *you.*
A: You'd better, waving that sweet ass of yours around like you do.
B: Now I know you been telling people you sucked my dick, but you don't have to lie. I mean, telling them it tastes like a lemon and all.
A: All I said was that if you'd pull your teeth I'd marry you.
B: Well, c'mon, let's get it on, I'm man enough if you're woman enough.

And so on, with no relief in sight. (Stodder 1979, 44; cf. the obscene Turkish duelling rhymes studied by Dundes *et al.* 1970, or the boy scout camp fire song analyzed by Mechling 1980, 43-6).

As Stodder points out, males who talk this way to each other would not dare show any signs of *real* tenderness. It might destroy their macho image. They might even allow themselves to be fellated by other males (i.e., dominate them sexually), yet they would deny being homosexual. Gagnon, reporting on the American male homosexual scene, says that "among adolescent and young adult delinquent and military groups, and among young men detached from family life, there are some who have sex with homosexual men for favors" (1977, 264). Yet, says Gagnon, these young men believe they are only "playing the queers," and "at no point before, during, or after the sexual act do these young men define themselves as homosexual or as experiencing or performing a homosexual act" (*ibid.*).

Perhaps the most common way for males to have intense and prolonged physical contact with one another is to engage in *sports.* Wrestling, judo, karate, boxing, football, ice hockey, soccer, roller derby, and rugby are examples which involve especially intense and violent physical contact. The contact is not overtly erotic of course. But, for one thing, the genitalia may play an explicit role, as when the martial arts instructor teaches his students how to castrate an opponent (when I was studying Korean Tae Kwon Do style karate I learned how to perform a very simple "front kick in the nuts," as well as a somewhat more complicated grab for the testicles – cf. also Legman 1975, 135). For another thing, the language and lore of sports can be very suggestive, sexually. Alan Dundes has demonstrated this for American football in his masterful paper "Into the Endzone for a Touchdown" (1980, 199-210).

Dundes observes, for example, that football players often congratulate or encourage their teammates with a pat on the buttocks, and that the center "presents" his hind quarters to the quarter[sic!]back while the latter rests his hand on them before the play begins. These affiliative actions of teammates contrast with the aggressive purpose of the game, which is to "penetrate" or make a "hole" in the opposing team's defense and to "score" by carrying the ball into the opposing "endzone." Dundes quotes professional player David Kopay, who says: "We are told to go out and 'fuck those guys'; to take that ball and 'stick it up their asses' or 'down their throats.' The coaches would yell, 'knock their dicks off,' or more often than that, 'knock their jocks off'" (*ibid.*, 207).

Another phenomenon of interest in the present context is the practice of male segregation (cf. Bullough 1976, 25ff.). In our own society the all-male prison is perhaps the best example of the kind of male segregation that encourages homosexual behavior (see Gagnon and Simon 1973, ch. 8, for an overview). The military also forces men to remain together for long periods, and thereby encourages homosexuality (see Hirschfeld's fascinating *Sexual History of the World War* [1941] for some examples). In other societies various forms of male segregation have been associated with homosexuality. Homosexual relations among males are documented for the ancient Spartans and Cretans, the Sedang-Moi of Indo China, the Batak of Sumatra, the Marind Anim, Kaluli, Sambia, and Keraki of New Guinea, and a few other societies which have or had *men's houses* (Ford and Beach 1951, 132, 177; Dover 1978, 192-3; Devereux 1967, 308-9; Money and Ehrhardt 1972, 130ff.; Vanggaard 1972, 35ff.; Davenport 1977, 156; Herdt 1981; 1982; Williams 1936, 158-9; Endleman 1981, 295-313; Schieffelin 1982; van Baal 1966, 148, 479, 488, 699-72; in their sample of 96 nonindustrial societies for which information was available, the Paiges [1981, 232] found that 31 [32.3%] had some major form of male segregation, such as a men's house, a male club, or sex-segregated living units). Sometimes the segregated males in the men's houses keep bullroarers, sacred flutes, or trumpets that women are not supposed to see (there is an enormous literature on these instruments — see especially Dundes 1980, 176-98; Legman 1968, 552; and Herdt 1982). During the "penis and flute" ceremony among Herdt's Sambia, for example, a sacred bamboo flute is inserted into the mouths of initiates in order to teach them the mechanics of fellatio (Herdt 1981, 233, 283; 1982, 61).

Information on the topic of institutionalized homosexuality is, incidentally, rather difficult to obtain. Sometimes the information is simply kept secret from the ethnographers. Herdt (1981) reports that he lived among the Sambia of Papua New Guinea for five months before discovering their elaborate cult of homosexual fellatio (which *all* males participate in before marriage). Even Herdt's designation "Sambia" is fictitious, because the natives did not want to end up being harassed by local missionaries and government patrol officers (cf. Keesing 1982, 10). One cannot but suspect that the available characterizations of homosexual practices in the literature on nonindustrial societies represent the mere tip of an iceberg. And secretive native informants are not the only ones to blame. For example, a standard reference work, *The Oxford Classical Dictionary* (Hammond and Scullard 1970) gives practically no indication of how important homosexuality was in ancient Greece (see Taylor 1954, 3-4, for further examples of repression of information about Greek pederasty). In the introduction to *Papuans of the Trans-Fly* (Williams 1936, xxxii) A.C. Haddon comments on the absence of references to sodomy in E.R. Riley's *Among Papuan Headhunters*, but adds: "... that proves nothing, as the publishers omitted a considerable amount of his manuscript." Broude (1981, 651-2) laments that "on the most basic level, data, regardless of quality or detail, are less available on homosexuality than they are for many other sex variables." Nevertheless, when we do have data, it is remarkable how prominent a role homosexuality plays in the overall social activities of a culture.

The men's houses of nonindustrial societies are of course extreme in their linkage of homosexuality to male social organization. Sodomy, fellation, and other homosexual practices are obviously not essential to the workings of such modern, twentieth-century organizations as the military, universities, corporations, the medical profession, the law, local, state, and national political groups, etc. Yet such organizations have in the past been primarily male hierarchies, and females have experienced great difficulty in entering them. Therefore we must suspect that some vestige of homosexual bonding between males is at least one factor that retards the sexual integration of these organizations. Women 'spoil it' for the men when they step into their midst and introduce new, *heterosexual* possibilities. Of course, an occasional female may be permitted entry and even upward mobility if she is willing to just be 'one of the boys.' For example, she may become adept at using obscenities — those linguistic forms which normally facilitate the eroticization of *male* relationships (cf. Rancour-Laferriere 1984). Or, she may express her 'male solidarity' in other ways. I know a woman professor who jokingly referred to a letter written by another woman as "weak, just like a woman!" (her very words — apparently without perceiving that the joke was on her).

On the other side, a man who accepts a woman into a previously all-male group may be able to do so only by behaving in a patronizing way. For example, the day my lawyer was admitted to the New York Bar, she was eight and three quarters months pregnant. Clearly, she did not look much like 'one of the boys,' and the presiding judge was so taken aback that he gallantly ordered her to go *first* in signing her name to the list of newly-admitted attorneys. A man can be lavish when the favors are his to give.

More typically, though, the male reaction is to actively thwart upward mobility of females in previously all-male organizations. In doing so a male not only enjoys a position of both dominating females and being a potential source of altruism to them (above, section 36), but is also free to continue participating in the sublimated homosexual relationships with his cronies. Male chauvinism, in short, is as much an expression of hidden homosexual impulses as it is an expression of disdain for the subordinate, altruism-eliciting sex.

The homosexual impulses, in turn, probably make it much easier for the males to cooperate with one another than would otherwise be the case. This is not to say that females do not themselves exploit homosexual impulses in the formation and maintenance of all-female groups. But I suspect that homosexuality plays a lesser role in this case. Females seem to be already adept enough at getting along with people (of either sex) not to require the extra cement of homosexuality. Both males and females develop basic social skills through early interaction with their mothers, but males seem to need the additional dose of sociality that real or sublimated homosexuality can provide.

In this connection it is interesting to observe that, according to Kinsey *et al.* (1965 [1953], 487) as much as 50% of American males (as opposed to 28% of females) had a homosexual experience by age 45, and about 37% of males (as opposed to 13% of females) even had homosexual experience "to orgasm." The more recent Hite statistics show that 43% of male respondents had experienced some form of homosexual interactions as boys (1981, 45), while only 17% of females had had some homosexual experience (1976, 395). On the basis of their extensive cross-cultural sample, Ford and Beach say: "It appears highly probable that human females are less likely than males to engage in homosexual relations" (1951, 133; cf. Gregersen 1982, 296). Also, males are more likely to have homosexual fantasies than females (G. Wilson 1978, 44).

The fact that, where it is measured, there is so much more homosexual contact among males than among females suggests, in my opinion, the workings of sexual selection in our hominid ancestry.

Zihlman and Tanner argued (see above, section 5) that ancestral hominid females preferred to mate with males who were cooperative and generally sociable rather than competitive and disruptive. Sociobiologically, such males were superior altruists. Behaviorally they were more like females than their reproductively less successful comrades ("Mothers chose to copulate most frequently . . . with males more *like themselves*" — Zihlman and Tanner 1976, 606 — italics added). But there is some reason to believe that such males also were more likely to have homosexual, bisexual, or psychologically androgynous inclinations, or carried genes predisposing to such inclinations.

One of the major tasks of sociobiology has been to explain how it is that some people are not genetically "selfish" enough to reproduce. What comes to the rescue is (among at least three other sociobiological explanations – Ruse 1981) the notion of kin selection: if it can be shown that homosexuals render substantial benefits to kin, then such benefits might enhance their own inclusive fitness as much as heterosexual reproduction would (Trivers 1974; Wilson 1975, 555; 1978, 146). Such an argument would of course be strengthened by evidence of genetic predisposition to homosexuality, and Wilson cites some of the twin studies which indicate (strongly or weakly, depending on who you consult – e.g., Ruse 1981; Adkins 1980, 401-3; Hutchinson 1959; Kirsch and Rodman 1982, 193) that there is an element of heritability in homosexuality (see also a critical review of recent attempts to link endocrine data with homosexuality – Meyer-Bahlburg 1980). Some other recent research, such as the path analysis of large homosexual and heterosexual populations performed by Bell *et al.* (1981) and the hormonal analysis of Gladue *et al.* (1984) tend to support the notion of a "biological" basis for adult sexual preference or what Ellis long ago called a "congenital predisposition" to homosexuality (1927-8, II, 83).

Let us consider the possibility that homosexuals render more altruism to kin than heterosexuals do. Of course a sexually mature boy who is being pedicated by or is fellating his bisexual elder is by sociobiological definition being an altruist, since he is surrendering personal fitness to others in refraining from sexuality that might result in offspring. He may even be enhancing the fitness of replicas of his own genes, since those who pedicate him may be more or less related to him, and his heterosexual restraint may facilitate their polygynous tendencies. Furthermore, his heterosexual day will come. His settling temporarily for only a homosexual outlet makes it more likely that he will successfully compete for females later (one characteristic of polygynous species, such as red-winged blackbirds or rhesus monkeys, is that sociosexual maturity is achieved later in males than in females – e.g., Daly and Wilson 1978, 258-9).

But I think there is more to it than that. I have already mentioned Freud's statement that "homosexual love is far more compatible with group ties [than heterosexual love]" (*SE* XVIII, 141). In an essay on paranoia, Freud says: "it is precisely manifest homosexuals . . . who are distinguished by taking a particularly active share in the general interests of humanity" (*ibid.*, XII, 61; cf. Fenichel 1945, 336). Ellis voices the opinion that "... among moral leaders, and persons with strong ethical instincts, there is a tendency toward the more elevated forms of homosexual feeling" (1927-8, II, 27). Ellis gives credit to Dante for having observed that "... homosexuality is especially common among men of exceptional intellect..." (*ibid.*, 26). Some of the famous homosexuals (or bisexuals) discussed by Ellis are: Erasmus, Leonardo da Vinci, Michaelangelo, Kleist, Humboldt, Francis Bacon,

Whitman, Wilde, Verlaine ... – an impressive list indeed!

If identification is one psychoanalytic reflex of what sociobiologists mean by altruism in humans (section E, above), then the supposedly greater degree of altruism in homosexuals should suggest a greater degree of identification in homosexuals as well. This is precisely what psychoanalysts claim: "in general, identification plays more of a role in homosexual love than in heterosexual love"; "Pregenital fixations . . . and the readiness to substitute identifications for object relationships are the necessary prerequisites [for homosexuality]" (Fenichel 1945, 337). The word "altruism" comes up again and again in Fenichel's discussion of homosexuality (see also Anna Freud 1966, 134).

Wilson points out that homosexuals in various societies have often played the roles of tribal advisor, shaman, berdache, peacemaker, matchmaker and other altruistic figures (cf. Kirsch and Rodman 1982, 191, 195; Churchill 1967, 81; Ruse 1981, 23; Ellis *ibid.*, 28ff.). Ruse (1981), citing the Harvard dissertation of J.D. Weinrich, notes that homosexuals are disproportionately represented in the acting profession. Actors, like shamans, matchmakers, etc. clearly possess highly developed social skills.

Also very adept at social interaction, though not necessarily homosexual in orientation, are those gender nonconformists that psychologists term "androgynous" (see Bem 1975; Heilbrun 1981). Ickes (1981) reviews studies which show that psychological androgyny facilitates interactional involvement. Safire *et al.* (1982) found evidence that androgyny is conducive to a satisfactory *hetero*sexual relationship.[127] I mention these findings on androgyny in connection with homosexuality because "if there is a biological basis for homosexuality, it probably accounts for gender nonconformity as well as for sexual orientation" (Bell *et al.* 1981, 217). Thus, if there was sexual selection for enhanced male social skills (translatable as kin altruism) in our ancestry, then both male homosexuality and male psychological androgyny would have been selected for into the bargain. Indeed, just as homosexuality is more common among males than among females, as we saw earlier, so too psychological androgyny is more likely in males than in females (see Heilbrun 1981, 69ff.). Overall, says Heilbrun, "men are more feminine than women are masculine" (*ibid.*, 190).

The empirical studies of homosexuality (summarized from a psychoanalytic viewpoint by Fisher and Greenberg 1977, Ch. V) indicate that the father of a future homosexual is typically perceived as unfriendly, threatening,

---

127.   Perhaps there is some overlap between measures of "androgyny" and measures of "extraversion." Eysenck (1976) did find correlation of extraversion with a more active and varied sex life.

or disappointing in some way. This seems to be true for homosexuals of both sexes, though the negative aspects of the father are somewhat different for male and female homosexuals, and there is great variability from individual to individual. My interpretation of these results is that faulty fathering, whatever the reason for it, places more of a developmental burden on mothering. In males, this means almost by default a greater strength of identification with the mother or with feminine values generally (see Fisher and Greenberg 1977, 243-45 for the experimental findings). In females, the consequence, in my view, is that the homosexual orientation which characterizes the adolescent girl anyway (the result of never breaking away from the mother as sharply as boys do) is not brought to a halt but is allowed, again by default, to flourish. For male homosexuality, then, it is a question of a greater than average identification with the mother, while for female homosexuality the identification with the mother is not any greater than usual. Now, if greater than average identification with the mother means adopting her altruistic mothering behavior to a greater than average extent, then *male homosexuality consequently means greater altruism.*

None of these developmental considerations preclude the operation of possible genetic determinants of sexual preference. As Bell *et al.* (1981, 218) point out, the unfavorable fathering that tends to be present in a homosexual's background could as likely result from the homosexual predisposition of the child as from the father's own behavior.

Actually, the possibility of reconciling a developmental model of homosexuality with a genetic model was recognized some time ago by G.E. Hutchinson, who suggested that

... the genotypes responsible for a tendency to paraphilia [including homosexuality] operate primarily on the rates and extent of development of the neuro-psychological mechanisms underlying the identification processes and other aspects of object relationships in infancy. Such an hypothesis would be in accord with a great deal of modern embryological genetics, in which the genetic control of rates of various processes rather than the control of the mere existence or non-existence of the processes is usual. Along these lines, it is to be noted that the variations to be explained are likewise not the clear-cut presence or absence of a trait, but its greater or lesser expression in action, when it may always be present as a verbally reportable subjective fantasy. The hypothesis also has the great merit of leaving the psychoanalytic theory, and in favorable cases the possibility of psychotherapy, untouched, though it provides a frame within which the theoretical model operates. (Hutchinson 1959, 87).

Yet other ways of taking both genetic and environmental factors into consideration are hypothesized by Michael Ruse:

Perhaps some forms of homosexuality are essentially a function of the genes, whereas other forms or manifestations require a significant environmental input. Genetically speaking, this is quite plausible. Suppose homosexuality were a function of the number of genes, i.e., if one had more than a certain number, then homosexuality would inevitably appear, but if one had less than that number, then a specific environmental input would be required to cause homosexuality. A person with none of the genes would not be homosexual whatever the input. This is a well-known phenomenon. The second possibility is that at least one form of homosexuality has a genetic base but still requires some kind of special environmental input. Without it, one is heterosexual. (Alternatively, some form or manifestation of heterosexuality might require some kind of special environmental input; without it, one is homosexual). (Ruse 1981, 18).

Which of the various proposals eventually prove correct (if any) is hard to predict. The reason I cite some of them here is to again falsify the widespread misconception that genes and environment are somehow mutually exclusive, and in particular to show that proponents of genetic models do not necessarily ignore developmental/environmental considerations.

To sum up: male homosexual inclinations, far from being "unnatural," seem to result in part from genes and possibly to have been selected for as a side-effect of sexual selection for altruistic behaviors. Obviously such a process could not have selected for *large* proportions of *exclusively* homosexual males. Such males would by definition have left no offspring. But altruistic homosexual males and males with some homosexual inclinations, that is, males whose youthful homosexual experience or whose adult bisexual practices would not preclude adult heterosexual copulatory vigilance — might well have been a result of sexual selection in the course of hominid evolution.

A final word on male circumcision. The Paiges argued that circumcision is a way of demonstrating loyalty to, or solidarity with kin-group members. Kin-group members are of course precisely the recipients of what sociobiologists mean by kin altruism. To demonstrate loyalty to kin is to signify ongoing kin altruism.

I argued, on the other hand, that circumcision is (among other things) one way of expressing homosexuality. But a sociobiological consideration of homosexuality leads, as we have seen, to altruism, especially kin altruism.

In other words, both the 1) *political* theory of circumcision put forth by the Paiges, as well as the 2) *psychoanalytic* conception of a homosexual basis in circumcision lead to the same 3) *sociobiological* result: kin altruism. One could hardly ask for better evidence of the correctness of all three approaches to circumcision.

48. The Threat of the Bloody Vulva

If to perform a circumcision is to bloody someone else's penis, to sexually avoid a menstruating woman is to escape bloodying one's own penis. The taboo on sexual (and other kinds of) contact with menstruating women is widespread. Haeberle (1978, 51) says that "from a purely medical standpoint, there is no reason why sexual intercourse should not take place at any time during the menstrual cycle." But to this day even in many sectors of civilized Western society a menstruating woman is regarded as "unclean" and sexually "untouchable." 31% of the men in Hite's anonymous general sample said they would not enjoy sex with a menstruating woman (1981, 1099). Derogatory expressions such as "the curse," "bad time," "on the rag," "weeping womb," "falling off the roof," "too wet to plough," "red plague" (American expressions – Rawson 1981, 181; Ernster 1975), "come off poorly" (British) as well as as the obscene intensifier "bloody" (also British) indicate how negative is the attitude toward menstruation in our supposedly advanced civilization. Such an attitude is obviously not very helpful to those women who have also to deal with the (at least in part[128]) physiologically generated premenstrual syndrome and/or dysmenorrhea.

Karen Paige reports that her

... survey of 352 unmarried college women showed that a large proportion of respondents endorsed the notion that sexual intercourse during menstruation would be personally embarrassing, unsanitary, repugnant to their male partners, and otherwise distasteful and unenjoyable. A sizable number also engaged in social practices similar to those observed among women in pre-industrial societies, such as avoiding bathing and swimming, taking special naps, and remaining at home during the menses. (Paige and Paige 1981, 275).

Paige also found that 52% of her sample of 102 married women "... had never had sex during menstruation" (ibid.). Morris and Udry report that "even in a highly educated sample of married couples where one might anticipate least adherence to tradition, intercourse is less frequent during menstruation" (1983, 180). These authors also find indications that wives, more so than husbands, want intercourse less during menstruation.

At various times in Western history and in various cultures around the

---

128. This hedge only mildly represents the current interpretative chaos in studies of the human menstrual cycle. See: Friedman *et al.* 1980, and particularly the volume edited by Friedman 1982, with its various contradicting theoretical positions on the psychology of the menstrual cycle.

world one finds beliefs that menstruating women can spoil crops, curdle mayonnaise, dim mirrors, cause flowers to wilt, drive bees from their hives, cause mares to miscarry, turn wine, beer, milk, etc. bad, spoil foods, cause sores, contaminate fishing and hunting gear, ruin weapons of combat, make sick people sicker, and make men insane, impotent, or even kill them (see Lederer 1968 and Hays 1964 for more examples).

In their survey of 99 nonindustrial societies for which the data are available, Paige and Paige (1981, 232) found that a total of 35 (35.4%) practiced some form of menstrual segregation of women (seclusion in special huts, separate rooms or parts of the household, etc.). 64 (64.6%) of the societies had some form of domestic, cooking, or personal taboo on menstruating women.

The obvious sociobiological observation to make on menstrual taboo is that both males and females do not lose any opportunity to replicate genes as a result of the taboo. Female hominids seem to have evolved from the one extreme of signalling when they are fertile to the other extreme of signalling when they are *not* fertile, and menstrual taboo seems to be a reinforcement of this signal. Perhaps there is an adaptive effect at work here. Perhaps not.

Women may use menstruation as an opportunity to rest, meditate, or socialize extensively with other women (Culpepper 1979). If they are secluded in menstrual huts and barred from the preparation of foods, they have the opportunity to rest from routine domestic work (Brown 1981, 590). Such resting is arguably adaptive. Janowsky *et al.* (1966, 283) go so far as to say there is "dangerously impaired behavior in menstruating women," and that perhaps "... menstrual taboos..., by limiting women's activities and contacts during menses, may constitute a worthwhile protection of the community, and so have positive survival value for their originating culture."

Males who avoid menstruating females could conceivably have more time and energy to attempt to inseminate other females,[129] to cooperate with other males in joint activities, to care for offspring, etc. Or, males who avoid menstruating women might simply be manifesting a concern for the reproductive potential of women, that is, the potential for women to get pregnant. Alexander (1979b, 167) says "it is even possible that the copious menstrual flow of women has evolved to be a signal of nonpregnancy." The Paiges, in their chapter on menstrual restrictions, make what is an essentially sociobiological or evolutionary hypothesis along these lines:

129. See Stephens 1962, 122, on the moderate correlation between extent of menstrual taboo and extent of polygyny. See also Morriss and Keverne 1974 on the putative advantage to the ancestral male when his mate suffers premenstrual tension, rebuffs him sexually, and thereby causes him to attempt to inseminate another female.

"... the regular appearance of menstrual bleeding after each pregnancy provides crucial evidence that a woman remains fertile. An obsessive concern with menstruation may well reflect men's need to assess women's ability to continue producing offspring" (1981, 209). Why a man "needs" to make this assessment is obvious in evolutionary perspective: the potential offspring in question are likely to be his offspring as well, i.e., to share genes with him as well as with his mate.

Let us now consider the psychoanalytic perspective. Freud believed that "primitive people cannot disassociate the puzzling phenomenon of this monthly flow of blood from sadistic ideas" (*SE* XI, 197). For example, Freud notes (following Frazer) that among the Monumbo of New Guinea the term applied to a menstruating woman is the same as that which describes a man who has just slain an enemy. Both are untouchable because both are bloodied. Mead (1975, 176) says that among the Manus menstruation is called "broken leg." Devereux reports that, among the Mohave Indians, "... men engaged in *aggressive* pursuits, such as warriors and hunters..., were especially prone to avoid contact with menstruating women" (1950, 239). Among the Malabar Coast natives a menstruating woman keeps a *knife* beside her, while the men believe that copulation with her would result in impotence (Gough 1955, 63).

In her discussion of a girl's experience of menarche, Simone de Beauvoir says that "just as the penis derives its privileged evaluation from the social context, so it is the social context that makes menstruation a curse" (1961 [1949], 295). Whether or not "social context" is the whole story, the parallelism that de Beauvoir makes is quite revealing: the anatomical area that is bloodied by menstruation is precisely where a penis *might* have been, had the girl been a boy. If the young girl was ever envious of the penis (see sect. 53), then the onset of menses must reactivate that envy and make her feel rather decisively "castrated." Throughout de Beauvoir's discussion of menarche the words "shame," "horror," "misfortune," "humiliation," etc. appear again and again. It is possible, though, that de Beauvoir has chosen as examples mostly girls who had particular difficulty in accepting the fact of their femaleness.

For it is males who are more likely to be made anxious by menstrual blood. In his cross-cultural study Stephens reports that "by far the dominant belief ... appears to be that menstruating women are dangerous to men. The reason usually given for such customs as the use of menstrual huts, the menstrual cooking taboo, or the menstrual sex taboo is that these avoidance-measures protect men" (1962, 96).

It is of course males, not females, who are expected (or expected not) to place their genital organ inside the apparently bleeding female genitalia.

But what exactly do males have to be protected against, given that there is no evidence that menstruating females are *objectively* dangerous?

According to Róheim (1945b, 174) "... the sight of the bleeding vagina produces castration anxiety in the male." Stephens assumes that

... the sight or thought of a person who bleeds from the genitals (a menstruating woman) is frightening to a person who has intense castration anxiety. It is a reminder of genital injury. Beyond this, I would not care to speculate too much about how the fear of this "reminder" is translated into institutionalized avoidance. I do assume that the various superstitions about the malignant power of menstruating women are projections or results of this fear-of-the-reminder-of-the-fantasied-expectation-of-genital-injury. Also, the avoidances are a way of "handling" or "doing something about" the fear. Quite possibly, the menstruating woman arouses phobic reactions in some men, analogous to phobias toward snakes, spiders, etc. (*ibid.*, 93).

A number of anthropologists and psychoanalysts take this position on menstrual taboo, i.e., regard it as, at least in part, one institutionalized way of dealing with the *male* castration anxiety aroused by menstrual bleeding (e.g., Montgomery 1974, 147; Devereux 1950; Lederer 1968, 25-9; Gough 1955). Thus the well known premenstrual tension, menstrual depression, and other menstrual problems sometimes suffered by females can be quite independent of any *female* "castration complex." As Thérèse Benedek says, anxiety dreams of menstruating women represent injury, "but whether the injury necessarily means castration in the sense of penis envy remains to be investigated in each case" (1959, 730).

One indicator that menstruation causes castration anxiety in males is the manner in which menstrual taboo is *violated*. When in a cultural context that encourages menstrual taboo a man deliberately engages in sexual relations with a menstruating woman anyway, his own *masculinity* is boosted. Thus Devereux's informants reported that "... some 'bad' (i.e., lewd) men did have intercourse with their menstruating sexual partners, and then went to swim in the river, in order to display their blood-stained genitalia to their friends, and to boast of having cohabited with a menstruating woman" (1950, 246). Legman gives several jokes and anecdotes in this vein, such as:

A travelling salesman propositions a young woman on a train. She objects mildly that she is "unwell," but allows him to come to her berth anyhow when he says, "That's all right; I don't mind. I used to be a Marine, and you know our motto: 'Through Mud and Blood to Glory!'" Waking up the next morning he finds the train stopped at a station. He sticks his head out the window and asks a small boy (or Negro), "What station is this?" "Birmingham, suh. Who hit you in de mouf?" (1975, 579).

Legman also reports that among the fraternal "Hell's Angels" a prestigious red wing patch is worn by those men who have performed public cunnilingus on a menstruating female in their group.

Paige and Paige (1981, 209-54) offer what they believe is an alternative to the psychoanalytic notion that menstruation causes castration anxiety. They establish that, in their large cross-cultural sample menstrual segregation practices (as well as related male segregation practices) are characteristic of societies with unstable economic resources and unstable political power among males. The Paiges interpret menstrual segregation as a way for males in these societies to "ostentatiously" refrain from intercourse with their mates and to leave them "unguarded" from other males (261):

The elaborate pollution practices of unstable societies can be interpreted as tactics of ritual disinterest in a wife's fertility that are part of a larger complex of tactics of ritual disinterest in wealth and power [e.g., potlatch]. A man's willingness to segregate his wife during her menstruation or to segregate himself from her throughout her reproductive span implies to others that his interest in the growth of his conjugal unit is not so complete as to preclude attention to social obligations and contractual agreements. His adherence to these customs reassures his affines and consanguines of his respect for their rights to share control over his wife's fertility and authority over her offspring and therefore of his continued allegiance toward the larger social group. (*ibid.*, 228).

Implicit in the Paiges' theory are the semiotic notions that 1) a wife's menstruation is a *sign* of her ongoing fertility, and 2) that a husband's ritual avoidance of her is a *sign* of his loyalty to the extraconjugal group.

From a sociobiological viewpoint a man who avoids his menstruating wife is, as it were, knocking down a straw man, since the wife is not able to conceive while menstruating anyway. The Paiges recognize this. A husband's disinterest would be more substantive if he avoided her while she were fertile. In societies which have a long postpartum sex taboo he does in fact avoid her when she is fertile. But since there is a cross-cultural correlation between long postpartum taboo and permitted polygyny (Stephens 1962; Saucier 1972; Daly and Wilson 1978, 289), then he may be recouping any losses due to postpartum avoidance by inseminating one or more other women.

The Paiges' analysis of menstrual taboo in nonindustrial societies is, I think, quite convincing but, as with their analyses of circumcision and defloration ceremonies, a psychoanalytic interpretation in terms of castration anxiety is not excluded. The Paiges direct most of their fire specifically at the psychoanalytic interpretation of menstrual taboo put forth by Stephens (1961; 1962). Stephens had hypothesized that childrearing conditions which aggravate castration anxiety — such as a long postpartum sex taboo which intensifies the mother-child relationship, punishment for rivalrous behavior toward the father, and punishment for childhood masturbation — should make it more likely that an adult, institutionalized manifestation of castration anxiety should exist, namely menstrual taboo. Stephens found that for the 55 societies for which there were adequate data, there was a highly significant association between his composite childrearing castration anxiety index and his menstrual taboo scale. Kline (1977, 74) commented that this association "... does seem [to be] impressive evidence for the concept of castration anxiety...."

Paige and Paige find fault with Stephens in three areas. First, they say that Stephens' childrearing index should be, but in fact is not correlated with three other factors — polygyny, patrilocal residence, and exclusive mother-child sleeping arrangements. These factors had been isolated by Whiting in his studies of *circumcision* (see above). But even if the three factors are assumed to be *indicative* of castration anxiety, there is no a priori psychoanalytic reason why they should be positively *correlated* with Stephens' childrearing index, and in any case Stephens had not said they should, nor was his theory the same as Whiting's theory.

Second, the Paiges found a sampling bias in Stephens' data. When his data are weighted to correct for the bias their own political-economic model proves to be statistically superior to the Stephens model.

Third, the Paiges discover that in their own data there is a *negative* correlation between menstrual (as well as male) segregation practices and what they say is "Whiting's crucial indicator of castration anxiety," i.e., circumcision. They conclude that "if segregation practices and circumcision both reflect unconscious anxieties about castration, then the two sets of rituals should be *positively* associated" (245, emphasis added). But they give no reason why they should be positively associated, and in fact there is no a priori psychoanalytic reason why they should be positively associated if they *both* signify the same thing, i.e., castration anxiety. Indeed, if both circumcision and menstrual taboo signify adult castration anxiety then it would make psychoanalytic sense for them *not* to typically occur together, since the occurrence of one would already be sufficient to signify adult castration anxiety. What could be said, from a psychoanalytic viewpoint, is that some social contexts encourage the signification of castration anxiety in adulthood by means of circumcision, and others by means of menstrual taboo, and only uncommonly is castration anxiety so aggravated by social conditions as to require *both* of the ritual signifiers in question (cf. the tendency for couvade and male transvestitism — each of them manifestations of feminine identity — *not* to occur together: Munroe 1980). This is not to mention that still other adult manifestations of castration anxiety are possible, such as the presence of castration motifs in folklore. The latter were included in Stephens' study, and their inclusion demonstrates that Stephens did not himself assume that menstrual taboo would have to be the only adult manifestation of castration anxiety.

In any case Paige and Paige have not demonstrated that menstrual taboos do not reflect castration anxiety, even if they have demonstrated that their political-economic model is superior to Stephens' specifically Oedipal model of the origin of menstrual taboo in nonindustrial societies. And as for industrial societies like our own, the Paiges also offer no counterevidence to a castration anxiety hypothesis, though they do present some convincing evidence that prevailing social attitudes about menstrual pollution can influence women's emotional responses to menstrual bleeding (274-5; cf. also the review in Rohrbaugh 1979, 56ff.).

49. From Castration Anxiety to Couvade

For every child a tooth.
Proverb

Whereas the Paiges found a negative correlation in the distributions of circumcision and menstrual segregation practices, Munroe, Munroe, and Whiting (1981; cf. Burton and Whiting [1961]) found a negative correlation in the distributions of circumcision and another reproductive ritual called *couvade*, which is a husband's imitative 'lying-in' and/or ritual abstinence from certain foods and activities around the time of his wife's delivery. The question that then arises is: if two things (menstrual segregation and couvade) are each negatively correlated (albeit in different samples) with a third thing (circumcision), might they themselves be related in some systematic way? To my knowledge, this question has not been explicitly addressed in the cross-cultural studies.[130] But if the tendency of menstrual segregation and circumcision to exclude each other indicates two different ways of males being preoccupied with castration, as I suggested above, then perhaps the tendency of couvade and circumcision to also exclude each other indicates the same preoccupation. In other words, perhaps couvade too is a manifestation of male castration anxiety?

Before tackling this question, a few words should be said about the definition and external manifestations of the practice in question. The term "couvade" was first used in English by E.B. Tylor in 1865 (288ff.). To simplify the etymology somewhat, the term is an anglicization of a now obsolete Basque area French word derived from *couver*, meaning 'to brood, hatch' (Partridge 1966, 290; Reik 1931, 27; Vol. I, 585 of the compact edition of the *Oxford English Dictionary*). The German equivalent is *das Männerkindbett* (as in Kunike 1911), literally 'men's childbed', though Bachofen (1943-67, VIII, 448) speaks of "*die Couvade.*" Russian scholars merely Russify, as English speakers merely anglicize, producing *kuvada* (as

---

130. Montgomery (1974) found an *inverse* relationship in her sample between numbers of restrictions on menstruating women and measures of the extent of participation by men in reproduction (including pre- and postpartum sex taboo, and participation of men in childbrith). To the extent that some of Montgomery's variables may be thought of as couvade, then an inverse relationship between menstrual taboo and couvade is suggested.

in vol. 23, 594 of the last Stalin years edition of the *Bolshaia sovetskaia entsiklopediia*).

One of the problems of dealing with couvade from a theoretical perspective is that widely differing practices in different societies are termed "couvade," depending on who the ethnographer is or what theoretical tradition the ethnographer is working in. Some, for example, restrict the term only to what a man does after his wife has given birth, such as taking the child into his bed, abstaining from various activities, and receiving the felicitations of friends. Others include the obviously imitative symptoms a man has before the child is born, such as his donning his wife's clothes, taking to his bed, and groaning with "sympathetic labor pains." Whether to include pre- and postpartum sex taboos also is a problem. Fine distinctions are made, such as "dietetic couvade," "classical couvade," "prenatal couvade," "postnatal couvade," "pseudocouvade," "pseudo-maternal couvade," etc. (for example: Hand 1957; Dawson 1929; Kroeber 1948, 543; Frazer 1910, IV, 255; Munroe *et al.* 1973; Reik 1931, 27-89). In the medical profession the term "couvade syndrome" is used (e.g., Trethowan 1972), and refers to somewhat less ritualized and perhaps less voluntary manifestations than the ethnographers' "couvade."

For present purposes I am simply going to lump together all the different practices under the rubric of "couvadish" behavior (or "couvadishness"). By this I mean all supernaturalistic and/or neurotic-psychosomatic phenomena in which a man,[131] before/during/after the birth of a child, engages in non-routine activities or manifests certain symptoms as a result of his association with the mother and/or child.[132] If the context is clearly anthropological, I may use the accepted anthropological term "couvade," and if the context is clinical I may use the medical term "couvade syndrome."

Couvadish behavior is remarkably common in today's hominids. It is not just a folkloric fantasy (though it *is* that too — see the entries "pregnant man" [T578], "man made to believe that he is pregnant" [J232] and "couvade" [T583.1] in the Aarne-Thompson index). Here is an example of the most typical symptoms:

---

131. I do not say "husband" here, because sometimes the mother's brother also observes couvade, as in the Wogeo (Hogbin 1943, 291). Trethowan (1972) cites occasional reports of couvade syndrome in the fathers of expectant daughters.

132. As for the specific scoring of couvade in the already mentioned cross-cultural study of Munroe *et al.* (1981), the following definition was used: "...if strong supernaturalistic observations were reported for the father, such that they involved his deviating from normal activities for more than half the time over a period of 1 day or longer, then a rating of intensive couvade observances was assigned" (625-6; nonintensive and couvade-absent cases were classed together).

A woman described how during the birth of her child her husband came to visit her. He came again the following day, after the child had been born, saying, "I wouldn't like to go through that again." He described how, on leaving the hospital the previous day, pains in his stomach had started and continued until the evening, when he vomited and felt better. This coincided more or less with the time the baby was born. She also added that during both her pregnancies her husband insisted on having a tooth extracted despite the dentist's opinion that his teeth were perfectly sound. (Trethowan 1972, 77).

Cases of nausea, vomiting, abdominal bloating, abdominal pains, heartburn, leg cramps, taking to bed, fatigue, food cravings, headaches, toothaches, styes, and dizziness in expectant fathers are all well documented in both the clinical literature on our own culture and in the anthropological literature on many other cultures (e.g., Hand 1957; Munroe and Munroe 1971; Trethowan and Conlon 1965; Trethowan 1972; Munroe and Munroe 1973; Munroe, Munroe, and Whiting 1973; Hogbin 1943; Lipkin and Lamb 1982). Trethowan and Conlon (1965) found that there was a significantly higher incidence of loss of appetite, toothache, and nausea and vomiting in a group of 327 expectant fathers than in a control group. Lipkin and Lamb (1982) found that 22.5% of 267 expectant fathers sought care for one or more symptoms (nausea, vomiting, abdominal pain, toothache, etc.) for which they had *not* sought care six months before or six months after their wives' pregnancies. Munroe *et al.* (1981, 619) state that "... male symptoms, including fatigue, food craving, vomiting, headaches, and dizziness, have been reported as present in all societies in which they have been asked about systematically ...." Trethowan (1972, 69) believes that Australia is the only continent where couvade as a ritual has *not* been observed. Couvade was already known to the ancients, judging from the writings of Strabo, Diodorus, Plutarch, and others. Marco Polo found it in Chinese Turkistan in the thirteenth century, and a French missionary observed it in northern Brazil in the seventeenth century.

Given such widespread distribution in time and space, it seems hardly likely that couvadishness can be accounted for as the result of cultural diffusion from one place (Dawson ventures the island of Cyprus as a point of origin – *ibid.*, 60). It is much more reasonable to assume, rather, that such behavior is one way for a male to respond to his *own* feelings at the thought that an important woman in his life is about to deliver, or has just delivered, a child.

I stress the word "own" because couvadish behavior gives such a distinct impression of selfishness or egocentrism.[133] It is, after all, the *woman*

133.   But I would not want to rule out the possibility that a man's couvadishness, without his knowing it, may even make a woman's pregnancy and delivery a more

who is having the baby, not the man. Yet it seems the man cannot bear to be left out. He insists on participating in some way, ritualistically or neurotically, consciously or unconsciously, even if in doing so he is telling the rest of the world about his personal problems.

One of the couvadish male's personal problems is, I think, his castration anxiety. For one thing, if the adult male had earlier feared that women themselves were 'castrated' creatures (above, section 44), then his imitation of a woman by means of his couvadish behavior should by definition raise the spectre of castration for him. For another thing, the act of childbirth is bloody and traumatic in itself, and is therefore interpretable to him as a kind of castration. Felix Boehm (1930, 456) observes that "all men find it overwhelming when they see for the first time the baby's head appearing from the vagina." Alexander (1923, 38ff.) regards birth as "a primal form of castration," and Otto Rank (1973 [1924], 20ff.) believes that castration anxiety is so pervasive precisely because it masks the "trauma of birth" that we have all experienced. In her analysis of the misfortunes of pregnant androgynes in Indian mythology O'Flaherty (1980, 300) says that "male pregnancy may be viewed as the positive aspect of a syndrome whose negative facet is manifest in self-castration...." Edwards (1984, 13) reports that in the Indonesian archipelago and in Malaya there is a widespread belief that the spirit of a female who has died in childbirth returns to castrate males.

It is quite natural for the egocentric male to associate childbirth with castration because the bloody mess that is the child separates from the woman's body precisely at that anatomical point where on *his* body there dangles a penis. Psychoanalysts have long been familiar with an equation made by little children, patients on the couch, native informants from other cultures, and others: *penis = baby* (*SE* XVII, 84, 128-33; XIX, 178-9; Klein 1977, 393, 419; Rank 1973, 39-40; Forrester 1980, 202-4; Chadwick 1925; Devereux 1950, 253; Ferenczi 1938, 23). Linguistic usage often supports this equation. In German, for example, "das Kleine" ('little one') can refer either to the penis or to a baby (*SE* XVII, 128). As we saw earlier, in many languages a penis often acquires a *personal* name ("Dicky," "Peter," etc.), while one of the first things that has to be done after a baby is born is to give it too a personal name. Furthermore, pet names for the penis are often diminutives, just as names for children are.

Robinson (1976, 174), speaking of the potential for orgasmic experience

---

positive experience than it would otherwise be. There are some indications that a man's participation in the delivery room helps a woman to enjoy the delivery (Hahn and Paige 1980, 166). My lawyer suggests that a husband's presence at delivery creates a situation where the wife is in charge for a change.

during childbirth, says: "One is inevitably reminded of the Freudian identification of the child with the penis. This seemingly extravagant psychoanalytic conception suddenly takes on an aura of plausibility when one learns that the child's passage through the vagina results in an experience not unlike orgasm."

In fact, regardless of the matter of orgasm, the parallel between what the erect penis does and the emerging fetus does is striking: they both have to pass through the same anatomical area, the vagina. In evolutionary terms, the structure of the hominid vagina has always been constrained to accomodate two — and only two — objects, the penis and the child (just as the structure of the penis and of the child [especially its cranium], as we saw earlier, have been under selective pressure vis-a-vis the structure of the vagina). The Freudian equation of penis and child may thus be said to reflect a very basic biological connection.

Greenberg and Fisher (1980; 1983) have conducted some experiments which, arguably, support the idea of an unconscious penis-baby equation. They found, for example, that pregnant women produced significantly more phallic imagery[134] in response to the Holtzman Inkblot Test than did non-pregnant women. Also, women scored significantly higher on phallic imagery when they were pregnant than when they were not pregnant. Women who masturbated, i.e., obtained sexual gratification without the help of a man's penis, tended to produce more phallic imagery during menstruation — a time when they could *not* be pregnant — than women who did not masturbate. Greenberg and Fisher also cite the abundant evidence (1983, 262) that women tend to dream about having boy babies rather than girl babies, and that they tend to be more pleased, less depressed, and less irritable when they give birth to boys (i.e., babies who *are* phallic) than when they give birth to girls.[135] All of these studies, by the way, concern women's, not men's attitudes toward penises and babies. However one may wish to interpret the

---

134. Responses were coded as "phallic" if they included such items as: elongated objects such as arrow, gun, cigar, rod, candle, rocket, flute, etc.; human body protrusions such as nose, chin, penis, finger, etc.; animal protrusions such as horns, antennae, claws, tail, etc.; phallic geographical formations such as mountain peak, stalagmite; "projective" motions, such as shooting, sticking out, towering, etc. (Greenberg and Fisher 1983, 280-1).

135. Cross-culturally, too, women seem to prefer to have boys than girls, and this preference can sometimes take rather graphic genital form. Among the Bolivian Siriono, for example, boys are called "penises" and girls are "vulvas" in the native language. Holmberg (1969, 202) says: "Males are definitely preferred. If asked the sex of her infant, a mother proudly holds up a boy and demonstrates his penis; if her infant is a girl, she contents herself merely with replying '*eréN*' ('Vulva,' i.e., female). A pregnant woman, too, always expresses a desire to give birth to a boy."

studies – and I think there will be much discussion of them in the future – they nonetheless do not have a direct bearing on couvadishness, which is an expression of men's rather than women's attitudes.

One of the most frequent of the couvadish themes in the ethnographic and anthropological literature has to do with sharp instruments. Rules and practices that involve the father in cutting, hacking, chopping, etc., or in avoiding these activities, can be found with monotonous regularity. Given that these themes concern primarily men, and given that the most important reproductive asset a man would not want to be cut off from is his penis, then I would say that they indicate castration anxiety.

A Melanesian Kurtatchi husband remains in seclusion, abstains from certain foods, does not do his normal chores, and does not handle *sharp tools*. On the final day of his couvade he enters his wife's seclusion hut and proceeds "... to *slash* at the infant as if he were about to *sever* its limbs and head" (Paige and Paige, 190, emphasis added). Among the Siriono of Bolivia it is imperative that the husband *cut* the newborn's umbilical cord as a signal of the commencement of couvade (Holmberg 1969, 179; Paige and Paige, *ibid.*, 191-2). The Araucanians of Chile believe that if an expectant father *cuts* his fingernails with scissors, a girl will be born, but with a knife a boy will be born (Montgomery 1974, 159). The Malay husband was not supposed to *shave* his head during his couvade (Crawley 1965, 178). Reik (1931, 31) cites a report of a Carib post-natal practice in which the relatives of the father "... *hack* the skin of this poor wretch with agouti teeth, and draw blood from all parts of his body ..." (italics added). Reik also quotes a description of an old Jewish practice in which a *sword* was laid at the head of a woman in childbed and was flourished about the bed for thirty nights in a row (*ibid.*, 58). In "male pregnancy" among the New Guinea Hua the stomach is said to burst when the *teeth* of the fetus erupt, and such "pregnancy" can be relieved by the administration of *cuts* (to the navel, lower back, or buttocks) which produce blood that is likened to menstrual blood (Meigs 1976, 395-8). The Dyak husband, like the Kurtatchi husband already mentioned, is not supposed to work with *sharp* instruments before the birth of his child (Reik 1931, 30). For the Black Carib it is specifically axes and machetes that are not supposed to be used (Munroe *et al.*, 1973, 51), while the Alor husband must refrain from digging and chopping (DuBois 1969, 32), which suggests that axes and shovels cannot be used. Hogbin (1943, 289) says the Wogeo husband must avoid the use of axes and knives.

Psychiatrist W. H. Trethowan (1972) says that *toothache* is one of the most frequent male pregnancy symptoms. It affected nearly 25% of the expectant fathers in his sample, while its occurrence in a control group was only 10% (cf. Stannard 1977, 324; Munroe *et al.* 1973, 57, report a 56%

incidence of toothache in their Black Carib sample). Folklorist Wayland Hand mentions not only the so-called "married man's toothache," but also reports on the ritualistic burning of a husband's cap or trousers after a wife's delivery in some parts of the American south (the phallic significance of hats is a psychoanalytic commonplace [*SE* V, 360-62], and the psychological equivalence of a man's trousers with his genitalia is confirmed by southern folk beliefs that wearing a husband's trousers or simply draping them over the marriage bed will help a woman get pregnant — see Hand, *ibid.,* 215, 225). In effect, the birth of the child equals the destruction of the husband's penis.

Though the various couvadish practices may be a way for a man to deal with his castration anxiety, I do not want to suggest that this is the whole story. Indeed, I doubt that it is even the major part of the story. The imitative element is so prominent that we would have to conclude that couvadish men *want* to be castrated if we did not recognize that there is also a more positive motive for couvadishness.

50. The Social Father as a Second Mother

> She who is called the child's mother is
> not its begetter, but the nurse of the
> newly sown conception. The begetter is
> the male, and she as a stranger for a
> stranger preserves the offspring....
> Apollo, in The Eumenides of *Aeschylus*

Already in 1861 Johann Jakob Bachofen recognized the element of identification in couvade and in couvade-like practices. He repeatedly uses the Latin
expression *"imitatio naturae"* and the German verb *"nachahmen"* ('to
imitate') in his discussion (Bachofen 1943-67 [1861], III, 626ff.). Though
Bachofen mistakenly believed that a primeval "mother-right" (*"Mutterrecht"*)
or "gynococracy" (*"Gynaikokratie"*) was the historical context for the
development of couvade, he nonetheless had considerable insight into its
psychological nature. Quite original is his overall notion of fatherhood as a
kind of fictitious motherhood. He speaks of "... the fiction whereby the
father is thought of and represented as a second mother [*als zweite Mutter*];"
"... the father is obliged to get past the fiction of the naturalness of motherhood [*muss durch die Fiktion der Naturwahrheit des Muttertums hin-
durchgehen*] in order to win recognition of a manhood which does not exist
in its own right" (ibid., 631). In other words, part of a man's very masculinity
seems to lie in the ability to appropriate certain motherly characteristics.
And apparently Bachofen understood couvade to be only one of the practices
whereby the father establishes himself as a "second mother."

In 1889 E. B. Tylor, in agreement with Bachofen, called couvade a
"farcical proceeding" (255) in which the father "... makes a ceremonial pretense of being the mother ..." (254). Tylor also agreed with Bachofen in
asserting that couvade can be a way of legitimizing ties between the father
and the mother's child. The tie of the father with the child is indeed prominent in a number of the practices, and often has a magical-sympathetic
character. But, as Crawley (1965 [1927], 185) says, in some cases "... the
most prominent feature is the sympathy between father and child, but in
couvade proper the chief feature is the taking over by the father of the
personality of the mother."

Bronislaw Malinowski, though he disputed much of what Bachofen had
to say, nonetheless adhered to Bachofen's conception of the imitative essence
of fathering:

The whole theory of paternity, its dependence upon a direct physiological bond between father and child or merely upon the bond indirectly established between father and offspring through marriage – this theory should be studied in functional connection with the various taboos, ritual observances, ceremonial, magical, economic and legal acts performed by the father at conception, during pregnancy and at childbirth. The famous custom of the *couvade* will naturally occur to every reader in this connection; the custom, that is, in which the husband mimics the pangs and vicissitudes of childbirth. But the *couvade*, if we place it in its setting of cognate phenomena, is but one of a whole series of customs which shows that the father has a number of legal and magical obligations to fulfil, and that, in performing them, he works for the welfare of his offspring and his wife. In other words, from the functional point of view, *all those customs which we might label as belonging to the couvade type are an exact parallel to those which establish cultural maternity.* (Malinowski 1962, 68-9, italics added).

Later Malinowski says that couvade makes sense if we assume that there is a "... tendency ... for the father to assimilate his role to that of his wife" (*ibid.*, 169). In *Sex and Repression in Savage Society* (1955 [1927]) he says that "... while we find that maternity is social as well as biological, we must affirm that paternity is determined also by biological elements, that therefore in its make-up it is closely analogous to the maternal bond" (190). Even an implicitly Darwinian, adaptive value to fathering in general, and couvade in particular, is suggested: "... it is of high biological value for the human family to consist of both father and mother ..." (*ibid.*, 189).

Another scholar to emphasize the similarity processes linking husband to wife in couvade is Bruno Bettelheim. In his book *Symbolic Wounds* (1954) Bettelheim sees couvade as only one of a variety of rituals – including circumcision, subincision, scarification, ritual transvestism, and other practices – which manifest "men's desire to participate in women's functions" (225). In couvade "the man wishes to find out how it feels to give birth, or he wishes to maintain to himself that he can" (211). Couvade is a "pretense" in which the man

... copies only the relatively insignificant externals and not the essentials, which, indeed, he cannot duplicate. Such copying of superficialities emphasizes the more how much the real, essential powers are envied. Women, emotionally satisfied by having given birth and secure in their ability to produce life, can agree to the couvade which men need to fill the emotional vacuum created by their inability to bear children. (*ibid.*).

I might add that the psychoanalyst Bettelheim, unlike most of his anthropologist-predecessors who theorized about couvade, was acquainted with some of the abundant, if neglected psychoanalytic literature on male envy of female reproductive functions, such as: Chadwick 1925; Zilboorg 1944;

Jacobson 1950. Other major psychoanalytic contributions in this area, which refer variously to "pregnancy envy," "vagina envy," "parturition envy," "envy of woman's procreative function," "envy of the breast," "womb envy," "vulva envy," and "woman envy"[136] include: Boehm 1930; Fromm 1951, 233ff.; Horney 1967 (1926), 60-1; Macalpine and Hunter in Schreber 1955, 381ff.; Klein 1975 (1957), 176-235 (esp. 201); Mack Brunswick 1940; Evans 1951; Jaffe 1977; Van Leeuwen 1966. In this literature we can read numerous direct expressions of the envy of female reproductive functions made by males. Boehm (1930) provides some examples:

"It vexes me that women have two openings in the lower part of their bodies, while men have only one. I envy them that." (451).

"When I was a boy and, I think, still when I was adolescent, I used when in the bath to squeeze my genitals in between my legs and press the upper part of my arms together so that they looked like a woman's bosom. (*ibid.*, 448).

"Mother, come quick. I've born a beautiful baby" (said by a three-year-old boy after he had been on the chamber pot — *ibid.*, 455).

Freud himself adduced some very clear evidence of such male envy in little Hans:

"... But you know quite well that boys can't have children." *Hans:* "Well, yes. But I believe they can, all the same." (*SE* X, 95).

Legman's *Rationale* includes many anecdotes that rely on the fantasy of "male motherhood," such as: "a homosexual with goiter on his neck starts knitting baby clothes" (1968, 600).

Of all the psychoanalysts who deal with the practice of couvade, it is Gregory Zilboorg who most explicitly and cogently advances the general thesis that fatherhood is basically a form of motherhood:

There is little doubt that this identification with the gravid and parturient woman has a deeper, magic wish-fulfillment value of earlier, more primitive strivings. I am inclined to believe that these strivings are coupled with envy and hostility — hence identification through illness — and that the same dynamic factors are responsible for the myth according to which Zeus took from the burning body of Semele the six-months-old foetus of Dionysus, sewed it up in his own loin, bore it to full term, and gave birth to the young god. Similarly, the birth of Athena from the head of Zeus is but another form of identification on the basis of the same type of envy. It is known

---

136. Solanas (1970, 6) prefers the term "pussy envy" — whereby she seems to defeat her own feminist purpose (why use a derogatory term for female genitalia?). Indeed the title of her book, *SCUM Manifesto* seems self-defeating (are feminists "scum"?).

that schizophrenics occasionally believe, and neurotics not infrequently have dreams, that a baby comes out of the penis – or the head. (Zilboorg 1944, 289).

I must submit that it was man who perceived himself biologically inferior, and it was this sense of inferiority and concomitant hostility that led to the phenomenon of *couvade* – a magic, compulsion-neurotic, hostile identification with the mother. *It is out of this identification with the mother that psychological fatherhood was achieved.* (*ibid.*, 290, emphasis Zilboorg's).[137]

In suggesting that "... fatherhood is a maternal trait of man ...," Zilboorg is (unwittingly) also making a significant sociobiological statement: a man who takes on the responsibilities of a father (pater) becomes a kind of 'mother' because he adopts the strategy of making a major long-term investment in offspring, *just as* real mothers do. At the level of proximate mechanisms, mothering turns out to be the major preadaptive device whereby fathering (in more than just the sense of being a genitor) becomes possible. The other major preadaptive device is the ability to imitate and to identify with somebody. But an imitation is not, of course, the real thing. A man cannot (without hormone injections) lactate, and he cannot gestate a fetus. Besides, his biological paternity is never quite as certain as her biological maternity is. So his 'motherhood,' i.e., his fatherhood, will always be somewhat of a sham. His mate's motherhood, on the other hand will never be a bogus 'fatherhood' (cf. Chodorow 1978, 11). There is plenty of talk about "male mothers" in the anthropological literature, but the concept of 'female father' does not exist. Similarly, ethologists speak of "allomothering," but there is no 'allofathering.' What a woman does from the point of conception on is simply *sui generis*. Motherhood just is what it is. It is free of the imitative or semiotic mystifications that fatherhood always perpetrates.[138]

As an example of just how far this male mystifying tendency can go, I would like to consider a case well known in the history of psychiatry.

---

137. See also Alice Balint's analysis (1926) of the cultural construct of the *pater familias*, which she interprets as basically a kind of metaphorical nursing mother. Harold Feldman, who mentions couvade in passing, argues that "...the father-image is a thin mask covering the image of the pre-Oedipal mother" (1955, 269; cf. Brown 1966, 77). The bits of philological evidence that Feldman introduces are particularly interesting, such as the fact that in Japanese "*chichi*" refers both to 'father' and to 'teats' or 'breast milk.' In his psychoanalytic study of the Old Testament, Roellenbleck (1974 [1949]) devotes a section to the images of Jahwe as a mother (80-84).

138. Throughout the present discussion it is understood that fathering as pseudo-mothering is above and beyond (though it also reinforces) *husbanding* as pseudo-mothering (above, section 23).

51. The Couvadishness of Herr Schreber

Some very interesting opinions on the ability to give birth are expressed by one Daniel Paul Schreber in a book entitled *Memoirs of my Nervous Illness* (1955, German original 1903). Schreber was a distinguished jurist who became mentally ill in 1893 shortly after taking up the post of president (*Senatspräsident*) of the Dresden Appeals Court. He eventually ended up in the Sonnenstein Asylum, where he remained for nearly nine years. Toward the end of his stay there he gathered together various notes and jottings from the earlier years and wrote his now famous *Memoirs*. Schreber considered this opus to be a "scientific treatise," but the many psychologists who have studied it since regard it as a very sophisticated attempt to build a rational world view out of a system of paranoid delusions.

Central to Schreber's argument is the idea that his body at certain times was transformed into a female body. The first hint of the transformation actually comes before his illness:

... one morning while still in bed (whether still half asleep or already awake I cannot remember), I had a feeling which, thinking about it later when fully awake, struck me as highly peculiar. It was the idea that it really must be rather pleasant to be a woman succumbing to intercourse. This idea was so foreign to my whole nature that I may say I would have rejected it with indignation if fully awake; from what I have experienced since I cannot exclude the possibility that some external influences were at work to implant this idea in me. (Schreber 1955, 63).

What is interesting about such a declaration is not so much its homosexual overtones as the fact that it comes just a few lines after the following statement:

After recovering from my first illness I spent eight years with my wife, on the whole quite happy ones, rich also in outward honours and marred only from time to time by *the repeated disappointment of our hope of being blessed with children.* (*ibid.*, italics added).

Later Schreber becomes quite graphic about his supposed female anatomy:

Twice at different times (while I was still in Flechsig's Asylum) I had a female genital organ, although a poorly developed one, and *in my body felt quickening like the first signs of life in a human embryo:* by a divine miracle God's nerves corresponding to male seed had been thrown into my body; in other words fertilization had occurred. (*ibid.*, 43, italics added).

Clearly, Schreber had the idea that he might be able to have a baby.

What made the Schreber case famous was not so much the publication of Schreber's *Memoirs* as it was the appearance of Freud's analysis of them in 1911 (*SE* XII, 3-82). In his analysis Freud establishes what has now come to be the basic psychoanalytic theory of paranoia. Freud argues, essentially, that the various delusions characteristic of paranoid schizophrenia are grounded in repressed homosexual impulses (cf. Schatzman 1973, 48-55, 94; Lacan 1966, 541-2; Rancour-Laferriere 1980, 199-201; Fisher and Greenberg 1977, ch. 6; Fenichel 1945, 427ff.). Schreber's paranoia probably did in fact have a homosexual basis, and Fisher's and Greenberg's review of the experimental studies of paranoia does show that "... the paranoid [as opposed to the normal person or the nonparanoid patient] has a unique pattern of reaction to anything that has the potential for conjuring up homosexual images" (268). The homosexual basis of paranoia does not, however, exclude other bases.

In Schreber's case there was, as Macalpine and Hunter put it, a "quest to procreate" (in Schreber 1955, 386). While institutionalized Schreber constantly imagined the existence of "souls" or "little people out of Schreber's spirit:"

... at that time I had the "God" or "Apostle" of these little people — that is to say presumably the aggregate of the rays which were derived from their states of Blessedness — as a soul in my body, more specifically *in my belly*. This little "God" or "Apostle" surpassed all other souls by virtue of a practical turn of mind — a fundamental trait of my own character (I cannot suppress some self-praise here) — so that in a way I recognized in him *flesh of my flesh and blood of my blood*. (*ibid.*, 112, italics added).

In this last expression ("*Fleisch von meinem Fleische und Blut von meinem Blute*") one can see the extent to which Schreber's fantasized creatures stand for some part ("practical turn of mind") of *himself* (at one point he even imagines that there once existed another Daniel Paul Schreber — *ibid.*, 86). In the anatomical specification of the location of these "little people" ("in my belly" — "*im Unterleibe*") it is clear that they emanate from a part of the body where babies would be thought to come from. Schreber says that "... my unmanning [*Entmannung*] will be accomplished with the result that by divine fertilization offspring will issue from my lap [*aus meinem Schosse*], or alternatively that great fame will be attached to my name surpassing that of thousands of other people much better mentally endowed" (*ibid.*, 214).

Although no real offspring ever did issue from Schreber's "lap," he nonetheless managed to make a record of the voices, that is, he managed to produce a different kind of offspring, the *Memoirs* themselves, so that the "unmanning" he felt he had to endure was not altogether in vain (cf. Macalpine and Hunter in *ibid.*, 406). Schreber is, as Macalpine and Hunter say, "the most frequently quoted patient in psychiatry" (Schreber 1955, 8). Whether Schreber himself consciously realized he would attain *this* kind of "immortality" is doubtful. He thought himself immune to death by violence or illness (*ibid.*, 212), and although he granted that his body would eventually die of "senility," he was certain that his "nerves" would be among the first to achieve a state of "Blessedness" ("*Seligkeit*") after death (*ibid.*, 213). On an unconscious level, however, Schreber must have realized what a magnificent, death-defying autoicon he had produced in the form of his *Memoirs*. Otherwise it would be very difficult to explain why he was so insistent about publishing them, in the face of resistance from his family as well as official censorship of several passages.

Freud was of course aware of the existence of fantasies of childbirth in males, and even discussed this matter in his paper on Schreber. Thus he says that "Dr. Schreber may have formed a phantasy that if he were a woman he would manage the business of having children more successfully" (*SE* XII, 58). Freud adds:

If the 'little men' whom Schreber himself finds so puzzling were children, then we should have no difficulty in understanding why they were collected in such great numbers on his head; they were in truth the 'children of his spirit' [cf. English "brainchild"]. (*ibid.*).

But these are only ancillary considerations in the context of Freud's overall analysis of the Schreber case. Freud saw Schreber's childbearing fantasies as merely the consequence of homosexual fantasies, rather than the other way around. No doubt the objective sequence of events — there must be intercourse before there is childbirth — influenced Freud in his reasoning. But there is, I think, a stronger influence. Freud is particularly anxious to avoid any idea of males wanting to give birth the way females do. For example, he dismisses couvade as "... probably intended to contradict the doubts as to paternity [in the sense of uncertain paternity] which can never be entirely overcome" (*SE*, IX, 223). Or, in his analysis of the "Rat Man," we find the following footnote:

As Lichtenberg says, 'An astronomer knows whether the moon is inhabited or not with about as much certainty as he knows who was his father, but not with so much certainty as he knows who was his mother'. A great advance was made in civilization when men decided to put their inferences upon a level with the testimony of their senses and to make the step from matriarchy to patriarchy. — The prehistoric figures which show a smaller person sitting upon the head of a larger one are representations of patrilineal descent; Athena had no mother, but sprang from the head of Zeus. (*SE*, X, 233).

Here, at the very moment Freud is introducing evidence that men (such as Zeus) might have liked to be able to have babies, he also feels obliged to say that a switch from "matriarchy" to patriarchy is a "great advance" (Bachofen's feelings precisely – see Bachofen 1943-67, III, 631). The value judgement is lurking not far in the background here. In effect: "it is *better* that descent be reckoned through one's father than through one's mother; if I (a male) cannot give birth to children, then at least I can take consolation in the fact that the children my wife gives birth to have my name, not hers."

Such consolation is in fact often taken in our own society, where a male will sometimes go so far as to give his child his first as well as his last name, producing a string of identically named males: John Smith, Sr., John Smith, Jr., John Smith III, etc. One doesn't hear of this being done to females (Mary Smith, Jr.?). In Lacanian terms, the obsession with the name of the father (*"nom du père"*) is a male problem, not a female one.[139]

---

139. I have of course neglected some important other aspects of the Schreber case, such as his castration anxiety which is expressed not only in his concern with *"Entmannung"* but in his great fear of "soul murder" (*"Seelenmord"*) – though the latter seems to be also a fear of loss of individuality and a concern with his inability to have children. I also have not mentioned the appalling biographical background to the *Memoirs*. Schreber's fantasies have been traced to actual abusive practices on the part of Schreber's father, Daniel Gottlieb Moritz Schreber (1808-61), who was a leading German pedagogue and medical doctor. Dr. Schreber, Sr., who might be thought of as a kind of sadistic Doctor Spock, advocated such things as: strapping children into bed to ensure that they remain supine and straight while sleeping; clamping one end of a strap to a child's hair, the other end to his underwear, so that any tilting of the child's head in a forward or sideways direction would cause a painful pulling of the hair; strapping children's jaws closed for periods of time supposedly in order to facilitate proper growth of the jaw and teeth (Schatzman 1973, 34-55; Niederland 1974, 49ff.).

52. A Man's Couvade Is Never Done

> The monkey is on his back and he feels it. Unlike his sister, he has no feminine base to return to to lick his wounds. He can't just comb his hair, he can't resort to "well, I can always be a mother."
> *James Neely*

The cross-cultural studies by Munroe *et al.*[140] established that couvade tends to occur in societies or in sectors of societies where there is close mother-infant contact. According to Munroe *et al.* (1981; cf. Munroe and Munroe 1971; 1973; Munroe *et al.* 1973) such close contact fosters intense cross-sex identification of a male child with the mother, and couvade is a way of enviously expressing the male's felt feminine identity later in life.

Munroe and Munroe (1971) found that those males in three selected cultures (United States, Black Carib, Logoli Bantu) who exhibit pregnancy symptoms are more likely to produce female-like responses on certain "covert" measures of sex identity than males who do not show the symptoms. For example, American males who show the symptoms are more likely to produce 'female' drawings on the Franck Drawing Completion Test and to watch television programs characteristically preferred by females than males who do not show the symptoms. Also, the majority of the American subjects who reported some father-absence in childhood belonged to the pregnancy symptom group. For the Black Carib sample, the longer subjects had lived without an adult male in the home during childhood, the more symptoms they experienced during their spouse's pregnancies.

There are many societies, particularly those which have "corporate patrilineages" (Munroe *et al.*) or "strong fraternal interest groups" (Paige and Paige), which tend *not* to have couvade, even though there is close mother-infant contact. These societies tend instead to have circumcision. I have already noted this statistical tendency for couvade and circumcision to be mutually exclusive (section 49). What I suggested then is that couvade and circumcision could be alternative expressions of the exaggerated male castration anxiety resulting from close mother-male child contact in those societies. Granted, it is more obvious that circumcision expresses castration anxiety than couvade does, because circumcision has to do directly with the male

---

140. But cf. the Paiges 1981, 207.

genitalia. We might say that castration anxiety is the 'major' underlying concern in circumcision, while it is 'minor' for couvade. What I want to suggest now is a parallel but reversed situation for underlying cross-sex identification. That is, given the close mother-infant contact in *both* the couvade-type and circumcision-type societies, one should expect an envy of/identification with the mother in both types of society. But since this envy/identification is already obvious for couvade, I will term it the 'major' underlying concern in couvade. What is less obvious is that circumcision-type societies should also be concerned with the envy of/identification with the mother, so I will term this concern 'minor' for such societies. Schematically:

	Castration Anxiety	Envy of/Identification with Mother
Circumcision-Type Societies	MAJOR	MINOR
Couvade-Type Societies	MINOR	MAJOR

But in what sense could envy of/identification with the mother be playing even a 'minor' role in societies which tend to circumcision?

Bettelheim argued, as we saw in section 46, that some forms of penile mutilation are essentially imitations of menstruation. But most of Bettelheim's examples are from Australia, and involve subincision rather than the more general practice of circumcision (though Bettelheim's examples do illustrate male identification with female functions).

The Paiges showed, on the other hand, that circumcision tends to be associated with strong fraternal interest groups, and Munroe *et al.* found an association of circumcision with corporate patrilineages. What I would like to suggest is that fraternal interest groups or corporate patrilineages (whether or not they occur in societies with penile mutilation) *themselves* express male envy of/identification with female reproductive function. In other words, a fraternal interest group or a corporate patrilineage is itself a metaphorical kind of mothering. By participating in and feeling at one with such a group a male is not technically practicing the custom of couvade, but he is nonetheless being couvadish.

The Paiges say that, "in societies with strong fraternal interest groups, the distribution of paternity rights is typically agreed upon before the birth of offspring through an explicit marriage bargain" (1981, 179). There is considerable male concern about "rights over a woman's reproductive capacity" in such societies. A pregnant woman may be subject to a variety of "maternal restrictions and ritual surveillance:"

Among the Tallensi, for example, a husband must be careful about the kinds of activities in which he engages during his wife's pregnancy so that he cannot be held responsible in any way for injury to her or the child. He avoids any connection with death, such as attendance at a funeral, and he may reduce the amount of time he devotes to subsistence activities. He also consults diviners to help prevent miscarriage and offers special sacrifices to his ancestors as a way of putting his wife in their care. The husband's close kinsmen keep watch over the pregnant woman to ensure that she does not overexert herself physically or break any of the food taboos she is supposed to observe. The husband's father consults a diviner, and he and the wife's father may both appeal to their ancestors for assistance. (*ibid.*, 184).

But some of this behavior is obviously couvadish, with other males besides the husband joining the husband in his superstitious activities. Or, consider some of the complicated marriage negotiations which take place among the African Taita:

... negotiations concerning the transfer of rights to women's fertility and the brideprice objects can take years. In some cases they are never entirely completed. For about two years before the husband takes the wife to his own household, certain rights are gradually transferred to him in return for certain livestock, foods, and services. For example, payment of the livestock portion of the brideprice explicitly allows the man rights to the wife's reproductive capacity; once that portion has been paid, her future offspring are recognized as his heirs and members of his lineage, his property will pass to her sons, and any brideprice obtained through her daughters' marriages belongs to him. Each animal presented during this and subsequent stages has special significance and involves different members of the kin group most intimately interested in the marriage.

The most important single animal transferred is an unborn heifer calf called *kifu*, or "womb." For this particular transaction to be considered complete, the calf must reach maturity and itself bear a calf. If it dies before giving birth, another heifer must be substituted. Between the time the heifer calf is born and the time it bears its own calf, the husband has certain rights and is a kind of "pater-elect." (*ibid.*, 181).

In addition to an overweening male concern with the woman's reproductive functions, we can also see here an explicit parallel between what the husband attempts to do and what the woman is truly capable of doing: the gift that *he* gives bears the name of *her* reproductive organ, namely, "womb." Nothing could be more couvadish.

The Paiges have demonstrated that strong fraternal interest groups are a reality, and that their activities are in large part aimed at asserting and defending paternity. But the hypothesis that such activities are quasi-maternal in nature is not at all excluded by the Paiges' data.

Not only corporate patrilineages and strong fraternal interest groups, but the very notion of patrilineal descent ought to be examined in this context. It is well known to anthropologists that patriliny is much more common, cross-culturally, than matriliny (Murdock 1949). This does not at first appear to make evolutionary sense, if we consider that maternity is always more certain and more obvious than paternity. Why do rules of descent not just follow the clearest course of genes, so that the various kinds of altruism prescribed by descent rules could also follow that course? Why does patriliny exist at all?

One reason is that women are not necessarily promiscuous, so that paternity is not necessarily in doubt. From a sociobiological viewpoint, it is generally more profitable for a male to be passing on his resources to his mate's children (patriliny) than to his sister's children (matriliny). Specifically, if female extramarital sex is minimal or even moderate, it is more advantageous genetically for a male to be living in a patrilineal society than in a matrilineal one (see Hartung 1986 for the relevant calculations). If he is living in a patrilineal society, female extramarital sex will be relatively restricted and probability of paternity will be high (*ibid.*).

Still, at a more proximate level, there has to be a mechanism (or mechanisms) making patriliny the more common variant. One of these mechanisms, I think, is the male's impulse to 'mother.' He is better able to act out this impulse with his mate and her children than with his sister and her children. If he is trapped with his mother, brother(s), sister(s), and other relatives in his natal family (the case in matrilineal societies), and if he is only minimally involved with his mate (making it easier for her to be promiscuous), then he is not going to get very involved with his mate's children. He is not going to feel he 'owns' them. He is not going to be very patrilineally oriented. On the other hand, though he is matrilineally oriented, his inclination to 'mother' his sister's children will be somewhat frustrated because there will be other adults around from the natal family doing the same thing (including perhaps his sister's mother, who he will never be able to outperform as a 'mother'). But in a patrilineal situation the man's wife will most likely be separated from *her* natal family (including her mother), so that she will be somewhat more inclined to accept 'mothering' for herself and for her children from him. It will be easier for him to feel a pride of 'ownership' in relating to his mate and offspring. So, all other things being equal, a patrilineal society will be a more auspicious environment for him to act out his 'maternal' impulses in.

In his recent book *Man, the Promising Primate*, Peter Wilson (1980) suggests that what is unique about the reproductive behavior of hominids, as opposed to other primates, is a special synthesis of the pair bond with the mother-child bond to yield the *father-child bond*:

The human extension of the primary bond [between mother and infant], together with the continuation and interdependence of that connecting the pair, creates a general situation whereby it now becomes possible for the two liaisons to overlap, to interact, and thereby to produce the possibility of a third relationship — that between adult male and infant.

This third relationship differs from the other two in that it is mediate, the product of the conjunction of the other two, which are immediately generated by the biological conditions of reproduction, nurture, and attraction. The relationship between an adult male and infant is possible only through their common connection with the adult female. The relation is premised not on the biological role of the male in the conception of the infant but only on the continuity if his relation to the female, which must be sufficient to overlap with her involvement in the primary bond. It is certainly more than likely that in the majority of instances the pair-bonded male is the genitor of the infant, but it is not necessary that he be so, and given that cultures exist even today that either do not recognize physiological paternity or give it no place in their ideas of reproduction, it is important that we recognize the real basis for the relationship. (Wilson 1980, 59-60).

But surely it cannot be an evolutionary accident that the social father or pater usually *is* the biological father or genitor. Like many anthropologists before him, Wilson interprets the cross-culturally common phenomenon of ignorance of physiological paternity as evidence that social paternity is somehow more "real," and that physiological paternity is somehow irrelevant. But ignorance of the biological facts of paternity in nonindustrial societies is merely part and parcel of the *general* ignorance that characterizes such societies. One would not argue, for example, that ignorance of the chemical composition of foods among nonindustrial peoples makes native food theories the "real basis" for nutrition. A native suffering from kwashiorkor is taking in too much carbohydrate and too little protein, no matter *what* the native *thinks* is happening. Furthermore, selection works just as inexorably against the genes of social fathers who are not also biological fathers as it works against the genes of kwashiorkor victims. There will admittedly always be a certain percentage of mismatching between pater and genitor in any given human population or society, but the selective pressures against the resulting cuckoldry (see section 6) will keep that percentage low. When Wilson says (65) that "... the 'invention' of the father is of necessity founded not on the biological facts of paternity...," he can only be speaking in the most proximate terms. Ultimately, the "invention" of fatherhood as a social convention *had* to be founded on the "biological facts of paternity."

Wilson goes on to say that the combination of the sexual pair bond with the primary mother-child bond is the very kernel of kinship structure in hominids:

The extension of the primary bond and the lengthening of the pair bond lead to a junction that is the elementary basis for a generalized social organization typical of the human species. For it is only then that kinship is possible, and with kinship we have the most flexible, generalized, and adaptable principle of group organization in the primate order. This principle provides the species with the means to organize groups of any (or almost any) size, from a minimal nuclear family to a maximal tribe, and according to any one of the number of possible specific forms. (*ibid.*, 60-1).

Non-hominid primates do not have kinship structures in the same sense that hominids do because the non-hominid male genitor does not occupy a "position complementary to that of the female" (64) and because there is no "... link between father and child [which] is created by passing to the child the male's relationship with the female ..." (*ibid.*). Unfortunately, Wilson does not give a very clear picture of the "complementary" relationship to the female upon which the male hominid's kinship with the child is based, or of how the "transfer" of the one relationship to the other is effected.[141] Wilson does discuss the hypersexuality that characterizes hominids (as opposed to many other primates), and points out that such hypersexuality has to be tempered by incest avoidance if kinship as a cultural artifact is going to be preserved. Also considered is the institution of marriage, which Wilson sees as a "social fact" entailing "... public recognition that the children of a particular woman will recognize one man rather than another as 'father'" (79). Wilson observes that even in those Carribean societies which are characterized by fluidity of sexual relations and relative lack of formal marriages there is always a "father" designated for every child. Wilson does not notice, incidentally, that the notorious reluctance of Carribean males to enter into a formal marriage relationship is more than compensated for by their equally notorious couvadishness (see, for example, Munroe and Munroe 1971).

Only toward the end of his book's appendix does Wilson hesitantly suggest that the mother-child bond is the proximate basis on which the social father's tie to the child — and kinship in general — is founded: "The natural, determinate female/offspring tie among all mammals remains a universal model, or at least a source, for the metaphor of kinship" (167). Had Wilson only considered the fact of male envy of female reproductive functions, and particularly the phenomena of couvade and the couvade syndrome, he might then have come right out and recognized the main thrust of his own argument: a male becomes paternal essentially by being maternal, i.e., by be-

---

141.   Earl Count is equally evocative, but ultimately also unclear when he says that the ancestral male acquired the status of husband by associating with a female and "..then acquiring a social interaction with the female's offspring by, so to speak, passing around the mother" (Count 1973, 102).

having in ways similar to the way his mate behaves (and to the way his mother whom she iconizes once behaved). More specifically, a male becomes paternal by rendering altruism to offspring (behaving in a nurturant fashion, offering emotional sustenance and physical protection, passing on inheritance, etc.), just as his mother rendered altruism to him and his mate renders altruism to her offspring.

There can be no doubt that, as Margaret Mead (1975[1949], 183ff.) and many other anthropologists have shown, human fatherhood is a "social invention:" "In every known human society, everywhere in the world, the young male learns that when he grows up, one of the things which he must do in order to be a full member of society is to provide food for some female and her young" (*ibid*, 189). But, on the one hand, sociobiology helps us to understand *why*, ultimately, the "social invention" of fatherhood should have been made: a male maximizes fitness by rendering altruism to some woman and her offspring, just so long as there is a reasonable likelihood that those offspring are also his. On the other hand, psychoanalysis offers a proximate explanation of *how* a male manages to accomplish this: he identifies with the mother-icon in his life (his mate) and acts possessively toward her (just as he once identified with his mother and was possessive about her). The result is that he behaves 'maternally' toward offspring likely to be his own.

Earlier I argued that one of the cultural manifestations of male 'mothering' is the prevalence of patriliny over matriliny. There are other cultural effects too, which have apparently not been deleterious to genes, and which may even have had some adaptive value for envious males. I have in mind, for example, the folklore and mythology about hermaphrodites and androgynes (male pregnancy is widespread in the religious and mythical texts of India — see O'Flaherty 1980, 28-9, 49-50, 55-7, 227-8, 299-300, 308-11; cf. Delcourt 1961, 67-72). Some of the envious male lore may depict birth from the female body but also require special male intervention, as in the Sambian initiatory myth in which the "first man" has breasts, is fellated by a woman, and enables her to give birth by cutting a vulva into her abdomen (Herdt 1981, ch. 8). Myths in which males are creators of the world, i.e., maternal icons (the American Indian earth-diver myth, the book of Genesis, the Chukchee myth of creation of the earth by defecation, and others) have been cogently psychoanalyzed by Dundes (1962). Dundes (1980, 173-5) also interprets the male figures of Santa Claus and the Easter Bunny — one has a big belly and both 'deliver' nice things — as 'mothers' in disguise.

Certain aspects of male initiation rites (not only circumcision) feature a transformation of males into 'mothers,' such as the ritualized separation of the initiates from their real mothers followed by their symbolic return to the 'womb' of the male collective and their 'rebirth' under the sponsorship of that collective (Eliade [1958] devotes much attention to this theme of male initiation, and Mead [1975] includes it in her chapter on "womb-envying patterns;" Bateson [1958] describes the various 'maternal' functions performed by the initiate's mother's brother in Iatmul scarification ceremonies; see also Dundes [1980], 182ff.; Bettelheim [1954], 214ff.; Gillison [1980]). There is also ritualized male transvestitism, such as the wearing of false breasts during *uli* ceremonies on New Ireland (Bettelheim 1954, 151), or a man's donning of women's rags in the Iatmul *naven* ritual to celebrate acts performed by his sister's child (Bateson, *ibid.*; see also Munroe 1980).

Most interesting, however, is the transformation of the procreative urge into a drive toward creativity generally. Though men cannot give birth to babies, they can produce such artifacts as poems, paintings, sculptures, mechanical gadgets, architectural designs, scholarly articles, novels, autobiographies, symphonies, etc. (not to mention books about sex!). This parallel has been noticed and been meaningfully discussed many times in the past by psychoanalysts and non-psychoanalysts alike, so I will not dwell on it (see: Chadwick 1925; Boehm 1930; Horney 1967 [1926], 54-70; Jaffe 1977; Stannard 1977; Jacobson 1950; Klein 1975, 201ff.; Dundes 1962; 1966; Lederer 1968; Legman 1968, 592-6; Montagu 1974, 43ff.; Stoller 1968, ch. 10). The only point I want to make is that women can do all these things too, even if they have been less motivated to, or have had less opportunity to as a result of their being *real* mothers and being restricted by male pseudomothers.

53. One Last Form of Envy

Before my female readers start to gloat too much over the sorry state of envious males, I should at least mention penis-envy. This phenomenon is in some sense the female counterpart of male envy of female reproductive functions. Unfortunately, some scholars tend to 'take sides' and argue explicitly or implicitly in favor of one form of envy over the other: either it is penis-envy or it is womb-envy, but not both (I have never heard anyone argue that neither one exists, incidentally). Others, however, recognize the existence of both envies (e.g.: Bettelheim 1954, 63, 250; Zilboorg 1944; Glover 1945, 107; Endleman 1981, 188; Horney 1967, 37-70). As Chodorow (1978, 152) points out, even some of the "dissident" analysts, such as Klein, Horney, Jones, Thompson, Chasseguet-Smirgel, and Stoller agree that women patients often express penis-envy, though they part company with Freud and some of the other more "orthodox" analysts (e.g., Deutsch, Abraham, Brunswick, Bonaparte) on how and whether penis-envy can be treated, clinically.

It is curious that no one seems to mind the idea that a *male* could envy another *male* his penis (e.g., Zelig 1927; Greenberg and Fisher 1983, 275), or that a *female* might envy another *female* who has just had a baby (e.g., Horney 1967, 45). It is when the envy crosses the boundary between the sexes that the theoretical fireworks begin.

Many behavioral phenomena in women have been partially or wholly attributed to an underlying penis-envy: kleptomania, vaginismus, attraction to amputees, the desire to have a baby, some forms of frigidity, tribadism, hysteria, feminism, nocturnal enuresis, female transvestitism, prostitution, nymphomania, dreams in which the dreamer admires a man's physical characteristics, etc. etc. Obviously, the relationship of each of these topics to penis-envy is a complicated and debatable matter, and I will not even begin to paraphrase the many arguments that have been advanced and disputed (some of the many conflicting views are expressed by: Freud, *SE*, XI, 204-5; XVII, 129-32; XIX, 178-9, 252-6; XXIII, 250-1; Abraham 1922; Brunswick 1940; Bonaparte 1953; Greenacre 1971; Deutsch 1944-5; Rado 1933; Moulton 1973; Millet 1970, 179ff.; de Beauvoir 1961, 254ff.; Sayers 1982, ch. 8; Zilboorg 1944; Thompson 1943; Horney 1967, 37-83; Marmor 1973; Fenichel 1945, 80-3, 90, 173, 229, 233, 244, 345, 494-5; Grossman and Stewart 1977; Hall and Van de Castle 1965; Eysenck and Wilson 1973, 166-7; Stoller 1979, 253; Chasseguet-Smirgel 1976; Rohrbaugh 1979, 96ff.; Greenberg and

Fisher 1980; 1983; Fisher and Greenberg 1977, 199-202, 248-50; Nathan 1981; and the references cited in these works). Because it is so difficult to find out how females really feel about the penis, many of the studies accept evidence of envy for masculine attributes as evidence for penis-envy. Or, conversely, penis-envy is often understood in the merely "symbolic" or metaphorical sense as signifying envy of other male attributes besides the penis, such as higher male social status, greater access to financial resources, greater physical strength of the male, etc. – all of which are obviously enviable in themselves. Neither approach, however, goes to the heart of the problem. If penis-envy exists, it is envy of the penis itself, for its own sake. All else is semiotic dodging.

Specific instances of penis-envy are fairly easy to find in both the clinical and anthropological literature:

That penis envy is manifested in the behavior of psychotics [among the South African Tembu and Fingo] ... is shown by female native patients standing up and pulling their labia apart and then urinating in a stream like a man, or carrying out the same procedure while lying on their backs. Again, they have been observed rolling up their dresses into pyramids and holding them projectingly in front of them, carrying out copulative dance movements towards other patients. (Laubscher 1937, 29-30).

... The African Chaga tradition, as taught *by* women *to* women, is that, formerly, the women had the penis and that she was deprived of it by mysterious horned beings. (Devereux 1960, 18; cf. Raum 1939, 557).

At the age of thirteen (a period when she was suffering from nervousness, depression, and loneliness) she began to menstruate. The facts of the sexual life now first became known to her. She also began to experience acute sexual desire before the onset of the periods; during one period of especially marked sexual restlessness she constructed a paper penis, without quite knowing its exact shape, and wore it; this gave her much satisfaction, and she felt that the organ belonged to herself rather than to another person. (Ellis 1927-8, VII, 438).

Lesbian couple C used the dildo in an attempt to simulate intercourse. The inserter strapped the dildo to her own pelvis just over the symphysis pubis, thus positioning the dildo in reasonable simulation of an erect penis. Dildo positioning was accomplished by a harnesslike belting arrangement that this couple provided for evaluation. After preliminary breast and genital stimulation of the insertee, the inserter penetrated her partner carefully and carried on in the pseudocoital connection in a male thrusting pattern. (Masters and Johnson 1979, 88).

... After musing sullenly a while, [she] added with an oddly sinister pursing of her mouth intended to be passed off as a smile: "Be reasonable. After all, what's the matter with the vagina dentata? It would be nice to get one and keep one [referring, with a look, to the penis]. When you eat a good meal, you don't expect to have to throw it up again right away." (Legman 1975, 435).

Eleanor E., 8;3, made a girl doll say: "Boys' ought not to be longer than girls'. Ours is short. Ours used to be longer. Hers (a girl doll's) used to be longer when she was a baby. When she got big, it got smaller." She was "sorry" that a boy's was longer and expressed the desire to have the same kind. (Conn and Kanner 1947, 48).

Enough examples. If only one of these is acceptable as a manifestation of penis-envy, then penis-envy exists. But the problem of how widespread penis-envy is remains. Despite the wealth of research on the subject we still do not know whether penis-envy (as opposed to generalized envy of males or of non-genital attributes of males) is as characteristic of females as, say, castration anxiety or envy of female reproductive functions is characteristic of males.

One of the important differences between female penis-envy and male envy of female reproductive functions is the way in which the envy is resolved. While the boy who envies his mother's ability to have babies will never literally be able to have babies (even if he becomes homosexual or has a trans-sex operation), a girl who envies her father his penis will later on actually be able to possess a man's (a father-icon's) penis within her vagina on a regular, if temporary basis (see the Legman example, above; also Horney 1967, 68-9). Indeed, if penis-envy is one of the reasons a woman desires to have a man regularly 'inside' her, then such envy might in fact be adaptive in the Darwinian sense, just as the hedonic aspect of female orgasm is adaptive. But there is not nearly as much psychological and cross-cultural evidence for the existence of female penis-envy as there is for the existence of female orgasm, and any argument about the possible adaptiveness of penis-envy would therefore be somewhat academic at present.

54. Semi-serious Coda

I have already summarized the main ideas of this book in the Preface (above, v-viii). There I indicated that the book would jump many fences because its subject, human sexuality, permeates so very many areas of human existence.

Indeed, it has been claimed by some that sex is everything. I do not subscribe to quite such an extreme position, however. I prefer the more moderate stance of those two great early twentieth-century sexologists, James Thurber and E.B. White:

> Sex is by no means everything. It varies, as a matter of fact, from only as high as 78 per cent of everything to as low as 3.10 per cent. The norm, in a sane, healthy person, should be between 18 and 24 per cent. In these hectic days, however, it is not unusual to hear even intelligent persons say, or imply, that sex is everything. (quoted from *Is Sex Necessary?*, 1929, 133-4).

What I hope to have explained is at least some of the whimsical variability that Thurber and White describe.

The flesh is semiotizable. It is not merely itself, but is capable of signifying something other than itself to interpreters. Sex is "everything" when the flesh is highly semiotized, and it is practically nothing when the flesh is not semiotized. The female orgasm, for example, can become "everything" for a young woman at a certain stage in her relationship with a man because it *indexes* that whole relationship for her. Or, a man's sexual potency can become "everything" to him at a certain stage in his relationship with a woman because it is a *sign* of the overall power dynamics of that relationship, and power can be very important to him.

Sex, then, is not "everything," except when certain signs operating in certain contexts make it so. These very contexts, however, are important in the evolutionary long run. It is evolutionarily important, for example, for a woman to 'know' whether she will receive parental assistance from the man she is copulating with, and insofar as her orgasm-signs indirectly signify this assistance, her momentary impression that "sex is everything" is adaptive in the Darwinian sense. Likewise, it is reproductively crucial for a man to 'know' whether he is rendering altruism in proportion to the control he is gaining, and the degree of his castration anxiety is a sign that helps him behave adaptively.

In other words, the signs of the flesh, and not only the flesh itself, are the product of natural selection. Sex will appear to be everything in precisely those situations where genes stand to benefit from the belief that sex is everything.

Bibliography

Abernethy, Virginia. (1974). "Dominance and Sexual Behavior: A Hypothesis," *American Journal of Psychiatry* 131, 813-17.

Abraham, Karl. (1922). "Manifestations of the Female Castration Complex," *International Journal of Psycho-Analysis* 3, 1-29.

Abraham, Karl. (1968). *Selected Papers of Karl Abraham, M.D.* New York: Basic Books.

Acton, William. 1871 (1857). *The Functions and Disorders of the Reproductive Organs in Childhood, Youth, Adult Age, and Advanced Life (5th ed.).* London: J. and A. Churchill.

Adams, D. B., A. R. Gold, A. D. Burt. (1978). "Rise in Female-Initiated Sexual Activity at Ovulation and its Suppression by Oral Contraceptives," *New England Journal of Medicine* 299 (21), 1145-50.

Adkins, E. K. (1980). "Genes, Hormones, Sex and Gender," *Sociobiology: Beyond Nature/Nurture?*, ed. G. Barlow, J. Silverberg. Boulder: Westview Press, 385-415.

Adler, Alfred. 1980 (1905-45). *Co-operation Between the Sexes: Writings on Women, Love and Marriage, Sexuality and its Disorders*, ed., tr. H. and R. Ansbacher. New York: Jason Aronson.

Aeschylus. 1970 (458 BC). *The Eumenides*. Englewood Cliffs, N.J.: Prentice-Hall.

Aitchison, Jean. (1976). *The Articulate Mammal: An Introduction to Psycholinguistics*. New York: McGraw Hill.

Alcock, John. (1980). "Beyond the Sociobiology of Sexuality: Predictive Hypotheses," *BBS* 3, 181-2.

Alexander, F. (1923). "The Castration Complex in the Formation of Character," *International Journal of Psycho-Analysis* 4, 11-42.

Alexander, Richard D. (1973). "Towards a Multidisciplinary View of Language: Some Biolinguistic Reflections," *Linguistische Berichte* 25, 1-21.

Alexander, Richard D. (1975). "The Search for a General Theory of Behavior," *Behavioral Science* 20, 77-100.

Alexander, Richard D. (1978). "Natural Selection and Social Exchange," *Social Exchange in Developing Relationships*, ed. R. L. Burgess and T. L. Huston. New York: Academic Press, 197-221.

Alexander, Richard D. (1979a). "Sexuality and Sociality in Humans and Other Primates," *Human Sexuality: A Comparative and Developmental Perspective*, ed. H. Katchadourian. Berkeley: Univ. of California Press, 81-97.

Alexander, Richard D. (1979b). *Darwinism and Human Affairs.* Seattle: Univ. of Washington Press.

Alexander, Richard D. and Gerald Borgia. (1978). "Group Selection, Altruism, and the Levels of Organization of Life," *Annual Review of Ecology and Systematics* 9, 449-74.

Alexander, Richard D. and K. M. Noonan. (1979). "Concealment of Ovulation, Parental Care, and Human Social Evolution," *Evolutionary Biology and Human Social Behavior: An Anthropological Perspective,* ed. N. A. Chagnon and W. G. Irons. North Scituate, Mass.: Duxbury Press, 436-53.

Alexander, Richard D., J. L. Hoogland, R. D. Howard, K. M. Noonan, and P. W. Sherman. (1979). "Sexual Dimorphisms and Breeding Systems in Pinnipeds, Ungulates, Primates, and Humans," *Evolutionary Biology and Human Social Behavior: An Anthropological Perspective,* ed. N. A. Chagnon and W. G. Irons. North Scituate, Mass.: Duxbury Press, 402-35.

Alland, Alexander. (1976). "The Roots of Art," *Ritual, Play, and Performance,* ed. R. Schechner, M. Schuman. New York: Seabury Press, 5-17.

Alland, Alexander. (1977). *The Artistic Animal: An Inquiry into the Biological Roots of Art.* New York: Doubleday.

Allen, M. R. (1967). *Male Cults and Secret Initiations in Melanesia.* London: Melbourne Univ. Press.

Aman, Reinhold and Friends. (1981). "What Is this Thing Called, Love? More Genital Pet Names," *Maledicta* 5, 41-4.

Andrew, R. J. (1964). "The Displays of the Primates," *Evolutionary and Genetic Biology of Primates,* ed. J. Buettner-Janusch. New York: Academic Press, II, 227-303.

Anon. (1891). *The Masculine Cross: or A History of Ancient and Modern Crosses and their Connection with Mysteries of Sex Worship.* Privately printed.

Anon. (1889). *Phallic Objects, Monuments and Remains.* Privately printed.

Aquinas, Thomas. (1945). *Introduction to Saint Thomas Aquinas,* ed. Anton Pegis. New York: Modern Library.

Austin, J. L. (1975). *How to Do Things with Words (2nd ed.).* Cambridge: Harvard Univ. Press.

Ayer, A. J. (1963). *The Concept of a Person.* New York: St. Martin's Press.

Ayim, Maryann. (1981). "The Implications of Sexually Stereotypic Language as Seen through Peirce's Theory of Signs," ms.

van Baal, J. (1966). *Dema: Description and Analysis of Marind-Anim Culture (South New Guinea).* The Hague: Martinus Nijhoff.

Bachelard, Gaston. (1942). *L'Eau et les rêves; essai sur l'imagination de la matière.* Paris: Libraire José Corti.

Bachofen, Johann Jakob. (1943-67). *Gesammelte Werke.* Basel: Schwabe, 10 vols.

Bachofen, Johann Jakob. (1967). *Myth, Religion and Mother Right,* tr. Ralph Manheim. Princeton, N.J.: Princeton Univ. Press.

Baer, Darius and Donald L. McEachron. (1982). "A Review of Selected Sociobiological Principles: Application to Hominid Evolution – I. The Development of Group Social Structure," *Journal of Social and Biological Structures* 5, 69-90.

Bak, Robert C. (1968). "The Phallic Woman: the Ubiquitous Fantasy in Perversions," *Psychoanalytic Study of the Child* 23, 15-36.

Baker, Robert. (1975). "'Pricks' and 'Chicks': a Plea for 'Persons'," *Philosophy and Sex*, ed. R. Baker and F. Elliston. Buffalo: Prometheus Press, 45-64.

Baker, Sidney J. (1950). "Language and Dreams," *International Journal of Psycho-Analysis* 31, 171-78.

Bakhtin, M. M. (1965). *Tvorchestvo Fransua Rable i narodnaia Kul'tura Srednevekov'ia i Renessansa*. Moscow.

Bakke, J. L. (1965). "A Double-Blind Study of Progestin-Estrogen Combination in the Management of the Menopause," *Pacific Medicine and Surgery* 73, 200-205.

Balint, Alice. (1926). "Der Familienvater," *Imago* 12, 292-304.

Balint, Alice. (1949). "Love for the Mother and Mother-Love," *International Journal of Psycho-Analysis* 30, 251-59.

Balint, Alice. 1954 (1931). *The Early Years of Life: A Psycho-Analytic Study*. New York: Basic Books.

Bamberger, Joan. (1974). "The Myth of Matriarchy: Why Men Rule in Primitive Society," *Woman, Culture, and Society*, ed. M. Z. Rosaldo and L. Lamphere. Stanford: Stanford Univ. Press, 263-280.

Bandura, Albert, and Richard H. Walters. (1963). *Social Learning and Personality Development*. New York: Holt, Rinehart and Winston.

Barash, David. (1977). *Sociobiology and Behavior*. New York: Elsevier.

Barash, David. (1979). *The Whisperings Within*. New York: Harper and Row.

Barash, David, and Mary Waterhouse. (1981). "Comment on Bixler 1981," *Current Anthropology* 22, 643-4.

Bardwick, Judith. (1971). *Psychology of Women: A Study of Bio-Cultural Conflicts*. New York: Harper and Row.

Bardwick, Judith and Elizabeth Douvan. 1972 (1971). "Ambivalence: the Socialization of Women," *Woman in Sexist Society: Studies in Power and Powerlessness*, ed. V. Gornick and B. Moran. New York: Mentor, 225-41.

Barkow, Jerome H. (1976). "Attention Structure and the Evolution of Human Psychological Characterstics," *The Social Structure of Attention*, ed. M. R. Chance and R. R. Larsen. New York: John Wiley, 203-219.

Barkow, Jerome H. (1978a). "Culture and Sociobiology," *American Anthropologist* 80, 5-20.

Barkow, Jerome H. (1978b). "Social Norms, the Self, and Sociobiology: Building on the Ideas of A. I. Hallowell," *Current Anthropology* 19, 99-118.

Barkow, Jerome H. (1980). "Sociobiology: Is This the New Theory of Human Nature?," *Sociobiology Examined*, ed. Ashley Montagu. Oxford: Oxford University Press, 171-197.

Bartell, Gilbert. (1971). *Group Sex: A Scientist's Eyewitness Report on the American Way of Swinging.* New York: Peter H. Wyden.

Bateman, A. J. (1948). "Intrasexual Selection in *Drosophila,*" *Heredity* 2, 349-68.

Bates, J. A. V. (1975). "The Communicative Hand," *The Body as a Means of Expression,* ed. J. Benthall and T. Polhemus. New York: Dutton, 175-194.

Bateson, Gregory. 1958 (1936). *Naven,* 2nd ed. Stanford, Calif.: Stanford Univ. Press.

Baumann, Hermann. (1955). *Das doppelte Geschlecht: Ethnologische Studien zur Bisexualität in Ritus und Mythos.* Berlin: Dietrich Reimer.

Baxtin, Mixail. 1971 (1929). "Discourse Typology in Prose," *Readings in Russian Poetics: Formalist and Structuralist Views,* ed. L. Matejka and K. Pomorska. Cambridge: MIT Press, 176-96.

Beach, Frank A. (1974). "Human Sexuality and Evolution," *Reproductive Behavior,* ed. W. Montagna and W. A. Sadler. New York: Plenum, 333-65.

Beach, Frank A. 1978 ($\approx$1974). "Human Sexuality and Evolution," *Human Evolution: Biosocial Perspectives,* ed. S. L. Washburn and E. R. McCown. Menlo Park: Benjamin/Cummings, 123-53.

Beals, Ralph L., Harry Hoijer, Alan R. Beals. (1977). *Anthropology,* 5th ed. New York: Macmillan.

de Beauvoir, Simone. 1961 (1949). *The Second Sex,* tr., ed. H. M. Parshley. New York: Bantam.

Beebe, Beatrice, Daniel Stern, and Joseph Jaffe. (1979). "The Kinesic Rhythm of Mother-Infant Interactions," *Of Speech and Time,* ed. A. Siegman, S. Feldstein. Hillsdale, N.J.: Lawrence Erlbaum, 23-34.

Bell, Alan P., Martin S. Weinberg, and Sue K. Hammersmith. (1981). *Sexual Preference: Its Development in Men and Women.* Bloomington: Indiana University Press, 2 vols.

Bell, Robert R. (1974). "Female Sexual Satisfaction and Levels of Education," *Sexual Behavior,* ed. L. Gross. Flushing, N.Y.: Spectrum Publications, 3-11.

Belote, Betsy. (1976). "Masochistic Syndrome, Hysterical Personality, and the Illusion of a Healthy Woman," *Female Psychology: the Emerging Self,* ed. S. Cox. Chicago: Science Research Associates, 335-48.

Bem, Sandra. (1975). "Sex Role Adaptability: One Consequence of Psychological Androgyny," *Journal of Personality and Social Psychology* 31, 634-43.

Bendix, Edward H. (1979). "Linguistic Models as Political Symbols: Gender and the Generic 'He' in English," *Language, Sex and Gender (=Annals of N.Y. Acad. of Sci. # 327),* ed. J. Orasanu, M. Slater, L. Adler. New York: New York Academy of Sciences, 23-39.

Benedek, Thérèse. (1959). "Sexual Functions in Women and their Disturbance," *American Handbook of Psychiatry,* ed. S. Arieti. New York: Basic Books, Vol. I, 727-48.

Benedek, Thérèse. (1968). "Discussion of Sherfey's Paper on Female Sexuality," *Journal of the American Psychoanalytic Association* 16, 424-48.

Bennett, Adrian. (1980). "Rhythmic Analysis of Multiple Levels of Communicative Behavior in Face-to-Face Interaction," *Aspects of Nonverbal Communication,* ed. W. Von Raffler-Engel. Lisse: Swets and Zeitlinger, 237-51.

Benshoof, Lee and Randy Thornhill. (1979). "The Evolution of Monogamy and Concealed Ovulation in Humans," *Journal of Social and Biological Structures* 2, 95-106.

Bentler, P. M. and W. H. Peeler. (1979). "Models of Female Orgasm," *Archives of Sexual Behavior* 8, 405-23.

Bergler, Edmund. (1935). "Some Special Varieties of Ejaculatory Disturbance Not Hitherto Described," *International Journal of Psycho-Analysis* 16, 84-95.

Bergler, Edmund. (1947). "Psychoanalysis of Writers and Literary Productivity," *Psychoanalysis and the Social Sciences* 1, ed. G. Róheim. New York: IUP, 247-296.

Bergler, Edmund, and Ludwig Eidelberg. (1933). "Der Mammakomplex des Mannes," *Internationale Zeitschrift für Psychoanalyse* 19, 547-83.

Bernard, Jessie. (1968). "The Status of Women in Modern Patterns of Culture," *Annals of the American Academy of Political and Social Science* 375, 3-14.

Bernard, Jessie. 1972 (1971). "The Paradox of the Happy Marriage," *Woman in Sexist Society: Studies in Power and Powerlessness,* ed. V. Gornick, B. Moran. New York: Mentor, 145-62.

Bernard, Jessie. (1981). *The Female World.* New York: The Free Press.

Berne, Eric. 1977 (1954). *Games People Play: The Psychology of Human Relationships.* New York: Grove Press.

Bettelheim, Bruno. (1954). *Symbolic Wounds: Puberty Rites and the Envious Male.* Glencoe, Illinois: The Free Press.

Bettelheim, Bruno. (1977). *The Uses of Enchantment: The Meaning and Importance of Fairy Tales.* New York: Vintage.

Bhattacharya, B. (1975). *Saivism and the Phallic World.* New Delhi: Oxford and IBH, 2 vols.

Biely, Andrey. 1959 (1913). *St. Petersburg,* tr. J. Cournos. New York: Grove Press.

Biller, Henry B. (1982). "Fatherhood: Implications for Child and Adult Development," *Handbook of Developmental Psychology,* ed. B. Wolman. Englewood Cliffs, N.J.: Prentice-Hall, 702-25.

Biller, Henry B. and Stephan D. Weiss. (1970). "The Father-Daughter Relationship and the Personality Development of the Female," *Journal of Genetic Psychology* 116, 79-93.

Bilz, Rudolf. (1940). *Pars pro toto: Ein Beitrag zur Pathologie menschlicher Affekte und Organfunktionen.* Leipzig: George Thieme.

Bischof, N. (1972). "The Biological Foundations of the Incest Taboo,"

Social Science Information 11, 7-36.

Bischof, N. (1975). "A Systems Approach toward the Functional Connections of Attachment and Fear," *Child Development* 46, 801-17.

Bixler, Ray H. (1981). "Incest Avoidance as a Function of Environment *and* Heredity," *Current Anthropology* 22, 639-54.

Black, Stephen L. and Colette Biron. (1982). "Androstenol as a Human Pheromone: No Effect on Perceived Physical Attractiveness," *Behavioral and Neural Biology* 34, 326-30.

Blum, Harold P. (1977). "Masochism, the Ego Ideal, and the Psychology of Women," *Female Psychology: Contemporary Psychoanalytic Views*, ed. H. P. Blum. New York: International Universities Press, 157-91.

Blumer, D., and E. A. Walker. (1975). "The Neural Basis of Sexual Behavior," *Psychiatric Aspects of Neurologic Disease*, ed. D. F. Benson, D. Blumer. New York: Grune and Stratton, 199-217.

Blumstein, Philip and Pepper Schwartz. (1983). *American Couples*. New York: William Morrow and Co.

Boehm, Felix. (1930). "The Femininity-Complex in Men," *International Journal of Psycho-Analysis* 11, 444-69.

Bonaparte, Marie. 1953 (1949). *Female Sexuality*, tr. E. Rodker. New York: International Universities Press.

Boorman, Scott A. and Paul R. Levitt. (1980). *The Genetics of Altruism*. New York: Academic Press.

Bordes, F. (1972). *A Tale of Two Caves*. New York: Harper and Row.

Bourke, J. G. (1891). *Scatologic Rites of All Nations*. Washington: W. H. Lowdermilk.

Bowlby, John. (1969). *Attachment and Loss, Vol. I: Attachment*. New York: Basic Books.

Bowlby, John. (1973). *Attachment and Loss, Vol. II: Separation*. New York: Basic Books.

Bowra, C. M. (1962). *Primitive Song*. Cleveland: World.

Boyd, R. and P. J. Richerson. (1976). "A Simple Dual Inheritance Model of the Conflict Between Social and Biological Evolution," *Zygon* 11, 254-62.

Brandes, Stanley. (1981). "Like Wounded Stags: Male Sexual Ideology in an Andalusian Town," *Sexual Meanings: the Cultural Construction of Gender and Sexuality*, ed. S. Ortner, H. Whitehead. Cambridge: Cambridge University Press, 216-39.

Brecher, Edward M. (1969). *The Sex Researchers*. Boston: Little, Brown and Co.

Briffault, Robert. (1931). *The Mothers: The Matriarchal Theory of Social Origins*. New York: MacMillan.

Briffault, Robert. 1952 (1927). *The Mothers: A Study of the Origins of Sentiments and Institutions*. New York: MacMillan, 3 Vols.

Brill, A. A. (1932). "The Sense of Smell in the Neuroses and Psychoses," *Psychoanalytic Quarterly* 1, 7-42.

Bronfenbrenner, U. (1960). "Freudian Theories of Identification and their Derivatives," *Child Development* 31, 15-40.

Broude, Gwen J. (1975). "Norms of Premarital Sexual Behavior," *Ethos* 3, 381-402.

Broude, Gwen J. (1981). "The Cultural Management of Sexuality," *Handbook of Cross-Cultural Human Development,* ed. Ruth Munroe, Robert Munroe, B. Whiting. New York: Garland STPM Press, 633-73.

Broude, Gwen J. and J. Greene. (1976). "Cross-Cultural Codes on Twenty Sexual Attitudes and Practices," *Ethnology* 15, 409-29.

Broughton, John M. (1981). "The Genetic Psychology of James Mark Baldwin," *American Psychologist* 36, 396-407.

Browe, Peter, S. J. (1936). *Zur Geschichte der Entmannung: Eine religions- und rechtsgeschichtliche Studie.* Breslau: Müller und Sieffert.

Brown, Judith K. (1981). "Cross-Cultural Perspectives on the Female Life Cycle," *Handbook of Cross-Cultural Human Development,* ed. Ruth Munroe, Robert Munroe, B. Whiting. New York: Garland STPM Press, 581-610.

Brown, Norman. O. (1947). *Hermes the Thief: The Evolution of a Myth.* Madison: University of Wisconsin Press.

Brown, Norman O. (1959). *Life Against Death: The Psychoanalytical Meaning of History.* New York: Vintage.

Brown, Norman O. (1966). *Love's Body.* New York: Vintage.

Brown, Penelope. (1980). "How and Why are Women More Polite: Some Evidence from a Mayan Community," *Women and Language in Literature and Society,* ed. S. McConnell-Ginet, R. Borker, N. Furman. New York: Praeger, 111-36.

Brown, Roger. (1973). *A First Language: The Early Stages.* Cambridge: Harvard University Press.

Brownmiller, Susan. (1975). *Against Our Will: Men, Women and Rape.* New York: Simon and Schuster.

Bruner, Jerome. (1972). "Nature and Uses of Immaturity," *American Psychologist* 27, 687-708.

Bruner, Jerome. (1975). "The Ontogenesis of Speech Acts," *Journal of Child Language* 2, 1-19.

Bruner, Jerome. (1982). "The Formats of Language Acquisition," *American Journal of Semiotics* 1 (3), 1-16.

Brunswick, Ruth Mack. (1940). "The Preoedipal Phase of the Libido Development," *Psychoanalytic Quarterly* 9, 293-319.

Bücher, Karl. 1924 (1896). *Arbeit und Rhythmus.* Leipzig: Emmanuel Reinicke.

Buckley, E. (1895). *Phallicism in Japan.* Chicago: University of Chicago Press.

Buffery, A. W. H. and J. A. Gray. (1972). "Sex Differences in the Development of Spatial and Linguistic Skills," *Gender Differences: Their Ontogeny and Significance,* ed. C. Ounsted, D. Taylor. London: Churchill Livingstone, 123-57.

Bullough, Vern L. (1973). *The Subordinate Sex: A History of Attitudes Toward Women.* Urbana: University of Illinois Press.

Bullough, Vern L. (1976). *Sexual Variance in Society and History.* New York: John Wiley & Sons.

Bunzl, M. and S. Mullen. (1974). "A Self Report Investigation of Two Types of Myotonic Response During Sexual Orgasm," *Journal of Sex Research* 10, 10-20.

Burgess, Ernest W. and Paul Wallin. (1953). *Engagement and Marriage.* Philadelphia: Lippincott.

Burian, Richard M. (1981-2). "Human Sociobiology and Genetic Determinism," *The Philosophical Forum* 13, 43-66.

Burley, Nancy. 1979. "The Evolution of Concealed Ovulation," *American Naturalist* 114, 835-58.

Burton, F. D. (1971). "Sexual Climax in Female *Macaca mulatta*," *Proceedings of the Third International Congress of Primatology.* Basel: S. Karger, Vol. 3, 180-91.

Burton, Roger V. and John Whiting. (1961). "The Absent Father and Cross-Sex Identity," *Merrill-Palmer Quarterly of Behavior and Development* 7, 85-95.

Campbell, Bernard. (1966). *Human Evolution: An Introduction to Man's Adaptations.* Chicago: Aldine.

Campbell, Bernard, ed. (1972). *Sexual Selection and the Descent of Man: 1871-1971.* Chicago: Aldine.

Campbell, Bernard. (1974). *Human Evolution: an Introduction to Man's Adaptations,* 2nd ed. Chicago: Aldine.

Campbell, Bernard. (1979). "Ecological Factors and Social Organization in Human Evolution," *Primate Ecology and Human Origins,* ed. I. Bernstein, E. Smith. New York: Garland STPM, 291-312.

Campbell, Donald. (1972). "On the Genetics of Altruism and the Counter-Hedonic Components in Human Culture," *Journal of Social Issues* 28, 21-37.

Campbell, Donald. (1975). "On the Conflicts Between Biological and Social Evolution and Between Psychology and Moral Tradition," *American Psychologist* 30, 1103-1126.

Cann, Rebecca and Allan Wilson. (1982). Letter to the Editor. *Science* 217, 303-4.

Cant, John G. H. (1981). "Hypothesis for the Evolution of Human Breasts and Buttocks," *American Naturalist* 117, 199-204.

Carey, Claude. (1972). *Les proverbes érotiques russes.* The Hague: Mouton.

Carini, Louis. (1970). "On the Origins of Language," *Current Anthropology* 11, 165-6.

Cavalli-Sforza, L. and M. Feldman. (1981). *Cultural Transmission and Evolution: a Quantitative Approach.* Princeton: Princeton University Press.

Caws, Peter. (1969). "The Structure of Discovery," *Science* 166, 1375-80.

Chadwick, M. (1925). "Über die Wurzel der Wissbegierde," *Internationale*

Zeitschrift für Psychoanalyse 11, 54-68.

Chagnon, Napoleon A. (1977). *Yanomamö, the Fierce People*, 2nd ed. New York: Holt, Rinehart and Winston.

Chance, M. R. A. (1961). "The Nature and Special Features of the Instinctive Social Bond of Primates," *Social Life of Early Man*, ed. Sherwood Washburn. Chicago: Aldine, 17-23.

Chasseguet-Smirgel, Janine. (1976). "Freud and Female Sexuality: the Consideration of some Blind Spots in the Exploration of the 'Dark Continent'," *International Journal of Psycho-Analysis* 57, 275-86.

Chesser, Eustace. (1957). *The Sexual, Marital and Family Relationships of the English Woman.* New York: Roy.

Chevalier-Skolnikoff, S. (1974). "Male-Female, Female-Female, and Male-Male Sexual Behavior in the Stumptail Monkey, with Special Attention to the Female Orgasm," *Archives of Sexual Behavior* 3, 95-116.

Chodorow, Nancy. 1972 (1971). "Being and Doing: a Cross-Cultural Examination of the Socialization of Males and Females," *Woman in Sexist Society: Studies in Power and Powerlessness*, ed. V. Gornick, B. Moran. New York: Mentor, 259-91.

Chodorow, Nancy. (1978). *The Reproduction of Mothering: Psychoanalysis and the Sociology of Gender.* Berkeley: University of California Press.

Chomsky, Noam. (1976). "On the Nature of Language," *Origins and Evolution of Language and Speech*, ed. S. Harnad, H. Steklis, J. Lancaster. New York: New York Academy of Sciences, 46-57.

Chomsky, Noam. (1978). "Language and Unconscious Knowledge," *Psychoanalysis and Language*, ed. Joseph H. Smith. New Haven: Yale University Press, 3-44.

Chomsky, Noam. (1979). "Human Language and Other Semiotic Systems," *Semiotica* 25, 31-44.

Churchill, Wainwright. (1967). *Homosexual Behavior among Males: a Cross-Cultural and Cross-Species Investigation.* New York: Hawthorn Books.

Clark, Grahame. (1977). *World Prehistory in New Perspective.* Cambridge: Cambridge University Press.

Clark, J. D. (1975). "Africa in Prehistory: Peripheral or Paramount?," *Man* 10, 175-198.

Clark, LeMon. (1970). "Is There a Difference Between a Clitoral and a Vaginal Orgasm?," *Journal of Sex Research* 6, 25-8.

Clark, Ruth. (1975). "What's the Use of Imitation?," *Journal of Child Language* 4, 341-358.

Clausen, J. A. (1966). "Family Structure, Socialization, and Personality," *Review of Child Development Research*, Vol. II, ed. M. L. Hoffman and L. W. Hoffman. New York: Russell Sage Foundation, 1-53.

Clutton-Brock, T. H. and P. H. Harvey. (1976). "Evolutionary Rules and Primate Societies," *Growing Points in Ethology*, ed. P. P. G. Bateson and R. A. Hinde. Cambridge: Cambridge University Press, 195-237.

Clutton-Brock, T. H. and P. H. Harvey. 1978 (1977). "Primate Ecology and Social organization," *Readings in Sociobiology*, ed. T. H. Clutton-Brock and P. H. Harvey. San Francisco: W. H. Freeman, 342-83.

Cohen, Percy. (1980). "Psychoanalysis and Cultural Symbolization," *Symbol as Sense*, ed. M. L. Foster, S. H. Brandes. New York: Academic Press, 45-68.

Coles, Claire D. and M. Johnna Shamp. (1984). "Some Sexual, Personality, and Demographic Characteristics of Women Readers of Erotic Romances," *Archives of Sexual Behavior* 13, 187-209.

Coles, J. M., and E. S. Higgs. (1975). *The Archaeology of Early Man*. Harmondsworth: Penguin.

Condon, W. S. (1980). "The Relation of Interactional Synchrony to Cognitive and Emotional Processes," *The Relationship of Verbal and Nonverbal Communication*, ed. M. R. Key. The Hague: Mouton, 49-65.

Condon, W. S. and W. D. Ogston. (1967). "A Segmentation of Behavior," *Journal of Psychiatric Research* 5, 221-35.

Condon, W. S. and L. W. Sander. (1974). "Neonate Movement is Synchronized with Adult Speech: Interactional Participation and Language Acquisition," *Science* 183, 99-100.

Conn, Jacob H. and Leo Kanner. (1947). "Children's Awareness of Sex Differences," *Journal of Child Psychiatry* 1, 3-57.

Constantine, Larry L. and Joan M. Constantine. (1973). *Group Marriage: A Study of Contemporary Multilateral Marriage*. New York: MacMillan.

Conway, Bertrand. (1929). *The Question Box: New Edition – Replies to Questions Received on Missions to Non-Catholics*. New York: Paulist Press.

Coombs, Robert H. and William F. Kenkel. (1966). "Sex Differences in Dating Aspirations and Satisfaction with Computer-Selected Partners," *Journal of Marriage and the Family* 28, 62-66.

Cooper, G. W. and L. B. Meyer. (1960). *The Rhythmic Strcuture of Music*. Chicago: University of Chicago Press.

Corballis, Michael C. and Michael J. Morgan. (1978). "On the Biological Basis of Human Laterality," *The Behavioral and Brain Sciences* I, 261-336.

Cornog, Martha. (1981). "Tom, Dick and Hairy: Notes on Genital Pet Names," *Maledicta* 5, 31-40.

Cott, Nancy F. (1978). "Passionlessness: an Interpretation of Victorian Sexual Ideology, 1790-1850," *Signs* 4, 219-236.

Coult, A. D. (1965). *Cross-Tabulation of Murdock's World Ethnographic Sample*. Columbia, Mo.: University of Missouri Press.

Count, Earl W. (1973). *Being and Becoming Human: Essays on the Biogram*. New York: Van Nostrand Reinhold.

Cowley, J. J., A. L. Johnson, B. W. L. Brooksbank. (1977). "The Effect of Two Odorous Compounds on Performance in an Assessment-of-People Test," *Psychoneuroendocrinology* 2, 159-72.

Cox, Marian R. (1892). *Cinderella: 345 Variants* (=Publications of the Folk-Lore Society, No. 31). Nendeln: Kraus Reprints (1967).

Crawley, Ernest. 1965 (1927). *The Mystic Rose,* rev. by T. Besterman. London: Spring Books.

Critchley, MacDonald. (1960). "The Evolution of Man's Capacity for Language," *Evolution After Darwin,* ed. Sol Tax. Chicago: University of Chicago Press.

Crook, John. (1972). "Sexual Selection, Dimorphism, and Social Organization in the Primates," *Sexual Selection and the Descent of Man 1871-1971,* ed. B. Campbell. Chicago: Aldine, 231-281.

Crook, John. (1977). "On the Integration of Gender Strategies in Mammalian Social Systems," *Reproductive Behavior and Evolution,* ed. J. Rosenblatt, B. Komisaruk. New York: Plenum, 17-38.

Crook, John. (1980). *The Evolution of Human Consciousness.* Oxford: Oxford University Press.

Crook, John. and J. S. Gartlan. (1966). "Evolution of Primate Societies," *Nature* 210 (5042), 1200-1203.

Crooke, William. (1896). *The Popular Religion and Folk-Lore of Northern India.* Westminster: Archibald Constable, 2 vols.

Crooke, William. 1951 (1917). "Serpent-Worship (Indian)," *Encyclopedia of Religion and Ethics,* ed. J. Hastings. New York: Charles Scribner's Sons, Vol XI, 411-19.

Crystal, David. (1979). "Prosodic Development," *Language Acquisition,* ed. P. Fletcher and M. Garman. Cambridge: Cambridge University Press, 33-48.

Cucchiari, Salvatore. (1981). "The Gender Revolution and the Transition from Bisexual Horde to Patrilocal Band: the Origins of Gender Hierarchy," *Sexual Meanings: the Cultural Construction of Gender and Sexuality,* ed. S. Ortner, H. Whitehead. Cambridge: Cambridge University Press, 31-79.

Culpepper, Emily E. (1979). "Exploring Menstrual Attitudes," *Women Look at Biology Looking at Women,* ed. R. Hubbard, M. Henifin, B. Fried. Cambridge: Shenkman Publishing, 135-61.

Cutler, Winnifred and Celso García. (1980). "The Psychoneuroendocrinology of the Ovulatory Cycle of Woman: a Review," *Psychoneuroendocrinology* 5, 89-111.

Daly, C. D. (1957). "The Psycho-Biological Origins of Circumcision," *International Journal of Psycho-Analysis* 31, 217-36.

Daly, Martin and Margo Wilson. (1978). *Sex, Evolution and Behavior.* North Scituate, Mass.: Duxbury Press.

Daly, Martin, Margo Wilson, and Suzanne J. Weghorst. (1982). "Male Sexual Jealousy," *Ethology and Sociobiology* 3, 11-27.

Danielli, James F. (1980). "Altruism and the Internal Reward System, or the Opium of the People," *Journal of Social and Biological Structures* 3, 87-94.

Daniels, Denise. (1983). "The Evolution of Concealed Ovulation and Self-Deception," *Ethology and Sociobiology* 4, 69-87.

Dart, R. A. (1959). "On the Evolution of Language and Articulate Speech," *Homo* 10, 154-165.

Darwin, Charles. (1859). *On the Origin of Species by Means of Natural Selection, or the Preservation of Favoured Races in the Struggle for Life.* London: Watts and Co.

Darwin, Charles. 1885 (1871). *The Descent of Man and Selection in Relation to Sex.* London: Murray.

Darwin, Charles. 1965 (1872). *The Expression of the Emotions in Man and Animals.* Chicago: University of Chicago Press.

Davenport, William H. (1977). "Sex in Cross-Cultural Perspective," *Human Sexuality in Four Perspectives,* ed. Frank Beach. Baltimore: Johns Hopkins University Press, 115-163.

Davis, Elizabeth Gould. (1971). *The First Sex.* New York: G. P. Putnam's Sons.

Davis, Martha, ed. (1982). *Interaction Rhythms: Periodicity in Communicative Behavior.* New York: Human Sciences Press.

Dawkins, Richard. (1976). *The Selfish Gene.* Oxford: Oxford University Press.

Dawkins, Richard. (1979). "Twelve Misunderstandings of Kin Selection," *Zeitschrift für Tierpsychologie* 51, 184-200.

Dawkins, Richard. (1983). "Opportunity Costs of Inbreeding," *Behavioral and Brain Sciences* 6, 105-6.

Dawson, Warren R. (1929). *The Custom of Couvade.* Manchester: University of Manchester Press.

Deacon, A. B. (1934). *Malekula: a Vanishing People in the New Hebrides.* London: George Routledge.

De Armond, Richard. (1971). "On the Russian Verb *ebat'* and some of its Derivatives," *Studies Out In Left Field: Defamatory Essays Presented to James D. McCawley,* ed. A. Zwicky, P. Salus, R. Binnick, A. Vanek. Edmonton: Linguistic Research, Inc., 99-107.

Deaux, Kay. (1976). *The Behavior of Women and Men.* Monterey: Brooks/ Cole.

De Beer, Gavin. (1962). *Embryos and Ancestors.* Oxford: Clarendon Press.

Degler, Carl N. (1974). "What Ought to Be and What Was: Women's Sexuality in the Nineteenth Century," *American Historical Review* 79, 1467-90.

Delcomyn, Fred. (1980). "Neural Basis of Rhythmic Behavior in Animals," *Science* 210, 492-8.

Delcourt, Marie. 1961 (1956). *Hermaphrodite: Myths and Rites of the Bisexual Figure in Classical Antiquity,* tr. J. Nicholson. London: Studio Books.

Deleuze, Gilles, and Felix Guattari. 1977 (1972). *Anti-Oedipus: Capitalism and Schizophrenia,* tr. R. Hurley, M. Seem, H. Lane. New York: Viking.

deMause, Lloyd. (1982). *Foundations of Psychohistory.* New York: Creative Roots.

Derogatis, Leonard R., Jon Meyer, Carol Dupkin. (1976). "Discrimination of

Organic versus Psychogenic Impotence with the DSFI," *Journal of Sex and Marital Therapy* 2, 229-40.

Desmond, Adrian J. (1979). *The Ape's Reflexion.* New York: Dial Press.

Deutsch, Helene. (1930). "The Significance of Masochism in the Mental Life of Women," *International Journal of Psycho-Analysis* 11, 48-60.

Deutsch, Helene. (1944-45). *The Psychology of Women.* New York: Grune & Stratton, 2 vols.

Devereux, George. (1939). "The Social and Cultural Implications of Incest Among the Mohave Indians," *Psychoanalytic Quarterly* 8, 510-33.

Devereux, George. (1950). "The Psychology of Feminine Genital Bleeding," *International Journal of Psycho-Analysis* 31, 237-57.

Devereux, George. (1958). "The Significance of the External Female Genitalia and of Female Orgasm for the Male," *Journal of the American Psychoanalytic Association* 6, 278-86.

Devereux, George. (1960). "The Female Castration Complex and its Repercussions in Modesty, Appearance and Courtship Etiquette," *American Imago* 17, 3-19.

Devereux, George. (1967). *From Anxiety to Method in the Behavioral Sciences.* The Hague: Mouton.

Devereux, George. 1969 (1947). "Mohave Orality: an Analysis of Nursing and Weaning Customs," *Man and His Culture: Psychoanalytic Anthropology after 'Totem and Taboo'*, ed. W. Muensterberger. London: Rapp and Whiting, 211-35.

Devereux, George. (1973). "The Self-Blinding of Oidipous in Sophokles: *Oidipous Tyrannos*," *Journal of Hellenic Studies* 93, 36-49.

Devereux, George. (1978). *Ethnopsychoanalysis: Psychoanalysis and Anthropology as Complementary Frames of Reference.* Berkeley: University of California Press.

Diamond, Milton. (1980). "The Biosocial Evolution of Human Sexuality," *BBS* 3, 184-6.

Dickemann, Mildred. (1979). "The Ecology of Mating Systems in Hypergynous Dowry Societies," *Social Science Information* 18, 163-95.

Dickemann, Mildred. (1981). "Paternal Confidence and Dowry Competition: a Biocultural Analysis of Purdah," *Natural Selection and Social Behavior*, ed. R. Alexander, D. Tinkle. New York: Chiron Press, 417-38.

Dickinson, R. L. and L. Beam. (1932). *A Thousand Marriages.* New York: Century.

Dinnerstein, Dorothy. (1976). *The Mermaid and the Minotaur: Sexual Arrangements and Human Malaise.* New York: Harper and Row.

Dixon, A. F. (1980). "Androgens and Aggressive Behavior in Primates: a Review," *Aggressive Behavior* 6, 37-67.

Dobzhansky, Theodosius. (1962). *Mankind Evolving.* New Haven: Yale University Press.

Dobzhansky, Theodosius, Francisco Ayala, G. Ledyard Stebbins, James W. Valentine. (1977). *Evolution.* San Francisco: Freeman & Co.

Dore, John. (1979). "Conversation and Preschool Language Development," *Language Acquisition*, ed. Paul Fletcher and Michael Garman. Cambridge: Cambridge University Press, 337-361.

Doty, Richard L. (1976). "Reproductive Endocrine Influences upon Human Nasal Chemoreception: a Review," *Mammalian Olfaction, Reproductive Processes, and Behavior*, ed. R. Doty. New York: Academic Press, 295-321.

Dover, K. J. (1978). *Greek Homosexuality*. London: Duckworth.

Dowling, Colette. (1981). *The Cinderella Complex: Women's Hidden Fear of Independence*. New York: Pocket Books.

Drabble, Margaret. (1969). *Thank You All Very Much*. New York: New American Library.

Dreizin, F. and T. Priestly. (1982). "A Systematic Approach to Russian Obscene Language," *Russian Linguistics* 6, 232-49.

Drummond, D. A. and G. Perkins. (1980). *Dictionary of Russian Obscenities*. Berkeley: Berkeley Slavic Specialties.

DuBois, Cora. 1969 (1944-1960). *The People of Alor: A Social-Psychological Study of an East Indian Island*. Cambridge: Harvard University Press.

Dundes, Alan. (1962). "Earth-Diver: Creation of the Mythopoeic Male," *American Anthropologist* 64, 1032-1051.

Dundes, Alan. (1966). "Here I Sit – a Study of American Latrinalia," *Kroeber Anthropological Society Papers* 34, 91-105.

Dundes, Alan. (1976). "Projection in Folklore: A Plea for Psychoanalytic Semiotics," *MLN* 91, 1500-1533.

Dundes, Alan. (1979). "Heads or Tails: a Psychoanalytic Study of Potlatch," *Journal of Psychoanalytic Anthropology* 2, 395-424.

Dundes, Alan. (1980). *Interpreting Folklore*. Bloomington: Indiana University Press.

Dundes, Alan, Jerry W. Leach and Bora Özkök. (1970). "The Strategy of Turkish Boys' Verbal Dueling Rhymes," *Journal of American Folklore* 83, 325-49.

Dworkin, Andrea. 1981 (1979). *Pornography: Men Possessing Women*. New York: G. P. Putnam's Sons.

Eakins, Barbara Westbrook and R. Gene Eakins. (1978). *Sex Differences in Human Communication*. Boston: Houghton Mifflin.

Eckland, Bruce K. 1982 (1968). "Theories of Mate Selection," *Social Biology* 29, 7-21.

Eco, Umberto. (1976). *A Theory of Semiotics*. Bloomington: Indiana University Press.

Edelheit, Henry. (1978). "On the Biology of Language: Darwinian/Lamarckian Homology in Human Inheritance (with Some Thoughts about the Larmarckism of Freud)," *Psychoanalysis and Language*, ed. J. H. Smith. New Haven: Yale University Press, 45-74.

Edwards, James W. (1984). "Indigenous Koro, a Genital Retraction Syndrome of Insular Southeast Asia: A Critical Review," *Culture, Medicine and Psychiatry* 8, 1-24.

Edwards, Stephen W. (1978). "Nonutilitarian Activities in the Lower Paleolithic: A Look at the Two Kinds of Evidence," *Current Anthropology* 19, 135-7.

Ehrenreich, Barbara and Deirdre English. 1979 (1978). *For Her Own Good: 150 Years of the Experts' Advice to Women.* Garden City: Anchor Books.

Eibl-Eibesfeldt, Irenäus. 1971 (1970). *Love and Hate – On the Natural History of Basic Behaviour Patterns,* tr. G. Strachan. London: Methuen.

Eibl-Eibesfeldt, Irenäus. (1975). *Ethology: The Biology of Behavior,* tr. Erich Klinghammer. New York: Holt, Rinehart and Winston.

Eibl-Eibesfeldt, Irenäus. (1979). "Human Ethology: Concepts and Implications for the Sciences of Man," *Behavioral and Brain Sciences* 2, 1-57.

Eissler, K. R. (1977). "Comments on Penis Envy and Orgasm in Women," *Psychoanalytic Study of the Child* 32, 29-83.

Eliade, Mircea. (1958). *Birth and Rebirth: the Religious Meanings of Initiation in Human Culture,* tr. W. Trask. New York: Harper and Brothers Publishers.

Eliade, Mircea. 1962 (1956). *The Forge and the Crucible,* tr. Stephen Corrin. New York: Harper & Brothers.

Eliade, Mircea. (1965). *Mephistopheles and the Androgyne: Studies in Religious Myth and Symbol,* tr. J. Cohen. New York: Sheed and Ward.

Eliade, Mircea. (1976). *Occultism, Witchcraft, and Cultural Fashions: Essays in Comparative Religions.* Chicago: University of Chicago Press.

Ellenberger, Henri. (1970). *The Discovery of the Unconscious: the History and Evolution of Dynamic Psychiatry.* New York: Basic Books.

Ellis, Havelock. 1914 (1894). *Man and Woman,* 5th ed. London: Walter Scott Publishing.

Ellis, Havelock. (1927-28). *Studies in the Psychology of Sex.* Philadelphia: F. A. Davis, 7 vols.

Elwin, V. (1968). *The Kingdom of the Young.* London: Oxford University Press.

Ember, Carol. (1978). "Men's Fear of Sex with Women: a Cross-Cultural Study," *Sex Roles* 4, 657-78.

Ember, Carol. (1981). "A Cross-Cultural Perspective on Sex Differences," *Handbook of Cross-Cultural Human Development,* ed. Ruth Munroe, Robert Munroe, B. Whiting. New York: Garland STPM Press, 531-80.

Endleman, Robert. (1981). *Psyche and Society: Explorations in Psychoanalytic Sociology.* New York: Columbia University Press.

Engels, Frederick. 1972 (1884). *The Origin of the Family, Private Property and the State in the Light of the Researches of Lewis H. Morgan.* New York: International Publishers.

Erikson, Erik. 1963 (1950). *Childhood and Society* (2nd ed.). New York: Norton.

Erikson, Erik. (1964). "Inner and Outer Space: Reflections on Womanhood," *Daedalus* 93, 582-606.

Ernster, Virginia. (1975). "American Menstrual Expressions," *Sex Roles* 1, 3-13.

Essock-Vitale, Susan and Michael T. McGuire. (1980). "Predictions Derived from the Theories of Kin Selection and Reciprocation Assessed by Anthropological Data," *Ethology and Sociobiology* 1/3, 233-43.

Etkin, W. (1954). "Social Behavior and the Evolution of Man's Mental Faculties," *American Naturalist* 88, 129-42.

Evans, Ihor (revisor). (1970). *Brewer's Dictionary of Phrase and Fable.* New York: Harper and Row.

Evans, William N. (1951). "Simulated Pregnancy in a Male," *Psychoanalytic Quarterly* 20, 165-78.

Eysenck, H. J. (1976). *Sex and Personality.* London: Open Books.

Eysenck, H. J. and Glenn Wilson. (1973). *The Experimental Study of Freudian Theories.* London: Methuen.

Eysenck, H. J. and Glenn Wilson. (1979). *The Psychology of Sex.* London: J. M. Dent and Sons.

Fairbairn, W. R. D. (1954). *An Object Relations Theory of the Personality.* New York: Basic Books.

Fairbanks, L. A. (1977). "Animal and Human Behavior: Guidelines for Generalization Across Species," *Ethological Psychiatry: Psychopathology in the Context of Evolution Biology,* ed. M. T. McGuire and L. A. Fairbanks. New York: Grune and Stratton, 87-110.

Farmer, J. S. and W. E. Henley, eds. (1890-1904). *Slang and its Analogues Past and Present.* Printed for subscribers only. 7 vols.

Farrell, B. A. (1981). *The Standing of Psychoanalysis.* Oxford: Oxford University Press.

Fedigan, Linda Marie. (1982). *Primate Paradigms: Sex Roles and Social Bonds.* Montreal: Eden Press.

Feldman, Harold. (1955). "The Illusions of Work," *Psychoanalytic Reivew* 42, 262-70.

Feldman, Philip and Malcolm MacCulloch. (1980). *Human Sexual Behavior.* New York: John Wiley & Sons.

Fenichel, Otto. (1945). *The Psychoanalytic Theory of Neurosis.* New York: Norton.

Fenichel, Otto. (1953). "The Psychology of Transvestitism," *Collected Papers of Otto Penichel, First Series.* New York: Norton.

Fenichel, Otto. 1954 (1936). "The Symbolic Equation: Girl = Phallus," *The Collected Papers of Otto Fenichel, Second Series.* New York: Norton, 3-18.

Ferenczi, Sandor. (1927). *Further Contributions to the Theory and Technique of Psycho-Analysis.* New York: Boni and Liveright.

Ferenczi, Sandor. 1938 (1924). *Thalassa: a Theory of Genitality,* tr. H. Bunker. New York: Psychoanalytic Quarterly, Inc.

Ferenczi, Sandor. 1972 (1919-1933). *Schriften zur Psychoanalyse.* Frankfurt: S. Fischer, Vol. II.

Ferguson, L. W. (1938). "Correlates of Woman's Orgasm," *Journal of Psychology* 6, 295-302.

Ferrier, Linda. (1978). "Word, Context and Imitation," *Action, Gesture and Symbol,* ed. Andrew Lock. New York: Academic Press, 472-83.

Ferro-Luzzi, Gabriella Eichinger. (1980). "The Female Lingam: Interchangeable Symbols and Paradoxical Associations of Hindu Gods and Goddesses," *Current Anthropology* 21, 45-68.

Field, Tiffany, Robert Woodson, Reena Greenberg, Debra Cohen. (1982). "Discrimination and Imitation of Facial Expressions by Neonates," *Science* 218, 179-81.

Firestone, Shulamith. (1970). *The Dialectic of Sex.* New York: William Morrow.

Fish, W. R., W. C. Young and R. I. Dorfman. (1941). "Excretion of Estrogenic and Androgenic Substances by Female and Male Chimpanzees with Known Mating Behavior Records," *Endocrinology* 28, 585-92.

Fisher, Helen E. (1982). *The Sex Contract.* New York: William Morrow.

Fisher, Seymour. (1973). *The Female Orgasm: Psychology, Physiology, Fantasy.* New York: Basic Books.

Fisher, Seymour. (1980). "Personality Correlates of Sexual Behavior in Black Women," *Archives of Sexual Behavior* 9, 27-35.

Fisher, Seymour and Roger P. Greenberg. (1977). *The Scientific Credibility of Freud's Theories and Therapy.* New York: Basic Books.

Fishman, Pamela. (1978). "Interaction: the Work Women Do," *Social Problems* 25, 397-406.

Flegon, A. (1973). *Za predelami russkikh slovarei.* London: Flegon Press.

Flew, Antony. (1967). "Immortality," *The Encyclopedia of Philosophy.* New York: Macmillan, and The Free Press. Vol. 4, 139-150.

Flinn, Mark. (1981). "Uterine vs. Agnatic Kinship Variability and Associated Cousin Marriage Preferences: an Evolutionary Biological Analysis," *Natural Selection and Social Behavior,* ed. R. Alexander, D. Tinkle. New York: Chiron Press, 439-75.

Fluehr-Lobban, Carolyn. (1979). "A Marxist Reappraisal of the Matriarchate," *Current Anthropology* 20, 341-59.

Flügel, J. C. (1924). "Polyphallic Symbolism and the Castration Complex," *International Journal of Psycho-Analysis* 5, 155-196.

Flügel, J. C. (1925). "A Note on the Phallic Significance of the Tongue and Speech," *International Journal of Psycho-Analysis* 6, 209-215.

Ford, C. S., and F. A. Beach. (1951). *Patterns of Sexual Behavior.* New York: Harper & Row.

Forrest, Tess. (1966). "Paternal Roots of Female Character Development," *Contemporary Psychoanalysis* 3, 21-38.

Forrester, John. (1980). *Language and the Origins of Psychoanalysis.* New York: Columbia University Press.

Foucault, Michel. 1980 (1976). *The History of Sexuality: Volume I, an Introduction,* tr. R. Hurley. New York: Vintage Books.

Foulkes, David. (1978). *A Grammar of Dreams.* New York: Basic Books.

Fox, Robin. (1972). "Alliance and Constraint: Sexual Selection in the

Evolution of Human Kinship Systems," *Sexual Selection and the Descent of Man 1871-1971*, ed. B. G. Campbell. Chicago: Aldine, 282-331.

Fox, Robin. (1980). *The Red Lamp of Incest.* New York: E. P. Dutton.

Frances, Susan J. (1979). "Sex Differences in Nonverbal Behavior," *Sex Roles* 5, 519-35.

Frazer, James G. (1910). *Totemism and Exogamy.* London and New York: MacMillan, 4 vols.

Frazer, James G. 1935 (1911-15). *The Golden Bough,* 3rd ed. London and New York: MacMillan, 12 vols.

Freedman, Daniel G. (1974). *Human Infancy: An Evolutionary Perspective.* New York: Wiley.

Freedman, Daniel G. (1979). *Human Sociobiology: a Holistic Approach.* New York: MacMillan.

Freeman, Derek. (1968). "Thunder, Blood, and the Nicknaming of God's Creatures," *Psychoanalytic Quarterly* 37, 353-399.

Freeman, Derek. 1969 (1967). "Totem and Taboo: a Reappraisal," *Man and his Culture: Psychoanalytic Anthropology after 'Totem and Taboo'*, ed. W. Muensterberger. London: Rapp and Whiting, 53-78.

Freud, Anna. 1966 (1936). *The Ego and the Mechanisms of Defense.* New York: IUP.

Freud, Sigmund. (1940-52). *Gesammelte Werke.* London: Imago, 18 vols.

Freud, Sigmund. (1953-1965). *The Standard Edition of the Complete Psychological Works of Sigmund Freud,* tr. under general editorship of J. Strachey. London: Hogarth, 24 vols. (= *SE* in text).

Friday, Nancy. 1975 (1973). *My Secret Garden: Women's Sexual Fantasies.* New York: Pocket Books.

Friedl, Ernestine. (1975). *Women and Men: an Anthropologist's View.* New York: Holt, Rinehart and Winston.

Friedman, R. C., ed. (1982). *Behavior and the Menstrual Cycle.* New York: Marcel Dekker. Inc.

Friedman, R. C., S. W. Hurt, M. S. Arnoff and J. Clarkin. (1980). "Behavior and the Menstrual Cycle," *Signs* 5, 719-38.

Friedman, S. M. (1952). "An Empirical Study of the Castration and Oedipus Complexes," *Genetic Psychology Monographs* 46, 61-130.

Friedman, Victor A. (1977). "Dostoevsky on the Meaning of Humanity," *Maledicta* 1, 40.

Friedrich, Paul. (1978). *The Meaning of Aphrodite.* Chicago: University of Chicago Press.

Fromm, Erich. (1951). *The Forgotten Language: an Introduction to the Understanding of Dreams, Fairy Tales and Myths.* New York: Rinehart and Co.

Gabow, S. L. (1977). "Population Structure and the Rate of Hominid Brain Evolution," *Journal of Human Evolution* 6, 643-65.

Gagnon, John H. (1977). *Human Sexualities.* Glenview, Illinois: Scott, Foresman and Co.

Gagnon, John H. and William Simon. (1973). *Sexual Conduct: the Social Sources of Human Sexuality.* Chicago: Aldine.

Gajdusek, Carleton. (1970). "Physiological and Psychological Characteristics of Stone Age Man," *Engineering and Science* 33, 26-33; 56-62.

Galdikas, Biruté. (1981). "Orangutang Reproduction in the Wild," *Reproductive Biology of the Great Apes,* ed. C. Graham. New York: Academic Press, 281-300.

Galdikas, Biruté and Geza Teleki. (1981). "Variations in Subsistence Activities of Female and Male Pongids: New Perspectives on the Origins of Hominid Labor Division," *Current Anthropology* 22, 241-56.

Gallup, Gordon G. (1982). "Permanent Breast Enlargement in Human Females: A Sociobiological Analysis," *Journal of Human Evolution* 11, 597-601.

Garrison, Robert J., V. Elving Anderson and Sheldon C. Reed. 1982 (1968). "Assortative Marriage," *Social Biology* 29, 36-52.

Gates, Anne and John L. Bradshaw. (1977). "The Role of the Cerebral Hemispheres in Music," *Brain and Language* 4, 403-31.

Gaulin, Steven J. C. and Alice Schlegel. (1980). "Paternal Confidence and Paternal Investment: a Cross Cultural Test of a Sociobiological Hypothesis," *Ethology and Sociobiology* 1, 301-9.

Gautier, J.-P. and A. Gautier. (1977). "Communication in Old World Monkeys," *How Animals Communicate,* ed. T. Sebeok. Bloomington: Indiana University Press, 890-964.

Gay, Peter. (1984). *Education of the Senses* (vol. I of *The Bourgeois Experience: Victoria to Freud*). New York: Oxford University Press.

Gebhard, Paul H. (1966). "Factors in Marital Orgasm," *Journal of Social Issues* 22, 88-95.

Gebhard, Paul H. (1970). "Postmarital Coitus Among Widows and Divorcees," *Divorce and After,* ed. P. Bohannan. New York: Doubleday, 81-96.

Geertz, Clifford. (1973). *The Interpretation of Cultures.* New York: Basic Books.

Gell, Alfred. (1979). "Reflections on a Cut Finger: Taboo in the Umeda Conception of the Self," *Fantasy and Symbol,* ed. R. H. Hook. New York: Academic Press, 133-48.

van Gennep, Arnold. 1960 (1908). *The Rites of Passage,* tr. M. Vizedom, G. Caffee. Chicago: University of Chicago Press.

Gerber, Albert B. (1981). *The Book of Sex Lists.* Seacus, N.J.: Lyle Stuart.

Geschwind, Norman. (1970). "The Organization of Language and the Brain," *Science* 170, 940-44.

Ghiselin, Michael T. (1974). *The Economy of Nature and the Evolution of Sex.* Berkeley: University of California Press.

Ghiselin, Michael T. (1980). "Is Sex Sufficient," *Behavioral and Brain Sciences* 3, 187-189.

Gibson, Kathleen. (1978). "Sociobiology, Brain Maturation, and Infantile Filial Attachment," *BBS* 1, 446.

Gill, Merton M. (1982). *Analysis of Transference, Vol. I.* New York: International Universities Press.

Gill, Merton M. and Irwin Z. Hoffman. (1982). *Analysis of Transference, Vol. II.* New York: International Universities Press.

Gillison, Gillian. (1980). "Images of Nature in Gimi Thought," *Nature, Culture and Gender,* ed. C. P. MacCormack, M. Strathern. Cambridge: Cambridge University Press, 143-73.

Gimbutas, Marija. (1974). *The Gods and Goddesses of Old Europe, 7000-3500 BC: Myths, Legends and Cult Images.* Berkeley: University of California Press.

Gladue, Brian A., Richard Green, Ronald E. Hellman. (1984). "Neuroendocrine Response to Estrogen and Sexual Orientation," *Science* 225, 1496-98.

Gladwin, Thomas and Seymour B. Sarason. (1953). *Truk: Man in Paradise (=Viking Fund Publications in Anthropology, Vol. 20).* New York: Wenner-Gren Foundation for Anthropological Research.

von Glaserfeld, Ernst. (1976). "The Development of Language as Purposive Behavior," *Origins and Evolution of Language and Speech,* ed. S. Harnad, H. Steklis, J. Lancaster. New York: New York Academy of Sciences, 212-226.

Glasser, Mervin. (1979). "Some Aspects of the Role of Aggression in the Perversions," *Sexual Deviation,* ed. I. Rosen. New York: Oxford University Press, 278-305.

Glick, B. S. and M. J. Raleigh. (1976). "On Gender Differences and the Origin of Language," *Current Anthropology* 17, 522.

Glover, Edward. (1945). "Eder as a Psycho-Analyst," *David Eder: Memoirs of a Modern Pioneer,* ed. J. B. Hobman. London: Gollancz, 89-116.

Goffman, Erving. (1971). *Relations in Public: Microstudies of the Public Order.* New York: Basic Books.

Goffman, Erving. 1979 (1976). *Gender Advertisements.* New York: Harper and Row.

Gogol, Nikolai. 1961 (1842). *Dead Souls,* tr. A. MacAndrew. New York: Signet.

Gogol, Nikolai. (1964). *The Collected Tales and Plays of Nikolai Gogol,* tr./ed. L. Kent. New York: Random House.

Goldberg, Daniel C., Beverly Whipple, Ralph E. Fishkin, Howard Waxman, Paul J. Fink, Martin Weisberg. (1983). "The Grafenberg Spot and Female Ejaculation: a Review of Initial Hypotheses," *Journal of Sex and Marital Therapy* 9, 27-37.

Goldberg, Steven. (1977). *The Inevitability of Patriarchy.* London: Temple Smith.

Goldfoot, D. A., H. Westerborg-van Loon, W. Groeneveld, A. Koos Slob. (1980). "Behavioral and Physiological Evidence of Sexual Climax in the Stump-Tailed Macaque (*Macaca arctoides*)," *Science* 208, 1477-9.

Goldman, Emma. 1972 (1917). "Marriage and Love," *The American Sisterhood,* ed. Wendy Martin. New York: Harper and Row, 224-33.

Goodale, Jane. (1971). *Tiwi Wives*. Seattle: University of Washington Press.

Goodall, J. van Lawick. (1967). "Mother-Offspring Relationships in Free-Ranging Chimpanzees," *Primate Ethology*, ed. D. Morris. Chicago: Aldine, 287-346.

Goodall, J. van Lawick. (1971). *In the Shadow of Man*. New York: Dell.

Goodall, J. van Lawick. (1976). "Continuities Between Chimpanzee and Human Behavior," *Human Origins: Louis Leakey and the East African Evidence*, ed. G. Isaac, E. McCown. Menlo Park: W. A. Benjamin, 81-95.

Goodall, J. van Lawick. (1981). Keynote Address to University of California Symposium on "Our Ancestors, Ourselves," Davis, California, 9 May 1981.

Goode, William J. (1963). *World Revolution and Family Patterns*. New York: Free Press of Glencoe.

Goode, William J. (1982). "Why Men Resist," *Rethinking the Family: Some Feminist Questions*, ed. B. Thorne, M. Yalom. New York: Longman, 131-50.

Goodland, Roger. (1931). *A Bibliography of Sex Rites and Customs*. London: George Routledge and Sons.

Goody, Jack. (1976). *Production and Reproduction: A Comparative Study of the Domestic Domain*. Cambridge: Cambridge University Press.

Goody, Jack and S. J. Tambiah. (1973). *Bridewealth and Dowry*. Cambridge: Cambridge University Press.

Gottdiener, Mark. (1977). "Unisex Fashions and Gender Role Change," *Semiotic Scene* I, No. 3, 13-37.

Gouet, Michel. (1971). "Lexical Problems Raised by some of the 'foutre'-Constructions," *Studies Out In Left Field: Defamatory Essays Presented to James D. McCawley*, ed. A. Zwicky, P. Salus, R. Binnick, A. Vanek. Edmonton: Linguistic Research, Inc., 79-85.

Gough, Kathleen. (1955). "Female Initiation Rites on the Malabar Coast," *Journal of the Royal Anthropological Institute* 85, 45-80.

Gough, Kathleen. (1975). "The Origin of the Family," *Toward an Anthropology of Women*, ed. R. Reiter. New York: Monthy Review Press, 51-76.

Gould, Stephen Jay. (1977). *Ontogeny and Phylogeny*. Cambridge: Harvard University Press.

Gould, Stephen Jay. (1979). "Panselectionist Pitfalls in Parker and Gibson's Model for the Evolution of Intelligence," *Behavioral and Brain Sciences* 2, 285-6.

Gould, Stephen Jay. (1980). "Sociobiology and the Theory of Natural Selction," *Sociobiology: Beyond Nature/Nurture?*, ed. G. Barlow, J. Silverberg. Boulder: Westview Press, 257-69.

Gould, Stephen Jay and Richard Lewontin. 1984 (1978). "The Spandrels of San Marco and the Panglossian Paradigm: A Critique of the Adaptationist Programme," *Conceptual Issues in Evolutionary Biology*, ed. E. Sober. Cambridge: MIT Press, 252-70.

Gove, Philip B., ed. (1971). *Websters Third New International Dictionary*.

Springfield, Mass.: G. and C. Merriam Co.

Gräfenberg, Ernst. (1950). "The Role of the Urethra in Female Orgasm," *International Journal of Sexology* 3, 145-8.

Graves, Robert. 1966 (1948). *The White Goddess: a Historical Grammar of Poetic Myth,* amended and enlarged edition. New York: Farrar, Straus and Giroux.

Gray, J. Patrick. (1984). "The Influence of Female Power in Marriage on Sexual Behaviors and Attitudes: A Holocultural Study," *Archives of Sexual Behavior* 13, 223-31.

Gray, J. A. and A. W. H. Buffery. (1971). "Sex Differences in Emotional and Cognitive Behaviour in Mammals Including Man: Adaptive and Neural Bases," *Acta Psychologica* 35, 89-111.

Gray, Louis H. 1951 (1917). "Eunuch," *Encyclopedia of Religion and Ethics,* ed. J. Hastings. New York: Charles Scribner's Sons, vol. 5, 579-84.

Green, Richard. (1979). "Biological Influences on Sexual Identity," *Human Sexuality,* ed. H. A. Katchadourian. Berkeley: University of California Press, 115-33.

Greenacre, Phyllis. (1971). *Emotional Growth: Psychoanalytic Studies of the Gifted and a Great Variety of Other Individuals.* New York: IUP, Vol. I.

Greenberg, Joseph, ed. (1963). *Universals in Language.* Cambridge: MIT Press.

Greenberg, Joseph. (1966). *Language Universals.* The Hague: Mouton.

Greenberg, Roger P. and Seymour Fisher. (1980). "Freud's Penis-Baby Equation: Exploratory Tests of a Controversial Theory," *British Journal of Medical Psychology* 53, 333-42.

Greenberg, Roger P. and Seymour Fisher. (1983). "Freud and the Female Reproductive Process: Tests and Issues," *Empirical Studies of Psychoanalytical Theories,* Vol. I, ed. J. Masling. Hillsdale, N.J.: Lawrence Erlbaum Associates, 251-81.

Greenson, Ralph. (1950). "The Mother Tongue and the Mother," *International Journal of Psycho-Analysis* 31, 18-23.

Greer, Germaine. (1972). *The Female Eunuch.* New York: Bantam.

Gregersen, Edgar A. (1977). "A Note on English Sexual Cursing," *Maledicta* 1, 261-68.

Gregersen, Edgar A. (1979). "Sexual Linguistics," *Language, Sex and Gender* (=*Annals of N.Y. Academy of Sciences 327*), ed. J. Orasanu, M. Slater, L. Adler. New York: New York Academy of Sciences, 3-19.

Gregersen, Edgar A. (1982). *Sexual Practices: the Story of Human Sexuality.* London: Mitchell Beazley.

Gregory, Richard. (1970). "The Grammar of Vision," *The Listener,* Feb. 19, 242-4.

Grossman, William I. and Walter A. Stewart. (1977). "Penis Envy: From Childhood Wish to Developmental Metaphor," *Female Psychology: Contemporary Psychoanalytic Views,* ed. H. Blum. New York: International Universities Press, 193-212.

Grusec, Joan E. (1981). "Socialization Processes and the Development of Altruism," *Altruism and Helping Behavior*, ed. J. Rushton, R. Sorrentino. Hillsdale, N.J.: Lawrence Erlbaum, 65-90.

Guillaume, Paul. 1971 (1926). *Imitation in Children,* tr. E. Halperin and B. Kaplan. Chicago: University of Chicago Press.

Guthrie, R. Dale. (1976). *Body Hot Spots: the Anatomy of Human Social Organs and Behavior.* New York: Van Nostrand Reinhold.

Guttentag, Marcia and Paul F. Secord. (1983). *Too Many Women? The Sex Ratio Question.* Beverly Hills, California: Sage.

Haeberle, Erwin. (1978). *The Sex Atlas.* New York: Seabury Press.

Haeckel, Ernst. (1866). *Generelle Morphologie der Organismen: Allgemeine Grundzüge der organischen Formen – Wissenschaft, mechanisch bergründet durch die von Charles Darwin reformierte Descendenz-Theorie.* Berlin: Georg Reimer, 2 vols.

Hahn, Susan Reed and Karen Ericksen Paige. (1980). "American Birth Practices: a Critical Review," *The Psychobiology of Sex Differences and Sex Roles,* ed. J. Parsons. Washington: Hemisphere Publishing, 145-75.

Haldane, J. B. S. (1955). "Animal Communication and the Origin of Human Language," *Science Progress* 43, 385-401.

Hall, Calvin and Robert L. Van de Castle. (1965). "An Empirical Investigation of the Castration Complex in Dreams," *Journal of Personality* 33, 20-29.

Hall, Edward T. (1976). *Beyond Culture.* Garden City: Doubleday/Anchor.

Halverson, H. M. (1938). "Infant Sucking and Tensional Behavior," *Journal of Genetic Psychology* 53, 365-430.

Hamburg, B. A. (1978). "The Biosocial Basis of Sex Difference," *Human Evolution: Biosocial Perspectives,* ed. S. L. Washburn, E. R. McCown. Menlo Park: Benjamin/Cummings, 155-213.

Hamilton, James W. (1966). "Some Dynamics of Anti-Negro Prejudice," *Psychoanalytic Review* 53, 5-15.

Hamilton, W. D. (1964). "The Genetical Evolution of Social Behavior," *Journal of Theoretical Biology* 7, 1-52.

Hamilton, W. D. (1970). "Selfish and Spiteful Behavior in an Evolutionary Model," *Nature* 228 (5277), 1218-20.

Hamilton, W. D. (1975). "Innate Social Aptitudes of Man: An Approach from Evolutionary Genetics," *Biosocial Anthropology,* ed. R. Fox. London: Malby Press, 133-55.

Hammel, E. A., C. K. McDaniel, K. W. Wachter. (1979). "Demographic Consequences of Incest Tabus: A Microsimulation Analysis," *Science* 205, 972-7.

Hammond, N. G. L. and H. H. Scullard. (1970). *The Oxford Classical Dictionary* (Second Edition). Oxford: Clarendon Press.

Hanby, J. P. (1974). "Male-Male Mounting in Japanese Monkeys (*Macaca fuscata*)," *Animal Behaviour* 22, 836-49.

Hand, Wayland D. (1957). "American Analogues of the Couvade," *Studies in Folklore,* ed. W. E. Richmond. Bloomington: Indiana University Press, 213-29.

Hanna, Judith Lynne. (1979). *To Dance Is Human: A Theory of Nonverbal Communication.* Austin: University of Texas Press.

Hannay, J. B. (1922). *Sex Symbolism in Religion.* London: privately printed, 2 vols.

Harcourt, Alexander. (1981). "Intermale Competition and the Reproductive Behavior of the Great Apes," *Reproductive Biology of the Great Apes,* ed. C. Graham. New York: Academic Press, 301-18.

Hardin, Garrett. (1978). "Nice Guys Finish Last," *Sociobiology and Human Nature: an Interdisciplinary Critique and Defense,* ed. M. Gregory, A. Silvers, D. Sutch. San Francisco: Jossey-Bass, 183-94.

Harding, Robert S. O. (1981). "An Order of Omnivores: Nonhuman Primate Diets in the Wild," *Omnivorous Primates: Gathering and Hunting in Human Evolution,* ed. R. S. O. Harding and G. Teleki. New York: Columbia University Press, 191-214.

Harding, Susan. (1975). "Women and Words in a Spanish Village," *Toward an Anthropology of Women,* ed. R. Reiter. New York: Monthly Review Press, 283-308.

Hariton, E. Barbara and Jerome L. Singer. (1974). "Women's Fantasies During Sexual Intercourse: Normative and Theoretical Implications," *Journal of Consulting and Clinical Psychology* 42, 313-22.

Harley, Diahan. (1982). Letter to the Editor. *Science* 217, 296.

Harnad, Stevan. (1976). "On Gender Differences and Language," *Current Anthropology* 17, 327-8.

Harrington, Charles. (1968). "Sexual Differentiation in Socialization and Some Male Genital Mutilations," *American Anthropologist* 70, 951-6.

Harris, Marvin. (1979). *Cultural Materialism: The Struggle for a Science of Culture.* New York: Random House.

Hart, Beth, Irma Hilton and Claudette Kunkes. (1982). "Teenage Pregnancy: Is Sexual Restraint an Effective Solution?," Paper presented at Eastern Psychological Association Meeting, Baltimore, 16 April, 1982.

Hartland, E. (1909-1910). *Primitive Paternity: The Myth of Supernatural Birth in Relation to the History of the Family.* London: David Nutt, 2 vols.

Hartland, E. 1951 (1917). "Phallism," *Encyclopedia of Religion and Ethics,* ed. J. Hastings. New York: Scribner's, Vol. IX, 815-31.

Hartung, John. (1986). "Matrilineal Inheritance: New Theory and Analysis," *Behavioral and Brain Sciences,* to appear.

Hartup, W. W. (1962). "Some Correlates of Parental Imitation in Young Children," *Child Development* 33, 85-96.

Hatfield, Elaine. (1982). "Passionate Love, Companionate Love, and Intimacy," *Intimacy,* ed. M. Fisher, G. Stricker. New York: Plenum, 267-92.

Hawkes, Jacquetta and Leonard Woolley. (1963). *Prehistory and the*

Beginnings of Civilization. New York: Harper and Row.

Hayes, C. (1951). *The Ape in our House.* New York: Harper and Brothers.

Hays, H. R. (1964). *The Dangerous Sex: the Myth of Feminine Evil.* London: Methuen.

Hazen, Helen. (1983). *Endless Rapture: Rape, Romance, and the Female Imagination.* New York: Charles Scribner's Sons.

Healey, Tim. (1980). "A New Erotic Vocabulary," *Maledicta* 4/2, 181-201.

Heath, Desmond. (1984). "An Investigation Into the Origins of a Copious Vaginal Discharge During Intercourse: 'Enough to Wet the Bed' – That 'Is Not Urine'," *Journal of Sex Research* 20, 194-215.

Heeschen, Volker, Wulf Schiefenhövel and I. Eibl-Eibesfeldt. (1980). "Requesting, Giving, and Taking: the Relationship Between Verbal and Nonverbal Behavior in the Speech Community of the Eipo, Irian Jaya (West New Guinea)," *The Relationship of Verbal and Nonverbal Communication,* ed. M. R. Key. The Hague: Mouton, 139-67.

Heger, Heinz. 1980 (1972). *The Men With the Pink Triangle,* tr., ed. D. Fernbach. London: Gay Men's Press.

Heilbrun, Alfred B., Jr. (1981). *Human Sex-Role Behavior.* New York: Pergamon Press.

Hemingway, Ernest. (1927). *The Short Stories of Ernest Hemingway.* New York: Modern Library.

Henley, Nancy. (1975). "Power, Sex, and Nonverbal Communication," *Language and Sex: Difference and Dominance,* ed. B. Thorne, N. Henley. Rowley, Mass.: Newbury House, 184-203.

Henley, Nancy. (1977). *Body Politics: Power, Sex, and Nonverbal Communication.* Englewood Cliffs, N.J.: Prentice-Hall.

Herdt, Gilbert H. (1981). *Guardians of the Flutes: Idioms of Masculinity.* New York: McGraw-Hill.

Herdt, Gilbert H. (1982). "Fetish and Fantasy in Sambia Initiation," *Rituals of Manhood: Male Initiation in Papua New Guinea,* ed. G. Herdt. Berkeley: University of California Press, 44-98.

Hermann, Imre. (1935). "The Use of the Term 'Active' in the Definition of Masculinity: a Critical Study," *International Journal of Psycho-Analysis* 16, 219-22.

Herter, Hans. (1932). *De Priapo.* Giessen: A. Topelmann.

Hetherington, E. Mavis. (1972). "Effects of Father-Absence on Personality Development in Adolescent Daughters," *Developmental Psychology* 7, 313-26.

Hewes, G. W. (1957). "The Anthropology of Posture," *Scientific American* 196, 123-132.

Hewes, G. W. (1961). "Food Transport and the Origin of Hominid Bipedalism," *American Anthropologist* 63, 687-710.

Hewes, G. W. (1974). "Language in Early Hominids," *Language Origins,* ed. R. Wescott. Silver Spring, Md.: Linstok Press, 1-33.

Hewes, G. W. (1976). "The Current Status of the Gestural Theory of Language

Origin," *Origins and Evolution of Language and Speech,* ed. S. Harnard, H. Steklis, J. Lancaster. New York: New York Academy of Sciences, 482-504.

Hewes, G. W. (1977a). "A Model for Language Evolution," *Sign Language Studies* 15, 97-168.

Hewes, G. W. (1977b). "Language Origin Theories," *Language Learning by a Chimpanzee: The Lana Project.* New York: Academic Press, 3-53.

Hilberman, Elaine. (1980). "Overview: The 'Wife-Beater's Wife' Reconsidered," *American Journal of Psychiatry* 137, 1336-47.

Hill, J. H. (1972). "On the Evolutionary Foundations of Language," *American Anthropologist* 74, 308-17.

Hinde, R. A. (1978). "Dominance and Role — Two Concepts with Dual Meanings," *Journal of Social and Biological Structures* 1, 27-38.

Hirschfeld, Magnus. 1941 (1929). *The Sexual History of the World War,* ed., tr. A. Gaspar *et al.* New York: Cadillac Publishing Co.

Hite, Shere. (1976). *The Hite Report: A Nationwide Study of Female Sexuality.* New York: Dell.

Hite, Shere. (1981). *The Hite Report on Male Sexuality.* New York: Alfred A. Knopf.

Hoch, Zwi. (1983). "The G Spot," *Journal of Sex and Marital Therapy* 9, 166-7.

Hockett, Charles F. (1960). "Logical Considerations in the Study of Animal Communication," *Animal Sounds and Communication,* ed. W. E. Lanyon and W. W. Tavolga. Washington: American Institute of Biological Sciences, 392-430.

Hockett, Charles F. and Robert Ascher. (1964). "The Human Revolution," *Current Anthropology* 5, 135-68.

Hoffman, Lois. (1972). "Early Childhood Experiences and Women's Achievement Motives," *Journal of Social Issues* 28, 129-55.

Hoffman, Martin. (1981). "The Development of Empathy," *Altruism and Helping Behavior,* ed. J. Rushton, R. Sorrentino. Hillsdale, N.J.: Lawrence Erlbaum, 41-63.

Hogbin, H. Ian. (1943). "A New Guinea Infancy: From Conception to Weaning in Wogeo," *Oceania* 13, 285-309.

Hogbin, H. Ian. (1970). *The Island of Menstruating Men: Religion in Wogeo, New Guinea.* Scranton, Pennsylvania: Chandler.

Hollender, Marc H., Lester Luborsky, Thomas J. Scaramella. (1969). "Body Contact and Sexual Excitement," *Archives of General Psychiatry* 20, 188-91.

Hollis, A. C. (1905). *The Masai.* Oxford: Clarendon Press.

Hollis, A. C. (1909). *The Nandi: Their Language and Folk-Lore.* Oxford: Clarendon Press.

Holloway, R. L. (1974). "The Casts of Fossil Hominid Brains," *Scientific American* 231, 106-115.

Holloway, R. L. (1976). "Paleoneurological Evidence for Language Origins,"

Origins and Evolution of Language and Speech, ed. S. Harnad, P. Steklis, J. Lancaster. New York: New York Academy of Sciences, 330-348.

Holmberg, Allan R. 1969 (1950). *Nomads of the Long Bow: the Siriono of Eastern Bolivia.* Garden City: Natural History Press.

Homans, George C. (1961). *Social Behavior: Its Elementary Forms.* New York: Harcourt, Brace and World.

Hopson, Janet. (1979). *Scent Signals: the Silent Language of Sex.* New York: William Morrow.

Horn, H. S. (1968). "The Adaptive Significance of Colonial Nesting in the Brewer's Blackbird *(Euphagus cynocephalus),*" *Ecology* 49, 682-94.

Horner, Matina. (1972). "The Motive to Avoid Success and Changing Aspirations of College Women," *Readings on the Psychology of Women,* ed. J. Bardwick. New York: Harper & Row, 62-7.

Horney, Karen. (1967). *Feminine Psychology.* New York: Norton.

Hosken, Fran. (1979). *The Hosken Report: Genital and Sexual Mutilation of Females,* 2nd ed. Lexington, Mass.: Women's International Network News.

Howard, Seymour. (1979). "The *Dresden Venus* and its Kin: Mutation and Retrieval of Types," *The Art Quarterly* 2, 90-111.

Hrdy, Sarah Blaffer. (1977). *The Langurs of Abu: Female and Male Strategies of Reproduction.* Cambridge/London: Harvard University Press.

Hrdy, Sarah Blaffer. (1979). "The Evolution of Human Sexuality: The Latest Word and the Last," *Quarterly Review of Biology* 54, 309-14.

Hrdy, Sarah Blaffer. (1981). *The Woman that Never Evolved.* Cambridge: Harvard University Press.

Huelsman, Ben R. (1976). "An Anthropological View of Clitoral and Other Female Genital Mutilations," *The Clitoris,* ed. T. P. Lowry and T. S. Lowry. St. Louis: Warren H. Green, 111-161.

Hugdahl, Kenneth and Ann-Christine Kärker. (1981). "Biological Vs. Experiential Factors in Phobic Conditioning," *Behaviour Research and Therapy* 19, 109-15.

Hunt, Morton. (1974). *Sexual Behavior in the 1970's.* Chicago: Playboy Press.

Hurwood, Bernhardt, ed. (1975). *The Whole Sex Catalogue.* New York: Pinnacle.

Hutchinson, G. E. (1959). "A Speculative Consideration of Certain Possible Forms of Sexual Selection in Man," *American Naturalist* 93, 81-91.

Huxley, Julian. (1942). *Evolution: The Modern Synthesis.* London: George Allen & Unwin.

Ickes, William. (1981). "Sex-Role Influences in Dyadic Interaction: a Theoretical Model," *Gender and Nonverbal Behavior,* ed. C. Mayo and N. Henley. New York: Springer Verlag, 95-128.

Illich, Ivan. (1982). *Gender.* New York: Pantheon Books.

Isaac, Glynn. (1976a). "Stages of Cultural Elaboration in the Pleistocene: Possible Archeological Indicators of the Development of Language Capabilities," *Origins and Evolution of Language and Speech,* ed. S. Harnad,

H. Steklis, J. Lancaster. New York: New York Academy of Science, 275-88.

Isaac, Glynn. (1976b). "The Activities of Early African Hominids," *Human Origins: Louis Leakey and the East African Evidence,* ed. G. Isaac and E. McCown. Menlo Park: W. Benjamin, 483-514.

Isaac, Glynn. (1978). "The Food-Sharing Behavior of Protohuman Hominids," *Scientific American* 238, 90-108.

Isaac, Glynn and Diana Crader. (1981). "To What Extent Were Early Hominids Carnivorous? An Archaeological Perspective," *Omnivorous Primates: Gathering and Hunting in Human Evolution,* ed. R. S. O. Harding and G. Teleki. New York: Columbia University Press, 37-103.

Isaac, Glynn and Richard E. F. Leakey, eds. (1979). *Human Ancestors.* San Francisco: W. H. Freeman.

Ivanov, V. V. (1974). "K predystorii znakovykh sistem," *Materialy vsesoiuznogo Simpoziuma po vtorichnym modeliruiushchim sistemam* 1/5, 81-7.

Ivanov, V. V. (1976a). "The Significance of M. M. Bakhtin's Ideas on Sign, Utterance, and Dialogue for Modern Semiotics," *Semiotics and Structuralism: Readings from the Soviet Union,* ed. H. Baran. White Plains, N.Y.: IASP, 310-67.

Ivanov, V. V. (1976b). *Ocherki po istorii semiotiki v SSSR.* Moscow: Nauka.

Jacobson, Edith. (1950). "Development of the Wish for a Child in Boys," *Psychoanalytic Study of the Child* 5, 139-52.

Jaffe, Daniel S. 1977 (1968). "The Masculine Envy of Woman's Procreative Function," *Female Psychology: Contemporary Psychoanalytic Views,* ed. H. P. Blum. New York: International Universities Press, 361-91.

Jaffe, Joseph, and Samuel W. Anderson. (1979). "Communication Rhythms and the Evolution of Language," *Of Speech and Time,* ed. A. Siegman and S. Feldstein. Hillsdale, N.J.: Lawrence Erlbaum, 17-22.

Jakobson, Roman. (1960). "Linguistics and Poetics," *Style in Language,* ed. T. Sebeok. Cambridge: M.I.T. Press, 350-77.

Jakobson, Roman. (1971). *Selected Writings: Vol. II – Word and Language.* The Hague: Mouton.

Jakobson, Roman. (1974). *Main Trends in the Science of Language.* New York: Harper and Row.

Jakobson, Roman. 1976 (1933). "What is Poetry?," *Semiotics of Art: Prague School Contributions,* ed. L. Matejka and I. Titunik. Cambridge: M.I.T, Press, 164-75.

Jakobson, Roman. n.d. "Life and Language," *Linguistics* 138, 97-103.

Jakobson, Roman, C. G. Fant, and Morris Halle. (1955). *Preliminaries to Speech Analysis.* Cambridge: M.I.T. Press.

Jakobson, Roman and Morris Halle.(1956). *Fundamentals of Language.* The Hague: Mouton.

Jakobson, Roman, and Linda Waugh. (1979). *The Sound Shape of Language.* Bloomington: Indiana University Press.

James, E. O. (1959). *The Cult of the Mother-Goddess.* New York: Barnes and Noble.

James, W. H. (1971). "The Distribution of Coitus Within the Human Intermenstrum," *Journal of Biosocal Sciences* 3, 159-71.

Janowsky, David S., Roderic Gorney, and Bret Kelley. (1966). "The Curse-Vicissitudes and Variations of the Female Fertility Cycle: Part II, Evolutionary Aspects," *Psychosomatics* 7, 283-7.

Janssen-Jurreit, Marie Louise. 1982 (1976). *Sexism: the Male Monopoly on History and Thought*, tr. V. Moberg. New York: Farrar, Straus, Giroux.

Janus, Sam, Barbara Bess, and Carol Saltus. (1977). *A Sexual Profile of Men in Power*. New York: Warner Books.

Jayne, Cynthia. (1981). "A Two-Dimensional Model of Female Sexual Response," *Journal of Sex and Marital Therapy* 7, 3-30.

Jaynes, Julian. (1976a). "The Evolution of Language in the Late Pleistocene," *Origins and Evolution of Language and Speech*, ed. S. Harnad, H. Steklis, J. Lancaster. New York: New York Academy of Sciences, 312-325.

Jaynes, Julian. (1976b). *The Origin of Consciousness in the Breakdown of the Bicameral Mind*. Boston: Houghton Mifflin.

Jensen, Gordon D. (1980). "Human Sociobiology: Sex-Typical Behavior Patterns," *Medical Sexology*, ed. R. Forleo, W. Pasini. Littleton, Mass.: PSG Publishing, 106-11.

Jespersen, Otto. (1925). *Mankind, Nation and Individual from a Linguistic Point of View*. Cambridge: Harvard University Press.

Jespersen, Otto. 1950 (1922). *Language: Its Nature, Development and Origin*. London: George Allen and Unwin.

Johanson, Donald and T. D. White. (1979). "A Systematic Assessment of Early African Hominids," *Science* 203, 321-330.

Johanson, Donald and Maitland Edey. (1981). *Lucy: The Beginnings of Humankind*. New York: Simon and Schuster.

Johnson, Miriam. (1975). "Fathers, Mothers and Sex Typing," *Sociological Inquiry* 45, 15-26.

Jolly, Alison. (1972). *The Evolution of Primate Behavior*. New York: Macmillan.

Jolly, Alison. (1979). "Feeding Versus Social Factors in Cognitive Evolution: Can't We Have It Both Ways?," *Behavioral and Brain Sciences* 2, 389-90.

Jonas, David and Doris Jonas. (1970). *Man-Child: A Study of the Infantilization of Man*. New York: McGraw Hill.

Jonas, David and Doris Jonas. (1975a). "Gender Differences in Mental Function: a Clue to the Origin of Language," *Current Anthropology* 16, 626-30.

Jonas, David and Doris Jonas. (1975b). "A Biological Basis for the Oedipus Complex: an Evolutionary and Ethological Approach," *American Journal of Psychiatry* 132, 602-6.

Jonas, Doris and David Jonas. 1980 (1975). *Sex and Status*. New York: Stein and Day.

Jones, Ernest. (1951). *Essays in Applied Psycho-Analysis*. London: Hogarth, Vol. II.

418   *Bibliography*

Jones, Ernest. (1953-7). *The Life and Work of Sigmund Freud.* New York: Basic Books, 3 vols.

Jones, Ernest. (1961). *Papers on Psycho-Analysis.* Boston: Beacon.

Jones, Ernest. (1964). "The Madonna's Conception through the Ear," *Essays in Applied Psychoanalysis.* New York: IUP, 266-357.

Jones, Ernest. 1971 (1951). *On the Nightmare.* New York: Liveright.

Jung, C. G. (1958). *Psyche and Symbol,* ed. V. de Laszlo. Garden City, N. Y.: Doubleday Anchor Books.

Jungers, William L. (1978). "On Canine Reduction in Early Hominids," *Current Anthropology* 19, 155-6.

Kagan, Jerome and J. Lemkin. (1960). "The Child's Differential Perception of Parental Attributes," *Journal of Abnormal and Social Psychology* 61, 440-47.

Kagan, Jerome and Howard Moss. (1962). *Birth to Maturity: a Study in Psychological Development.* New York: John Wiley and Sons.

Kakar, Sudhir. (1978). *The Inner World: a Psycho-analytic Study of Childhood and Society in India.* Delhi: Oxford University Press.

Kane, F. J., M. A. Lipton, and J. A. Ewing.(1969). "Hormonal Influences in Female Sexual Response," *Archives of General Psychiatry* 20, 202-9.

Kanowitz, Leo. (1969). *Women and the Law: the Unfinished Revolution.* Albuquerque: University of New Mexico Press.

Kaplan, Helen S. and Erica Sucher. (1982). "Women's Sexual Response," *Women's Sexual Experience: Explorations of the Dark Continent,* ed. M. Kirkpatrick. New York: Plenum Press, 3-16.

Katchadourian, Herant and Donald Lunde. (1972). *Fundamentals of Human Sexuality.* New York: Holt, Rinehart and Winston.

Keesing, Roger M. (1982). "Introduction," *Rituals of Manhood: Male Initiation in Papua New Guinea,* ed. G. Herdt. Berkeley: University of California Press, 2-43.

Keith, Arthur. (1948). *A New Theory of Human Evolution.* London: Watts.

Kelley, Ann E. and Louis Stinus. (1984). "Neuroanatomical and Neurochemical Substrates of Affective Behavior," *The Psychobiology of Affective Development,* ed. N. Fox, R. Davidson. Hillsdale. N.J.: Lawrence Erlbaum Associates, 1-75.

Kempton, Willett. (1980). "The Rhythmic Basis of Interactional Microsynchrony," *The Relationship of Verbal and Nonverbal Communication,* ed. M. R. Key. The Hague: Mouton, 67-75.

Kendon, A. (1970). "Movement Coordination in Social Interaction: Some Examples Described," *Acta Psychologica* 32, 100-125.

Kennell, J. H. and M. H. Klaus. (1979). "Early Mother-Infant Contact: Effects on the Mother and the Infant," *Bulletin of the Menninger Clinic* 43, 69-78.

Kent, R. D. and John C. Rosenbek. (1982). "Prosodic Disturbance and Neurologic Lesion," *Brain and Language,* 15, 259-91.

Kephart, William M. (1967). "Some Correlates of Romantic Love," *Journal of Marriage and the Family* 29, 470-74.

Kerckhoff, Alan C. (1974). "The Social Context of Interpersonal Attraction," *Foundations of Interpersonal Attraction,* ed. T. Huston. New York: Academic Press, 61-78.

Key, Mary Ritchie. (1975). *Paralanguage and Kinesics (Nonverbal Communication).* Metuchen, N. J.: Scarecrow Press.

Key, Mary Ritchie. (1977). *Nonverbal Communication: a Research Guide and Bibliography.* Metuchen, N. J.: Scarecrow Press.

Key, Mary Ritchie. (1980). "Language and Nonverbal Behavior as Organizers of Social Systems," *The Relationship of Verbal and Nonverbal Communication,* ed. M. R. Key. The Hague: Mouton, 3-33.

Khattab, Aziz. (1981). "Treatment of Anorgasmia (Frigidity) in 106 Egyptian Women," *Fifth World Congress of Sexology, Jerusalem, June 21-26, 1981* (abstracts), p. 63.

Kidd, Kenneth K., Brigitte A. Prusoff, Donald J. Cohen. (1980). "Familial Pattern of Gilles de la Tourette Syndrome," *Archives of General Psychiatry* 37/12, 1336-39.

Kiell, Norman. (1976). *Varieties of Sexual Experience.* New York: IUP.

Kimura, Doreen. (1979). "Neuromotor Mechanisms in the Evolution of Human Communication," *Neurobiology of Social Communication in Primates,* ed. H. Steklis, M. Raleigh. New York: Academic Press, 197-219.

King, Glenn. (1980). "Pair Bonding and Proximal Mechanisms," *BBS* 3, 191-2.

King, James C. (1980). "The Genetics of Sociobiology," *Sociobiology Examined,* ed. Ashley Montagu. Oxford: Oxford University Press, 82-107.

Kinsey, Alfred C., W. B. Pomeroy and C. E. Martin. (1948). *Sexual Behavior in the Human Male.* Philadelphia: W. B. Saunders.

Kinsey, Alfred C., W. B. Pomeroy, C. E. Martin, Paul H. Gebhard. 1965 (1953). *Sexual Behavior in the Human Female.* New York: Pocket Books.

Kiparsky, Paul. (1976). "Historical Linguistics and the Origin of Language," *Origins and Evolution of Language and Speech,* ed. S. Harnad, H. Steklis, J. Lancaster. New York: New York Academy of Sciences, 97-103.

Kirk-Smith, M. and D. A. Booth. (1977). "Effects of Androstenol on Sexual and Other Social Attitudes," *Proceedings of the Sixth International Symposium on Olfaction and Taste,* ed. J. Magnen, P. MacLeod. London: Information Retrieval, 485.

Kirsch, John A. W. and James Eric Rodman. (1982). "Selection and Sexuality: the Darwinian View of Homosexuality," *Homosexuality: Social, Psychological, and Biological Issues,* ed. W. Paul, J. Weinrich, J. Gonsiorek, M. Hotvedt. Beverly Hills: Sage, 183-95.

Kleiman, D. G. (1977). "Monogamy in Mammals," *Quarterly Review of Biology* 52, 39-69.

Klein, Ernest. (1971). *A Comprehensive Etymological Dictionary of the English Language.* Amsterdam: Elsevier.

Klein, Melanie. (1949). *The Psycho-Analysis of Children,* tr. Alix Strachey. London: Hogarth.

Klein, Melanie. (1975). *Envy and Gratitude, and Other Works, 1946-1963.* London: Hogarth.

Klein, Melanie. (1977). *Love, Guilt and Reparation and Other Works, 1921-1945.* New York: Dell.

Kleinbaum, Abby Wettan. (1983). *The War Against the Amazons.* New York: McGraw-Hill.

Klimek, David. (1979). *Beneath Mate Selection and Marriage: the Unconscious Motives in Human Pairing.* New York: Van Nostrand Reinhold.

Kline, Paul. (1977). "Cross-Cultural Studies and Freudian Theory," *Studies in Cross-Cultural Psychology, Vol. I,* ed. N. Warren. New York: Academic Press, 51-90.

Kline-Graber, Georgia and Benjamin Graber. (1976). *Woman's Orgasm.* New York: Popular Library.

Klopfer, Peter. (1977). "Communication in Prosimians," *How Animals Communicate,* ed. T. Sebeok. Bloomington: Indiana University Press, 841-50.

Knapp, Mark. (1978). *Nonverbal Communication in Human Interaction* (2nd ed.). New York: Holt, Rinehart and Winston.

Knight, Richard Payne and Thomas Wright. 1957 (1786, 1866). *Sexual Symbolism: A History of Phallic Worship.* New York: Julian Press.

Koedt, Anne. 1973 (1968). "The Myth of the Vaginal Orgasm," *Radical Feminism,* ed. A. Koedt, E. Levine, A. Rapone. New York: Quadrangle Books, 198-207.

Koford, C. B. (1963). "Group Relations in an Island Colony of Rhesus Monkeys," *Primate Social Behavior,* ed. C. Southwick. Princeton, N.J.: Van Nostrand, 136-152.

Kohlberg, Lawrence. (1966). "A Cognitive-Developmental Analysis of Children's Sex-Role Concepts and Attitudes," *The Development of Sex Differences,* ed. E. Maccoby. Stanford: Stanford University Press, 82-173.

Köhler, Wolfgang. 1959 (1917). *The Mentality of Apes,* tr. E. Winter. New York: Vintage.

Kohut, Heinz. (1971). *The Analysis of the Self.* New York: International Universities Press.

Kolb, Bryan and Ian Q. Whishaw. (1980). *Fundamentals of Human Neuropsychology.* San Francisco: W. H. Freeman.

Konner, Melvin. (1981). "Evolution of Human Behavior Development," *Handbook of Cross-Cultural Human Development,* ed. Ruth Munroe, Robert Munroe, Beatrice Whiting. New York: Garland STPM Press, 3-51.

Konner, Melvin. (1982). *The Tangled Wing: Biological Constraints on the Human Spirit.* New York: Holt, Rinehart and Winston.

Kowalski, G. W., rapporteur. (1980). "Reports of Three Group Discussions: Group Two," *Morality as a Biological Phenomenon,* ed. Gunther Stent. Berkeley, University of California Press, 231-52.

Krafft-Ebing, Richard. 1929 (1886). *Psychopathia Sexualis,* tr. and adapt. F. J. Rebman. Chicago: Login Brothers.

Kramarae, Cheris. (1981). *Women and Men Speaking: Frameworks for*

Analysis. Rowley, Mass.: Newbury House.

Kramer, Cheris. (1975). "Women's Speech: Separate but Unequal?," *Language and Sex: Difference and Dominance,* ed. B. Thorne and N. Henley. Rowley, Mass.: Newbury House, 43-56.

Kramer, Cheris. (1977). "Perceptions of Female and Male Speech," *Language and Speech* 20, 151-61.

Krantz, Grover S. (1982). "The Fossil Record of Sex," *Sexual Dimorphism in Homo Sapiens: a Question of Size,* ed. R. L. Hall. New York: Praeger, 85-105.

Krebs, D. (1970). "Altruism – an Examination of the Concept and a Review of the Literature," *Psychological Bulletin* 73, 258-302.

Kroeber, A. L. (1948). *Anthropology: Race, Language, Culture, Psychology, Prehistory.* New York: Harcourt, Brace and Co.

Kronhausen, Phyllis and Eberhard Kronhausen. (1968). *The First International Exhibition of Erotic Art.* Copenhagen: Kronhausen.

Kronhausen, Phyllis and Eberhard Kronhausen. (1970). *Erotic Bookplates.* New York: Bell.

Kropotkin, Peter. 1972 (1902). *Mutual Aid: A Factor in Evolution,* foreword by Ashley Montagu, with "The Struggle for Existence" by T. H. Huxley appended. New York: Garland Publishing.

Kundera, Milan. (1981). *The Book of Laughter and Forgetting,* tr. M. Heim. New York: Penguin.

Kunike, Hugo. (1911). "Das sogenannte 'Männerkindbett'", *Zeitschrift für Ethnologie* 43, 346-63.

La Barre, Weston. (1962). *They Shall Take Up Serpents: Psychology of the Southern Snake Handling Cult.* Minneapolis: University of Minnesota Press.

La Barre, Weston. (1964). "The Snake-Handling Cult of the American Southeast," *Explorations in Cultural Anthropology,* ed. W. H. Goodenough. New York: McGraw-Hill, 309-33.

Lacan, Jacques. (1966). *Ecrits.* Paris: Seuil.

Lacan, Jacques. 1977 (1966). *Ecrits: A Selection,* tr. Alan Sheridan. New York: W. W. Norton.

Ladas, Alice Kahn, Beverly Whipple and John Perry. (1982). *The G Spot and Other Recent Discoveries about Human Sexuality.* New York: Holt, Rinehart and Winston.

Laferrière, Daniel. (1976a). "The Writing Perversion," *Semiotica* 18, 217-233.

Laferrière, Daniel. (1976b). "The Subject and Discrepant Use of the Category of Person," *Versus* 14, 93-104.

Laferrière, Daniel. (1977a). *Five Russian Poems: Exercises in a Theory of Poetry.* Englewood, N. J.: Transworld.

Laferrière, Daniel. (1977b). "What is Semiotics?," *Semiotic Scene* 1, 2-4.

Laferrière, Daniel. (1978). *Sign and Subject: Semiotic and Psychoanalytic Investigations Into Poetry.* Lisse: Peter de Ridder Press.

Laferrière, Daniel. (1979). "Making Room for Semiotics," *Academe,* 435-40.
Laferrière, Daniel. (1980). "The Teleology of Rhythm in Poetry," *Poetics and Theory of Literature* 4, 411-50.
Laing, R. D. (1960). *The Divided Self: An Existential Study in Sanity and Madness.* Baltimore: Penguin.
Lakoff, George and Mark Johnson. (1980). *Metaphors we Live by.* Chicago: University of Chicago Press.
Lakoff, Robin. (1975). *Language and Woman's Place.* New York: Harper and Row.
Lakoff, Robin. (1977). "Women's Language," *Language and Style* 10, 222-47.
Lamb, Michael. (1982). "Why Swedish Fathers Aren't Liberated," *Psychology Today,* Oct., 74-7.
Lamendella, John T. (1976). "Relations Between Ontogeny and Phylogeny of Language: A Neorecapitulationist View," *Origins and Evolution of Language and Speech,* ed. S. Harnad, H. Steklis, J. Lancaster. New York: New York Academy of Sciences, 396-412.
Lancaster, Jane. (1975). *Primate Behavior and the Emergence of Human Culture.* New York: Holt, Rinehart, Winston.
Lancaster, Jane. (1979). "Sex and Gender in Evolutionary Perspective," *Human Sexuality: A Comparative and Developmental Perspective,* ed. H. Katchadourian. Berkeley: University of California Press, 51-80.
Lancaster, Jane B. and R. B. Lee. (1965). "The Annual Reproductive Cycle in Monkeys and Apes," *Primate Behavior: Field Studies of Monkeys and Apes,* ed. I. DeVore. New York: Holt, Rinehart and Winston, 486-513.
Lane, H. U., ed. (1980). *The World Almanac and Book of Facts 1981.* New York: Newspaper Enterprise Association.
Langer, Susanne. (1953). *Feeling and Form.* New York: Charles Scribner's Sons.
Langer, Susanne. (1972). *Mind: An Essay on Human Feeling.* Baltimore: Johns Hopkins University Press, 2 vols.
Langley, Roger and Richard C. Levy. (1977). *Wife Beating: the Silent Crisis.* New York: E. P. Dutton.
Lanpo, Jia. (1980). *Early Man in China.* Beijing: Foreign Languages Press.
LaPlanche, Jean and J.-B. Pontalis. (1973). *Vocabulaire de la Psychanalyse.* Paris: P.U.F.
Lasswell, Harold D. 1960 (1930). *Psychopathology and Politics.* New York: Viking Press.
Latimer, B. M., T. D. White, W. H. Kimbel, D. C. Johanson, C. O. Lovejoy. (1981). "The Pygmy Chimpanzee Is Not a Living Missing Link in Human Evolution," *Journal of Human Evolution* 10, 475-88.
Laubscher, B. J. F. (1937). *Sex, Custom, and Psychopathology.* London: George Rutledge and Sons.
Lausberg, H. (1960). *Handbuch der literarischen Rhetorik.* Munich: Hueber, 2 vols.
Lea, Henry Charles. 1957 (1939). *Materials Toward a History of Witchcraft.*

New York: Thomas Yoseloff, 3 vols.

Leacock, Eleanor Burke. (1981). *Myths of Male Dominance.* New York: Monthly Review Press.

Leakey, Richard E. (1981). *The Making of Mankind.* New York: E. P. Dutton.

Leakey, Richard E. and Roger Lewin. (1978). *People of the Lake: Mankind and Its Beginnings.* Garden City: Anchor Press.

Lederer, Wolfgang. (1968). *The Fear of Women.* New York: Harcourt, Brace, Jovanovich.

Lee, Marjorie. (1973). *Erotic Fantasies of Women.* New York: Pinnacle Books.

Lee, Richard B., and Irven DeVore, eds. (1968). *Man the Hunter.* Chicago: Aldine.

Leghorn, Lisa and Katherine Parker. (1981). *Woman's Worth: Sexual Economics and the World of Women.* Boston: Routledge and Kegan Paul.

Legman, G. (1968). *Rationale of the Dirty Joke,* 1st series. New York: Grove Press.

Legman, G. (1975). *No Laughing Matter (=Rationale of the Dirty Joke,* 2nd series). New York: Breaking Point.

Lehiste, Ilse. (1977). "Isochrony Reconsidered," *Journal of Phonetics* 5, 253-63.

Leites, Nathan. (1979). *Interpreting Transference.* New York: W. W. Norton.

Le Magnen, J. (1952). "Le phénomènes olfacto-sexuels chez l'homme," *Archives des sciences physiologiques* 6, 125-60.

Le May, M. (1976). "Morphological Cerebral Asymmetries of Modern Man, Fossil Man, and Nonhuman Primate," *Origins and Evolution of Language and Speech,* ed. S. Harnad, H. Steklis, J. Lancaster. New York: New York Academy of Sciences, 349-66.

Lenneberg, Eric. (1967). *Biological Foundations of Language.* New York: John Wiley.

Leonard, Laurence, Richard Schwartz, M. Folger, and M. Wilcox. (1978). "Some Aspects of Child Phonology in Imitative and Spontaneous Speech," *Journal of Child Language* 5, 403-15.

Leonard, Marjorie R. (1966). "Fathers and Daughters," *International Journal of Psycho-Analysis* 47, 325-34.

Lesser, Simon O. (1963). "The Image of the Father," *Art and Psychoanalysis,* ed. Wm. Phillips. Cleveland: World Publishing, 226-46.

Lessing, Doris. (1970). *Martha Quest.* New York: New American Library.

Lester, Barry M. (1984). "Infant Crying and the Development of Communication," *The Psychobiology of Affective Development,* ed. N. Fox, R. Davidson. Hillsdale, N. J.: Lawrence Erlbaum Associates, 231-58.

Leutenegger, Walter. (1974). "Functional Aspects of Pelvic Morphology in Simian Primates," *Journal of Human Evolution* 3, 207-22.

Leutenegger, Walter. (1977). "A Functional Interpretation of the Sacrum of *Australopithecus africanus,*" *South African Journal of Science 73,* 308-10.

Leutenegger, Walter. (1978). "Scaling of Sexual Dimorphism in Body Size and Breeding System in Primates," *Nature* 272, 610-11.

Lévi-Strauss, Claude. 1967 (1963). *Structural Anthropology*, tr. C. Jacobson and B. G. Schoepf. Garden City: Doubleday Anchor.

Lévi-Strauss, Claude. 1969 (1949). *The Elementary Structures of Kinship*, trans. J. H. Bell, J. R. von Sturmer, R. Needham. Boston: Beacon.

Levin, R. J. (1981). "The Female Orgasm – a Current Appraisal," *Journal of Psychosomatic Research* 25, 119-33.

Levin, Samuel. (1977). *The Semantics of Metaphor*. Baltimore: Johns Hopkins University Press.

Levine, Stephen B. (1982). "A Modern Perspective on Nymphomania," *Journal of Sex and Marital Therapy* 8, 316-24.

Lewin, B. (1933). "The Body as Phallus," *Psychoanalytic Quarterly* 2, 24-47.

Lewin, Roger. (1983a). "Fossil Lucy Grows Younger, Again," *Science* 219, 43-4.

Lewin, Roger. (1983b). "Were Lucy's Feet Made for Walking?," *Science* 220, 700-702.

Lewis, Helen Block. (1976). *Psychic War in Men and Women*. New York: New York University Press.

Lewis, J. M. (1969). "Impotence as a Reflection of Marital Conflict," *Medical Aspects of Human Sexuality* 3/6, 73-8.

Lieberman, Philip. (1975). *On the Origins of Language*. New York: MacMillan.

Lieberman, Philip. (1977). "The Phylogeny of Language," *How Animals Communicate*, ed. Thomas Sebeok. Bloomington: Indiana University Press, 3-25.

Lifton, R. J. (1976). *The Life of the Self: Toward a New Psychology*. New York: Simon and Schuster.

Lipkin, Mack, and Gerri S. Lamb. (1982). "The Couvade Syndrome: an Epidemiologic Study," *Annals of Internal Medicine* 96, 509-11.

Lippert, John. (1979). "Sexuality as Consumption," *The Women Say/The Men Say*, ed. E. Shapiro, B. Shapiro. New York: Delta, 51-5.

Litewka, Jack. (1977). "The Socialized Penis," *For Men Against Sexism: a Book of Readings*, ed. J. Snodgrass. New York: Times Change Press, 16-35.

Livingstone, Frank B. (1962). "Reconstructing Man's Pliocene Pongid Ancestor," *American Anthropologist* 64, 301-5.

Livingstone, Frank B. (1969). "Genetics, Ecology, and the Origins of Incest and Exogamy," *Current Anthropology* 10, 45-62.

Lockard, Joan. (1980a). "Speculations on the Adaptive Significance of Self-Deception," *The Evolution of Human Social Behavior*, ed. J. Lockard. New York: Elsevier, 257-75.

Lockard, Joan. (1980b). "Studies of Human Social Signals: Theory, Method and Data," *The Evolution of Human Social Behavior*, ed. J. Lockard. New York: Elsevier, 1-30.

Lockard, Joan. (1980c). "The Biological Synthesis of Behavior." *The Evolu-*

tion of Human Social Behavior, ed. J. Lockard. New York: Elsevier, 297-318.

Loewald, Hans. (1980). *Papers on Psychoanalysis*. New Haven: Yale University Press.

Lomax, Alan, ed. (1968). *Folk Song Style and Culture*. Washington, D. C.: American Assoc. for Advancement of Science, Publication No. 88.

Lomax, Alan. (1982). "The Cross-Cultural Variation of Rhythmic Style," *Interaction Rhythms: Periodicity in Communicative Behavior*, ed. M. Davis. New York: Human Sciences Press, 149-74.

Lombardo, William, Gary Cretser, Barbara Lombardo, Sharon Mathis. (1983). "Fer Cryin' Out Loud — There Is a Sex Difference," *Sex Roles* 9, 987-95.

Lopreato, Joseph. (1981). "Toward a Theory of Genuine Altruism in *Homo Sapiens*," *Ethology and Sociobiology* 2, 113-26.

Lorand, Sandor. (1939). "Contribution to the Problem of Vaginal Orgasm," *International Journal of Psycho-Analysis* 20, 432-8.

Lorenz, Konrad. (1943). "Die angeborenen Formen möglicher Erfahrung," *Zeitschrift für Tierpsychologie* 5, 235-409.

Lorenz, Konrad. (1971). *Studies in Animal and Human Behavior*, trans. R. Martin. Cambridge: Harvard University Press, vol. II.

Lorenz, Konrad, 1977 (1963). *On Aggression*, tr. M. K. Wilson. New York: Bantam.

Lovejoy, C. Owen. (1981). "The Origin of Man," *Science* 211, 341-50.

Lowe, Walter, Arthur Kretchmer, James Petersen, Barbara Nellis, Janet Lever, and Rosanna Hertz. (1983). "The Playboy Readers' Sex Survey, Part Four," *Playboy* 30, 130-203.

Lowie, Robert H. (1920). *Primitive Society*. New York: Liveright.

Lowie, Robert H. (1922). "Myths and Traditions of the Crow Indians," *Anthropological Papers of the American Museum of Natural History* 25, 1-308.

Lowry, Thomas P., and Thea Snyder Lowry, eds. (1976). *The Clitoris*. St. Louis: Warren H. Green.

Lullies, R. (1931). *Die Typen der griechischen Herme*. Königsberg: Privatdruck (privately printed).

Luria, A. R. (1966). *Human Brain and Psychological Processes*. trans. B. Haigh. New York: Basic Books.

Luria, Zella. (1979). "Psychosocial Determinants of Gender Identity, Role, and Orientation," *Human Sexuality*, ed. H. Katchadourian. Berkeley: University of California Press, 163-93.

Lynn, David. (1969). *Parental and Sex-Role Identification*. Berkeley: McCutchan.

Lynn, David. (1974). *The Father: His Role in Child Development*. Monterey: Wadsworth.

Lynn, David. (1979). *Daughters and Parents: Past, Present, and Future*. Monterey: Wadsworth.

Lyons, John. (1977). *Semantics*. Cambridge: Cambridge Univ. Press, 2 vols.

Maccoby, Eleanor. (1966). "Sex Differences in Intellectual Functioning," *The Development of Sex Differences,* ed. E. Maccoby. Stanford, Calif.: Stanford University Press, 25-55.

Maccoby, Eleanor and Carol Nagy Jacklin. (1974). *The Psychology of Sex Differences.* Stanford: Stanford University Press.

MacCulloch, J. A. 1951 (1917). "Serpent-Worship (Introductory and Primitive)," *Encyclopedia of Religion and Ethics,* ed. J. Hastings. New York: Charles Scribner's Sons, Vol. XI, 399-411.

MacLean, Paul. (1962). "New Findings Relevant to the Evolution of Psychosexual Functions of the Brain," *Journal of Nervous and Mental Disease* 135, 289-301.

MacLean, Paul. (1964). "Mirror Display in the Squirrel Monkey, *Saimiri sciureus,*" *Science* 146: 950-952.

MacLean, Paul. (1965). "New Findings Relevant to the Evolution of Psychosexual Functions of the Brain," *Sex Research: New Developments,* ed. J. Money. New York: Holt, Rinehart, and Winston, 197-218.

MacLean, Paul. (1970). "The Triune Brain, Emotion and Scientific Bias," *The Neurosciences: Second Study Program,* ed. F. O. Schmidt. New York: Rockefeller University Press, 336-49.

MacLean, Paul. (1973a). *A Triune Concept of Brain and Behavior.* Toronto: University of Toronto Press.

MacLean, Paul. (1973b). "New Findings on Brain Function and Sociosexual Behavior," *Contemporary Sexual Behavior. Critical Issues in the 1970s,* ed. J. Zubin, J. Money. Baltimore: Johns Hopkins Univ. Press, 53-74.

MacLean, Paul. (1975). "Brain Mechanisms of Primal Sexual Functions and Related Behavior," *Sexual Behavior: Pharmacology and Biochemistry,* ed. M. Sandler and G. Gessa. New York: Raven Press, 1-11.

MacLean, Paul. (1976). "The Imitative-Creative Interplay of Our Three Mentalities," *Astride Two Cultures: Arthur Koestler at 70,* ed. H. Harris. New York: Random House, 187-213.

MacLean, Paul. (1982). "The Co-evolution of the Brain and Family," *Anthroquest (The L.S.B. Leakey Foundation News)* 24, 1, 14-15.

MacLean, Paul. (1984). "Evolutionary Psychiatry and the Triune Brain," *Psychological Medicine* 14.

Mahler, Margaret, Fred Pine, Anni Bergman. (1975). *The Psychological Birth of the Human Infant: Symbiosis and Individuation.* New York: Basic Books.

Maisch, H. 1972 (1968). *Incest,* tr. C. Bearne. New York: Stein and Day.

Major, Brenda. (1981). "Gender Patterns in Touching Behavior," *Gender and Nonverbal Behavior,* ed. C. Mayo and N. Henley. New York: Springer Verlag, 15-37.

Malinowski, Bronislaw. (1929). *The Sexual Life of Savages in North-Western Melanesia.* London: George Routledge and Sons.

Malinowski, Bronislaw. 1955 (1927). *Sex and Repression in Savage Society.* New York: New American Library.

Malinowski, Bronislaw. (1962). *Sex, Culture, and Myth.* New York: Harcourt, Brace and World.

Malson, Lucien/Jean Itard. (1972). *Wolf Children/The Wild Boy of Aveyron.* London: NLB.

Mann, Alan E. (1981). "Diet and Human Evolution," *Omnivorous Primates: Gathering and Hunting in Human Evolution,* ed. R. S. O. Harding and G. Teleki. New York: Columbia Univ. Press, 10-36.

Marcus, Steven. (1966). *The Other Victorians: a Study of Sexuality and Pornography in Mid-Nineteenth Century England.* New York: Basic Books.

Margolin, Gayla. (1982). "A Social Learning Approach to Intimacy," *Intimacy,* ed. M. Fisher, G. Stricker. New York: Plenum, 175-201.

Mark, V. H. and F. R. Ervin. (1970). *Violence and The Brain.* New York: Harper and Row.

Marler, Peter and Richard Tenaza. (1977). "Signaling Behavior of Apes with Special Reference to Vocalization," *How Animals Communicate,* ed. T. Sebeok. Bloomington: Indiana University Press, 965-1033.

Marmor, Judd. 1973 (1968). "Changing Patterns of Femininity: Psycho-analytic Implications," *Psychoanalysis and Women,* ed. J. B. Miller. New York: Brunner/Mazel, 191-206.

Marshack, Alexander. (1971). *The Roots of Civilization.* New York: McGraw Hill.

Marshack, Alexander. (1976). "Some Implications of the Paleolithic Symbolic Evidence for the Origin of Language," *Current Anthropology* 17, 274-82.

Marshack, Alexander. (1977). "The Meander as a System: the Analysis and Recognition of Iconographic Units in Upper Paleolithic Compositions," *Form in Indigineous Art,* ed. P. Ucko. Canberra: Australian Institute of Aboriginal Studies, 286-317.

Marshack, Alexander. (1981). "On Paleolithic Ochre and the Early Uses of Color and Symbol." *Current Anthropology* 22, 188-191.

Marshall, Donald S. (1971). "Sexual Behavior on Mangaia," *Human Sexual Behavior,* ed. Donald S. Marshall and Robert C. Suggs. New York: Basic Books, 103-162.

Marshall, Eliot. (1983). "A Controversy on Samoa Comes of Age," *Science* 219, 1042-5.

Martin, M. Kay and Barbara Voorhies. (1975). *Female of the Species.* New York: Columbia University Press.

Martin, Wendy, ed. (1972). *The American Sisterhood: Writings of the Feminist Movement from Colonial Times to the Present.* New York: Harper and Row.

Martindale, Colin. (1977). "Syntactic and Semantic Correlates of Verbal Tics in Gilles de la Tourette's Syndrome: a Quantitative Case Study," *Brain and Language* 4, 231-47.

Martyna, Wendy. (1980). "The Psychology of the Generic Masculine," *Women and Language in Literature and Society,* ed. S. McConnell-Ginet,

R. Borker, N. Furman. New York: Praeger, 69-78.

Masters, William H. and Virginia Johnson. (1970). *Human Sexual Inadequacy*. Boston: Little, Brown.

Masters, William H. and Virginia Johnson. (1979). *Homosexuality in Perspective*. Boston: Little, Brown and Co.

Masters, William H. and Virginia Johnson. 1980 (1966). *Human Sexual Response*. New York: Bantam.

Mauss, Marcel. 1967 (1925). *The Gift*, trans. I. Cunnison. New York: W. W. Norton.

Mawson, C. O. Sylvester, ed. (1963). *Roget's University Thesaurus*. New York: Barnes and Noble.

May, Robert. (1966). "Sex Differences in Fantasy Patterns," *Journal of Projective Techniques and Personality Assessment* 30, 576-86.

May, Robert. (1980). *Sex and Fantasy: Patterns of Male and Female Development*. New York: W. W. Norton.

Maynard Smith, John. (1978). *The Evolution of Sex*. Cambridge: Cambridge University Press.

Maynard Smith, John. (1980). "The Concepts of Sociobiology," *Morality as a Biological Phenomenon*, ed. G. Stent. Berkeley: University of California Press, 21-30.

Maynard Smith, John and G. A. Parker. (1976). "The Logic of Asymmetric Contests," *Animal Behavior* 24, 159-75.

Mayr, Ernst. (1961). "Cause and Effect in Biology," *Science* 134, 1501-6.

Mayr, Ernst. (1982). *The Growth of Biological Thought*. Cambridge: Harvard University Press.

McConnell-Ginet, Sally. (1980). "Linguistics and the Feminist Challenge," *Women and Language in Literature and Society*, ed. S. McConnell-Ginet, R. Borker, W. Furman. New York: Praeger, 3-25.

McCulloch, Warren. (1965). *Embodiments of Mind*. Cambridge: MIT Press.

McEachron, Donald L. and Darius Baer. (1982). "A Review of Selected Sociobiological Principles: Application to Hominid Evolution – II, The Effects of Intergroup Conflicts" *Journal of Social and Biological Structures*, 5, 121-39.

McGrew, W. C. (1981). "The Female Chimpanzee as a Human Evolutionary Prototype," *Woman the Gatherer*, ed. F. Dahlberg. New Haven: Yale University Press, 35-73.

McGuinness, Diane. (1980a). "Male and Female Choice in Human Sexuality," *BBS* 3, 194-5.

McGuinness, Diane. (1980b). Review of Symons 1979. *Journal of Social and Biological Structures* 3, 311-16.

McHenry, Henry M. and Peter S. Rodman. (1980). "Bioenergetics and the Origin of Hominid Bipedalism," *American Journal of Physical Anthropology* 52, 103-6.

McLennan, John. (1865). *Primitive Marriage*. Edinburgh: Adam and Charles Black.

McMillan, Julie R., A. Kay Clifton, Diane McGrath, Wanda S. Gale. (1977). "Women's Language: Uncertainty or Interpersonal Sensitivity and Emotionality?," *Sex Roles* 3, 545-59.

Mead, Margaret. 1963 (1935). *Sex and Temperament in Three Primitive Societies.* New York: Morrow.

Mead, Margaret. 1975 (1949). *Male and Female: A Study of the Sexes in a Changing World.* New York: William Morrow.

Mechling, Jay. (1980). "The Magic of the Boy Scout Campfire," *Journal of American Folklore* 93, 35-56.

Meerloo, Joost and Marie Coleman. (1951). "The Transference Function: A Study of Normal and Pathological Transference," *Psychoanalytic Review* 38, 205-21.

Megaw, J. V. S. (1968a). "Problems and Non-problems in Palaeo-organology: a Musical Miscellany," *Studies in Ancient Europe,* ed. J. M. Coles, D.D.A. Simpson. Bristol: Leicester University Press, 333-58.

Megaw, J. V. S. (1968b). "The Earliest Musical Instruments in Europe," *Archaeology* 21, 124-32.

Meigs, Anna S. (1976). "Male Pregnancy and the Reduction of Sexual Opposition in a New Guinea Highlands Society," *Ethnology* 15, 393-407.

Meiselman, Karin C. (1978). *Incest: a Psychological Study of Causes and Effects with Treatment Recommendations.* San Francisco: Jossey-Bass.

Mellen, Sydney L. W. (1981). *The Evolution of Love.* San Francisco: W. H. Freeman.

Melotti, Umberto. (1981). "Towards a New Theory of the Origin of the Family," *Current Anthropology* 22, 625-38.

Meltzoff, Andrew and M. Keith Moore. (1977). "Imitation of Manual and Facial Gestures by Human Neonates," *Science* 198, 75-8.

Messenger, J. C. (1971). "Sex and Repression in an Irish Folk Community," *Human Sexual Behavior,* ed. D. S. Marshall and R. C. Suggs. New York: Basic Books, 3-37.

Meyer-Bahlburg, Heino F. L. (1980). "Homosexual Orientation in Women and Men: a Hormonal Basis?," *The Psychobiology of Sex Differences and Sex Roles,* ed. J. E. Parsons. New York: Hemisphere/McGraw-Hill, 105-30.

Michael, R. P., P. R. Bonsall, and M. Kutner. (1975). "Volatile Fatty Acids, 'Copulins', in Human Vaginal Secretions," *Psychoneuroendocrinology* 1, 153-63.

Michael, R. P., and R. W. Bonsall. (1979). "Hormones and the Sexual Behavior of Rhesus Monkeys," *Endocrine Control of Sexual Behavior,* ed. C. Beyer. New York: Raven Press, 278-302.

Midgley, Mary. (1978). *Beast and Man: The Roots of Human Nature.* Ithaca: Cornell University Press.

Mill, John Stuart. 1906 (1869). *The Subjection of Women.* London: Longmans, Green, and Co.

Miller, A. R. (1969). "Analysis of the Oedipal Complex," *Psychological Reports* 24, 781-2.

Miller, Casey and Kate Swift. (1976). *Words and Women*. New York: Anchor/ Doubleday.

Miller, W. R. (1964). "The Acquisition of Formal Features of Language," *American Journal of Orthopsychiatry* 34, 862-7.

Millett, Kate. (1970). *Sexual Politics*. New York: Doubleday.

Milton, Kay. (1979). "Male Bias in Anthropology," *Man* 14, 40-51.

Mitchell, G. (1979). *Behavioral Sex Differences in Nonhuman Primates*. New York: Van Nostrand Reinhold.

Mitchell, G. (1981). *Human Sex Differences: A Primatologist's Perspective*. New York: Van Nostrand Reinhold.

Mitchell, Juliet. (1974). *Psychoanalysis and Feminism*. New York: Random House.

Mohr, J. W., R. E. Turner, and M. B. Jerry. (1964). *Pedophilia and Exhibitionism*. Toronto: Univ. of Toronto Press.

Moncrieff, R. W. (1966). *Odour Preferences*. London: Leonard Hill.

Moncrieff, R. W. (1970). *Odours*. London: Willam Heinemann Medical Books.

Money, John. (1961). "Sex Hormones and Other Variables in Human Eroticism," *Sex and Internal Secretions*, ed. W. C. Young. Baltimore: Williams and Wilkins, vol. II, 1383-1400.

Money, John. (1975). "Ablatio Penis: Normal Male Infant Sex-Reassigned as a Girl," *Archives of Sexual Behavior* 4, 65-72.

Money, John. (1980). *Love and Love Sickness: the Science of Sex, Gender Difference, and Pair-Bonding*. Baltimore: Johns Hopkins University Press.

Money, John and Anke Ehrhardt. (1972). *Man and Woman, Boy and Girl*. Baltimore: Johns Hopkins University Press.

Montagu, M. F. Ashley. (1937). *Coming into Being Among the Australian Aborigines*. London: George Routledge and Sons.

Montagu, M. F. Ashley. 1962 (1960). "Time, Morphology, and Neoteny in the Evolution of Man," *Culture and the Evolution of Man*, ed. M. F. Ashley Montagu. New York: Oxford University Press, 324-342.

Montagu, M. F. Ashley. (1967). *The Anatomy of Swearing*. New York: Macmillan/London: Collier-Macmillan.

Montagu, M. F. Ashley. (1971). *Touching: The Human Significance of the Skin*. New York: Harper and Row.

Montagu, M. F. Ashley. (1974). *The Natural Superiority of Women*. New York: Collier MacMillan.

Montagu, M. F. Ashley, ed. (1980). *Sociobiology Examined*. Oxford: Oxford University Press.

Montagu, M. F. Ashley and Floyd Matson. (1979). *The Human Connection*. New York: McGraw-Hill.

Montgomery, Rita E. (1974). "A Cross-Cultural Study of Menstruation, Menstrual Taboos, and Related Social Variables," *Ethos* 2, 137-70.

Moore, Burness E. (1977). "Psychic Representation and Female Orgasm,"

Female Psychology: Contemporary Psychoanalytic Views, ed. H. Blum. New York: International Universities Press, 305-30.

Morgan, Elaine, 1973 (1972). *The Descent of Woman*. New York: Bantam.

Morgan, Lewis H. (1877). *Ancient Society*. Chicago: Charles H. Kerr.

Morris, Desmond. (1967). *The Naked Ape: A Zoologist's Study of the Human Animal*. New York: McGraw-Hill.

Morris, Desmond. 1973 (1971). *Intimate Behavior*. New York: Bantam.

Morris, Desmond. (1977). *Manwatching: A Field Guide to Human Behavior*. New York: Harry N. Abrams.

Morris, Desmond, Peter Collett, Peter Marsh, and Marie O'Shaughnessy. (1979). *Gestures: Their Origins and Distribution*. New York: Stein and Day.

Morris, Naomi M. and J. Richard Udry. (1983). "Menstruation and Marital Sex," *Journal of Biosocial Science* 15, 173-81.

Morriss, Gillian M. and E. B. Keverne. (1974). "Premenstrual Tension," *The Lancet* 7892, 1317-18.

Moulton, Janice. (1975). "Sex and Reference," *Philosophy and Sex*, ed. R. Baker and F. Elliston. Buffalo: Prometheus Books, 34-44.

Moulton, Ruth. 1973 (1970). "A Survey and Reevaluation of the Concept of Penis Envy," *Psychoanalysis and Women*, ed. J. B. Miller. New York: Brunner/Mazel, 207-30.

Mowrer, O. H. (1950). "Identification: A Link Between Learning Theory and Psychotherapy," *Learning Theory and Personality Dynamics*, ed. O. H. Mowrer. New York: Ronald, 573-616.

Muensterberger, Warner. 1969 (1955). "On the Biopsychological Determinants of Social Life," *Man and His Culture: Psychoanalytic Anthropology After 'Totem and Taboo'*, ed. W. Muensterberger. London: Rapp and Whiting, 81-99.

Mundinger, Paul. (1980). "Animal Cultures and a General Theory of Cultural Evolution," *Ethology and Sociobiology* 1, 183-223.

Mundkur, Balaji. (1983). *The Cult of the Serpent: an Interdisciplinary Survey of Its Manifestations and Origins*. Albany: State University of New York Press.

Munroe, Robert L. (1980). "Male Transvestitism and the Couvade: a Psycho-Cultural Analysis," *Ethos* 8, 49-59.

Munroe, Robert L., and Ruth H. Munroe. (1971). "Male Pregnancy Symptoms and Cross-Sex Identity in the Three Societies," *Journal of Social Psychology* 84, 11-25.

Munroe, Robert L. and Ruth H. Munroe. (1973). "Psychological Interpretation of Male Initiation Rites: the Case of Male Pregnancy Symptoms," *Ethos* 1, 490-98.

Munroe, Robert L., Ruth H. Munroe, and John W. M. Whiting. (1973). "The Couvade: a Psychological Analysis," *Ethos* 1, 30-74.

Munroe, Robert L., Ruth H. Munroe, John W. M. Whiting. (1981). "Male Sex-Role Resolutions," *Handbook of Cross-Cultural Human Development*, ed. Robert Munroe, Ruth Munroe, B. Whiting. New York: Garland STPM Press, 611-32.

Murdock, George P. (1937). "Comparative Data on the Division of Labor by Sex," *Social Forces* 15, 551-553.

Murdock, George P. (1949). *Social Structure.* New York: MacMillan.

Murdock, George P. (1950). "Family Stability in Non-European Cultures," *Annals of the American Academy of Political and Social Science* 272, 195-201.

Murdock, George P. (1957). "World Ethnographic Sample," *American Anthropologist* 59, 664-87.

Murdock, George P. (1967). *Ethnographic Atlas.* Pittsburgh: University of Pittsburgh Press.

Murdock, George P. and Douglas R. White. (1969). "Standard Cross-Cultural Smaple," *Ethnology* 8, 329-69.

Murphy, Robert F. (1959). "Social Structure and Sex Antagonism," *Southwestern Journal of Anthropology* 15, 89-98.

Murphy, Robert F. (1960). *Headhunter's Heritage: Social and Economic Change among the Mundurucú Indians.* Berkeley: University of California Press.

Murphy, Robert F. (1977). "Man's Culture and Woman's Nature," *Annals of the New York Academy of Sciences* 293, 15-24.

Murray, Henry. (1955). "American Icarus," *Clinical Studies of Personality*, ed. A. Burton, R. Harris. New York: Harper and Brothers, 615-41.

Murray, R. D. (1980). "The Evolution and Functional Significance of Incest Avoidance," *Journal of Human Evolution* 9, 173-8.

Murstein, Bernard I. (1982). "Marital Choice," *Handbook of Developmental Psychology*, ed. B. Wolman. Englewood Cliffs, N. J.: Prentice-Hall, 652-66.

Musaph, George and Herman Abraham. (1977). "Frigidity or Hypogyneismus," *Handbook of Sexology*, ed. J. Money and H. Musaph. Amsterdam: Elsevier/North Holland, 873-7.

Mussen, Paul and Nancy Eisenberg-Berg. (1977). *Roots of Caring, Sharing, and Helping.* San Francisco: W. H. Freeman.

Nadler, Ronald D. (1981). "Laboratory Research on Sexual Behavior of the Great Apes," *Reproductive Biology of the Great Apes*, ed. C. Graham. New York: Academic Press, 191-238.

Napier, J. R., and P. H. Napier. (1967). *A Handbook of Living Primates.* New York: Academic Press.

Naso, Publius Ovidius. 1955 (8 AD?). *Metamorphoses*, tr. M. Innes. London: Penguin.

Nathan, Sharon G. (1981). "Cross-Cultural Perspectives on Penis Envy," *Psychiatry* 44, 39-44.

Needham, Rodney, ed. (1973). *Right and Left: Essays on Dual Symbolic Classification.* Chicago: Univ. of Chicago Press.

Neel, James V. (1970). "Lessons from a 'Primitive' People," *Science* 170, 815-22.

Neely, James C. (1981). *Gender: the Myth of Equality*. New York: Simon and Schuster.

Neisser, U. (1967). *Cognitive Psychology*. New York: Appleton-Century Crofts.

Neisser, U. (1976). *Cognition and Reality*. San Francisco: W. H. Freeman.

Neubauer, Peter. (1960). "The One-Parent Child and His Development," *Psychoanalytic Study of the Child* 15, 286-309.

Neumann, Erich. (1955). *The Great Mother: An Analysis of the Archetype*, tr. R. Manheim. Princeton: Princeton University Press.

Newman, Philip L. and David J. Boyd. (1982). "The Making of Men: Ritual and Meaning in Awa Male Initiation," *Rituals of Manhood: Male Initiation in Papua New Guinea*, ed. G. Herdt. Berkeley: University of California Press, 239-85.

Newton, Niles. (1973). "Interrelationships Between Sexual Responsiveness, Birth, and Breast Feeding," *Contemporary Sexual Behavior*, ed. J. Zubin and J. Money. Baltimore: JHUP, 77-98.

Niederland, William. (1974). *The Schreber Case: Psychoanalytic Profile of a Paranoid Personality*. New York: Quadrangle/New York Times Book Co.

Niederland, William. (1976). "Psychoanalytic Approaches to Artistic Creativity," *Psychoanalytic Quarterly* 45, 185-212.

Nilsen, Don L. F. (1981). "Sigma Epsilon Xi: Sex in the Typical University Classroom," *Maledicta* 5, 79-91.

Nobile, Philip. (1977). "The Root of All Evil," *Cosmopolitan*, Nov., 272-5.

Nunberg, Herman. (1947). "Circumcision and Problems of Bisexuality," *International Journal of Psycho-Analysis* 28, 145-79.

Oakley, K. P. (1950). *Man the Tool-Maker*. London: Trustees of the British Museum.

Oakley, K. P. 1962 (1951). "A Definition of Man," *Culture and the Evolution of Man*, ed. A. Montagu. New York: Oxford Univ. Press, 3-12.

Offit, Avodah. (1977). *The Sexual Self*. Philadelphia: J. B. Lippincott.

Offit, Avodah. (1981). *Night Thoughts: Reflections of a Sex Therapist*. New York: Congdon and Lattès.

O'Flaherty, Wendy Doniger. (1980). *Women, Androgynes, and Other Mythical Beasts*. Chicago: University of Chicago Press.

Ojemann, George A. and Catherine Mateer. (1979). "Cortical and Subcortical Organization of Human Communication: Evidence from Stimulation Studies," *Neurobiology of Social Communication in Primates*, ed. H. Steklis and M. Raleigh. New York: Academic Press, 111-31.

Older, Jules. (1981). "Falling in Boinng Again," *New England Journal of Medicine* 305, 1583-4.

Olearius, Adam. 1967 (1647). *The Travels of Olearius in Seventeenth-Century Russia*, tr. S. Baron. Stanford: Stanford University Press.

Oliven, John F. (1974). *Clinical Sexuality: a Manual for the Physician and the Professions*. Philadelphia: J. B. Lippincott.

Oppenheimer, John R. (1977). "Communication in New Word Monkeys,"

How Animals Communicate, ed. T. Sebeok. Bloomington: Indiana Univ. Press, 851-89.

Ortner, Sherry. (1974). "Is Female to Male as Nature Is to Culture?," *Woman, Culture, and Society,* ed. M. Z. Rosaldo and L. Lamphere. Stanford: Stanford Univ. Press, 67-87.

Ortony, Andrew, ed. (1979). *Metaphor and Thought.* Cambridge: Cambridge University Press.

Packer, C. (1979). "Inter-Troop Transfer and Inbreeding Avoidance in *Papio anubis,*" *Animal Behaviour* 27, 1-36.

Paige, Karen Ericksen and Jeffery M. Paige. (1981). *The Politics of Reproductive Ritual.* Berkeley: University of California Press.

Papoušek, Hanuš, and Mechthild Papoušek. (1979). "Early Ontogeny of Human Social Interaction: Its Biological Roots and Social Dimensions," *Human Ethology,* ed. M. von Cranach *et al.* Cambridge: Cambridge Univ. Press, 456-78.

Parker, Sue Taylor and Kathleen Rita Gibson. (1979). "A Developmental Model for the Evolution of Language and Intelligence in Early Hominids," *Behavioral and Brain Sciences* 2, 367-408.

Parlee, Mary Brown. (1979). "Conversational Politics," *Psychology Today,* May, 48-56.

Parsons, Talcott, and Robert F. Bales. (1955). *Family, Socialization and Interaction Process.* Glencoe, Ill.: Free Press.

Parsons, Talcott, and Edward Shils, eds. (1951). *Toward a General Theory of Action.* Cambridge: Harvard University Press.

Partridge, Burgo. (1960). *A History of Orgies.* New York: Crown Publishers.

Partridge, Eric. (1966). *Origins: a Short Etymological Dictionary of Modern English.* New York: MacMillan.

Passingham, R. E. (1982). *The Human Primate.* San Francisco: W. H. Freeman.

Pasternak, Boris. (1958). *Safe Conduct, An Autobiography and Other Writings.* New York: New Directions.

Peirce, Charles Sanders. (1965-66). *Collected Papers of Charles Sanders Peirce,* eds. Charles Hartshorn, Paul Weiss, and Arthur Burks. Cambridge: Harvard University Press, 8 vols.

Penzer, N. M. (1952). *Poison-Damsels and Other Essays in Folklore and Anthropology.* London: Privately Printed.

Persky, H., H. I. Lief, D. Strauss, W. R. Miller, C. P. O'Brien. (1978). "Plasma Testosterone Level and Sexual Behavior of Couples," *Archives of Sexual Behavior* 7, 157-173.

Pfeiffer, John E. (1978). *The Emergence of Man* (3rd ed.). New York: Harper and Row.

Philips, Susan. (1980). "Sex Differences and Language," *Annual Review of Anthropology* 9, 523-44.

Piaget, Jean. 1962 (1945). *Play, Dreams and Imitation in Childhood,* tr. C. Gattegno and F. Hodgson. New York: Norton.

Piaget, Jean. (1977). *The Essential Piaget*, ed. H. Gruber and J. Vonèche. New York: Basic Books.

Pilbeam, D. R. (1975). "Middle Pleistocene Hominids," *After the Australopithecines*, ed. K. Butzer, G. Isaac. The Hague: Mouton, 809-865.

Plath, Sylvia. (1971). *The Bell Jar*. New York: Harper and Row.

Plath, Sylvia. (1981). *The Collected Poems*. New York: Harper and Row.

Ploog, Detlev W. and Paul D. MacLean. (1963). "Display of Penile Erection in Squirrel Monkey (*Saimiri sciureus*)," *Animal Behaviour* 11, 32-9.

Pomeroy, Sarah B. (1975). *Goddesses, Whores, Wives, and Slaves: Women In Classical Antiquity*. New York: Schocken Books.

Popper, Karl R. 1959 (1934). *The Logic of Scientific Discovery*. New York: Basic Books.

Popper, Karl, R. and John C. Eccles. (1977). *The Self and Its Brain*. Berlin: Springer International.

Prangishvili, A. S., A. E. Sherozia and F. V. Bassin, eds. (1978). *Bessoznatel'-noe: priroda, funkcii, metody issledovanija/The Unconscious: Nature, Functions, Methods of Study*. Tbilisi: Metsniereba, 4 vols.

Preston, James J., ed. (1982a). *Mother Worship*. Chapel Hill: University of North Carolina Press.

Preston, James J. (1982b). "New Perspectives on Mother Worship," *Mother Worship*, ed. J. Preston. Chapel Hill: University of North Carolina Press, 325-43.

Pribram, Karl. (1962). "The Neuropsychology of Sigmund Freud," *Experimental Foundations of Clinical Psychology*, ed. Arthur Bachrach. New York: Basic Books, 442-468.

Pribram, Karl. (1971). *Languages of the Brain: Experimental Paradoxes and Principles in Neuropsychology*. Englewood Cliffs, N. J.: Prentice Hall.

Pribram, Karl. (1978). "The Linguistic Act," *Psychoanalysis and Language*, ed. J. Smith. New Haven: Yale University Press, 75-98.

Pribram, Karl and Merton Gill. (1976). *Freud's "Project" Reassessed*. New York: Basic Books.

Prost, J. H. (1980). "Origin of Bipedalism," *American Journal of Physical Anthropology* 52, 175-89.

Proust, Marcel. 1981 (1913-27). *Remembrance of Things Past*, tr. C.K.S. Moncrieff, T. Kilmartin, A. Mayor. New York: Random House, 3 vols.

Pruscha, H. and M. Maurus. (1976). "The Communicative Function of Some Agonistic Behavior Patterns in Squirrel Monkeys," *Behavioral Ecology and Sociobiology* 1, 185-214.

Pulliam, H. Ronald and Christopher Dunford. (1980). *Programmed to Learn: an Essay on the Evolution of Culture*. New York: Columbia University Press.

Pumphrey, R. J. (1953). "The Origin of Language," *Acta Psychologica* 9, 219-239.

Quàng Phúc Dóng. (1971a). "English Sentences Without Overt Grammatical Subject," *Studies Out in Left Field: Defamatory Essays Presented to*

James D. McCawley, ed. A. Zwicky, P. Salus, R. Binnick, A. Vanek. Edmonton: Linguistic Research, Inc., 3-10.

Quàng Phục Dòng. (1971b). "A Note on Conjoined Noun Phrases," *Studies Out in Left Field: Defamatory Essays Presented to James D. McCawley*, ed. A. Zwicky, P. Salus, R. Binnick, A. Vanek. Edmonton: Linguistic Research, Inc., 11-18.

Racker, Heinrich. (1968). *Transference and Countertransference*. New York: International Universities Press.

Rado, Sandor. (1933). "Fear of Castration in Women," *Psychoanalytic Quarterly* 2, 425-75.

von Raffler-Engel, Walburga. (1980). "The Unconscious Element in Intercultural Communication," *The Social and Psychological Contexts of Language*, ed. R. St. Clair, H. Giles. Hillsdale, N. J.: Lawrence Erlbaum, 101-29.

Rainwater, Lee. (1966a). "Crucible of Identity: the Negro Lower-Class Family," *Daedalus* 95, 172-216.

Rainwater, Lee. (1966b). "Some Aspects of Lower Class Sexual Behavior," *Journal of Social Issues* 22, 96-108.

Rancour-Laferriere, Daniel. (1978). "The Identity of Gogol's Vij," *Harvard Ukrainian Studies* 2, 211-34.

Rancour-Laferriere, Daniel. (1979a). "Speculations on the Origin of Visual Iconicity in Culture," *Ars semeiotica* 2, 173-85.

Rancour-Laferriere, Daniel. (1979b). "Some Semiotic Aspects of the Human Penis," *Versus* 24, 37-82.

Rancour-Laferriere, Daniel. (1980). "Semiotics, Psychoanalysis, and Science: Some Selected Intersections," *Ars semeiotica* 3, 181-240.

Rancour-Laferriere, Daniel. (1981). "Sociobiology and Psychoanalysis: Interdisciplinary Remarks on the Most Imitative Animal," *Psychoanalysis and Contemporary Thought* 4, 435-526.

Rancour-Laferriere, Daniel. (1982a). *Out From Under Gogol's Overcoat*. Ann Arbor: Ardis.

Rancour-Laferriere, Daniel. (1982b). "All the World's a Vertep: the Personification/Depersonification Complex in Gogol's *Soročinskaja jarmarka*," *Harvard Ukrainian Studies* 6, 339-71.

Rancour-Laferriere, Daniel. (1984). "The Boys of Ibansk: A Freudian Look at Some Recent Russian Satire," *Psychoanalytic Review*. To appear.

Rank, Otto. (1932). *The Myth of the Birth of the Hero and Other Writings*. New York: Alfred A. Knopf.

Rank, Otto. 1952 (1909). *The Myth of the Birth of the Hero*, trans. F. Robbins and Smith Ely Jelliffe. New York: Robert Brunner.

Rank, Otto. 1973 (1924). *The Trauma of Birth*. New York: Harper Torchbooks.

Raum, O. F. (1939). "Female Initiation Among the Chaga," *American Anthropologist* 41, 554-65.

Rawson, Hugh. (1981). *A Dictionary of Euphemisms and Other Doubletalk*. New York: Crown Publishers.

Reage, Pauline. 1965 (1954). *The Story of O*, tr. S. d'Estrée. New York: Ballantine Books.

Rector, Frank. (1981). *The Nazi Extermination of Homosexuals*. New York: Stein and Day.

Reed, Evelyn. (1975). *Woman's Evolution: From Matriarchal Clan to Patriarchal Family*. New York: Pathfinder Press.

Reich, Wilhelm. 1969 (1930). *The Sexual Revolution: Toward a Self-Governing Character Structure*. New York: Farrar, Straus and Giroux.

Reik, Theodor. (1931). *Ritual: Psychoanalytic Studies*. London: Hogarth Press.

Reik, Theodor. (1941). *Masochism in Modern Man*, tr. M. Beigel, G. Kurth. New York: Farrar, Straus and Co.

Reik, Theodor. (1950). "The Fear of Touch," *Neurotica* 6, 3-10.

Reik, Theodor. (1963). "The Three Women in a Man's Life," *Art and Psychoanalysis*, ed. Wm. Phillips. Cleveland: World, 151-64.

Reiter, Rayna, ed. (1975). *Toward an Anthropology of Women*. New York: Monthly Review Press.

Restak, Richard M. (1979). *The Brain: The Last Frontier*. New York: Warner Books.

Reynolds, Peter C. (1981). *On the Evolution of Human Behavior: the Argument from Animals to Man*. Berkeley: University of California Press.

Reynolds, V. 1974 (1968). "Kinship and the Family in Monkeys, Apes, and Man," *Man in Adaptation: The Biosocial Background*, 2nd Edition, ed. Yehudi Cohen. Chicago: Aldine, 138-49.

Rheingold, H. L. and D. F. Hay. (1980). "Prosocial Behavior of the Very Young," *Morality as a Biological Phenomenon*, ed. G. S. Stent. Berkeley: University of California Press, 93-108.

Rich, Adrienne. (1977). *Of Woman Born*. New York: Bantam.

Richman, Bruce. (1976). "On Gender Differences and the Origin of Language," *Current Anthropology* 17, 523-4.

Richman, Bruce. (1980). "Did Human Speech Originate in Coordinated Vocal Music?," *Semiotica* 32, 233-44.

Ridley, Mark and Richard Dawkins. (1981). "The Natural Selection of Altruism," *Altruism and Helping Behavior*, ed. J. Rushton and R. Sorrentino. Hillsdale, N.J.: Lawrence Erlbaum, 19-39.

Riencourt, Amaury de. (1974). *Sex and Power in History*. New York: David McKay.

de River, J. Paul. (1958). *Crime and The Sexual Psychopath*. Springfield, Illinois: Charles C. Thomas.

Rizley, Ross. (1980). "Psychological Bases of Romantic Love," *On Love and Loving*, ed. K. S. Pope "and associates." San Francisco: Jossey-Bass, 104-13.

Robbins, Rossell Hope. (1959). *The Encyclopedia of Witchcraft and Demonology*. New York: Crown.

Robinson, Bryan W. (1976). "Limbic Influences on Human Speech," *Origins and Evolution of Language and Speech*, ed. S. Harnad, H. Steklis, J. Lancaster. New York: New York Academy of Sciences, 761-771.

Robinson, Paul. (1969). *The Freudian Left: Wilhelm Reich, Geza Roheim, Herbert Marcuse.* New York: Harper & Row.

Robinson, Paul. (1976). *The Modernization of Sex.* New York: Harper & Row.

Robson, K. S. (1967). "The Role of Eye-to-Eye Contact in Maternal-Infant Attachment," *Journal of Child Psychology and Psychiatry* 8, 13-25.

Roe, A. (1963). "Psychological Definitions of Man," *Classification and Human Evolution*, ed. S. L. Washburn. Chicago: Aldine, 320-31.

Roellenbleck, Ewald. 1974 (1949). *Magna Mater im alten Testament: Eine psychoanalytische Untersuchung.* Darmstadt: Wissenschaftliche Buchgesellschaft.

Róheim, Géza. (1932). "Psycho-Analysis of Primitive Cultural Types," *International Journal of Psycho-Analysis* 13, 2-224.

Róheim, Géza. (1934). *The Riddle of the Sphinx, or Human Origins.* London: Hogarth Press.

Róheim, Géza. (1943). *The Origin and Function of Culture.* New York: Nervous and Mental Disease Monographs (69).

Róheim, Géza. (1945a). "Aphrodite, or the Woman with a Penis," *Psychoanalytic Quarterly* 14, 350-90.

Róheim, Géza. (1945b). *The Eternal Ones of the Dream.* New York: International Universities Press.

Róheim, Géza. (1950). *Psychoanalysis and Anthropology: Culture, Personality and the Unconscious.* New York: International Universities Press.

Rohner, Ronald P. (1976). "Sex Differences In Aggression: Phylogenetic and Enculturation Perspectives," *Ethos* 4, 57-72.

Rohrbaugh, Joanna Bunker. (1979). *Women: Psychology's Puzzle.* New York: Basic Books.

Rosaldo, Michelle Z. and Louise Lamphere, eds. (1974). *Woman, Culture, and Society.* Stanford: Stanford University Press.

Rosenblatt, Paul C. (1974). "Cross-Cultural Perspective on Attaction," *Foundations of Interpersonal Attraction*, ed. T. L. Huston. New York: Academic Press, 79-95.

Rosenthal, Robert, Judith A. Hall, M. Robin DiMatteo, Peter L. Rogers, Dane Archer. (1979). *Sensitivity to Nonverbal Communication: the Pons Test.* Baltimore: Johns Hopkins University Press.

Rossi, Alice. (1977). "A Biosocial Perspective on Parenting," *Daedalus* 106, 1-31.

Roszak, Betty, and Theodore Roszak. (1969). *Masculine/Feminine: Readings in Sexual Mythology and the Liberation of Women.* New York: Harper and Row.

Roth, Walter E. (1897). *Ethnological Studies Among the North-West-Central Queensland Aborigines.* Brisbane: Edmund Gregory, Government Printer.

Roy, Maria, ed. (1982). *The Abusive Partner: an Analysis of Domestic*

Battering. New York: Van Nostrand Reinhold.

Rubin, Gayle. (1975). "The Traffic In Women: Notes on the 'Political Economy' of Sex," *Toward an Anthropology of Women*, ed. R. Reiter. New York: Monthly Review Press, 157-210.

Rubin, Zick. (1974). "From Liking to Loving: Patterns of Attraction in Dating Relationships," *Foundations of Interpersonal Attraction*, ed. T. Huston. New York: Academic Press, 383-402.

Rubin, Zick, Letitia Anne Peplau, and Charles T. Hill. (1981). "Loving and Leaving: Sex Differences in Romantic Attachments," *Sex Roles* 7, 821-35.

Ruse, Michael. (1979). *Sociobiology: Sense or Nonsense?* Dordrecht, Holland: D. Reidel.

Ruse, Michael. (1981). "Are There Gay Genes? Sociobiology and Homosexuality," *Journal of Homosexuality* 6, 5-34.

Rushton, J. Philippe and Richard M. Sorrentino. (1981). "Altruism and Helping Behavior: An Historical Perspective," *Altruism and Helping Behavior*, ed. J. Rushton and R. Sorrentino. Hillsdale, N. J.: Lawrence Erlbaum, 3-16.

Russell, Bertrand. 1957 (1929). *Marriage and Morals.* New York: Liveright.

Sachs, Curt. (1937). *World History of the Dance.* trans, B. Schonberg. New York: W. W. Norton.

Sackeim, Harold A. (1983). "Self-Deception, Self-Esteem, and Depression: the Adaptive Value of Lying to Oneself," *Empirical Studies of Psychoanalytical Theories*, ed. J. Masling, vol. I. Hillsdale, N. J.: Analytic Press, 101-57.

Sade, Donald Stone. (1968). "Inhibition of Son-Mother Mating Among Free-Ranging Rhesus Monkeys," *Science and Psychoanalysis* 12, 18-38.

Sade, Donald Stone. (1980). "Human Sexuality: Hints for an Alternative Explanation," *BBS* 3, 198-9.

Sadie, Stanley. (1980). *The New Grove Dictionary of Music and Musicians.* London: MacMillan, 20 vols.

Safir, Marilyn P., Yochanan Peres, Myrna Lichtenstein, Zwi Hoch, and Joseph Shepher. (1982). "Psychological Androgyny and Sexual Adequacy," *Journal of Sex and Marital Therapy* 8, 228-40.

Sagan, Carl. (1977). *The Dragons of Eden: Speculations on the Evolution of Human Intelligence.* New York: Random House.

Sahlins, M. D. (1965). "On the Sociology of Primitive Exchange," *The Relevance of Models for Social Anthropology*, ed. M. Banton. London: Tavistock, 139-236.

Sahlins, M. D. (1976). *The Use and Abuse of Biology.* Ann Arbor: Univ. of Michigan Press.

Sanday, Peggy Reeves. (1981). *Female Power and Male Dominance.* New York: Cambridge Univ. Press.

Saucier, J. F. (1972). "Correlates of the Long Postpartum Taboo: A Cross-Cultural Study," *Current Anthropology* 13, 238-49.

De Saussure, Ferdinand. 1973 (1915). *Cours de linguistique générale*. Paris: Payot.

Savage-Rumbaugh, E. Sue, Duane M. Rumbaugh, Sally Boysen. (1979). "Chimpanzees and Protolanguage," *Behavioral and Brain Sciences* 2, 396-7.

Savage-Rumbaugh, E. Sue, and Beverly J. Wilkerson. (1978). "Socio-sexual Behavior in *Pan paniscus* and *Pan troglodytes*: A Comparative Study," *Journal of Human Evolution* 7, 327-344.

Savage-Rumbaugh, E. Sue, Beverly J. Wilkerson, and Roger Bakeman. (1977). "Spontaneous Gestural Communication Among Conspecifics in the Pygmy Chimpanzee (*Pan paniscus*)," *Progress in Ape Research* ed. G. H. Bourne. New York: Academic Press, 97-116.

Sayers, Janet. (1982). *Biological Politics; Feminist and Anti-Feminist Perspectives*. London: Tavistock Publications.

Scaife, M. and J. Bruner. (1975). "The Capacity for Joint Visual Attention in the Infant," *Nature* 253 (5489), 265-6.

Scarf, Maggie. (1980a). *Unfinished Business: Pressure Points in the Lives of Women*. Garden City: Doubleday.

Scarf, Maggie. (1980b). "The Promiscuous Woman," *Psychology Today*, July issue, 78-87.

Schapera, I. (1940). *Married Life in an African Tribe*. London: Faber and Faber.

Schatzman, Morton. (1973). *Soul Murder*. London: Allen Lane.

Schieffelin, Edward L. (1982). "The *Bau A* Ceremonial Hunting Lodge: an Alternative to Initiation," *Rituals of Manhood: Male Initiation in Papua New Guinea*, ed. G. Herdt. Berkeley: University of California Press, 155-200.

Schlegel, Alice. (1972). *Male Dominance and Female Autonomy: Domestic Authority in Matrilineal Societies*. New Haven: Human Relations Area Files Press.

Schlegel, Alice and Herbert Barry, III. (1980). "The Evolutionary Significance of Adolescent Initiation Ceremonies," *American Ethnologist* 7, 696-715.

Schmidt, Karl. (1881). *Jus Primae Noctis: Eine geschichtliche Untersuchung*. Freiburg: Herder.

Schreber, Daniel Paul. 1955 (1903). *Memoirs of My Nervous Illness*. trans. and intro. Ida Macalpine and Richard Hunter. London: W. M. Dawson.

Schreber, Daniel Paul. 1973 (1903). *Denkwürdigkeiten eines Nervenkranken*. Wiesbaden: Focus-Verlag.

Schultz, J. H. (1966). *Organstörungen und Perversionen im Liebesleben*. München: E. Reinhardt.

Schulz, Muriel. (1975). "The Semantic Derogation of Woman," *Language and Sex: Difference and Dominance*, ed. B. Thorne, N. Henley. Rowley, Mass.: Newbury House, 64-75.

Schur, Max, and Lucille B. Rivto. (1970). "The Concept of Development and

Evolution in Psychoanalysis," *Development and Evolution of Behavior: Essays in Memory of T. C. Schneirla*, ed. L. R. Aronson. San Francisco: W. H. Freeman, 600-19.

Schwartz, Bernard J. (1955). "The Measurement of Castration Anxiety and Anxiety over Loss of Love," *Journal of Personality* 24, 204-19.

Scott, George Ryley. (1966). *Phallic Worship*. London: Luxor Press.

Sears, Robert, Lucy Rau, and Richard Alpert. (1965). *Identification and Child Rearing*. Stanford: Stanford University Press.

Sebeok, Thomas. (1976a). "Iconicity," *Modern Language Notes* 91, 1427-56.

Sebeok, Thomas. (1976b). *Contributions to the Doctrine of Signs*. Bloomington: Indiana Univ. Press.

Sebeok, Thomas. (1981). *The Play of Musement*. Bloomington: Indiana University Press.

Segraves, R. T., H. W. Schoenberg, C. K. Zarnis, J. Knopf and P. Camic. (1981). "Discrimination of Organic Versus Psychological Impotence with the DSFI: a Failure to Replicate," *Journal of Sex and Marital Therapy* 7, 230-8.

Seidenberg, Robert and Karen DeCrow. (1983). *Women Who Marry Houses: Panic and Protest in Agoraphobia*. New York: McGraw-Hill.

Seligman, M. E. P. 1972 (1971). "Phobias and Preparedness," *Biological Boundaries of Learning*, ed. M. Seligman and J. Hager. New York: Appleton-Century-Crofts, 451-62.

Seligman, M. E. P. and J. L. Hager, eds. (1972). *Biological Boundaries of Learning*. New York: Appleton-Century-Crofts.

Semenov, Yu. I. (1979). "More on Marxism and the Matriarchate," *Current Anthropology* 20, 816-20.

Shapiro, A. K., E. Shapiro, H. L. Wayne, J. Clarkin, and R. Bruun. (1973). "Tourette's Syndrome: Summary of Data on 34 Patients," *Psychosomatic Medicine* 35, 419-35.

Shapiro, Evelyn and Barry M. Shapiro, eds. (1979). *The Women Say/The Men Say*. New York: Delta.

Sheldon, Ann. (1970). Letter to Editor, *Village Voice*, Dec. 17, 4.

Shepher, Joseph. (1971). "Mate Selection among Second Generation Kibbutz Adolescents and Adults: Incest Avoidance and Negative Imprinting," *Archives of Sexual Behavior* 1, 293-307.

Shepher, Joseph. (1978). "Reflections on the Origin of the Human Pair-Bond," *Journal of Social and Biological Structures* 1, 253-64.

Shepher, Joseph. (1983). *Incest: A Biosocial View*. New York: Academic Press.

Sherfey, Mary Jane. 1972 (1966). *The Nature and Evolution of Female Sexuality*. New York: Random House.

Shettel-Neuber, Joyce, Jeff B. Bryson, Leanne E. Young. (1978). "Physical Attractiveness of the 'Other Person' and Jealousy," *Personality and Social Psychology Bulletin* 4, 612-5.

Shields, William M. and Lea M. Shields. (1983). "Forcible Rape: an Evolutionary Perspective," *Ethology and Sociobiology* 4, 115-36.

Shlezinger, O. A. (1900). "Skoptsy," *Entsiklopedicheskii slovar'*, ed. I. Andreevskii, K. Arsen'ev, F. Petrushevskii. St. Petersburg: Brokgauz-Efron, vol. 30 (half-vol. 59), 223-27.

Short, R. V. (1977). "Sexual Selection and the Descent of Man," *Reproduction and Evolution*, ed. J. H. Calaby and C. H. Tyndale-Biscoe. Canberra: Australian Academy of Science, 3-19.

Short, R. V. (1979). "Sexual Selection and Its Component Parts, Somatic and Genital Selection, as Illustrated by Man and the Great Apes," *Advances in the Study of Behavior* 9, 131-58.

Short, R. V. (1981), "Sexual Selection in Man and the Great Apes," *Reproductive Biology of the Great Apes*, ed. C. Graham. New York: Academic Press, 319-41.

Shulman, Alix. (1972). "Organs and Orgasms," *Woman in Sexist Society: Studies in Power and Powerlessness*, ed. V. Gornick, B. Moran. New York: Mentor, 292-303.

Sigusch, Volkmar and Gunter Schmidt. (1971). "Lower-Class Sexuality: Some Emotional and Social Aspects in West German Males and Females," *Archives of Sexual Behavior* 1, 29-44.

Silk, J. (1978). "Patterns of Food-Sharing Among Mother and Infant Chimpanzees at Gombe National Park, Tanzania," *Folia primatologica* 29, 129-41.

Silverstein, Michael. (1976). "Shifters, Linguistic Categories, and Cultural Description," *Meaning in Anthropology*, ed. K. Basso, H. Selby. Albuquerque: University of New Mexico Press, 11-55.

Singer, Irving. (1974). *The Goals of Human Sexuality*. New York: Schocken.

Sipes, R. G. (1973). "War, Sports, and Aggression: an Empirical Test of Two Rival Theories," *American Anthropologist* 75, 64-86.

Slater, Philip E. (1968). *The Glory of Hera: Greek Mythology and the Greek Family*. Boston: Beacon.

Slocum, Sally. (1975). "Woman the Gatherer: Male Bias in Anthropology," *Toward an Anthropology of Women*, ed. R. Reiter. New York: Monthly Review Press, 36-50.

Smith, Dennis Craig, William Sparks, and Candice Kurstin-Young. (1981). *The Naked Child*. Saratoga, California: Century Twenty One Publishing.

Smith, Peter K. (1976). "On Gender Differences and the Origin of Language," *Current Anthropology* 17, 524.

Smith, Raymond T. (1973). "The Matrifocal Family," *The Character of Kinship*, ed. J. Goody. Cambridge: Cambridge University Press, 121-44.

Smith, W. John, Julia Chase and Anna Katz. (1974). "Tongue Showing: A Facial Display of Humans and Other Primate Species," *Semiotica* 11, 201-246.

Snow, Catherine E. (1979). "Conversations with Children," *Language Acquisition*, ed. Paul Fletcher and Michael Garman. Cambridge: Cambridge University Press, 363-75.

Solanas, Valerie. (1970). *SCUM (Society for Cutting Up Men) Manifesto.* New York: Olympia.

Solzhenitsyn, Alexander. (1973). *The Gulag Archipelago 1918-1956: an Experiment in Literary Investigation, I-II* (tr. T. Whitney). New York: Harper and Row.

Sontag, Susan. (1972). "The Double Standard of Aging," *Saturday Review,* Sept. 23, 127-34.

Spector, Jack. (1972). *The Aesthetics of Freud: a Study in Psychoanalysis and Art.* New York: Praeger.

Spencer, Baldwin and F. J. Gillen. (1927). *The Arunta: A Study of a Stone Age People.* London: MacMillan, 2 vols.

Sperber, Hans. (1912). "Über den Einfluss sexueller Momente auf Entstehung und Entwicklung der Sprache," *Imago* I, 405-453.

Spiro, Melford. (1982). *Oedipus in the Trobriands.* Chicago: University of Chicago Press.

Spiro, Melford and Roy D'Andrade. (1967). "A Cross-Cultural Study of Some Supernatural Beliefs," *Cross-Cultural Approaches,* ed. C. S. Ford. New Haven: HRAF Press, 196-206.

Spuhler, James N. (1979). "Continuities and Discontinuities in Anthropoid-Hominid Behavioral Evolution: Bipedal Locomotion and Sexual Receptivity," *Evolutionary Biology and Human Social Behavior: an Anthropological Perspective,* ed. N. Chagnon and W. Irons. North Scituate, Mass.: Duxbury Press, 454-61.

Stam, James H. (1976). *Inquiries into the Origin of Language: the Fate of a Question.* New York: Harper & Row.

Stamps, July A. and Robert A. Metcalf. (1980). "Parent-Offspring Conflict," *Sociobiology: Beyond Nature/Nurture?,* ed. G. Barlow, J. Silverberg. Boulder: Westview Press, 589-618.

Stanley, Julia. (1977). "Paradigmatic Woman: the Prostitute," *Papers in Language Variation,* ed. D. L. Shores and C. Hines. University, Alabama: University of Alabama Press, 303-21.

Stannard, Una. (1977). *Mrs Man.* San Francisco: Germain Books.

Stärcke, August. 1921 (1910). "The Castration Complex," *International Journal of Psycho-Analysis* 2, 179-201.

Stark, Werner, 1976-8. *The Social Bond: An Investigation Into the Bases of Law-Abidingness.* New York: Fordham University Press.

Steinem, Gloria. (1972). "What It Would Be Like If Women Win," *The American Sisterhood,* ed. W. Martin. New York: Harper and Row, 183-88.

Steklis, Horst. (1976). "On Gender Differences and Language," *Current Anthropology* 17, 328-9.

Steklis, Horst. (1980). "Problems of Comparative Primate Sexuality," *BBS* 3, 199-200.

Steklis, Horst and Stevan Harnad. (1976). "From Hand to Mouth: Some Critical Stages in the Evolution of Language," *Origins and Evolution of Language and Speech,* ed. S. Harnad, H. Steklis, J. Lancaster. New

York: New York Acad. of Sciences, 445-55.

Steklis, Horst and Michael Raleigh. (1979). "Requisites for Language: Interspecific and Evolutionary Aspects," *Neurobiology of Social Communication in Primates*, ed. H. Steklis, M. Raleigh. New York: Academic Press, 283-314.

Stephens, William N. (1961). "A Cross-Cultural Study of Menstrual Taboos," *Genetic Psychology Monographs* 64, 385-416.

Stephens, William N. (1962). *The Oedipus Complex: Cross-Cultural Evidence.* New York: Free Press of Glencoe.

Stephens, William N. (1963). *The Family in Cross-Cultural Perspective.* New York: Holt, Rinehart and Winston.

Stern, D. N. (1974). "Mother and Infant at Play: the Dyadic Interaction Involving Facial, Vocal, and Gaze Behaviors," *The Effects of the Infant on Its Caregiver*, ed. M. Lewis & L. Rosenblum. New York: Wiley, 187-213.

Stern, Jack and Randall Susman. (1983). "The Locomotor Anatomy of *Australopithecus afarensis*," *American Journal of Physical Anthropology* 60, 279-317.

Stern, Mikhail and August Stern. (1980). *Sex in the USSR.* New York: Times Books.

Sternglanz, S. H., J. L. Gray, M. Murakami. (1977). "Adult Preferences for Infantile Facial Features: an Ethological Approach," *Animal Behaviour* 25, 108-115.

Stilwell, Donald L. (1976). "Anatomy of the Human Clitoris," *The Clitoris*, ed. T. P. Lowry and T. S. Lowry. St. Louis: Warren H. Green, 9-21.

Stockard, Jean and Miriam H. Johnson. (1979). "The Social Origins of Male Dominance," *Sex Roles* 5, 199-218.

Stodder, Jim. (1979). "Confessions of a Candy-Ass Roughneck," *The Women Say/The Men Say*, ed. E. Shapiro, B. Shapiro. New York: Delta, 40-44.

Stoehr, Taylor. (1979). *Free Love in America: a Documentary History.* New York: AMS Press.

Stoller, Robert J. (1968). *Sex and Gender: Volume I, The Development of Masculinity and Femininity.* New York: Jason Aronson.

Stoller, Robert J. (1976). *Sex and Gender: Volume II, the Transsexual Experiment.* New York: Jason Aronson.

Stoller, Robert J. (1979). *Sexual Excitement: Dynamics of Erotic Life.* New York: Pantheon Books.

Strage, Mark. (1980). *The Durable Fig Leaf: a Historical, Cultural, Medical, Social, Literary, and Iconographic Account of Man's Relations with His Penis.* New York: William Morrow and Co.

Strassmann, Beverly I. (1981). "Sexual Selection, Paternal Care, and Concealed Ovulation in Humans," *Ethology and Sociobiology* 2, 31-40.

Strauss, Anselm. (1946). "The Influence of Parent-Images Upon Marital Choice," *American Sociological Review* 11, 554-59.

Strauss, Erwin W. (1966). *Phenomenological Psychology.* New York: Basic Books.

Stürup, Georg K. (1972). "Castration: the Total Treatment," *Sexual Behaviors: Social, Clinical, and Legal Aspects*, ed. H. Resnik, M. Wolfgang. Boston: Little, Brown and Co., 361-82.

Sulloway, Frank. (1979). *Freud: Biologist of the Mind*. New York: Basic Books.

Suppes, P. and H. Warren. (1975). "On the Generation and Classification of Defence Mechanisms," *International Journal of Psycho-Analysis* 56, 405-14.

Suslick, Alvin. (1963). "The Phallic Representation of the Voice," *Journal of the American Psychoanalytic Association* 11, 345-359.

Swacker, Marjorie. (1975). "The Sex of the Speaker as a Sociolinguistic Variable," *Language and Sex: Difference and Dominance*, ed. B. Throne and N. Henley. Rowley, Mass.: Newbury House, 76-83.

Symons, Donald. (1979). *The Evolution of Human Sexuality*. Oxford: Oxford Univ. Press.

Symons, Donald. (1980). "Précis of *The Evolution of Human Sexuality*," *BBS* 3, 171-214.

Symons, Donald. (1982). "Another Woman That Never Existed," *Quarterly Review of Biology* 57, 297-300.

Tannahill, Reay. (1980). *Sex in History*. New York: Stein and Day.

Tanner, Nancy. (1974). "Matrifocality in Indonesia and Africa and Among Black Americans," *Woman, Culture, and Society*, ed. M. Z. Rosaldo and L. Lamphere. Stanford: Stanford Univ. Press, 129-56.

Tanner, Nancy. (1981). *On Becoming Human*. Cambridge: Cambridge University Press.

Tavris, Carol. (1982). *Anger: the Misunderstood Emotion*. New York: Simon and Schuster.

Tavris, Carol, and Carole Offir. (1977). *The Longest War: Sex Differences in Perspective*. New York: Harcourt Brace Jovanovich.

Tavris, Carol, and Susan Sadd. (1977). *The Redbook Report on Female Sexuality*. New York: Delacorte.

Taylor, G. Rattray. (1954). *Sex in History*. New York: Vanguard Press.

Tennov, Dorothy. (1979). *Love and Limerence: the Experience of Being in Love*. New York: Stein and Day.

Terman, Lewis M. (1938). *Psychological Factors in Marital Happiness*. New York: McGraw-Hill.

Terman, Lewis M. (1951). "Correlates of Orgasm Adequacy in a Group of 556 Wives," *Journal of Psychology* 32, 115-172.

Thass-Thienemann, Theodore. (1973). *The Interpretation of Language*. New York: Jason Aronson, 2 vols.

Thiessen, Del and Barbara Gregg. (1980). "Human Assortative Mating and Genetic Equilibrium: an Evolutionary Perspective," *Ethology and Sociobiology* 1, 111-40.

Thompson, Clara. (1943). "'Penis Envy' in Women," *Psychiatry* 6, 123-5.

Thompson, Spencer K. (1975). "Gender Labels and Early Sex Role Development," *Child Development* 46, 399-47.

Thompson, Stith. (1929). *Tales of the North American Indians*. Bloomington: Indiana University Press.

Thompson, Stith. (1955-8). *Motif-Index of Folk-Literature*. Bloomington:
Indiana University Press, 6 vols.

Thompson, William Irwin. (1981). *The Time Falling Bodies Take to Light*.
New York: St. Martin's Press.

Thorne, Barrie and Nancy Henley, eds. (1975a). *Language and Sex: Difference and Dominance*. Rowley, Mass.: Newbury House.

Thorne, Barrie and Nancy Henley. (1975b). "Difference and Dominance:
an Overview of Language, Gender, and Society," *Language and Sex:
Difference and Dominance*, ed. B. Thorne and N. Henley. Rowley, Mass.:
Newbury House.

Thornhill, Randy and Nancy Wilmsen Thornhill. (1983). "Human Rape:
an Evolutionary Analysis," *Ethology and Sociobiology* 4, 137-73.

Thurber, James and E. B. White. (1929). *Is Sex Necessary?: or, Why You
Feel the Way You Do*. New York: Harper and Brothers.

Tiger, Lionel. (1969). *Men in Groups*. New York: Random House.

Tiger, Lionel. (1979). *Optimism: the Biology of Hope*. New York: Simon
and Schuster.

Tiger, Lionel and Robin Fox. (1971). *The Imperial Animal*. New York:
Holt, Rinehart & Winston.

Tikh, N. A. (1970). *Predystoriia obshchestva*. Leningrad: Izdatel'stvo Lenin-
gradskogo Universiteta.

Trethowan, W. H. (1972). "The Couvade Syndrome," *Modern Perspectives
in Psycho-Obstetrics*, ed. J. G. Howells. Edinburgh: Oliver and Boyd,
68-93.

Trethowan, W. H. and M. F. Conlon. (1965). "The Couvade Syndrome,"
British Journal of Psychiatry 111, 57-66.

Trevarthen, Colwyn. (1979). "Instincts for Human Understanding and for
Cultural Cooperation: Their Development in Infancy," *Human Ethology*,
ed. M. von Cranach *et al.* Cambridge: Cambridge University Press, 530-71.

Trevarthen, Colwyn, and Penelope Hubley. (1978). "Secondary Intersubjec-
tivity: Confidence, Confiding and Acts of Meaning in the First Year,"
Action, Gesture and Symbol, ed. Andrew Lock. New York: Academic
Press, 183-229.

Tripp, C. A. (1975). *The Homosexual Matrix*. New York: Signet.

Trivers, R. L. (1971). "The Evolution of Reciprocal Altruism," *Quarterly
Review of Biology* 46 (1), 35-57.

Trivers, R. L. (1974). "Parent-Offspring Conflict," *American Zoologist* 14,
249-264.

Trivers, R. L. 1978 (1972). "Parental Investment and Sexual Selection,"
Readings in Sociobiology, ed. T. H. Clutton-Brock and P. H. Harvey.
San Francisco: W. H. Freeman, 52-97.

Turke, Paul W. (1984). "Effects of Ovulatory Concealment and Synchrony on Protohominid Mating Systems and Parental Roles," *Ethology and Sociobiology* 5, 33-44.

Turner, G. (1884). *Samoa*. London: MacMillan.

Tutin, Caroline and Patrick McGinnis. (1981). "Chimpanzee Reproduction in the Wild," *Reproductive Biology of the Great Apes*, ed. C. E. Graham. New York: Academic Press, 239-64.

Tuttle, Russell, ed. (1975a). *Socioecology and Psychology of Primates*. The Hague: Mouton.

Tuttle, Russell, ed. (1975b). *Primate Functional Morphology and Evolution*. The Hague: Mouton.

Tuttle, Russell. (1981). "Paleoanthropology without Inhibitions," *Science* 212, 798.

Tylor, Edward Burnet. (1865). *Researches into the Early History of Mankind and the Development of Civilization*. London: John Murray.

Tylor, Edward Burnet. (1874). *Primitive Culture*. Boston: Estes and Lauriat.

Tylor, Edward Burnet. (1889). "On a Method of Investigating the Development of Institutions: Applied to Laws of Marriage and Descent," *Journal of the Anthropological Institute of Great Britain and Ireland* 18, 245-72.

Uddenberg, Nils. (1974). "Psychological Aspects of Sexual Inadequacy in Women," *Journal of Psychosomatic Research* 18, 33-47.

Udry, J. Richard and Naomi M. Morris. (1968). "Distribution of Coitus in the Menstrual Cycle," *Nature* 220, 593-6.

Umiker-Sebeok, Jean. (1981). "The Seven Ages of Woman: A View from American Magazine Advertisements," *Gender and Nonverbal Behavior*, ed. C. Mayo and N. Henley. New York: Springer-Verlag, 209-52.

Urdang, Lawrence. (1981). "I Wanna Hot Dog For My Roll," *Maledicta* 5, 69-76.

Vance, E. B. and N. N. Wagner. (1976). "Written Descriptions of Orgasm: a Study of Sex Differences," *Archives of Sexual Behavior* 5, 87-98.

Van den Berghe, Pierre. (1978). *Man in Society: A Biosocial View*. New York: Elsevier.

Van den Berghe, Pierre. (1979). *Human Family Systems: An Evolutionary View*. New York: Elsevier.

Van den Berghe, Pierre. (1983). "Human Inbreeding Avoidance: Culture in Nature," *Behavioral and Brian Sciences* 6, 91-123.

Van den Berghe, Pierre, and D. Barash. (1977). "Inclusive Fitness and Human Family Structure," *American Anthropologist* 79, 809-23.

Van den Berghe, Pierre, and G. M. Mesher. (1980). "Royal Incest and Inclusive Fitness," *American Ethnologist* 7, 300-317.

Vanggaard, Thorkil. 1972 (1969). *Phallós: a Symbol and Its History in the Male World*. New York: International Universities Press.

Van Leeuwen, Kato. (1966). "Pregnancy Envy in the Male," *International Journal of Psycho-Analysis* 47, 319-24.

Vasmer, Max. (1953-58). *Russisches etymologisches Wörterbuch*. Heidelberg: Winter, 3 vols.

Vilensky, J. A., G. W. Van Hoesen, A. R. Damasio. (1982). "The Limbic System and Human Evolution," *Journal of Human Evolution* 11, 447-60.

Voinovich, Vladimir. (1979). *The Life and Extraordinary Adventures of Private Ivan Chonkin*, tr. R. Lourie. New York: Bantam.

Vygotsky, Lev. 1962 (1934). *Thought and Language*. trans. & ed. E. Hanffmann and G. Vakar. Cambridge: MIT Press.

Vygotsky, Lev. 1968 (1925). *Psikhologiia iskusstva*. Moscow: Izdatel'stvo Iskusstvo.

Waddington, C. H. (1960). *The Ethical Animal*. London: Allen and Unwin.

Wagner, Gorm and Richard Green. (1981). *Impotence: Physiological, Psychological, Surgical Diagnosis and Treatment*. New York: Plenum.

Walker, Alice. (1982). *The Color Purple*. New York: Harcourt Brace Jovanovich.

Wallace, B. and A. M. Srb. (1964). *Adaptation*. Englewood Cliffs: Prentice-Hall.

Walsh, Robert H. and Wilbert M. Leonard. (1974). "Usage of Terms for Sexual Intercourse by Men and Women," *Archives of Sexual Behavior* 3, 373-6.

Walster, Elaine and G. William Walster. (1978). *A New Look at Love*. Reading, Mass.: Addison-Wesley.

Wang, William S-Y. (1976). "Language Change," *Origins and Evolution of Language and Speech*. New York: New York Academy of Science, 61-72.

Washburn, S. L. (ed.). (1961). *Social Life of Early Man*. Chicago: Aldine.

Washburn, S. L. (1969). "An Ape's-Eye View of Human Evolution," *Evolutionary Anthropology*, ed. Hermann Bleibtreu. Boston: Allyn & Bacon, 89-98.

Washburn, S. L. and C. S. Lancaster. 1973 (1968). "The Evolution of Hunting," *Man in Evolutionary Perspective*, ed. C. L. Brace and J. Metress. New York: John Wiley, 57-69.

Washburn, S. L. and E. R. McCown, eds. (1978). *Human Evolution: Biosocial Perspectives*. Menlo Park, Ca.: Benjamin-Cummings.

Waugh, Linda. (1982). "Marked and Unmarked: a Choice Between Unequals in Semiotic Structure," *Semiotica* 38, 299-318.

Weatherhead, Patrick and Raleigh Robertson. (1979). "Offspring Quality and the Polygyny Threshold: 'The Sexy Son Hypothesis'," *American Naturalist* 113, 201-8.

Webb, Peter. (1975). *The Erotic Arts*. Boston: New York Graphic Society.

Webster, Paula. (1975). "Matriarchy: a Vision of Power," *Toward an Anthropology of Women*, ed. R. Reiter. New York: Monthly Review Press, 141-56.

Weiner, A. B. (1979). "Trobriand Kinship from Another View: the Reproductive Power of Women and Men," *Man* 14, 328-48.

Weinrich, James D. (1977). "Human Sociobiology: Pair-Bonding and Resource Predictability (Effects of Social Class and Race)," *Behavioral Ecology and Sociobiology* 2, 91-118.

Weiss, Robert S. (1982). "Attachment in Adult Life," *The Place of Attachment in Human Behavior*, ed. C. Parkes and J. Stevenson-Hinde. New York: Basic Books, 171-84.

Weisstein, Naomi. 1972 (1968). "Psychology Constructs the Female," *Woman in Sexist Society: Studies in Power and Powerlessness*, ed. V. Gornick, B. Moran. New York: Mentor, 207-24.

Weitz, Shirley. (1977). *Sex Roles: Biological, Psychological, and Social Foundations*. New York: Oxford Univ. Press.

Welsford, Enid. 1951 (1917). "Serpent-Worship (Teutonic and Balto-Slavic)," *Encyclopedia of Religion and Ethics*, ed. J. Hastings. New York: Charles Scribner's Sons, vol. XI, 419-23.

Wentworth, Harold and Stuart Flexner. (1975). *Dictionary of American Slang* (2nd suppl. edition). New York: Thomas Y. Crowell.

Wescott, Roger (ed.). (1974). *Language Origins*. Silver Spring, MD.: Linstok Press.

Wescott, Roger. (1976). "Protolinguistics: The Study of Protolanguages as an Aid to Glossogonic Research," *Origins and Evolution of Language and Speech*, ed. S. Harnad, D. Steklis, J. Lancaster. New York: New York Academy of Sciences, 104-116.

Westermarck, Edward. (1922). *The History of Human Marriage* (5th ed.). New York: Allerton, 3 vols.

Westoff, Charles F. (1978). "Marriage and Fertility in Developed Countries," *Scientific American* 239(6), 51-57.

White, Gregory L. (1980). "Inducing Jealousy: a Power Perspective," *Personality and Social Psychology Bulletin* 6, 222-7.

White, Gregory L. (1981). "Some Correlates of Romantic Jealousy," *Journal of Personality* 49, 129-47.

White, Tim D. (1980). "Evolutionary Implications of Pliocene Hominid Footprints," *Science* 208, 175-6.

Whiting, Beatrice. (1965). "Sex Identity Conflict and Physical Violence: a Comparative Study," *American Anthropologist* 67, 123-40.

Whiting, Beatrice, and John Whiting. (1975). *Children of Six Cultures: a Psycho-Cultural Analysis*. Cambridge: Harvard Univ. Press.

Whiting, John. (1964). "Effects of Climate on Certain Cultural Practices," *Explorations in Cultural Anthropology*, ed. W. H. Goodenough. New York: McGraw-Hill, 511-44.

Whiting, John, Richard Kluckhohn, and Albert Anthony. (1958). "The Function of Male Initiation Ceremonies at Puberty," *Readings in Social Psychology*, ed. E. Maccoby, T. Newcomb, E. Hartley. New York: Holt, Rinehart and Winston, 359-70.

Whiting, John and Beatrice Whiting. (1975). "Aloofness and Intimacy of Husbands and Wives: a Cross-Cultural Study," *Ethos* 3, 183-207.

Whitney, William Dwight. (1878). *The Life and Growth and Language*. New York: D. Appleton.

Whitten, Richard G. (1982). "Hominid Promiscuity and the Sexual Life of

Proto-Savages: Did *Australopithecus* Swing?," *Current Anthropology* 23, 99-101.

Whyte, Martin King. (1978a). "Cross-Cultural Codes Dealing with the Relative Status of Women," *Ethnology* 17, 211-37.

Whyte, Martin King. (1978b). *The Status of Women in Preindustrial Societies.* Princeton: Princeton Univ. Press.

Wickler, W. (1966). "Ursprung und biologische Deutung des Genital Präsentierens mannlicher Primaten," *Z. Tierpsychol.* 23, 422-437.

Wickler, W. (1967). "Socio-Sexual Signals and their Intra-specific Imitation among Primates," *Primate Ethology*, ed. D. Morris. London: Wiederfield and Nicolson, 69-147.

Wickler, W. 1972 (1969). *The Sexual Code: The Social Behavior of Animals and Men.* Garden City: Doubleday.

Wilden, Anthony. (1972). *System and Structure: Essays in Communication and Exchange.* London: Tavistock.

Williams, F. E. (1936). *Papuans of the Trans-Fly.* Oxford: Clarendon Press.

Williams, George C. (1966). *Adaptation and Natural Selection: A Critique of Some Current Evolutionary Thought.* Princeton: Princeton University Press.

Williams, George C. (1975). *Sex and Evolution.* Princeton: Princeton University Press.

Williams, Juanita. (1977). *Psychology of Women: Behavior in a Biosocial Context.* New York: Norton.

Williams, Leonard. (1967). *The Dancing Chimpanzee.* New York: W. W. Norton.

Wilson, Edward O. (1975). *Sociobiology: The New Synthesis.* Cambridge: Harvard University Press.

Wilson, Edward O. (1976). "Sociobiology: A New Approach to Understanding the Basis of Human Nature," *New Scientist* 70, 342-45.

Wilson, Edward O. (1977). "Biology and the Social Sciences," *Daedalus* 106, 127-140.

Wilson, Edward O. (1978). *On Human Nature.* Cambridge: Harvard Univ. Press.

Wilson, Edward O. and C. J. Lumsden. (1981). *Genes, Mind, and Culture: the Coevolutionary Process.* Cambridge: Harvard University Press.

Wilson, Glenn. (1978). *The Secrets of Sexual Fantasy.* London: J. M. Dent and Sons.

Wilson, Peter J. (1980). *Man, the Promising Primate: the Conditions of Human Evolution.* New Haven: Yale Univ. Press.

Wilson, Wayne J. (1981). "Five Years and 121 Dirty Words Later," *Maledicta* 5, 243-55.

Wind, Jan. (1976). "More on Gender Differences and the Origin of Language," *Current Anthropology* 17, 745-8.

Winner, Ellen. (1979). "New Names for Old Things: The Emergence of Metaphoric Language," *Journal of Child Language* 6, 469-91.

Winnicott, D. W. (1960). "The Theory of the Parent-Infant Relationship," *International Journal of Psycho-Analysis* 41, 585-595.

Wolf, A. P. (1970). "Childhood Association and Sexual Attraction: a Further Test of the Westermarck Hypothesis," *American Anthropologist* 72, 503-15.

Woolf, Virginia. 1978 (1931). *The Waves*. New York: Harcourt, Brace, Jovanovich.

Wormhoudt, Arthur. (1949). "The Unconscious Identification Words – Milk," *American Imago* 6, 57-68.

Wright, Kristina, Delwood Collins, Paul Musey and John Preedy. (1981). "Comparative Aspects of Ape Steroid Hormone Metabolism," *Reproductive Biology of the Great Apes*, ed. C. E. Graham. New York: Academic, 163-190.

Yando, Regina, Victoria Seitz, and Edward Zigler. (1978). *Imitation: A Developmental Perspective*. Hillsdale, N. J.: Lawrence Erlbaum Associates.

Yates, Gayle Graham. (1975). *What Women Want: the Ideas of the Movement*. Cambridge: Harvard University Press.

Yates, Sybille. (1930). "An Investigation of the Psychological Factors in Virginity and Ritual Defloration," *International Journal of Psycho-Analysis* 11, 167-84.

Yeats, William Butler. (1959). *The Collected Poems of W. B. Yeats*. New York: Macmillan.

Young, Frank W. (1965). *Initiation Ceremonies: a Cross-Cultural Study of Status Dramatization*. Indianapolis: Bobbs-Merrill.

Young, J. Z. (1978). *Programs of the Brain*. Oxford: Orford Univ. Press.

Zaborowski, M. (1896). "La circoncision, ses origines et sa répartition en Afrique et à Madagascar," *Anthropologie* 7, 653-75.

Zelig, Leonard. (1927). "Male Penis-Envy: a Personal Approach," *International Psychopath* 7, 666-7.

Zihlman, Adrienne. (1978). "Women in Evolution, Part II: Subsistence and Social Organization among Early Hominids," *Signs* 4, 4-20.

Zihlman, Adrienne. (1981). "Women as Shapers of the Human Adaptation," *Woman the Gatherer*, ed. F. Dahlberg. New Haven: Yale University Press, 75-120.

Zihlman, Adrienne and Nancy Tanner. (1976). "Women in Evolution, Part I: Innovation and Selection in Human Origins," *Signs* 1, 585-608.

Zihlman, Adrienne, Lynda Brunker. (1979). "Hominid Bipedalism: Then and Now," *Yearbook of Physical Anthropology* 22, 132-62.

Zilboorg, Gregory. (1944). "Masculine and Feminine," *Psychiatry* 7, 257-96.

Zimmerman, Don H. and Candace West. (1975). "Sex Roles, Interruptions and Silences in Conversation," *Language and Sex: Difference and Dominance*, ed. B. Thorne and N. Henley. Rowley, Mass.: Newbury House, 105-129.

Zimmerman, Frank. (1951). "Origin and Significance of the Jewish Rite of Circumcision," *Psychoanalytic Review* 38, 103-12.

Zolla, Elémire. (1981). *The Androgyne: Fusion of the Sexes.* London: Thames and Hudson.

Zubin, Joseph and John Money, eds. (1973).*Contemporary Sexual Behavior: Critical Issues in the 1970's.* Baltimore: JHUP.

Zuckerman, Marvin. (1971). "Physiological Measures of Sexual Arousal in the Human," *Technical Report of the Commission on Obscenity and Pornography*, dir. W. Cody Wilson. Washington: U. S. Govt. Printing Office, I, 61-101.

Zuckerman, Solly. (1932). *The Social Life of Monkeys and Apes.* London: Kegan Paul, Trench, and Trubner.

Zuckerman, Solly. (1933). *Functional Affinities of Man, Monkeys and Apes.* New York: Harcourt, Brace.

General Index

grooming, 86, 210, 218
Grossman, W., 385
Grunberger, R., 346
Grusec, J., 209
Guillaume, P., 27
guilt, 141, 155, 163, 172, 206, 211, 261, 282, 284, 313
Guthrie, R., 114, 165, 198, 248, 249, 298, 339
Guttentag, M., 56, 255, 280
gynocracy, *see:* "matriarchy"
Gypsies, 180

habitat, 33-34, 49, 50, 57
Haddon, A., 349
Haeberle, E., 355
Haeckel, E., 11, 36
Hager, J., 6
Hahn, S., 365
Haldane, J., 21, 217, 233
Hall, C., 385
Hall, E., 240, 244
Halle, M., 28, 29
Halverson, H., 339
Hamburg, B., 38, 66, 199
Hamilton, J., 48
Hamilton, W., 16, 20, 21, 22, 203, 217, 220
Hammel, E., 156
Hammond, N., 162, 349
Hanby, J., 275
Hand, W., 363, 364, 368
Hanna, J., 236, 238
Harcourt, A., 57
Hardin, G., 6
Harding, R., 34
Harding, S., 173, 229
harem, 50, 99, 178, 261, 309
Hariton, E., 281
Harnad, S., 215, 229
Harrari, 100
Harrington, C., 331
Harris, M., 9
Hart, B., 132
Hartland, E., 119, 122, 303
Hartley, D., 29
Hartung, J., 380
Harvey, P., 20, 22, 56, 57
Hatfield, E., 145

Hawaiians, 122, 146
Hawkes, J., 119
Hay, D., 209
Hays, H., 250, 262, 311, 321, 342, 356
Hazen, H., 281
Healey, T., 224, 254, 292, 303, 317
Heath, D., 99
Hebrews, 179, 332
hedonic function of female orgasm, 71-72, 104-7
Heeschen, V., 218
Heger, H., 346
Heilbrun, A., 352
hemicastration, 98, 308
Henley, N., 164, 249, 253, 254
Henley, W., 224
Herdt, G., 295, 324, 348, 383
Hermann, I., 277
hermaphrodite, 188-89, 293, 311, 365, 383
Hertz, R., 278
Hetherington, E., 127
Hewes, G., 35, 49, 215, 216, 217, 222, 226, 228, 233, 238
Hilberman, E., 281
Hill, J., 219, 232
Hinde, R., 276
Hindus, 290, 311, 322
Hippocrates, 13, 307
Hirschfield, M., 348
Hite, S., 64, 65, 73, 74, 76, 80, 82, 97, 99, 101, 102, 104, 109, 164, 280, 292, 350, 355
Hoch, Z., 64
Hockett, C., 199, 215, 298
Hoffman, I., 141
Hoffmann, M., 210
Hogbin, H., 333, 339, 363, 364, 367
Hoijer, H., 52
Hollender, M., 118
Holloway, R., 33, 234
Hollis, A., 341
Holmberg, A., 366, 367
Homans, G., 253
home base, 57-8, 160, 192, 195, 196-97, 305
hominids, *passim*
Homo erectus, 57, 235
homogamy, 89, 144-45, 147, 243

181, 212, 277, 280, 306, 333, 357, 383, 384
meanders, 234-35
Mechling, J., 347
Meerloo, J., 142
Megaw, J., 236
Meigs, A., 319, 333, 367
Meiselman, K., 126, 146, 148, 154, 156, 217
Mellen, S., 51, 56, 58, 59, 151, 160, 164, 196, 199, 200, 216, 217, 219, 247, 298
Melotti, U., 51
Meltzoff, A., 26
Menomini, 224
menstrual cycle, 54-55, 69-72, 161, 355
menstrual taboo, 151, 328, 355-62
menstruation, 139, 261, 281, 293, 333, 355-62, 366, 378, 386
Mesher, G., 59, 146
Messenger, J., 74, 76, 77
metaphor, 29ff., 276
Metcalf, R., 22, 204
Meyer, L., 235, 239
Meyer-Bahlburg, H., 351
Michael, R., 38, 54
Midgley, M., 20, 205, 206
milk, *see:* breasts
Mill, J., 29
Mill, J.S., 262, 280
Miller, A., 126
Miller, C., 253
Miller, W., 28
Millet, K., 279, 280, 385
mimicry, 16, 32
Minankabau, 123
misogyny, 194, 250, 261ff.
Mitchell, G., 58, 229, 276
Mitchell, J., 203, 307
Mohave, 98, 138, 291, 357
Moncrieff, R., 39, 40
money, 148, 151, 152, 158-67, 173, 212, 218, 283. *see also:* altruism, exchange
Money, J., 38, 64, 106, 170, 189, 196, 271, 309, 348
Mongo, 340
Mongol Tartars, 41
monogamy, 50-62, 63, 66, 67, 89, 106, 123, 139, 141-45, 150-53, 166, 170,

177, 193ff., 221, 246, 314, 320
Montagnais-Naskapi, 285, 286
Montagu, A., 5, 6, 58, 110, 120, 207, 220, 223, 240, 242, 248, 250, 256, 333, 384
Montgomery, R., 358, 362, 367
Monumbo, 357
Moore, B., 64, 284
Moore, M., 26
Morgan, E., 298
Morgan, L., 119, 121, 123
Morgan, M., 228
Mormons, 59
Morris, C., 3
Morris, D., 32, 35, 37, 58, 66, 72, 95, 111, 112, 114, 160, 165, 166, 180, 181, 197, 198, 199, 218, 249, 250, 269, 291, 298, 315
Morris, N., 54, 355
Morriss, G., 356
Mosher, C., 76
Moss, H., 142
mother, 15, 26, 27, 28, 30, 37, 46, 50, 91, 102, 116-24, 128-49, 153, 154-55, 163, 166-7, 176, 190-214, 216, 219, 228-31, 243, 252, 260-67, 274, 279, 287-97, 316, 319, 320, 321, 325, 328, 329, 334, 350, 353, 356, 359, 360, 362-84
mother goddesses, 121-24
mother-in-law, 168-74, 304
Moulton, J., 81
Moulton, R., 385
Mowrer, O., 26, 129, 134
Muensterberger, W., 114
Mullen, S., 74
Mundinger, P., 219
Mundkur, B., 271, 272, 322
Mundurucú, 268, 311, 318
Munroe, Robert, 193, 334, 335, 338, 360, 361, 363, 364, 367, 377, 378, 382, 384
Munroe, Ruth, 361, 364, 377, 382
Murdock, G., 51, 146, 152, 153, 159, 279, 380
Muria, 79, 122, 303, 318
Murphy, R., 161, 164, 268, 278, 280, 318, 327
Murray, R., 146, 324

Daniel Rancour-Laferriere was originally trained as a biologist and is now Professor of Russian at the University of California, Davis. He is the author of *Sign and Subject, Out from Under Gogol's Overcoat*, and *The Mind of Stalin*, and the editor of *Russian Literature and Psychoanalysis*.